Infant/Toddler Care and Education

In every child there is something precious that is in no other.

SECOND EDITION

Infant/Toddler Care and Education

MARGARET G. WEISER, ED.D.

Professor, Early Childhood Education
University of Iowa

Merrill, an imprint of
Macmillan Publishing Company
New York

Collier Macmillan Canada, Inc.
Toronto

Maxwell Macmillan International Publishing Group
New York   Oxford   Singapore   Sydney

Cover Photo: Bob Daemmrich, The Image Works.

Administrative Editor: Linda A. Sullivan
Production Editor: Mark J. Opperwall
Art Coordinator: Vincent A. Smith
Photo Editor: Gail Meese
Cover Designer: Russ Maselli

This book was set in Souvenir and Univers

Macmillan Publishing Company
866 Third Avenue, New York, NY 10022

Collier Macmillan Canada, Inc.

Library of Congress Catalog Card Number: 90–61993
International Standard Book Number: 0–675–21318–5

Printing: 3 4 5 6 7 8 9
Year: 3 4

To my daughter Margie and my son Rob,
who introduced me to the challenge and excitement of the infant/toddler years

Foreword

Although the sharpest rise in enrollment in the early childhood field is for children younger than three years, many college and university training programs offer no courses to help prepare personnel to work in these programs. Furthermore, if they do, the instructor is hard-pressed to find a decent text to use—one that is both scholarly and practical, comprehensive yet specific. With the publication of this book, at least the second of those problems is solved. To build a comment on the charming Egyptian proverb with which Peg Weiser begins her own preface, I would like to reassure her that there is now less need for anyone else to write a book on the care and education of infants and toddlers. She has given us the one we need for the nineties.

Writing about educare for infants and toddlers is not easy. Young children are so indivisible into the separate categories in which we sometimes think and write—health, intelligence, social competence, emotional stability, and the like—that writing about their development is especially difficult. One simply cannot pour out everything at once, and the effort to avoid doing so can be frustrating. Dr. Weiser has managed this conflict by showing, at the beginning, just what little children need. Thus,

she manages to present the whole child at the outset, and the reader never loses sight of that. As she examines development in all of these integrated areas, we never forget that she is writing about little children, not psychological processes.

As one who has become a history buff, and one who has discovered in the classroom over the years just how unaware of the distinguished history of early childhood and of the identity of our heroines and heroes many of today's students and practitioners are, I was delighted to find the history of early education right up front. Early childhood appears to be "rediscovered" every decade or so—with the eighties being at least the second time around during my active career—and this brief reminder of where our major concepts and practices have come from is extremely valuable. Persons who work with infants and toddlers are writing the history of the future, so it is valuable for them to begin their own learning with at least a brief history of the past.

The comprehensive coverage in this book may well be its strongest point. All too many books prepared primarily for teachers and educarers give short shrift to the health needs of the young child and to procedures necessary to maintain healthful conditions in the environment. Likewise, many books prepared for health care professionals ignore the need to create an environment that is growth fostering as well as sanitary. The early childhood professional has to develop some of the surveillance skills of the sanitation worker and many of the nurturing practices of the nurse. Trainees will find many helpful and life-saving techniques described in these pages. Indeed, chapter 6, The Health Component, should become a handbook for guiding daily activities with the children so as to ensure health maintenance as a vital component of overall development.

But I suppose I must admit that what I like best about the book is its adoption of the word I want to see become the name of our field: *educare*. Although most people would agree that one cannot educate an infant/toddler without also offering care and protection, our semantic habits imply that we think we can. Many people still go to great lengths to make a distinction between *early childhood education* and *day care* (or *child care*). And why should they not try to do so? After all, what we have called early childhood education has had general public support—if anybody paid attention to it at all, that is. Not so for day care. Although child care has for many years offered one of the most vital types of family support ever designed within the broad field of human services, it has somehow been stigmatized by the general public, and to some extent snubbed by professionals. But no more. Now that roughly two-thirds of all mothers of children under six and slightly more than one-half of all mothers of children under three are employed, the stigma is lifting and professionals are clamoring to get on the bandwagon. And for the little children involved, this is good.

So it is gratifying to see a book written about the *educare* of infants and toddlers and about the training of personnel who will become *educarers*. It will be read with pleasure and gratitude for years to come.

Bettye Caldwell

Preface

We have fallen on difficult times.
Children no longer obey their parents;
everyone wants to write a book.
　　　　　　—Ancient Egyptian Proverb

We are still trying to get children to obey their parents, and it does seem as though many persons want to write a book. My desire to write this book (a major revision of *Group Care and Education of Infants and Toddlers*) has been strengthened by the statements of three well-known early childhood authorities.

According to Alice Honig,

> In the past few years, there has been a sharp rise in the needs for infant/toddler care but a singular dearth of teachers trained specifically for under threes and a scarcity of teacher-trainers specialized for the preparation of infancy teachers (1990, p. 63).

Infant/Toddler Care and Education is designed to help meet the training needs of preservice and inservice teachers and caregivers for the under threes. Although many excellent publications about early childhood education exist, few include the beginning months and years of a child's life. The text also serves as a guide for the human services personnel who monitor and license infant/toddler programs.

The second reason for this book is to reinforce the concept of *educaring* as the appropriate description of what infant/toddler caregivers and teachers do. Both Magda Gerber and Bettye Caldwell consistently use the term *educaring*, and the term is used as far away as South Africa and New Zealand! Caldwell has stated that the terms *infant care* and *infant education* cannot describe two separate activities because programs for the very young are "both educational and protective" (1986a, p. 7). I use the term *educarer* to describe the caregiver/teacher because it so aptly describes the role of the adult in a center-based program, in a family day-care home, and in the child's own home with his or her parent or guardian.

The third authority is the National Association for the Education of Young Children, an organization of over 72,000 members (1990) who are closely involved in early childhood education and care for children from birth to eight and their families. The Association's position statement (Lally, Provence, Szanton, & Weissbourd, 1987) and publications about infants and toddlers provided the rationale and support for the recommended theory and practices.

The demand for nonmaternal infant/toddler care and education has reached crisis proportions. Over half of the mothers of babies under one year enter or reenter the work force, and the percentage rises each year. It has been projected that four out of every five infants will be in out-of-home programs by year 2000. Obtaining accurate figures on the number of babies who need but do not have out-of-home care is not possible today. Programs licensed to serve 12 or 15 children report waiting lists of 50, 60, or 70, and stop adding names when enrollment within a year or two is improbable. A few employers and public school systems are attempting to meet the needs (see chapter 11), but there will not be enough programs under any kind of sponsorships, nor enough educarers to staff the programs, for years to come. We will continue to read about babies being stowed under the counter in stores where mothers are clerking, or left in locked cars in a factory's parking lot, or left at home alone, with a slightly older sibling, or at the home of a neighbor who may or may not be committed to or knowledgeable about educaring.

As we approach the 21st century, the need for qualified personnel in infant/toddler care and education will become even greater. Not only will a need exist for educarers who have day-to-day contact with children and their families, but also a need for knowledgeable directors of centers, knowledgeable child-care consultants to monitor and license programs, and persons to train the educarers. This book has been written to help meet this need.

As is true of most worthwhile endeavors, we need to know where we have been in order to understand where we are and where we hope

to go. Without an acceptance of the importance of the very early years, there would be no reason to pursue the topic of the care and education of infants and toddlers beyond the usual instructions given in the typical manual for babysitting. Unlike many methods textbooks, this one concerns itself first with the evaluation of the importance and significance of the very early years; from there the emphasis shifts to the current state of the art in very early care and education, and on recommendations for current and future programs. The knowledge gained from this information and the participation in a practicum situation will enable the student to become a competent educarer of very young children.

The text is divided into five sections. Part One provides the historical development of very early childhood education and a summary of what has been learned about early child development and early learning. Part Two presents the developmental (or educational) curriculum and addresses the planned nurturance of young children's cognition, language, social competency, and motor competency. Part Three presents the care and protection curriculum, and includes detailed information about the health, nutrition, and safety components of a program. Part Four includes the physical, experiential, and human environments recommended for a high quality program. Part Five describes the essential partnerships with parents, and the emerging partnerships with public education and business. Typical days for four young children show parent-educarer-child partnerships in action. The section concludes with examples of national partnerships and the why's and how's of child advocacy.

The role of the educarer is emphasized in all sections of the book. For the sake of ease in reading, the example of T. Berry Brazelton has usually been followed in using the masculine pronoun to refer to the child and the feminine pronoun to refer to the educaring person.

I am indebted to the children and educarers at the Early Childhood Education Center at the

University of Iowa and Kindercampus in Iowa City, for the photographs of children and edu-carers. Special mention is made of Jane Dunlap Carver, who wrote the descriptions of typical days in the lives of three children at the center, and of Jane Kaplow Rosenthal, who explained the concept and related experiences of a primary caregiving structure. They both served as head teachers in the Center's infant/toddler program.

Appreciation for support and encouragement is also extended to Jeanne Tack and Beth Kemp of Kindercampus, and to Mary Rose Mazure, who described a typical day in her family day-care home. Special acknowledgment is given to Alfred Healy, M.D., director of the University of Iowa's Division of Developmental Disabilities, for his critique of the health information. I especially thank Bettye Caldwell for contributing the foreword. Comments from the following people helped make this a better book: Geri Ash, Cuyahoga Community College; Rhoda Chalker, Florida Atlantic University; Kathleen Elson, Orange Coast College; Christine Hazen-Askew, University of Connecticut; John Hranitz, Bloomsburgh University of Pennsylvania; Earline Kendall, Belmont College; Oralie McAfee, Metropolitan State College; and Linda Ruhmann, San Antonio College.

Few photographs would have appeared in the text without the expertise of Lida Cochran and Cal Mether, both from the University of Iowa. And of course, there would have been no typed manuscript without the patience of my secretary, Connie Barthelman.

Margaret G. Weiser

Contents

Infant/Toddler Care and Education

ONE

The Very Early Years

It has taken a long, long time for us to agree that children have rights just like adults have rights, and that adults are responsible for making certain that the rights of children are honored.

Both the rights and the responsibilities are defined and described in the United Nations' *Convention on the Rights of the Child,* adopted in 1989. These rights include adequate nutrition, housing, recreation, and medical services; free primary education; special treatment, education, and care if handicapped; and protection from any form of discrimination regardless of race, color, sex, religion, or nationality (Convention, 1989, March). These rights are described in nonlegalistic terms in the publication of Children's Defense International—USA titled *In the Child's Best Interest* (Castelle, 1990).

You will be able to trace the historical development of these rights, as well as the status of young children, as you read chapter 1, The Importance of the Very Early Years: Historic and Current Perspectives. It was not until the 1960s that our attention was focused on the infant/toddler years. The research findings of Hunt (1961) and Bloom (1964) led to the appreciation of the

importance of these beginning years, and the development of the pioneer programs in the 1960s and 1970s indicated that at last our infants and toddlers were being looked at as persons with their own rights. The 1986 enactment of the *Education of the Handicapped Act Amendments* (P.L. 99–457) indicated our national concern for very young handicapped children. We in the United States have made considerable progress in the care and education of infants and toddlers (and preschoolers), but there remain many challenges before the rights identified in the Convention will be a reality.

Chapter 2, Very Early Child Development and Learning, contains an overview of selected child development theories and the typical sequence of behavior for infants and toddlers, with special attention being given to the prerequisites for and development of very early learning.

These first two chapters lay the groundwork for the remainder of the text, which presents suggestions and guidelines for our efforts toward the achievement of these universal rights for infants and toddlers in nonmaternal care. We can do this by providing high quality infant/toddler care and education.

Historic and Current Perspectives

All the flowers of all the tomorrows are in the seeds of today.
Chinese proverb

What is a baby worth? As individuals, we each have our personal opinion. Societies also have public policies about the worth of babies. Today some countries are actively encouraging more and more births; others are limiting the number of allowable births per family unit. But the true worth of a baby is in the minds and hearts of each one of us. In the United States there are many tangible indications that we highly value our youngest citizens: special baby food; designer clothes for the birth-to-three group; literally hundreds of books on child-rearing and teaching your baby to read, count, and solve problems; and highly paid speakers who claim to have the answers to "how to do" almost anything related to infants and toddlers and preschoolers. We are indeed a child-centered society, at least on the surface.

We have reason to believe that babies and young children have been treasured by society even from the very beginnings of human history. Archeologists have found numerous artifacts representing pregnant women (but not children), and anthropologists have concluded that the legal and religious sanctions of marriage came into being solely for the protection of children. Children assured the continuation of the race.

Written history reveals that recognition of the importance of the early years of life has been sporadic. It has taken many forms and has frequently been selective rather than universal. The values, attitudes, and goals of societies determine the place of the young child in their midst. Depending on their time and place in history, some children have been valued as future soldiers, some as future philosophers and kings, and many as potential wage earners; others have been viewed as liabilities, even disasters. Almost always, boys have been more highly valued than girls. Until the 19th century all children were viewed as miniature or incomplete adults, and their importance was determined solely by their anticipated adult roles. Childhood was brief and of little account—a period of marking time.

In spite of the various views about young children, the popular assumption is that

3

throughout history young children have been cared for and nurtured within the family at least until they were old enough to join the work force—which may have been as young as 5 years of age. However, this was not the case. The coming of civilization meant that upper-class women, at least, assigned the role of nurse and caregiver to servants or to slaves. Old Testament prophets felt the need to tell mothers it was their duty to nurse their children; in the second century A.D. Plutarch strongly admonished mothers to nurse their young. In 1633, Comenius (the "father" of early childhood education in Czechoslovakia) maintained that babies received not only alien milk, but alien morals from the wet nurse. In the 1700s Rousseau stated that there would be a reform in morals and no lack of citizens for the state if mothers would nurse their own children. At that time, it was estimated that of the 21,000 children born in Paris each year, 1,400 were nursed by their mothers or wet nurses in their homes, 2,600 were placed in suburban nursery care, and the remaining 17,000 were sent into the country to be cared for by professional wet nurses. The children sometimes stayed as long as 12 years!

In the United States the owners of Southern plantations customarily assigned the nursing and rearing of their young children to their slaves. During the same time period, the apprentice system was based on families rearing and training children other than their own, while sending their own children to other families.

In 20th century America, especially during times of national stress, very young children have been cared for by others either in the home or outside the home while mothers work or receive job training. It might be assumed that voluntarily assigning the nursing and care of very young children to persons outside the immediate family implies an unawareness of the importance of these beginning months and years. It is also evident that, despite the hue and cry about the sanctity of the home for the rearing of its young, such has never existed as a universal phenomenon.

To a very large degree, any historical review of attitudes involves the drawing of inferences from happenings and writings and is always subject to some misinterpretation. The story of the evolution of the recognition of the importance of the very early years presents two additional difficulties: First, very young children have been only occasionally viewed as important enough to write about. Second, the word *infant* has been used to refer to varying age ranges, from the first 7 years of life—"in this age it cannot talk well or form its words perfectly, for its teeth are not yet well arranged or firmly implanted" (Le Grand Proprietaire, 1556, cited in Aries, 1962, p. 21)—to the entire span of years preceding adulthood. There was no term to distinguish between child and adolescent in 17th century France; *enfant* was used for both. As recently as 1824, a father wrote of his "infant" daughter, about 10 years old. Today the first years of compulsory schooling in Britain are housed in the "infant school," which serves children aged 5 through 7 years. However, within these limitations, a selected review of history does reveal the evolution of the importance accorded the very early years.

ANCIENT TIMES TO THE MIDDLE AGES

Greece

Greece was the site of the beginnings of Western civilization, and some note was made of young children even in the days of antiquity. In the eighth century B.C. Spartan children were less the offspring of their parents than the property of the state, and immediately after birth were inspected for physical fitness by a citizens' committee. Those deemed not fit were tested by being exposed to the elements of the mountains in northern Greece—a test that would probably have killed even a healthy baby. Those infants deemed fit were almost immediately immersed in the life we now call Spartan, a life away from home, with no tenderness or nurturing, a life designed from the start to teach obedience, military prowess, and stamina. Healthy children did have value, but only as future soldiers or as mothers of future soldiers.

The peak of Sparta's civilization was the military crushing of Athens, about 404 B.C. Out of Athenian shame and turmoil came the first educational theorists, Plato and Aristotle, both of whom recognized the importance of the early years in the formation of good persons and good citizens. Plato's *Republic* contains guidelines for the leadership training of the future guardians of the political state, including provisions for the regulation of marriage and procreation. All children of free men were to be removed at birth from their parents and reared by state-supported nurses, but all other adult citizens were also charged with the protection and education of all the children. Plato's major concern for the very young child was the formation of character, and he admonished the nurses to tell stories that presented only the human virtues and to ignore the ancient myths and legends that contained violence, lust, and passion. Historically, Plato is the first known writer to acknowledge the critical period of infancy. In the *Dialogues* he quotes Socrates as saying:

> The beginning is the most important part of any work, especially in the case of a young and tender thing; for that is the time at which the character is being formed and the desired impression is more readily taken. . . . Anything that he receives into his mind at that age is likely to become indelible and unalterable.

Plato's goals were twofold: (1) to train a wise ruling class, and (2) to free parents from the demands of child care so that they might actively meet their civic responsibilities. The motivating force was obviously not good child care. (We have not made much progress. When it exists at all, government interest in child care is still for the benefit of adults who need to be employed or trained for future employment.)

Plato (428–348 B.C.) concerned himself with the ideal; his recommendations were far removed from the customs of his time and were never put into practice; however, the *Republic* is the first great educational classic in historical time. Aristotle (384–322 B.C.) dealt with the real and based his guidelines for the upbringing of small children on direct observation of children and "other young animals." He recommended a regime of more milk and less wine; physical movement exercises; exposure to cold temperatures (with a view to future military service); minimal association with slaves; and censored tales and stories. Children up to the age of 7 years were to be reared at home by their mothers or nurses, under the guidance of a children's tutor who made certain that the stories told, the language used, and the games played were moral and appropriate for future citizens. Until the age of 5 there were no prescribed studies or tasks, because the necessary physical exercise would occur naturally during periods of free play. Unlike Plato's proposal, Aristotle's educational system was designed only for the male children of free citizens.

Plutarch (A.D. 46–120), although best known for *Parallel Lives,* also recommended appropriate methods of child-rearing. Like Plato, he was concerned with parenting, warning against cohabitation with courtesans and concubines, and urging the husband's abstinence from wine when he approached his wife. Mothers of newborns were advised to feed their infants and nurse them themselves. Immediately after birth, they were to manipulate the child's limbs so that they would grow straight. This advice was in direct opposition to the customs of the times, when not only the Greeks but also the Romans and the Jews wrapped their infants tightly in swaddling bands. Frequently even the infant's head was protected by a pointed, close-fitted cap that also covered the ears and the back of the neck. Swaddling is an ancient practice that has continued throughout the centuries in many parts of the world. It is simply the wrapping of the child with strips or bands of cloth, in some cases so tightly that little or no movement is possible. Swaddling as such is not practiced in the

United States, but our babies are often wrapped snugly in hospital nurseries and are "tucked in" tightly in their cribs at home. The modern Chinese swaddle their babies tightly for the first month but leave legs and feet free.

Plutarch further admonished parents to be very selective in choosing the foster mothers, nursemaids, or young slaves who would be nurses and servants or companions of young children. They were to be Greeks who were moral and distinct in their speech.

Plutarch was a firm believer in the virtues of early habit training (behavior modification!) and described the first recorded animal research study on learning. Apparently, Lycurgus took two puppies and reared them in different ways in an attempt to show the positive effects of habit training on future performance. At a gathering of the Spartan lawgivers, he demonstrated the results by putting the two dogs down in front of a dish of food and a live rabbit. One dog immediately ran after the hare; the other gobbled up the food. When the lawgivers did not understand, Lycurgus explained, "These dogs are both of the same litter, but they have received a different bringing-up, with the result that one has turned out a glutton and the other a hunter. In regard to habits and manners of life, let this suffice" (Moralia, cited in Ulich, 1954, p. 92).

The Roman Empire

While the early Greeks were concerned with lofty ideals and philosophy, the Romans were bound to the practical matters of daily living and the governing of an ever-growing number of conquered peoples of diverse cultures and races. Unlike the Greeks, the early Romans depended on the power of the home as the site of learning to honor the gods, the family, and the country. We know little beyond this, although Quintilian (A.D. 35–95) offered some very specific suggestions about the education of very young children. No doubt, the great empire fell before the suggestions were put into practice. He believed that most, if not all, children of free

men were quick to reason and ready to learn, and therefore the father should plan his son's education from the moment of birth. Once again, the custom of assigning the direct care of little children to other than the natural mother becomes apparent:

> Above all see that the child's nurse speaks correctly. . . . It is the nurse that the child first hears, and her words that he will first attempt to imitate. And we are by nature most tenacious of childish impressions. . . . It is the worst impressions that are most durable (Institute of Oratory, cited in Ulich, 1954, p. 104).

Quintilian also expressed dissatisfaction with the common practice of teaching the names and order of the letters before teaching their shapes, and suggested that young children be given sets of ivory letters to play with. After the children could recognize and differentiate the shapes, they were to be supplied with wooden boards on which the letters had been cut out so that the mistakes that occurred with wax tablets could not happen. After the child had progressed to syllables and words, he would then copy lines containing sound moral lessons, which would contribute to character formation.

Similar advice about an infant's training and education was offered in A.D. 403 by Jerome, who also recommended boxwood or ivory letters as playthings, and the letter shapes supplied so that there would be no mislearning. Jerome's concern was to nurture souls for a future world. Christianity had begun to supplant the concerns for military strength and political administration, and the names of the apostles and the patriarchs from Adam downward were to be the first learned words. A glimpse of the customs of the day is contained in the following excerpt from a letter addressed to a Roman matron who wished to raise her infant daughter as a virgin dedicated to Christ:

> Let her very dress and garb remind her to whom she is promised. Do not pierce her ears or paint her face dedicated to Christ with white lead or rouge. Do not hang gold or pearls about her neck

or load her head with jewels, or by reddening her hair make it suggest the fires of ghenna (Principal Works of St. Jerome, cited in Braun & Edwards, 1972, p. 23).

The only other indication we have of the value of very young children in these centuries, an indication much more direct than the advice and various guidelines previously referred to, is the passing of the Roman law in A.D. 318 proclaiming infanticide a criminal act. Nonetheless, infanticide continued to be practiced without much condemnation until the 18th century, and it continues today in one form or another.

The Middle Ages

The idea of childhood completely disappeared during the Middle Ages—although of course there were children! As soon as the swaddling bands were removed (at 9 to 12 months), infants were dressed just like the men or women of their social class. Because of superstition and lack of medical knowledge or hygiene, only one child of every two or three lived to adulthood, and the Church began the immediate baptism of all infants to save them from eternal damnation before they died.

The Middle Ages were indeed the Dark Ages. Europe was torn by wars and hunger, leaving little time or inclination for tenderness, individuals, or grandiose plans concerning education and child-rearing. The major contribution of the period was the safekeeping of the ancient literary works, preserved and copied by the monks in the monasteries, and it was to these writings that the noblemen of the Renaissance turned for guidance. Because Plato and Aristotle had planned education for the elite of their societies, the education of the Renaissance was directed toward the male children of noble parentage. The young male child of rank was considered precious because he promised the continuation of the family, but even he was not allowed childhood. Swaddling was discarded at 4 to 6 months of age; both girls and boys were then dressed in lace-edged petticoats, full-

skirted frocks with full real sleeves (as well as false sleeves to be used as leading strings to control the child's efforts to walk), aprons, bibs, and lace-edged bonnets. This was the mode of dress (minus the leading strings) for the remainder of a girl's life. The boys were "breeched" at age 5 or 6 years, but over the breeches wore a floor-length doublet with added false hanging sleeves. Under the doublet were a matching petticoat and decorative underpetticoats. With minor changes, this, too, became the lifetime mode of dress.

WESTERN EUROPE

Thirteenth to Eighteenth Centuries

Chivalry and royalty. Chivalry came into being near the close of the Middle Ages (A.D. 1200–1400). Knighthood was in flower and involved a new gentleness, an esteem for women and young children, and an intense interest in the childhood of Jesus, who until then had been pictured as a stern, child-sized adult with little compassion. (Neither artists nor anyone else had any interest in studying children.)

By the end of the 15th century the Christ child began to appear lifelike. By this time artists had begun to study the anatomy of children, and both body proportions and facial features became more realistic. From this religious interest in the baby Jesus evolved an interest in all young children, which unfortunately went to extremes. In many cases children became objects of amusement.

As was formerly the case, as soon as they left the infant stage, children were immediately immersed in all facets of adult life. An account of the beginning years in the life of Louis XII of France highlights this total immersion. The Dauphin was born in 1601, and the royal physician kept detailed records of his charge's activities and development. Before 17 months of age, the Dauphin played with the "usual toys": a hobbyhorse, a windmill, a top; at 17 months of age Louis could play the violin and sing at the same

Madonna and child. (GIOTTO; National Gallery of
Art, Washington; Samuel H. Kress Collection;
date: probably c. 1320/1330)

time, as well as play mall (similar to our game
of golf). By the age of 2 years, Louis started to
talk, and his tutors made him pronounce the
syllables separately. He was also taken to the
King's apartments where he danced and sang
with the adults, although he still played his child-
ish games. When he was 2 years, 7 months he
was given a doll collection; and at 2 years and
9 months, he was moved from his cradle to his
own bed. At age 3 years, 4 months, he could
dance all the adult dances and was taught to
read. At age 4, he was taught to write, and
started to learn Latin, but still played with dolls.
By age 5 or 6 he practiced archery and played
cards, chess, and countless parlour games (Aries, 1962, pp. 62–65).

Not only was young Louis a source of
amusement, but precocious as well! Few chil-

dren, of course, were heirs to thrones. For most,
childhood was brief, with even the small toddlers joining their families in weeding, planting,
and harvesting.

Comenius. These were the conditions into
which Comenius (1592–1670) was born—a
time when parents were nonsolicitous of little
ones, or so they appeared, because the fate of
the infant could just as easily be death as life,
and one could not allow oneself to become too
emotionally attached. Comenius dared to suggest that not only was there an identifiable stage
of growth from infancy until 6 years of age, but
also that there was an appropriate educational
curriculum for this stage. Such a startling proposal was too revolutionary and too removed
from everyday life to be accepted during his lifetime. However, some 300 years later he was
acclaimed as the father of early childhood education, at least by his native Czechoslovakia.
Today his recommendations for teaching very
young children are put into practice in home
intervention programs, day-care centers, nursery schools, and kindergartens in Western Europe and the United States. Comenius proposed
an educational ladder, beginning with a school
"at the mother's knee," not an actual school,
but one that should exist in every household. He
even outlined a detailed curriculum for mothers,
including the training of the senses, rudimentary
facts, and vocabulary development.

We especially remember Comenius for his
introduction of the picture book as the more appropriate way of helping children learn (as opposed to pages of print). The picture book is
now a mainstay in all programs for young children. Comenius was the first advocate for very
early education since the times of Plato and Aristotle. Unlike them, he recommended that education include both boys and girls from all socioeconomic classes, starting at birth.

Locke. John Locke (1632–1704), a contemporary of Comenius, was concerned with the
education of upper-class boys. Locke's view of

the newborn's mind as an empty slate, a blank sheet of paper, led him to the conclusion that very early experiences made impressions of lasting importance. Unfortunately, he considered mothers too soft with their children, and recommended a tutor from the earliest months. Locke, although unmarried and childless, was colonial America's favorite philosopher. He counseled,

> Would you have your son obedient to you, when past a child? Be sure then to establish the authority of a father, as soon as he is capable of submission, and can understand in whose power he is. If you would have him stand in awe of you, imprint it in his infancy (Bremner, 1970, p. 132).

Locke described a baby of his time as:

> rolled and swathed, ten or a dozen times round; then blanket upon blanket, mantle upon that; its little neck pinned down to one posture; its head more than it frequently needs, triple-crowned like a young page, with covering upon covering; its legs and arms as if to prevent that kindly stretching which we rather ought to promote . . . the former bundled up, the latter pinned down; and how the poor thing lies on the nurses lap, a miserable little pinioned captive (Cunnington & Buck, 1965, p. 103).

Although historians call this period the Renaissance, the reawakening of scientific thought and mathematical and astronomical knowledge included no consideration whatsoever of child development. At the end of the 1600s, early childhood was an almost nonexistent stage of life, and the voices of Comenius and Locke were not even heard, let alone heeded. The young child was considered either innately bad or morally asleep. Comenius totally rejected the idea of innate badness and attributed morality to education and firm (not harsh) discipline; Locke maintained that the infant was born with no predisposition toward anything.

Eighteenth and Nineteenth Centuries

It is essential to keep in mind the great differences between the writings and recommendations about child-rearing in any period of history and the harsh realities of the times. During the first half of the 18th century one out of every three infants was abandoned, and the infant mortality rate in the foundling homes reached as high as 80%.

Rousseau. In the 18th century an idea was reintroduced that toppled the European world . . . and is still creating reverberations. First hinted at in early Greece and Rome then set forth in Locke's writings in the 17th century, it appeared full bloom in Rousseau's *Social Contract,* first published in 1762. The idea? The people are more important than their rulers.

We in early childhood education owe our appreciation also for other startling ideas expressed by Rousseau in *Emile or Treatise on Education* (1892):

> Everything is good as it comes from the hands of the Author of Nature. . . . Our instruction begins when we begin to live; our education begins with our birth. . . . Should not the education of a child begin before he speaks and understands (pp. 1, 9, 27)?

The very young child has at last appeared, and is naturally good, no longer tainted by original sin. The child no longer requires punishment to be rid of the evil one, but rather is good, at least until society and education introduce their artificial ways. Both the *Social Contract* and *Emile or Treatise on Education* had a tremendous impact. The French Revolution erupted the year after Rousseau died; harsh discipline has virtually disappeared from the schools of the world.

Rousseau dignified the first 5 years of life as a recognizable and important stage of development, proclaiming that children should be treated as children, not as irrational animals or miniature adults. He argued that children had their own ways of seeing, thinking, and feeling, and that their appropriate education was natural growth in a natural environment. His ideas constituted the beginnings of child study as a discipline and incorporated the concept of the young child as an active, searching organism who learned through play and living, with minimal interference from adults. Perhaps most important is Rousseau's fundamental concept, developed partially by Comenius, that childhood is a time important in and of itself, during which childlike behavior is appropriate.

Fortunately for the children, Rousseau advocated breast-feeding by the natural mother, fresh air, and loose clothing. As the result of his writings many mothers discarded the swaddling bands and nursed their infants instead of immediately sending them to a wet nurse. Even the paintings of this period depict the ideal nature of the child.

Pestalozzi. This concept was further reinforced by Pestalozzi (1746–1827). Not only did he agree with the natural unfolding of childhood, but also he reemphasized the role of the home and the "mother's knee" in the early education of the child. According to Pestalozzi, if education in the schools was to have real value,

Hobby horse. (Kindercampus, Iowa City; Date: c. 1990)

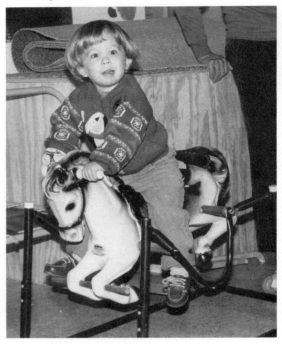

The Hobby Horse. (AMERICAN; National Gallery of Art, Washington; Gift of Edgar Williams and Bernice Chrysler Garbisch; Date: c. 1840)

it should imitate the methods in the home. In *How Gertrude Teaches Her Children* (1801/ 1898) he outlined his educational premise: sense impressions lead to awareness, and awareness forms the foundations of language and academic skills. He stated that

> very great harm is done to the child by taking it away from home too soon and submitting it to artificial school methods. The time is drawing near when methods of teaching will be so simplified that each mother will be able not only to teach her children without help, but continue her own education at the same time (Braun & Edwards, 1972, p. 56).

Within a span of only 40 years we not only have the young child as an identifiable, whole human being, but we also have the blueprint for modern early childhood education and for the home-based education of very young children. The educational innovations of Comenius,

Rousseau, and Pestalozzi made the child interesting as a focus for educational attention, but scientific study of the child itself was necessary in order to formulate a theory of child development based on empirical analysis. We owe the introduction of the child as subject for such study to Darwin's *On the Origin of the Species* (1859). Almost all of American child psychology is derived from the comparative studies of Darwin, whose observations of the infant and child led him to his theory of the descent of man. Darwinian theories are biological. Some 50 years later Sigmund Freud introduced the notion that stages of development are sequential and occur in a biologically predetermined order.

Froebel.   However, prior to Darwin and Freud, Froebel had pulled together the previous thinking and added some of his own in his major work published in 1826 (*The Education of Man: The Art of Education, Instruction, and Training*), which he put into practice in his kindergarten in 1837. His first school was attended by some 50 children who ranged in age from 1 to 7 years. (Even today in Europe "kindergarten" designates group education for children from 3 to 6 or 7 years of age, unlike our own adaptation for 5 year olds only.) The first volume of the *Education of Man* gives specific information about the very early years:

> Disregard about the value of earlier, and particularly the earliest, stages of development with reference to later ones, prepares for the future teacher and educator of the boy difficulties which it will be scarcely possible to overcome. . . . The child, the boy, man, indeed, should know no other endeavor but to be at every stage of development wholly what this stage calls for (pp. 29–30). . . . From a very early period . . . children should never be left too long to themselves on beds or in cradles without some external object to occupy them. . . . It is advisable to suspend in a line with the child's natural vision, a swinging cage with a lively bird. This secures occupation for the sense, and the mind, profitable in many directions (p. 49). . . . Even very small children, in moments of quiet, and particularly

when going to sleep, will hum little strains of songs they have heard; this, too, . . . should be heeded and developed even more in melody and song. Undoubtedly this will soon lead in children to a self-activity similar to that attained in speech, and children whose faculty of speech has been thus developed and trained, find, seemingly without effort, the words for new ideas, peculiar associations and relations among newly discovered qualities (p. 71). . . . Let us live with our children; then shall we begin to grow wise, to be wise. . . . Living with our children implies on our part sympathy with childhood, adaptability to children, and knowledge and appreciation of child-nature; it implies genuine interest in all that interests them, . . . it implies seeing ourselves with the eyes of a child, hearing ourselves with the ears of a child, judging ourselves with the keen intuition of a child (p. 89).

Pat-a-cake, in S. E. Blow (1895). (*The songs and music of Friedrich Froebel's Mother Play.* New York: D. Appleton, p. 35)

Froebel added to the growing number of books for mothers: *Mother-Play and Nursery Songs* is the source of many of the finger plays, action songs, and stories used in early childhood classes throughout the world. Also, many of the toys and manipulatives used by young children today are closely related to the wooden building blocks and different colored balls of yarn that he devised as playthings. (Froebel advised teachers to wash the yarn balls at least once a year!) To Froebel, also, we owe the introduction of women, instead of men, as teachers of young children.

Apparently Froebel's philosophy had few immediate followers in the educational system of the late 1890s. A female principal of a New York City school was evaluated in 1893 as excellent for her 25 years of service. She believed that

> what the child knows and is able to do on coming to school should be entirely disregarded, that he should not be allowed to waste time, either in thinking or in finding his own words to express his thoughts, but that he should be supplied with ready-made thoughts as given in a ready-made vocabulary (Rice, cited in Braun & Edwards, 1972, p. 97).

This happy thought leads us to the United States.

THE UNITED STATES

Eighteenth Century

Puritanism. From the earliest colonial days to the 20th century young children were taught the alphabet and the rudiments of reading and writing in the home. Childhood, as a unique part of human life, had no advocate and no protection against the railings of religious leaders such as Jonathan Edwards, who wrote in 1740:

> All are by nature the children of wrath, and heirs of hell. . . . As innocent as children seem to be to us, [yet they] are young vipers, and are infinitely more hateful than vipers, and are in a most miserable condition . . . and they are naturally

very senseless and stupid, being born as the wild asses colt, and need much to awaken them (Bremner, 1970, p. 139).

Such a violent opinion of very young children had definite overtones for early child-rearing. In addition, the prevailing belief that original sin caused illness delayed serious attempts at the prevention and treatment of both childhood and adult maladies. The most important medical advance in the early 19th century was the smallpox vaccination. It was not until 1880 that the American Medical Association established its pediatric section. In 1881 silver nitrate prophylaxis was placed in the eyes of the newborn for the first time as a blindness preventative.

Fortunately, not all early Americans agreed with Jonathan Edwards. We have been told that "one of the most precious flowers of Puritanism" was a girl born in 1708 in Boston. At the age of 2 she knew her letters, spoke distinctly, and told many stories from the Scriptures. At age 3 she recited the catechism and many psalms, and read "distinctly"; at age 4 she "asked many astonishing questions about divine mysteries. As her father was president of Harvard College, it may be inferred she had an extended reading course" (Glubok, 1969, p. 112).

Nineteenth Century

Children as economic assets. Until the beginning of this century young children of affluent white parents were treasured and educated. Other young children were valued also, but as economic assets to their families or owners. Adam Smith reported on child power as the nation's wealth:

> A numerous family of children, instead of being a burden, is a source of opulence and prosperity to the parents. . . . A young widow, with four or five young children, who, among the middling or inferior ranks of people in Europe would have so little chance for a second husband, is there [North America] frequently counted as a sort of fortune. The value of children is the greatest of

all encouragement to marriage (Bremner, 1970, pp. 169–170).

In the South, slave children were economic assets. They were legally equated with the off-spring of tame and domestic animals, and as objects of property; they were administered by the owner.

Children of the "savages". What about the children of the "savages" of America? A Belgian Jesuit missionary described the child-rearing practices of Plains Indians in a letter to his niece written in 1851. In the mid-1800s the only "school" for the Indian children was the example of their elders. The father had charge of the boys; the girls were the mother's responsibility. These native Americans paid great attention to the children's physical development, and plunged the newborn several times into water to build up the child's resistance, regardless of the season of the year. Someone other than the mother cared for the baby for the first week. When the child was returned home, she was fastened securely onto a cradle-board, which was used until she was able to walk. The cradle was hung inside the lodge or outside on the branch of a tree, close by the other family members. When the family traveled, the baby went right along in the cradle hung from the saddle-bow, out of the rider's way but with no danger (Bremner, 1970). It might appear that "savage" child-rearing was more humane than that espoused by Jonathan Edwards.

The dame schools. Not all "nonsavage" mothers in the 18th and 19th centuries had the time or inclination to rear and teach their young children. Many sent their infants and toddlers to a neighbor, usually a poor widow or dame, for their "day care." The "dame schools" thrived in New England, where their quality was as varied as the widows or dames who ran them. Lucy Larcom (1889) was one of the more fortunate children; she described her dame school as follows:

Aunt Hannah used her kitchen or her sitting room for a schoolroom, as best suited her convenience. We were delighted observers of her culinary operations and other employments. If a baby's head nodded, a little bed was made for it on a soft comforter in the corner, where it had its nap hour undisturbed. But this did not often happen; there were so many interesting things going on that we seldom became sleepy. Aunt Hannah was very kind and motherly, but she kept us in fear of her ferule, which indicated to us a possibility of smarting palms. The ferule was shaped much like the stick with which she stirred her hasty pudding for dinner,—I thought it was the same,—and I found myself caught in a whirlwind of family laughter by reporting at home that 'Aunt Hannah punished the scholars with a pudding-stick'. There was one colored boy in school, who did not sit on a bench like the rest, but on a block of wood that looked like a backlog turned endwise. Aunt Hannah often called him a 'block-head', and I supposed it was because he sat on that block. Sometimes, in his absence, a boy was made to sit in his place for punishment for being a 'blockhead' too, as I imagined. I hoped I should never be put there. Stupid little girls received a different treatment,—an occasional rap on the head with the teacher's thimble; accompanied with a half-whispered, impatient ejaculation, which sounded very much like "Numskull!" . . . I began to go to school when I was about two years old. . . . But I learned my letters in a few days, standing at Aunt Hannah's knee, while she pointed them out in the spelling-book with a pin, skipping over the 'a b abs' into words of one and two syllables, thence taking a flying leap into the New Testament, in which there is concurrent family testimony that I was reading at the age of two and a half years (pp. 42–44).

Apparently young future kings had no corner on precocity.

During the 19th century, many manuals on the proper methods of child-rearing appeared, and the stage of early childhood was firmly acknowledged in the New World. Another change of importance: judges began to override the traditional rights of fathers in custody cases, placing the welfare of the child as top priority. At that

Baby in Wicker Basket. (Joseph Whiting STOCK;
National Gallery of Art, Washington; Gift of Edgar
William and Bernice Chrysler Garbisch; Date:
c. 1840)

time it was universally assumed that a child's
future welfare depended on a mother's care.

How far have we progressed in the recognition of the importance of the early years? With
due appreciation for the thoughts and writings
of theorists and educators from England,
France, Switzerland, Czechoslovakia, and Ger-
many, we have accorded the young child status
as a subject for scientific inquiry and the early
childhood period as a stage in human development with age-specific behaviors and needs.
At the beginning of the 20th century, the American debt to Europe was considerable.

Twentieth Century

During the 20th century the United States has
faced disastrous wars, periods of depression and
inflation, baby booms, and zero population
growth. We have also accumulated a diverse

collection of social welfare and health programs,
which contain minimal focus on the very young
child per se. The longest-lived democratic experiment is still suffering from growing pains,
but one of the positive facets of the experiment
is our growing acknowledgment of the significance of the very early years of human life.

Child studies. Changes in all aspects of child
study were discernible by 1910. The first revolutionary factor was the measurement of intelligence and the assessment of human variability.
Galton was convinced that the major differences
in babies were hereditary, but Binet maintained
that the intelligence of children (that is, their capacity to learn) could be increased by stimulation. His original scale contained 55 tests arranged according to the year in which the
majority of normal children acquired each skill
or ability. According to his findings, most children by the age of 3 years could (1) point to
facial features; (2) repeat two digits; (3) enu-
merate objects in a picture; (4) give their last
name; and (5) repeat a sentence of six syllables.

In the 1920s and 1930s the issue of infant
and young child development was being debated, but only in the halls of academia. At Yale,
Dr. Arnold Gesell maintained that environment
had very little effect; it was the child's individual
biological characteristics that made the difference. Gesell (1923, 1940) did some extremely
important foundation work on the sequential development of young children. He produced a set
of developmental schedules that have been in
widespread use ever since. The Bayley Test of
Infant Development, the Cattell Test, and the
Denver Developmental Test are based on the
work of Gesell.

At Clark University during the Gesell period, John Watson emphasized the exclusive importance of the environment on the development of children. He believed in rigid training in
habits, and claimed that he could turn any child
into a thief, a fireman, a scholar, or an administrator by manipulating the child's environment. He advised parents not to hug or kiss or

Baby in crib. (Kindercampus,
Iowa City; Date: c. 1990)

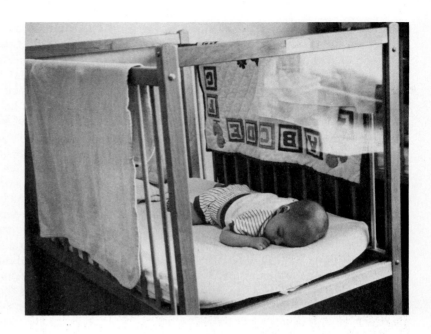

cuddle their infants, and to establish the habit of feeding at prescribed times, rather than on demand. The result was many frustrated babies and many distressed parents who had to endure listening to their babies cry (Watson & Watson, 1928). His theories are completely opposed to our current theories, which emphasize the building of a trusting relationship between caregiver and child.

At the same time, Skeels and his colleagues at the University of Iowa were working in an overcrowded orphanage where they discovered two little girls (aged 13 and 16 months old chronologically) who showed considerable retardation. It was decided that the girls should be moved to a less crowded institution, since "nothing" could be done for them. They were moved into a home for "feebleminded" adolescent girls and older women. A few months later, Skeels returned to the home for the feebleminded and found two bright, alert little girls, not at all mentally retarded as they had seemed months before. They even tested in the normal range of intelligence. What had happened? The toddlers had been "adopted" by the older girls

on the ward, who rocked them, played with them, and talked to them; in other words, they showered them with attention and stimulation. As a result, Skeels then purposely transferred an experimental group of 13 orphanage children, all under 3 years of age, and all considered "unsuited for adoption" (the current term is *mentally retarded* or *disabled*), to the same institution for older girls and women. The 10 girls and 3 boys had no gross physical handicaps, but their mental development was seriously retarded. One or two children were placed in each ward, and again the women and ward attendants became attached to "their" children, and gave them almost constant attention and encouragement. This personal interest was the unique feature of the experimental setting. The 13 children were observed until they were 4½ years of age; final tests of mental development showed an IQ score change from +7 to +58 points; none had failed to show some gain. In the contrast group still in the orphanage only one child had any gain in IQ points (+2); negative change ranged from -8 to -45 points. But the best was yet to come. Skeels conducted a follow-up study some 30 years later; his findings are summarized in Table 1–1. The contrast in outcomes highlights the first significant indication of the effect of very early environmental experience. What happens before the age of 3 can make a difference!

Unfortunately, the original study received much criticism. Critics claimed that the study was not well done, that tests were not given correctly, and that the statistical analysis was wrong. Such criticisms were not justified. The academic world apparently was not yet ready to accept new ways of thinking about the early years, early experiences, and the nature of intelligence.

During World War II the whole issue of the importance of the early years received little attention, but in the late 1940s and into the 1950s, researchers began to discover that the infant had a number of capabilities that could be studied. It was learned that very young infants could discriminate among visual stimuli, visually track a slowly moving object, and react to tactile experiences. Infants were found to listen to a soft rattle or a caregiver's voice, and to have different reactions to female and male voices. As a result, it was conjectured that the infant constantly received and reacted to stimuli, and with

Table 1–1
Adult Status of Skeels' Subjects

Experimental (N = 13)	Contrast (N = 12)
All reached adulthood, 11 in adoptive homes.	One subject died in the institution. None had been adopted.
All were self-supportive; none showed need for psychiatric or economic support	Four were without occupation; others worked as dishwashers, part-time food service helpers; one as a typesetter.
Mean grade completed: 12.0	Median grade completed: 2.75

each stimulus reaction, the infant's brain stored experience for future learning.

More studies followed in the next two decades, all of which added to the documentation of the significance of the very early months and years of life. It has been conjectured by some researchers that foundations of behavior, personality, and cognitive structures are established by the age of 3 years, and that these basic structures regulate the child's current and future views of himself and of his encounters with the world. If the child has been discouraged from exploration or deprived of consistent care and affection during the first 3 years, he or she apparently constructs a defensive shield against the world that is difficult to penetrate. This protective mechanism does not seem to form if the young child has engaged in consistent reciprocal human relationships. Therefore the maturational view of development has been revised because it does not include reciprocal relationships; the "blank slate" view has been replaced, because it ignores the child's own predispositions and readinesses for relationships and interactions.

The findings of these more recent researchers might have remained in the psychological journals had not two major publications appeared in the 1960s. Hunt (1961) conclusively ended the contention that the development of intelligence was predetermined by genes and therefore fixed. He suggested that the environmental encounters that children have are especially important during the early years of development. In 1964 Bloom reported his analysis of over 1,000 longitudinal studies of the development of human characteristics. He did *not* conclude, as is the oft-quoted statement, that a child develops 50% of his or her intelligence by age 4. What he did conclude was that in terms of intelligence measured with a standardized instrument at age 17, about 50% of that development had taken place by age 4. That distinction is very important.

Numerous studies have shown a consistent finding of no relationship between socioeconomic status and IQ test scores at 15 months, and significant correlations between socioeconomic status and IQ test scores by 3 years of age. Kagan (1971) has reported on discernible differences in patterns of attention and reaction to visual and auditory stimuli as early as 8 months of age. White and Watts (1973) classified 1 and 2 year olds as "competent" or "not competent," using a list of psychological characteristics. They followed the development of the two groups of children, and their original classification proved accurate at the end of a year. Teachers of 3- and 4-year-old children from less advantaged backgrounds have become increasingly aware that many of these children have already suffered a decrease in both motivation to learn and expectations for success, apparently never to be regained. One of the oft-cited reasons for the mixed success of the federally funded compensatory programs is that probably they did not start soon enough. Newspapers recently reported a study of Israeli nursery school children indicating that even the most intense educational effort starting at age 3 failed to achieve effective integration of the disadvantaged children with their peers, intellectually or socially. The results of the study indicate that deprivation has measurable effects during the first 3 years of life.

Pioneer programs. In the United States, programs for very young children first received the attention of professional educators in the 1920s. Harriet Johnson described her all-day program for toddlers (14 months and older) in *Children in the Nursery School* (1928/1972), and in *School Begins at Two* (1936). Two year olds again appeared in the literature in Woodcock's *Life and Ways of the Two-Year-Old* (1941). A beautiful example of a comprehensive child-care program operated during the World War II years at the Kaiser Child Service Centers. It served older children as well as infants and toddlers, and contained many special innovative features, which should be included in our center-based programs today (Stolz, 1978).

The work of Bettye Caldwell and Julius Richmond in the Children's Center at Syracuse University, starting in 1968, initiated our present positive position regarding infant-toddler care and education by contradicting the conventional wisdom that would not even consider other than in-home care by the biological or surrogate mother. Mary Elizabeth Keister operated a demonstration center for the daytime care of infants and toddlers at the University of North Carolina at Greensboro, and described her program in *"The Good Life" for Infants and Toddlers* (1970). Willis and Ricciuti at Cornell University, New York, followed soon after with *A Good Beginning for Babies* (1975), which describes their 3-year program.

Up until the early 1970s, the emphasis was on the child, although the federally sponsored model programs all included parents to some degree. The prevalent assumptions about parents were (1) an infant program was essentially a child-care program to provide opportunities for mothers to engage in activities other than child-rearing, or (2) child-rearing was too important to be left to parents alone. Just as Caldwell and Richmond (1968a) blazed a trail by offering evidence that quality infant-toddler child care did not necessarily disturb the mother-child attachment, others began programs in which the emphasis was either on the parent(s), or shared by parent(s) and child. These include Gordon's Parent Education Program, Karnes's Home Intervention Program, the Family Development Research Program by Lally and Honig, Levenstein's Mother-Child Program, and Schaefer's Infant Education Research Project. These are described in many government documents (all received federal funds), and accounts of each are included in *The Preschool in Action* by Day and Parker (1977), copies of which are in most college or university libraries. The major result of these programs was the professional acceptance of the concept that parent education and significant involvement are essential to the quality and effectiveness of any infant-toddler program. Most if not all of these programs are no longer in existence because of new priorities for federal funds, but they each serve as models for exemplary practices.

The new priority is early intervention in the lives of young handicapped children from birth to 5 years of age. Because of the increase in federal funding, it is anticipated that all states will be serving all the eligible children aged 3 to 5 by fiscal year 1991 at the latest. It is hoped, because of the government's incentive plan, that many states will also "develop and implement a statewide, comprehensive, coordinated, multidisciplinary interagency program of early intervention services for handicapped infants and toddlers and their families" (P.L. 99–457, Part H, cited in Berman & Szanton, 1989, p. 89). Covered in the proposed plan are infants and toddlers who are experiencing developmental delays, or who have a diagnosed physical or mental condition that could result in a developmental delay, or who are at risk for having substantial delays. (Silverstein, 1989). Although the provision of such services is at the discretion of each state, it is probable that programs for nonhandicapped infants and toddlers will be asked to mainstream one or more children in the days to come. Safford (1989) suggests that one to four handicapped infants and toddlers may be satisfactorily included in a group of 8 to 12 children.

The full text of Part H of the Public Law 99–457 is contained in appendix A. The law was enacted in October 1986 and by September 1989 all fifty states were involved in the Part H program.

This review would not be complete without mention of the Kramer Project in Little Rock, Arkansas (Caldwell & Rorex, 1977; Elardo & Caldwell, 1974). The Project put into practice Caldwell's convictions about a truly developmental approach to the care and education of children from 6 months of age through their elementary school years. Not only were the baby, toddler, and preschool classes held in the public school facility, but there were many multi-age activities for children from 6 months to 12 years

during, before, and after the regular school day. The program for the young children was not a watered-down version of kindergarten or preschool, but moved forward from birth. This, too, was a trailblazer, but few school districts have followed in Caldwell's footsteps. Even today we are debating the advisability of a 4-year-old prekindergarten, and only a very few schools even consider an infant-toddler program. The typical school infant-toddler program provides child care for the children of teenage mothers so the mothers may complete their high school education.

The last two programs worthy of mention are not child-care programs per se, but indicate changing societal views. The Parents as Teachers project, (Meyerhoff & White, 1986; White, 1988b; Zigler, 1988), offered in every school district in Missouri, and the RIE (Resources for Infant Educarers) project in California (Gerber, 1981) are both designed to help parents of children from birth to 3 years of age give their children the best possible start in life.

Today and tomorrow. There are still questions, but there are many answers about the infant-toddler care and education practices that contribute to quality programs. There has been a substantial increase in the number of centers and day-care homes that serve very young children, but there has been more than a substantial increase in the numbers of families who desperately need child-care alternatives.

Have policymakers taken heed of both the research findings about quality and the critical needs of young families? Although we have been described as a child-centered society, our actions do not match our words. We are making a slow recovery from the 1971 veto of child-care legislation, and the withdrawal of federal responsibility for child-care standards in the early 1980s. Our recovery needs to move more swiftly. Reports of the Children's Defense Fund note national trends toward (1) the feminization of poverty; (2) the rise in the number of teen parents; (3) the surge in the number of mothers of young children in the workforce; and (4) the increasing challenge for low-income families to attain economic self-sufficiency. Political and public opinion will determine the continuation or the reversal of these trends. Each one of them highlights our critical need for child care. The countries in Western Europe have long recognized the need, and most of them provide support in the form of parental leaves and/or networks of child-care centers and family homes.

The last item in this brief review of the current state of affairs is a new conception of the term *care*. Both psychologists and educators have reinforced the notion that children, even from birth, are learning from every experience and every environment, whether planned or incidental. Therefore, *education* is an integral part of child *care*. This is especially true in the case of infants and toddlers, whose curricula take place primarily during the routines of caregiving. In our country, both Bettye Caldwell and Magda Gerber use the word *educarer* to describe the person involved in the care and accompanying education of young children. In South Africa, the Grassroots *Educare* Trust is delivering care and education to the children and their families under the sponsorship of the Bernard van Leer Foundation. The term is gradually being accepted, as more persons come to believe that you can't deliver care without teaching, and you can't teach very young children without providing care. The emphasis of this book is the essential coordination of care and education for infants and toddlers.

GOALS AND OBJECTIVES

Approaches to Goal Setting

Eighty years ago the question of goals for infants and toddlers in group settings would not have been asked. Of course many children were being cared for by persons other than their parents, but the issue was not given attention by society as a whole. Forty years ago the classic Bowlby report *Maternal Care and Mental Health* (1951)

introduced the ideas of maternal deprivation, early emotional frustration, multiple mothering, and the negative effects of the institutionalization of very young children. The impact of this publication was reinforced by a second World Health Organization report, *Deprivation of Maternal Care: A Reassessment of Its Effects* (1962), in which it was stated that the effects of multiple nonindividualized caregiving in an institution without a primary caregiver would be quite different from the effects of multiple caregiving that was supplemental to the usual upbringing by the child's parent(s) in the home. This report also noted that truly individualized caregiving during day care would be more likely to foster attachments than multiple caregiving. A careful reading of both reports leads us to the young child's need for dependable love, and the conclusion that even though day care means regular separation from the mother, it does not mean maternal separation. The concept of *primary caregiver*, introduced in 1962, is a major requirement in quality programs today. Even 20 years ago, the daytime care of infants and toddlers outside the home by a nonrelative existed, but was still not acknowledged in public policy. Family day-care homes were invisible; just the woman down the block who cared for kids.

Today child care is no longer a cottage industry, and no longer exclusively a social welfare concern. It is a recognized profession that is attempting to meet a recognized need. The major delivery systems are family day-care homes and center-based programs. Regardless of the location or the number of children and families served, the first step in the delivery of a quality program is the agreement on the goals and objectives for the program.

Until very recently, out-of-home care was custodial, and the provider was frequently described as a baby-sitter. Even today there are persons who still believe that infants need no more than food, rest, and a little rocking and cuddling. When the baby starts to toddle, just remove the breakables and let her go. And when the adult has had enough, plop the baby into the crib or playpen. This is not an exaggeration—in 1986 over half the licensed centers were not required to state their philosophy or goals, and only two states required such a statement from family day-care providers (Morgan, 1987, Table 6).

Today we have an abundance of information about children's needs and characteristics, about the importance of the early years, and about the disastrous effects of custodial care. Today there is no excuse for having care and protection as the *primary* goals for out-of-home services for children.

Whatever child development information has been offered to parents of very young children is equally appropriate for teachers and caregivers of young children. Child-rearing advice is equally applicable to parents and to teachers/caregivers. However, some modifications are necessitated by the logistics of having more children and more adults in child-care centers. Centers may be homelike, but they are not home.

It is hoped that parents and teachers of very young children agree on the goals and objectives for their children. We all have glibly verbalized "the growth and development of the total child" as a goal many times, but have recognized and acted on the phrase's total meaning in too few instances. The very nature of the goal is too global to enable us to plan the specific encounters of specific children that will encourage and enhance the growth and development of the total child in a group situation.

Goals for the care and education of very young children may be expressed in global terms or in varying degrees of specificity. They may come from various points of reference: universal goals, as in the *United Nation's Convention on the Rights of the Child;* goals of parents as a total group; and goals determined by the characteristics and needs of the children. Goals are also stated in terms of the hoped-for accomplishments of the centers themselves, which go beyond the confines of the daily program and setting for the children.

Universal Goals

Goals for authoritarian societies have been stated in simple, direct terms: "the new Soviet man" (the Soviet Union) or "a good party member" (People's Republic of China). Definitions of these terms are relatively straightforward, and therefore it is relatively easy to plan and program the care and education of their children. However, universal success in meeting these goals is open to question. It is considerably more complex to plan child care and education in democratic societies because of emphasis on the individual and respect for cultural pluralism. In spite of societal and cultural differences, however, there seem to be universal goals of parents for their children regardless of their geopolitical location or culture.

1. The physical survival and health of the child. . . .
2. The development of the child's behavioral capacity for economic self-maintenance in maturity.
3. The development of the child's behavioral capacities for maximizing other cultural values—e.g., morality, prestige, wealth, religious piety, intellectual achievement, personal satisfaction, self-realization—as formulated and symbolically elaborated in culturally distinctive beliefs, norms, and ideologies (Levine, 1974, p. 56).

Can these be helpful in formulating goals for infant-toddler care and education? Certainly there is no disagreement with the goal for the physical survival and health of the children, nor should there be disagreement about the development of the child's behavioral capacities for economic self-maintenance or for the other cultural values. The foundations of achieving all these goals are laid in the first few years of life: attitudes toward exploring, questioning, and learning; expectations of success or failure; and defense mechanisms for physical or psychological abuse. These universal goals contain some indication of our responsibilities toward young children, but again they are too global for specific planning.

Goals to Meet Children's Needs

Although professional persons and children's centers express their goals and objectives in different words and with different emphases, they all speak to at least some of the needs of the young child. A quality center attempts to meet all of them. A custodial center stops at meeting the physical needs—care and protection—reminiscent of the institutional environments of former years, which are still being referred to in arguments against infant-toddler day care. In the 1973 edition of *The Infants We Care For,* goals for the first two years of life were identified as the development of a healthy body, an active mind, and wholesome feelings (Dittmann, 1984).

Ira Gordon (1975) addressed the issue of goals for very young children by stating,

> Homes or institutions must not only meet physical needs, but also attend to intellectual needs through stimulation, reasoning, rewards for attainment, direct face-to-face language interaction, and to emotional needs through a single, consistent mothering one who is affectionate and responsive, and sees the child as a unique individual (p. 45).

The needs of children that must be met to reach the goal of growth and development of the total child might be stated as follows. All children need

1. An environment that is
   a. physically safe, clean, and healthful (including nutritious food)
   b. emotionally warm and supportive; trust-supporting
   c. comfortable and functional
   d. rich in sensorimotor and social experiences
   e. available for extensive exploration, manipulation, and discovery of objects
   f. available for social relationships with adults and other children
   g. consistent and predictable
2. Primary (or significant) attachment(s) to one or a few loving adults who
   a. respect uniqueness in temperament, state, and developmental stage
   b. meet dependency needs, both social and physical, as well as encourage increasing independence
   c. frequently initiate physical, social, and verbal contacts with the child
   d. respond to and reinforce the child's physical, social, and verbal behavior most of the time (always would be ideal)
   e. "program" experiences, interactions, and materials appropriate to children's individual current levels of functioning
   f. are consistent and predictable
3. Stimulation that is
   a. self-initiated
   b. other-initiated
   c. object- or environment-initiated
4. Self-determined cycles of activity, rest, and relaxation
5. A sense of trust and security, leading to a sense of autonomy, effectiveness, and competence
6. Freedom and opportunity to develop at one's own pace, accompanied by adult and environmental support and guidance toward self-control, responsibility, and mastery

These are innate needs of all young children, whether in or out of a group setting. Living in a group imposes additional ones:

7. Learning to live happily away from the family group and home setting for part of the day
8. Learning to modify personal needs or desires, or at least delay their gratification, upon occasion

9. Learning to establish and enjoy personal relationships with nonfamily members

Developmental Goals

Honig (1976) lists the following developmental tasks for children in their very first years: increasing the variety and sophistication of prehension skills; intercoordinating information received; developing the concept of object permanence; increasing the degree of intentionality and the understanding of causal relationships; learning to imitate; improving cognitive skills involving classification, polar concepts, and seriation; learning language; developing large muscle skills; learning ever finer sensory discriminations and skills; and internalizing first a sense of trust, then a sense of autonomy and initiative.

Huntington, Provence, and Parker (1973) summarize the developmental goals of a child from birth to 3 years in the following manner:

1. Gaining increasing control of his body systems; development of regulatory physiologic mechanisms; gross and fine motor development and coordination.

2. Increasing awareness of self as a separate identity; a sense of self involving who and what he is.

3. A sense of effectiveness and competence; a sense of controlling his destiny at least to a limited extent—the opposite of powerlessness and sense that no matter what he does it makes no difference.

4. The ability to communicate needs, wants, feelings and ideas; the use of verbal and non-verbal methods of communication; the development of a sense of being understood.

5. The ability to take initiative, to be curious and exploratory, the ability to act.

6. To have hope and faith and a belief that the world is, by and large, a good place.

7. The ability to trust others and be trustworthy; to develop a sense of responsibility.

8. The ability to give and receive from other people; to be appropriately dependent and appropriately independent; to cooperate with others and to respect others.

9. The ability to be flexible and open to new ideas, new feelings and new people.

10. The ability to think, to remember, to order, to perceive, to categorize, to learn, to be creative in intellectual processes, to attend, to observe, to inspect and investigate, to reflect.

11. The development of skills, and techniques for gaining skills.

12. To be motivated to broaden knowledge of self, others, the inanimate world and the world of ideas; to explore and to discover.

13. The ability to control impulses when appropriate or to express them when appropriate; to be able to affirm and to negate; to exclude, to postpone; to hold on and let go; to follow rules and to believe in their importance (p. 16).

Admittedly, these are expressed in more or less global terms, but they are a direct reflection of the body of knowledge known as *child development*.

Another approach to goals or objectives is to use children's feelings and attitudes as the frame of reference. The goals listed in Figure 1–1 were written from this perspective.

Goals to Meet Societal Needs

When we think in terms of what children need to learn, instead of what children need, we introduce an element of society- and culture-related values, expectations, and realities.

Harriet Johnson pioneered group day care and education for very young children. Her report of the Nursery School in New York City describes the very beginnings of the developmental-interaction approach to early childhood education for which Bank Street College and Barbara Biber are now well known. The written report contains no goals per se; however, John-

Figure 1–1

Goals for Young Children in a Group Setting

A. Positive feelings about self
  1. I *am*.
  2. I *can*.
B. Positive feelings about others
  1. About adults
    a. They love me.
    b. They enjoy me.
    c. They take care of me when I need care.
    d. They help me when I need help, but they also encourage me to do things by and for myself.
    e. I like "big people."
  2. About other children
    1. I like to be near or with them.
    2. They like to be near or with me.
C. Positive feelings about the world
  1. The world is full of interesting things to see, hear, touch, and find out about.
  2. The world is full of interesting people to see, hear, touch, and find out about.
  3. I can learn about the world and the things and people in it.

son did offer various children's accomplishments at the end of the experiment, which have been reworded into the goals listed below. They are both far-sighted and near-sighted. They reflect the view toward child development that prevailed in the early decades of the 20th century, and therefore do not give sufficient emphasis to cognitive or intellectual abilities. Nevertheless, they are of value in this review, as well as being historically important. The implied goals are the following:

1. To learn to live happily away from the intimate contact with the family

2. To establish enough motor control so that the approach to the physical environment is with "readiness and confidence"

3. To go through a day with the least possible amount of direction and dictation

4. To establish interests and explore them independently

5. To share in the life of a social group and to modify demands in relation to their peers.

Positive feelings about self: I am! I can! (Kindercampus, Iowa City)

Of course there is a classic listing of developmental tasks by Havighurst (1952) that includes (for the very early years) learning to walk, talk, take solid foods, control elimination of body wastes, relate emotionally to other persons, distinguish right from wrong, and form simple concepts of social and physical reality. The accomplishment of these tasks is greatly influenced by the persons and objects in the child's world. This positive influence is what is meant by nurture, and you will note that the word *nurturing* has replaced the word *teaching* in the following parts, especially in Part Three, The Care and Protection Curriculum.

More current statements of the goals of early care and education are offered in many reports of theory, research, and model programs. Gewirtz (1971) suggests the global goal "to stimulate and enhance development of the child's behavior systems in socially desirable ways" (p. 173) and also offers a more specific list of generally valued behaviors:

1. bodily skills, gross and fine movements
2. social responsiveness
3. speech and language skills
4. self-reliance
5. freedom from fear or anxiety
6. emotional independence
7. perseverance
8. ability to acquire information about the environment
9. tolerance for delay of reinforcement (p. 203).

Goals for Centers

The last point of reference for the determination of goals is that of the center itself. Center goals may focus on the needs and characteristics of infants and toddlers, that is, to meet physiological needs, to provide for optimal development, or to create an environment that provides security, safety, and happiness. The Learning Center in Philadelphia operates under the primary goal of creating a familylike atmosphere with a secure relationship between each child and the caregivers, and attempts to meet this goal by providing a male and female caregiver for each group of 10 children, from infancy to 4 years of age.

Many programs reported in the literature have been established as demonstration or research centers, and their goals reflect these broader purposes. The Children's Center at Syracuse University (SUNY) was established in the 1960s as a demonstration day-care program for infants and toddlers, and one of its main goals was the evaluation of group day care for very young children on an objective rather than a clinical basis. The profession owes much to this endeavor, because one of their evaluations showed that, at least for their population of children and families, there were no negative effects resulting from maternal separation for many hours during each day. Apparently, mother-child attachments were not disrupted or minimized by the child's regular attendance at an all-day center-based program. Needless to say—but necessary to point out—the Children's Center was an example of a very high quality program; therefore, a generalization of this finding to many centers in existence today is not valid. Many so-called developmental day-care settings seem to stress *either* warm interpersonal relations *or* encouragement of curiosity and beginning cognitive and language skills, but rarely both.

Because of the discouraging long-range results of many of the early education models designed for 3- and 4-year-old economically or culturally disadvantaged children in the late 1960s and early 1970s, some infant-toddler programs were established to remediate "deficits." Most of these have been part-day programs, designed specifically for developing readiness for the academic content of the primary grades, but a few have attempted to educate parents as teachers of their own children, with excellent results. National attention is now being focused on handicapped or "at risk" infants and toddlers. The major goals of these programs are the early identification and remediation of the handicapping condition(s), and the programs are either part-day, whole-day, or in the child's own home.

In addition to meeting the needs of children, centers and family day-care homes must meet the varying needs of parents. They may include adjusting the hours to meet the working schedules of parents, providing a morning or evening meal, or offering a listening ear and support in a problem situation. They include sharing information about the child, about the program, and about community and governmental resources. How to meet these and other needs are considered in the following chapters.

SUMMARY

The status of very young children has slowly evolved from that of no recognition or value to considerable recognition and value. This change has been traced from ancient times to the early Christian era, when children were valued as souls for a future world. The *child* actually disappeared until the early 17th century when Comenius and Locke "discovered" the importance of the very early years, although their ideas drew little attention. In the 18th century Rousseau dignified the first 5 years of life, and introduced the idea of *childhood* as different from small-sized adulthood. In the 19th century Pestalozzi and Froebel were the pioneer practitioners in early childhood education, and taught young children with methods much more appropriate than the customary rote teaching in Latin and Greek. The theories and/or practices of Comenius, Rousseau, Pestalozzi, and Froebel have had considerable impact on pedagogical methods in Europe and the United States. Today the importance of the very early years, and the value of very young children, are recognized and accepted by professionals in the fields of psychology, medicine, human services, and education. However, societal commitment, at least in the United States, is not yet unanimous.

For those agencies and persons committed to the establishment of quality programs for young children, the question of goals and objectives is a first consideration. The excitement and activity in the 1960s and 1970s resulted in many program descriptions and related goal statements. These have been studied and some have been put into practice in more recent programs. All agree that young children deserve the best that we can provide, wherever they spend their time, at home, in a center-based program, or in a family day-care home. Also, based on experience and expert opinion, we now recognize the important, even essential, role of parent's involvement in the very early care and education of their children. An important part of this role is a mutually agreeable philosophy and goal statement. Although parents and caregivers alike probably agree on the global goal of *the growth and development of the total child,* this goal offers little guidance for planning specific encounters and activities for individual children.

A goal statement not only states what a center or family day-care home hopes to accomplish, but it gives a clear indication of an educational philosophy. Programs that state their philosophy in specific terms, and that actively pursue specific goals, have a more positive, measurable impact than programs that do not. There are various approaches to goals, and aspects of all of them may be included in any particular statement. However, there can be no universal statement of specific goals that can be applied to all the programs for infants and toddlers, because what we want for an individual child and what we do with an individual child are influenced by cultural values, religious values, socioeconomic conditions, scientific knowledge, and government policies. These change over time, from culture to culture, and from family to family.

Stated goals for infant-toddler programs are sometimes necessary for state licensing purposes, but are always necessary for the delivery of a quality program, be it housed in a family day care or a center.

SUGGESTED ACTIVITIES AND QUESTIONS

1. Visit a center and/or family day-care home that serves children up to 3 years. Observe the program and talk with the director or educarer about their goals and objectives for the program and the children. Ask about the possibility of mainstreaming.

2. Review the licensing standards for your state. In particular, look for any mention of a requirement for a statement of goals or of program characteristics.

3. Start a clipping collection of newspaper or popular magazine articles about infant-toddler (or other) child care.

4. Have an in-class debate (or raise the issue among your friends) about the use of public funds to (1) subsidize a parent so that he or she might stay at home with a young child; (2) subsidize child care for young children whose parents are employed out of the home; and (3) determine if no public funds should be used for either (1) or (2).

5. Compare the lives of the upper-class children in the 13th to 18th centuries with the "super babies" of today.

SUGGESTED READINGS

Historic Perspectives

Aries, P. (1962). *Centuries of childhood.* New York: Random House.

Braun, S. J., & Edwards, E. P. (1972). *History and theory of early childhood education* (2nd ed.). Belmont, CA: Wadsworth.

Cunnington, P., & Buck, A. (1965). *Children's costume in England.* New York: Barnes & Noble.

Downer, M. (1970). *Children in the world's art.* New York: Lothrop, Lee & Shepard.

Glubok, S. (Ed.). (1969). *Home and child life in colonial days.* New York: Macmillan.

Greenleaf, B. (1978). *Children through the ages: A history of childhood.* New York: McGraw-Hill.

Grotberg, E. (Ed.). (1977). *200 years of children.* Washington, DC: Department of Health, Education, and Welfare.

Johnson, H. M. (1936). *School begins at two.* New York: New Republic.

Johnson, H. M. (1972). *Children in "the nursery school."* New York: Agathon. (Originally published in 1928)

Kessen, W. (Ed.). (1965). *The child.* New York: John Wiley & Sons.

Larcom, L. (1889). *A New England girlhood.* Boston: Houghton Mifflin.

McGraw, M. (1941). *The child in painting.* New York: Greystone Press.

Monroe, W. S. (Ed.). (1892). *Comenius' School of Infancy: An essay on the education of youth during the first six years.* Boston: D. C. Heath. (Originally published 1633)

Osborn, D. K. (1980). *Early childhood education in historical perspective.* Athens, GA: Education Associates.

Pestalozzi, J. H. (1898). *How Gertrude teaches her children* (2nd ed.). (L. Holland & F. Turner, Trans.). Syracuse, NY: Bardeen. (Original work published 1801)

Rousseau, J. J. (1893). *Emile, or Treatise on education* (W. Payne, Trans.). New York: D. Appleton. (Original work published 1762)

Steinfels, M. (1973). *Who's minding the children? The history and politics of day care in America.* New York: Simon & Schuster.

Ulich, R. (1954). *Three thousand years of educational wisdom* (2nd ed.). Cambridge, MA: Harvard University Press.

Woodcock, L. P. (1941). *Life and ways of the two-year-old.* New York: Dutton.

Current Perspectives

Abt Associates (1979). *Executive summary. Children at the center: Final report of the National Day Care Study.* Washington, DC: Department of Health, Education, and Welfare.

Auerbach, S. (Ed.). (1978). *Creative centers and home.* New York: Human Sciences Press.

Berman, C., & Szanton, E. (Eds.). (1989). *The intent and spirit of P.L. 99–457: A sourcebook.* Washington, DC: National Center for Clinical Infant Programs.

Bronfenbrenner, U. (1974). *A report on longitudinal evaluations of preschool programs:* Vol. 11. *Is early intervention effective?* (pp. 21–39). (DHEW Publication No. [OHD 75–25]). Washington, DC: U.S. Government Printing Office.

Caldwell, B. (1971). Day care: A timid giant grows bolder. *National Elementary Principal, 51,* 74–78.

Castelle, K. (1990). *In the child's best interest: A primer on the U.N. Convention of the Rights of the Child* (3rd ed.). East Greenwich, RI: Foster Parents Plan International and New York: Defense for Children International–USA.

Cataldo, C. (1983). *Infant and toddler programs.* Reading, MA: Addison-Wesley.

Children's Defense Fund. (Annual Editions). *A children's defense budget.* Washington, DC: Author.

Clarke-Stewart, A. (1982). *Day care.* The Developing Child Series. Cambridge, MA: Harvard University Press.

Colbert, J. (Ed.). (1980). *Home day care: A perspective.* Chicago: College of Education, Roosevelt University.

Day, M. C., & Parker, R. K. (Eds.). (1977). *The preschool in action.* Boston: Allyn & Bacon.

Denenberg, V. (1970). *Education of the infant and young child.* New York: Academic Press.

Dickerson, M., & Ross, M. K. (1985). Acting on what we know: Child care. In K. J. Swick & K. Castle (Eds.), *Acting on what we know: Developing effective programs for young children.* Little Rock, AR: Southern Association on Children under Six.

Dittmann, L. L. (Ed.). (1968). *Early child care—The new perspectives.* New York: Atherton.

Dittmann, L. L. (Ed.). (1984). *The infants we care for* (rev. ed.). Washington, DC: National Association for the Education of Young Children.

Elardo, R., & B. Pagan. (1972). *Perspectives on infant day care.* Orangeburg, SC: Southern Association for Children under Six.

Endsley, R., & Bradbard, M. (1981). *Quality day care. A handbook of choices for parents and caregivers.* Englewood Cliffs, NJ: Prentice-Hall.

Evans, E. B., & Saia, G. E. (1973). *Day care for infants: The case for infant day care and a practical guide.* Boston: Beacon Press.

Fosburg, S., & Hawkins, P. (1981). *Final report of the National Day Care Home Study.* Vol. 1. Cambridge, MA: Abt Books.

Frost, J. (Ed.). (1977). *Developing programs for infants and toddlers.* Washington, DC: Association for Childhood Education International.

Galinsky, E., & Hooks, W. (1977). *The new extended family: Day care that works.* Boston: Houghton-Mifflin.

Garcia, R. (1985). *Home centered child care: Designing a family day care program.* San Francisco: Children's Council of San Francisco.

Gewirtz, J. L. (1971). Stimulation, learning, and motivation principles for daycare settings. In E. H. Grotberg (Ed.), *Day care: Resources for decisions* (pp. 173–226). Washington, DC: Office of Economic Opportunity.

Godwin, A., & Schrag, L. (1988). *Setting up for infant care: Guidelines for centers and family day care homes.* Washington, DC: National Association for the Education of Young Children.

Grotberg, E. H. (Ed.). (1971). *Day care: Resources for decisions.* Washington, DC: Office of Economic Opportunity.

Gutierrez, M., & Derman-Sparks, L. (1989). Beginnings: Working with 2-year-olds. In L. Derman-Sparks & the A.B.C. Task Force, *Anti-Bias curriculum: Tools for empowering young children* (ch. 3). Washington, DC: National Association for the Education of Young Children.

Keister, M. E. (1970). *A review of experience: Establishing, operating, evaluating a demonstration nursery center for the daytime care of infants and toddlers, 1967–1970.* Greensboro, NC: University of North Carolina. (ERIC Document Reproduction Service No. ED 050 810; PS 004 666).

Keyserling, M. D. (1972). *Windows on day care: A report on the findings of members of the National Council of Jewish Women on day care needs and services in their communities.* (ERIC Document Reproduction Service N. ED 063 027).

Lally, J. R., & Honig, A. S. (1975). Education of infants and toddlers from low-income and low-education backgrounds: Support for the family's role and identity. In B. Z. Friedlander, G. M. Sterritt, & G. E. Kirk (Eds.), *Exceptional infant.* Vol. 3 (pp. 285–303). New York: Brunner/Mazel.

Lambie, D. Z., Bond, J. T., & Weikart, D. P. (1975). Framework for infant education. In B. Z. Friedlander, G. M. Sterritt, & G. E. Kirk (Eds.), *Exceptional infant.* Vol. 3 (pp. 263–303). New York: Brunner/Mazel.

Lazar, I., Hubbell, V. R., Murray, H., Rosche, M., & Royce, J. (1977). *The persistence of preschool effects: A long-term follow-up of fourteen infant and preschool experiments.* Final report (18-76-07843) to the Administration on Children, Youth, and Families, Office of Human Development Services, Department of Health, Education, and Welfare.

Leavitt, R. L., & Eheart, B. K. (1985). *Toddler day care: A guide to responsive caregiving.* Lexington, MA: Lexington Books.

Lurie, R., & Neugebauer, R. (1982). *Caring for infants and toddlers.* Vol. I & II. Redmond, WA: Child Care Information Exchange.

Modigliani, K., Reiff, M., & Jones, A. (1987). *Opening your door to children: How to start a family day care program.* Washington, DC: National Association for the Education of Young Children.

Morgan, G. (1987). *The national state of child care regulation 1986.* Watertown, MA: Work/Family Directions.

National Center for Clinical Infant Programs. (1986). *Infants can't wait.* Washington, DC: Author.

National Center for Clinical Infant Programs. (n.d.). *Who will mind the babies?* Washington, DC: Author.

Provence, S., Naylor, A., & Patterson, J. (1977). *The challenge of daycare.* New Haven, CT: Yale Press.

Robinson, N. M., Robinson, H. B., Darling, M. A., & Holm, G. (1979). *A world of children: Day care and preschool institutions.* Monterey, CA: Brooks/Cole.

Roby, P. (Ed.). (1973). *Child care—Who cares?* New York: Basic Books.

Ruopp, R., Travers, J., Glantz, F., & Coelen, C. (1979). *Children at the center.* (Final report of the National Day Care Study, Vol. 1). Cambridge, MA: ABT Associates.

Squibb, B. (1980). *Family day care: How to provide it in your home.* Cambridge, MA: Harvard Common Press.

UNICEF and the rights of the child. (1974). UNICEF/6601 #5203. New York: United Nation's Children's Fund.

Zigler, E. F., & Gordon, E. W. (1982). *Day care: Scientific and social policy issues.* Boston: Auburn House.

2

Early Development and Learning

Before I got married I had six theories about bringing up children; now I have six children and no theories.

Lord Rochester (1647–1680)

Child development is easily defined as the study of how children develop, yet the experts in the field maintain that "child development" defies precise definition. We might therefore suspect that our simple answer is not so simple after all. Like most simple answers to questions about human beings, the definition involves an in-depth investigation of which fundamental questions need to be asked. It is important not only to ask the questions but also to find the answers. It is essential for all persons in any responsible relationship with young children to know how and why children develop the way they do. They can then plan experiences and environments, both in and out of the home, that are relevant and appropriate for maximizing the potential of young children.

There is also a need for widespread understanding about the normal range in the date of onset of certain developmental landmarks. For example, there are reliable reports of children learning to walk at 7 or 8 months of age, but a large number of perfectly normal children do not learn to walk before they are 15 or even 18 months of age. We therefore need to ask and answer the following: What characteristics result because of membership in the human race? In a specific family? Under all or just some environmental conditions? Are there individual differences? Why? How do these determinants of growth and development interact and modify one another?

The first part of this chapter is designed to offer clues to some of the answers, but it will no doubt lead to more questions. It serves two functions, depending on the background knowledge of the reader. It will serve either as an introduction to theories of child development or as a review of selected developmental theories. In either case, it is necessary background information for planning the care and education of very young children.

The newborn appears totally helpless and dependent, and frequently has a physical appearance only a mother could love! This new person many times protests entrance to the world loudly and vigorously, but apparently the inevitable is soon accepted. Within 5 or 6 days the infant is able to respond to visual, auditory, and tactile stimulation with strong preferences and dislikes. This new baby is capable of selecting stimuli to which to respond or ignore, to physically withdraw from an external cause of pain, or to react with total body movement to internal distress. Almost immediately, an infant can lift or turn his head in order to avoid suffocation, reflexly grasp objects with hands and feet, visually track a slowly moving object, locate a small object with the mouth when touched near the mouth, and suck. All physiological systems of a human being are in working order at the time of a normal birth; not only does the newborn have potential for humanness, the newborn *is* human. Very soon after birth (some say while still in the womb) the baby's education begins.

Burton White (1975), a leader in child development, maintains that

> the period that starts at eight months and ends at three years is a period of primary importance in the development of a human being. To begin to look at a child's educational development when he is two years of age is already much too late (p. 4).

White and his colleagues have presented evidence to show that many skills and abilities of the "competent" 6 year old are also part of the behavioral repertoire of advanced 3 year olds. Such abilities include: (1) using adults as resources for information, food, and assistance; (2) leading and following age-peers; (3) expressing emotions of affection, hostility, and pride; (4) using expressed language extensively and meaningfully; (5) recognizing discrepant happenings or appearances; (6) anticipating consequences; and (7) attending to more than one thing simultaneously or in rapid succession. "The 10- to 18-month period of life is in effect a critical period for the development of the foundations of competence" (White & Watts, 1973, p. 245). It is a temptation for casual readers to interpret White's many writings as meaning "all is over" by 3 years of age, and, indeed, the

implication is there. The accepted position is to agree that the early years are important—as are the other years. Jerome Kagan contends that developmentalists have overemphasized the psychological significance of the early years. "All periods in development, from conception through adolescence, are critical periods in which the child requires the care and attention of loving adults as well as other environmental nutrients in order to ensure optimal development" (Zigler & Turner, 1982, p. 180). White's most recent publication (1988b) describes his New Parents as Teachers project in Missouri, and in it he presents the same abilities as distinguishing qualities of the outstanding three- to six-year-old child (pp. 185–195). He continues to insist on the importance of the very early months and years.

Competence (or its absence) is directly attributable to a unique composite of influential agents at work in the child's development. This uniqueness holds true not only in differentiating the competent from the not so competent, but also in differentiating individuals within each of these categories. The first and primary principle of child development is just this: *Each child is unique because of a unique biological inheritance (excepting monozygotic multiple births) in combination with a unique life experience from the time of conception.*

We are all so matter-of-fact about children (they are born and they seem to grow without much effort) that we overlook the miracle that takes place each time a child is conceived, born, and reaches adulthood. A sense of wonder comes from increased knowledge about the many-sided components of child development, and should be enhanced by each personal contact with a child.

NORMATIVE-MATURATIONAL THEORIES

Historically, when the young child was even considered, it was usually in the guise of a miniature adult, and little or no concern or thought was given beyond that. We might attribute William Shakespeare the honor of being the first "ages and stages" theorist. The following is from *As You Like It:*

All the world's a stage,
And all the men and women merely players:
They have their exits and their entrances;
And one man in his time plays many parts,
His acts being seven ages. At first the infant,
Mewling and puking in the nurse's arms.
And then the whining school-boy, with his satchel
And shining morning face, creeping like snail
Unwillingly to school . . .

Shakespeare apparently did not view infants or young children with much pleasure! The real breakthrough in the consciousness of the evolution of human growth and development came with the publication of Darwin's *On the Origin of the Species* (1859) and *Expression of the Emotions in Man and Animals* (1873). As noted by Kessen (1965), for at least 50 years "the developing human being was seen as a natural museum of human phylogeny and history; by careful observation of the infant and the child, one could see the descent of men" (p. 115). Interestingly enough, Darwin never intended that his theory of survival of the fittest be applied socially—and probably not even biologically—to humans. Nevertheless, the impact of Darwinian theory led to the totally new field of child observation and inquiry.

AFFECTIVE DEVELOPMENT

Sigmund Freud

Sigmund Freud, a doctor of medicine, applied the theories of evolution to stages of human development, maintaining that stages were sequential and biologically determined. He assigned stages of personality development to the ages of human life: (1) the first year, the oral stage, with pleasure as the motivation; (2) the second and third years, the anal stage, encompassing a growing awareness of self and a beginning awareness of societal demands; (3) the

third and fourth years, the phallic stage, with its concern with sexual identity, approval from others, and the testing of aggressive behavior. Freud's influence is still alive and well in the United States, particularly in psychoanalytic fields.

The issue of the emergence of all types of identity (not just sexual) has never been felt more keenly. Identity is a uniquely human characteristic, a natural by-product of human experience. In its Report to the President, the U.S. National Commission on the International Year of the Child points out that

> there are many types of identity—family, ethnic and cultural, religious, political, economic, physical, sexual, and intellectual. Identity involves aspects of a person's being. Research during the past decades has firmly established the validity of the concept of the uniqueness of each individual. And more recent evidence strongly indicates that the foundation for this individual unique identity is established in the early years (1980, p. 19).

Each human being has an identifiable sense of identity, but not every human being has a favorable and realistic sense of identity.

Erik Erikson

Erik Erikson's theory of personality development outlines the maturational sequence involved in the emergence of identity. The knowledge he has given to child development theory is somewhat unique in that it is a rational presentation rather than a systematic developmental theory. Erikson presented his theory at the Midcentury White House Conference on Children and Youth in 1950, and since then his theory has been accepted by virtually all persons involved in the care and education of children, as well as by researchers and theoreticians. According to Erikson, in each stage of child development there is a central problem that has to be solved, at least temporarily, if the child is to proceed positively to the next stage. Some central problems may never be totally resolved. Each conflict appears in its purest form at a particular stage. The central problems of very early childhood are trust versus distrust, autonomy versus doubt and shame, and initiative versus guilt.

Trust versus distrust. The first component of a healthy personality is a sense of trust, which develops from the child's satisfying experiences during the first 18 months of life. Having biological needs anticipated and met by others with consistency and continuity, gaining control over one's body movements, and experiencing pleasurable encounters with objects and persons all assure the baby that the world is a dependable place. The baby's trust-mistrust problem is symbolized in the game of peek-a-boo. In this game, which infants begin to like at about 4 months of age, an object disappears and then reappears. There is a slightly tense expression on the infant's face when the object "goes away"; its reappearance is greeted by wiggles and smiles. Only gradually does a baby learn that things continue to exist even when out of sight, and only gradually does a baby learn that there is order and stability in the universe. Piaget called this a sense of "object permanence." Studies of mentally ill individuals and observations of infants who have been grossly deprived of affection and attention suggest that trust is an early-formed and important element. It is a common finding of psychological and social investigations that individuals having a "psychopathic personality" were so unloved in infancy that they had no reason to trust the world or humanity.

For most infants in our society a sense of trust is not difficult to come by. Psychologists tell us that primary caregivers (usually mothers) create a sense of trust in a child not by the particular techniques they employ, but by the sensitiveness with which they respond to the child's needs. A sense of trust is the most important building block in a healthy personality, and it emerges at the most vulnerable period of a child's life (birth to about 18 months).

Autonomy versus doubt and shame. Much of the child's energy during the next 2 years will be focused on the need to establish autonomy. The positive outcome is self-control without loss of self-esteem; the unfavorable outcome is doubt and shame. This is the period of muscle system maturation and the resulting ability to coordinate a number of action patterns, such as walking, talking, manipulating objects, holding on, and letting go. Although some psychologists have concentrated particularly on bladder and bowel control during this period, the ramifications of developing and establishing autonomy cover a much wider area. The child needs to develop a sense of adequacy and self-reliance. The child must experience over and over again that he is a person who is permitted to make choices. At the same time the child must learn some of the boundaries of self-determination. Not only are some objects out of reach, but also there are some adult commands that are strongly enforced.

The American way of life is based on the premise that individuals have the right to be in control of their lives, to have personal opinions and, more important, to express them. Therefore we actively encourage the young child's sense of adequacy and self-reliance. The solving of this conflict between autonomy versus doubt and shame is forcefully met for the first time between 18 months and 3 years of age. However, much of our normal life span involves its continuing resolution, as circumstances change, and as we adapt to societal expectations for our behavior.

Initiative versus guilt. By the ages of 4 and 5 years, having established a trust in the world and the persons and objects in it, and having asserted one's sense of personhood, the young child looks beyond present reality to future possibilities. This is the time for all kinds of learning—about the various roles and functions of adults, about social relationships with agemates and others, and about the usefulness and pleasure of imagination, particularly when projects dreamed up are either physically impossible or not permitted. Children at this age are beginning to feel guilty even for mere thoughts (the beginnings of conscience are in evidence).

These first three stages—developing a sense of trust, a sense of autonomy, and a sense of initiative—are probably the most important for personality development. The following stages are *accomplishment* (or industry) *versus inferiority* (5 years to puberty); *identity role versus role confusion* (adolescence); *intimacy versus isolation* (adulthood and relationships); *generativity versus stagnation* (parenthood and/ or creativity and productivity); and *ego identity versus despair* (old age and a sense of satisfaction with one's accomplishments). The first three stages are also the most important for the emergence of a sense of identity.

A sense of identity. The beginnings of a sense of self originate in the infant's body through countless experiences involving touch, sight, hearing, smelling, and movement. The knowledge that things exist outside oneself is gradually achieved, and the infant's sense of separateness continues to emerge as certain actions elicit response from the environment. Another aspect of identity emerges with a change in the infant's attachment to the significant person(s) from one based on need and need gratification (during the first 6 months) to one based on love (second 6 months). Attaining the physical skills of locomotion firmly establishes the sense of separateness, and by the time the child is 2½ years old there is no remaining question of personhood and identity. The various identities relevant to each person (family, ethnic, religious, economic, physical, and intellectual) are quite firmly established by the age of 6 years.

The drive toward and the pleasure in achieving a sense of one's identity is well illustrated by the following description of a momentous event in the life of young Tommy.

The Players: Tommy, age 3½
Older sister
Mother

Scene: A restaurant, where all three are seated at a table. Mother and big sister have just given their orders for lunch to the waitress.
Action: Waitress to Tommy, "And what would you like?"
Mother to waitress, "Oh, I'll order for him."
Waitress, ignoring mother, repeats her question to Tommy, looking squarely at him.
Big sister to waitress, "He's too little, I'll order for him," and then to Tommy, "What do you want?"
Waitress, ignoring big sister, repeats her question to Tommy.
Tommy to waitress: "A hamburger."
Waitress to Tommy: "Do you want everything on it—lettuce, tomato, pickle, onion, mustard, ketchup?"
Tommy to waitress: "Everything."
Waitress leaves, Tommy turns to mother, and exclaims, "Hey Mommy, she thinks I'm real!"

Every child is "real," and must be so recognized and treated.

PHYSICAL-BEHAVIORAL DEVELOPMENT

Arnold Gesell

Many of the major tests of early development currently in use are drawn from the work of Dr. Arnold Gesell, who founded the Yale Clinic for Child Development in 1911, and who was one of the first to use scientific procedures to study children over a period of time. He agreed with Freud in his biological and behavioral approach to child development. His studies describe age-related behaviors by years, and emphasize the divergent and convergent aspects of development. Grotberg (n.d.) explains Gesell's theory as follows:

> The various aspects of human growth and development, i.e., physical, intellectual, social and emotional, are divergent in terms of rate and harmony, and are periodically convergent into nodal stages, when the different aspects are in harmony. Gesell saw the divergent stages and ages as causes for conflict and disorder in the child's behavior, and the convergent or nodal stages and

ages as sources of order and harmony in the child's behavior (p. 398).

On the basis of his early research on 109 middle-class families in Connecticut, Gesell and his colleagues produced an instrument for use in screening children for gross normality. Revised editions of the test have been in wide use ever since.

Until recently, the normative data of Gesell and his associates have been considered appropriate for use in testing. However, there is now considerable questioning about the appropriateness of the norming sample (white, middle-, and upper-class children), because of the increasing numbers of children in our centers and schools who are not white, and who are not middle- or upper-class. The Gesell instruments do not meet the American Psychological Association's standards for either reliability or validity. Nonetheless, the Gesell and Amatruda Developmental Screening Inventory (Knobloch & Pasamanick, 1974) is one of the major tools used by pediatricians to identify very young children who are physically or mentally disabled.

Although Gesell's interpretation of the basic determinant of development (i.e., maturation) has been substantially revised by more recent studies, his age norms have stood the test of time. In very condensed form, the following sequence of development exemplifies Gesell's approach to child development.

By the end of the first 28 weeks, the infant has eye control, holds her head erect and steady, and reaches out for, grasps, transfers, and manipulates things.

By age 52 weeks, the child uses his fingers with adult precision, and stands and walks with support. In the second year the child learns to walk and run, articulate words, control bowel and bladder functions, and has a rudimentary sense of personal identity. Between 2 and 3 years of age the child can speak in sentences to articulate thoughts. He tries to understand the environment and to obey cultural demands. He

is no longer an infant (Knoblock & Pasamanick, 1974).

The notion of normal development has been derived from certain patterns of behavior appearing at certain ages (or ranges of age). Knowing when new behaviors and abilities can be expected is indeed helpful for program and environmental planning, whatever the setting. However, a word of caution is necessary. At best, developmental charts contain lists of behaviors normally present at the given chronological age for age for only 50% of the children. The other 50% are either ahead of or behind the norm. It therefore should be evident that the setting of realistic expectations, and the provision of appropriate activities can be achieved only when each child is viewed as an individual with unique characteristics, including a unique developmental time table.

In the normative-maturational theory, each stage is a direct reflection of the individual's maturational level at the time. The stages form an invariant sequence through the maturational unfolding of a series of innate biological patterns. Illustrative of the educational implications of this approach is the "hands-off" theory of instruction. For instance, teachers of reading will wait until the child is "ready" according to the normal developmental readiness time; they ignore the possible influential agents of the child's previous experiences and interests, and the variety of methods and materials available for use. For the teacher (or educarer) of an infant, a strict interpretation of the maturational theory would mean leaving the child in his crib, because the timetable says he is not yet ready to crawl or walk.

Over years of observation and study, other psychologists and medical personnel have formulated a list of developmental sequences of motor behaviors, which do not specify ages, but do indicate directions of normal development. These directions are as follows:

1. Cephalocaudal, or from head to toe

2. Proximo-distal, or from the center of the body to the outer extremities

3. Mass to specific, or from generalized to specific movements

4. Gross motor to fine motor, or from large muscles to fine (or small) muscles

5. Maximum to minimum muscle involvement, or from whole body movement to the specific muscles needed for a task

6. Bilateral to unilateral, or the development of a preference for right or left (adapted from O'Donnell, 1969)

These developmental directions are universal, given normal environmental conditions and absence of disability.

Even though agreement has been reached on the directions, the norms have been memorized with little or no understanding of the range of normal variation. If "the book" says a certain behavioral item appears on the average of 15 months but with a range of 12 to 18 months, parents are disappointed if their child does not exhibit the behavior at the stroke of 12 months and are alarmed if such behavior does not appear by 15 months. Gesell's infant schedules are still used by many professional persons for the evaluation of a child's progress, particularly during the first year of life.

"Normal" Development

Over the last 25 years an impressive body of research data and knowledge has been accumulated that indicates wide differences in various aspects of development in children. We now know that the inner laws of physical development are considerably influenced by amount of sleep, habits of elimination, amount and character of food intake, amount of fluid intake, and degree and kind of physical activity. Attitudes, fatigue reactions, stability of personality, and changes in mental development play important roles as well. The results of this research lead

to the second child development principle: *Heredity and environment never operate as separate entities; neither can exert an influence without the other.*

COGNITIVE AND MENTAL DEVELOPMENT

The major breakthrough on age-related intellectual functioning was the Binet method of age scaling developed in 1907. Binet's approach resulted in widely accepted age norms for the development of mental abilities, although his prime concern was to identify retarded children for placement in institutions. He did not theorize about mental development, but he did help expand our understanding of age-related intellectual functioning. We turn to the writings of Jean Piaget for the most fully developed theory of the development of mature cognitive thought to date.

Jean Piaget

Piaget was less interested in precise ages than in sequential stages, which are qualitatively discrete. He saw mental growth as an extension of biological growth, governed by the same principles and laws. He emphasized the normative aspects and attempted to identify those mental structures that hold true for individuals and for the human species. Like Gesell, Piaget maintained that an understanding of normal development is a prerequisite for an understanding of differences between individuals, but his concept of development stressed the role of the child's experience, as opposed to Gesell's concept of maturation. Piaget assumed that developmental change is based both on biological processes of maturation, and on the experiences of an active subject who gains knowledge by acting on the world and by utilizing the feedback from his actions to construct increasingly complex schemata, or mental structures.

If we accept the definition of intelligence as the ability to adapt to and make sense out of the environment (there are other equally appropriate definitions), it is logical to accept the theory that the development of this ability passes through a series of maturational stages.

Piaget's taxonomy of developmental periods of major developmental epochs includes many so-called stages, substages, and subperiods, and his writings are inconsistent as to both numbers and names of stages, substages, and so on, from one publication to the next. However, he has consistently designated three major periods of intellectual development from birth to maturity.

Sensorimotor intelligence (birth to 2 years). There are six major stages in this period, with a few substages scattered throughout. Essentially, each child begins as a totally egocentric, uncoordinated neonate who engages only in reflexlike activities (from which Piaget says intelligence begins) to a child who acts intentionally and who can solve problems through actions that indicate some remembrance of past actions and new combinations of past experiences. At the culmination of the sensorimotor period, the child can: (1) imitate quite complex actions of persons and objects, whether visibly perceptible or remembered; (2) truly pretend or make-believe; (3) remember and think about actions, rather than simply perform them; (4) infer a cause, given only its effect and foresee an effect, given its cause; and (5) recognize that an object is a thing (or person) apart, subject to its own laws of displacement and action. The child has progressed from total egocentrism (a consideration of the world from only a personal point of view) to an awareness of separateness and both self-identity and "other-identity." As the child moves toward an ability to symbolize, the next period is entered.

Preoperational thought (2 to 7 years). In Piagetian terms, an *operation* is the mental manipulation of an object or event. It necessitates the use of logic. The very young child does not yet seem capable of applying logic in conclusions or explanations of happenings. This child might be described as: (1) completely egocentric, but very curious; (2) able to use language as a social tool and for communicating needs or desires; and (3) ready with an explanation for everything. The characteristics of a child's preoperational thinking during these years are of particular importance in planning educational programs.

1. The child is unable to think from any point of view except her own, and is unable to imagine how it would be (or look) from another point of view or perspective.

2. The child is greatly influenced by what is perceived at a given moment, and will pass judgments on what is perceived, rather than on past experiences. The child concentrates on one variable only, usually the variable that stands out visually.

3. The child cannot understand that an object can have more than one attribute or quality and consequently belong in more than one classification.

4. The child pays little or no attention to another person's thoughts or language.

Concrete and formal operations (7 years to maturity). During the major portion of the elementary school years, the child appears to have a fairly stable and systematic mental framework with which to understand the world of objects and events. Piaget describes objects and events that are seen and experienced as *concrete*. The mental operations of a child from 7 to 11 or 12 years are tied to reality. As children move into adolescence, they are able to deal effectively both with the real and the abstract world.

· · ·

It should be noted that Piaget's material on sensorimotor development is scattered throughout a number of books and articles. Primary sources include *The Origins of Intelligence in*

Children (1936/1952) and *Play, Dreams, and Imitation in Children* (1962). It should also be noted that while Gesell obtained his data from groups of highly advantaged children, and therefore has received criticism, Piaget's data on sensorimotor development was obtained almost exclusively from his own three children. He has also received criticism for this. With the exception of the specificity of ages for particular accomplishments, however, Piaget's theory has held firm since it was first introduced in the United States, in spite of numerous attempts to upset the invariance of the stages. Nonetheless, Piaget's theory is not in itself adequate to explain human development and behavior.

"Ages and Stages" Re-evaluated

Most modern theorists have concluded that age per se is not a good criterion for establishing developmental stages. Even Piaget admits that, although his stages always succeed one another, accelerations or delays will occur with differences in social environment and past experiences. With the current evidence that discredits the concepts of predetermined development and fixed intelligence, and the proposals that the early years are the most influential for intellectual growth, the traditional faith in maturational theory is a serious question. Developmental theory based on maturation is useful, but incomplete. The related assessment instruments and scales are of help in stating sequences of development and will reveal gross handicaps. In individual cases the scales seem to underestimate abilities of some and are of little help in predicting later intellectual abilities of others. A poignant reminder of the recent change of direction in developmental theories may be inferred from the obvious omission of any reference to the maturational-normative point of view in the 1970 (and later) editions of the *Manual of Child Psychology* (Mussen).

Individual differences. A popular thought about individual differences before the 1960s

1960s was essentially that of predetermination by genetic and hereditary influences. As McClearn (1964) noted, however, even limiting the theory to

> genetic homogeneity has pitfalls beyond count; the number of possible genotypes far exceeds the number of persons now living, plus those who have ever lived, in all human history. Excepting identical twins and other identical multiple births, each human being is a unique and unrepeatable event (p. 472).

It should not be surprising, therefore, that each baby even from the same parents is a unique individual. Parents often remark on the differences between their own children; a second child may well have a very different temperament from the firstborn.

Bettelheim (1987) neatly describes the progress made over the last thirty years by stating "The psychological studies which establish behavioral norms for various age groups neglect the innumerable individual differences which make each child unique" (p. 35). Child development researchers Thomas, Chess, and Birch (1963/1980), in a longitudinal study over 30 years ago, first identified these differences. They found that children have different styles of functioning, or differences in temperament at birth or shortly thereafter. These differences in temperament have been summarized by Brazelton (1987) as follows:

Activity
amount of movement

Rhythmicity
regularity of need—predictable or nonpredictable

Adaptability
how a baby adjusts to the new and different

Approach
initial reaction of a baby to people or things coming toward her

Threshold
intensity of sound, touch, or sight at first response

Intensity
amount of response to a stimulus

Mood
pleasant, joyful, friendly behavior contrasted with unpleasant, crying, unfriendly responses

Distractibility
degree to which an event can attract the attention of the baby away from what she is doing

Persistence
degree to which an activity is continued even when other interests or obstacles are presented (pp. 30–31)

According to Brazelton, extremes of these differences are neither good nor bad in themselves; they are perceived as good or bad by the family and the caregiver.

The original Thomas, Chess, and Birch study (1963/1980) was continued until the children reached adolescence, with the finding that about 65% of the children had been reliably categorized soon after birth. In other words, the ratings had remained relatively stable throughout the study (Thomas, Chess, Birch, Hertzig, & Korn, 1983).

Not only do the studies in child development reveal individual differences, but studies from neurology, neuropsychology, biochemistry, and anatomy all add to the range of natural differences. We need to go one step further. Not only do these differences derive from specific genes and the resulting characteristics, but "new individual patterns emerge from the interaction of these tendencies . . . (and) different individual aspects of the environment interacting with the infants' own patterns contribute to new outcomes" (Murphy, Heider, & Small, 1986, p. 7).

Perhaps the safest prediction is that an immense variety of differences will be found in any group of young children. Implications of their existence are of particular importance to parents, caregivers, and educarers. Not only will individual children react in individual ways to the same environmental influence, but a particular child's response will usually determine the related behavior of the significant persons in the child's life. A simple example will illustrate this important concept.

Imagine two infants in a child-care center or family day-care home. One of them is active and alert, and consistently seeks adult attention by babbling and smiling and wiggling all over when an adult approaches. The other is less active, less vocal, and less responsive to the approach of an adult. We might describe these infants as "active" and "reflective." Most adults are drawn to active children and will engage in mutual vocalizations and movements, and both baby and adult will share a pleasurable experience. The reflective child, for a variety of reasons, may need as much or even more attention, but will usually receive less, and thus a cycle is started that may result in the child's withdrawal, or even apathy in extreme cases.

The message is clear: The same expectations and approaches should not be applied to all children—even infants and toddlers. Each child's reaction pattern must be understood, respected, and accommodated.

Before the classic study of Thomas, at al. (1963), such personality variables as motivation, anticipation, curiosity, and expectations were considered to be inherited characteristics. As the result of their studies and the studies of others we have concluded that these variables are learned from the very first weeks and months of life. The medium for learning is the reciprocal interaction between child and environment. Therefore, our third child development principle is: *Growth and development occur when a child is engaged in mutually fulfilling actions with other persons.*

In our efforts to learn and put into practice our knowledge of child development, let us not lose our sense of wonder, as expressed by Pablo Casals:

Do you know what you are?
You are a marvel.
You are unique.
In all the world there is no other child exactly
    like you.

In the millions of years that have passed there
has never been a child like you.

And look at your body—what a wonder it is!
Your legs, your arms, your cunning fingers,
the way you move!

You may become a Shakespeare, a Michelangelo,
a Beethoven
You may have the capacity for anything.
Yes, you are a marvel.

VERY EARLY LEARNING: PREREQUISITES AND DEVELOPMENT

The research that serves as the basis for much of the information and the recommended practices in this and succeeding chapters has been quite recent. Until the 1960s (or even the 1970s), it had been assumed that early learning was the result of classical conditioning, as theorized by John Watson and B. F. Skinner. Classical conditioning is a process in which a subject (child, animal, bird, etc.) is trained to make an automatic response to a specific event (word or other sound, light, movement). One typical research example is the encouragement of a baby to turn his head or to suck at the sound of a buzzer. Baby is encouraged with the use of a reward after he behaves in the desired manner. These rewards are called reinforcers, and their use supposedly will increase the number of times baby will respond correctly. Travers (1985) indicates "that the conditioning of infants has turned out to be rather difficult" (p. 164), and that "there is difficulty in distinguishing whether learning has taken place through reinforcement, because the infant seems capable of using these responses for adaptive purposes from birth" (p. 165).

Today this view has been replaced with the recognition that the human organism is equipped to learn, is programmed to learn, and is an active participant in learning. One can find little basis for the belief in classical conditioning in the following description of the young child's learning accomplishments:

- A *newborn* will try to listen and look at his environment, sometimes learning to suck his thumb in his struggle to pay attention to the world instead of his empty stomach.
- A *four-month old* is "falling in love" with the human world and begins to offer radiant smiles to parents and a few special caregivers.
- An *eight-month old* can communicate with purposeful signals when she wants to be picked up, cuddled or protest her lunch menu. If the caregiver responds appropriately, the baby learns that her actions have a predictable effect.
- A *toddler's* behavior becomes increasingly organized and assertive as a complex sense of self emerges. Unlike the newborn, who can only cry when hungry, a 16-month old uses his cognitive, social and emotional skills to "figure out" how to get his needs met as he takes his mother's hand, pulls her to the refrigerator, motions to her to open the door and points to his favorite food.
- A *two-year old* is not only learning to use language, run, and scribble but also is learning to create ideas and to reason, as well as to concentrate on and persist at a task in the face of difficulties. Children as young as 18 months of age are learning to recognize and label feelings and may even exhibit understanding of the emotional intentions of others.
- A *three-year old* is already learning to think logically, know what is real and what is "pretend," how to control impulses, maintain positive self esteem, concentrate and learn. The ability of most three-year olds to employ logic in disagreements with a parent and develop friendships reveals dramatically their expanding cognitive and emotional worlds (The National Center for Clinical Infant Programs, 1986, p. 4).

Most children progress in this manner, and will achieve the expected developmental milestones presented in appendix B. The big question for us is "How?" How do very young children achieve these milestones? How do young children learn?

All learning is initiated by sensory stimulation. The first responses are involuntary reflex actions, but during the first few months, movements become voluntary, and the infant can explore by himself, and can relate himself to his world. Exploring stimulates learning, and each new bit of learning increases the potential for more learning.

Sensation and Perception

All learning has its groundwork based in early sensory development and perception. The child is born with receptor organs that initially introduce the sensations in his immediate world. He is also born with motor equipment that soon enables him to visually focus, and to turn his head toward the source of sound. Gradually the impressions from the visual and auditory modalities are enhanced with tactual information. These impressions are mentally organized and stored. Piaget calls these stored impressions *sensorimotor schemata.* As the infant encounters new impressions (or sensations), these schemata are revised and changed in order to incorporate the new impressions.

Sensory reception is the term used to describe the mechanical intake of a stimulus. It is dependent on the full development of the structures of the sense organs—eyes, ears, nose, mouth, skin. These organs are activated and refined by external objects or happenings; this activation is called *sensation,* and it requires stimulation, but does not require previous learning or experience. The newborn receives sensations from sensory stimulation from the moment of birth. There have even been some indications that sensations might be received in utero.

Perception is a meaningful experience initiated by sensory stimulation. It is achieved when a new sensation combines with a former sensation, and a beginning meaning or understanding results. Infants build their store of meanings by exploring and manipulating the objects in their environment.

A simple example will illustrate the difference between sensation and reception. When very young children look at the front of a house,

they see the visible parts. Sensation has occurred. When older children look at the same house, they see the same visible parts, but they mentally fill in the parts they don't see by drawing on their past experiences with houses. They *perceive* a whole house, front and back, sides, and rooms and furniture inside.

Perception is midway between sensation and thought. Sensation requires present stimulation but no previous experience. Perception requires previous sensations in addition to present stimulation. It involves such mental activities as recognition, association, interpretation, and an understanding of relationships. Thought grows out of many perceptions. It does not require present stimulation, but it does require past sensations, perceptions, and experiences. Few, if any, specific experiences

> have unalterable and inevitable long-term effects . . . infant experiences do affect the way children are affected by later experiences and even the nature of the experiences they are likely to have. There is no simple long-term continuity in development; instead we are constantly reshaped by our experiences (Lamb & Campos, 1982, p. 235).

Fortunately, newborns are equipped to learn. They arrive with sensitivities for seeing, hearing, tasting, smelling, touching, and feeling. Infants are able to perceive, move, communicate, imitate, and remember. They are innately curious, and they like to play. These are the abilities and characteristics that are the tools for learning, and the educarer responds, mediates, and initiates interactions that capitalize on them. The educarer teaches, but not in the traditional way of transmitting facts and knowledge. It is this traditional interpretation of the act of teaching that has led to the "how-to-teach-baby" materials that are readily available in drug stores, supermarkets, and bookstores. Most of these are "cookbooks," with specific directions to follow. The activities are focused on a single specific skill, and frequently ignore many of the baby's natural ways of learning. A growing body of research findings indicate that learning begins with perception—the process of receiving information through the sensory systems—and not with skill-focused activities.

The Sensory Systems

In ancient times, Aristotle argued that there were "five 'windows of the soul' through which an individual could understand small explorations of the surrounding world" (Travers, 1985, p. 28). Much later, Charles Darwin claimed there were 12 "windows" or senses. Samples (1976) claims there are 20 or more. Actually the specific number of senses depends on how they are grouped. For example we now know that each sense (i.e., vision) is made up of a number of differing receptors of sensation. We also have learned that there are receptors of sensations from the outside world, and also of sensations about happenings within the body (i.e., hunger or thirst pangs as well as sense organs that help us maintain balance). The receptors of all these

sense organs transform one form of energy into another (the light we see is transformed into nerve impulses, which are transmitted to the brain). This is why we speak of *sensory systems* instead of *senses.*

Our concerns here are limited to the receptors, or receivers, of information from the outside world.

Seeing. Normal newborns arrive with the ability to see, and very soon they can focus, perceive depth and dimension, and can visually track a moving object within a range of about 8 to 12 inches. They can even see all the colors, but until about 6 months of age, they prefer to look at patterns with highly contrasting colors. Simple designs of black against white are the most appealing. However, although the human face does not usually contain sharp color contrast, nor is its design simple, it is by far the most attention-receiving of all the things in the baby's immediate environment. We have all noted a

Using all the senses. (Early Childhood Education Center)

Can you see me? (Early
Childhood Education Center)

baby's solemn intense gaze into the adult's face
during nursing times from the very first days.

Visual fixation, or sustained attention, to
other "objects" appears in the third or fourth
week, and may last as long as several minutes
during the second month. It is at this time that
visual perception begins to play a primary role
in the infant's learning.

Hearing. It has long been observed that the
very young startle at loud and/or sudden
noises—actually a fetus in the last trimester will
respond to a loud sound. Musick and Householder (1986) state that "newborns react to all
the major characteristics of sound—pitch, loudness, timbre, and rhythm—but are the most responsive to sounds within the range of the human voice" (p. 176). Some observers claim that
an infant can recognize his own name, and the
voices of his mother and father by the end of the
first week.

There is still much to be learned about the
development of the more complex auditory
skills, although there is agreement that human
hearing is particularly receptive to speech
sounds from early infancy. Even newborns will
consistently turn their heads toward the sound
of a voice, and they more readily turn to their
primary caregiver's voice than to any other. In
most cases, this primary caregiver is the mother.

In the second or third week a new reaction
to a relatively strong auditory stimulus appears,
in terms of the inhibition of general motor activity. This is auditory fixation, and like visual fixation, it plays a primary role in the child's learning. Fixation of any sensory receptor is the
forerunner of attention, and is essential to any
learning act.

Touching. The sense of touch is the earliest to
develop in the human embryo (from conception
to the end of the eighth week). Therefore we
should not be surprised to learn that the infant
seems to be programmed for early touch or tactual stimulation. What may be surprising is the
importance of skin-to-skin contact. "Cuddling,
nuzzling, and lap snuggling give babies the cour-
age to go forth and tackle some of the more
difficult early adventures of learning" (Honig,
1982, p. 9). Studies of failure-to-thrive infants
in the "best" homes as well as in hospitals and
other institutions have led Ashley Montagu to
conclude that

> what the child requires if it is to prosper . . . is to
> be handled, and carried, and caressed and cud-
> dled, and cooed to, even it it isn't breast-fed. It
> is the handling, the carrying, the caressing, the
> caregiving, and the cuddling that we would here
> emphasize, for it would seem that even in the
> absence of a great deal else, these are the reas-
> suringly basic experiences the infant must enjoy
> if it is to survive in some semblance of health.
> Extreme sensory deprivation in other respects,
> such as light and sound, can be survived, as long
> as the sensory experiences of the skin are main-
> tained (1986, pp. 99–100).

Cuddling is part of educaring.
(Kindercampus)

Brazelton (1984b) groups the various functions served by touch as passive (being touched), self-touching, and active. Included under passive touching are: pain, alerting, stimulating, communicating, and controlling. Self-touch is useful in exploration, self-stimulation, and self-control. Active touching is used to explore, alert another, communicate, emphasize, and/or calm another.

Certainly the tactual exploration and manipulation of objects (and pets and people) are essential for cognitive development. Psychological safety comes from feeling attached or connected to others, and the connection is established by physical touching. As we have learned, the touching equipment exists long before the baby is born, and is in working order from the moment of birth. Babies get the tactile stimulation they need if their caregivers are genuinely friendly, loving, and demonstrative.

Tasting-smelling. There are mixed research findings about the newborn's ability to differentiate tastes and smells, but it is generally ac-

cepted that these systems are well developed in the full-term newborn. According to Travers (1985), the taste-smell system is highly trainable, and children can learn to enjoy tastes and odors that may at first seem objectionable. The sense of smell is very difficult to investigate, but we have learned that when smell, touch, and temperature are ruled out, there are four taste sensations: sweet, sour, salty, and bitter.

Tastes and smells may be pleasing or displeasing and at times they may serve in our survival. A good rule of thumb for very young children who are inclined to taste everything is that if it doesn't smell good or taste good, don't eat it. Perhaps this is best taught through the adult modeling exaggerated reactions to pleasant and unpleasant stimuli.

Summary of the sensory systems. Children learn about their world by seeing, hearing, touching, tasting, and smelling. Fortunately, these are built-in abilities that do not have to be learned (or taught). Sensory stimulation encourages brain development, memory, and at-

What does the smell tell you?
(Early Childhood Education
Center)

tention span. It makes the infant's world concrete, understandable, and interesting, thereby motivating him to seek out even more discoveries. The senses keep us in touch with the world, and they are essential for learning from the very first days.

However, after the first few weeks, utilization of the sensory systems depends to a large extent on the developing ability to move.

Perception and Movement

Without the ability or opportunity to move, the sensations that are received would have little or no meaning.

Exploration and manipulation. Exploration of this large world begins with visual exploration of the small world of the breast of the mother during the first nursing sessions. Travers (1985) reports that coordinated searching movements are apparent in the first weeks of life, and that the newborn

> sees the world as filled with objects that have identities, but the shapes have no meaning for

the infant, and they cannot have until they are acted upon, by grasping, mouthing, banging, turning over, hitting, throwing, and by performing all the actions that a baby can perform in its quest for understanding and mastery of the physical world (pp. 151–152).

As infants explore and manipulate objects, they increase their perceptions; they are actually building their sensorimotor intelligence with their hands. Observations of infants from 6 to 12 months have shown that they alternate mouthing and looking; they hold an object in one hand while fingering it with the other, they rotate objects with one or both hands, and they transfer objects from hand to hand (Ruff, 1984). It does seem logical that the infant who does not finger, rotate, or transfer objects very much will not learn much about object properties, which means they will be less able to categorize, which in turn will inhibit or slow their language and cognitive development (Ruff, McCarton, Kurtzberg, & Vaugh, 1984).

These essential initial and continuing explorations depend on movement; it is not possible to separate movement from perception. Some psychologists claim that perception both initiates and regulates movement—that even the beginning actions are purposeful.

Exploration soon involves manipulation, and both are necessary to learn about objects—what they are like and what they can do. If we analyze any task or concept down to its basic parts, we will begin to understand the necessity for repeated and varied explorations and manipulations. Kamii and DeVries (1978) suggest that the young child learns about a ball (or ball-ness) in the following manner:

> It is only by dropping the ball on the floor, rolling it, throwing it into the air, throwing it against the floor, throwing it against the grass, throwing it against a wall, varying the force applied, trying to catch it, chasing it down a stairway, kicking it, and so forth, that the child can come to know the ball (p. 234).

Too many adults expect children to learn by visual stimulation only. It is true that the identification of colors is a visual discrimination, but identification and understanding of sizes, shapes, weights, and space depend on vision, exploration, manipulation, and movement.

Perception is not developed in isolation but in the course of manipulations and interactions with physical objects. Motor behaviors correct or reinforce the perceptions triggered by sensations. We have long recognized the cumulative effects of first-hand experiences involving sensory and motor activities. Piaget also recognized these beginning experiences and called them sensorimotor intelligence. Our debt to him is not that he discovered the importance of sensorimotor learning, but that he popularized the idea. His writings describe, in fine detail, such learnings in the lives of his own children and the children attending the Montessori school next to his Institute in Geneva, Switzerland. His writings have been interpreted as attributing all the knowledge gained by the very young child to the child's actions; it is true that he paid little attention to the persons in the child's life-space. Perhaps this is because many Swiss preschools, and particularly those that follow the Montessori method, intentionally minimize the instructional

role of the adult (directress). They also emphasize individual activity rather than social activity. Sensorimotor learning is a primary mode of early learning, but it is not the only mode.

After the child becomes acquainted with objects (What are they? What are they like?) and manipulates them (What can I do with them or to them?), he begins to play.

Play. Play is not a frivolous activity; it is an essential part of the child's natural life. The oft-quoted statement that "play is child's work" is the adult's attempt to legitimize play as part of the daily program, and the word *work* implies there is a conscious purpose or objective. But our little ones have no objective; they are just exploring and experimenting. They expect no end product; their motivation is simply to find out.

Play starts with what children are capable of doing. New babies soon explore visually, and they respond to sounds. Social reinforcement even at the beginning stages is very important, because there can be no separation of play activities and playfulness from learning. Current play research and theory emphasize the value of play for the development of cognition, language, and the intellectual functions; they also emphasize the personal, social, and cultural functions.

Interest in, and appreciation of the role of play in the young child's total development is relatively recent. The current position is that play should be the basic ingredient of the awake hours in the life of the infant and toddler (and preschooler). The basis for play is the exploration and manipulation development just described. Further comments in some detail are included in each of the chapters in Part Two, The Developmental Curriculum. Play is not only the result of the initial actions of the baby, it also is based on the infant's ability to imitate.

Imitation

Imitation is the ability to reproduce behavior observed in someone or something. To be able to imitate, a person must be able to perceive and to engage in purposeful motor activity. We really don't know how or when true imitation happens. Some researchers have claimed that a 1-hour-old infant imitated an adult who stuck out his tongue (Meltzoff & Moore, 1977); others express doubts about this, and suggest the behavior was coincidental. Piaget (1936/1952) states that imitation is active and intentional toward the end of the sensorimotor stage.

We do know that facility in imitation develops out of an interaction between two partners in which the older one provides the infant with feedback related to the infant's own behavior. Early motor imitation is usually limited to one bit of behavior; early verbal imitation is usually limited to a single syllable (or repetitions of the single syllable). We also know that the ability to imitate is a necessary first step toward modeling behavior or language patterns. Of course, before the infant or toddler can duplicate or approximate a behavior pattern, she must be able to do the actions involved, and have some control over her movements. Motor skill ability combined with the ability to imitate enable the child to model the higher level motor patterns in the preschool years (Musick & Householder, 1986).

From 6 months on, imitation of age-appropriate actions is a powerful force in learning, and appears to be the most powerful motivation for behavior.

In addition to the development of motor and communication skills, all social learnings during the very early years result from the imitation of the behavior of significant others, both age-peers and older. It is possible, of course, to teach "please" and "thank you" through imitation, if the use of the words leads to a reward (reinforcer). But the words are meaningless unless they represent an attitude of respect and consideration of others. The words and their meaning are best learned by the observation of consistent adult behaviors, including but not limited to verbalization. Even the simple social rituals of greeting when children are delivered to and picked up from the center or family day-care home are important in "teaching" social behavior. Unfortunately, in too many instances, the adults greet one another and chat on an adult level while ignoring the child. This is an easy routine to follow, and must be consciously avoided. Why? It tells the child that only grown-ups are important, and that he is not important.

Imitation appears to be the most powerful motivator for behavior throughout childhood and definitely during young adulthood. Underneath it all during the very young years is the child's natural curiosity.

Curiosity and Attention

Even before the baby is physically able to imitate (or even reach out) he is searching for answers with his whole being. He has arrived with a need to find out about the world. Everything is new to the newborn, and many things are new to the infant and toddler. They are all curious. Their learning does not depend on or need external incentives if their curiosity needs are recognized and satisfied. These needs are recognized and satisfied by the true educarer.

The educarer's responsibility is three-fold: to design and furnish the physical environment so that it invites exploration; to provide the opportunity for child-initiated exploration; and to direct the child's curiosity (or attention) to pertinent factors in the environment. Even very young children will attend to individual objects or actions. We can predict and therefore somewhat control the focus and duration of attention if we consider the following guidelines.

1. Infants pay attention to what they can see or hear. After the first 5 or 6 months, these sensory systems are quite similar to those of an adult.

2. There are individual differences in the amount of attentiveness, and young children are more attentive at some times than at other times. Attentiveness is directly related to feelings of physical well-being and psychological safety.

3. The degree of attentiveness is directly related to the intensity of the stimulus. Loud noises and bright colors attract more initial attention than do subdued noises and colors. Intense sights and sounds may attract the child's attention but will not necessarily hold it. The physical environment should not be overwhelming. Understimulation has the same result as overstimulation. It is probably impossible to accurately state age-appropriate intensities for normal children because of their individuality. Experience with each child is the best guide.

4. Although the attributes that hold a child's attention have not been specifically identified, it has been observed that sustained attention is influenced by associations with previous perceptions. Even the very young infant has a store of early perceptions. Hungry babies stop crying when they hear approaching footsteps. The toddler's attention is attracted when she hears her name or the voices of her parents, and is totally inattentive when she hears the voices of another child's parents.

5. The young child's attention is influenced by the degree to which the event or object matches his previous perceptions. A totally new experience frequently causes him to either ignore or withdraw from the encounter. A totally new experience may even frighten. The child's attention is attracted and held by happenings or objects that are only moderately different from the expected.

These guidelines tell us that we should build on (or from) the familiar. Novelty may be introduced into a familiar environment by changing the pictures on the wall or bulletin board, by rearranging or moving an interest center, and by adding and taking away toys and other objects available for investigation. Some flexibility in the day's schedule also introduces a difference in a familiar routine. A balance between the familiar and the unfamiliar is particularly important for infants and toddlers.

SUMMARY

Although the newborn appears totally helpless and dependent, studies of early child development and early learning have shown that he already has many of the prerequisites for growth and development. The rapid changes during the first years are truly miraculous.

The accumulated body of research findings have led to three major principles of early child development.

1. Each child is unique because of his unique biological inheritance combined with unique life experiences from the moment of conception.

2. Heredity and environment do not operate as separate entities; neither can exert an influence without the other.

3. Growth and development occur when a child is engaged in mutually fulfilling actions with other persons.

Normal children have the essential tools for learning, either at birth or shortly thereafter. The sensory systems are activated by both internal and external happenings. In a short time random sensations are internalized and are organized into perceptions. These percepts, or mental images, are the result of exploration, manipulation, play, and imitation, with the concurrent motor skill development. Underlying all learning is the child's innate curiosity.

As wonderful as the infant's abilities and characteristics are, they need to be nurtured and encouraged by persons and environments that are sensitive to the infant's needs and internal drives. This is the essence of educaring—a sensitive combination of teaching and caring.

SUGGESTED ACTIVITIES AND QUESTIONS

1. Observe an infant and a toddler in a group setting, using the Developmental Milestones chart in appendix B as a reference. Note what milestones have been reached, and those that are just appearing.

2. Observe two or more infants or toddlers of the same chronological age. In what ways are they similar? In what ways are they different?

3. Visit and evaluate a program for infants and/or toddlers, using the guidelines contained in part two (Developmentally Appropriate Care for Children from Birth to Age 3) in either the 1986 or 1987 edition of *Developmentally Appropriate Practice* edited by S. Bredekamp of the National Association for the Education of Young Children.

4. Send for information about infant toddler growth and development from your county extension service or your state's Department of Human Services. Request a list of available information from the Superintendent of Documents, U.S. Government Printing Office, Washington, DC 20402.

5. Visit a local toy store. Select three items designed for infants and/or toddlers. Evaluate them in terms of appropriateness for sensory and/or motor development, using the information in this chapter and appendix B.

6. Start an index card file for appropriate toys and activities for infants and toddlers.
Group them according to
sensory receptive: seeing, hearing, touching, tasting and smelling
motoric: gross and fine motor
curiosity and attention
Your card file should grow as you continue your studies, and as you have hands-on experiences with very young children.

SUGGESTED READINGS

Ames, L. & Ilg, F. L. (1980). *Your two year old.* New York: Dell.

Ames, L. & Ilg, F. L. (1983). *Your one year old.* New York: Dell.

Ames, L. B., Gillespie, C., Haines, J., & Ilg, F. L. (1979). *The Gesell Institute's child from one to six.* New York: Harper & Row.

Anselmo, S. (1980, Fall). Children learn about their senses. *Day care and early education, 8,* 42–44.

Anselmo, S. (1987). *Early childhood development: Prenatal through age eight.* Columbus, OH: Merrill.

Appleton, T., Clifton, R., & Goldberg, L. (1975). The development of behavioral competency in infants. In F. D. Horowitz (Ed.), *Review of child development research.* Vol. 4. Chicago: University of Chicago Press.

Baldwin, A. L. (1980). *Theories of child development* (2nd ed.). New York: John Wiley.

Belsky, J., & Most, R. K. (1982). Infant exploration and play: A window on cognitive development. In J. Belsky (Ed.), *In the beginning: Readings on infancy.* New York: Columbia University Press.

Bower, T. G. R. (1977). *The perceptual world of the child.* Cambridge, MA: Harvard University Press.

Bower, T. G. R. (1982). *Development in infancy* (2nd ed.). San Francisco: W. H. Freeman.

Brazelton, T. B. (1969). *Infants and mothers.* New York: Dell.

Brazelton, T. B. (1987). *What every baby knows.* Reading, MA: Addison-Wesley.

Brown, C. C. (Ed.). (1984). *The many facets of touch.* Skillman, NJ: Johnson & Johnson Baby Products Company.

Bybee, R. W., & Sund, R. B. (1982). *Piaget for educators* (2nd ed.). Columbus, OH: Merrill.

Charlesworth, R. (1987). *Understanding child development* (2nd ed.). Albany, NY: Delmar.

Chess, S., Thomas, A., & Birch, H. G. (1976). *Your child is a person.* New York: Penguin.

Church, J. (1973). *Understanding your child from birth to three: A guide to your child's psychological development.* New York: Random House.

Crain, W. C. (1980). *Theories of development: Concepts and applications.* Englewood Cliffs, NJ: Prentice-Hall.

Deci, E. L., & Ryan, R. M. (1982). Curiosity and self-directed learning: The role of motivation in education. In L. G. Katz (Ed.), *Current topics in early childhood education.* Vol. IV. Norwood, NJ: Ablex.

Dittmann, L. L. (Ed.). (1984). *The infants we care for* (rev. ed.). Washington, DC: National Association for the Education of Young Children.

Elkind, D. (1976). *Child development and education: A Piagetian perspective.* New York: Oxford University Press.

Ellis, M. J. (1984). Play, novelty, and stimulus seeking. In T. D. Yawkey & A. D. Pellegrini (Eds.),

Child's play: Developmental and applied (pp. 203–218). Hillsdale, NJ: Erlbaum.

Erikson, E. H. (1982). The life cycle completed. New York: W. W. Norton.

Fenson, L., Kagan, J., Kearsley, R. B., & Zelazo, P. R. (1976). The developmental progression of manipulative play in the first two years. Child Development, 47, 232–236.

Fishbein, H. D. (1984). The psychology of infancy and childhood: Evolutionary and cross-cultural perspectives. Hillsdale, NJ: Erlbaum.

Gesell, A. (1975). The first five years of life (rev. ed.). New York: Harper Brothers.

Gesell, A., Ilg, F., Ames, L. B., & Rodell, J. (1974). Infant and child in the culture of today (rev. ed.). New York: Harper & Row.

Ginsburg, H., & Opper, S. (1979). Piaget's theory of intellectual development (2nd ed.). Englewood Cliffs, NJ: Prentice-Hall.

Gordon, I. J. (1975). The infant experience. Columbus, OH: Merrill.

Gottfried, A. E. (1983, November). Intrinsic motivation in young children. Young Children, 39, 64–73.

Haith, M. M. (1980). Rules that babies look by: The organization of newborn visual activity. Hillsdale, NJ: Erlbaum.

Hellmuth, J. (Ed.). (1967). Exceptional infant. Vol. 1. The normal infant. Seattle: Special Child Publications.

Honig, A. S. (1981). Recent infancy research. In B. Weissbourd & J. S. Musick (Eds.), Infants: Their social environments. Washington, DC: National Association for the Education of Young Children.

Horowitz, F. D. (1982). The first two years of life; Factors related to thriving. In S. G. Moore & C. R. Cooper (Eds.), The young child: Reviews of research. Vol. 3 (pp. 15–34). Washington, DC: National Association for the Education of Young Children.

Kagan, J., Kearsley, R., & Zelazo, P. (1980). Infancy. Cambridge, MA: Harvard University Press.

Labinowicz, E. (1980). The Piaget primer: Thinking, learning, teaching. Menlo Park, CA: Addison-Wesley.

Lamb, M. E., & Campos, J. J. (1982). Development in infancy: An introduction. New York: Random House.

Leach, P. (1983). Babyhood (2nd ed.). New York: Knopf.

LeBoyer, F. (1982). Loving hands. New York: Knopf.

McCall, R. B. (1974). Exploratory manipulation and play in the human infant. Monographs of the Society for Research in Child Development, 39 (Serial No. 155).

McCall, R. B. (1979). Infants: The new knowledge. Cambridge, MA: Harvard University Press.

Mehler, J., & Fox, R. (Eds.). Neonate cognition: Beyond the blooming buzzing confusion. Hillsdale, NJ: Erlbaum.

Murphy, L. B. (1972). Infant's play and cognitive development. In M. W. Piers (Ed.), Play and development. New York: W. W. Norton.

Mussen, P. H., Conger, J. J., Kagan, J., & Huston, A. (1984). Child development and personality (6th ed.). New York: Harper & Row.

Neubauer, P. B. (1968). The third year of life: The two-year-old. In L. L. Dittmann (Ed.), Early child care: The new perspectives. New York: Atherton Press.

Olson, G. M., & Sherman, T. (1983). Attention, learning, and memory in infants. In P. H. Mussen (Ed.), Handbook of Child Psychology. Vol. 2. Infancy and developmental psychobiology. New York: John Wiley.

Osfosky, J. D. (Ed.). (1979). Handbook of infant development. New York: John Wiley & Sons.

Patent, D. H. (1988). Babies. New York: Holiday House.

Pavenstedt, E. (1968). Development during the second year: The one-year-old. In L. L. Dittmann (Ed.), Early child care: The new perspectives. New York: Atherton Press.

Provence, S. (1968). The first year of life: The infant. In L. L. Dittmann (Ed.), Early child care: The new perspectives. New York: Atherton Press.

Richards, M. (1980). Infancy. New York: Harper & Row.

Rosenblatt, D. (1977). Developmental trends in infant play. In B. Tizard & O. Harvey (Eds.), The biology of play. Philadelphia: Lippincott.

Rosenblith, J. F., & Sims-Knight, J. E. (1985). *In the beginning: Development in the first two years.* Monterey, CA: Brooks/Cole.

Salapatek, P., & Cohen, L. (Eds.). (1987). *Handbook of infant perception.* Vols. 1 & 2. New York: Academic Press.

Sameroff, A. J., & Cavanagh, P. L. (1979). Learning in infancy: A developmental perspective. In J. D. Osofsky (Ed.), *Handbook of infant development.* New York: John Wiley & Sons.

Singer, D. G., & Revenson, T. A. (1978). *How a child thinks: A Piaget primer.* New York: New American Library.

Smart, M. S., & Smart, R. C. (1987). *Development and relationships* (3rd ed.). New York: Macmillan.

Sophian, C. (Ed.). (1984). *Origins of cognitive skills: The 18th annual Carnegie Symposium on Cognition.* Hillsdale, NJ: Erlbaum.

Stone, J. L., Smith, H. T., & Murphy, L. B. (1973). *The competent infant—Research and commentary.* New York: Basic Books.

Thomas, A., & Chess, S. (1977). *Temperament and development.* New York: Brunner/Mazel.

Thomas, A., Chess, S., Birch, H. G., Hertzig, M. E., & Korn, S. (1983). *Behavioral individuality in early childhood.* New York: New York University Press.

Travers, R. M. W. (1985). *Training human intelligence: Developing exploratory and aesthetic skills.* Holmes Beach, FL: Learning Publications.

Wachs, T. D., & Gruen, G. E. (1982). *Early experience and human development.* New York: Plenum Press.

Wadsworth, B. J. (1984). *Piaget's theory of cognitive and affective development* (3rd ed.). New York: Longman.

Watson, M. M., & Jackowitz, E. R. (1984). Agents and recipient objects in the development of early symbolic play. *Child Development, 55,* 1091–1097.

White, B. L. (1985). *The first three years of life* (rev. ed.). New York: Simon & Schuster.

White, B. L., Kaban, B., & Attanucci, J. (1979). *The origins of human competence: The final report of the Harvard Preschool Project.* Lexington, MA: Lexington Books.

Willemsen, E. (1979). *Understanding infancy.* San Francisco: W. H. Freeman.

Zelazo, P. R., & Leonard, E. L. (1983). The dawn of active thought. In K. W. Fischer (Ed.), *Levels and transitions in children's development* (pp. 37–50). New Directions for Child Development, No. 21. San Francisco: Jossey-Bass.

TWO

The Developmental Curriculum

Information about child care regulations in the fifty states has been compiled by Morgan (1987). She found that 34 states had program requirements for infants and toddlers in family day care and/or centers, although most of these states had minimal requirements.

However, "more than 90% of family day care homes are operating outside any regulatory system" (Corsini, Wisensale, & Caruso, 1988, p. 17). We cannot assume anything, therefore, about the vast majority of family day-care homes.

An example of a minimal program requirement is found in the 1988 licensing regulations from the Iowa Department of Human Services.

A child care center serving children two weeks to two years must provide an environment which protects the children from physical harm, but is not so restrictive as to inhibit physical, intellectual, emotional and social development. . . . Stimulation shall be provided through being held, rocked, played with and talked with individually several times each day (p. 18).

The nine states having detailed infant/toddler program requirements (in 1986) were Arkansas, Illinois, Maine, New Jersey, Oregon, Rhode Island, Tennessee, West Virginia, and Wisconsin. Because of the recent growing atten-

tion being given to our youngest children, it is probable that more states either have moved or are moving in the direction of more detailed program requirements for infants and toddlers.

It is generally recognized that licensing requirements state the barest minimum of good practices. In the curriculum section of *Accreditation Criteria & Procedures of the National Academy of Early Childhood Programs* (1984), the following standards are included.

B–6. Staff members continually provide learning opportunities for infants and toddlers, most often in response to cues emanating from the child. Infants and toddlers are permitted to move about freely, exploring the environment and initiating play activities. Curriculum for very young children involves providing a stimulating environment for children to explore and manipulate. Nonmobile children should be carried by staff and their position should be changed frequently so that they can observe different aspects of the environment (p. 13). B–11. Routine tasks are incorporated into the program as a means of furthering children's learning, self-help, and social skills. Routines such as diapering, toileting, eating, dressing, and sleeping are handled in a relaxed, reassuring, and individualized manner based on developmental needs. . . . Young children are constantly learning and much learning takes place during daily activities. Young children gain a sense of their own identity and self-worth from the way in which their bodily needs are responded to and satisfied (p. 14).

These standards are included in the criteria for center accreditation by the National Academy, and therefore are required only for those centers applying for accreditation.

The following chapters contain the information necessary to ensure a high quality infant-toddler program, regardless of its location (home or center).

For our purposes, learning starts at birth, although there is research evidence that a fetus in utero can learn to respond to certain sounds, and to remember them after birth. Learning, therefore, takes place throughout the entire life span. Some researchers claim that the first 2 or 3 years of life are the most important for learning. The more universal opinion, however, is that each stage is important, and that appropriate experiences in each stage lead to learning in that stage and also lay the foundation for optimal learning in the next stage. The goal of infant/toddler educaring is to maximize the learnings during that stage and to lay the foundation for the preschool years.

You perhaps remember Topsy in *Uncle Tom's Cabin*. Topsy "just growed" and did a remarkable job of it. However, "just growing" is not enough. Although there may be times in a high quality program when the children just grow, these times are limited to sleep time. During all the awake times the infants and toddlers are learning in their own unique ways.

The normal newborn arrives with sensitivities for seeing, hearing, tasting, smelling, touching, and feeling. Infants are able to perceive, move, communicate, imitate, and remember. They are innately curious, and they like to play. These are the abilities and characteristics that enable children to learn. Their learning is enriched by their interactions with responsible and responsive educarers in an appropriate environment whether in family day care or a center.

The chapters in Part Two present information about this learning in cognitive and language skills, social skills, and motor skills.

Chapter 3 discusses the necessity of goal setting as a first step in planning a program, and suggests that the main cognitive goal for infants and toddlers should be that each one becomes an enthusiastic learner. Prerequisites for enthusiastic learning are a positive concept of self, motivation to learn, and both environmental and human stimulation. The first learnings are achieved by exploration and experimentation, action and interaction, and imitation. The very young child's learning grows out of his developing skills in language and play.

Chapter 4 focuses on the nurturing of *social competency,* a term used to describe the personal and social skills expected of the 3 year old. The child progresses from her knowledge of self to knowledge of others to her relationships with others. Suggested approaches for teaching acceptable social behaviors are included as well as for the problem behaviors of aggression, temper tantrums, biting, and stranger anxiety. Both conversation skills and social play skills have an important role in the development of social competency.

Chapter 5 discusses the nurturing of motor skill development. Activities are suggested that are appropriate for the developmental stages of both gross and fine motor skills, and for their coordination in selected play activities, especially block play. Of course, motor skills are basic to the self-help skills of dressing and grooming, feeding and eating, and toileting.

The topics covered in the next chapters are interdependent. Their arbitrary separation has been done for ease in presentation and understanding. However, our interactions with infants and toddlers will frequently combine some or all of them.

3

Nurturing Cognitive and Language Development

I hear and I forget; I see and I remember; I do and I understand.
Chinese proverb

A child is born with the essential tools for learning: the sensory systems and an insatiable curiosity. The first 3 years are devoted primarily to sensorimotor activities and the resulting satisfaction of some of the curiosity drive. If all goes well by age 3 the child will begin to have the capacities for reflection, manipulating ideas, and understanding quite complicated verbal expressions. Individuality and imagination are developing.

It has been said that the child learns more during the first 3 years than during any other 3-year period of life. Even though this cannot be verified, no one can deny that the rate of learning is spectacular. This learning is usually referred to as *cognitive development.*

Although the proverb at the beginning of this chapter applies to persons of all ages, it has the most significance for the early years of human life. Learning by doing is the primary mode of learning for infants and toddlers. Most persons agree with this. But if these children learn by doing, what is the role of the educarer? Perhaps good infant-toddler caregivers and

teachers are just good baby-sitters. Many persons in the larger community think this is the case. These are the same persons who are critical of many programs for preschoolers. They ask, "Why preschool, if all they do is play?" Teachers of young children should be prepared to respond to the issues of teaching (or educaring) versus babysitting, and learning versus play, as well as other issues involved in developmentally appropriate educaring. Education during the first 3 years is the first link in the educational chain.

GOAL SETTING

The setting of goals is the appropriate first step in planning any program. Without goals, a program goes willy-nilly like a rudderless boat. The program may contain all kinds of opportunities for learning, but without a preconceived direction, the time and energy of both adults and children will have less than optimal results.

The setting of goals for an infant-toddler learning program is more difficult than the traditional setting of goals for an academic kindergarten or the primary grades. Teachers of the very young cannot state that the child will learn colors, shapes, letters, and numerals. They cannot offer a program designed to teach reading, writing, and arithmetic. They cannot even state that the child will learn the social skills of sharing and cooperation.

Child development specialists are inclined to base their programs on developmental milestones, and to design programs to enhance the achievement of these milestones. Educators and psychologists are inclined to base their programs on societal expectations for later academic achievement. The model programs for very young children fall into one of the above designs. To date, we do not have conclusive evidence that one is significantly better than the other.

Perhaps it is the parents of the infants and toddlers who are the best goal-setters. However, experience has shown that it is difficult to find a group of parents who agree on goals for their children in any specific center or family day-care home. It is not unusual to find a mother and father in the same family who disagree about the goals for their own children. In addition, there is a relationship between goals and economic status, and between goals and cultural or ethnic status. Some groups are more oriented to academic readiness, obedience, and "good manners." Other groups are more concerned about individuality, creativity, and social relationships.

There can be a compromise approach to educational goal-setting that involves both parents and staff members. In this approach the staff take the lead instead of the parents. All persons involved in the delivery of the program (directors, educarers, aides, nurse, social workers, etc.) should initially explore the full range of goals suggested by the experts in the field and by their own value systems. They select the most appropriate goals, and from this list they select those goals that are achievable in their particular situation. These appropriate, achievable goals are then presented to the parents for discussion. The parents are asked to choose from them, or to list them in terms of their own priorities. It is possible in this way to arrive at mutually agreeable goals for the cognitive program, and in particular, for the cognitive development of the children in the program.

Regardless of the actual method used to choose the goals, the foundation for all cognitive goal-setting should be the current knowledge about cognitive development. Unfortunately, it is difficult to define. According to Copple, DeLisi, and Sigel (1982), the best approach is to describe "changes in children's knowledge and thinking skills and the way these are organized and used in dealing with problems" (p. 3). The knowledge and thinking skills during the first 3 years of life are derived primarily from sensorimotor experiences. Knowledge is also obtained from strong messages directed to the child verbally by the nearby adult ("No!" or "Don't touch!"). The most recent interpretation of Piaget's theory is based on the idea that each child constructs his own knowledge. In other words, the child learns from his own activity and reflections; he learns nothing when he is simply told with words.

Katz (1988) has identified four levels of learning in early childhood education as knowledge, skills, dispositions, and feelings. Knowledge and skills are necessary to get meanings from objects and events and persons. A disposition is simply wanting to find out, the motivation for learning. Feelings, of course, are the result of the physical and social environments in which the child lives. Ideally, these environments are relaxed, enjoyable, and appropriately stimulating.

Hayward (1987) describes two kinds of cognitive learning:

> direct exposure to environmental events, and mediated learning experience. Some mediated learning experience is necessary for all children, but the amount, quality, intensity, frequency, and duration of what is needed for adequate cog-

nitive development will vary as a function of individual differences in children (p. 3).

The mediator, of course, is the educarer, who knows the individual infants and toddlers well enough to decide on the amount, quality, intensity, frequency, and duration of what is needed for each child. This is more than a small responsibility for anyone in an early childhood program.

Howard Gardner (1985) has expanded our traditional ideas about cognitive development and general intelligence by identifying six types of intelligence. According to his theory, all human beings have varying degrees of linguistic, musical, logical-mathematical, spatial, bodily kinesthetic, and personal intelligences.

The nurturing and enhancing of these intelligences takes place in the home and the surrounding culture, and in the agencies dedicated to education, usually the school, but in our case the infant-toddler program. To meet the needs of these developing intelligences, our programs should include activities and experiences in all these areas, and not focus on one or two of them. Many of our infant-toddler programs seem to forget the overall goal of development of the "total" child.

Basic to any theory is the development of cognition, and the goals for the cognitive development of young children should be drawn from what we know about how very young children learn.

The research findings about infant learning have been summarized by Sameroff and Cavanagh (1979). Up until that time, infant learning had been considered to be synonymous with conditioning. The reviewers raised questions about this definition, and along with more recent researchers, theorized that the answer might not be so simple. Nonetheless, good research in the 1980s (Blass, Granchrow, & Steiner, 1984; DeCasper & Carstens, 1981; Rose & Slater, 1983) has supported the "conditioning = infant learning" theory. Most recently, Caruso (1988) has suggested that remembering can take place

without understanding, and therefore we must distinguish between the two. "If learning in infancy is broadly defined as coming to know about and make sense of the world, then understanding must be seen as the key factor in this process" (p. 64).

There are three basic steps in learning as understanding:

1. They take in information with their senses. This is frequently accomplished by a combination of seeing, hearing, and moving (the most important senses), and smelling, tasting, and touching.

2. They process information. As their senses explore the people, events and things in their environment, children remember, organize the information, attach meaning to it, and figure out uses for each new learning achievement.

3. They use information. If children have received information from their environment through their senses, and if they have remembered and attached meaning to the information they have received, they are able to behave in a way that tells us what they have learned. The behavior may be motoric (what they do) or verbal (what they say).

These basic steps in learning are the basic steps in cognitive development, and they contain the clues for program development. We want children to learn about their physical environments, and to learn from them; we want children to learn about their social environments, and to learn from them; we want children to learn about their own bodies, and to control their movements.

The main cognitive goal for infants and toddlers is that each one becomes an enthusiastic learner. In so doing, we will be teaching that both living and learning are satisfying and exciting.

This "learning how to learn" will not occur unless certain conditions are present. These conditions, or prerequisites, for learning are all related to the child's disposition or motivation to learn.

MOTIVATION TO LEARN

Motivation Defined

Motivation is an intrinsic quality; stimulation is an extrinsic quality. Therefore the term *motivation* is misused when teachers are admonished to motivate their children to learn. According to Samples (1975):

> I cannot motivate you (although I can move you to action), and you cannot motivate me (although you can arouse my motivation). . . . What school teachers generally think of as motivation is what psychologists call stimulation. . . . Stimulation is something I can do to you and you can do to me, but in terms of motivation the actual inner drive that is created in each one of us and that provides us with the impetus to do something has to come from within ourselves (p. 136).

Teachers of infants and toddlers are fortunate indeed. Their children are motivated by an innate curiosity, one of the essential tools of learning. We would hope that these children have not yet had their curiosity suppressed for the sake of a smooth routine or an exaggerated view of safety precautions or for the adults' convenience. Teachers do not need to stimulate curiosity. They do need to arrange for its continuation. Studies of human infants who are satisfied with their lives suggest that

> they are avid seekers of information who scan their environment, make fine distinctions, and prefer certain types of complex stimuli. Children appear to be biologically programmed to seek, explore, and respond to gain increased information and competence in dealing with their environment (Coopersmith, 1975, p. 18).

Even with this biological programming, teachers cannot sit back and let baby "just grow." Motivation to learn has a somewhat elusive quality. Although it comes with the baby, it

can actually be eliminated, or at least driven underground, unless baby has the security and stability of a positive concept of self.

A Positive Concept of Self

Self-concept is learned, and the learning begins at birth. By the time most children have reached their third birthday they have learned two of the most complex tasks to be confronted during their lifetime: to walk and to talk. The other children (excluding those with developmental delays) very possibly have not learned to walk or to talk because their early environment discouraged their attempts to learn. Lack of psychological support leads to a negative concept of self, which leads to fear, anxiety, and noticeable withdrawal from the normal activities. The time and energies of these children have been focused on developing their defense mechanisms, instead of seeking new challenges. Defense mechanisms of infants and toddlers include regression to earlier behaviors, denial, and withdrawal. Murphy (1962) and Murphy and Moriority (1976) report that young children develop characteristic ways of coping that remain fairly consistent over childhood. The necessity of an early positive concept of self should not be questioned.

It is appropriate here to mention two extensive studies of public school systems, even though the children involved were well beyond the infant-toddler age period. The Coleman study (1966) found that only two factors made a difference in school achievement. These were not the traditional factors of class size, teacher preparation, or per-pupil expenditure. They were the *child's sense of self-worth* and the *child's socioeconomic background.* The second study by Platt (1974), involving school children from 20 countries, resulted in essentially the same findings. Although neither the public schools nor child-care centers can control the socioeconomic factors in a child's life, they can and must help each child develop feelings of self-worth. This development should occur during the first 3 years, long before the children attend elementary school.

This period may even be a critical one. Attitudes toward self determine openness to new experiences. They determine approaches to and relationships with other persons. They influence the intrinsic motivation to learn.

There are few research studies concerning the developing feelings of self-worth in very young children. The research findings and statements of expert opinion are usually directed toward the elementary school years. Coopersmith (1975) has no reservation when he states "children with high self-esteem perform better and will do less poorly in their schoolwork" (p. 96). There are research conclusions that indicate that the kindergarten child's feelings about self are a better indication of reading readiness than are the scores on intelligence tests (Wattenberg & Clifford, 1964). More recently, it has been found with preschool children that a quality preschool program apparently results in more positive concepts, more positive attitudes toward learning, and toward life itself, even at age 19, 15 years after the preschool experience (Berrueta-Clement, Schweinhart, Barnett, Epstein, & Weikart, 1984). Perhaps no more need be written here about the importance of a positive self-concept, except that most educators and psychologists agree about its influential role.

Our immediate concern is how to teach positive self-concepts. The following episodes, which were observed in an infant-toddler center, highlight a few of the recommended teaching techniques. How many of these techniques can you find? There are at least 16 of them.

EPISODE 1

Four-month old Margie was sitting contentedly in the infant seat playing intently with some bells that were strung above her just within her reach. She was batting the bells, looking quite pleased with the resulting sounds. Suddenly her mood completely changed. She arched her back, began kicking her feet and waving her arms wildly. She began to whimper and continued whimpering until one of the caregivers came to her and said, "Margie, you must be tired of sitting in your chair." The caregiver unfastened the restraining belt and moved Margie from the chair to the adult-sized rocking chair. The bottle of formula was ready. Margie nestled into the caregiver's arms and greedily sucked the bottle. Her eyes were wide open and were focused on the caregiver's face as she talked softly to Margie during the feeding. Margie's body was very still as she concentrated on sucking and gazing into the caregiver's eyes. After about 5 minutes the caregiver removed the bottle, placed Margie in a sitting position on her lap, and patted her firmly on the back. After a clearly audible bubble, the caregiver resumed Margie's feeding and began to gently rock. Margie finished the bottle, her eyes still glued to her caregiver's face. After a few more pats (and another bubble), Margie was placed on her tummy on a blanket in front of a long low mirror fastened to the baseboard of the wall. She promptly rolled over, smiled at the caregiver, and then began to smile at herself in the mirror.

EPISODE 2

Eighteen-month-old John has been greeted by a caregiver after waking from his nap. The caregiver tended to his emotional and physical needs by caressing, kissing, holding, changing, dressing, and getting his lunch. After eating eagerly, and just as eagerly washing his hands, John walked to the caregiver and raised his arms saying "up!" The caregiver responded, "Let's go play," and swooped John up in his arms. John smiled and giggled. He was put down on the floor where he began to play with a pull toy near the caregiver. John gradually moved away, after giving the caregiver a smile.

EPISODE 3

Thirty-month-old Tommy was having a bad time. He and the other children were on the outside playground on a gusty, nippy day. Every time an-other gust of wind came, he would start to scream, look terrified, and run for the storage shed in the corner of the playground. The teacher would pick him up, and talk and comfort him while standing inside the shed. When the wind died down, Tommy went back out to play. After two such episodes, the teacher suggested that he stay in the shed and play for awhile. She put a sleeping bag on the floor so he could pretend he was camping out. She also opened the window shutters so that he could see out and watch the other children at play. As soon as he heard an-other gust of wind he would back into the corner of the shed. The teacher stayed with him most of the time. When she did leave to attend to other children, she returned every few minutes to check on Tommy. A trash truck backed into the pick-up area on the other side of the fence. With this new excitement and noise, Tommy ventured outside the shed and seemed to forget the wind, but it was at his back. After the truck left, he started to cry again. The teacher suggested they both back into the wind, and soon they were both playing "backing up into the wind." In a minute it was time to go inside. Tommy ran happily into the cen-ter with the rest of the children.

Each episode contains teaching techniques appropriate to both the ages and the personal-ities of the individual children. Each episode in-cludes teaching and learning a positive self-con-cept. In each instance, there was an educarer who cared enough to respond to signals appro-priately and affectionately. As the result of the adult-child interactions, each child in his or her own way felt acceptance and love in the day-care setting.

Attitudes toward self are learned in the same way attitudes toward other persons, experi-ences, things, and places are learned. They are the result of consistent responses from things, experiences, or persons. Attitudes can be strengthened, weakened, or destroyed. The re-sponsibility of the educarer is to strengthen each child's concept of self. It is not difficult, if we

remember that desirable attitudes result from emotionally satisfying experiences. We also need to remember that even very young chil-dren are not fooled by superficial words of praise or demonstrations of physical affection. Adults must be genuinely interested and con-cerned; they must involve themselves in the child's activities; they must appreciate what the child is doing and can do. Educarers offer sup-port in times of stress and encouragement in times of uncertainty.

There is a subtle but important difference between encouragement and praise. Praise is external recognition given to the child for a suc-cessful performance. It is intended to motivate and to stimulate further performance. However, praise can have harmful side effects. It might suggest to children that their value or relation-ship to the praiser is dependent on success. En-couragement is not dependent on success or achievement. All of us need encouragement when we have not succeeded. Encouragement may take many forms in an infant-toddler cen-ter. "Try again" is appropriate some times. At other times the teacher can rearrange the envi-ronment or objects in it to enable the child to succeed. Also, comforting words and temporary redirection (e.g., the sleeping bag for Tommy) are powerful encouragers.

Motivation and Basic Needs

Maslow (1943) is sometimes called the father of the needs theory of human motivation. He con-tends that basic needs are arranged in hierar-chical order, and that the emphasis on one need grows out of the satisfaction of a previous need. Maslow's list of basic needs can be adapted to very young children in the following manner:

1. Needs relating to physiological survival and well-being: food, water, oxygen, clothing, shelter, hygiene, and health care.

2. Needs relating to physical safety and psy-chological security in the environment: Young children show strong reactions when

they are suddenly disturbed or startled by loud noises, flashing lights, or other intense stimuli. They are upset by rough handling and by loss of physical support. They perceive danger when their world is unorganized and unstructured and therefore unpredictable. Even a physical illness may be threatening to the very young child and can lead to a feeling of loss of safety.

3. Needs relating to love and belongingness: All children (even the "unlovable") need to be loved, cared for, attended to, and given emotional support. Human love needs include both receiving and giving love.

4. Needs relating to self-esteem or self-worth: Infants and toddlers need to be accepted, appreciated, and valued as individuals. They also need to achieve and to be independent. Of course, achieving and independence are closely related to, and somewhat determined by, the developmental stages. Nonetheless, very young children have these needs and constantly strive to meet them under normal circumstances. Satisfaction of the self-worth need leads to self-confidence and a positive concept of self.

5. Need to know and to understand: Curiosity is readily observable in any infant or toddler. The need to know (or to learn) is as basic a need as are the needs for physical well-being and emotional satisfaction. The need to know is activated only when these other needs have been met. It will be expressed automatically and naturally if the teacher(s) have adequately met the prerequisite needs. A satisfied need no longer motivates behavior, and the child is freed to attempt to satisfy the next higher need.

Motivation and Stimulation

Many theories have been forwarded in an attempt to analyze what motivates humans to learn. Some claim that basic drives of hunger, thirst, and sex spur us to action. Others suggest love and a sense of belongingness as learning incentives. Still others rely on a planned system of rewards and punishments. Robert White (1968) emphasizes the need for competence as the basic motivation. He includes three characteristics of the competence need: (1) the need for activity, (2) the need for mastery, and (3) the need for excitement and stimulation.

Behaviors directed by these needs are readily observable. Very young children continually explore their surroundings by moving, touching, grasping, lifting, pulling, pushing, dropping. Young children are active whenever the opportunity is there. They do not need external stimulation to cause or provoke activity. Young children strive for mastery. Picture the baby just learning to grasp and later learning to let go. Watch the toddler work and work and work to master "chair-sitting." She backs up and plops, usually on the floor a foot away from the chair. She starts again, this time facing the chair and putting her hands on the chair, thereby gaining tactual knowledge of its location. She twists and turns her body so that one hand remains on the chair seat while she backs up again, and tentatively sits down on the front edge of the chair. She wriggles back into position and shows pure delight at her mastery of chair-sitting. The moment of delight is short-lived, and she now attempts mastery without hand-help. When finally successful, her beaming face and loud chuckles prove without a doubt that she has satisfied her need for mastery. No one had offered a gold star or a cookie; no one had instructed or consciously demonstrated. Such intrusive actions might even have led to loss of interest in the activity.

The third characteristic, the need for excitement and stimulation, is the characteristic that has resulted in controversy regarding desirable techniques for teaching very young children. According to Bromwich (1977), "the term infant stimulation is misleading and should not be used in identifying educational programs appropriate for young infants" (p. 81). Brazelton (1979) tells parents that so much cognitive development goes on in a young child *who is being nurtured properly* that any artificial or imposed stimulation is superfluous. Actually, "stimulating" a baby is just a natural part of caring for the baby. Talking to baby, responding to baby's gestures or sounds, and playing with baby— these are the appropriate and fun ways to encourage the development of cognition. In an interview on a National Public Radio broadcast, Burton White (1979) said that "almost anything the kid does is enough to move the child forward."

Cognitive development is related to a match between the child's developmental level and the quantity and quality of environmental stimulation (Hunt, 1961). The child shows interest in objects and events that are mildly discrepant from previous experiences. Too much discrepancy will result in noninterest or even avoidance. Too little (or no) discrepancy produces boredom and even apathy when continued over a period of time. Previous experiences, natural abilities, and chronological age all influence the child's developmental level. It is for this reason that norms of cognitive development are questionable when applied to an individual beyond the first birthday.

Environmental stimulation. Infants generally receive large amounts of environmental stimulation from the time of birth. Therefore there is no need for imposing a specially designed infant program. However, there is a need for observing each baby to discover the optimal environmental match. Programs that are not related to individual behavior or temperamental patterns, as well as to maturational changes and needs, could interfere with cognitive development. Reciprocity of interaction is the cornerstone for optimal development. If the child is allowed the opportunity to explore and interact with a varied environment, he will encounter novel or discrepant stimuli that introduce new learnings. It is now thought that stimulation that proceeds in a somewhat predictable order will lead to formation of the basic concepts of object permanence and causality. However, given the appropriate environment, the child must be given freedom to pace his own encounters with stimuli.

General guidelines for planning the stimulation in the physical environment follow the stages of sensorimotor development during the first 2 years. During the first month, baby responds primarily to stimuli relating to the innate reflexes. These include the sucking and rooting behaviors related to hunger and thirst, and the crying and other vocal behaviors related to discomfort or stress. After the first month, baby's reflexive behaviors begin to be modified by sensory experiences. All stimuli possess novelty when first presented. The environment now should contain a variety of sights, sounds, textures, and shapes. Baby will smile at some and will gaze at others for a long time. Now is the time to use bright patterned sheets, crib mobiles within visual range, decals on the inner sides of the crib, and pictures on the wall. Soft rhythmic music both stimulates and soothes. There is no substitute for an educarer's song or hum. This is also the time to place rattles and different toys and textured objects in baby's hand and to offer help in grasping (wrap baby's fingers around the object). Baby should accomplish a firm grasp by 4 months of age and then will start to adjust the grasp to the specific object. The ability to integrate seeing, reaching, and grasping has not yet developed. Sometime during the fifth or sixth month, baby will be intrigued by an attractive object just beyond reach and will attempt to reach it. Continuing frustration is nonproductive, and the object should be moved close enough for baby to be successful. The mobile objects should be within reach, and therefore safe for baby to grasp.

When the baby's position in the crib is changed periodically (this should happen well before the sixth month), he gains a whole new perspective of his world. An even larger perspective with many new stimuli is opened up when baby is placed on the floor. Intentional

Integrated seeing, reaching, and grasping. (What is wrong in this picture? The answer is in chapter 8.)

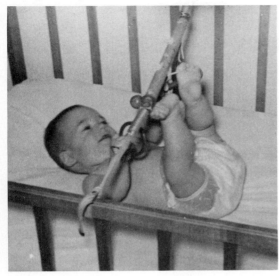

behavior is observable between 6 and 12 months of age when baby becomes mobile and able to reach a desired object. The sequence of behaviors will be continued in a later section, Exploration and Experimentation.

Selected principles about the stimulation qualities of the physical environment include the following:

1. The best environment at one stage of development is not the best at another stage. The rattles and toys that intrigue the 6 month old have lost their fascination for the 1 year old, who is beginning to enjoy the banging of real pots and pans. The child who is toddling (or walking) is attracted to objects with removable parts, and to manipulative toys, push-and-pull toys, and small cube blocks, but only when she is not working on the mastering of walking skills. By the time the third birthday occurs, the child is ready to encounter the world.

2. The best physical environment is one that provides encounters and experiences with a variety of objects that can be investigated and manipulated with a minimal number of restrictions. To assure challenging stimulation for children at different developmental levels, there must be an even wider range of stimuli.

3. Optimal stimulation occurs when events or objects are mildly discrepant from previous experiences. The experiences of any parent or teacher of very young children testify to this principle. The well-known story of a trip to the zoo is a good example. The adults are intrigued by the bizarre make-up of the giraffe, the 3 year old is intrigued with the different kind of knob on the entrance gate, and the 1 year old is busy attending to the crinkly candy wrapper on the ground. The giraffe was too different from previous experiences with animals to create much interest at all on the part of the young children.

Human stimulation. No matter how varied the physical environment, the young child will not go beyond a certain developmental stage in learning if only an enriched environment is provided. The physical environment needs an adult to serve as mediator between the child and the environment. Adults mediate by structuring the child's interactions, by giving emotional support and encouragement, and by providing stimulation by playing with and talking to the child. Because young children differ in their responsiveness to stimuli, an educarer must vary the quantity, the quality, and the pace of stimulation. For example, very young babies are more visually attracted to bright colors and bright color contrasts than they are to differences in size or shape, and this knowledge should be used in arranging the physical environment. The environment should also be arranged so the child can learn that specific actions have specific results. Crying leads to comfort, pulling a toy produces sounds, and playing an instrument produces music or rhythm.

Horowitz (1969) suggests that the retardation found in children who had been raised in institutions might be the result of the poor match between the environment and the children's individual needs. When a few adults are responsible for the care of too many young children, individual differences are more difficult to accommodate. In order to facilitate a good match between the child's abilities and the physical environment, educarers need to be alert, enthusiastic, and genuinely interested in what the child is doing. When this is the case, they are more likely to interact with the child in a meaningful way. Genuine interest does not involve pressure to achieve. An optimal match implies that the child is not being pushed or overstimulated. An optimal match ensures enjoyable learning.

Adults in day-care centers and homes can profit from a study of Burton White's (1972) findings about parents who produced competent 3 year olds. Not only were the parents genuinely interested in their children's activities, but also most parent-child interactions occurred at the child's request. In addition, these parents engaged in frequent conversations related to what the child was doing at the time. White concluded that exposure to live language directed toward the child's understanding level is related to the development of competence. Language from a radio or television set does little to develop a child's competence. White (1980) summarizes his recommendations to parents as follows.

> Newly crawling infants should be given maximum access to the house. They should be allowed to practice their climbing and other emerging motor skills. For most of their waking hours, they should have easy access to people who have a very special love for them. These people should talk to them about what they are focusing on at the moment, using ordinary language. They should lavish affection, encouragement, and enthusiasm on the baby, thereby intensifying her interest and excitement in learning. They need not make use of elaborate educational toys or programs (p. 3).

There's no stopping her! (Early Childhood Education Center)

Bronfenbrenner (1978) reinforces this recommendation when he states "in order to develop, a child needs the enduring, irrational involvement of one or more adults" (p. 773).

Educaring responsibilities include the initiation and mediation of stimulation and response to the child's behaviors. The adult initiates stimulation by holding, cuddling, playing with, and talking to the child. Physical contact continues to be important until the child's growing sense of independence no longer permits it.

Other suggestions for appropriate stimulation include making available appropriate materials and experiences, manipulating situations to elicit a response, and encouraging the child to try to solve his own problems.

The teaching event described in Episode 4 illustrates one example of manipulating a situation in order to elicit an appropriate intellectual response.

EPISODE 4

The teacher was seated at the table with three children, from 2 to 3 years of age. They were placing colored cube-blocks on color-matched squares on a game board. Each card contained squares of only one color; there were blocks of three colors from which to choose. Dottie joined the group, but did not appear to understand the game. She watched the others, and then began to place blocks of any color on the card with yellow squares. The teacher noticed and said, "Can you put a yellow block on top of a yellow place?" Dottie did so immediately. The teacher gave reinforcement by saying "good" and then led her a step further. "Now can you put a yellow block on all the yellow places?" Dottie correctly completed the yellow card, and asked for a card of a different color. She happily completed this one independently.

As mediator, the educarer regulates the amount, intensity, variety, and complexity of stimulation, as well as its timing and background conditions. As an agent of response, the adult responds to and interacts with the child's behavior instead of merely doing things to and for her. Caregivers who pride themselves on having well-behaved but passive babies who grow into toddlers who never get dirty or noisy deny these children their opportunities to become intelligent. Even when infant-toddler centers are somewhat stimulating, if the primary concern is for efficient routine care, the results may include delayed motor skills, delayed social language, and abnormal passivity, all of which are cumulative.

Three more principles of stimulation may be added.

4. Each child should be given the freedom to choose those stimuli that are interesting at any particular moment.

5. Each child should be free to investigate and interact with the stimulus according to the child's timetable of development, not to the teacher's timetable for teaching.

6. In order to reach the developmental potential in learning, each child needs a genuinely interested adult who will initiate and mediate stimulation, and will respond to and interact with the child.

Motivation to learn is an intrinsic quality. It is also an elusive and highly personal quality. It is dependent on the fulfillment of basic needs, a positive concept of self, and appropriate interactions with both the physical and the human environment. The most powerful force for learning at all ages is the inner sense of excitement that results from having learned something by and for one's self. This excitement is all the stimulation needed by our infants and toddlers. It is the primary motivator of all learning.

BEGINNING INTELLIGENCE AND LEARNING

Definitions and Development

Piaget is frequently given credit for the idea of sensorimotor intelligence, although the importance of such intelligence and learning has been recognized for more than 100 years.

The word *sensorimotor* implies the coordination of sensory and motor functions. Actually, it is difficult to clearly separate the two, because sensory perceptions are instrumental in all motor acts, whether consciously or unconsciously. The infant who is beginning to reach successfully has achieved precise visual perception and is now concentrating on the motor act of reaching and grasping. The abilities of looking, reaching, grasping, and the control of arm and hand are involved in the final ability. As soon as the baby is successful once, he will repeat and repeat, visibly enjoying his new skill. Soon he will tackle new challenges, and over time will succeed in using objects together, putting one inside another, stacking one on top of another, and maybe even throw one, just to see what happens. This is *not* the time to say "No throwing" or "Stop that"; this is the time to show appreciation of baby's new ability, and perhaps redirect his throws, if he continues.

Sensorimotor intelligence is intelligence in action. It may be said that the child "reasons" and "thinks" with his body. There is no real thought in the traditional sense of the word.

The next step is representational intelligence, which is necessary for mental thought but not for "action" thought. Representation is the ability to function symbolically, to remember past experiences, and to anticipate future ones. The coordination of representational ability and language ability leads to conceptual thinking. According to Flavell (1963), Piaget likened sensorimotor intelligence to a

> . . . slow motion film which represents one static frame after another, but can give no simultaneous and all-encompassing purview of all the frames. Representational thought, on the other hand, through symbolic capacity has the potential for simultaneously grasping, in a single internal epitome, a whole sweep of separate events. It is a much faster and mobile device which can recall the past, represent the present, and anticipate the future in one temporarily brief, organized act (pp. 151–152).

A milestone in the progression from action thought to mental thought is that of goal-oriented behavior. The very beginnings can be observed at age 10 to 11 months, when the child is manipulating different objects or toys in different ways. He squeezes a rubber toy, swings or bangs a rattle, and drops or rolls a ball. These manipulations are simple, but they are of great significance in cognitive development. As the result of exploration and experimentation with objects, the child's perceptions and motor activities lead to goal-oriented behavior. During this period, the visual characteristics of objects are of more importance than the tactile or auditory characteristics. Visual perception maintains its prime importance during the second and third years. It is the combination of recognizing that one's own actions have results and discriminating between effective and ineffective actions that determines the level of goal-directed behavior achieved by age 3 years.

The progression of perceptuomotor (sensorimotor) development, involving motor control, prehension, and manipulation skills is outlined in Table 3–1.

Another milestone is the conceptualization of object permanence. Numerous normative studies have led to the following description of its development. Abilities during the first 4 months include recognition and anticipation of events and smooth visual tracking of objects. The infant visually follows an object as it is hidden, but shows no surprise when a different object appears in its place. Between 4 and 7 months the baby will show surprise when the reappeared object is not the same one that was hidden, but will not look for a hidden object. From 7 to 10 months, the baby acts puzzled if a different object is pulled from the hiding spot, and will search for a hidden object if the actual hiding has been observed. By the end of the first year, the child will continue looking for the hidden object in the same place it was first found, even if the adult has been observed while moving it to another hiding place. During the second year, the child will extend the search and will achieve success in finding the object in the last place it was hidden, ignoring the temporary hiding spots. Object permanence has now been solidly conceived, and the road to the mental representation of objects is opened. The child's initial ability to represent mentally an object does not include the ability to classify on the basis of more than one characteristic. Even the 3-year-old child is perception dominated, and will attend to one visual perception only (usually length and not width, or amount of space covered and not the number of objects occupying that space). The child under 3 or 4 years of age will not group objects according to adult logic. Child logic leads to groupings based on the child's former experiences with the objects.

The cognitive landmarks related to child-object relationships and representational competence are summarized in Table 3–2. Implications of goal-oriented behavior are included,

Table 3—1
Progression of Perceptuomotor Development*

Age	Motor Control	Prehension and Manipulation
By 4 months	Control of eye muscles and movement	Hand watching Objects brought to mouth Hand-swiping Beginning reaches for seen objects
By 7 months	Control of head and arms	Successful reaching Palmar grasp
By 10 months	Control of trunk and hands	Refined grasp Partial thumb opposition Fingering holes in pegboard
By 12 months	Control of legs	Placing pegs in pegboard Opening and closing boxes
2nd year	Walking and running	Holding crayons; scribbling Building cube towers Using spoon Using trial and error with form board
3rd year	Jumping, climbing, balancing Integration of large and fine motor skills	Making visual comparisons between holes and objects of form boards before intentional insertion

*Adapted from Appleton, Clifton, and Goldberg, 1975, pp. 131–134.

with the child moving from random actions to purposeful ones.

As is the case with all statements of age-expected behaviors, environmentally adequate conditions are necessary. As is also the case, an enriched environment that includes competent educarers will enable the child to reach certain stages before the normative age. One example concerns the visual and tactual differentiation of shapes. If toys have been well sequenced, babies under 1 year can successfully work with form boards. The sequence of learning shapes progresses as follows: one circle; two circles; one square; two squares; one triangle, one circle, and one square; one square and one triangle.

Intelligence is but one aspect of adaptation to the environment, but it seems to attract the most interest in discussions of the education of even the youngest infant. It is true that mental functions derive from motor actions on concrete objects. Motor actions derive from sensation and perception, and result in exploration and experimentation with objects.

Exploration and Experimentation

Infants are visually responsive to their environments from the moment of birth, and visual interest rapidly increases. They are able to scan (explore) and track briefly at two days. Older

Table 3–2

Cognitive Landmarks Related to Object Exploration and Representational Competence

Age (months)	Child-object relationships	Means-end	Representation
0–3	Undifferentiated action	Random	
3–9	Beginning repertoire of action specific to object By 9 months, object permanence	Repeats actions that please	At end of 9 months, will imitate own actions
9–12	Knows functional use of common objects (to play with, to drink from)	Idea that an object can be used to do something else	Imitates adult's action, if the act is already in baby's repertoire
12–18	Knows functional use of more objects; may combine objects	Understands there are tools or intermediaries, including people, to achieve goal	Imitates new behaviors; starts to associate object or event with representation of another object or event (e.g., adult gets coat, baby says "go bye-bye.")
18–24	Relates to objects; will use one to represent another (block as car, tissue as dolly blanket)	Makes more use of tools and persons	Object or event is represented by a word (true internal representation); demonstrates deferred imitation of action occurring up to 2 weeks ago (usually household activities)

infants respond not only in terms of perceptual characteristics, but in terms of their meaning. For instance, photographs of human faces hold a special interest by four months. With further visual experience, babies begin to construct a variety of fundamental schemes or concepts. Their increasing memory ability enables them to notice and study discrepancies from a previously perceived object or event.

Physical contact with objects enables the infant to acquire many more types of information: weight, flexibility, temperature, and other properties of objects. "This combination of visual and manual exploration makes an inestimable contribution to infants' developing conceptions of the world" (Fenson, 1985, p. 32).

Actions that can be performed on objects to make them move (or react) include pulling, pushing, rolling, kicking, jumping, blowing, sucking, throwing, swinging, balancing, and dropping. Kamii and DeVries (1978) suggest the following criteria for the selection of appropriate objects:

(a) the child must be able to produce the movement by his own action, (b) the child must be able to vary his action, (c) the reaction of the object must be observable, (d) the reaction of the object must be immediate (pp. 8–9).

Such objects will enable the child to progress from random exploration (sucking, shaking, squeezing) to experimentations in producing desired effects or object reactions. Even after baby has used a spoon for eating, she will use it as a noisemaker by banging it on a table. Indeed, all kinds of things can be done with a spoon, as shown in Episode 5.

EPISODE 5

Timmy, aged 15 months, was playing near the water table, where four 2 to 3 year olds were playing. He wandered over, peeked in, and ran his hands through the water. He reached in and grabbed a spoon, which kept his attention for the next 5 minutes. First, he splashed it in the water. Then he put a spoonful of water in his mouth. He stuck out his tongue and rubbed the back of the spoon on it. He stooped down and tried to dig the carpet with it. Next, he found a small plastic container in the water table. He banged the spoon against it, put the spoon in it, and used it as a

A light beach ball meets the criteria for objects to manipulate. (Kindercampus, Iowa City)

rattle. Then he pointed the spoon at John, who was walking by. Then he used the spoon as a "weapon"—he hit John with it!

Timmy's actions showed a mix of "adult-appropriate" and "toddler-appropriate" uses for a spoon. The episode came to an end before John had a chance to react, when the teacher announced that it was time to go outside.

Forman and Hill (1984) describe a similar learning possibility at the sand table.

Within any single activity, such as digging in the sand table, the child may have numerous encounters with events that are educational. The child may discover, for example, that a spoon handle makes different marks in the sand than the bowl of the spoon does. He may also learn that his playmate Jenny cannot see an object on his side of the sand bucket, that he can dig to the bottom of the sand table, and that he enjoys his play more if he takes a few minutes to negotiate sharing the shovels with his playmates (p. 3).

Both the spoon and sand experiences are educational and increase the child's knowledge base.

Exploratory activities and suggested objects for the first 12 to 15 months include the following:

1. Looking and inspecting—mobiles, stabiles, pictures, photographs of known persons and places, magazines, catalogs, cloth books, safety mirrors, living people (considered as objects by the child)

2. Listening—metronome, ticking clock, bells on booties, variety of rattles, musical kicking toys, music boxes, records or tapes of music and familiar sounds, people's activities, verbalizations

3. Touching and fingering—hand-sized objects differing in texture, shape, edges; miniature copies of large objects; piano keys and guitar strings; simple form boards and shape-sorting boxes; people

4. Turning—book and magazine pages

5. Hammering and pounding—drum or other percussion instruments; wooden pegboard with 1-inch thick pegs or dowels; cube blocks; modeling materials such as clay or play dough

6. Emptying and filling—sand, water, buckets, blocks, containers, nesting toys, one- or two-piece puzzles

7. Threading—wooden beads, empty thread spools, heavy cord or shoelaces

8. Opening and shutting—doors and drawers, boxes; pots and pans with lids

9. Stacking and knocking down—cube blocks, color cones

10. Picking up—counters, bottle caps, checkers, cotton balls, paper scraps

11. Twisting—knobs and switches; lock and lever boards

12. Bouncing—mattresses; "baby bouncers" (preferably people)

13. Rolling and retrieving—balls, beanbags, round bell rattles

14. Dropping—spoons, cereal bowls, anything loose

15. Scribbling—crayons, newspaper, paper bags

16. Creeping or crawling through or under—boxes, barrels, classroom furniture

17. Pulling and perhaps pushing—pull-string wagon, toy animals on wheels, wheelless wooden cars and trains, pop-beads

A similar listing of appropriate objects for 15- to 36-month-old children would be very long indeed. Sources of suggestions include infant-toddler curriculum and activity books readily available in book stores and even at the supermarket. The best source may be the curriculum resource center connected with a college, an area education agency, or a branch of Community Coordinated Child Care (the 4-C's).

During this age range the recommended activities will grow in number as well as in complexity of small motor abilities. For instance, hammering and pounding have been replaced by the use of carpentry tools on a sturdy small workbench. Walking, running, jumping, and climbing will replace creeping and crawling, requiring climbing equipment both indoors and outside, jumping or tumbling mats, tricycles, and lots of space. The stacking and knocking down of small blocks will progress into building with cartons and boxes, hollow blocks, and full and half-unit blocks. The pull-string wagon has been relegated to "babies," and replaced with wagons and wheelbarrows to pull and push and to carry things and children. Now there is a fascination in vehicles that work, such as trucks that dump or carry freight.

Jigsaw puzzles are academic readiness materials. Do you know why? (Kindercampus, Iowa City)

Books, books, and more books.
(Early Childhood Education
Center)

Crayon scribbling has developed into "writing" on the chalkboard as well as on paper, finger and easel painting, drawing with felt-tip pens, and making collages out of pasted scraps. The single objects for touching and fingering are replaced with multi-objects and interlocking toys (log cabins, erector sets, connected trains), wind-up toys, hand or finger puppets, design blocks and mosaics, as well as toys, books, or clothes designed to teach self-help skills. Magnetic boards with brightly colored shapes, flannel boards with pieces of felt, picture puzzles of four to twelve pieces, and picture lotto games all enhance perceptual, manipulative, and representational skills. The addition of an infant bathtub or small water table (water 2 to 3 inches deep) will extend tactual experiences.

Role-playing has been added to the toddler's repertoire of activities. Therefore it is necessary to provide child-sized housekeeping equipment, dress-up clothes of all kinds, and washable baby dolls and doll equipment.

The provision of selected objects in sequence will even enhance the emerging literacy skills of toddlers. These are included not as an argument for teaching baby to read but as the appropriate means for preparing the child for much later learning-to-read activities. Reading-related objects for exploration are listed in the order of their presentation.

1. Catalogs and magazines to look at, to touch and finger, to mouth, and otherwise explore

2. More catalogs, magazines, and cloth books

3. "First" books with pictures of everyday objects (sturdy cardboard pages, perhaps protected by transparent stick-on material)

4. Photographs or books containing photographs of persons and objects in baby's life, including the infants and toddlers in the program

5. "Sense" books that call for touching or smelling

6. Picture books, ABC books, illustrated nursery rhyme books, pop-up books

7. Alphabet and number books

8. Books containing simple stories with which the child can identify

9. Books, books, and more books

The exploration and manipulation of objects other than books also have clear-cut implications for later reading (and writing) endeavors, as well as representational competence.

The development of numerical concepts also has its foundation in the early years. These are closely related to the exploration and manipulation of objects. Object exploration is an important (but not the only) part of the infant-toddler curriculum. Its importance has been noted by designers of many intervention programs for 3 and 4 year olds who have been identified as educationally disadvantaged. Some of these programs have included the same kinds of activities and opportunities for object exploration that are recommended for infants and toddlers in group care and education programs. Moore et al. (1975) offer a satisfactory concluding statement for this discussion of exploration and experimentation.

> A specific, concrete base for learning comes from the freedom to explore and discover a relatively predictable environment and to manipulate actively the materials in it. This active involvement with even relatively simple surroundings is more productive of mental development than continual sensory stimulation which reduces arousal level and produces a long-range dulling effect. Material enrichment and equipment are less necessary than accepting and responsive people for an environment conducive to learning (p. 92).

Action and Interaction

The child is no longer viewed as a passive receiver of information, which means that learning does not result only from being in an enriched environment. The child acts on the environment, and the environment is designed to react to the child. The environment, of course, includes living persons as well as objects. An expectation for future interactions develops out of this action-reaction sequence. For example, at 4 months of age, the infant smiles more readily at an "object" that smiles in return. This is a beginning learning that the world is a predictable place.

This view of learning emphasizes interaction. It implies that a maturational view of de-

velopment is not the total answer, because maturational theory allows no room for reciprocal interactions. Maturation is a necessary condition for development and learning, but it does not provide the motivation for learning. The child's experiences, including interactions, are important and necessary to genetic tendencies and environmental influences. From the moment of birth these two are interacting. They modify the adaptational pattern of the baby as well as that of the significant persons in the baby's life space. Different components of the physical environment also direct baby's growth and development. A highly active baby may be limited in space exploration (for the convenience of the adult) but given many toys and play objects within that space. Another equally active baby may be given free rein to explore a wide area, with only a few toys. Would this make a difference? Probably. The space-limited baby will concentrate on the mastery of available objects. The space-free baby will gain exploration-of-space skills, but perhaps will not master specific objects in the same time period.

Interactions between child and object and child and adult have been stated or implied repeatedly in the preceding statements. It is the reciprocal interplay that binds the child to the world of people and things. Recognition of this fact leads to the issue of adult/child ratio. Adults with too many children cannot be effective as teachers, caregivers, or educarers. For the individualized reciprocal exchanges necessary for learning, the adults must have time for each child, and interest in the child's interests at the moment. The actions and responses (resulting in interactions) presented in Table 3–3 give examples of their development from birth until 3 years of age.

Imitation

Although there have been a few studies that have indicated that infants can imitate "tongue-sticking-out" and other facial expressions within the first few days of life, these apparently are

Imitation in a group setting.
(Kindercampus)

pseudo-imitations (Piaget's term), and they disappear. The overall evidence about imitation still points to the appearance of real imitations toward the end of the first year (White, 1988a). From this time period, imitation appears as a very powerful motivation for behavior throughout the childhood years. It is both active and intentional.

Imitation provides a shortcut to many learnings at all ages. Froebel ("father of the kindergarten") was correct in 1893 when he wrote "what the child imitates, he begins to understand" (cited in Baker, 1989, p. 21). Simple fingerplays and action rhymes using the fingers are fun ways to encourage the development of imitation skills, and therefore cognitive skills. Fingerplays are short verses or stories that can be dramatized by finger or hand motions. Good collections of fingerplays are available at any bookstore or library. The children's department of many public libraries distribute their own collections at little or no cost. A beginning list of books of fingerplays and simple songs is included in the suggested readings at the end of the chapter.

Because imitation is such a strong motivator in young children, the teacher's repertoire of values and behaviors must be worthy of imitating. Children will imitate those persons with

whom they identify. This is clearly shown in Episode 6.

EPISODE 6

Bobby and Clara, both 2 years, 10 months old, were sitting close on the floor. Their "conversation," which was too quiet to be overheard, came to an abrupt end when Bobby hit Clara. Clara began to cry. She continued crying and loudly announced "I don't like it when Bobby does that!" Her perfect imitation of a teacher's verbal response to aggression rang out loud and clear. There was a dramatic pause in the classroom activities as teachers and children alike realized that Clara was "teacher" for a moment.

All social learnings during the early years are developed out of the imitation of significant others. Of course, it is possible to teach "please" and "thank-you" by rote, if the adults insist on the words and provide a tangible reinforcer. But "please" and "thank you" are more than meaningless words to be used when needed. They represent an attitude of respect and consideration of others in social relationships. The words and their meanings are best learned by the imitation of consistent adult behaviors, including but not limited to verbalization.

Table 3–3

Selected Actions and Interactions

Age	Infant-Toddler	Educarer
0–3 months	Makes baby noises; gurgles and coos	Imitates, uses in conversation, makes new sounds with changes in pitch
	Engages in mouth play	Allows baby to chew her hand; kisses baby's hand; lets baby grab a finger or two
	Shows surprise at a change in the usual	Makes faces and different vocal sounds
	Moves arms and legs	Pushes gently on soles of baby's feet; raises and lowers baby's arms
	Responds to rhythmic sounds or movements	Dances with baby in her arms; gently rocks the baby
	Visually explores	Provides things to look at (patterns, bright colors, movement) and persons to look at
3–6 months	Plays with food	Supplies finger foods
	Recognizes familiar things	Provides stability in objects and persons
	Shows surprise at novelty in the context of the familiar	Gradually introduces slightly different objects and persons and activities
	Engages in object play and power play	Provides toys that do something as a result of the child's action
	Is excited by movement and rhythm	Dances, sings, and plays with baby; bounces baby on her knees, holds baby up in the air
	Enjoys predictable excitement	Plays "this little piggy," "pat-a-cake," "rock-a-bye baby"
	Explores environment visually and tactually	Provides objects to look at and touch; positions baby in visual range of ongoing activities
6–12 months	Explores visually, tactually and motorically	Permits reasonable and safe exploration; introduces new objects; places baby in different locations in the room
	Imitates new sounds or sights	Converses with vocalizations, verbalizations, and facial expressions, including funny faces and sounds
	Wants an audience	Is a frequent observer and appreciative responder; makes "mirror" faces
	Enjoys total body movement	Gently roughhouses
	Enjoys predictable surprises	Plays "peek-a-boo" and "hear-a-boo"
	Enjoys fun and games	Makes baby laugh; plays with baby
12–24 months	Explores sensually and motorically	Adds new objects to investigate, such as pegboards, containers to fill and empty, doors and drawers to open and close, balls, modeling materials, crayons and paper; also "field trips" to other rooms or the nearby outdoors

Table 3–3
continuing

Age	Infant-Toddler	Educarer
12–24 months (continued)	Likes to put together and take apart, to fill and empty	Provides pop-beads, blocks for stacking, train cars that hook together, nesting toys, one-to-three-piece puzzles
	Likes to hide and look for	Plays hide-and-seek games; pretends to lose things, including the toddler; supplies corners or big boxes for toddler to hide in
	Likes to test his/her strength	Plays tug-of-war
	Likes to chase and be chased	Chases and "runs" from the child
	Enjoys people and simple social rituals	Engages in verbal and action messages associated with "hello" and "good-bye"
	Tests social behaviors and imitates the actions of others	Provides opportunities to observe others; gradually introduces interaction with other children: includes toddler in small-group activities (two or three), and adult activities when possible and feasible
	Enjoys pretending	Provides realistic toys; dress-up clothes; baby dolls; stuffed animals; blocks and boxes; simple child-sized housekeeping equipment
	Tests his motor abilities	Provides opportunities to run, throw, climb, hit, jump, march, and balance
24–36 months	Likes to explore	Enlarges the environment for exploration and provides field trips to other parts of the building and in the adjoining neighborhood. Allows unhurried times for exploration and investigation
	Likes to make things	Provides unit blocks, "tools" (hammers, soft wood, paper, paste), small interlocking blocks, beads to string, puzzles, pegboards, materials to make into musical instruments
	Likes to test his physical prowess	Increases the complexity and opportunities in the 12–24 month list; provides an obstacle course; balance beam; set of two or three steps; appropriate trampoline; balls of all sizes
	Imitates and represents	Provides opportunities for role-playing, including objects and toys that may but do not necessarily represent their real counterparts. Introduces imitation games such as "Simon says"; uses many fingerplays and action songs
	Enjoys people	Plans for and encourages participation in small group activities of many kinds, some of which are adult-directed

Toward the end of the second year, children will incorporate imitations in their dramatic play. The housekeeping corner is proof of the influence of parents and teachers on a child's behaviors and developing attitudes. It is an interesting side note that children rarely imitate the play of adults. For whatever reason, it is the work of adults that is reflected in their behaviors. (Perhaps adults play only when children are somewhere else.)

Teachers of very young children recognize that the ability to imitate progresses in stages. The first imitative behavior is noted when an infant assimilates the crying of other infants. It is common knowledge in an infant center or nursery that crying is contagious. Babies cry when others are crying. They also stop crying when others stop. This may (or may not) be imitative behavior.

Next, the infant imitates actions or sounds of a significant adult, but only if the adult has first imitated the child's own actions or sounds. Deliberate imitations of sounds and movements follow, but they are limited to those already in the child's repertoire, and are visually or auditorially perceptible. In the last stage (about 18 months), the child's ability to remember (or represent) enables imitation of actions or sounds not immediately perceptible. The child begins to imitate the actions and sounds of objects as well as those of persons. This ability has been called symbolic functioning, and it is the beginning of the make-believe world. Pretending reaches its peak during the preschool years (ages 3 to 5).

The activity of stringing beads is a usual activity in the toddler curriculum. It involves imitation in almost every step. A description of a suggested learning sequence follows.

1. From a group of wooden beads, similar in color and shape, the educarer demonstrates stringing the beads onto a shoelace with a firm tip.

2. Baby imitates the action, using a pincer grasp to pick out beads from the same group.

3. The educarer gives baby time to explore and manipulate.

4. When baby has conquered the art of bead stringing, the educarer adds beads of a second color (but the same shape) and strings beads of alternating colors.

5. Baby imitates.

6. The educarer again gives baby time to explore and manipulate the beads.

7. The educarer adds beads of a third color, and so on.

After beads of more than one color (or shape, which should be added later) are being used in a pattern set by the educarer, it is worthwhile to let the toddler make up patterns for the educarer to copy.

THE ROLE OF PLAY IN COGNITIVE DEVELOPMENT

Thirty years ago, the learning activities (exploration and experimentation, actions and interactions, and imitation) would have been viewed as "just play." Today we know that during the infant-toddler stage play is the best medium for learning.

Exploration and Play

The first important discovery for our purposes was that exploration and play are similar, but also different. According to Johnson, Christie, and Yawkey (1987), "exploration occurs when the child seemingly asks the question 'What does this object do?'; play happens when the child seemingly asks the question 'What can I do with this object?'" (p. 51). Both questions are prompted by the child's natural curiosity, and the answering actions may appear to be either exploration or play. However, the questions indicate a difference in purpose. When young children play, they bypass the traditional use of an object, and use it in whatever way they choose. Exploration is primarily a sensorimotor activity, and involves perception and movement. Play also involves perception and movement, but it is also closely related to the cognitive abilities that have been described as preoperational.

Burtt and Kalkstein (1981) have traced the stages from beginning explorations to play during toddlerhood as follows:

> *Birth to 1½ mos*
> Learning comes from looking
>
> *1½ to 3½ mos*
> Hands get into the act
>
> *3½ to 5½ mos*
> Reach and grasp experiences
>
> *5½ to 8 mos*
> Experimenting with cause and effect
>
> *8 to 14 mos*
> Exploring places and examining things
>
> *14 to 24 mos*
> Play! The work of toddlerhood

Of course, many play activities continue to have elements of exploration, and much exploration is playful.

As a result of his review of research on play and learning in infancy, Caruso (1988) stated, "It is now widely assumed that play and exploration have a central role in the adaptability, learning, cognitive development, socioemotional development, and early education of the young child" (p. 53).

Play and Cognitive Development

A brief overview of research findings about the role of play in cognitive development provides the evidence that playing is important for opti-

Getting acquainted with object characteristics. (Early Childhood Education Center)

mal cognitive development. Play enables children to practice and consolidate newly acquired mental skills (Piaget, 1962); and play activities, especially make-believe play, lead to the development of abstract thought (Vygotsky, 1976). Positive relationships have been found between IQ scores and levels of play (Johnson, Ershler, & Lawton, 1982); training in how to play has resulted in gains in IQ scores (Saltz, Dixon, & Johnson, 1977), and these gains appear to last (Christie, 1983). The studies that investigated the relationship of IQ scores to play abilities involved children older than infants and toddlers, but it is only reasonable to assume that these children had opportunities to play during these early years.

Pretend, or make-believe play, is a favorite activity of toddlers, and begins as early as 12 months. According to McCune (1986) it is in full flower by age 3. In the beginning there is the simple substitution of pretend objects for real ones; the play is usually solitary, and the pretend objects most closely resemble the real ones. Toward the end of the third year, pretend play becomes dramatic or even sociodramatic, and the pretend objects are not necessarily realistic (Saltz & Saltz, 1986). The ability to pretend is one more indication of the child's development from the sensorimotor to the preoperational stage of cognitive development.

Play contributes to cognitive development in a number of ways:

1. It provides the opportunity for children to practice new skills and functions.
2. It provides the opportunity for children to act on objects, and to experience events.
3. It enables children to change reality to symbolic representations.
4. It consolidates previous learning.
5. It enables children to learn how to learn—through curiosity, invention, persistence, and other factors.

Play also contributes to the development of language. And, play is relaxing and fun!

LANGUAGE: ITS DEVELOPMENT AND NURTURANCE

Language Development

Probably no aspect of child development has received as much attention during recent years as the development of language, although much remains to be learned. Language is more complicated than previously imagined. Language as communication will be explored in some detail in the next chapter, Nurturing Social Competency, but language as the production of speech is the focus here.

For an understanding of language development, just as for cognitive development, we need to recognize and understand the various speech and language subskills. These include pragmatics (how and when to communicate), semantics (word meanings, which are not only definitions but also the correct use and place of the utterance), syntax (usually called grammar, or the rules of language usage), morphology (inflection as well as content), and phonology (speech sounds and patterns).

These are technical terms, and may seem far removed from our focus on infant-toddler learning, but the acquisition of each subskill is based on the development and experiences of the very early months and years. Bates (1976) writes that the acquisition of pragmatic skills begins with pointing and reaching, vocalizations, and eye gaze (attention). The eye gaze is apparent during the first weeks of life; the other behaviors emerge around the 10th month, and lay an important foundation for language development. Semantic relations are apparent in the child's first two-word combinations, such as "more duce" or "no want" (Bloom & Lahey, 1978). These two-word utterances also show a beginning knowledge of syntax, or word order. The stringing of two or three words together in a crude but appropriate way is achieved by age 2. Beginning sentences (containing a subject and verb) such as "I go-ed" or "I wented" show that eager learners are internalizing the rules of morphology. Listening to adult speech will gradually teach them the forms of the irregular verbs and plurals (ran instead of "runned," men instead of "mans"), and by age 4, most children will speak in grammatically correct full sentences, and will produce nearly all the sounds of their native language. The detailed sequence of the development of these language subskills is in appendix C.

Another way to follow the development of language focuses on the skills of listening, vocalization, and verbalization with meaning.

Baby spends the first year learning to listen—this involves attending, selecting, memorizing, recalling, and matching—skills that are basic to all learning, and especially learning to talk. The infant also begins to practice sound-making. At first these are limited to discomfort and comfort sounds. Babbling begins at about 8 weeks. In babbling the infant is making sounds for the fun of making and hearing them. At 5 to 6 months, babbling develops into vocal play, and sounds are used for a reason: to get attention, to say "No!", to say "I'm hungry!" At 8 months, babbling develops another feature, inflection. Baby's voice begins to rise and fall, apparently indicating questions or statements or expressions of surprise. Now the babbling closely resembles adult sound-making.

The first year is really a prelanguage state, focusing on a readiness to listen. The second year is a prespeech state, focusing on a readiness to speak. By the 12th month, baby can understand some words, and soon will speak some words, usually a command ("mum" for "I want milk") or words of recognition ("goggie" for dog).

Two other kinds of vocalizations appear in the baby's second year: jargon and echolalia. Jargon is a stream of unintelligible jabber that usually develops between the 12th and 15th month. This is more than sound-play; the child jabbers intentionally, "talking" to toys and to familiar persons. Jargon reaches its peak at 18 months, when another form of sound-making appears. Echolalia is the child's parrotlike echoing of the speech he hears. Echolalia goes like this:

> "Baby want some milk?"
> "Want some milk?"
> "Here is your cup."
> "Here cup."

Babies seem to do this without thinking; apparently their attention is elsewhere. Fortunately for the peace-of-mind of the adults, echolalia seldom lasts beyond age 2½.

The 2 year old talks in simple compound sentences. Pronunciation is often faulty, rhythm hesitant, and speech may be interspersed with unintelligible jargon. A 2 year old's ability to grasp the meaning in long bursts of sound has now progressed to the point where a two-part spoken direction, such as "Please get the book and bring it to me," can be followed without adult gestures. The toddler can identify familiar objects when they are named (and can name some of them) and can imitate sentences of two or more words, which are understandable. One dramatic sign of progress is ability to learn a new word after hearing it just once.

The 3 year old has too much to say to rely on jargon and gesture alone, and will use words socially to tell you what she thinks and wants. She talks so fast and so much that you would have to follow her about with a tape recorder to keep track of her progress.

As is true with any other developmental sequences there is significant variation in the age of the onset of a wide variety of language abilities during the first 3 years of life. White (1985) states that the onset of meaningful speech can happen anywhere from 7 months to the second birthday. In most cases, the earlier onset is the result of an attentive and responsive educarer.

Language does not equal communication; language is what is said, and communication is the sharing or giving of information, feelings, and attitudes.

Language and Story-Reading

"Books that encourage children to respond to the story because of interesting and exciting language help stimulate language growth. Participation stories, poetry and rhymes, and song books help immerse children into language" (Glazer, 1989, p. 23). One year olds, 2 year olds and 3 year olds love to share books with an adult, especially when there is a one-to-one ratio. One of the very specific goals for any infant-toddler program should be that each child each day shall share a book with an adult. In order to achieve this goal, educarers should ask for volunteers to come in for story-reading time.

Parents of the children, senior citizens, even primary grade children all are possible volunteers, but Strickland and Taylor (1989) suggest that parents are the most appropriate story-readers and should be encouraged to participate. All parents who share books, regardless of ethnic and educational backgrounds, socioeconomic levels, geographic locations, "often expand and extend the content of the stories in natural and meaningful ways. Parents seem to sense when such expansions are necessary, or when an unembellished reading is the best way to share a particular story" (Strickland & Taylor, 1989, p. 30).

Experience has shown that many adults, including parents, are reluctant to read aloud to young children. Glazer (1989) makes the following suggestions for reading to infants and toddlers:

1. Hold the child on your lap in a cozy manner. Put your arms around the child, and together hold the book as you read the story. If the book is a song (Go tell Aunt Rhody, Go tell Aunt Rhody) with repetitive language, reading the repetitive passage once or twice should entice the child to read it with you each time it appears in the text. Very young children will make sounds that follow the tempo, intonation, and pitch used by the adult.

2. When reading to a group of children, sit as they do, on the floor, on a rug, or in a small chair. Use books with repetitive rhyming text. Read the story, and as you approach the language that repeats, look at the children. Begin the repetitive, rhyming sequence slowly suggesting that you need them to help you say it. Have the children repeat the sequence each time it appears in the text (pp. 24–25).

Participation books, such as *Pat the Bunny* (Kunhardt, 1940) and *Pat the Cat* (Kunhardt, 1984) and the Spot books (Hill, 1980, 1981, 1984, 1985, 1986, 1987a, 1987b), are enjoyable, and involve the child (or children) in a fun way. Repetitive stories that rhyme *(The Ginger-*

bread Man, This is the House that Jack Built) enable the children to anticipate the language and to become part of the activity. When should books be introduced? "As soon as a child can grasp a book . . . there should be a book to grasp" (Cullinan, 1989, p. 39). Sturdy books with durable pages are available that withstand chewing, dribbles, and other mishandlings.

Resources for children's literature for infants and toddlers are included in the Suggested Readings for chapter 4 (Nurturing Social Competency).

Language and Play

Young children play with all aspects of language (Kuczaj, 1985), from the first babbling to playing games with the intentional misuse of a word. Weir (1962) found that young children frequently play with different forms and rules of language. They play with sounds by repeating strings of nonsense syllables, with syntax by systematically substituting words of the same grammatical category, and with semantics by intentionally distorting meaning through nonsense and jokes (Johnson et al., 1987, p. 17). According to Cazden (1981) this language play helps children to perfect newly acquired language skills and increases their awareness of linguistic rules. Garvey (1984) claims that language is a helping device that furthers social play, which sometimes includes play with noises and sounds, play with the linguistic system, spontaneous rhyming and word play, play with nonsense and fantasy, and play with conversation.

Language and Cognition

Of equal importance is the interrelationship between cognition and language. Actually, there are specific cognitive prerequisites for learning language. These include the ability (and willingness) to attend; the ability to imitate body movements and vocal behavior; knowing that something exists when it moves out of view (object permanence); and the ability to achieve a desired goal by some means (means-end relationships). These prerequisites are the basis of much of language development as outlined.

Language and learning theorists differ in their views about the relationship of language and cognition. Gerald Gratch maintains that thought and language interact and mutually influence one another; Bloom argues that thought and language are interdependent and overlapping; and Fischer and Corrigan theorize that language development is a large set of partially overlapping, strictly defined skills, including listening, speaking, concept formation, and social interaction (Reilly, 1980).

There are differences in the theories about the details of language and cognitive development, and their interrelatedness; however, the consensus of these and other experts is that the development and achievements in language and cognition are closely related. This is expressed most strongly by Genishi (1986) who states, "The child's language learning proceeds from action or experience to concept to words, and not from word to concept to experience" (p. 18).

SUMMARY

The meanings underlying the Chinese saying "I hear and I forget; I see and I remember; I do and I understand" have been presented and expanded as they refer to the cognitive development of infants and toddlers. Perhaps the main message of this chapter is that young children learn by doing, and they learn better when the "doing" is guided and encouraged by a responsive educaring person.

The basis of the setting of goals for the cognitive development of very young children is two-fold: (1) the mutual agreement of the parents and the educarers, and (2) the current knowledge about how very young children learn. The basic steps in the learning process are (1) taking in information with the senses; (2) processing the information; and (3) using the information.

A vital prerequisite for learning is the disposition to learn (motivation). Motivation is dependent on a positive concept of self, the satisfaction of basic needs, and appropriate stimulation from the physical and human environments. The activities that encour-

age early learning are exploration and experimentation, action and interaction, and imitation. As young children develop and mature, they move from just looking to total body and mind involvement with the objects and persons in their environment. Infants and toddlers are action-oriented. It is the responsibility of the educarer to introduce activities and materials at the appropriate times, and to interact with the child and the child's actions. Because imitation also plays an important part in the child's development, the adult's behaviors must be worthy of imitating.

Play is the most appropriate medium for the cognitive development of very young (and older) children. Playing with something is the next step after getting to know something, and is related but not limited to the exploration of objects. Pretend or make-believe play is a more advanced type of play, and develops rapidly in the second and third year. Its appearance is one indication that the young child is progressing from the sensorimotor to the preoperational stage of cognitive development.

Play contributes to cognitive development in several ways: (1) it provides the opportunity for children to act on objects, to experience events, and to practice new skills; (2) it enables children to change reality to symbols; and (3) it encourages children's learning how to learn.

The development of language is really the development and integration of several language subskills. These are pragmatics, semantics, syntax, morphology, and phonology. These skills of mature language usage have their roots in the experiences of the early months and years.

Language skills also include listening, vocalization, and verbalization with meaning. Very young infants play with sounds; older infants and toddlers play with sounds, syntax, and semantics. Playing with language is encouraged by educarers who talk to children, respond verbally to children, share books and language activities with children, and who play with children.

The development of language and cognition are very closely related.

SUGGESTED ACTIVITIES AND QUESTIONS

1. Observe a very young child at play. List the learnings that are possible from one or more play episodes.

2. Describe one adult-planned experience that will foster development in each of Gardner's intelligences during the infant/toddler years.

3. Explain the difference between exploration and play.

4. Based on the information given about how infants and toddlers learn, what is your opinion of television watching as part of an infant toddler program?

5. Start an index card file for fingerplays and action games appropriate to use with infants and toddlers.

SUGGESTED READINGS

Resources for Fingerplays

Brown, M. (1980). *Finger rhymes.* New York: Dutton.

Brown, M. (1985). *Hand rhymes.* New York: Dutton.

Brown, M. (1987). *Play rhymes.* New York: Dutton.

Glazer, T. (1973). *Eye winker, Tom tinker, Chin chopper.* Garden City, NY: Doubleday.

Glazer, T. (1983). *Music for ones & twos: Songs and games for the very young child.* Garden City, NY: Doubleday.

Glazer, T. (1988). *Tom Glazer's treasury of songs.* Garden City, NY: Doubleday.

Graham, T. L. (1986). *Fingerplays and rhymes for always and sometimes.* Atlanta, GA: Humanics.

Grayson, M. F. (1962). *Let's do fingerplays.* New York: David McKay.

Matterson, E. (1971). *Games for the very young: Finger plays and nursery games.* New York: American Heritage Press.

Poulsson, E. (1983). *Finger plays for nursery and kindergarten.* New York: Lothrop.

Scott, L. B. (1983). *Rhymes for learning times.* Minneapolis: Denison.

Chapter-related

Ackerman-Ross, S., & Khanna, P. (1989). The relationship of high quality day care to middle-class 3-year-olds' language performance. *Early Childhood Research Quarterly, 4* (1), 97–116.

Anisfeld, M. (1984). *Language development from birth to three.* Hillsdale, NJ: Erlbaum.

Ault, R. L. (1983). *Children's Cognitive development* (2nd ed.). New York: Oxford University Press.

Baghban, M. (1984). *Our daughter learns to read and write: A case study from birth to three.* Newark, DE: International Reading Association.

Baker, B. R. (1989). Learning experiences through fingerplays. *Day Care and Early Education, 16* (3), 21–26.

Baldwin, D. A., & Markman, E. M. (1988). Establishing word-object relations: A first step. *Child Development, 60* (2), 381–398.

Bjorklund, D. F. (1989). *Children's thinking: Developmental function and individual differences.* Belmont, CA: Wadsworth.

Borden, G. J., & Harris, K. S. (1980). *Speech science primer.* Baltimore: Williams and Wilkins.

Bromwich, R. M. (1977). Stimulation in the first year of life? A perspective on infant development. *Young Children, 32* (2), 71–82.

Brown, C. C., & Gottfried, A. W. (Eds.). (1985). *Play interactions: The role of toys and parental involvement in children's development.* Pediatric Round Table 11. New York: Johnson & Johnson Baby Products.

Bruner, J., & Sherwood, V. (1976). Peekaboo and the learning of role structures. In J. Bruner, A. Jolly, & K. Sylva (Eds.), *Play: Its role in development and evolution* (pp. 277–285). New York: Basic Books.

Burchinnal, M., Lee, M., & Ramey, C. (1989). Type of day care and preschool intellectual development in disadvantaged children. *Child Development, 60,* 128–137.

Burtt, K. G., & Kalkstein, K. (1981). *Smart toys for babies from birth to two.* New York: Harper & Row.

Belsky, J. (Ed.). (1982). *In the beginning.* New York: Columbia University Press.

Caldwell, B. (1988). Word processing, baby style. *American Baby, 1* (8), 58, 65.

Caruso, D. A. (1988). Play and learning in infancy: Research and implications. *Young Children, 43* (6), 63–70.

Cazden, C. (Ed.). (1981). *Language in early child-hood education* (rev. ed.). Washington, DC: National Association for the Education of Young Children.

Chance, P. (1979). *Learning through play.* Pediatric Round Table 3. New York: Johnson & Johnson Baby Products.

De Villiers, J. G., & De Villiers, P. A. (1979). *Early language.* Cambridge, MA: Harvard University Press.

Engel, R. (1968). *Language motivating experiences for young children.* Van Nuys, CA: DFA Publishers.

Flavell, J. H. (1985). *Cognitive development* (2nd ed.). Englewood Cliffs, NJ: Prentice-Hall.

Forman, G. E., & Hill, F. (1984). *Constructive play: Applying Piaget in the preschool* (rev. ed.). Menlo Park, CA: Addison-Wesley.

Gardner, H. (1983). *Frames of mind: The theory of multiple intelligences.* New York: Basic Books.

Garvey, C. (1984). *Children's talk.* Cambridge, MA: Harvard University Press.

Genishi, C. (1988). Children's language: Learning words from experience. *Young Children, 44* (1), 16–23.

Goelman, H., Oberg, A. A., & Smith, F. (Eds.). (1984). *Awakening to literacy.* Exeter, NH: Heinemann.

Golinkoff, R. M. (Ed.). (1983). *The transition from prelinguistic to linguistic communication.* Hillside, NJ: Erlbaum.

Gopnik, A. (1988). Three types of early words: The emergence of social words, names and cognitive-relational words in the one-word stage and their relation to cognitive development. *First Language, 8* (22), 47–70.

Gordon, I. J. (1975). *The infant experience.* Columbus, OH: Merrill.

Honig, A. S. (1984, Winter). Why talk to babies? *Beginnings, 3–6.*

Ibuka, M. (1980). *Kindergarten is too late!* New York: Simon & Schuster.

Johnson, J. E., Christie, J. F., & Yawkey, T. D. (1987). *Play and early childhood development.* Glenview, IL: Scott, Foresman.

Kimmel, M. M., & Segal, E. (1988). *For reading out loud! A guide to sharing books with children.* (rev. and exp. ed.). New York: Delacorte.

Languis, M., Sanders, T., & Tipps, S. (1980). *Brain and learning: Directions in early childhood education.* Washington, DC: National Association for the Education of Young Children.

McGee, L. M., & Richgels, D. J. (1990). *Literacy's beginnings: Supporting young readers and writers* (chs. 2, 3, 4). Boston: Allyn & Bacon.

Moore, T. E. (Ed.). (1973). *Cognitive development and the acquisition of language.* New York: Academic Press.

Murphy, L. B. (1973). Infant's play and cognitive development. In M. W. Piers (Ed.), *Play and development.* New York: W. W. Norton.

Osofsky, J. D. (Ed.). (1979). *Handbook of infant development.* New York: Wiley.

Owens, R. E. (1984). *Language development: An introduction.* Columbus, OH: Merrill.

Piaget, J. (1955). *The language and thought of the child.* New York: Meridian.

Piaget, J. (1976). *The psychology of intelligence.* Totowa, NJ: Littlefield, Adams. (Especially chapter 4).

Pines, M. (1982, Feb.). Baby, you're incredible. *Psychology Today, 16* (2), 48–53.

Reilly, A. P. (1980). *The communication game: Perspectives on the development of speech, language, and non-verbal communication skills.* Pediatric Round Table 4. New York: Johnson & Johnson Baby Products.

Rogers, C. S., & Sawyers, J. K. (1988). *Play in the lives of children.* Washington, DC: National Association for the Education of Young Children.

Rubin, R. R., Fisher, J. J., & Doering, S. G. (1980). *Your toddler.* New York: Macmillan.

Seefeldt, C. (Ed.). (1986). *Early childhood curriculum: A review of current research.* New York: Teachers College Press.

Segal, M., & Adcock, D. (1985). *Your child at play: Two to three years: Growing up, language and the imagination.* New York: Newmarket.

Spodek, B. (Ed.). (1982). *Handbook of research in early childhood education.* New York: Free Press.

Sponseller, D. (Ed.). (1974). *Play as a learning medium.* Washington, DC: National Association for the Education of Young Children.

Sutton-Smith, B. (Ed.). (1979). *Play and learning.* New York: Gardner Press.

Taylor, D., & Strickland, D. (1986). *Family storybook reading.* Portsmouth, NH: Heinemann.

Thoman, E. B., & Browder, S. (1987). *Born dancing.* New York: Harper & Row.

Trelease, J. (1985). *The read-aloud handbook.* New York: Penguin.

Trelease, J. (1989). *The new read-aloud handbook* (2nd rev.). New York: Penguin.

Waite-Stupiansky, S. (1989). Language develops as children play. *Pre-K Today, 3* (4), 32–34.

White, B. L. (1988). *Educating the infant and toddler.* Lexington, MA: Lexington Books.

Wood, B. S. (1981). *Children and communication: Verbal and nonverbal language development* (2nd ed.). Englewood Cliffs, NJ: Prentice-Hall.

Yawkey, T. D., & Pellegrini, A. D. (Eds.). (1984). *Child's play: Developmental and applied.* Hillsdale, NJ: Erlbaum.

Yawkey, T. D., & Trostle, S. L. (1982). *Learning is child's play.* Provo, UT: Brigham Young University Press.

Nurturing Social Competency

The difference between a lady and a flower girl is not how she behaves, but how she is treated.

Eliza Doolittle in *My Fair Lady*

We have learned that the very young child develops as a cognitive being. We also know that the young child develops as a social being who experiences satisfactions and frustrations, joy and anger, and serenity and anxiety. These feelings are part of being human, and the child's feelings toward himself and others are a strong influence on all areas of his development, including cognitive. Sroufe (1979) states that the "affective (emotional) life is the meaning and motivational system that cognition serves. . . . Emotional growth and experience and affective expression contribute vitally to cognitive and social development" (p. 462). Yarrow (1979) summarizes the recent research on infant social development as follows:

> It is likely that these social-developmental characteristics are closely dependent on the attainment of a number of perceptual and cognitive skills. Differentiation of the self from the environment is dependent at least partly on the child's awareness that he can have an effect on the environment. . . . The growth of social discrimina-

tion is probably tied in with the development of basic perceptual discriminations, not only in the visual and auditory modalities but in the tactile, kinesthetic, and olfactory as well. The development of trust is closely related to the growth of contingency awareness and the capacity for mental representation of objects and persons in their absence—that is, object and person permanence (p. 904).

The Goals for Young Children in a Group Setting (in chapter 1 Figure 1–1) included (1) positive feelings about self; (2) positive feelings about others; and (3) positive feelings about the world. These positive feelings are achievable even before age 3. When they have been internalized, the child becomes socially competent.

THE DEVELOPMENT OF SOCIAL COMPETENCY

Definitions

Can you define social competency? We usually can recognize a socially competent person

83

(charming, poised, articulate, friendly) but a precise definition is difficult to put into words. A general definition might describe an individual's everyday ability in dealing with his or her environment. In very early childhood education, the definition might be a listing of the personal and social behaviors that we hope children will develop by age 3.

Landmarks of Personal-Social Development

The following sequence of personal-social development is based on the assumption that all is going well in the young child's life.

0–1 mo.	Primary identification with mother or mother-substitute; interested in faces
1 mo.	Is quieted by touch; responds to speech
2 mo.	Turns head toward speaking voices; spontaneously produces responsive smiles
3 mo.	Is quieted by a voice; cries when adult leaves; shows anticipation
4 mo.	Adjusts position in anticipation of being lifted; nonselective smiling; aware of strange situations
5 mo.	Is quieted by voice or caress; disturbed by strangers; smiles at other children; dislikes being left alone
6 mo.	Can distinguish between friendly and angry talking; holds arms up to be picked up; recognizes familiar people; smiles only at recognized persons
7 mo.	Reacts to image in mirror; differentiates known and unknown people
8 mo.	Pats and smiles at own mirror image; interested in other children's play; begins to imitate movements and sounds
9 mo.	Is developing preferences for people and objects; knows

	mother; possible separation anxiety
10 mo.	Imitates movements of other children; responds to pat-a-cake and peek-a-boo
11 mo.	Strives for attention; will repeat a behavior for an appreciative audience
12 mo.	Enjoys watching other children, but the ability to play considerately with anyone else is still far in the future. The playmate may be pushed or bitten or sat on! The playmate has not been mentally separated from objects-to-be-explored
12–18 mo.	Learns that some actions please adults and that others do not; tests limits of caregivers; pursues new relationships and is less shy toward strangers
18–24 mo.	Begins to understand "mine"; other children are still explored. Murphy and Leeper (1976) suggest that 1 to 2 year olds will benefit by occasionally playing with other children (4 or 5 year olds) instead of always with other toddlers. Not only do the older children model more mature interaction skills, but also the toddler will not have to fend off the aggressive attacks that are likely to come from peers. Of course the older children may be dictatorial, and supervision is advisable. Toward the end of the second year, the toddler may offer a toy to another child. At this point, the realization that a child is not an object has been achieved
24–30 mo.	Engages in solitary play and spends a lot of time watching other children. May engage in occasional parallel play as well as some physical/aggressive acts
30–36 mo.	The number of social interactions increases, although they

may be negative or destructive. Usually unwilling to share toys, but during the next months, a preschooler will begin to play co-operatively. The importance of having a friend soon follows

The Development of Social Competency

The basis of these personal-social developments is social cognition, which is the first of three steps in the development of social competency (Lewis & Brooks-Gunn, 1979). During the early years, social cognition is "the relationship between three aspects of knowledge: (1) knowledge of the self; (2) knowledge of others; and (3) knowledge of one's relations to others" (p. 2).

The second step, or process, in the development of social competency is the acquisition of skills and techniques for initiating and responding to persons and social events. The third step involves the development of appropriate reactions that undergird and motivate social behavior.

These steps are easily adapted for the infant-toddler years.

SOCIAL COGNITION

Knowledge of Self

As long ago as 1934, George Mead wrote that the major outcome of socialization was the development of self.

One of the many surprises that came out of the first years of the Head Start programs was that many low-income 4 year olds had no visual knowledge of their *selves*. The director of one of the centers tells of taking a group of children to the market to buy fruit for their afternoon snack. As they started their return walk to the center, some of them were reluctant to leave the sidewalk in front of the store, where they were seeing their full-length reflection in the plate glass store window. They had discovered their visual

selves, and were excited. As the result of many similar episodes, a new goal was added for all Head Start programs: the development of self-awareness as the basis for self-esteem and self-confidence. How did the teachers work toward this goal? They provided full-length mirrors so the children could see all of their selves (a triple mirror that gives front, side, and back views is ideal). They took a full-length picture of each child and attached it to the child's personal cubby. They made up songs and games that included the children's names. They used the child's name in face-to-face conversation. They made an effort to establish a warm friendship with each child, and with the child's family. They were constantly reminded of this new goal by a poster hanging in the classroom that stated "Each day, each child will go home with his head held a little bit higher."

These Head Start children had missed an essential learning in their pre-Head Start years; they had no knowledge of self. Today's infants and toddlers can learn their selves, and the learning starts at birth. The Head Start suggestions are equally appropriate for younger children.

"Who am I?". Self-knowledge is learned through interactions and relationships with persons in the social world, just as object-knowledge is learned through interactions and relationships with things in the physical world. Indeed, the exploration and manipulation of objects not only gives information about the objects, but it gives much information about one's self. "I can reach . . . I can grasp . . . I can let go . . . I can make something happen!" This expectation of making something happen is a significant landmark not only in the growth of competence, but also in the development of a positive self-concept.

Although it is difficult to distinguish between *self* and *self-concept*, we do know that a sense of self is a prerequisite for the formation of self-concept. Both are learned from the same interactions and relationships, and both are closely related to body image. Body image (or perception of one's body) is determined by adult attitudes and reactions to normal behaviors such as the child's exploration of his own body and the bodies of others, thumbsucking, masturbation, and the routines of diaper changing and toileting. The first real awareness of *self* as a separate entity develops out of the quality of care and personal trustworthiness experienced by the infant through his caregivers (Erikson, 1964).

Another prerequisite for a positive self-concept is a basic sense of trust in persons, and in a predictable physical environment. These are also necessary for the later achievements of autonomy and initiative, both of which further deepen the child's view of self as distinct from others.

It is difficult to give a specific age for the accomplishment of the concept of self. Probably the first attempt was by Ames (1952), who traced the development of verbalized concepts of self, starting at age 2. She found that typical remarks of 2 year olds included "Me . . . mine . . . me want . . . me do it." Brazelton (1974) notes that a 2 year old "knew what was 'his' and what belonged to someone else. He called his toys 'mine' and Mark's 'his'" (pp. 151–152). Musick and Householder (1986) report that the second year of life brings about the emergence of sense of self, and the recognition of the self as a separate individual. This period also contains the beginnings of the sense of autonomy or independence. The 2 year old has wants and ideas of his own, and makes them known in assertive ways! In former days this stage was known as the *terrible twos;* today we say *terrific twos,* because the 2 year old has developed from a helpless dependent babe to an independent being, capable of purposeful activity and behavior.

Nurturing "Who am I?". Action games, songs, and fingerplays all help young children become aware of parts of themselves and of themselves as persons who can do things. For the younger toddlers, activities involving the larger body parts are more suitable than fingerplays. Beginning favorites include the following:

Jack-in-the-Box
Jack-in-the-box
Sit so still
   (Children squat or stoop down, placing
   hands overhead as cover.)
Won't you come out?
Yes I will!
   (Children open their hands and jump up.)

Here is a Ball
Here is a ball,
   (Fingers of both hands touch to form first
   ball.)
Here is a bigger ball,
   (Bowed arms with fingers touching, form the
   second ball.)
And here is the biggest ball of all
   (Arms form biggest ball, no fingers touching.)
Now let us count the balls we made:
One,
Two,
Three.
   (Repeat making balls, showing increasing
   size.)

Rain
Rain in the green grass,
   (Bend hands at wrists, wiggle fingers for
   rain.)
And rain in the tree,
   (Raise both hands for tree.)
Rain on the roof top,
   (Make roof above head with palms down.)
But not on me.
   (Point to self.)

After the toddlers have some idea of the names and motions of the various body parts, as well as a beginning ability to follow directions, they are introduced to the various action songs and games. Following directions at this point is mostly imitating the teacher's actions. Traditional favorites include the following:

Teddy Bear
Teddy Bear, Teddy Bear, turn around.
Teddy Bear, Teddy Bear, touch the ground.

Teddy Bear, Teddy Bear, climb the stair.
Teddy Bear, Teddy Bear, hop into bed.
Teddy Bear, Teddy Bear, turn out the light.
Teddy Bear, Teddy Bear, blow a kiss
   "Goodnight!"

Ring Around a Rosy

Ring around a rosy,
A pocket full of posies.
Ashes, ashes,
All fall down!
(The children form a circle, holding hands, and
  skip around until the word "down", when
  they squeal and fall down on the rug.)

The Mulberry Bush

1. Here we go round the mulberry bush,
   The mulberry bush, the mulberry bush,
   Here we go round the mulberry bush,
   So early in the morning.

2. This is the way we wash our clothes,
   So early Monday morning.

3. This is the way we iron our clothes,
   So early Tuesday morning.

4. This is the way we scrub the floor,
   So early Wednesday morning.

5. This is the way we mend our clothes,
   So early Thursday morning.

6. This is the way we sweep the house,
   So early Friday morning,

*7. This the way we bake our bread,
   So early Saturday morning.

*8. This is the way we go to church,
   So early Sunday morning.

(The children join hands and skip around in a
circle. Beginning with the second verse, they
act out the words of the song.)

Action songs and games might be called
bodyplays. Fingerplays come into their own as
toddlers begin to gain control over their finer
muscle movements. Such all-time favorites in-

---

*Some children and their families go to church on Saturday,
and some do not go at all. Also, some families wish complete
separation of religion and the center program. Adjustments
might be made in the last two verses to meet the needs and
wishes of the families in a particular center.

clude Open, shut them, Eentsy weentsy spider,
Here is a beehive, Five little squirrels, and Two
little blackbirds. (Refer to the previous chapter
for sources of fingerplays.)

Most important, however, in teaching "Who
am I?" is the use of the child's name whenever
talking to or about the child. Adults must consciously refrain from using "honey" or "swee-
tie" when talking to individual children. In addition, self-awareness is enhanced when teacher
mentions such things as "John is wearing red
socks today" or "Mary washed her hands all by
herself."

The use of children's names when talking to
or about them is an important part of teaching
"Who am I?" First names or nicknames, however, are only half a name! A 2 year old may
know his name is Sam, but that will be of little
help if he is ever separated from the group or
family members. When Sam knows that his
name is Sam Jones, he can be of some assistance when he is found. Soon after learning his
full name, he can learn his street address or at
least the name of the town or section of town
where he lives. By 3½ or 4 years of age children
should also know their phone numbers.
Our hesitance toward having children learn by
rote memory should not apply to this kind of
information.

If the parents of the children agree, birthday
parties and "King" and "Queen" for the day
activities serve to celebrate the specialness of
each child. (Some parents do not want their children to engage in celebrations of any kind, and
their opinions must be honored.) Conversations
about each child's favorite color or food, or
about pets, a new baby, or family outings all
help children get to know themselves. Full-
length pictures of individual children, of the
group of children in the child-care group with
the staff members, and with their families posted
on bulletin boards or included in teacher-made
picture books further increase the understanding of "Who am I?"

It is possible, and it happens all too frequently, to completely negate the "I am some-

body" learnings at the times of arrival and departure from the center. Visualize the following and its unspoken message to Jonathan:

EPISODE 7.

Mrs. Andrews and 1-year-old Jonathan arrive at the center breathlessly at 7:45 A.M. Mrs Andrews must punch in on the time clock by 8:00 at her job across town or have her pay docked. Mrs. Andrews: "Hi, Ruth, here's the baby. I've got to run. Oh—I'll be a little late tonight. I have a doctor's appointment after work." Ruth (as she takes Jonathan from Mrs. Andrews): "I hope nothing is wrong. Don't forget we close at 6." Mrs. Andrews: "O.K.," and she rushes off.

Poor Jonathan! He had no more status than a sack of potatoes! Unfortunately, the end of the day is typically just as rushed as the beginning—working mothers or fathers have to grocery shop, get dinner, do the laundry, and tend to other children. It is conceivable that Jonathan both starts and ends his day like a bag of potatoes!

Knowledge of Others (Adults) and Related Skills

It is interesting to note that Moore's 1982 review of research about prosocial behaviors in the early years did not include any studies of children under the age of 3. Less than 10 years later, we were convinced that even very young infants are tuned in to what their significant adults are doing, saying, and perhaps even thinking! It is these adults who set the standards, both consciously and unconsciously, for the young child's behavior and attitudes, and for the child's developing sense of self.

There has been much research about mother-child relationships, but up until now there has been a very limited amount of research on father-child relationships during the infancy stage, although the importance of the father's role in the development of older children has been well documented. We have learned that infants prefer fathers to strangers,

but they also prefer mothers to fathers. Perhaps this preference will change as more fathers become involved in regular and consistent caregiving.

An example of these changing attitudes is shown by book titles. Klaus and Kennell's 1976 publication is titled *Maternal-Infant Bonding;* their second edition in 1982 is titled *Parent-Infant Bonding.* Their research demonstrated that "early involvement of fathers with newborns leads to the same positive changes in interaction patterns over time that were found with early involvement of mothers" (Anselmo, 1987, pp. 106–107). The tie from infant to parent is called attachment.

Attachment. Attachment is "an affective bond built upon learning and dependent upon cognitive development" (Musick & Householder, 1986, p. 331). It has been an area of much research interest since the idea was first introduced by Bowlby in 1958, and greatly elaborated by him in 1982. According to Bowlby's theory, infants form social attachments primarily by having personalized contact with adults, which goes beyond the routine caregiving activities.

There has long been a fear that infants whose mothers are employed are emotionally less secure than babies whose mothers are more available. This fear originates from observations of children raised in institutions who were greatly damaged emotionally. But those children were deprived of the continuous and consistent care of any nurturing adult. According to Clarke-Stewart (1989), an infant whose mother is employed is not deprived of her love—he is simply deprived of some of her time. Numerous studies have shown that infants of employed mothers are no less likely to become attached to their mothers than infants of homemaker mothers.

Most research studies have focused on the mother-child attachment, but it has also been found that infants can form additional attachments with one or two sensitive and responsive caregivers in a group setting. Rubenstein and Howes (1979) suggest that high quality day care does not reduce the parent-child attachment. They found that infants in day care show the same degree of preference for their parents as those who are home reared. Robertson's review of day-care studies (1982) leads to the same conclusion, that of "no difference between day care and home care children in the preferential attachments they exhibit towards their mothers" (p. 53).

However, the debate continues. In the September 1986 issue of *Zero to Three,* Belsky states that "entry into care in the first year of life is a 'risk factor' for the development of insecure-avoidant attachments in infancy" (p. 7). His statement resulted in a violent protest and severe criticism of his alleged manipulation of the data, and the weaknesses in the studies he chose to report on (Chess, 1987; Phillips, McCartney, Scarr, & Howes, 1987). In spite of this controversy, the realities of American life indicate that infant day care is here to stay. It is our responsibility and challenge to provide the very best educaring for children in out-of-home centers and family day-care homes. The practices and activities involved in the very best educaring are presented in chapter 10.

The major period for social attachment is from 9 to 12 months of age. The quality of the attachment relationship is a product of learning and of countless experiences. Gonzalez-Mena and Eyer (1980) recommended a relationship that is "respectful, responsive, and reciprocal" (p. 12). When nonfamilial educarers are sensitive, responsive, and consistent, attachments are formed with them in addition to a firm attachment to the mother. During the first half of the second year, the child moves out "into the world" with her interests and explorations. This, of course, leads to separateness from the educarer, a necessary step in the formation of self-concept. This "moving out" was beautifully described by Kierkegaard in 1846. His description brings to life the transition from attachment to separateness.

The loving mother teaches her child to walk alone. She is far enough from him so that she cannot actually support him, but she holds out her arms to him. She imitates his movements, and if he totters, she swiftly bends as if to seize him, so that the child might believe he is not walking alone. . . . And yet, she does more. Her face beckons like a reward, an encouragement. Thus, the child walks alone with his eyes fixed on his mother's face, not on the difficulties in his way. He supports himself by the arms that do not hold him and constantly strives toward the refuge in his mother's embrace, little suspecting that in the very same moment he is emphasizing his need of her, he is proving that he can do without her, because he is walking alone (Sroufe, 1979, p. 462).

It is very possible that baby's first steps will be in an infant-toddler group setting. The responsive educarer will adopt this mother's attitudes and actions and sense of excitement.

Transitions from home to group setting. Infants are born ready to communicate with others. They usually learn to communicate most frequently and most effectively with their mothers (or mother-substitutes). When baby is left with someone who does not "speak" the same language, baby is left without a communication partner. This happens when babies under 6 months are placed in out-of-home care. All efforts must be made to enable the new caregiver to get to really know the baby as soon as possible. The frequent smiles of the baby should elicit warm responses (physical and vocal) from the responsive caregiver, and—voila!—a new communication partnership has begun. An outstanding description of the development of a communication partnership is the focus of *Born Dancing* by Thoman and Browder (see suggested reading list at the end of the chapter).

During the second 6 months, this same partnership must develop. Ideally, the mother can arrange her other commitments so that she and the new caregiver can share the baby's care in the new surroundings. If mother can stay long enough for the new caregiver to become a person familiar to the baby, many emotional upsets can be avoided. The best situation, of course, would be to have the caregiver spend time at baby's home, interacting with both mother and baby, before the beginning attendance in the group setting. Unfortunately, the best is rarely possible. It is included here to emphasize the importance of a gradual transition for baby from one primary caregiver to another, and from one setting to another.

When gradual transition cannot occur because of other demands on the parent or the educarer, it has been found that "mothers who inform their children that they are leaving and/or will return shortly, and also give their children instructions as to what to do in their absence, have children who are most likely to play and least likely to cry" (Powell, 1989, p. 43). There is no magic age when the child will understand this message, but we do know that understanding precedes oral expression, and it is possible that the soothing tones of mother's voice may have the desired effect even before total comprehension is achieved.

Young children (and even adults) not only develop social attachments, but they also develop deep nonhuman attachments, perhaps with a live kitten, or a stuffed teddy bear or a ragged blanket or even a pacifier. These nonsocial items are called *transitional objects*. For many young children, blankets and soft toys become a way of easing the transition from an excitable state to a more calm state (Mahalski, 1983). Transitions from home to child-care program, or even from awake-time to rest-time, are eased if the child has something familiar to fondle. These "security blankets" usually become most important around 2½ years of age, "probably because somewhere between the second and third year, many children begin to acquire the skills necessary for relating emotionally to others beyond the primary people in their lives" (Jalongo, 1987, p. 4). However, babies usually choose their "loveys" sometime during the first 12 to 18 months. Transitional objects

usually include teddy bears, blankets, cloth diapers, or dolls, but there is a wide range of choices, including pot holders, old fur coats, and toy fire trucks! (Berg, 1989).

From adults to peers. White (1985) observed that the social abilities usually achieved during the second year include getting and holding the attention of adults, using adults as resources, expressing affection and mild annoyance to adults, and showing pride in personal accomplishment. During the third year the child will turn his attention to his peers. His social behavior with them will include leading and following, expressing affection and annoyance, and beginning to compete, especially with an older sibling.

Knowledge of Others (Peers) and Related Skills

The young child's developing sense of other children is a recent research interest. In a review of the research on children's social cognition, Forbes (1978) proposes four stages in the development of a cognitive sense of other:

1. Early fusion between self and other
2. Initial recognition of other's continued existence at about 10–12 months of age
3. Development later in infancy of a rudimentary sense that the other has independent inner states
4. Awareness by middle or late childhood that others have personal histories and general life circumstances that contribute to their inner states of the moment (p. 129)

Detailed observations of infants during their first year have shown that their initial question is not "Who are you?" but "What is it and what can I do with it or to it?" When babies become mobile, they approach one another because of their attraction to a new and different object. Sometimes two babies will collide because of a mutual attraction to the same toy or other object. Infants may play side by side, may tug each other's hair and clothes, and may handle the same objects, but there seems to be little recognition of the aliveness of one another. This is shown clearly in the following episode.

EPISODE 8

Mary (10 months) is sitting on the floor, playing with pop-beads, close to Shelley (9 months) who is lying on the rug. Neither child seems aware of the other. Mary starts to swing her arms, and drops her "necklace," which lands on Shelley's arm. At this moment, both babies stop short and fix their attention on one another. Mary reaches over to retrieve the beads, drops them again, starts to wave her arms, and accidentally hits Shelley. There is no observable reaction from Shelley, who has been watching Mary attentively. Mary suddenly stops her arm waving and gazes at Shelley. She leans over and puts her face directly in front of Shelley's. She puts out her hand and touches Shelley's hair, eye, nose, and mouth, gurgling and cooing the whole time. Shelley returns a small "coo," and they both touch noses several times. Shelley starts to kick her legs, and moves back. Mary sits up and resumes playing with the beads. Both babies ignore each other once again.

These initial getting-to-know-you behaviors will gradually lead to the realization that one does not act the same toward a peer as toward a new toy. Mary and Shelley had already spent several months at the day-care center and were probably more at ease with their investigations than babies who had not yet been in a group setting. Lois Murphy's observation of Colin's first days in a nursery school (1956) offers the same getting-to-know-you behaviors at an older age. Colin was 2 years, 9 months old when he was taken to the nursery school.

Colin progressed quickly from a quiet, friendly, watching relationship on the first few days to actively hugging the other children. The hugging seemed to be in an excess of friendliness and was only mildly aggressive. Having started hugging he didn't know how to stop, and usually just held

on until he pulled the child down to the floor. This was followed very closely by hair pulling. He didn't pull viciously, but still held on long enough to get a good resistance from the child (p. 12).

When babies have been in a happy group setting from their earliest months, there are indications of beginning social interactions with peers toward the end of the first year. The 1 year old is aware that a peer is someone who both initiates and responds to social behaviors. Once discovered, this awareness develops at a rapid pace, although all does not go smoothly.

EPISODE 9

Two-year-old Jimmy was contentedly playing with a toy telephone in the middle of the playroom floor. Mark, also 2 years old, decided he had to have that particular phone. (There were two more on the toy shelf.) Mark grabbed the phone and pushed Jimmy down. Jimmy screamed. Mark ran to the playhouse with Jimmy in hot pursuit. The teacher arrived on the scene, and held Jimmy's arm to get his attention. She tried to calm Jimmy by talking to him slowly and directly and holding him close. "Jimmy, you took a little fall. Are you alright?" Jimmy continued to sob. His attention was on Mark. The educarer took Jimmy over to Mark and said, "Jimmy, Mark, let's play a game with the phone together. I'll start first." She pretended the phone rang, answered it, and said, "Yes, Mark is right here." She handed the phone to Mark who started an imaginary phone conversation. The educarer withdrew, and both boys happily took turns with the phone.

This incident and the educarer's response give a clue to appropriate methods of discipline for toddlers, and will be referred to later in that context. At this time, it serves to point up the negative or destructive interactions that are to be expected sometimes in children who are learning the complexities of social behavior. Aggressive encounters between young children rarely last more than a minute. Often they are completed and apparently forgotten within 30 seconds. Common and normal behaviors during these episodes are pushing, pulling, pinching, and throwing relatively harmless objects. Two and 3-year-old children have little understanding of the rights or desires of other children. They also have little capacity to express their feelings verbally (Feldman, 1975).

Teachers of toddlers have observed enough instances of cooperative play among 2 year olds to question the usual description of their social interactions as egocentric and noncooperative. Laboratory stories by Rheingold, Hay, and West (1976) demonstrated that sharing is a characteristic of children 18 months of age and younger. The child's sharing was defined as: (1) showing—directing a person's attention to a toy by pointing; (2) giving—releasing a toy in a person's hand or lap; and (3) partner play—manipulating a toy given to someone else and still in the possession of the other. Incidental observations of younger children revealed that sharing by pointing, showing, and giving occurred in babies as young as 10.1 months. The incidents reported involved sharing with mother, father, and experimenter (all adults). The study shows that very young children exhibit social behaviors much sooner than has been traditionally expected. These children had been reared at home. It is reasonable to expect that these "early" ages for sharing behaviors would exist in a group setting as well.

Rubin (1980) agrees: "By the time children are two and a half years old, they are able to manage interactions with one another that contain, in fledgling form, all the basic features of social interaction among older children or adults—sustained attention, turn-taking, and mutual responsiveness" (p. 16–17).

Press and Greenspan (1985) suggest a sequential pattern in the development of a friendship as follows:

- Attraction, usually toward a toy held by another child

- Exploration (touching, mutual gazing, handing of objects back and forth)
- Explorative aggression of another child (hair pulling, poking, grabbing an object or toy) and passivity by the other child—perhaps he is surprised or excited, or is not sure how to react
- Cooperative "refereed" play, in the presence of a buffering adult
- Unbuffered, reciprocal, and imitative play without objects
- Sharing objects (the beginning of true cooperative play)
- Discovery and shared humor
- Early cooperative, representational play together

If the educarer refers to the above sequence, he or she will recognize the role of attraction in the first social approaches, will encourage it, will understand the importance of person-exploration and will not inhibit it (unless there is a possibility of bodily harm), will join in an activity as referee or buffer during the initial stages of playing together, and will join in early attempts at humor.

THE NURTURING OF APPROPRIATE SOCIAL BEHAVIORS

Throughout history, the teaching of appropriate social behaviors has ranged from very severe physical or psychological abuse to the intentional ignoring of an unacceptable behavior. An example of intentional ignoring is contained in Episode 9. The teacher ignored Mark (the aggressive child), attended to Jimmy (the victim), and initiated an associative play interaction.

Piagetian theory suggests that children under the age of 4 or 5 years are not able to reason, but the key time for learning how to handle aggressive drives is between 2 and 3 years of age (Lourie, 1973). How can we teach, if our young children are unable to reason? One approach is found in the principles of behavioral psychology, which rely on behavioral management to teach acceptable behaviors.

Behavioral Management and Aggression

For young children aggressive behavior is currently defined as that which "has the capacity to hurt or injure or damage, regardless of intent" (Caldwell, 1977, p. 6). There are at least two types of aggression. One is hostile and involves an intent to hurt another person or an object. In Episode 9, should it be assumed that Mark pushed Jimmy down because he wanted to hurt him? Was the act premeditated? The other kind of aggression, according to Feshback (1970), is instrumental aggression. The child wants to get or retrieve something and there is a block in the attempt (the "block" in the episode was Jimmy). Instrumental aggression can be viewed as an assertion of self-interest. It is quite possible that Mark's primary concern over possession of the telephone completely eclipsed his developing cognizance that Jimmy was another human, and that pushing him down was a normal reaction to an object in the way of a goal. The intent to hurt should never be assumed in the infant-toddler group.

The educarer applied principles of behavioral psychology in her approach (or nonapproach) to Mark. She completely ignored Mark immediately after the incident, devoted all her attention to Jimmy. In a few moments, when both she and Jimmy returned to the scene and the educarer engaged both boys in play, she was subtly reinforcing Mark for his nonaggression after the pushing down. The three principles of teaching that are useful in helping children stop unacceptable behaviors are:

1. Remove all positive reinforcement for the behavior.

2. Ignore a child who is not behaving acceptably. This ignoring is especially effective if the educarer immediately attends to (rein-

forces) the child when the unacceptable behavior stops.

3. Structure unpleasant consequences for a particularly unacceptable behavior. In this instance, the educarer assumed lack of intent to hurt and also knew the usual developmental sequence of social behaviors. She did not consider Mark's behavior "particularly unacceptable" for his age.

The incident finished happily, but the learning had just begun. In order to increase the frequency of an acceptable behavior, the following guidelines for teaching behavior have been derived from the principles of learning. The sequential steps are:

1. Careful observation to determine what toys, activities, or forms of attention are reinforcing for the child.

2. Arranging the environment so that the child can observe significant persons performing the desired behavior. (One educarer is looking at a book; a second adult approaches and says, "May I look at the book, please?" First educarer responds, "I'm not finished reading it. Would you like to read it with me?" or even "I'm not finished with it, but I'll give it to you when I am finished.") Note: It would be next to impossible to structure such a situation with the other toddlers, although such interactions do sometimes occur. The best way for a child to learn a new behavior response is to observe it in another child. Our teaching should not wait for happenstance, however. Children do imitate behaviors that receive observable reinforcement, and we therefore do not limit our positive reinforcement only to those who specifically need it.

3. Immediate reinforcement for increasingly successful steps in the right direction (usually called "shaping"). (In Mark's case, a successful step in the right direction might be to come close to a child playing with a

truck and to stand close by to watch. An observant educarer might say, "I like the way you are waiting for your turn.")

4. Immediate reinforcement (within 3 seconds) for each successful performance of the desired behavior. ("You asked for the truck nicely, Mark. Good asking!").

5. Giving verbal cues or suggestions to help the child identify situations where the new behavior is appropriate and to serve as a reminder. ("Maybe if you asked Terry for the trike, he would let you have a turn .")

6. Gradual decrease in reinforcement when the child has mastered the behavior and is performing it at appropriate times.

One or two final comments should be made before we leave Jimmy and Mark. If an uninformed observer had watched (1) Mark grabbing the phone and pushing Jimmy down and (2) the adult's complete ignoring of Mark immediately afterward, the observer would feel justified in saying, "that teacher lets kids get away with everything!" At the very least the observer would classify the adult as very permissive. The educarer was neither permissive nor did she use any form of punishment. She taught in the appropriate way for the situation.

One of the most valuable conclusions of the classic longitudinal study of child-rearing patterns (Sears, Macoby, & Levin, 1957) is as follows:

> The way for parents to produce a non-aggressive child is to make it abundantly clear that aggression is frowned upon, and to stop aggression when it occurs, but to avoid punishing the child for his aggression. Punishment seems to have complex effects. While undoubtedly it often stops a particular form of aggression, at least momentarily, it appears to generate more hostility in the child and lead to further aggression outbursts at some other time or place. . . . The most peaceful home is one in which the mother believes aggression is undesirable . . . and who relies mainly on non-punitive forms of control (p. 266).

This philosophy is equally appropriate in child-care centers or family day-care homes, and has been reemphasized by Bettye Caldwell (1977).

One last word about aggression. It is now thought that providing clay to pound on, or a doll or pillow to pummel, or a tree to kick is *not* the way to reduce the frequency of aggressive behaviors toward persons. "Contrary to popular beliefs, children encouraged to behave aggressively toward inanimate objects are likely to try out their aggressive skills learned in these situations on their peers" (Roedell, Slaby, & Robinson, 1976, p. 11). This conclusion has been well documented by several research psychologists (Borke, 1972; Chandler & Greenspan, 1972; Grusec, 1974; Hoffman, 1972).

Other Problem Behaviors

Temper tantrums. After a child has adequate language to communicate his needs and desires, he should no longer resort to temper tantrums to express frustration or unmet needs. Infants and toddlers have not yet reached that stage, and "occasional tantrums on the part of 1- and 2-year-olds are quite normal circuits . . . even in the most reasonable homes and child care settings" (Discipline: Are Tantrums Normal?, 1988, p. 35).

Temper tantrums are the ultimate in negativism. They can be eliminated by using the three principles of teaching included in the presentation of behavioral management and aggression. The child is removed from the group, so that he receives no attention from the other children or adults (Principle No. 1); the adult, after moving the child, ignores him completely (Principle No. 2); the teacher immediately pays attention to, and invites the child back to the group as soon as he is under control (Principle No. 3). If the tantrum continues, a natural consequence very probably could be missing snack or outdoor play or music or whatever is next on the schedule. If the timing of the daily schedule does not match the need, the adult might rearrange the schedule on the spur of the moment. However, a time-out of even a minute is a very long time for a child under 3 years of age. Probably he will be ready to rejoin the group before even a spur-of-the-moment change can be put into action. The American Academy of Pediatrics (1989) recommends that removal from the scene of the tantrum be used only in case of tantrums that are too violent to ignore.

Brazelton (1974) maintains that tantrums are necessary and appropriate at around 12 to 15 months of age. He defines a tantrum "as a reflection of the inner turmoil of decision-making that one is faced with when decisions become one's own" (p. 21). There is no punishment that will calm this inner turmoil.

A tantrum can be a frightening experience for a very young child; he is temporarily out of control, and loses all sense of reality. What is needed is a nearby compassionate adult who offers psychological security, as well as physical affection and verbal soothing as soon as possible. Nothing can be gained by attempting to reason with the child. The most quieting and reassuring environment is away from the group where he can gradually regain control with the support of a responsive adult.

As children get older, there is a subtle change in the stimulus for tantrum behavior. The tantrum becomes an intentional means of obtaining one's way when it conflicts with expectations or requests. If adults allow themselves to be manipulated in this way, the frequency and duration of the tantrums will increase because they have been reinforced. Educarers who know their children can tell the difference between the inner-turmoil and the manipulative tantrum, and can therefore respond appropriately. An appropriate response to the intentional tantrum is prompt removal from the group with as little commotion as possible. In this instance, the adult's role is to teach acceptable behavior, not to support unacceptable behavior. It is taught by the complete absence of all reinforcement (attention) from both children and adults. Close

adult supervision is necessary, however, to prevent any self-inflicted injury.

Biting. Biting is a usual occurrence in a toddler group, and there is nothing necessarily wrong with the child who bites, unless it happens regularly. But even the occasional biting episode usually creates a great deal of turmoil and emotion. Bettye Caldwell (1988) estimates "that about one child in 20 or 25 will be a problem biter at some time during the infant/toddler period" (p. 138). Caldwell (1988) also prescribes the most appropriate action to take.

> Probably the best way for an adult to deal with biting is with firm and non-negotiable removal of the child from the setting in which the deed occurred. While swooping up a child and removing her from the room, the teacher can say something like "I will not let you do that. You may not stay in the same room with the other children if you are going to bite." When the child is released from the ensuing isolation, there is probably no point in nagging her with "Now if you bite Mary again, you're going right back in this room with the door closed" (p. 140).

The true educarer does not stop here. Children have reasons for biting, just as they have reasons for hitting out and for throwing a tantrum. A brief review of possible reasons will include

- Infants and toddlers are learning to hold and let go of their parents, their toys, their bowel movements. Sometimes they "hold" with their teeth.

- Toddlers are developing autonomy, and sometimes a bite gives them power over the other child (or adult).

- Babies use their senses to learn, and tasting (or perhaps biting) is one of the expected exploratory actions.

- Infants and toddlers are teething, and need the comfort of something to chew on.

- Infants and toddlers are just beginning to learn how to approach their peers, and may poke, pull hair, or bite as a way of establishing contact.

- Infants and toddlers are exploring cause and effect relationships. What an exciting effect happens when they bite!
- All young children need attention, and negative attention is better than none at all.
- All young children have feelings of anger and frustration, and bite because they don't know what else to do.

(adapted from Miller, 1984)

Do not be dismayed if a few of the children under your care bite you or the other children. It is not necessarily a reflection of poor adult skills or techniques. A recent report of bite injuries at a very high-quality, child-care center (Solomons & Elardo, 1989) found 224 bites over a 42-month period. September was the "bitingest" month, and the majority of bites during any day occurred between 10 A.M. and noon.

One word of caution: If a child continues biting, bites viciously, or bites and then smiles, seek professional help, and/or explore the possibility that the child may need an environment with fewer children and more one-on-one adult attention.

Aggressive behaviors (tantrums, hitting, biting) almost always are the result of a toddler's overwhelming frustrations. We may not be able to prevent all of them, because of possible outside sources of frustrations and stress. But we can control the conditions in our child-care environments, and therefore minimize the number of outbursts. Leavitt and Eheart (1985) suggest that we need to be sure toddlers

1. are involved and interested in activities of their own choosing
2. understand what behavior is expected and are encouraged when behaving appropriately
3. are kept out of overwhelming situations
4. have an adult's help, but not interference

5. aren't unnecessarily thwarted by too many adult restrictions (p. 67).

Stranger anxiety. Although not a "problem" in the same meaning as aggression or tantrums or biting, stranger anxiety is an upsetting emotion for the young child, and can be lessened or even eliminated given the proper conditions.

Most people expect all young children to experience stranger anxiety, but this is not the case. If baby has had experiences with many people (family members, neighbors, even unfamiliar persons) there will be little or no stranger anxiety. Much depends on how the strange person approaches the baby. If the mother is present and the approach is gradual, the anxiety level is markedly decreased. The recommended approach is one in which the newcomer pays no attention to baby, but engages in friendly conversation with the mother. Baby's curiosity will soon overcome uncertainty, and he will approach and "explore" the stranger. The stranger's welcoming response will initiate a social interaction, and the stranger is no longer "strange." The following incident illustrates the resolution of the stranger anxiety of a 2½ year old, who solved the problem for herself, with the guidance of an educaring mother.

EPISODE 10

Carol could talk of nothing else but her desire to see Santa Claus. Mother and Carol made a special trip downtown to one of Santa's headquarters, and joined the line of other adults and children. But when Carol's turn came, she burst into tears and clung to her mother. They both moved away, and after Carol had calmed down, her mother said, "Just watch." They watched for awhile at a safe distance.

During the next week, Carol and mother saw several Santas as they went in and out of stores Christmas shopping, and one evening Carol saw Santa on a television program.

Eight days after the first encounter, Carol announced, "I want to go to see Santa Claus." She and her mother again went to Santa's headquarters and joined the line. When Carol's turn came, she jumped up on his lap and happily responded to his questions, "What is your name? . . . What do you want for Christmas?" Her answer to both questions was "Two in August!" He laughed and gave her a hug and a candy cane. Carol hurried back to her mother, visibly pleased with the whole affair.

So many good things happened in this story, and all of them happened because the mother did not pressure, scold, or ridicule her daughter's anxiety and fear. Mother gave Carol the time and the opportunity to solve the problem for herself, and the little girl made a giant step forward.

Brazelton (1978) has suggested that the infant's strong reactions to strangers are really "peaks of intense curiosity, and that they accompany spurts of learning about new areas of his world" (p. xv). The educarer can lessen the usual fears and thereby enhance the child's learning from the experience.

Acceptance of Differences

An important part of social learnings is the positive acceptance of differences. Derman-Sparks (1989) reports that awareness of gender, skin color, and obvious physical disabilities is one of the 2 year old's accomplishments. There are "signs of pre-prejudice in the form of discomfort with physical differences" (p. 23) as early as 2½ years. Children become aware of these differences by themselves, but they are totally dependent on the adults in forming attitudes of positive acceptance.

Educarers must integrate anti-bias content into the environment and into the daily activities. Suggestions offered by Derman-Sparks (1989) include providing paints, crayons, magic markers, paper, chalk, and play dough in different skin shades; including dolls and figures that represent men, women, and children from a variety of racial backgrounds and physical features; and

singing simple songs or reciting rhymes in more than one language. Such suggestions are of little use unless the educarer makes positive comments and answers questions truthfully. Even a puzzled expression on the face of a 2 year old should be viewed as a question that needs an answer. The educarer takes the lead from such looks or tentative touches and puts into words the child's implied question and the explanation, such as "children have many different colors of skin, but we all like to play together," or "Johnny is learning to talk with his hands; let's all learn to say some words in his language."

Carefully selected children's books will answer some of the questions. The children's books listed in the suggested readings at the end of this chapter are appropriate for 2 and 3 year olds. They tell of anti-bias interactions between children or between animals. It is most important that the stories introduce and/or reinforce the idea that "different" does not mean bad or wrong.

PUNISHMENT AND DISCIPLINE

Punishment per se need not be addressed when the topic is the socialization of the child under the age of 3. Punishment has no place in a group or home setting for infants and toddlers. These children do not "misbehave"; they behave in ways that lead to their learning. Misbehavior, like beauty, lies in the eyes of the beholder. Somehow, even the adults who encourage the children to explore and experiment with physical objects in the environment do not extend their encouragement or even their permission to explore personal and social behaviors.

It is easy to get tangled in a jumble of words when we think about punishment and discipline. There are almost as many definitions of the words as there are teachers of young children. I am defining punishment as an act by an adult that is intended to physically or psychologically hurt the child (a slap, a spank, a shake, or abusive language). These acts are mistakenly viewed as teaching acts. They do teach, but they do not teach the hoped-for learnings. They do not even teach the child "to mind."

The young child who has been removed from positive reinforcement probably views the removal as punishment. The adult should view the removal as a teaching act. It helps the child learn which behaviors are acceptable and which are not. Even so, removal from reinforcement should be a last resort that is used infrequently in the infant-toddler age group.

The process of socialization (rule-learning) does not proceed in a straight line. A zigzag line is the usual sequence. The child tests limits, adults, and the other children. When the initial testing is frustrated, the testing behaviors may intensify. But if the limits are consistently enforced, the testing behaviors will soon decrease in number and intensity. If the adult gives in, the testing is reinforced and will continue.

The popularization of the phrase "terrible twos" has sometimes led adults to overlook the positive growth of this stage. In the first place, any coined phrase or label tends to blur the individuality of the child. Any label, therefore, is deceiving and dangerous. Second, every 2 year old—it might be said that every person regardless of age—wants and needs to be self-assertive. During the early years, self-assertion is a part of the establishment of self-identity and autonomy. This drive is most easily observable in the child's use of the word "no." Brazelton defines the child's "no" as "a fragile barrier behind which a child this age can hide. If he is taken too literally, he will be surprised and disappointed" (1974, p. 101). When a child says "no" outloud he has asserted his ability to make a decision. Most frequently the child's decision will coincide with the adult's, as shown in Episode 11.

EPISODE 11

Two-year-old Karen was busily engaged in caring for her doll baby right before lunch time. The educarer approached, saying "Let's go to the sink, Karen, and I'll help you wash your face and hands." Karen: "No!" The educarer smiled, took Karen by the hand, and said "Come on Karen, it will only take a minute, and then it's time to eat. Let's go." Karen smiled, and teasingly pretended a reluctant walk over to the sink. Her reaction to the cool water on her face and hands was one of delight. Karen even had to be reminded that the other children needed a turn, also.

If an educarer had reacted in a completely opposite way ("Don't you say 'no' to me, young lady!") a serious confrontation of wills would have followed. Adults rarely win a serious clash with young children. They wear out and give in. In so doing, they make certain that future confrontations will occur.

When adults follow the suggested principles of teaching they are in control of the situation, and the child is subconsciously assured of a sense of security. The overall sense of trust is reinforced, because the adult's behavior is predictable and consistent. However, the teaching sequence presented so far is not complete. If an alternative to crying or breath-holding or tantrums is not offered the child, we have not taught an acceptable way to obtaining one's wants. We leave an empty spot in the child's repertoire of behaviors. Specific alternatives cannot be suggested for each incidence each time and for each child. The following statements have proved useful and indicate the general philosophy:

> Blocks are to build with.
> Hammers are to pound nails with.
> Dolls are to be played with.
> You may color on the paper, or you may find something else to do.
> You may leave the playground walking or I'll carry you.

How much better than "Don't throw the blocks" or hammers or dolls, etc.; how much better than nagging a child to come in from the playground. Our job is to teach, and we teach by providing an alternative.

Adults are prone to dismiss a child's clinging behaviors (to skirt or pants or legs) as a bid for attention, and they react in one of two ways. They give the attention, thus reinforcing the child's techniques of getting attention, or they say "Stop it" or Get away," giving the child neither the needed attention nor an acceptable alternative. A positive way to respond to the attention-seeking child is to say "I know you want me to hold you, but I won't hold you until you stop hanging on (or crying, or whining) and ask me to hold you." If the child is too young to ask verbally, suggest she raise her arms up, or even lead her through the action. Immediately reinforce, and pick up the child. According to Brazelton (1974) almost 75% of the infants are able to make word demands by 1 year of age:

> The first words are the simple vowels attached to an explosive consonant. As the exploration of such speech sounds proceeds, the baby senses that certain ones . . . produce a more rewarding response from the environment. He quickly learns their value and by nine months of age has fixed them as producible responses (p. 3).

There are many nonverbal ways of showing attention to a child. These include smiling, nodding, establishing eye contact, watching a child's activities with interest, really listening to a child's language, helping the child when appropriate, and making a physical contact. It is frequently the case in a group setting that an educarer may be involved with one or more children, and yet want to attend to another one. This is why the above suggestions should be part of the educarer's repertoire of attending behaviors. Whenever possible, a direct interaction involving language is preferable. Note the educarer's verbal interaction with Melissa while she was busily engaged with Luther in "a day in the life of Luther" in chapter 12.

Limits in an infant-toddler group should be confined to the three major ones: (1) you may not hurt yourself; (2) you may not hurt someone else; and (3) you may not hurt the materials or equipment. These limits must be consistently enforced in order for learning to take place.

Pertinent to all adult behaviors in teaching (disciplining) a young child is the statement that a child who is never shouted at never learns to shout at others. It can be applied to hitting or

biting or kicking equally as well. We can learn from the experiences at the Enep'ut Day-Care Center in Fairbanks, Alaska, where "at all times, the children . . . are held, picked up, carried around, tickled, fondled, and most of all, listened to" (Butler, 1973, p. 18). Eskimo adults are models of gentleness; their children grow up as gentle to others as their parents and teachers were to them. In an atmosphere of acceptance, encouragement, trust, respect, joy, and fellowship, children can function as friends and playmates. Such an atmosphere is well described in the "typical" days in chapter 12.

The educarer's goal for discipline in this center where these children spent many hours each day was to provide an environment that was rich in positive self-concept, concern for one another, and the security of equitable treatment. To meet this objective, the focus is on desired behaviors by educarer attention, facial expression, tone of voice, and verbal interaction. Educarers point out to children what it is about their behavior that is likable: "I like the way you hold your glass with both hands. It really helps you drink without spilling." "That's a careful way to go down the slide. You waited for David to be out of the way. Thanks, Jean." An educaring adult also supports social compatibility. "I can tell that Julie likes you, John. You make her laugh when you talk to her." "Tammy is feeding the doll right now. Let's look on the shelf and see if you can find one too." "I like the way you are building together. It's fun to build with a friend." Adult requests include reasons, and are carefully worded to avoid confrontations. "Books are to read. When you tear out the pages, we can't read the whole story. The pages need to stay in the book." "It is time to go to the bathroom. Would you rather walk or be carried?"

I suspect that when adults observe a basketball or football game, they "behave" basketball or football. These same adults would not yell or stamp their feet in a post office or library. Little children can be taught to act in accordance with whatever behaviors are deemed acceptable and desirable in a group setting. Barker (1968) concludes that the principal determinant of behavior is the nature of the situation that the child or adult perceives himself or herself to be in. The nature of the situation is in the hands of the educarers, and the situation should contain reasonable and definite limits, clear-cut guidelines, and a few necessary taboos.

Appropriate techniques for discipline with infants and toddlers involve distraction, substitution of alternative activity, and a change of subject. In all instances we must enable the child to "save face."

The Group for the Advancement of Psychiatry (1973) summarizes the position expressed here:

> Good discipline is a positive force directed toward what the child is allowed to do rather than what he is forbidden to do. It is based mainly on mutual love and respect. In childhood it has to be reinforced with teaching, firmness, and reminder (p. 74).

SOCIALIZATION AND COMMUNICATION

Children become socialized during the 8- to 36-month period. This is the time when they enter the world of people, and

> they must learn how to ask for help, how to cooperate, how to deal with prohibitions, and so on. Adults teach these and other basic social skills precisely during the period when language is developing most rapidly. Furthermore, social skills are taught by adults through the medium of language (White, 1988a, p. 21).

Long ago, Ben Franklin wrote, "Teach your child to hold his tongue; he'll learn fast enough to speak." Perhaps in his day when children were to be seen and not heard, his advice was appropriate. Today our responsibility is to both see and hear children, and to take an active role in encouraging and increasing their abilities to communicate and converse.

During the infant's first months, the educarer's role is that of a conversational partner, even though the baby is prelinguistic. In later months, the adult(s) continue in a speaking partnership, and by the time the toddler is in the last half of the second year, his peers will become limited speaking partners. Without such partners (adults and children), the development of language is impossible.

Development of Communication Skills

Infants start to communicate from birth. By one signal or another, babies let the world know they are hungry or uncomfortable or fatigued. Although babies can neither walk nor talk, they communicate in a forceful manner. The frantic pulling-up and stretching out of legs is readily understood as meaning "I have a pain in my tummy." For the first 3 months, baby's responses to the self-state and the other-than-self state are reflexive: smiling, grasping, gazing, and orienting to sound. These all give messages to the educarer. The child, therefore, learns that these reflex actions are signals, because the adult responds to them. The cry is also a reflex response during the first few months, and is neither controlled or designed to exploit the educarer. Bell and Ainsworth (1972) found that mothers who respond to their babies' cries and other signals have babies who cry less often and for shorter periods of time at 1 year of age. They also noted that the babies who cry least are more mature in ways to get attention and are more independent at 1 year than are the babies who are left to "cry it out." Cries soon become cause-specific, and can be differentiated by a caregiver as hunger or pain or fatigue cries.

Between the third and ninth month, baby becomes more active in using signals to communicate. Baby will look and smile, will usually follow the educarer's line of regard, will respond to adult vocalizations, and begins to anticipate events, as in peek-a-boo. Also during this period, baby coos, gurgles, and laughs, and makes many vocal sounds. Osgood (1957) claims a baby can make all possible sounds; McNeill (1970) and Ingram (1976) say nearly all. All babbling starts around 6 months and reaches its peak between 9 and 12 months. Baby has developed conversational skills even before 9 months. Baby learns to engage the attention of the educarer by vocalizing or crying. The adult responds with attention, and the baby responds by smiling, quieting, grasping, and so on. Before reaching the first birthday, baby has made a remarkable discovery: certain sounds result in certain reactions from caregivers. Sounds such as ma-ma-ma-ma have no meaning for baby, but they certainly create an excitement in the adult. Baby repeats the syllables because they evoke pleasure, thereby initiating the first social conversation. It is the educarer's feedback that leads baby to the attachment of meaning to sound experiments such as ma-ma and da-da. If no one responds to these or other sounds, the baby loses interest in trying new ones and will remain content with babblings and other vocalizations. The child will eventually stop even these, because no one gave any indication that sounds can communicate meaning. The advice of Huntington and colleagues (1973) is that the infant-toddler environment must supply:

- a relatively small number of adults having continuing, focused and affectively meaningful relationships with the child; adults who encourage reciprocal interactions.

- frequent contacts with adults and other children, contacts that are predominantly gratifying, expressive and warm.

- verbal interaction; a "speaking partner." Sound alone does not stimulate speech development; verbal exchanges do. Free and open verbal communication is essential (p. 9).

Toward the end of the first year, babbling contains variation in intonation and perhaps even a word or two. A stream of babbling sounds like talking with meaning. Pflaum-Connor (1978) observed

a puzzled three-and-a-half year old listening intently to a baby with this pseudo-language. Finally the older child said that the baby was funny because she sounded like she was saying something but it did not come out like talk (p. 25).

Until recently, research on language acquisition has been directed toward the production of sounds, the length of word utterances, and the size of vocabulary at different ages. For instance, at age 1 year, baby uses one or two words meaningfully, and by age 2, the average number of vocabulary words is 272. An average is often misleading because of the very large range of vocabulary size, even at age 2. We know that in favorable conditions, a 3-year-old child understands most of the words that are used in everyday adult conversations and is able to produce many of them.

The current emphasis in research on language acquisition is directly applicable to infant-toddler programs. Activity, motor involvement, and play are significant in the establishment of a language system. There are numerous studies of early utterances that support the idea that meaning is gained through actions. An early language development program, therefore, should provide opportunities for the action-development of meanings before and during the expectations for verbal expressions. Children always know more than they can verbalize. They need continuing opportunities to engage in both monologues and dialogues with adults who are involved active listeners as well as talkers. Certainly, the labeling of an object that has been learned motorically will greatly enlarge communication. *Ball,* for example, depending on eye focus, intonation, and gestures, may mean: "This is my ball. . . . Where is the ball?. . . I want to play ball. . . . Play ball with me. . . . I found the ball." (Languis, Sanders, & Tipps, 1980).

Between 9 and 12 months there appears a primitive intention to communicate, although baby is still preverbal and prelanguage. Baby will deliberately try to get the educarer's attention by vocalizing and using eyes and gestures. A concurrent understanding is the differentiation of self from object or other person. At 12 months, babies may not be very articulate, but they understand most of what is said to them and will babble and jabber in response.

Development of Conversation Skills

Sometime between 9 and 18 months the toddler moves from prelinguistic communication to intentional one-word utterances with a purpose. They are directed to a responder in order to (1) satisfy needs, (2) exert control over the responder's behavior, (3) express self-awareness, (4) ask why, (5) play or pretend, (6) inform, or (7) ask for help (Halliday, 1975). These may be considered social utterances because they are addressed to someone, and they request a response of some kind. These utterances are frequently accompanied by gestures of pointing, showing or giving objects, or an indication of "give it to me." The combination of word, intonation, and gesture is usually correctly interpreted. Therefore the sequence of a conversation is established (baby points to cookie, caregiver gives baby cookie, baby vocalizes, caregiver verbalizes in return). Occasionally two one-word utterances will be offered sequentially with a pause in between ("car . . . bye-bye"). The sequence shows a beginning insight into word and meaning relationships. Not all intentional utterances are addressed to persons. Children will practice the labeling of an object and will repeat words they or others have said. In other words, they practice talking.

From 18 to 24 months, the major gestures are still used, but the toddler makes sequential or adjacent utterances that sometimes deal with past events and objects not immediately perceivable. "Truck go" is not a story yet, but it is important for conversation. During this period the child seems to recognize that listeners may have different conversational needs. For instance, how the child talks to his mother is dif-

ferent from how he talks to a stranger. The child seems aware of previously shared information or experiences and adjusts the choice of words accordingly. It appears that the child is able to relate past experiences, but this is because the familiar adult structures the conversation. According to Halliday (1975), the child engages in a verbal dialogue before the age of 2 years:

> Dialogue can be viewed as essentially the adoption and assignment of roles. The roles in question are social roles, but of a special kind: they exist only in and through language, as communication roles—speaker, addressee, respondent, questioner, persuader, and the like (p. 48).

The child knows that when a question is asked, an answer is expected. Also, the child knows that a conversation can be initiated with a question. The roots of these conventions are in the ritualized turn-taking games of caregiver and child.

Young children combine words intentionally sometime between 18 and 24 months of age. They seem to be sensitive to the adult conventions for ordering words in sentences. This is the first grammatical rule they will learn. Children talk about actions, what happened to what, who does what, locations, recurrences, and nonexistence. Sample utterances include: "We go bye-bye. . . . Mommy outside. . . . More milk. . . . Soup all gone" (de Villiers & de Villiers, 1979).

The 2 year old's language is not always used in conversations or interactions with others. The following episode illustrates the fact that Elaine did not wish an interaction, but that she was willing and able to respond to the questions of an adult.

EPISODE 12

Elaine (2 years old) is playing in the kitchen corner of the toddler playroom. An educarer is tending to the caged rabbit, about 10 feet away. She asks, "What are you cooking Elaine?" She casually answers "ot dog," and continues getting out the utensils and ingredients. The adult moves close and asks, "Do you need any help?" Elaine shakes her head "no," and works diligently, pouring, measuring, and mixing in the bowl. The educarer asks, "Did you get your hot dogs cooked?" Elaine replies "Almost." Then from a wooden block she pours another imaginary ingredient into the bowl. "Sh sh sht." She carefully measures a spoonful from an empty spice box and adds it to the mixture. "You tell me when the hot dogs are done, O.K.?" Elaine continues making her hot dogs and then, "Done. Ot." She puts her materials away and joins the educarer for a story.

Elaine apparently felt no desire to share her activity with anyone else—she was alone in the kitchen corner, and matter-of-factly refused the adult's offer to help.

Although not an example of child-child interaction, the next episode illustrates a growing social awareness of other persons' feelings.

EPISODE 13

The educarer was sitting on the floor, reading to a group of five children, all around the age of 2 years. Sadie, aged 17 months, began to cry. Educarer: "Sadie, why are you crying? Can you tell me what's wrong?" Sadie didn't answer, and continued her crying. The educarer asked, "Does anyone know why Sadie is crying?" Jeff (28 months) suggests "Maybe she's hungry." Tom (24 months) says "Is she tired?" Jeff adds, "Maybe she wants to be picked up." The adult picks up Sadie and puts her on her lap. Sadie stops crying, and the story continues.

Although the cause for Sadie's crying was not discovered, it is easy to attribute it to her "youth"—17 months is very young to be expected to listen contentedly to a story when part of a group containing four other children.

From age 2 the child builds on the communication accomplishments of the first 2 years. During the third year, the number of conversations in adult-child interactions multiplies rapidly, with rapid changes in topics. In child-child relationships, the monologue predominates and there are few real dialogues. Children typically use three- and four-word utterances.

The conversation tasks, in addition to grammar and vocabulary, are internalized. Children consider the perspective of the listener and the give-and-take rules of conversation. The child is learning to distinguish a referent from alternatives. An adult should supply a referent such as "I want the truck," not just "I want it." The child must learn when he can presuppose information, because what we choose to say is based on the presupposed information known by the other. "Peter is lost" could refer to another child, a stuffed animal, even to an Uncle Peter. In this case, Peter was a live pet rabbit. The child presupposes that the listener already has that information. Other rules that make utterances acceptable in conversations include: don't interrupt; don't bore people; answer questions when asked; be truthful; be relevant; and use the common courtesy phrases, such as "please" and "thank you." These rules are not always put into practice in everyday living, by either children or adults.

McAfee (1967) gives some excellent suggestions for the teacher's language when working with Mexican-American children. They apply equally well to the teachers of infants and toddlers. She suggests that teachers speak in complete sentences, and that they be specific in their use of words (not "over there" but "under the chair"). It is also helpful if a word denoting a classification is used whenever possible. For instance, "The *animals* in the cage are bunnies," or "The blocks are all the same *color*—red."

Most of the developmental research has been confined to the child's first 3 years. It has been noted, however, that the conversations of 3- and 4-year-old children resemble adult conversations in that a single topic is continued over several successive utterances. It has been observed that 4-year-old children modify their speech as a function of the age of the listener. The 4 year olds used simpler and shorter sentences when talking with 2 year olds than when talking with adults. Other researchers have noted that children around age 4 years include direct or indirect hints in their language: "My mother always lets me have *two* cookies!" I have observed these same behaviors in children who were under the age of 3 in a day-care center. These children had been in day care for more than 2 years. It is quite logical to expect a more mature approach to communication by language in children who have been in group situations over a period of time.

Language in an infant-toddler program is developed primarily as a means of intentional communication. Bretherton and Bates (1979) describe the following sequence of the development of such communication:

- Behaviors designed to attract the attention of an adult ("showing off")
- At about 9 months, gestures (giving, showing, pointing) to communicate
- By 13 months, use of both vocal and gestural symbols to recognize, categorize, identify, name, and communicate about events in the world (Example: child uses words for cup or bottle, and also pretends to drink from an empty cup or bottle)
- True dialogue separate from action appears toward the end of the second year.

Nurturing Conversation Skills

There seems to be total agreement among researchers of early language development that highly stimulating mother-child interactions with children from birth to 2½ years old are a major predictor of child language development (Goelman, 1986). It has proven to be most difficult to evaluate caregiver-child interactions in group settings because of the many other influences (size of group, age of children, staff/child ratio) in centers or family day-care homes. Nonetheless, it seems reasonable to state that the same highly stimulating caregiver-child interactions would also enhance child language development.

Social competency and communication? They are mutually dependent, and they develop side by side. But to enrich the communication, the conversation, there must be more than just talk or gesture. As Dorothy Butler writes,

> None of us can endlessly initiate speech; we run out of ideas, or just plain get sick of it. The lives of babies and toddlers, even favored ones, are limited. The experience just isn't there to provide the raw material for constant verbal interaction without inevitable boredom on the child's part and desperation on the adult's. But if books are added . . . (1983, p. 7).

The value of children's books as a stimulus for communication and conversation cannot be overstated. Of course reading to children (the experts say children should be read to from the very first day of life!) has so many good results in all areas of development that it should be included as often as possible in any infant-toddler program. The emphasis here is on the power of a shared book to enhance conversation and adult-child relationships, and therefore to encourage the development of social competency. Dinsmore (1988) offers the reasons for introducing books to infants, and concludes the list by saying, "Most important, the interaction of reading and sharing books provides the opportunity for physical closeness—holding, talking, smiling, loving—so critical to an infant's emotional and intellectual growth" (p. 216).

Resources for choosing appropriate books for infants and toddlers are listed in the suggested readings for this chapter in a special section.

One last word about young children's literature:

> The satisfactions of literature should not be the province of a privileged few. Children are universally entitled to meaningful experiences with memorable books. As educators, we have an obligation to familiarize children with many different picture books and to convince adult skeptics about the benefits of children's experiences with literature (Jalongo, 1989, p. 4).

The best teachers of language are the natural language models (educarers, parents, volunteers) who actively participate. Most if not all of the published language stimulation programs for very young children do not match the child's needs or development. Interest in labeling colors or numerals does not exist, except to please a pressuring adult. Educarers need not spend time, money, or effort in direct language instruction. They should devote their time and effort in talking about things that are happening, that have happened recently, and that will happen soon; and, of course, in book sharing. Basic to language activity is the understanding that children learn to communicate verbally by talking and responding to another's talking. Of course this applies to the shared storytime, as well as to daily conversations. Children should be engaged in an active role. How? Ask "what" questions rather than yes/no questions. Encourage speculation about what is happening, or what might happen, and give verbal feedback to any ideas or comments. Not only will this enrich language and cognitive development, but it is another step toward social competency.

Social Competency and Play

Playing is important for optimal cognitive development, but it also has a key role in social development. It is through play that "children can acquire many important social skills such as turn taking, sharing, and cooperation, as well as the ability to understand other people's thoughts, perceptions, or emotions" (Johnson et al. 1987, p. 99). The learning of these skills is achieved through appropriate modeling and reinforcement on the part of the significant adults in the infant/toddler's daily experience. It is the responsibility of the educarer to teach the skills of sharing, cooperation, helping, and other forms of altruistic behavior (Radke-Yarrow, Zahn-Waxler, & Chapman, 1983). Learning these social skills will prepare the toddler for active engagement in social play with peers.

Solitary play—contented and satisfied. (Early Childhood Education Center)

Development of social play. Just as there are stages in development from exploration of objects to the actual play with objects, there are also steps or stages in the development of social play. The classic description of Parten's stage theory (1932) has stood the test of time. Children move through these stages:

1. *Solitary*—no ability or desire to play with others. Another child is viewed as a plaything to explore, and perhaps to poke or pinch.

2. *Parallel*—two or more children occupy adjacent space and take pleasure in each others presence but engage in unrelated play. Parallel play is the least mature form of social participation.

3. *Associative*—two or more children are in adjacent spaces and are engaged in the same activity (making mud pies, pushing trucks in the sand box, stacking blocks), but with no true interaction.

4. *Cooperative*—two or more children discuss plans for play, assign roles or actions, and

Parallel play: You can stay, but I'll play by myself.
(Kindercampus, Iowa City)

develop their play together. Children make up their own rules, which may be continuously changed.

5. *Games with rules*—two or more children play a game, following superimposed rules.

Although games with rules are considered to be the most advanced stage in the development of social play, these games have their beginnings in the give-and-take interactions of caregiver and infant. Certainly rules are followed in the simple game of peek-a-boo.

Until recently, most professionals accepted the notion that children younger than 2 years were capable only of solitary and onlooker activity (Geismar-Ryan, 1986), and apparently ignored the findings of investigations during the 1930s (Bridges, 1933; Buhler, 1933; Maudry & Nekula, 1939), which provided evidence that infants as young as 6 months did direct behaviors toward each other, and that behaviors became increasingly social throughout the first year. Research and observations during the 1970s and 1980s have convinced us now that the begin-

Beginnings of associative play.
(Kindercampus, Iowa City)

nings of social interactions with peers is evident during the first year (Cataldo, 1983; Hartup, 1982; Willis & Ricciuti, 1975). Infants as young as 12 months engage in the simplest type of pretend play (sleeping, eating, drinking, and talking on the phone). These actions are inner-directed. Outer-directed or symbolic play sequences are observable at about 18 months. It is true, however, that the dominant play activities during the first 12 to 18 months are sensorimotor.

Symbolic and role-play. Symbolic (or representational) play appears sometime during the second year. The play has shifted from random banging, waving, or pushing, to using things as objects with practical purposes. Fein (1979) describes the development of symbolic play in the following way:

> Initially, the play is self-directed, but soon it becomes other-directed; the child begins to feed a doll or another person, at times indicating that a social relationship between giver and receiver is being represented. At first the play requires objects similar to those actually used in real life, but soon increasingly dissimilar objects can be substituted, such as a piece of wood for a doll, a stick for a horse. . . . And while symbolic play is initially solitary, by three years of age it becomes a collaborative social effort (p. 2).

In symbolic play, young children move in and out of the roles and events with which they are most familiar. Although they are pretending momentarily, they frequently need to touch base with reality and real objects. The environment for symbolic play may be no more than a few wooden or cardboard boxes of various sizes, or simple block structures or enclosed spaces, or a simple toddler-sized housekeeping corner. The housekeeping corner should be simple because crude play equipment will draw on the imagination of the child (or children). A cardboard or wooden carton suddenly becomes a stove when it is equipped with empty spools as knobs to turn on and off. The first housekeeping corner should include a stove, shelves, and table and chairs.

Accessories to enhance child-initiated play include plastic or metal cups and plates of various sizes, perhaps some child-sized eating utensils, a plastic pan for a sink, child-sized broom and dust pan, doll bed and dolls, and a play telephone.

Early symbolic play episodes are usually imitations of adult activities. Sweeping the floor, shoveling snow, raking leaves, unloading grocery bags and putting away the (empty) boxes and cans, washing the table, preparing and serving a meal, and washing the dishes all require the coordinated use of arms and hands. Finer coordinations are involved in caring for a baby doll: feeding, rocking, washing, spanking, and tucking into bed.

Uhde (1983) suggests that infants and young toddlers be surrounded with objects used by the adults with whom they are very familiar:

1. Baby dolls/blankets
2. Dishes
3. Stuffed animals like dogs and cats
4. Pull toys (such as dogs which they can take for a walk)
5. Push toys like lawn mower, vacuum cleaner, broom
6. Flat shoes that fit over their own shoes
7. Pocketbooks filled with keys, large plastic circles (for money) etc. (p. 16)

When simple role-playing activities begin to appear (about age 2), add items that represent their expanding world. They are beginning to imitate the actions of peers and "significant adults in their play activities as well as acting out the roles of their parents. A two-year-old will quickly become the new baby and even making sucking actions as he pretends to drink a bottle" (p. 16). We now should add a variety of dress-up clothes, both male and female, large sturdy jewelry, small people dolls and furniture, and empty food containers and plastic food.

Role-playing is important for learning about self and others. Children frequently try out parental behaviors (usually punishment of some kind) while at the same time they are trying to handle their own feelings of powerlessness. Role-playing is also a precursor of sociodramatic play. According to Smilansky (1968), advantaged 3-year-old children

> demonstrate in their play all the basic components of sociodramatic play. They undertake roles and imitate in action and verbally the role figures; they use make-believe to change the function of objects to evoke imaginary situations and to describe nonperformed activities; they interact with other children (mostly one or two only) whenever they have an opportunity, and cooperate in the elaboration of the theme; they are able to sustain the game for relatively long periods (p. 40).

The 3 year olds who have attended a high-quality infant-toddler program in a center or a family day-care home should be "advantaged" because of their experience with trained educarers in an environment designed to guide and encourage their social and cognitive development. With these conditions, symbolic and/or pretend play will be well established by age 3 and the children will be engaging in social play activities including some sociodramatic play.

SUMMARY

There is a close relationship between cognitive development and social development during the infant/toddler years. The child's feelings toward self and toward others, both adults and peers, strongly influence all other aspects of development. If these feelings are positive, the child will have social competence appropriate for his developmental age.

Steps in the development of social competency are social cognition, the acquisition of skills and techniques for initiating and responding to persons and social events, and the development of appropriate reactions that undergird and motivate social behavior. Social cognition (step one) is the relationship among three aspects of knowledge: knowledge of the self; knowledge of others, and knowledge of one's relations to others. These knowledges are learned through interactions and relationships with other persons.

Perhaps the most researched area in social development is that of mother-child attachment. With few exceptions, researchers have found that the attachment to mother is not diminished by attendance at an infant/toddler program, and that children may form strong attachments with one or two caregivers in addition to their primary attachment.

The emotional upsets usually accompanying the transition from home care to group care can be eased by the appropriate, nonthreatening attitudes of both parent and caregiver. These transitions are best achieved after the infant has become comfortable with the "new" adult in the presence of the mother. Less traumatic are the expected transitions from interest in self to interest in adults to interest in peers, which may occur fleetingly during the first year, but are firmly in place by age 3.

The redirection of "problem" behaviors (aggression, tantrums, biting, and stranger anxiety) is another component of teaching social competency. The two main teaching efforts focus on the reinforcement of acceptable behavior and the suggestions of alternate behaviors to achieve the child's purposes. In many instances, however, children will learn from one another if they are left alone to cope with their peers. Actually, it is not best to have a "well-behaved" group. These young children are striving for independence and are going through negativism and ambivalence. If inappropriately strict controls are imposed, the children will be stressed, and may return to babyhood to combat the strain of "being good." Punishment (a slap, spank, shake, or abusive language) should never be a part of behavior management during the infant-toddler years.

The achievement of social competence is dependent on the abilities to communicate and engage in conversation (by gesture and later by language), and the abilities to engage in social interactions in the context of play with adults and peers. If all has gone well in the life of a 3 year old, the child will have the skills necessary to engage in positive and productive social play interactions, and will be socially competent.

SUGGESTED ACTIVITIES AND QUESTIONS

1. Observe the infants and/or toddlers in a group setting. Can you identify the stage of social play development in each child? Do you see the same child engaging in more than one stage?

2. Describe why the games of peek-a-boo and hide-and-seek should be included in the activities of an infant/toddler program. Even these simple games progress from simple to complex. What is the appropriate sequence for each?

3. Recall an incident in your life for which you were punished. Do you consider the punishment appropriate, or can you suggest other techniques that might have been more positive?

4. Start a card file of children's books appropriate for the very early years. If you have the opportunity, read one or more of them to an infant or toddler. Do more than read it, try to involve the child in some appropriate way.

SUGGESTED READINGS

Anti-bias Children's Books

Adoff, A. (1973). *Black is brown is tan*. New York: Harper & Row.

Bang, M. (1983). *Ten, nine, eight*. New York: Greenwillow.

Behrens, J. (1985). *I can be a truck driver*. Chicago: Childrens Press.

Bellet, J. (1984). *A-B-C-ing: An action alphabet*. New York: Crown.

Brenner, B. (1973). *Bodies*. New York: Dutton.

Brown, M. W. (1942). *Runaway bunny*. New York: Harper & Row.

Burningham, J. (1973). *Mr. Grumpy's motor car*. New York: Crowell.

Church, V. (1971). *Colors around me*. Chicago: Afro-American Publishing.

Corey, D. (1983). *You go away*. New York: Greenwillow.

Feeney, S. (1980). *A is for aloha*. Honolulu: University of Hawaii Press.

Feeney, S. (1985). *Hawaii is a rainbow*. Honolulu: University of Hawaii Press.

Greenberg, P. (1981). *I know I'm myself because*. New York: Human Sciences Press.

Greenberg, P. (1988). *Rosie and Roo*. Washington, DC: Growth Program Press.

Greenfield, E. (1978). *Honey, I love and other poems*. New York: Crowell.

Henriod, L. (1982). *Grandma's wheelchair*. Niles, IL: Whitman.

Iwamura, K. (1984). *Ton and Pon*. New York: Bradbury.

Jonas, A. (1982). *When you were a baby*. New York: Greenwillow.

Kempler, S. (1981). *A man can be. . . .* New York: Human Sciences Press.

Martin, B., Jr. (1970). *I am freedom's child*. Oklahoma City: Bowmar.

Martin, B., Jr. (1983). *Brown bear, brown bear, what do you see?* New York: Holt, Rinehart & Winston.

McGovern, A. (1969). *Black is beautiful*. New York: Scholastic.

Ormerod, J. (1981). *Sunshine*. New York: Lothrop, Lee & Shepard.

Parish, P. (1984). *I can, can you?* New York: Greenwillow.

Rockwell, H. (1976). *My nursery school*. New York: Greenwillow.

Steptoe, J. (1974). *My special best words*. New York: Viking.

Turner, G. (1990). *Colors*. New York: Viking.

Vincent, G. (1982). *Ernest and Celestine*. New York: Greenwillow.

Weissman, J. (1981). *All about me/Let's be friends*. Mt. Rainier, MD: Gryphon.

Resources for Children's Literature

Barton, B. (1986). *Tell me another: Storytelling and reading aloud at home, at school, and in the community*. Portsmouth, NH: Heinemann Educational Books.

Boegehold, B. D. (1984). *Getting ready to read*. New York: Ballantine.

Butler, D. (1983). *Babies need books*. New York: Atheneum.

Cascardi, A. (1985). *Good books to grow on*. New York: Warner Books.

Dinsmore, K. E. (1988). Baby's first books. *Childhood Education, 64,* (4), 215–219.

Dzama, M., & Gilstrap, R. (1983). *Ready to read: A parent's guide*. New York: Wiley.

Fisher, J. J. (1986). *Toys to grow with infants and toddlers.* New York: Putnam.

Jalongo, M. R. (1989). *Young children and picture books: Literature from infancy to six.* Washington, DC: National Association for the Education of Young Children.

Lamme, L. L. (1980). *Raising readers: A guide to sharing literature with young children.* New York: Walker.

Larrick, N. (1980). *Children's reading begins at home.* Winston-Salem, NC: Starstream Products.

Oppenheim, J., Brenner, B., & Boegehold, B. D. (1986). *Choosing books for kids: Choosing the right book for the right child at the right time.* New York: Ballantine Books.

Taylor, D., & Strickland, D. C. (1986). *Family storybook reading.* Portsmouth, NH: Heinemann Educational Books.

White, D. (1984). *Books before five.* Portsmouth, NJ: Heinemann Educational Books.

Chapter-related

American Academy of Pediatrics (1989). *Temper tantrums: A normal part of growing up.* (Brochure). Elk Grove Village, IL: Author.

Asher, S. R., & Gottman, J. (Eds.). (1981). *The development of children's friendships.* Cambridge, MA: Harvard University Press.

Belasco, L. (Ed.). (1989, Oct.). Dealing with a biter. *Parents, 64* (10), 38, 40.

Berg, B. J. (1989, July). "My blankie and me." *Parents, 64* (7), 94–98, 100.

Bloom, L., Beckwith, R., & Capatides, J. B. (1988). Developments in the expression of affect. *Infant Behavior and Development, 11* (2), 169–186.

Brazelton, T. B. (1969). *Infants and mothers: Differences in development.* New York: Dell.

Brazelton, T. B. (1974). *Toddlers and parents: A declaration of independence.* New York: Dell.

Brazelton, T. B. (1981). *On becoming a family: The growth of attachment.* New York: Delacorte/Seymour Lawrence.

Brazelton, T. B. (1987). *What every baby knows.* Reading, MA: Addison-Wesley.

Brazelton, T. B., & Yogman, M. W. (Eds.). (1986). *Affective development in infancy.* Norwood, NJ: Ablex.

Bretherton, I. C. (Ed.). (1984). *Symbolic play: The developmental psychology of social cognition.* New York: Academic Press.

Bretherton, I., & Bates, E. (1979). The emergence of intentional communication. *New Directions in Child Development, 4,* 81–100.

Bruner, J., & Sherwood, V. (1975). Peek-a-boo and the learning of rule structures. In J. Bruner, A. Jolly, & K. Sylva (Eds.), *Play: Its role in development and evolution* (pp. 277–285). New York: Basic Books.

Buss, A. H., & Plomin, R. (1984). *Temperament: Early developing personality traits.* Hillsdale, NJ: Erlbaum.

Caldwell, B. M. (1977). Aggression and hostility in young children. *Young Children, 32* (2), 4–13.

Caldwell, B. M. (1988). It's not nice to bite. *Working Mother, 11* (11), 138, 140.

Derman-Sparks, L., & A. B. C. Task Force. (1989). *Anti-bias curriculum: Tools for empowering young children.* Washington, DC: National Association for the Education of Young Children. (Especially chapter 3)

Derman-Sparks, L., Higa, C., & Sparks, B. (1980). Children, race and racism: How race awareness develops. *Interracial Books for Children Bulletin, 11* (3 and 4).

Discipline: Are tantrums normal? (1988, September). *Young Children, 43* (6), 35–40.

Dunn, J. (1977). *Distress and comfort.* The Developing Child Series. Cambridge, MA: Harvard University Press.

Eheart, B. K., & Leavitt, R. L. (1985). Supporting toddler play. *Young Children, 40* (3), 18–22.

Field, T. M., & Fox, N. A. (Eds.). (1985). *Social perception in infants.* Norwood, NJ: Ablex.

Friedberg, J. (1989). Helping today's toddlers become tomorrow's readers: A pilot parent participation project offered through a Pittsburgh health agency. *Young Children, 44* (2), 13–16.

Geismar-Ryan, L. (1986). Infant social activity: The discovery of peer play. *Childhood Education, 63* (1), 24–29.

Goelman, H. (1986). The language environments of family day care. In S. Kilmer (Ed.), *Advances in Early Education and Day Care, 4,* 153–179.

Greenspan, S., & Greenspan, N. T. (1985). *First feelings: Milestones in the emotional development of your baby and child.* New York: Viking.

Harris, K. H., & Wallick, M. M. (1976). Books to begin on. *Dimensions, 5* (1), 4–9, 26.

Hartup, W. H. (1982). Peer relations. In C. B. Kopp & J. B. Krakow (Eds.), *The child: Development in a social context.* Reading MA: Addison-Wesley.

Haswell, K., Hock, E., & Wenar, C. (1982). Techniques for dealing with oppositional behavior in preschool children. *Young Children, 37,* 13–18.

Hay, D., Ross, H., & Goldman, B. D. (1979). Social games in infancy. In B. Sutton-Smith (Ed.), *Play and Learning* (pp. 83–107). New York: Gardner.

Honig, A. S. (1986). Stress and coping in children (Parts I and II). *Young Children, 41* (4), 50–63; (5), 47–59.

Howes, C. (1989). Infant child care. *Young Children, 44* (6), 24–28.

Ilg, F. L., Ames, L. B., & Baker, S. M. (1981). *Child behavior: Specific advice on problems of child behavior* (rev. ed.). New York: Harper & Row.

Jalongo, M. R. (1987). Do security blankets belong in preschool? *Young Children, 42* (3), 3–8.

Kagan, J. (1981). *The second year: The emergence of self awareness.* Cambridge, MA: Harvard University Press.

Kaplan, L. J. (1978). *Oneness and separateness: From infant to individual.* New York: Simon & Schuster.

Lamb, M. E. (1981). The development of social expectations in the first year of life. In M. E. Lamb & L. R. Sherrod (Eds.), *Infant social cognition: Empirical and theoretical considerations.* Hillsdale, NJ: Erlbaum.

Lamb, M. E., Thompson, R. A., & Frodi, A. M. (1982). Early social development. In R. Vasta (Ed.), *Strategies and techniques of child study.* New York: Academic Press.

Maccoby, E. E. (1983). Social-emotional development and response to stressors. In N. Garmezy & M. Rutter (Eds.), *Stress, coping, and development in children.* New York: McGraw-Hill.

McAfee, O. (1967). The right words. *Young Children,* (23), 74–78.

Miller, P., & Garvey, C. (1984). Mother-baby role play: Its origins in social support. In I. Bretherton (Ed.), *Symbolic play: The development of social understanding.* New York: Academic Press.

Moore, S. G. (1982). Prosocial behavior in the early years: Parent and peer influences. In B. Spodek (Ed.), *Handbook of Research in Early Childhood Education* (pp. 65–81). New York: Free Press.

Murphy, L. B. (1974). Coping, vulnerability and resilience in childhood. In G. V. Coehlo, D. A. Hamburg, & J. E. Adams (Eds.), *Coping and adaptation.* New York: Basic Books.

Murphy, L. B., & Moriarty, A. E. (1976). *Vulnerability, coping and growth.* New Haven: Yale University Press.

O'Connell, B., & Bretherton, I. (1984). Toddler's play, alone and with mother. In I. Bretherton (Ed.), *Symbolic play: The development of social understanding.* New York: Academic Press.

Powell, D. R. (1989). *Families and early childhood programs.* Washington, DC: National Association for the Education of Young Children.

Press, B. K., & Greenspan, S. I. (1985). Ned and Don: The development of a toddler friendship. *Children Today, 14* (2), 24–29.

Radke-Yarrow, M., Zahn-Waxler, C., & Chapman, M. (1983). Children's prosocial dispositions and behavior. In P. H. Mussen (Ed.), *Handbook of child psychology* Vol. 4 *Socialization, personality, and social development* (4th ed.) (pp. 469–545). New York: Wiley.

Robertson, A. (1982). Day care and children's responsiveness to adults. In E. F. Zigler & E. W. Gordon (Eds.), *Day care: Scientific and social policy issues* (pp. 152–173). Boston: Auburn House.

Rogers, C. S., & Sawyers, J. K. (1988). *Play in the lives of children.* Washington, DC: National Association for the Education of Young Children.

Rogers, F. (1984). The past and present is now. *Young Children, 39,* 13–18.

Rosenblatt, D. (1977). Developmental trends in infant play. In B. Tizard & D. Harvey (Eds.), *Biology of play* (pp. 33–44). London: Heinemann.

Ross, H. S., & Kay, D. A. (1980). The origins of social games. In K. H. Rubin (Ed.), *Children Play* (pp. 17–31). San Francisco: Jossey-Bass.

Schaffer, H. R. (1984). *The child's entry into a social world.* Orlando, FL: Academic Press.

Segal, M. (1985). *Your child at play: Birth to one year.* New York: Newmarket.

Segal, M., & Adcock, D. (1981). *Feelings.* Atlanta: Humanics.

Segal, M., & Adcock, D. (1985a). *Your child at play: One to two years.* New York: Newmarket.

Segal, M., & Adcock, D. (1985b). *Your child at play: Two to three years.* New York: Newmarket.

Smith, C. A. (1982). *Promoting the social development of young children: Strategies and activities.* Palo Alto, CA: Mayfield.

Sroufe, L. A. (1979). Socioemotional development. In J. D. Osofsky (Ed.), *Handbook of infant development* (pp. 462–516). New York: Wiley.

Stern, D. N. (1985). *The interpersonal world of the infant.* New York: Basic Books.

Stone, J. G. (1978). *A guide to discipline* (rev. ed.). Washington, DC: National Association for the Education of Young Children.

Thoman, E. B., & Browder, S. (1987). *Born dancing: How intuitive parents understand their baby's unspoken language and natural rhythms.* New York: Harper & Row.

Thoman, E. B., & Trotter, A. (Eds.). (1978). *Social responsiveness of infants.* Pediatric Round Table 2. New York: Johnson & Johnson Baby Products.

Tronick, E. Z. (Ed.). (1982). *Social interchange in infancy.* Baltimore: University Park Press.

Tronick, E., & Adamson, L. (1980). *Babies are people: New findings on our social beginnings.* London: McMillan.

Weissbourd, B., & Musick, J. (Eds.). (1981). *Infants: Their social environments.* Washington, DC: National Association for the Education of Young Children.

White, B. L. (1988). *Educating the infant and toddler.* Lexington, MA: Lexington Books.

Willis, A., & Ricciuti, H. (1978). *A good beginning for babies: Guidelines for group care.* Washington, DC: National Association for the Education of Young Children.

Yawkey, T. D., & Pellegrini, A. D. (Eds.). (1984). *Child's play: Developmental and applied.* Hillsdale, NJ: Erlbaum.

5

Nurturing Motor Skill Development

Motor development is also mental development.
                                        Ira J. Gordon

The maturational viewpoint of the development of physical (motor) skills is that they unfold naturally in an appropriate environment. Evidence seems to reinforce this concept—apparently all normal children walk, climb, and run without instruction. Research in the 1930s and 1940s by McGraw, Gesell, and others, using the co-twin experimental design in which one twin received enriched motor experiences and the other sat in a crib, provides evidence that motor skills do unfold. McGraw (1954) concluded that Johnny, the "enriched" twin, and Jimmy, who received no exercise or movement experience, did not differ. Both boys learned to walk, run, climb, and so on. Walking, running, and climbing are the phylogenetic motor skills. They are common to the species. It can be reasonably argued that they require very little stimulation for their appearance.

There is a quantum leap, however, in the argument that all motor skills develop naturally. How many of you have an under-par golf score, or can hit a winning tennis serve? Does the ballerina's arabesque just develop? Does the foot-ball punter's kick just develop? Of course not. Efficient, skillful movement must be learned and then practiced over and over again.

There should no longer be any questioning of the importance of the early years for all components of development. The importance of the environment, including interacting objects and persons, has been accepted in relation to the learning of cognitive skills. Recent research is leading to the same conclusion about the learning of motor skills. As a result, there is a relatively new component of the curriculum called movement education. It is designed to teach motor skills and to provide specific movement experiences for children of all ages.

A survey of the journal articles and books written by persons involved in physical and recreational education results in the following list of the values of movement:

• Movement is a medium to get in touch with ourselves. Moving provides a concrete, sensorily rich experience with ourselves. It leads to self-awareness. Descartes wrote "I think—

therefore I am." A paraphrase might be "I move—therefore I am."

- Movement is a medium for the development of a positive sense of self. The ability to move in various ways is the first major development in the young child's life. A sense of mastery through physical actions is achieved long before mastery in language, social relationships, or cognition. Carefully planned movement experiences present challenges that can be met successfully. Physical development progresses rapidly in the early years. It deserves our attention. Body image is an important factor in feelings about self.

- Movement is a medium for self-expression. Young children do not need to have speaking, writing, or drawing skills to express their feelings of joy, anger, or sadness when they have been taught nonverbal communication skills.

- Movement is a medium for learning about the environment. The exploration, manipulation, and interaction components of learning have already been stressed in all kinds of learning. Piaget, among others, believed that movement is the foundation for cognitive learning. Although infants and toddlers learn much by sensory observation, their ability to move greatly enhances their observational data. Each episode in the preceding chapters has been heavily dependent on the children's ability to move purposely.

- Movement is a medium for interacting with others. The interactions of infants and toddlers are primarily physical. Their social and language skills are just beginning to play a role in their encounters with people.

- Movement is important for its own sake. To learn to move skillfully is to learn to enjoy living. All early play episodes are based on some ability to move and to interact with movement.

As children grow and develop they must acquire skill in managing two essential elements—their bodies and objects. Body management is first and foremost in importance. Although children have their own unique rate of development, there are two patterns that all children follow in acquiring body management skills.

Body control begins initially in the head and neck region and progresses along the spine into the torso. This is known as the cephalocaudal process. Second, body management skills are acquired "proximodistally" (that is, body control proceeds from control of the whole to control of the specific parts). Manipulation skills involving the hands progress from the use of the arm as a unit, to the use of the hand, then the palm, and finally the use of fingers and thumbs (Gober & Franks, 1988).

Although we speak of motor development, control of posture and movement cannot develop without ongoing sensory information. Kinesthetic feedback provides a strong reinforcement for the baby to continue his own movement. Pressure receptors that are activated by body weight against a surface lead to postural righting reactions that are necessary for the fundamental organization of movement. The light touch that starts with the young infant's tentative exploration of clothing and blankets is vital for later exploration of texture, form, and shape. It is matched with visual impressions as a base for eye-hand coordination. Even the temperature of a surface can determine the quality of movement. Increasing control gradually brings about the smoothness of control that we recognize as normal coordinated movement. It is obvious "that the infant engages in a great deal of perceptual behavior before the onset of accurate movement capabilities" (Cratty, 1982, p. 30).

Fine coordination—the ability to draw with a crayon, to write with a pencil, or to play a musical instrument—is also dependent on postural control or the ability to stabilize the body in space. The hand cannot function without the shoulder maintaining the arm in an appropriate position. A step cannot be taken without a subtle change of weight and the ability to sustain the body weight briefly and securely on one leg and foot so that the opposite one is able to move freely (Nelson, 1988).

GROSS MOTOR SKILLS

Development

The milestones in gross motor development are as follows:

1. *Rolling:* the first voluntary rolling is from the tummy-lying position to the back-lying position (about 3 months)

2. *Sitting:* child can sit without support at about 6½ months, but getting into a sitting position voluntarily does not occur until about 9 months

3. *Creeping and crawling:* crawling occurs first, at about 7 months, and creeping soon follows

4. *Standing and walking:* most children are able to pull themselves to a standing position at about 9 months, but it may take several more months before they can stand without any kind of support. Most children do not start to walk until they are about 13 or 14 months. Walking backward starts at 19 months, and step climbing at about 21 months

5. *Running:* the first attempts are seen at about 18 months, but "true" running occurs sometime between the age of 2 or 3 years

6. *Jumping:* the first kind of jump is an exaggerated step with one foot from an elevated level. After some skill has been achieved in walking and running, the child can handle a 2-foot takeoff from an elevated level at 2 to 2½ years

7. *Hopping:* not until age 4

8. *Galloping and skipping:* about 4 or 5 years

9. *Climbing:* "after learning to walk, the child will climb up and down stairs in an upright position but will usually lead with the same foot, thereby 'marking time' for a moment on each step (about 3 years of age)" (Zaichkowsky, Zaichkowsky, and Martinek, 1980, p. 39–40)

10. *Balance:* at about 3 years of age most children can maintain balance on one foot for 3 to 4 seconds.

11. *Ball skills—throwing and catching:* before age 2, a child may throw a ball with two hands in a very crude manner. By 3½, children throw with body rotation and arm range. Catching is more difficult; at about 3½ children will attempt to catch a ball by holding their arms straight out in front of their body.

There are three key principles that should direct any instruction or guidance in the development of motor skills. They need to be remembered as you study (and put into practice) the exercises and activities that follow.

1. A wide variety of movement experiences will lead to better learning of more movement responses. Refining of skills comes later. The early years (birth to 6 years) should be filled with variety.

2. Movement tasks should be developmentally appropriate. Infants and toddlers will be in various substages of the prelocomotor and locomotor phases. Tasks and activities should be planned that encourage the continued development of these skills. They should incorporate flexibility of choice. For example, beanbags and balloons as well as balls of various sizes should be provided when the children are learning to catch.

3. Movement tasks should be staged so that children can solve them without adult help (interference). Learning to do somersaults might start with a child being asked to roll over a small rolled-up mat or even a large ice cream carton. Throwing to hit a target might start with "Can you throw the ball to me?"

Children need time and practice to learn the skills of movement. They need time and freedom to explore, manipulate, and interact with their physical bodies. They learn motor skills in the same way they learn cognitive and social skills. It is the educarer's responsibility to provide the environment and the challenge. Teachers of children of all ages often fail to include the nonlocomotor skills of bending, stretching, twisting, turning—all the movements done in place. They are just as important as the locomotor skills.

The movement learnings of infants and toddlers cover a wide range of activities. At first, the child is moved by a teacher or caregiver. Before the age of 3, the child should be moving independently and efficiently.

Physical Fitness

Immediately after birth the infant is able to lift her head unsteadily for a second or so, kick her legs, grasp with her fingers when the palm of her hand is touched, and grasp with her toes when her foot is touched. When held in an upright position, the infant can move forward with crossed legs, and will use toes and feet to push against a surface. Baby will even try to climb when held against a caregiver's body. These physical/motor activities are the reflexive behavior repertoire of the normal full-term baby. For the most part they are involuntary. Some of these activities fade out and are replaced later by intentional activities.

As is true with each facet of development and learning, guided stimulation and encouragement are required for optimal progress in motor skill development.

"Moving" the baby. At first baby usually lies on his tummy on a firm mattress, which should absorb movement and support the body. The prone position helps baby learn to help himself. Baby learns to raise his head through the strength of the back muscles; he realizes success

as he sees more of the surroundings, and he breathes more deeply and more quietly. Even during the first few days, baby's position in the bed should be changed, and baby should be carried and held in different positions. Above all, baby needs freedom to move—no tight diapers or swaddling bands, and a room temperature that requires as little clothing as possible. The debate about swaddling continues. It is possible that swaddling is relaxing and adds to a sense of security for some babies. As is true with almost everything, there is a happy middle-of-the-road position. It is a certainty that infants need unswaddled freedom during their waking times. Because the sense of movement is sensitized by the skin receptors, baby should be held closely, and cradled slowly and quietly, against bare skin if possible. Kinesthesia (perception of one's own movements) is strengthened when baby moves freely during the bath also. The water temperature should not be more than 88° F, because warmer water decreases the impulses to move.

First steps in "teaching" baby to move include carrying baby in different positions (on hip, on the back, horizontally, vertically). Holding baby over one's shoulder in an upright position increases the amount of quiet alert time of the newborn, and rocking the baby is a time-honored custom and pleasure for both rocker and baby.

In the desire to do what is best for the infant, many parents and educarers have introduced structured exercise and fitness programs for infants as young as 1 day old! These programs ignore two basic facts: (1) infant bones are softer (and therefore more fragile) than mature bones, and (2) the ability to sit, stand, and walk is primarily dependent upon maturation.

> Programs that promote the idea of producing super fit babies by starting structured programs at birth are nothing more than an opportunity for some professionals who know little about infant development to take advantage of the gullibility of parents and caregivers who are anxious to provide the very latest and best for their infants (Dinsmore, 1989, p. 1).

A recent policy statement from the American Academy of Pediatrics (Committee on Sports Medicine) states the position that programs with structured activities and exercise equipment do not promote early physical development and may even cause harm, such as dislocating baby's shoulder or elbow. Michael Nelson, chairman of the Committee on Sports Medicine, states "From a biomechanical point of view, an infant or young child does not move efficiently enough to stimulate the cardiorespiratory system to gain fitness levels above and beyond what he or she would achieve in normal, active, unstructured play" (Eastman, 1989, p. 46).

Jumper seats (used during the fourth, fifth, and sixth months) move the baby toward independent orientation of self in addition to strengthening the leg and foot muscles needed for walking. The seats should be hung in such a way that the child can push up off the floor or ground with his feet or the tips of his toes. Jumper seats are *not* baby-sitters. They should be used for short periods of time, and only as long as baby is actively using them.

Rocking and swinging have commonalities in movement and sensation. Ideally, babies have been rocked from the very first time they were picked up for feeding. Introduction to the swinging motion starts when the baby is held around the torso and swung gently (and carefully) up and down. Babies can also sit on a caregiver's folded hands to be swung between her legs. After the first year, children enjoy hanging onto an adult's hands and being swung back and forth and up and down.

All of these rhythmical movements through space should be accompanied by rhymes or songs.

Rock-a-bye baby, on the tree top,
When the wind blows, the cradle will rock,
When the bough breaks, the cradle will fall,
And down will come baby, cradle and all.
(Rock the baby until the word "fall." Then let
the baby fall slightly backward, and bring
back to a sitting position on the last line.)

Bouncing the baby is fun, too. Place the baby on your lap (or knee or leg) and bounce up and down so that baby:

Rides a cock horse to Banbury Cross
To see a fine lady upon a white horse.
With rings on her fingers and bells on her toes,
She shall have music wherever she goes.

Baby moves. By 6 months or so, babies should be traveling—rolling, creeping, or scooting. Soon after they will be able to crawl. The sheer ability to move is exhilarating in itself. Even so, some babies need encouragement. All babies react to moving objects: they will crawl after a rolling ball, a "crawling" adult, or another child. They may even push a ball away from themselves, for the challenge of going after it. The educarer builds on this interest by rolling the ball in different directions, sometimes close and sometimes further away from the child. The more the child learns to follow a motion in different directions and to recognize different speeds, the more competent the child will become.

When crawling ability is well established, a new challenge is to crawl over the rungs of a ladder placed down on the floor. Crawling up and down a sturdy ramp with an incline of about 12 inches is also recommended. A more advanced crawl is required when baby is placed in a cardboard box and encouraged to crawl out. Even 2 and 3 year olds are tempted to crawl under an obstacle or through a narrow opening, because they are attracted to challenge. Educarers create additional challenges by letting children crawl through their straddled legs, through a hoop held vertically, or a tunnel on the floor.

By 8 or 9 months, children may be pulling themselves to a standing position. An educarer can place a toy or bit of food on a chair or table (of appropriate height) and call the child's attention to it. If the child is having difficulty, the adult can offer index fingers for him to grasp and pull himself up. If necessary, transfer his hands to the edge of the chair or table and allow him to reach the object. The next step, of course, is to stand unsupported. As the child's leg muscles gain strength, and when she is standing and holding onto a piece of furniture or equipment, she can be offered a toy or two to occupy her hands so that she will release her hold. Another way of encouraging standing alone is to support the child lightly with your hands by his sides and gradually remove your hands. The child should be praised immediately when he stands independently. In this "exercise," the educarer should support the child, rather than have the child hold onto her.

The last milestone of the infant stage is the first step, at first with support and then independently. These first hesitant steps may be encouraged by having the child hold onto the lowered handles of a buggy or stroller. The child can hang on, push, and walk, all at the same time. The toddler may not understand what is expected at first. If this is the case, the adult should stand behind the child, place the child's hands on the handles, and gently push both child and vehicle until the child goes it alone. The buggy or stroller might hold some blocks or toys to give it some weight so that it will not tip over easily.

With the increased attention given to infants and toddlers who have observable handicaps, or who are developmentally delayed, there has been a proliferation of developmental scales or assessment instruments, most of which contain many suggestions for age-appropriate motor activities. Appendix D describes some of these instruments.

Nurturing Gross Motor Skills

Once a child has learned to walk, many adults seem to take large muscle development for granted. They let Topsy "just grow." They assume that Topsy will learn to run, skip, hop, and climb. These are the adults who view outdoor playtime as a time to use excess energy (children) and to catch up on the latest gossip

(adults). It is true that most children develop these abilities with little or no instruction *if they* are provided with encouragement, appropriate equipment, space, and time and opportunity to practice their developing skills.

The toddler moves instead of relying on an adult to do the moving. At first the sheer joy of independent moving is almost overwhelming to the child. The child and the adults should be equally excited. Although the first "moving" is not coordinated or efficient, it is an accomplishment that changes an infant into a child.

Walking and running. The prerequisites for walking include an upright posture and a satisfactory progression through the creeping-crawling stage. A few children neither creep nor crawl, but suddenly stand up and attempt to walk.

If the baby has been active during the first year, good posture will be the natural result.

A mature walking skill usually develops through the following steps: creeping-crawling; standing with support and then without support; stepping with support and then without support. This skill is learned naturally: babies do not need to be placed in walkers in order to learn how to walk, or to learn faster. Indeed, walkers delay the natural progression of prewalking skills. They take time from the development of the creeping and cruising movements that help establish the rhythmic patterns of leg movements and the coordinated arm and leg movements. Babies will walk when their bodies and nervous systems are developmentally ready. Many educarers encourage toddlers to go barefoot as one way of encouraging good walking and healthy feet.

During the second year, walking becomes an insatiable need and is constantly practiced. The skills become automatic during the second and third years. Now is the time to provide obstacle courses that include low objects to climb over, large crates or tunnels to crawl through, a table or other large object arranged so that the child must turn sideways to get through, and any other similar challenges. Obstacle courses are both development-nurturing and fun, and can be used both indoors and outside.

Running ability develops out of coordinated walking. It requires sufficient leg strength to propel oneself upward and forward with one leg, and enough balance to accommodate the body weight on one foot when landing. At first, children will walk fast with feet spread far apart and hands at waist level. This fast walking will be stiff and awkward, and may be accompanied by many falls. But practice makes perfect, and children will practice on their own initiative. Soon the child will run with the hands held below the waist and the head leaning forward in front of the rest of the body. A mature run is achieved when the head is held high and the arms swing alternately at the sides. It may not be accomplished by age 3, because all toddlers are "top-heavy" with prominent tummies and "sitters"; all toddlers are inclined to toe out in an effort to balance themselves. This is normal. However, if the 2 to 3 year old continues the duck-like walk, the child should be referred to a pediatrician, because this is the prime time to prevent future knock-knees, flat feet, and sagging backs (Brazelton, 1974).

At the infant-toddler stages, preliminary walking and running skills are encouraged by games of people-chasing and ball-chasing. Marching in place, and then around a space, with arms swinging, will help the arm movements develop. Whenever possible, walking and running activities are best without shoes, and on a variety of surfaces.

When the children are developing a smooth, coordinated walk (and later), the following activities are useful and appropriate.

WALKING THE TRACKS

First crawl over the rungs of a ladder placed on the floor or ground. Then step over ladder rungs. Walk forward and beside the ladder on right and left sides. Walk backward close to the ladder sides. Walk backward in the between-rung spaces. Walk forward on the rungs. Walk backward on the rungs. (Note: not all 3 year olds can manage rung-walking.) An adult must always be close enough to the child and ladder to give physical support or assistance when needed.

In the above as well as the following activities young children may get started in one of several ways. It is preferable to let the children discover instead of having an adult demonstrate the desired activity, or even to make verbal suggestions. The unexpected appearance of a ladder on the floor will lead the more adventurous children to explore its possibilities and even perhaps crawl or walk over the rungs. Others will soon follow, if they are ready developmentally. Imitation of another child's activities motivates to a much greater degree than imitation of an adult's actions. The educarer should wait to see if it will happen before intruding, directing, or even suggesting. In this instance, the educarer is a close-by active observer. Former knowledge and present observation of individual children should enable the educarer to offer suggestions or support only when needed. Whenever a child indicates a psychological or physical need for an adult hand to hold, it should be available and readily offered. But *never* deprive a child of a sense of accomplishment in a job done "all by myself." After a period of experimentation, the adult may suggest a new or different approach, such as walking close to the outside, or walking backward, and so on.

The ladder activities and those that follow should be "taught" in the same way. In the examples that contain different activities around the same theme, the activities have usually been presented in the order of difficulty. The final activity in each category may take weeks (or months) to be achieved. In the "ladder" sequence, crawling over the rungs may be accomplished in the 12- to 15-month period, and walking between the rungs in the 12- to 18-month period. The ability to walk backward and sideways may come around 18 months. The difficulty of walking backward between the rungs may delay this particular pattern for several more months.

FOLLOWING THE PATH

The first path may be a straight line, two or three feet wide, on the floor delineated by large hollow blocks or cardboard boxes. As the toddlers become more mature walkers and less wobbly, the width of the path may be decreased as well as the height of the sides. By 30 months of age, most children can successfully walk on a path 8 inches wide. The path at this point (or before) may be formed by two parallel lines of masking tape on the floor. Also during the second year, the path may be curved or angled so that children must change their forward motion in order to stay within the parallel lines. The path may also be indicated by lengths of cord or rope stretched knee high, thigh high, or waist high. Three-year-old children can be expected to walk on a 1-inch path. All of these path-walkings are equally appropriate for outdoor play. The children can crawl, walk, tiptoe, roll, and even run on a masking tape or chalk path. They will be challenged, perhaps, to walk backward on a one-inch path but may not succeed.

WALKING THE PLANK

Related to path-walking is walking on a balance beam. The beam or plank is first laid on the floor, and the children first crawl and then walk on it from one end to the other. It can be gradually raised, perhaps an inch at a time, up to 4 to 6 inches. Walking backward on a beam may not be achieved by age 3. Children 20 to 24 months old will probably be able to travel sideways using a closed step pattern. If the beam is wide enough, children can pretend to be four-legged animals and move forward and return backward. When the children have achieved a sense of confidence in walking the beam, they might be asked to walk forward with their arms held straight from the shoulders or with the arms straight up over their heads. In the very beginning, however, children

will probably walk the plank with one foot on and one foot off.

CROSSING THE RIVER

Large paper cut-outs of various sizes and shapes may be taped to the floor, serving as flat rocks on which to cross the river without getting wet. Cut-out paper footprints accomplish the same thing when traveling on "dry land." If the room is carpeted, hollow blocks placed close together also serve as stepping stones. On the outside playground, ideally in a nonslippery area, children will sometimes line up their own stepping stones (large blocks) and play follow the leader.

WALKING THE DOTS

The teacher may place large paper dots on the floor in straight or curving lines or at sharp right angles. Children follow the path by stepping on the dots.

TIPTOE THROUGH THE TULIPS

This time the paper cut-outs serve as tulips, and in order to walk through the garden, one must avoid stepping on the flowers. Some children will be able to tiptoe by 18 months. Children at this age are not yet able to represent or symbolize. Therefore, it might add to the fun to use paper tulips or other flowers. Vinyl cut-outs will outlast construction paper cut-outs many times over. For those children who have not yet conquered the skill of tiptoeing, a cookie or toy may be placed on a table or window sill just high enough to necessitate rising on tiptoes.

MERRY-GO-ROUND

Tape a large circle on the floor. Play follow-the-leader in walking on the line, beside the line, straddling the line, both frontward and backward. Moving up and down during the walking activities is an additional accomplishment in body coordination and control.

SQUATTER'S RIGHTS

Children stand erect with feet together and hands on hips. They bend their knees to a squatting position, then stand tall again. (The jack-in-the-box action game turns this into fun instead of exercise.) Squatting seems to be a natural position for young children. It is the stretch up that is important.

GIRAFFE WALK
The children stretch their arms overhead, clasping their hands together forming a giraffe's head and neck. They imitate a giraffe's movement by walking with knees stiff. Arms and trunk may sway slightly, but they must point upward. Children may also walk on tiptoes for the giraffe walk.

LEG SWING
Children hold onto back of a chair or railing with one hand and stand on one foot. They swing their free leg forward and backward. An arm swing should accompany the leg swing.

MOVING DAY
A self-initiated activity in which a child may carry, or use a wagon or cart to move, all the blocks (or toys, cars, dolls, etc.) from one place to another, and probably back again.

Movement and music. Rhythmical walking and other movement activities should frequently be directed by musical sounds or rhythms. One of the goals for an early childhood music curriculum (McDonald & Simons, 1989) is "learning to move expressively and rhythmically. The research . . . reveals that, for most young children, listening to music means moving to music. The development of rhythmic competency not only enables children to enjoy music, but also helps them to understand it more fully" (p. 59). It also enables them to move rhythmically and with increased coordination. The "rocking, patting, touching and moving with children to the beat" (p. 60) during the physical caregiving should be a part of every infant's day. For the twos and threes, Weikart (1985) suggests that the children first do an activity without any music. "If the children are going to pat their legs and then their heads, for example, do the sequence

several times until all of them can do it comfortably. Then add music" (p. 2).

The use of recordings, drum or tambourine beats, or piano accompaniment can direct the pace of the actions, and can indicate when to stop and start. Taking giant steps and baby steps around the room or outdoor play area will increase coordination and control. Twos and threes may be able to play statues (move to music and freeze in position when the music stops). Their statues will not be very stable, but the activity is fun.

Climbing and jumping. The ability to climb stairs with alternating feet (with no support) is achieved sometime before the third birthday. Descending stairs independently is more difficult and will be conquered after the fourth birthday.

It is possible in these times of apartment living that some toddlers do not have an opportunity to practice step-climbing skills. Therefore steps of some kind should be provided in the day-care center or home. A set of sturdy, free-standing steps backed up against a wall, or a combination step-platform-slide is recommended.

The baby who is creeping or crawling is also interested in climbing and can climb onto a step or platform 6 inches off the floor. Climbing is an all-fours (hands and feet) movement, and therefore is a natural outgrowth of crawling. Children are exhilarated by being up high and looking down for a change. They have not yet learned to be afraid, and therefore need sturdy objects to climb on and nearby supervision. The supervision should not prevent the child from testing, however. Toddlers should be free to attempt "daring" feats. The report of the following observation, written by a nearby adult, illustrates both the challenge of climbing and appropriate supervision.

EPISODE 14
Kathy (10 months) was quietly sizing up the long stairway leading to the upstairs hallway. She hiked herself up the first step, looked up again,

Climbing, the hard way. (Kindercampus, Iowa City)

conquered the next one, rested a minute, and then crawled to the very top. She surveyed her world (including the teacher at the bottom of the steps). She turned herself around carefully, and after several complicated body movements, she felt her way backward and arrived at the first step down in 5 minutes. She negotiated the next one in half the time, and continued downward slowly. Her beaming face shown with her sense of accomplishment when she arrived back down.

The "appropriate" supervision was the availability of the adult who wisely refrained from saying "Be careful," or "That's too high." There was no distraction whatsoever, as Kathy devoted her total being to her self-set task.

By the first birthday, most babies are able to climb on and off chairs and other furniture several feet high. They can manage climbing intervals of about 12 inches and show much ingenuity in reaching higher levels. Low stepladders or combinations of block-chair-table will offer appropriate climbing opportunities, unless one of the rules is "no climbing on the table." In a normally developing child, climbing is even less of a teaching responsibility than walking. The problem is to keep the toddler from climbing! In the early stages of climbing, the action itself is the goal. By age 2 or 2½ climbing

becomes purposeful. The child will use an object as a climbing-off space to reach even higher levels. After reaching the heights, there may be cries of frustration over the inability to get down. Young children and kittens have much in common in this respect. Therefore many opportunities for safe climbing should be provided to enable children to learn for themselves what they can and cannot do.

The first jump, maybe. (Early Childhood Education Center)

Jumping really begins when a toddler has climbed up and wants to get down. Preparatory exercises include crouching, squatting, using arms for balancing on a balance beam, and using the legs together for hopping. If a climber indicates uncertainty about getting down, the adult can grasp both her hands and lift her off and down quickly, directing her to keep legs somewhat bent. A soft landing spot is best (rug, mattress, grassy spot). The child will rapidly progress from relying on two adult hands, to one adult hand, to the security of an adult close by, to complete independence. The best height for safe jumping is about half the child's height.

Many of the walking activities lend themselves to jumping also. Children may jump over a rope or yardstick on the floor, which is then gradually raised; over cracks in the sidewalk; or in and out of the "pond" (masking tape circle on the floor). Bouncing on a flexible board and then jumping off lends excitement and challenge to other jumping activities.

Throwing and catching. Throwing and catching activities are usually thought of in terms of balls and beanbags. But baby starts to throw soon after he discovers that a dropped spoon or cereal bowl causes a commotion. Prethrowing skills are the grasp-and-release motions, which progress to intentional releasing (or dropping), and then throwing just to see what happens or as a release for frustration. Random throwing is not toward anything. The throwing itself is important. Dropping can be led to a goal-oriented behavior, as baby drops clothespins, blocks, or buttons, into large-mouthed containers. In the first stages, each child should have his or her own objects and a container to drop them in. Gradually child and container can be moved further apart, necessitating the need for aimed throwing with the application of some force.

Sometime around the first birthday, the educarer can sit on the floor behind a seated child and can help the child push a ball away. After the child gets the idea, they can face each other for a beginning game of ball-rolling. Once a child has internalized the idea of needed force, all kinds of throwing opportunities are available. Balls and beanbags may be rolled or thrown across taped lines, circles, or squares, into wastebaskets, or to the educarer or another child.

A beginning throw. (Early Childhood Education Center)

Lightweight beach balls are best as beginning balls. Gradually the size of the balls may be decreased down to tennis ball size. As the balls become more hand-sized, children should be shown over- and underhand approaches to throwing. As was suggested earlier, educarer and child can throw the ball together, so that the child gets the feel of the motions. Games such as ring toss help refine throwing skills. The upright legs of an overturned chair serve as well as any purchased piece of equipment. At first the child may simply drop the rings in the right place, and then gradually back away. Aiming a ball or beanbag toward a target is a little more advanced. The target must be such that the child can see the result (a container in which the object stays) rather than a hoop or target board that the ball contacts only momentarily.

Catching is harder than throwing. Balloon-tapping and catching give the child the opportunity to coordinate catching motions with body position. A balloon-pass game will initiate catching movements, with children standing in a circle and passing the balloon from one to another. Using two balloons at the same time will ensure the involvement of each child without much waiting for a turn. Later the same game can be played with balls, first passing them, and then throwing them to children in a spread-out circle.

Balls are favorite playthings during the second year, and teachers and children should have lots of ball games. A 2 year old will also walk up to a large ball on the floor or ground and kick it.

It takes several years to refine throwing and catching skills. The suggested activities lay the foundation skills.

FINE MOTOR SKILLS

The coordination of gross and fine motor skills proceeds rapidly through the second and third years of life. The beginnings are laid during the first few months of life.

A move from whole-hand grasp to . . . (Kindercampus)

a pincer grasp. (Kindercampus, Iowa City)

The First Year

During the first 7 to 9 months, baby has progressed from grasping with whole hands or palms to grasping and picking up small objects with the thumb and index finger (pincer grasp). Adults encourage the initial steps by first placing an object (plastic keys, rattle, small squeeze toy) in baby's hand and closing his fingers around it and then removing her hand. Another object can be substituted for the first one. Later, two objects may be offered at the same time. The child should have the opportunity to use both hands, either singly or together. In other words, toys should be offered from each side, instead of always from the right or left side. Baby will probably be able to grasp and release an object before his first birthday. If there is a reluctance to let go, sometimes the request ''Please give it to me'' will trigger the release. The development of the pincer grasp in a normal child needs no more encouragement than a few bits of dry cereal spread on a tray or table, or a few crumbs on the floor. Dust balls are also intriguing. If baby needs help, a one-time ''walking through'' with educarer's hand over the baby's should initiate the independent action. As soon as baby is able to grasp (around 7 or 8 months), a crayon may be placed in her hand with her fingers wrapped around it. Together the educarer and baby can mark on a piece of paper. It is premature to instruct or show baby the ''right'' way to hold the crayon. The grasping and holding on are sufficient at this stage.

Adults sometimes postpone the introduction of fingerplays and action games until baby can imitate or initiate the called-for motions. This postponement overlooks some opportunities for fun, and for a beginning awareness and interest in hands and fingers. In addition to the traditional nursery rhymes and made-up jingles that are used since baby's early weeks, fingerplays and motion games should be included in the daily activities. As was the case in the early activities for gross motor development, the educarer either demonstrates or moves baby in response to rhythms and words. A few examples are sufficient to start thinking about others.

1. Teacher recites:
    Knock on the door (tap baby's forehead)
    Peek in (lift baby's eyelid)
    Lift the latch (tilt baby's nose)
    Walk in (put baby's finger in mouth)
    Go way down cellar and
    Eat apples (tickle baby under chin).

2. The teacher makes a fist and shows one finger at a time while baby watches:
   Here is a beehive—where are the bees?
   Hidden away where nobody sees!
   Soon they come creeping out of the hive—
   One! Two! Three! Four! Five!

3. The teacher pulls baby's arms back and forth, while singing "Row, row, row your boat."

4. The teacher moves baby's arm with his, while going through these motions:
   Over there the sun gets up (extend arm horizontally),
   And marches all the day (raise arm slowly),
   At noon it stands right overhead (point straight up),
   At night it goes away (lower arm slowly).

5. Again with teacher's help:
   These are grandmother's glasses (make finger circles at each eye)
   This is grandmother's hat (both hands over head)
   This is the way she folds her hands (fold hands)
   And puts them in her lap (all four hands in baby's lap).

6. Arms are raised, and then lowered while moving fingers to represent raindrops:
   Pitter-patter, pitter-patter,
   Hear the rain come down,
   Pitter-patter, pitter-patter,
   All around the town.

If such games as these are introduced to baby motorically as well as verbally, baby will soon begin to imitate the motions, and a developmental milestone will have been reached. Sources of finger- and action plays are included in the suggested readings of chapter 3.

As you know by now, the baby's drive to explore seems to be all-encompassing. This drive can be channeled so that baby is introduced to classification skills, or at least to rela-tionships. Objects provided should have some connection to one another. Self-care items include a comb, brush, washcloth, empty powder can, and a spoon and cup. Food-related items include cooking spoons, measuring spoons and cups, egg beaters, and pots and pans with lids. Even babies under 1 year of age are intrigued by toys that react, or do something, and toys or objects with simple parts that move.

Of course, the most fascinating game of all is grasping and dropping, soon followed by intentional dropping and then throwing. Around the first birthday, baby can drop clothespins into a container with a 2-inch opening. Old fashioned wooden clothespins may be slid over the rim of a round container so that baby will learn a pulling-off action in addition to the dropping. Later, a plastic-lidded, large coffee can with a slit cut in the lid is a perfect receptacle for buttons and the like. Further refinement of finger muscles comes when spring-type clothespins are introduced.

In a group situation there cannot always be a one-to-one interaction between educarer and child. Indeed, baby needs time alone periodically. One self-teaching piece of equipment can be a collection of many small objects (too large to mouth) of a variety of shapes, sizes, and textures placed in a container with a wide opening. A gallon ice cream can works well. The objects should be changed periodically so that baby's interest will continue. Natural curiosity along with the skills of grasping and manipulating are the only motivation necessary. This collection of miscellaneous small objects will turn into the activity boxes described later.

By the end of the first year, babies are beginning to recognize at least one shape visually and tactually. The circle is the appropriate first shape, and with a little maneuvering it can be dropped through a matching hole in the top or side of a box. The first form board or box should contain a round hole and a square hole. Squares are much more difficult to drop in because they require some rotation to fit into the hole.

The Second and Third Years

No doubt balloons and large balls and beanbags have been enjoyed for several months. By the time baby is 15 or 16 months old, ping pong balls can be handled with some degree of success. They are light weight and easily thrown. They are not easy to catch, but they are fun to chase.

The toddler has also been manipulating the colored small cube blocks, stacking them and knocking them over with much glee. Some nesting toys are good stackers also if they have lids. The educarer can demonstrate stacking progressively smaller ones. Stacking activities lead to size awareness and discrimination, size comparisons, and eye-hand coordination. They also provide the opportunity for language development if there is a stacking partner. Stacking is a readiness skill for ordering and seriating activities. Almost any set of objects can be used: different-sized toothpaste boxes, detergent boxes, candy boxes, paper cups and plates, even shoes (doll, baby, child, adult).

When children can order objects from little to big, labels can be introduced. "This one is little, this one is big, this one is the biggest," etc. The game should be started with two objects, one big and the other little. Gradually in-between-sized objects can be introduced. Matching objects of the same size should also start with just two sizes, with the in-between sizes gradually added. As soon as possible, the child should be moved from manipulative ordering and matching to pointing, and then to verbalizing in response to "Show me the biggest one" and so on. The containers that have been used for ordering should be used in the sandbox or the water table for the experiments that will reinforce the notion that biggest is really biggest because it holds more than any of the others.

Sorting games can use all kinds of homemade materials, starting with large bowls, cans, or milk cartons, and progressing to TV dinner trays and egg cartons. Actual objects can be taped in the corner of each section to give a visual direction to the sorting. Pasted-on paper cut-outs may also indicate the desired color or shape or size. Later, line drawings or pictures can provide the clues.

Beginning educarers face many time-consuming tasks and learnings. If they have a collection of homemade teaching-learning tools in advance, they will be able to devote their time and energies to their children and to the program itself. It is difficult to store large cardboard boxes, or even coffee cans, but it is both practical and advisable to begin collecting pictures. Mounted pictures can be used in a number of ways: for matching, sorting, and grouping, lotto games, language development, story-telling, and beginning symbolization skills. A good assortment of pictures, line drawings, and silhouettes will supply sets for matching by color, size, and shape, by relationships (e.g., fork and spoon), by function (e.g., things we wear, things we ride on, things we eat), and by location (e.g., indoors or outdoors, kitchen or bedroom, zoo or farm). There is a very important caution about using pictures, however. They are appropriate and useful *only* after the child has had many real experiences with the ideas and concepts in planned and incidental activities.

When a child is able to sit, stand, walk, reach, and retrieve, that child is freed to become an individual and to make use of developing social and intellectual abilities. It is during these first 3 years that motor abilities and patterns of movement should be developed, so that the preschooler is freed from physical limitations on further and expanded activities.

COORDINATION OF MOTOR SKILLS

The older toddler is glorying in his mastery of body movements and control, and should be given ample opportunity (time and space) to put them to use and to enjoy them. The older toddler is also becoming socially aware of other children and is beginning to realize the benefits of cooperation and "togetherness," but on a limited basis. One of the several techniques of building on this social awareness and of extending the already-present motor skills is the introduction of action games and circle activities.

Action Games and Circle Activities

One of the traditions of early childhood education is the use of group activities that require movement, following directions, and paying attention. At first they are led by the educarer, but then an individual child may assume the teaching role. The following games are samples of those that should be a part of every toddler program. In each of them the children stand in a circle, facing inward, and move through the called-for actions.

Reach for the Ceiling
Reach for the ceiling
Touch the floor,
Stand up again
Let's do more.
Touch your head,
Then your knee,
Up to your shoulder,
Like this . . . see?
Reach for the ceiling
Touch the floor,
That's all now—
there isn't anymore.

I'm a Little Teapot
I'm a little teapot, short and stout.
Here is my handle; here is my spout.
  (place left hand on hip for handle, and raise right arm with palm down.)
When I get all steamed up then I shout,
"Tip me over and pour me out!"
(Bend over toward the right.)

The following games call for a leader and a small group of children. Children should be leaders occasionally for the fun of it. When the adult is the leader, the suggested actions can challenge the children's motor skills more than the child leader will.

COPY CATS
The leader engages in any physical action—walking frontward, backward, and sideways; marching; crawling; hopping; turning around; stooping—with the children following behind copying the actions. Sometimes two simultaneous actions can be presented to make the copying more challenging. Walking on all fours, flopping as a rag doll, and animal walks are other suggested movements.

THE TALKING DRUM
The adult will be the first drummer, but all the children should be given the opportunity. The game is to move as the drum directs: fast, slow, loudly, softly, fast and softly, slow and loudly, etc.

MARCHING
Children face educarer, and imitate her marching in place, with arms swinging. Educarer should face the children. It is helpful to tie a colored piece of yarn on the educarer's right shoe, and on each child's left wrist and shoe.

GUESSING GAME
One child (with eyes closed) is in the center of the circle of children. Children repeat the verse, and stand tall or stoop low when appropriate. At the end of the verse, the adult motions to the children to be tall or small, and the child in the center guesses.

We're very, very tall
We're very, very small
Sometimes tall, sometimes small
Guess what we are now.

A HUNDRED WAYS TO GET THERE
Children watch as one child walks or crawls or runs around the room. Children then imitate. There might be pillows or blocks scattered on the floor to make an indoor obstacle course.

Awareness of body parts and movements is a necessary understanding for the young child. Such awareness helps the child to recognize body limits and its position in space in relation to other objects.

GETTING TO KNOW ME

Children should lie flat on their backs on the floor. The educarer calls out names of body parts, and the children raise the named part. The adult can also call out the names of paired body parts (arms, hands, legs, feet) and the children raise both together.

ANGELS IN THE SNOW

This activity gets progressively harder, and not all 3 year olds will be able to do the variations. Children should lie flat on their backs on the floor (or in the snow), with their arms down at the sides. Keeping the arms touching the floor, children slowly move them out and up until they are above the head with backs of hands touching. Then children move their feet apart as far as possible (touching the floor). Bring arms and legs back together. Children repeat, moving arms and legs at the same time.

Variations: move one arm at a time; one leg at a time; move left arm and left leg; move right arm and right leg.

Games like the above contribute to motor coordination and perception, both of which are forerunners of academic readiness. The components of motor perception are:

1. Body image—the complete awareness of its potential for movement and performance
2. Laterality—the awareness of two sides of the body
3. Directionality—the projection of the body into space in all directions
4. Balance—the stability produced by maintaining an equal distribution of weight on all sides of the body
5. Temporal projection—behavior made up of synchrony (the harmonious working together of body parts), rhythm (recurrent actions at ordered intervals), and sequence (arrangement of events in time)

Eye-Hand Coordination

To become motorically competent, one must be able to coordinate and integrate all body actions. One of the most important is the coordination of eyes and hands. We cannot teach it, but when the infant is ready, we can help it along.

At first, the hands alone make an interesting "toy," but the infant soon puts them to use, and swipes at a swinging object with the hand closest to it. Sometime around 2½ months his tight fists uncurl, and the open hands just ask for something to hold. Rattles or other toys that make a sound attract the baby's attention and will lead to the connection between what his eyes see and what his hands do. Also about this time, things to swipe at lead him to discover that his action results in both movement and sound. By 4 months, swiping isn't enough; touching is important. Leach (1981) cautions,

> Adults who hold toys out to babies at this stage often spoil their practice by mistake. The glancing backwards and forwards from toy to hand to toy takes so long that the adult gets sorry for the baby and puts it in his hand. Have patience. Don't help him until he has actually touched the object he wants. Then he needs to have it put in his hand so that his pleasure in having touched the toy can be increased by having actually *got* it (p. 177).

Baby needs lots of practice, and if we supply interesting things to look at and reach out for and grab, eye-hand coordination will soon be accomplished.

At 6 to 7 months, baby uses hands to explore objects beyond just grabbing and putting into his mouth. He begins to develop interest in textures. At the same time he is learning to use different parts of his arms separately, and also different parts of his hands. Now he points and pokes. He uses a pincer grasp to retrieve the smallest crumb. By 1 year, he has discovered how to hold on to and how to let go.

All babies start out using both hands with equal ease, although preference in handedness,

Scribbling with whole-arm movements. (Early Childhood Education Center)

footedness, and eyedness are set in the child's brain at birth. Until about 2 years, babies may use a particular hand for a particular thing, and dominance is quite evident by the second year. Although we can model right-handedness (if we are right-handed), we should never pressure the child to use the hand he is not inclined to. The hemisphere of the brain that controls handedness also controls language, and there is evidence that insistence on hand-preference-changing results in later language problems.

Sometime during the second year, educarers can further eye-hand coordination by providing activities and materials with this goal in mind.

Scribbling with a crayon or a felt-tip pen on paper, or with chalk on a chalkboard leads to a desire (and ability) to make the marker do certain things. Every infant-toddler environment should have a child-reachable chalkboard. Using it encourages full-arm movements using elbows and shoulders as well as wrists, hands, and fingers. The child should use both hands together as well as each hand individually. Chalk can be fastened to a long piece of string attached to the wall or chalkboard frame.

For reasons of their own, some children reject using chalk as a scribbling instrument. If this happens, the educarer can cover the entire chalkboard with chalk (using its side) and ask the child to erase some of it with arms or palms, using large circular motions.

After the children have engaged in chalkboard drawing, they can be encouraged to draw a line between dots placed progressively farther apart, but never so far that the child cannot reach while standing still. We are working for directional movements of the arms and hands, with the child's body at the center of the task. Children can trace straight lines, curves, or circles with each hand, moving their hands and arms but not the trunk. An adaptation of follow-the-leader can incorporate chalkboard drawing. The teacher draws a line, the child follows, the teacher draws another, and so on. A more advanced dot game can be introduced in this way, with the teacher drawing lines between dots that will form a recognizable shape (circle, square, triangle). The next step, of course, is to draw arrows between the dots so that the children do not rely on direct imitation. The more advanced dot games may not be successful before the age of 3 years, but they can be introduced playfully as one more way to encourage the ability to imitate.

Pegboards can be used in the same way. The educarer may place two pegs as end points for horizontal, vertical, and diagonal lines. After a child has filled in the missing pegs and formed a continuous line, a line of the same direction can be drawn on paper with crayon or on the chalkboard.

Paper, chalkboards, and even pegboards may be considered two dimensional. Their use should come only after considerable time has been spent in working with three-dimensional objects (blocks, toys). The transfer from three to two dimensions is not automatic and must not be rushed.

Playing catch with balloons or keeping a balloon in the air by gently tapping it with both hands and then either hand requires the coordination of eye-hand muscles, in addition to the

larger muscles. Dropping objects into various-sized containers, putting disks through slots, matching shape inserts with form boards or shape boxes, joining pop-beads, stacking rings, hammering pegs, throwing beanbags to a target or in a container—these are examples of the activities that help consolidate the desired eye-hand control and coordination.

A room full of infants and toddlers is a room filled with motion. The actions, both random and intentional, are directed toward practicing developed motor skills and learning new ones. It is the practice that is important, and good teachers capitalize on the child's innate need to move by guiding the movements in increasingly coordinated patterns.

Play

Motor development is promoted by action, and young children at play are involved in motor ac-

Taxi, anyone? (Early Childhood Education Center)

tions. Running, climbing, riding wheeled toys, chasing balls, and playing in the sandbox are all influential in the development of gross motor skills and their coordination. Fine motor skills are exercised and developed through activities that involve cutting and pasting, crayoning, and painting; table games and puzzles; and pouring water, sand, rice, or cornmeal in and out of containers.

Play as learning. Play is the vehicle used in infant-toddler teaching and learning. It is the means by which the young child discovers and learns. Play involves stimulation, exploration, experimentation, manipulation, action, and interaction.

In more recent years there has been an emphasis on the role of play in the development of intellectual abilities. Arnold (1971) tells parents that "your child becomes teachable through play" (p. 29). Fowler (1980) reminds teachers that the "most obvious function of play is the production of learning" (p. 144). Phrases such as these and others ("play is serious business"; "play is children's work") have been interpreted as references to learning. Elkind (1988) questions the labeling of children's play as work, because many persons view play as fun and work as learning. Certainly, the little ones work at learning how to dress themselves, how to handle eating utensils, how to follow directions. But they also learn social behaviors, new or extended concepts, and knowledge of self and others as they play. Perhaps we should change the phrase "play is children's work" to "children learn through both play and work." So many issues, including the issue of play, seem to follow a pendulum course, and opinions swing from one extreme to the other. It has always been recognized that playing enhances motor skill development. Up until the 1950s play was viewed as essential for both social skill development and emotional stability. I suspect the current emphasis on play as an intellectual exercise is partly a reaction to society's desire for instant observable results. I also suspect that those persons who

are stressing the seriousness of play are attempting to counteract this societal concern for intellectual results by stressing the intellectual or academic learnings in any play episode. Their goal may not be to identify play as an academic tool per se, but to ensure the inclusion of play as an essential component in any program for young children. The problem stems from the general misinterpretation of the terms *teaching* and *learning*.

Early play activities. Sutton-Smith and Sutton-Smith (1974) suggest games that are appropriate for educarers (and parents) and their infants and toddlers as follows:

Birth to 3 Months

1. Imitate baby, make baby noises
2. Alternate noises with baby (gurgles)
3. "Baby talk" (long vowels and high pitch)
4. Make clown faces
5. Poke out your tongue
6. Let baby pull your finger

3 to 6 Months

1. Make baby laugh
2. Do gymnastics with baby (bounce on bed, turn upside down)
3. Blow raspberries on baby's body
4. Play "pretend" walking, "pretend" standing
5. Let baby pull your hair
6. Play "This Little Pig" (induce anticipation)

6 to 12 Months

1. Roughhouse
2. Grab and give up (give and take)
3. Play peek-a-boo (locate object or person)
4. Bury baby under blanket
5. Ride camel (parent on all fours, baby on parent's back)
6. Make baby laugh (sound, touch, social, and visual stimuli)

1 to 2 Years

1. Chase, be chased
2. Hide thimble (object permanence)
3. Empty, fill
4. Play catch
5. Play "phony" birthdays (birthday of the center, of the pet hamster)
6. Have tug-of-war. (cited in Johnson et al., 1987, pp. 96–97)

The dramatic play of older twos and threes was included in chapter 4, and of course this type of play depends on motoric actions and abilities, in addition to helping in the development of social competency.

The most traditional play objects in early childhood education are blocks, which also require motoric actions and abilities.

Block play. Blocks teach best when the children are allowed to explore, discover, and manipulate on their own. Playing with blocks will enhance all areas of a child's development.

Throughout the early years the child should have access to a variety of blocks, each providing a different sensory input. Blocks of foam, cloth, rigid plastic, cardboard, and wood all send different messages to the child, and need somewhat different handling. Not only should the block materials differ, but blocks should also differ in size, shape, color, texture, weight, sound, and perhaps even smell.

Blocks are first introduced in the form of empty frozen juice cans or plastic dairy containers that are good for stacking up and knocking down. Lightweight but sturdy cardboard boxes or blocks are great for lugging and piling. Oversized plastic snap blocks call for finer motor skills (Oppenheim, 1984).

A simple set of unit blocks (these are hardwood blocks whose sizes are fractions and multiples of a carefully designed unit block) should be a part of every infant/toddler setting, because unit block building "develops both large and

small motor coordination and sensitive eye-hand integration" (Cartwright, 1988, p. 44).

As is true with all learning and development, block behaviors progress through a developmental sequence. The findings of two early studies (Bates & Learned, 1954; Johnson, 1933) and more recent descriptive accounts (Bjorklund, 1978; Hirsch, 1984; Rudolph, 1973) agree on the following sequence:

1. Blocks are carried from place to place
2. Blocks are used for building rows (either horizontal or vertical, with much repetitious building)
3. "Buildings" are expanded by bridging (two blocks with a space between them, connected by a third block over the top of the space)
4. Blocks are used to enclose space
5. Beginning symmetry and balance
6. Naming of structures for dramatic play. Earlier structures may have been named, but the names were at random
7. Buildings are recognizable as models of actual structures. Dramatic play rapidly increases around the block structures

The sequence will come to life in the following episodes.

EPISODE 15

Shelly, almost 18 months old, has never been in the block corner before. She is getting acquainted with the unit blocks. There are other children present in the corner, but she is oblivious of anyone as she bangs the blocks on the floor, shakes them, moves them from one hand to the other, and carries four of them, one by one, to another part of the room. She returns to the block corner to watch the other children play.

Shelly is learning the properties of the wooden blocks and their relationship to her. They are an appropriate size to handle and carry, and their shape and solidity appear to be unchanging. The next time she comes to the block corner, she may manipulate some more, and she also may start to line them up or stack them. She is not yet socially ready to interact with other children, but is interested in their activities.

EPISODE 16

Danny (2½ years) has been attending the center for only a week. Because he has had at-home experience with blocks, he spends much of his free time in the block corner as he gradually adjusts to being part of a group. He stacks blocks of two different sizes and builds horizontal roadways on the floor. He rebuilds these same structures many times. He is careful to place the blocks exactly on top of each other and is discovering that it works

best when a larger block is on the bottom of the tower. He plays near, but not with, the other builders. Yesterday he labeled a single block "truck" and today he "parks" a block next to a larger one, which he labels "garage."

EPISODE 17

Three-year-old Carrie is busy with trial-and-error experimentation to get blocks to fit together without falling. She is able to build enclosures and bridges, imitating other children's structures. Marie joins Carrie, and they each build a house close to the other's. There is some verbalized planning "Now I need a roof," but there is little verbal conversation. However, the girls are sharing the blocks amiably.

Beginning block play with a friend. (Early Childhood Education Center)

Children between the ages of 2 and 3 years achieve much satisfaction from block play, whether it be carting them from one place to another or building with them. Blocks are satisfying because there is a tangible end product that is always "right."

Particular attention is given here to the values of hardwood unit blocks. Many programs are inclined to spend less money and purchase a playset of blocks. Playsets may represent a farm or a circus ring or a gas station, and therefore limit the kind of play they suggest. A set of unit blocks can be a farm today, a circus tomorrow, a gas station the next day, and a multitude of other things in the days and years to come. The initial investment is high, but it is worthwhile. An introductory set of unit blocks should be provided for children by the time they are 2 years of age. They require careful supervision. A beginner's set usually consists of eight basic shapes and 32 pieces. The shapes should be proportioned to the basic block unit, measuring $2\frac{3}{4}''$ by $5\frac{1}{2}''$ by $1\frac{3}{4}''$. Additional blocks should be purchased periodically. They become increasingly important throughout the early childhood years. Building with unit blocks incorporates both small and large muscles.

Other kinds of blocks are equally useful in an infant-toddler center. Hollow wooden blocks and large bricklike cardboard blocks suggest episodes of dramatic play. These blocks are especially suitable for very young children because they involve the use of large muscles. Large and small blocks can be homemade with a little time and effort. The first building blocks can be made from two half-gallon milk cartons, one inserted in the other. These are light in weight and fairly sturdy. They may be painted with one or two coats of acrylic paint or covered with contact paper. Satisfactory blocks of all sizes and shapes can be made from cardboard boxes with a little practice—and a great deal of compact stuffing. Even toothpaste, tissue, and cereal boxes can be made geometrically true and therefore stackable. They are light in weight, do not hurt little fingers or toes when

they topple, and can be handled easily. Although not as useful as building blocks, larger cardboard boxes or cartons serve as ready-made houses or private nooks, and are excellent for climbing in and out of. With opposite ends cut off, they make excellent tunnels to crawl, walk, run, or ride through, depending on their size.

Smaller wooden, plastic, or foam rubber cubes, attribute blocks, parquetry blocks, and Lego blocks all require fine motor coordination. Their use can be unstructured or structured. Some 3 year olds are able to build structures using Lincoln logs, thereby making good use of their eye-hand coordination skills.

There can be no question regarding the benefits of block play for the development of coordinated motor movements. All block play requires manipulation of some kind. The picking up of small blocks with a pincer grasp and building a stack or tower develop fine motor control as well as eye-hand coordination. When children squat to pick up a large block, lift it, and stand to make a higher tower, they are utilizing larger muscles. When block-roads are made for walking on, children learn to balance their entire bodies while moving. When pathways are delineated by lengths of parallel blocks with space in between two rows, children walking the path will learn control as well as spatial awareness. A large assortment of blocks is a necessary component in any infant-toddler center.

Sensorimotor manipulations are the dominant play activities during the first 12 to 18 months. Shelly's "getting-to-know-blocks" (Episode 15) is a good example. Sometime during the second year a new play form emerges: symbolic play. Simple block structures or enclosed spaces offer the environment for this new form of play.

Activity boxes. Activity boxes for infants and toddlers are a popular item in child-care centers in Israel, and should become a popular and useful item in our own group settings. "An activity box is a container of every day objects that have a purposeful relationship to each other in functions, color, or material" (Suskind & Kittel, 1989, p. 46). They can be used as transitional activities, as portable learning centers, and as conversation starters, and they are a good means for encouraging children to initiate and explore on their own. The boxes themselves may be shoe boxes or small cardboard boxes, gallon ice cream containers, lunch boxes, or whatever. The contents may be as simple as blue and red objects for sorting, spools for stacking and rolling, or cloth materials of different textures or designs for tactile or visual discrimination. The selection of contents is determined by the developmental status of the children, and may range from simple to complex. In some ways, these activity boxes are related to the collections of dress-up clothes or kitchen utensils that encourage dramatic role-playing, but their purpose is more toward the development of exploration and manipulation (motor abilities) and the beginnings of concepts (cognitive abilities).

We have seen that children learn motor skills through "play."

Children also learn motor skills through "work."

SELF-HELP SKILLS

Self-help skills are those skills that are used daily, require repetitive actions, and lead toward independence from adults. They include the skills of dressing, grooming, toileting, and eating. The routines of learning and teaching these skills take up a large proportion of the awake hours of the infants. Good educarers use these routine times for language, cognitive, social, and emotional development, in addition to motor development. Many of the adult-infant interactions center around the routines of diapering, dressing, and feeding. There is a striking change of emphasis as the baby enters the toddler stage and all kinds of investigative opportunities are available. It is during the toddler stage, also, that the foundation skills for independent dressing,

grooming, eating, and toileting are taught. It is not the intention here to present detailed task analyses of the self-help skills. Detailed descriptions of each skill can be found in any of a number of teaching guides for use with young handicapped children.

Typical infants and toddlers appear to develop the skills as a result of the combination of maturation, imitation, adult encouragement, and a few techniques that have proved to be helpful.

Independent Dressing

Infants pay no attention whatsoever to getting dressed; indeed, their reaction is to wiggle and kick when an adult tries. But as soon as they can move their arms and legs purposefully, they can be of some help, if the adult helps them put arms in armholes and feet and legs in pants. The toddler, on the other hand, can put on and take off his hat, mittens, and socks, and can almost dress and undress himself with some adult direction. However, buttons create a problem.

Completely independent dressing and undressing should not be expected by the third birthday. Many of the activities during the first 3 years will give practice in the beginning skills. These predressing skills are encouraged by handling Nerf balls, beanbags, and sponges; by putting buttons in the slot of a coffee can lid or pennies in a bank; by unraveling yarn or crepe paper that has been wrapped around one's body; by stringing beads or cereal; by dressing up (and down) in dress-up clothes; by dressing and undressing dolls; by tossing a ring onto someone's arms or legs; by removing clothespins clipped onto the edge of a carton or one's clothing; by putting a sack or puppet on one's hand; and by lowering a Hula Hoop or innertube over one's head and all the way down the body.

Children will begin to cooperate with their dressing sometime around their first birthday. They will duck their heads for a pullover shirt, start to put one arm through the sleeve, and put out both feet for one shoe. As adults dress the baby, they should talk about what they are doing, labeling parts of the body as well as articles of clothing—"Now we'll put the shoe on your foot. . . . Your arm goes in here. . . . "If the shirt or dress is a pullover, baby can put hands into the armholes so that the teacher can pull it on, fitting the neck opening over and down under the head. Pants with elastic waists are best; wide hooks are easier than snaps; and a wide belt with a single-prong buckle is best. Iron-on appliques or some other mark should be applied to the fronts of the garments. The easiest way to introduce pulling on pants is to sit the toddler on a low chair, gather the pant legs into "doughnuts," and lay them on the floor just in front of the child's feet. His job is to step into the holes; yours is to ease the doughnuts around his toes and ankles. Both of you grasp the top of the pants and pull up together.

Socks are fun because they have heels. Again make a doughnut, with the child stepping into the holes, and the teacher bringing the sock to and over the heel. The toddler can pull the sock up the leg. Tube socks (socks without heels) might be used when the toddler is first ready to do it himself. Midway between the first and second birthday, children will imitate others by pulling off hats or shoes. Even double knots are not childproof. The adult can untie the laces, but let the toddler loosen them (good eye-hand training). The parents might supply an extra set of laces, which will be needed before the shoes are outgrown or worn out. White glue will help stiffen frayed ends that have lost their tips. By the second birthday, children can remove shoes (if untied), socks, and pants independently. They will still put two feet into one pant leg and hats on backward. They can put shoes on (not always on the correct feet) and can put socks on (sometimes the heel will be on top). Shoes can be color-coded with a dot of paint, or with different colored shoelaces. Only one shoe need be marked with a color. At this stage children

will also help pulling up and pushing down pants.

Children do not usually conquer buttoning by their third birthday, but they may be able to manipulate a sturdy zipper if it has a large tab, or if a large paper clip or metal ring has been fastened onto the original tab.

Clothes one or two sizes too large help immensely when the child is trying to conquer the skills of independent dressing. Velcro fasteners instead of shoe laces or buttons also lead to independence.

Grooming

Toothbrushing and handwashing are two essential grooming (and health) aids in the daily lives of very young children. Unfortunately they are sometimes overlooked.

Until toddlers have developed the coordination needed for purposefully using a soft toothbrush, their teeth and gums should be wiped clean with a damp cloth. Baby teeth arrive before the baby is able to understand "swish out your mouth," but a drink of water after each meal or snack will help remove food particles from between the teeth. At about 18 months, children should be provided with their own toothbrushes, but adults will need to do much of the actual brushing for several months to come.

Handwashing, or at least handwashing by the educarer, should be part of the daily routine from the very beginning. Hands should be washed before each snack and meal, as well as when the children come in from outdoor play, and after toileting. Prewashing skills are involved in every instance of water play: washing dolls, play dishes, and tables; finger-painting with soap suds, and playing with water or snow. Handwashing can be made special by having a dot of fragrant hand lotion to rub in after hands are dried. Liquid soap in a dispenser is easier to handle and more hygienic than a loose cake of soap.

Feeding and Eating

Information about bottle-feeding (not really a self-help skill) is given in the following chapters dealing with health and nutrition. The first item in the self-help component of feeding and eating is spoon-feeding.

Spoon-feeding. There is no need to introduce pureed or semisolid foods before 5 or 6 months, in spite of our apparent desires to rush baby into adulthood. A 5 or 6 month old will suck pureed foods from a spoon and can swallow them without choking. The educarer should use a spoon with a small, shallow bowl. It should be placed in baby's mouth from either side, with a slight downward pressure to counteract a tongue thrust. Baby will "chew" between 6 to 8 months if given soft foods such as banana pieces, mashed potatoes, or cottage cheese. By the first birthday, baby will lick food off a spoon, or lick an ice cream cone. Baby will learn to lick crumbs off the corners of his mouth if a bit of peanut butter is placed on the corner. Sometimes watching himself in a mirror will help him find the food with his tongue.

After the baby can self-feed with fingers, it is time to introduce eating with a spoon. Before then, while an adult is feeding him, there may be less interference if he has a spoon to hold during the process. When teaching baby to use a spoon, the adult and baby can first work through the motions together. A dish with a suction cup on the bottom will make it easier for the child to scoop with a spoon. Foods that stick to the spoon (mashed potatoes, applesauce) are easiest in the beginning stages. Loose foods such as peas or corn present additional challenges, and should be delayed for awhile. A fork should not be introduced until baby can chew solid foods, which should be cut into small pieces before serving.

Drinking. Between 6 to 8 months, baby will be able to hold the formula bottle, but this is no

reason not to hold him during feeding times. A small cup can be introduced now. Some babies like two-handled cups, and some do not want any handles at all. A small cup with a spouted cover is the best first cup. The cover may be removed at 10 to 12 months.

Feeding problems. There are probably fewer feeding problems in a group setting than there are in the individual homes. Meals should definitely not become battles in either place. During the second year, eating gets mixed up with the self-assertion drive, and a child may refuse whole meals or refuse any but the most familiar foods. This becomes a feeding problem only if the adults turn it into one. An environment that accepts temporary refusals to eat and in which other children are eating will diminish the child's protests very shortly. According to Brazelton (1974), "one good meal a day in the second year is about par for the course" (p. 62). Educarers and parents together can ensure the child's getting the equivalent of one good meal without much fuss.

Toileting

Toileting is a learning like all other learning in that it is a gradual process, with different stages at different times. First, the toddler must understand what we want him to do; then he must realize when he is *about* to urinate, not already doing it; third, he must get himself to the nearest bathroom; fourth, he has to be able to remove his clothing and sit on the potty or toilet; finally he must relax his sphincter muscles and let the urine come out (Rubin, Fisher, & Doering, 1980).

Brazelton (1974) suggests:

This developmental step can be treated like others, like those of feeding himself or of making choices about clothing. We can wait for him to learn at his own pace. . . . To treat toilet training differently from all of the child's other tasks places undue emphasis on it. It becomes a focus for attention. He uses it for rebellion, for negativism, to tease those around him. . . . The saddest part of pressing him to conform is that he loses the pleasure and excitement of achievement from mastering each step for himself (p. 143–144).

Problems arise when training is started too early or too late, or when the adults are pressuring for success. Fortunately, there are indications for toilet-training readiness, and these are not usually achieved until the child is 2 years old, or older, although he may indicate by motions or words his need to go to the toilet before that time.

During the first year, the infant urinates every few hours, usually has bowel movements after meals, stops his activity when having a bowel movement, and notices when his pants are wet. The toddler has his bowel movement in the toilet, and will look at and touch it; he knows ahead of time when he needs to go to the toilet, and will sometimes tell the adult, but often has "accidents."

How do we know the appropriate time to start toilet training? Signs of readiness are: (1) regularity; (2) awareness of self as the source; (3) ability to communicate; and (4) a dry diaper for more than an hour. By the time these indications of readiness are observed, the child will be far enough past the original excitement of walking that he is willing to sit still for short periods of time, and his voluntary sphincter control has developed.

The adults must be "ready" also. If the attitude of the adult is negative, hostile, or suggests rejection, the adult is not ready. If the adult's eagerness for success results in anxiety or tension, the adult is not ready.

Before training begins, the toddler should feel comfortable in the bathroom, and can even try out sitting on the potty chair or child-sized toilet with his clothes on, just to get the feel of it. The child should be able to sit with his feet on the floor so there is no fear of falling.

Just as teachers comment on any performance, the simple statement that "Eddie is having a BM in his diapers" will call Eddie's attention to the activity. Because he knows the teacher is interested in what he is doing, he will start to tell her when he is feeling the sensation, and he can be led to the toilet. For the first few times, the toilet should not be flushed until the child leaves.

Control of the bowels is achieved first. These movements are less frequent than urination and cause more internal pressure.

The same matter-of-fact approach should be used for bladder training: "Jean is wet" . . . "Jean is wetting now." When children are aware that they are the source of the puddle, they may point to it or even get a cloth to wipe it up.

"Toilet training, when initiated, shall follow a prescribed, sequential plan that is developed and coordinated with the parent's plan for implementation in the home environment" (Cohen, 1989, VII–2). During the training period, children should be placed on the toilet right after a meal or nap when success might be anticipated. Putting them into training pants will be a psychological help when they are ready for bladder training. In the beginning, however, diapers are still best during nap time.

Brazelton (1974) suggests waiting to begin training until after age 2. For the impatient, there are quicker training methods.

> Two behaviorists (Azrin & Foxx, 1981) suggest that children over twenty months of age can be taught to use the potty by imitation and rewards. The success rate is high for daytime dryness, but two-thirds of the children who were trained in this manner continue wetting at night (Anselmo, 1987, p. 260).

Children are not intrinsically motivated to be toilet trained. They submit to it primarily to gain the love and approval of persons who are significant in their lives. Cooperation between home and center is very important. Parents and educarers should agree as to the initial starting time, to the approach to be used, and to the words to be used. It can be suggested to the parents that the child might observe them in the bathroom, and also that the child wear clothes that are easy to remove. Of course the parents should provide a spare set of clothes, and most centers also keep extras on hand. There should be accurate exchanges of information about the progress being made in both locations.

A last word of advice from Brazelton (1974) is

> don't use the guards which are commonly provided on seats for training little boys, to divert their urine. Sooner or later the child gets hurt by them as he climbs on or off the pot, and it may slow up the training process. They serve no necessary purpose anyway, for he will be intrigued with the process of holding down and aiming his penis into the pot, as soon as he realizes that he can make noise that way (p. 144).

The adult's role is somewhat easier in an infant/toddler setting with mixed ages, or even with children older than 3 years. The younger children have a natural inclination to identify with older children in the learning of a new skill, and may imitate many behaviors, including toileting.

SUMMARY

The specialists in physical and recreational education have agreed to the following listing of the values of movement. Movement is a medium (1) to get in touch with ourselves; (2) for the development of a positive sense of self; (3) for self-expression; (4) for learning about the environment; (5) for interacting with others; and (6) that is important for its own sake.

As children grow and develop, they must acquire skill in managing their bodies and in managing objects. Body management is first in importance. Body control begins in the head and neck region and progresses along the spine into the torso. It proceeds from control of the whole to control of the specific parts. The control of body posture and movement

depends on sensory feedback, both kinesthetic and visual.

During the infant/toddler years, gross motor skills progress from rolling to sitting to creeping-crawling to standing to walking to running and jumping. These skills are best learned when they are provided for in the normal routines of group living. The smooth co-ordination of these locomotor skills is enhanced by accompanying musical sounds or beats. Climbing and jumping and throwing and catching are movement activities that develop after the child is a somewhat coordinated walker. Of course, even before the first birthday, climbing is sometimes an extension of creeping or crawling.

The fine motor skills develop from swiping to grasping with whole hands to picking up small objects with a pincer grasp (thumb and index finger), which, of course, enables the child to manipulate objects, first at random, and then purposefully.

Coordination of gross and fine motor skills can be encouraged by action games and circle activities, by playing "catch," and by the appropriate use of various art materials. Active play, especially play with blocks for gross motor skills, and play (or exploration and manipulation) with objects in activity boxes for fine motor skills, is the most appropriate approach to movement education during these early years.

Motor skills are very important and necessary for the learning of the self-help skills of independent dressing and grooming, feeding and eating, and toileting. They are best taught in an accepting environment by persons who are significant in the lives of the children.

SUGGESTED ACTIVITIES AND QUESTIONS

1. Explain the relationship of the development of motor skills, social skills, and cognitive skills.

2. Why were art activities introduced in this chapter on motor skill development?

3. What is meant by the statement "Children learn through both play and work"? Give examples of play as learning, and of work as learning.

4. Observe toddlers, focusing on the self-help skills.

5. Add to your picture collection by including pictures that illustrate various kinds of motor skills.

SUGGESTED READINGS

Badger, E. (1981). *Infant/toddler: Introducing your child to the joy of learning.* Toys'n Things Press, c/o Resources for Child Caring Inc., 906 N. Dale, St. Paul, MN 55103.

Cataldo, C. Z. (1983). *Infant and Toddler programs: A guide to very early childhood education* (ch. 3). Reading, MA: Addison-Wesley.

Chance, P. (1979). *Learning through play.* Pediatric Round Table 3. New York: Gardner Press.

Clare, C. (1977). *Creative movement for the developing child* (rev. ed.). Belmont, CA: Fearon.

Cole, J. (1989). *Your new potty.* New York: Morrow.

Curtis, S. (1982). *The joy of movement in early childhood.* New York: Teachers College Press.

Diem, L. (1974). *Children learn physical skills,* Vol. 1 (Birth to 3 years). Washington, DC: American Alliance for Health, Physical Education, and Recreation.

Dinsmore, K. E. (1989). The fallacies and dangers of baby exercise programs. *Focus on infancy, 1* (3), 1–2. (ACEI Division for Infancy).

Fein, G., & Rivkin, M. (Eds.). (1986). *The young child at play: Reviews of research.* Vol. 4. Washington, DC: National Association for the Education of Young Children.

Flinchum, B. (1975). *Motor development in early childhood: A guide for movement education with ages 2–6.* St. Louis, MO: Mosby.

Foxx, R. M., & Azrin, N. H. (1973). Dry pants: A rapid method of toilet training children. *Behavior Research and Therapy, 11,* 435–442.

Fucigna, C., Ives, K. C., & Ives, W. (1982). Art for toddlers: A developmental approach. *Young Children, 37* (3), 45-51.

Gonzalez-Mena, J., & Eyer, D. W. (1980). *Infancy and caregiving* (Ch. 7). Palo Alto, CA: Mayfield.

Gordon, I. J. (1977). *Baby to parent to baby: A guide to developing parent-child interaction in the first twelve months.* New York: St. Martin's Press.

Gordon, I. J., Guinagh, B., & Jester, R. E. (1971). *Child learning through child play: Learning activities for two and three year olds.* New York: St. Martin's Press.

Hirsch, E. S. (Ed.). (1984). *The block book* (2nd ed.). Washington, DC: National Association for the Education of Young Children.

Hoben, A. (1989). Our thoughts on diapering and potty training. *Young Children, 44* (6), 28–29.

Johnson, H. M. (1933). *The art of block building.* New York: John Day.

Keogh, J., & Sugden, D. (1985). *Movement skill development.* New York: Macmillan.

Lansky, V. (1984). *Toilet training.* New York: Bantam.

Leavitt, R. L., & Eheart, B. K. (1985). *Toddler day care; A guide to responsive caregiving* (ch. 2). Lexington, MA: Lexington Books.

Mack, A. (1978). *Toilet learning: The picture book technique for children and parents.* Boston: Little, Brown.

Malina, R. M. (1982). Motor development in the early years. In S. G. Moore & C. Cooper (Eds.), *The young child: Reviews of research.* Vol. 4 (pp. 211–230). Washington, DC: National Association for the Education of Young Children.

Matterson, E. (1971). *Games for the very young: Finger plays and nursery games.* New York: American Heritage Press.

O'Brien, M., Porterfield, J., Herbert-Jackson, E., & Risley, T. R. (1979). *The toddler center: A practical guide to day care for one- and two-year-olds.* Baltimore: University Park Press.

Oppenheim, J. F. (1985). *Kids and play.* (ch. 1–4). New York: Ballantine.

Rubin, R., Fisher, J., & Doering, S. (1980). *Your Toddler.* New York: Macmillan.

Segal, M. (1985). *Your child at play: Birth to one year.* New York; Newmarket.

Segal, M., & Adcock, D. (1985a). *Your child at play: One to two years.* New York: Newmarket.

Segal, M., & Adcock, D. (1985b). *Your child at play: Two to three years.* New York: Newmarket.

Sinclair, C. B. (1978). *Movement of the young child ages two to six.* Columbus, OH: Merrill.

Sparling, J., & Lewis, I. (1979). *Learningames for the first three years.* New York: Walker.

Sullivan, M. (1982). *Feeling strong, feeling free: Movement exploration for young children.* Washington, DC: National Association for the Education of Young Children.

Sutton-Smith, B., & Sutton-Smith, S. (1974). *How to play with your children (and when not to)*. New York: Hawthorn.

Watrin, R., & Furfey, P. H. (1978). *Learning activities for the young preschool child*. New York: D. Van Nostrand.

Weikart, P. S. (1985). *Movement plus music*. Ypsilanti, MI: High/Scope.

Williams, C. K., & Kamii, C. (1986). How do children learn by handling objects? *Young Children, 42* (1), 23–26.

THREE

The Care and Protection Curriculum

One of the ironies of the current emphasis on the developmental care and education of very young children is an apparently decreasing emphasis on the health and safety components in any child-care setting, whether in a group center or in a family day-care home. For instance, many center goal statements are prefaced in the following manner: "Assuming health and safety provisions have been made, our goals are . . . ", and the stated goals are directed toward the encouragement of the cognitive and social-emotional development of the children. We cannot assume anything so vital; we just might be throwing out the baby with the bath water.

The care and protection curriculum includes the health, nutrition, and safety of children and their educarers and merits as detailed attention as the developmental or educational curriculum in the behavioral, social-emotional, and cognitive domains. Ideally, the health and safety components should be so well known and internalized that the adults' conscious attention is freed to focus on the developmental aspects of the program.

Just as we cannot assume that the health and safety needs will be met by the adults—even conscientious, loving adults—we should not assume that group living for very young children automatically increases the risks of accidents or illness. It is very possible that such risks can be minimized in a quality center.

The chapters in Part Three present the essential components of the care and protection curriculum designed for the group care of infants and toddlers.

6

The Health Component

The health of the people is really the foundation upon which all their happiness and their powers as a state depend.

Benjamin Disraeli (1877)

HEALTH GOALS

The American Academy of Pediatrics (1980) has proposed national child health goals as follows:

- All children should be wanted and born to healthy mothers.
- All children should be born well.
- All children should be immunized against the preventable infectious diseases for which there are recommended immunization procedures.
- All children should have good nutrition.
- All children should be educated about health and health care systems.
- All children should live in a safe environment.
- All children with chronic handicaps should be able to function at their optimal level.
- All children should live in a family setting with an adequate income to provide basic needs to

ensure physical, mental, and intellectual health.
- All children should live in an environment that is as free as possible from contaminants.
- All adolescents and young people should live in a societal setting that recognizes their special health, personal, and social needs.

(Copyright © American Academy of Pediatrics, 1980)

Although the United States is the only industrialized nation that has not adopted in principle or practice the right to health care for all children, we in very early childhood care and education can meet at least six of these national goals. Many parents (and some educarers) think that the health of children suffers when mothers work away from the home, and child care is provided away from the home. The research findings are mixed. The most recent study (Illnesses in day care children, 1989) shows that hospitalizations were more frequent for illnesses contracted by children under 3 who were enrolled in child-care centers than those cared for in family day-care homes and in their own homes. The greatest number of hospitalizations were for ear infections, followed by bronchitis and stomach problems.

We now have the know-how, some data, and in most cases the essential support systems to provide preventive and corrective health care to our infants and toddlers in an effective and systematic way. Such a provision is an essential component of every center and day-care home.

It is only in the last half of the 20th century that group care and education of very young children could be recommended. The discovery of vaccines and antibiotics has virtually wiped out the dangers of serious illnesses and epidemics of childhood diseases. But the bad news is that more than 40% of children under age 4 have not received the complete basic series of immunizations (National Association of Children's Hospitals and Related Institutions, 1989).

What do we want in terms of health for our very young children? We want to improve every child's present functioning and we want to help ensure every child's future health. Day-care providers cannot meet these goals in isolation from the parents, from professional health persons and resources, or from the community at large. The most often quoted statement of health goals for children in day care was first published in the series of day-care handbooks sponsored by the former Office of Child Development and written by Dr. Frederick North in 1973. It reads as follows:

I. To improve a child's present function by:
   A. Finding all existing health problems through:
      (i) Accumulating records of past health and immunization status.
      (ii) Considering the observations of classroom teachers and other staff.
      (iii) Performing screening tests; including tuberculin, hematocrit or hemoglobin, vision testing, hearing testing.
      (iv) Interviewing the child and his parents about his current and past health and function.
      (v) Performing a physical examination as part of a complete health evaluation.
   B. Remedying any existing problems through:
      (i) Applying whatever medical or dental treatments are necessary.
      (ii) Arranging for rehabilitative services, special education, and other forms of continuing care.
      (iii) Applying mental health principles in the classroom or group.
II. To ensure a child's future health by:
   A. Providing preventive services including:
      (i) Immunization against infectious diseases.
      (ii) Fluoride treatment to prevent tooth decay.
      (iii) Health education for children and parents.
      (iv) Introducing the child to a physician and dentist who will be responsible for his continuing health care.
      (v) Assuring that the day care setting and the home provide a safe and stimulating environment.
   B. Improving the health of all members of the child's family through:
      (i) Calling attention to family health needs.
      (ii) Introducing the family to health care services, and to sources of funds for these services.
   C. Improving the health of the community in which the child lives through:
      (i) Increasing the awareness and concern of professionals and the gen-

eral population with the health problems of children.

(ii) Stimulating and providing new resources for health care.

(iii) Making existing health resources more responsive to the special needs of children and parents (p. 8).

I would like to add another subgoal for an infant-toddler center. This goal rarely appears in a formal statement. It is to prevent, or at least minimize, the child's resistance to medical procedures or medical persons. Causes of such resistance may be "natural" ones, such as the stranger anxiety syndrome so often evidenced in the months after the first half-year of life. No doubt the white lab coat or uniform emphasizes the strangeness of this new person. Perhaps this is the reason why doctors, nurses, and others who work with young children have discarded their usual attire and dress in street clothes. It would seem that this defeats the purpose. Our efforts to teach a child that the nurse or doctor is a friend will be effective only if the nurse or doctor is dressed in some distinguishing manner and acts like a friend.

Other causes of violent resistance include letting the child "get away" with such behavior, lack of trust in the world and the people in it, and lies or threats. Such statements as "We are just going shopping" (but ending up at the doctor's office), and "It won't hurt" (when it will) naturally build resistance to health care. It is a recognized fact that children, even under the age of 3, understand both the words and actions of other persons and behave accordingly. Their inability to verbally express emotion does not preclude their ability to express emotion in other ways. When the circumstances warrant it, the approach to health care or health personnel might be an appropriate topic for discussion with parents.

These goals can be met in an infant/toddler center or a family day-care home.

GOAL I: TO IMPROVE A CHILD'S PRESENT FUNCTION

HEALTH POLICIES AND FORMS

Preliminary Planning

Each center or group of centers (or family day-care providers) should involve persons and organizations in planning their health component to ensure that *their* health program is tailored to meet the needs of *their* children, and that it uses the available community resources and does not duplicate already existing services. In order to achieve the comprehensive goals as set forth, the health program must be planned by professionally competent persons who are dedicated to bringing high quality health services to all children. This planning must take place well before the day-care program begins and children are enrolled.

A single individual should bear the responsibility for planning and carrying out the health program. This person might be a pediatrician, a public health physician, or a general practitioner with particular interest in and concern for the health of very young children. This person may volunteer services or be paid as a part- or full-time employee or consultant of one large center or several smaller ones. It is wise strategy to include as many relevant organizations and individuals as possible during the planning stages. Those who are involved early in the planning are more likely to cooperate in the implementation of the program. In addition to pediatricians or interested physicians, consider child psychiatrists and psychologists and their organizations; dentists and dental associations, speech and hearing personnel and their associations; hospital administrators; county and state medical societies; and local, regional, and state health officers. Although not usually included in a day-care health planning committee, the local fire marshal is not only an expert on fire prevention, but also on all procedures related to any disaster such as tornado, flood, and hurricane. Nonphysician health personnel, such as the pediatric nurse practitioner and the medical assistant in pediatrics are increasing in numbers and are valuable allies for day-care centers. And let us not ignore the essential role of the parents of the children to be enrolled. They often know a great deal about what community resources are available and which meet expected standards. Parents can give valuable input as to the feasibility of any plan proposed by "experts."

Keeping in mind the health goals of all children in day care and the various kinds of expertise held by any or all of the above resources, it is possible to formulate a health policy statement for an individual infant-toddler day-care center (and, or course, for a center serving older children as well). The example of the health policy in Figure 6–1 is the result of a group endeavor by health professionals, a multidisciplinary advisory council including selected staff members, selected parents, and references to current editions of relevant publications of the American Academy of Pediatrics, the Child Welfare League of America, and the American Public Health Association.

As new standards are introduced, the health policy (and other policies) must be updated. The draft standards of the American Public Health Association and the American Academy of Pediatrics (Cohen, 1989) contain the current thinking about health and safety standards for center-based care and group and family day care. They also include the provisions necessary for the integration of disabled or "at-risk" children into care settings of nondisabled peers.

Implementation

As stated previously, a single individual should have the responsibility for planning and carrying out the health program. However, unless this person is one of the paid employees of the center, he or she should not be expected to continue with the time-consuming administration of the health program on a routine basis. The outsider

Giving medication with TLC instead of a "spoonful of sugar." (Early Childhood Education Center)

who has agreed to assist in the formulation of a health policy and perhaps in setting up the implementation of the policy should then be relieved of the ongoing implementation. The role of the health professional becomes that of consultant in case of emergencies or when revisions are needed in policy or practice. Many centers employ a registered nurse or pediatric nurse practitioner (PNP) on a part- or full-time basis for the regular delivery of the health component. Others have been able to employ a person who qualifies as both a registered nurse or PNP and an educarer. This arrangement would appear to be both practical and ideal, depending on the number of children enrolled. However, specific guidelines and time allotments must be agreed on in writing as to the health component and the educaring component. It is a common occurrence to use such a person as almost a "permanent substitute" in the classroom, thereby allowing too little time for the health component of the program. Sometimes the services of a visiting nurse may be obtained once or twice a week. If this is the case, there needs to be someone in the center who holds current certifications in first aid and pediatric CPR and who will assume the major responsibility for the daily delivery of health services. This person must be able to recognize the signs of childhood illnesses, and would have responsibility for contacting community resources and the medical consultant and for parent-center relationships with regard to health issues. This person may also be designated to give any medications. Three important and sometimes difficult tasks to be performed are: (1) being sure every child receives the routine tests, health evaluations, and immunizations; (2) being sure that every child who is found to have a health problem receives the necessary evaluation and treatment, as specified in a child's individualized plan of services if one exists; and (3) being sure that every child (and family) is introduced to a physician who can be responsible for the child's future care. In very small centers or family day-care homes, the director, owner, or head teacher might assume these tasks, or there might be a division of labor; however, one person should be the coordinator and carry the responsibilities. This person probably will also fill the role of the coordinator of procedures in suspected child abuse and neglect cases.

Admission Procedures

Admission policies and their related forms will vary from center to center and from one day-care home to another. Regardless of location, number of children served, or sponsorship, each center or home should have an initial information-sharing meeting.

The informational meeting. The initial meeting provides the opportunity for the center

representative to explain the program, hours, meal service, facilities, and other information. Ideally, each parent visited the center and had such a discussion before deciding on enrolling the child. Even if this has been the case, many items bear repeating. In addition, each family will have questions of their own. It is a big and important decision to assign the care and education of a very young child to someone other than a family member in a location other than the home. Even when outside care for the child is essential, for whatever reason, many parents are plagued with guilt feelings.

A staff member's willingness to spend an unhurried time period and to answer or discuss any and all relevant items is the first important part of the mental health component of the center's program. The bond between the parents and their infant or toddler is very close. Even before young children can understand the meaning of words, they can sense their parents' fears or doubts, and are adversely affected by them. Therefore we do whatever possible to allay these fears or doubts in the minds of the parents. This is one reason why the initial interview is so important. Another purpose of the interview is to obtain background information about the child that will make the transition from home to center as smooth as possible.

When possible, the educarer who will assume major responsibility for the child is the best person to talk with the parent(s). It seems to be the custom in the larger centers to assign admission procedures to the director or nurse as an efficient use of time. If this is the system in a particular center, it is absolutely essential that the parent(s) and the responsible educarer also have an unhurried period when they can discuss mutual concerns to minimize any doubts the parents may have.

The admission interview. Shortly before the child begins regular attendance, the parent(s) and educarer should meet again, this time for the purpose of obtaining developmental information about the child. Responses should be

Figure 6–1

Sample Health Policy for an Infant-toddler Child-care Center

10. Administration

The health program will be the joint responsibility of the Center staff and professional health consultants. Periodic reviews of the health program will be undertaken to ensure its implementation and to assess the need for modification or revision. The health policies relate to both children and adults involved in the Center.

20. Admission policies

Parents are required to provide the following information for each child enrolled:

21. Information about the child's previous and current developmental history.

22. A statement from a licensed health practitioner that:

    a. Describes any special precautions for diet, medication, or activity.

    b. States that the child has received immunizations in accordance with recommendations of the U.S. Public Health Service or the American Academy of Pediatrics. (These immunization requirements may be waived or modified according to the code of an individual state.)

    c. States that the child has received a health assessment in accordance with the standards of the American Academy of Pediatrics, or the EPSDT National Recommended Health Assessment Plan.

    22.1 The above statement for each child must be on record within 60 days of admission, and must be updated according to the American Academy of Pediatrics, or the EPSDT National Recommended Health Assessment Plan.

    22.2 Smallpox vaccinations are no longer routine in the United States. However, any infant receiving smallpox vaccine will be excluded from attendance at the Center until the scab has fallen off.

23. Verification that the child has received a tuberculin skin test at the time of, or preceding, the measles immunization, with adequate follow-up for positive reactors.

24. Source of the child's regular health care (pediatrician, physician, or health resource responsible for on-going health care), including name, address, and phone number. Also an authorization signed by the parent(s) or guardian for emergency treatment of the child.

25. Name, address, and telephone number of persons in addition to parent(s) or guardian who have agreed to accept responsibility for the child if the child becomes ill and the primary caregivers cannot be contacted.

30. Health supervision

31. *Center staff responsibility*

    31.1 It shall be the responsibility of the director (or designated staff) to supervise the administration of medication. Nonprescription medications will be given with signed authorization of the parent. Prescription medication must:

    a. Be prescribed by a physician.

    b. Contain the following information on the container:
Child's name
Physician's name
Name of medication
Directions for administering
Duration it is to be given.

    c. Be accompanied by a written request and authorization by parent or guardian. Records of these prescriptions and authorization will be maintained on file. The Center will maintain a record of the dates and hours the medications are given, as well as the staff member who administered the medication. All medications are to be kept in locked cabinets out of children's reach and in a separate location from where food is stored or prepared.

    31.2 It shall be the responsibility of the director (or designated staff) to integrate the health components of the Individualized Family Service Plan (PL. 99–457) in care plans for the children covered by the plan.

    31.3 A staff member shall regularly seek to meet with the parent(s) or guardian to share a summary of the information on the child's growth, development, behavior, nutritional habits, and any special problems. The parents will provide reports of interval immunization and health care and evaluation the child has received. The list of names of professional health persons or resources, as well as the parent(s) or guardian, will be brought up to date. Recommendations should be developed by the parent(s) or guardian and the staff for the child so that there will be a coordinated program of care in the Center and home.

    31.4 There shall be daily communication on problems of diet, illness, and behavior between parent(s) or guardian and staff.

    31.5 Staff shall provide information to parents as needed concerning child health services available in the community, and shall assist parents in obtaining the health services.

    31.6 A screening program will be implemented for each child for the purpose of recognizing

Figure 6–1
continuing

health impairments. The program includes a minimum of (a) periodic vision screening, (b) periodic hearing testing, (c) periodic weight and growth measurements.

31.7 Children will be assisted in acquiring knowledge and health practices appropriate to their age and development. Consultation with parents will allow reasonable consistency in handling the child between the home and the Center. This includes information about promoting good dental health (daily care, early dental inspection, adequate nutrition, fluoridation, and salvage of injured teeth).

32. *Sanitary procedures*

32.1 The Center will provide facilities and promote the practice of washing hands and face before and after meals, and hands after using toilet facilities and after outdoor activities.

32.2 Wet or soiled clothing shall be changed promptly. An adequate emergency supply will be available at the Center.

32.3 Soiled disposable diapers will be placed in a lined, covered step can. Soiled cloth diapers will be put in a plastic bag, securely tied, then put into a larger, labeled, plastic bag to go home.

33. *Staff in-service training health goals*

33.1 To develop increasing ability to appraise the health status of children.

33.2 To develop increasing ability to recognize deviations (either behavioral or physical) from group and individual health status.

33.3 To be knowledgeable about appropriate community health resources.

33.4 To promote the use of preventive and corrective measures in interactions with parents.

33.5 To teach positive health and safety behavior by example and instruction of children and their parent(s) or guardian.

40. Management of child who appears ill

41. A child who appears tired, ill, or upset will be given the opportunity to rest in a quiet area under frequent observation. Center staff will give the child an appropriate health appraisal, involving, for instance, measurement of temperature, assessment through observation and responses from the child regarding symptoms, general appearance, appetite, and activity level. Parents will be notified either during the day or at the end of the day, at the discretion of Center staff.

42. If a child appears acutely ill and uncomfortable, parents will be informed and asked to seek medical care as soon as possible. If parents cannot be contacted, Center staff will contact the individuals designated as per #24.

43. A child may be cared for at the Center during minor illness at the discretion of the parents and the staff.

44. Any child who frequently requires seclusion and health observation for fatigue, illness, or emotional upset will be discussed with the parents and a complete medical evaluation will be suggested. The Center staff will provide the family with a complete report of the observations of the child. If the special needs of the child cannot be met at the Center, the Center retains the right to disenroll the child.

45. Parents will be notified if their child has been exposed to a communicable disease. When isolated cases occur, children may be asked to remain at home during the time when they are most likely to develop the disease. This may help to prevent rapid spread of the disease. Parents will be told what symptoms to expect.

46. Readmission to the Center following illness is dependent on the individual child's diagnosis and should be a mutual responsibility of parents and Center staff. When the protection of the other children is involved, the director may have the prerogative of requiring a physician's certification of health before the child reenters the Center.

47. Medical consultation will be available to the director to aid in establishing policies for management of current illness or threat of illness.

50. Management of accidents

51. The center nurse or other appropriate persons (local or state social service or health department personnel) shall evaluate the physical facility at least semiannually to determine that it is reasonably free from common hazards, including lead. Daily vigilance will be maintained to "police" the environment.

52. All staff members working with children will be given instruction in first aid principles, including control of bleeding, management of seizures, administration of artificial respiration, cardiopulmonary resuscitation, and splinting of fractures.

53. The Center nurse will assist the staff in developing routine procedures for the treatment of minor injuries. These procedures shall be written and posted with the first aid materials. The current First Aid Chart from the American Academy of Pediatrics will be used as the basic first aid reference.

54. There shall also be written, posted procedures for disaster (including fire), ingestion of poison, and the management of more serious injuries. First aid measures and the procedures to be followed in bringing children to emergency medical care shall also be posted. (First aid measures for more serious accidents will be primarily based on the cur-

Figure 6–1
continuing

rent edition of *School Health: A Guide for Physicians,* American Academy of Pediatrics.)

55. The Center will negotiate arrangements with the local hospital emergency facilities to provide emergency medical care.

56. First aid supplies will be maintained in the Center.

57. If a child has an accident during the day, the parent or designated responsible person shall be notified. A record of accident or injury shall be kept in the child's permanent health form. Records of accidents shall be reviewed by the medical consultant and staff, semiannually.

60. Employee health

61. An employee with a disease that can be transmitted represents a threat to the health of the children

and the other adults. The most important considerations are tuberculosis and hepatitis. All employees, volunteers, and others, including food handlers, housekeepers and van drivers, should be screened for tuberculosis and hepatitis. The form of screening is dependent upon conditions in the community.

62. Employees will be told that they may not be in contact with children or food service at times when they have respiratory infections, skin infections, or other types of communicable disease.

63. A health examination by a physician will be required before the first day of activities at the Center and should be annually updated. The signed examination form will become part of the employee's file.

recorded in an organized way. The kinds of information desired are suggested in the Background Information form (appendix E). Even though many parents are capable of reading the questions and writing the answers, the center-parent relationship is enhanced when the questions and answers are discussed face-to-face. Parents like to talk about their children. They should be given the opportunity to do so.

At the time of the admission interview or within 60 days of admission, parents are required to provide a statement from a licensed health practitioner describing any special precautions for diet, activity, or medication. An additional statement is also required certifying that the child has received a health assessment in accordance with the standards of the American Academy of Pediatrics (AAP), the EPSDT National Recommended Health Assessment Plan, or the U.S. Public Health Service, including immunization status. The current AAP's recommended schedule for active immunization of normal infants and children is as follows:

Age	Immunization
2 mo.	DTP–Diphtheria and Tetanus toxoids combined with pertussis vaccine
2 mo.	OPV–Oral poliovirus vaccine
4 mo.	DTP; OPV
6 mo.	DTP; OPV is optional
15 mo.	MMR–Measles, mumps, rubella
18 mo.	DTP; OPV
24 mo.	HBPV–Haemophilus b polysaccharide vaccine

(Adapted, AAP, 1987)

Because recommendations are updated frequently and new vaccines are developed, a pediatrician's advice is always necessary. For instance, there has now been a recommendation to require a first measles shot to be given at 9 months in high-risk areas because of a large increase in numbers of cases. Also, the HBPV (or Hib) vaccine was not included in the AAP recommendations appearing in the first edition of this text. A very new vaccine (PRP-D), which replaces the HIB, can be safely administered at 18 months (Shelov, 1989). Because the situation changes rapidly, it is essential for parents and educarers to have professional advice.

No vaccine is 100% effective in each child. However, "if enough children in a given area are immunized, the whole group is protected because each child has less chance of coming into contact with the disease" (Shelov, 1989, p. 44).

As with any medication or immunization, there are always risks and side effects to be considered along with the potential benefits. The risk of permanent damage or death is negligible, when one considers how many children would be seriously damaged or would die without the vaccine. This fact has been recognized by the United States Congress through passage of the Vaccine Compensation Act of 1988.

Not all states require immunizations before or soon after enrollment for infants and toddlers. A few may require it for these children in center programs, but not in family day-care homes.

The *Manual of Policies and Procedures: Day Care Centers* from California has detailed requirements for immunizations for enrollment in elementary and secondary schools, and in child-care centers, day nurseries, nursery schools, and development centers (but not for family day care). However, they allow the following exemptions:

1. A physician provides a written statement that immunization is not indicated and specifies the duration of the exemption if it is temporary.
2. The parents provide a written statement that immunization is contrary to their personal or religious beliefs.
3. Such written statements shall be maintained in the center for as long as the child is enrolled (1987, Section 101320.1).

Experience and our nation's policy of civil rights have necessitated such an exemption policy.

Immunization information must be given to the parents. They must know first of all for what reasons immunization is advised for their child. It is a good thing to explain to them what measles or poliomyelitis really mean, and what ravages they caused before immunization was known. They must also be told:

- where and when their children can be immunized

- what effect the immunization will have
- the recommended date for the next injection, with emphasis on the fact that it is necessary in order to complete the child's protection

Other Policies and Forms

Information about the health professional or resource responsible for the ongoing health care of the child may be easily recorded on an index card, and is another essential part of the child's folder. At the same time, parents should fill in a "release of child to adult other than parent" form. Although the parents may have every intention of *always* picking up their child at the end of each daily session, unforeseen happenings may prevent this on occasion. No child-care center should release a child to *anyone* other than the primary caregiver, usually the parent(s) or guardian, unless such written permission is given. At all times we must ensure the child's safety. This policy is particularly important during this period of time when child custody cases and "kidnappings" by one parent occasionally occur. This same precaution is one of the reasons for requesting a "consent for photographs," which may or may not be given. The child's enrollment is not affected by this, however. Such a form might be worded as in Figure 6–2.

A "consent for travel" form, when secured at the time of enrollment, will save future last minute arrangements. An example is found in Figure 6–3.

The above forms are indirectly related to the health and safety components of a day-care center or home. Of direct relationship to the health and safety component is an authorization for emergency treatment of the child. This authorization is a must. Ideally, it will never have to be used. Because of its seriousness and the possible liabilities that may be involved, it is not phrased in casual terms, but in a formal style, such as that shown in Figure 6–4 (p. 156).

Figure 6–2
Consent for photographs.

ABC Day Care Center

CONSENT for PHOTOGRAPHS

I/we consent _____ do not consent _____ to photographs being taken of my/our child, _____

_____ , at the ABC Day Care Center to be used for informational, scientific, or

publicity purposes.

This authorization shall remain effective from the time of enrollment until August 1, 19 _ , and will be updated

each August thereafter that my/our child is enrolled in the ABC Day Care Center.

_____
Father

_____
Mother

_____
Legal Guardian

_____
Date

Executed forms and information that should be part of every child's folder in any day-care center or home include the following:

1. Statement from a licensed health practitioner or health resource that:
   a. describes special health precautions for the child
   b. states that the child has received appropriate immunizations
   c. states that the child has received a health assessment
   d. verifies that the child has received a tuberculin skin test
2. Statement of the source of the child's regular health care
3. Statement of authorization of emergency treatment

Optional but highly recommended forms or information include the following:

1. Release of child to adult other than parent
2. Consent for photographs

Figure 6–3
Consent for travel.

ABC Day Care Center

CONSENT for TRAVEL

I/we consent _____ do not consent _____ that my/our child, _____

_____ , be taken by the ABC Day Care Center on its various field trips away from the school premises.

This authorization shall remain effective from the time of enrollment until August 1, 19 ____ , and will be updated

each August thereafter that my/our child is enrolled in the ABC Day Care Center.

_____
Father

_____
Mother

_____
Legal Guardian

_____
Date

---

3. Consent for travel
4. Background information about child

Information Exchanges

The responsibilities of the center staff include periodic information exchanges with each child's primary caregiver(s) about that child's growth, development, behavior, nutritional habits, and any special problems. In turn, the parents or guardian will provide reports of interval immunization and health care and evaluation that the child has received. Forms signed at the time of enrollment should be updated. Any changes that have immediate application should be made immediately rather than waiting to set up an appointment. Frequently, parents will wish to add to the list of persons who may pick up the child, for instance, as car pools are formed or as conditions at home change.

In addition to these exchanges on either an immediate or scheduled basis, there should be daily communication between the parent or guardian and the educarer at the center. This may be no more than a greeting and "How are things going?" However, building into the pro-

Figure 6–4
Authorization to consent to emergency treatment.

ABC Day Care Center

AUTHORIZATION TO CONSENT TO EMERGENCY TREATMENT OF MINOR

I/we, the undersigned, parent(s) of _____ , a minor, do hereby authorize the Director of the ABC Day Care Center, or the Director's authorized representative, as agent for the undersigned, in case of emergency, to consent to any x-ray examination, anesthetic, medical, or surgical diagnosis or treatment and hospital care that is deemed advisable by, and is to be rendered under the general or special supervision of any physician and surgeon on the Medical Staff of _____ Hospital, whether such diagnosis or treatment is rendered at the office of said physician or at said hospital. We further authorize the aforesaid agent to consent to any emergency dental services that may be deemed advisable by and are rendered under the supervision of dentists on the staff of the _____ Hospital.

It is understood that this authorization is given in advance of any specific diagnosis, treatment, hospital care, or dental services being required but is given to provide authority and power on the part of our aforesaid agent to give specific consent to any and all such diagnosis, treatment, hospital care, or dental services that the aforementioned physician, surgeon, or dentist in the exercise of his/her best judgment may deem advisable.

In the event any medical services are rendered to my/our child pursuant to this authorization to consent, I/we request that the Director of the ABC Day Care Center notify my/our family physician.

Physician _____

Address _____

Telephone Number _____

This authorization shall remain effective from the time of enrollment until August 1, 19 __ , and will be updated each August thereafter that the aforesaid minor is enrolled in the ABC Day Care Center, _____
_____ .
      address

_____
Father

_____
Mother

_____
Legal Guardian

_____
Date

Arrival at the center; baby is ready to join his friends. (Early Childhood Education Center)

gram the requirement of daily person-to-person contact ensures the opportunity for the exchange of more vital information when necessary. A good rule to enforce is that the parent or other authorized adult personally deliver the child to the educarer. The picture clearly shows that this mother is well satisfied with her arrangements for day care, as she delivers her baby. Note that the baby's attention has already been drawn to the on-going activities of the earlier arrivals. The rule of personal pick-up at the end of the day is equally valid. There are definite positive gains derived from this individualized pick-up and delivery system, in addition to providing an opportunity for exchange of information.

Further suggestions and comments about parent-center sharing of information, health and otherwise, will be presented in chapter 11.

Community Health Resources

Almost every community will have available many health resources. The day-care health coordinator and the policy planning committee should investigate each source of funds and services. These sources include:

- Private practitioners of medicine, dentistry, psychology
- Health departments—city, county, regional, state
- Clinics run by hospitals, medical schools, or other agencies
- Prepaid medical groups
- Neighborhood health centers
- Comprehensive child health centers
- Dental service corporations
- Special voluntary or public agencies, usually concerned with a single category of disease or handicap
- State *Children with Special Health Care Needs* programs, limited to certain categories of illness
- Medical assistance under Medicaid (funds for diagnostic and treatment services for a wide range of health problems for poor children)
- Community mental health programs
- County department of social services
- Community colleges or universities for screening, staff development
- State day-care training offices

- State sanitation office
- Preventive dentistry programs
- Area health education centers
- Area education associations
- Red Cross, especially for caregiver instruction in first aid and related fields
- County extension agents, especially for nutrition education
- Hospital emergency rooms

The day-care program may contract with existing agencies to provide some or all of the health services, but responsibility for the quality and coordination of these services remains with the day-care center staff.

Giving such a list as the above to parents who inquire about (or need) funds or services is worthless. Only the day-care center or its health coordinator can make this list meaningful by personal contact and investigation of each health resource with regard to the needs of the children enrolled. Some of the resources listed above are nonexistent in a specific community, and some of the resources provide services only for certain categories of children or for certain problems. It is very possible that some of the resources are not available to children below the age of 3 years. Keeping these limitations in mind, the list is a good starting point for on-the-scene investigation.

Knowing the location of support systems and telling parents what they might find and where is merely the first step. For a wide range of reasons, it may be necessary for the center's health coordinator, director or the child's educarer to encourage the parents to make the initial contact; or the center personnel themselves may need to make contact for the parent and child, setting up an appointment, actually providing transportation, and perhaps providing care for siblings. It is said that love is a many-splendored thing. A quality infant-toddler care center is a many-splendored thing also. Its inherent responsibilities go far beyond the onsite

delivery of care and education to young children.

SCREENING AND ASSESSMENT

Scheduling of Health Examinations

Any child may develop a new health problem at any age. The AAP's *Guidelines for Health Supervision* (1988a) recommended a health examination at the following times:

By	1 month	12 months
	2 months	15 months
	4 months	18 months
	6 months	24 months
	9 months	36 months

If the above schedule is followed, a child would receive 10 health evaluations by the time he was 3 years old. Few parents, especially those who do not have a family physician, arrange for these examinations on their own initiative after 18 to 25 months. The center's health coordinator can suggest and recommend, but has neither the right nor the authority to force parents to follow the schedule. The coordinator can only require the initial health evaluation and immunizations at the time of enrollment, and a statement from a physician for readmittance after absence caused by some illnesses or diseases.

Screening

However, the center or family day care can serve as a screening agent. Of course, the health coordinator can weigh and measure, but it is the educarer in daily contact with the children who can screen by observation during the normal activities. Most centers serving children below the age of 3 may not have access to the services of organizations or persons who periodically screen children for vision or hearing.

Vision. The prevalence of eye problems in infants and very young children is not known. Observable conditions such as unusual sensitivity to light, excessive tearing, inflammation, difficulty with focusing, and especially the deviation of one eye are causes for concern. A visit to an ophthalmologist should be recommended. Sometimes the educarer is in a better position than the parents to question the child's ability to see because she spends many hours with the child and with other children of the same age. The child's failure to notice and pick up small objects at the age when he or she should be practicing newly achieved prehension skills is also cause for concern.

Hearing, language, speech. Even before 6 weeks of age, an infant will alert to a spoken word and will respond to vocalizations by attending behaviors. By 6 to 9 months a baby with normal hearing will turn her head toward a soft, familiar sound. At 12 months she should understand simple directions (for instance to point to a familiar object), use jargon, and perhaps say one or two true words. If an infant's ability to perform any of the above is questionable, a recommendation for referral should be made. As in the case of possible vision problems, purposeful observation by the educarer may uncover suspicions of possible hearing impairment that have not been noted by the parents. Sometimes deafness in children is not detected until after 2 years of age, which is extremely unfortunate. The optimal time for learning language is from birth to 2 to 3 years. The same age period is optimal for teaching children to communicate with alternative methods.

According to the Committee on Standards of Child Health Care (AAP, 1977), the child with normal language-speech development should:

babble by age 6 months; try to imitate simple words (echolalia); and say two to three meaningful, but distorted words by 12 months. At 24 months this child should: follow at least a one-stage verbal command without gesture cues (e.g., "pick up the block"); spontaneously name familiar objects or body parts; and say meaningful sentences of two or more words. By 3 or 4

years of age a child should be speaking in complete sentences of 4 to 5 words for social purposes (p. 12).

There may be some misarticulation of speech sounds and some sound or word repetition. Both of these occurrences frequently correct themselves—unless undue attention is paid them by well-meaning adults.

Other developmental signposts. If the child does not play such games as peek-a-boo, pattycake, or wave bye-bye at the age of 1; if the child does not imitate adults doing routine housekeeping chores by age 2 or 3; if the child does not enjoy playing alone with toys, pots and pans, sand, and so on by age 3—recommendation for referral is in order. If a child does not react to his own name when called by age 1; is unable to identify hair, eyes, ears, nose, and mouth by pointing to them by age 2; does not understand simple stories told or read by age 3—recommendation for referral is in order.

A trained, experienced educarer can intuitively sense that something is amiss in the life of an infant or toddler, just as an experienced kindergarten teacher can correctly assess a 5 year old's readiness to read without a standardized instrument. The educational and medical professions, however, rely on standardized assessment tools to validate their intuitions. This is as it should be. There is a need for a recognized technique for screening and assessment and for any subsequent diagnosis, remediation, and treatment procedures. A widely used screening procedure is the Denver Developmental Screening Test, which is valid as a screening tool up to age 6 if it is used as designed. It seems to be a better instrument for children under age 3 years. It does not yield a definitive evaluation or a diagnosis if a problem exists, but it was not designed to do either.

If time and staff are available, it is desirable to screen all the children; if time and staff are at a premium, which is all too often the case, the children whose behavior or progress is questionable or abnormal should be evaluated with an instrument such as the Denver Developmental Screening Test. If the caregiver's suspicions are substantiated, the child should be referred to the appropriate education agency (state, area, or local). The education agencies in many states have both personnel and funds to evaluate the progress and development of children *under* the age of 3. They will plan and arrange the delivery of an appropriate program, if necessary, either in the child's home or in a group setting. Each community has an established process or local custom; it is the day-care provider's responsibility to learn about the local referral system. If the area or local education agency deems it necessary, or if it is not authorized to work with children under the age of 3, the logical referral for suspected developmental disabilities is to a pediatrician in the community.

Comments. Caregivers must never forget that they are not trained to accurately screen, assess, or diagnose any developmental problems. These persons may also mistakenly suspect as a developmental problem traits in a child that are purely racial or cultural in nature. Children have been mistakenly labeled as developmentally disabled, and their future development and education have been negatively influenced by such a label. The role of the educarer in any center or family day care is to recommend a referral for a child about whom there may be questions. It is not to diagnose or label. However, the entire series of processes (screening, assessment, diagnosis, and treatment) must take place if the health program is to be effective. The suspicions of an educarer may be the first step in this vital sequence of events.

GOAL II: TO ENSURE A CHILD'S FUTURE HEALTH

CHILDHOOD DISEASES

Shots and Drops

When full-term babies are born, they have a natural protection from many diseases. This pro-

tection wears off sometime during the first 6 to 12 months. When that happens, there is only one thing to do: get special shots and drops that stimulate the body to produce the antibodies that take the place of the natural protection that has worn off. These are the immunizations previously referred to; they are sometimes called vaccinations or inoculations.

Immunizations are made from very small amounts of the material that cause a specific disease. They are injected into the body (shots) or taken by mouth (drops). The body reacts to the vaccine by producing antibodies, which build up in the body and protect it for a long time. As a result of an immunization, some children may have a low fever, a mild rash, or soreness at the shot spot. Children may be tired, cross, or fussy, and may have little appetite. These are fairly common reactions, and should not last for more than 1 or 2 days. If a child has a more serious reaction, the parents should be notified, and a doctor called. These normal reactions are a small price to pay when compared with the reactions and results of the preventable childhood diseases.

Until very recently, there have been a very few cases of serious allergic reactions to the DPT (diphtheria, pertussis, tetanus) vaccine. These reactions include seizures, brain damage, or even death. But it has now been shown that a standard blood test given before the DPT injection can be used to identify the children who are likely to have these reactions. If parents object to your admission requirement for immunizations out of fear of a possible serious reaction, suggest they speak to their health professional about the blood test.

Vaccine-Preventable Diseases

Diphtheria. Diphtheria is an infection that usually develops in the throat, with early symptoms of sore throat, chills, slight fever, and headache. It is described as "a severe, often life-threatening infection of the tonsils, throat, larynx, trachea, or skin . . . which produces a thick, tenacious membrane that can cause suffocation" (Andersen, Bale, Blackman, & Murph, 1986, p. 17). It is most likely to strike children under 15 years of age, and is most harmful to the very young. It is caught by breathing in germs that the sick person throws out when coughing or sneezing. It can also be spread by a carrier—a person who carries the germ in his or her body for a long time without getting sick.

Diphtheria germs produce a strong poison that spreads through the body and affects nerves and heart muscles. It can result in heart failure and pneumonia, and even death. Fortunately, the almost universal use of the vaccine has decreased the number of reported cases from 200,000 between 1900 and 1925 to five in the year 1983 in the United States.

Pertussis (Whooping Cough). Pertussis is most likely to strike children under the age of 7. Infants have no natural protection against this disease. Andersen et al. (1986) describe it as "a life-threatening disease . . . characterized by fits of coughing, which culminate in a high-pitched 'whoop' as air is taken in. . . . Before the widespread use of the vaccine, over 7,000 deaths occurred annually, and seventy percent of these deaths occurred in children under 1 year old" (p. 18).

Whooping cough is spread through the air when the sick person coughs and sneezes. It begins like a common cold, but develops into violent coughing fits within 1 or 2 weeks. It can lead to pneumonia and convulsions. These conditions are most likely to occur in the very young. Pertussis can cause death in babies under 6 months of age.

Tetanus. Tetanus (or lockjaw) can strike people at any age whenever they have a dirty wound, and babies are born with little, if any, protection. It "is a potentially fatal neurological disease characterized by severe, painful muscle spasms. . . . [It] usually occurs as a result of contamination of a wound by soil, dust, or animal feces" (Andersen et al., 1986, p. 18).

Tetanus is spread by germs coming into the body through an open wound, sometimes as small as a pinprick, but more usually a deep cut such as those made by nails or knives. When you see baby playing in the dirt, or in a sandbox used by pets as a litter box, beware!

The germs grow fast in closed or dirty wounds, and make a strong poison that attacks the nervous system. At first, the child may be fussy or cross, and have a headache with a stiff jaw and neck. Later, the child (or adult) will have a hard time swallowing, and will have painful muscle spasms in the back, neck, face, and throat. These spasms (convulsions) may lead to breathing and heart problems. A person with tetanus has an even chance of living or dying.

Poliomyelitis. Polio is a "viral disease that usually causes only a mild febrile illness or no symptoms at all. . . . In 1–2 percent of cases, paralytic polio develops, resulting in permanent paralysis or death" (Andersen et al., 1986, p. 22). It is contagious. It starts with fever, headache, vomiting, sore throat, and sometimes severe muscle pain and stiffness in the neck, back, and legs. In the years before the discovery and widespread use of the polio vaccine, the disease often led to paralysis in the arms, legs, throat, and chest, and even to death. There is no cure for polio.

Measles. Measles (or rubeola), is different from rubella (German or 3-day measles), which is most dangerous to unborn babies during their early months. It is easily caught by breathing in bits of the measles virus that the sick person throws out when coughing, sneezing, or even talking. Measles usually strike young children after the first 6 months of life, and last about 2 weeks. It begins with symptoms like those of a bad cold—severe cough, chills, watery light-sensitive eyes, and a temperature that may rise at high as 105°F. A few days later a red rash appears, and fades away in 7 to 10 days.

Catching measles used to be considered a normal part of childhood, like skinned knees.

We now know there may be serious complications, and children should be immunized at the appropriate time.

Mumps. "Mumps is a viral disease of childhood [usually between 5–10 years of age] that commonly causes fever and headache, along with swelling and tenderness of the salivary glands" (Andersen et al., 1986, p. 21). These glands are located between the ears and the jaws. It is spread by contact with persons who have mumps, and by eating or drinking with the same utensils. Mumps may cause sterility in teenage and adult males.

Rubella (German measles). "Rubella is a viral disease of childhood that causes mild fever, rash, and swollen lymph nodes behind the ears and at the back of the head and neck. . . . [It] is such a mild disease in young children and adults, were it not for its devastating effects on the fetus, vaccination programs would not be necessary" (Andersen et al., 1986, p. 21). If a pregnant woman catches rubella during the first 3 months of her pregnancy, her baby stands a great chance of being born with heart problems, deafness, blindness, or mental retardation. The woman has an even greater chance of losing her baby.

Hemophilus Influenza Type B (Hib). Hemophilus influenza type b (Hib) is the most common cause of bacterial meningitis in infants and young children. Studies suggest that the risk of Hib disease is greater for those children who attend day-care centers. Over half of the cases occur between 6 and 12 months of age, and 15% between 18 and 24 months. The vaccine is a relatively new breakthrough, and is frequently given as a single injection with the DPT vaccine. The American Academy of Pediatrics recommends that all children receive the current vaccine by age 2. Children in day care, who are at greater risk for Hib, should be vaccinated at 18 months or younger.

Common Infections in Infant/Toddler Groups

Very young children are especially vulnerable to certain infections because of their small size and their anatomic relationships. There is only a short distance between locations in the body where infectious agents are normally found and are harmless, and the locations where these same agents cause disease. Very young children are also especially vulnerable to certain infections because of their developmental behaviors, for example, they enjoy playing in the dirt, sand, and mud. They also frequently have scrapes or cuts that allow easy entry of foreign substances. Young children mouth anything and everything, and are seemingly oblivious to the difference between edible and nonedible substances. The likelihood of infection is also increased by the close contact of others in a group setting.

Upper respiratory infections. Anyone in frequent contact with very young children knows that upper respiratory infections are by far the most common illness. Common respiratory viral illnesses are colds, influenza, and roseola. Colds are somewhat mild infections, and are caused by many different viruses. The contagious period is over when there is no fever. Influenza is also caused by viruses, and is usually accompanied by high fever, chills, coughing, and muscle aches. A person (child or adult) with influenza will probably feel too ill to leave home, although the contagious period is over once the fever has gone. Roseola is another high-fever viral infection; when the fever is gone, a body rash appears. The disease is contagious until the rash disappears. These infections can lead to a middle ear infection (known technically as otitis media). It has been estimated that half of all children develop a middle ear infection by the time they reach 12 months of age. In all, some 90% will have had such infections by age 6.

The middle ear, that portion that lies behind the eardrum, is subject to infection when it doesn't drain properly. The eustachian tube, which normally serves as a way for fluid to drain from the middle ear, might become blocked during a cold, sore throat, or other type of infection. Children under the age of 6 have small, short, almost horizontal eustachian tubes, and Pizzo and Aronson (1976) suggest that feeding position may be a factor in middle ear disease.

> Breast fed infants are normally held in an inclined position in which the child's ear and eustachian tube openings are slightly elevated above the mouth and throat. With bottle feeding in the hands of a person unaware of the problem and almost inevitably with bottle propping and self-bottle feeding in bed, the child is placed on his back, which favors the entry of liquid and/or the secretions from the nasopharynx through the eustachian tube into the middle ear. Since the secretions of the nasopharynx normally contain some bacteria and viruses which are not welcome visitors to the middle ear, the potential for middle ear problems is greatly increased (p. 62).

There is a significant relationship between otitis media and hearing loss and subsequent language delays and disabilities. We need to be on the alert for possible symptoms in children who have any sort of respiratory infection, and for any sign of reduction in hearing. A vaccine is not yet available, and antibiotics do not always work. Many times small tubes can be inserted in the eardrum to drain off the fluid.

Gastrointestinal infections. Also quite frequent in an infant/toddler group setting are gastrointestinal infections, accompanied by diarrhea and/or vomiting.

> In general, attack rates for diarrheal illness are highest in children less than two years of age. Toddlers in diapers, with their combination of dubious hygiene and unimpaired mobility, pose a particular hazard. . . . The responsibility for outbreaks of diarrhea does not rest solely with the toddlers. A number of epidemics have been associated with inadequate physical facilities and

Safe drinking water is one key to good health. (Early Childhood Education Center)

> major lapses in personal and environmental hygiene. This is especially disconcerting, given our knowledge that hand washing alone is effective in reducing the spread of diarrhea (Trumpp & Karasic, 1983, p. 223).

Hepatitis A refers to inflammation of the liver. It is transmitted by the fecal-oral route and the young children infected with it "usually are asymptomatic, or have non-specific illness. . . . The risk of clinical illness is greatest for adults having regular contact with one- or two-year-old children in diapers" (Trumpp & Karasic, 1983, p. 223). Hand washing, especially after changing diapers, is the most important hygienic measure. Hepatitis B has not proven to be a problem in early child care.

Diarrhea is no doubt the most distasteful illness to be encountered in a child-care center.

There is no specific treatment other than increasing the intake of clear liquids and decreasing or eliminating the intake of milk and solid foods (biekost). The infection is transmitted by personal contact. Thorough handwashing and careful disposal of infected materials are essential. If the condition persists for more than 2 days, if there is a high fever (+102°F), or extreme loss of fluids, a physician should be called. It can be an emergency situation.

Common rashes. Rashes of various kinds are the third most frequent health problem in the infant-toddler group. Rashes have a variety of causes, ranging from chemicals used at home or in the center, to wearing apparel, to medicines, plants, and some foods. Heat and fungi are also agents. A rash may also indicate any of a long list of illnesses such as measles, chicken pox, and scarlet fever. If a rash covers most of the body, the cause is probably internal, either an infectious disease or an allergy.

If the rash is localized, the cause is usually direct contact with an irritating substance. Rashes appear frequently on the infant and toddler whose skin is more tender and sensitive than an adult's. They are usually transitory when caused by an external agent and if treated appropriately. Most localized rashes are accompanied by discomfort and itching but leave no permanent scars. Of course, scratching increases the likelihood of infection, which in turn may cause scarring.

Heat rash and *diaper rash* are most usually found in very young children. Although they are not communicable, they increase the chance for skin infections and should be treated promptly. Because diaper rash seems to be always a problem, the following care procedure is included.

1. Change the diapers as soon as baby wets or soils. If a baby's bottom is extremely sore, he will cry or fuss when he needs changing, because the urine and stool will sting and hurt. (Ideally, a baby is always changed when needed. If educarers are conscientious about checking at regular intervals, this ideal can almost be met.)

2. Clean genital area and buttocks twice daily with a hexachlorophene soap (Zest or Dial) and dry thoroughly before rediapering.

3. If ointment or cream has been ordered by the nurse or doctor, apply after the buttocks have been washed and thoroughly dried. Powder is never recommended because of the possibility of inhalation.

4. Expose the buttocks to the air two or three times during the day by removing the diaper completely for 20 to 30 minutes. On warm sunny days the baby can be taken outside undiapered.

5. In case of a severe rash, remove plastic pants during the daytime (two or three diapers folded together will help prevent too much "leak").

6. If nondisposable diapers are used (a real nuisance in a child-care center), presoak them for at least 30 minutes before washing in 1 gallon of water and ½ cup of vinegar. Wash them only with soap, not a detergent.

7. A pediatrician should be contacted if the urine has a foul odor, is dark colored or bloody, or if the amount is small when fluid intake is good.

Impetigo is highly communicable, either by direct contact or when skin abrasions or insect bites are present. Hot, humid weather encourages outbreaks of impetigo. Children with impetigo need not be isolated or kept from the center, but there should be an increased emphasis on personal cleanliness and hygiene. The infected children should be referred to a health professional.

Fifth disease. *Fifth disease* (*Erythema infectiosum*) is a communicable disease causing redness of the skin. According to Schmitt (1987), "staying home is unnecessary because the infection is very mild or minimally contagious" (p. 316). It is included in this survey only because it is causing significant personnel problems in early-child–care centers in some parts of the country.

Parasites. Infections caused by parasites not only cause extreme discomfort for the infected child, but their appearance also seems to create a sense of revulsion that is psychologically damaging to the child. Also, parasites are not particular. They appear in elite private centers as well as in publicly supported centers.

Severe itching of the scalp frequently indicates head lice (pediculosis). Small white particles (the eggs) are attached to the hair shaft, usually close to the scalp and behind the ears. The particles may look like dandruff; the lice themselves are dark brown. Personal hygiene, including the thorough cleaning of combs, brushes, clothing, and bedding, is a must, but is not sufficient. Reinfestation or transmittal to anyone who comes into close physical contact with the affected child may occur easily. Head lice are not as dangerous as strep throat, but they are just as contagious. They reached epidemic status in the 1980s. Infected children may be readmitted to the center after application of an insecticide prescribed by a physician.

The most common skin disease is probably scabies caused by small mites that burrow underneath the skin. This results in red bumps and severe itching. Again, personal hygiene, as well as thorough washing or even boiling of clothing, bedding, and towels is essential. The child with suspected scabies or head lice should be referred for treatment.

Ringworm of the scalp or body is a fungal infection and results in a raised reddened circle on the skin. It is transmitted through personal contact, and is communicable as long as the fungi are present. Ringworm on the scalp results in small circular patches, sometimes associated with an area of baldness. The hair becomes dull, brittle, and breaks near the root. Wearing a protective cap and taking a prescribed oral medicine usually result in healing, and the child so treated need not be isolated. Again, it is essen-

tial to practice personal hygiene to avoid infecting others. Ringworm in places other than the scalp shows up as flat, circular lesions with raised edges. It necessitates thorough bathing with soap and water with removal of the scabs and crusts. A physician should prescribe ointment or oral medication. Children infected with ringworm may attend the center if they are under a physician's care.

Comments. In no way should the above list of infections be considered all-inclusive. Geographic location, living conditions, community sanitation, and home and center practices all influence both the incidence and the spread of infectious diseases. Selection of the problems described was based on personal experience and on recommendations of nurses and others involved in infant-toddler day care. It is hoped that none of the readers of this text will repeat my embarrassing mistake when I saw my first case of ringworm on the neck of a young boy. I assumed that the red oval was the result of a human bite!

Much of the information about infectious diseases was adapted from the Report of the Committee on Infectious Diseases (AAP, 1988c), a copy of which should be in every child-care center or home. It presents the current position of the American Academy of Pediatrics.

Chronic Illnesses

In an Infant/Toddler Group. With the increase in federal incentives for programs for children from birth through 2 years (PL 99-457), and the results of modern technology, it is possible that an infant/toddler center or family day-care home will be asked to include a child (or children) suffering from a chronic illness or even a life-threatening chronic disease. These children frequently lead seemingly normal lives with periodic episodes of trips to the clinic or hospital. Many of them do not look sick and may not act sick, making it easy to forget that they may be fragile and may need extra attention. These children may be suffering from allergies, asthma, heart problems, epilepsy and other seizure disorders, sickle-cell anemia, or diabetes. They may need medication or health treatment on a predetermined schedule, which will include the times when they are at the center or family day-care home.

Rules for Medication. The following suggested policy for the administration of medication has been adapted from the policy of the Iowa Department of Public Instruction's Rules of Special Education (1985).

> *Medications.* Each early childhood center or family day-care home shall establish written policies concerning the administration of prescribed medication by staff during its hours of operation. Medications shall not be administered unless the following requirements are met:

1. *Directed by physician.* A statement of the physician's directions specifying frequency, amount, and method of administration signed by the physician must be filed at the center or family day-care home.

2. *Reactions and side effects.* A physician's description of anticipated reactions to and possible side effects of the medicine must be filed at the center or family day-care home.

3. *Proper labeling.* The medicine shall be kept in the original prescription container, which shall be labeled with:
   a. name of child
   b. name of medicine
   c. directions for use
   d. name of physician
   e. name and address of pharmacy
   f. date of prescription

4. *Parent's written consent.* A parental signature on a statement requesting and authorizing child-care personnel to administer the medicine in accord with the prescription

shall be filed at the center or family day-care home.

5. *Administering medication.* The person responsible for administering the medication shall have ready access to a review of the information regarding the medication filed at the center or family day-care home.

6. *Record of administration.* Each time a medicine is administered a record shall be maintained to include the child's name, date, time, and signature of the person administering the medicine.

7. *Security.* Each center or family day-care home shall designate in writing the specific locked and limited access space within each center or family day-care home to store pupil medication.
   a. In each center, access to medication locked in a designated space shall be under the authority of the health coordinator.
   b. In each family day-care home, access to medication locked in a designated space shall be under the authority of the health coordinator or family day-care provider.

If the educarer has any concern about a medication or how to administer it, she should call the doctor for verification. It is necessary that the substance be in its original container. The parents should request two containers from the pharmacist, one for the center or family day-care home, and one for home. If only one container is labeled, the parents should take the responsibility of the unlabeled one at home.

HIV Infection (AIDS)

The virus known as HIV sometimes causes illnesses designated as AIDS (acquired immunodeficiency syndrome) and ARC (AIDS-related complex). The virus was first detected in 1980, and to date there has been no vaccine developed, and no cure for the disease. AIDS is a disease that can damage the brain and destroy the body's ability to fight off illness. It does not kill, but it allows other infections to invade the body, and these infections kill. One percent of the reported cases have been infants who were infected by their mothers. Because blood screening procedures were started in 1985, the young children in today's infant/toddler programs can no longer be infected by unsafe blood transfusions.

The big question facing persons in early childhood education (and education at all levels) is that of permitting or denying participation in a group setting for the child who has been infected by the HIV virus. The unanimous medical opinion is that casual contact with AIDS patients does not place an individual at risk for getting the infection. The current AAP position is that the danger of a child (or adult) contracting AIDS from another child is virtually nonexistent. There is no reason to screen children before enrollment in an infant/toddler program, preschool, or public school, although they should be excluded temporarily if an outbreak of an infectious disease (i.e., measles) is imminent. This is to protect the child with AIDS, whose resistance to infections is low.

Although there is a growing belief that the AIDS condition is transmitted only by blood, sexual contact, and intravenous injections, and *not* by contact with urine or feces, vomitus, or saliva, there remains a widespread fear of transmission among educarers and other persons in close contact with children suffering from AIDS. The procedures for diaper changing and handwashing (see Recommended Practices) are health-promoting procedures and represent the best thinking at this time.

New information about the medical and social aspects of AIDS appears almost daily. For up-to-date information, call the National AIDS Hotline 1-800-342-AIDS. For printed information (for yourself or the parents of the children

in your care), send for the following. The copies are free.

"What you should know about AIDS"
(an 8-page pamphlet)
America Responds to AIDS
P.O. Box 23961
Washington, DC 20026-3961

"Surgeon General's Report on AIDS"
(35 pages)
Surgeon General's Report on AIDS
P.O. Box 23961
Washington, DC 20026-3961

Include your name and address, and indicate the number of copies you would like (up to 1,000).

DISEASE PREVENTION AND CONTROL

Prevention by Immunization

The Surgeon General established health goals with an immunization goal for 1990 of 90% of all children having completed the basic immunization series listed previously by age 2. "The nation will not reach this objective or even come close. In 1985 a smaller percentage of children age two and younger were fully immunized . . . than in 1980" (Children's Defense Fund, 1988, p. 66). Perhaps we in very early childhood can help reverse this downward trend.

Diphtheria, pertussis, tetanus, polio, measles, rubella, mumps, and hemophilus influenzae type b (Hib) may be prevented in an infant/toddler group by requiring immunizations of all the children attending. Immunization records should be kept on file and periodically reviewed and updated.

Control of Other Diseases

The following information about the control of selected diseases has been adapted from Andersen et al. (1986) and *Health in Day Care: A Manual for Health Professionals* (AAP, 1987).

Diseases spread by respiratory secretions. These include colds, otitis media, and Hemophilus influenzae type b. They are spread easily in a day-care program, and isolation of infected children does not seem to reduce their spread. Careful hand washing by children and adults after direct contact with secretions may help reduce the spread. If a case of Hib is diagnosed in a day-care program, an antibiotic is usually recommended for the persons in the household and child-care program who have been in contact with the child to help prevent spread of the infection.

Diseases spread by direct contact. These include cytomegalovirus (CMV), which research has shown to be extremely prevalent among very young children who are becoming mobile, curious, and sociable, and who put everything in their mouths. Nearly everyone acquires CMV infection sooner or later. It usually occurs without symptoms and is rarely of consequence for the infected child or adult (except a pregnant woman). Isolation is not necessary. Good hygiene significantly lowers the risk of transmitting the infection.

Herpes simplex is a viral infection transmitted by direct contact. Individuals are considered contagious while skin lesions are present in the mouth, on the skin, or on the genitals. A "cold sore" is the common symptom for this infection. Children with active herpes sores on the mouth or skin should be excluded from day care until the sores are all crusted over.

Careful handwashing of children and adults is a must. Caregivers should use gloves if direct contact with the sores is unavoidable.

Diseases spread by fecal-oral transmission. Infectious diarrhea is particularly prevalent in large centers and in infant/toddler centers. Children who are not yet toilet trained are the most susceptible. They mouth objects, wipe their noses with their hands, put their hands into their own and other children's mouths, and into their diapers. Objects such as teething rings and

pacifiers should be used by one child only, and should be sanitized if dropped or otherwise contaminated. A recommended solution is 1 part household bleach to 10 parts water; it should be freshly made daily. Careful handwashing, especially after diaper changing, is the most important hygienic measure. The usual causes of diarrhea are a parasite called giardia lamblia (a leading cause among children in a day-care center, and treatable); a bacteria, salmonella (spreading through feces, or from contaminated poultry, raw milk, and pet turtles); and another bacteria, shigella (individuals with this infection should be excluded from day care).

Hepatitis A, a virus, poses a major health risk in day-care centers. There is no effective treatment, and efforts are aimed at preventing the disease through good hygiene.

Diseases spread through body fluids. The diseases that deserve our attention in this category are Hepatitis B and AIDS/HIV infection.

Hepatitis B is not highly contagious, and transmission is not likely to occur under normal hygienic conditions, although "care should be taken that the blood of infected individuals or carriers never comes into contact with open wounds of other children or adults" (Andersen et al., 1986, p. 106). Routine disinfecting measures will kill the virus, and a vaccine is available.

AIDS education is necessary for everyone. There have been many misunderstandings among adults about the admission of children to group settings who are HIV-infected or who are subject to infections because of AIDS. Both physical and psychological damage to the infected children and their families have been inflicted because of lack of knowledge and fear of the unknown.

The Center for Disease Control recommends that children with AIDS or ARC be allowed to attend their usual schools or day care centers and be placed in foster homes in unrestricted settings. Children with AIDS are at greater risk of acquiring an infection from their peers; and peers are at minimal risk of contracting AIDS from them. The AIDS child needs to be careful about contracting colds, chicken pox, and other common childhood diseases (Center for Disease Control, 1985, August 30).

The American Academy of Pediatrics (Task Force on Pediatric AIDS) (1988b) reinforces this recommendation about admitting infected children, as does the National Association for the Education of Young Children (1989).

Suggestions for educarers when with an AIDS child include: (1) change diapers only while wearing disposable gloves; (2) wear gloves for tending to cuts or other secretions; (3) protect your own open sores against secretions from any child; and (4) do not allow the child to be immunized while in your care (immunization in AIDS children may cause problems due to the damaged immune system (Raper & Aldridge, 1988).

It is very possible that some of these children may be too weak or too ill to attend the infant/toddler program. For those who do attend, the toys and items handled by them and the soiled surfaces should be cleaned with the sanitizing solution ("1 tablespoon bleach to 1 quart water if no blood present or 1 part bleach to 10 parts water for cleaning blood spills") (National Association for the Education of Young Children, 1989, 51).

Also, the necessity of careful handwashing cannot be overemphasized.

PROCEDURES AND ISSUES FOR CONTROL AND MANAGEMENT

Recommended Practices

Handwashing. It would be difficult to ignore the necessity of careful handwashing after reading the previous information. Even though correct handwashing has been found to be the most effective method of preventing disease, 16 states do not even mention it in their regulations for center-based programs. Of the 34 states that do include it, only 21 specify a certain procedure.

Of these some merely say "soap and water" (Morgan, 1987).

A complete and specific procedure is found in *Healthy Young Children: A Manual for Programs* (Kendrick, Kaufmann, & Messenger, 1988) published by the National Association for the Education of Young Children. Their recommended procedure is presented in Figure 6–5.

Diaper changing. The same manual contains specific directions for changing diapers, presented in Figure 6–6.

Clues to the Possibility of Illness

The lack of verbal language does not limit the infant's ability to tell us he isn't feeling well. Changes in usual behavior, loss of appetite, fever, vomiting or diarrhea, all indicate that something is not right. When nonverbal children hurt, their behavior will tell us so. If they have a sore throat, they may drool more than usual, and may breathe through their mouth. If the child has an earache, he or she may pull on the ear or hold the head to one side. A child with legs pulled up toward the chest, and clenched fists, may have a tummyache. If an arm or leg hurts, the child may hold the arm or may limp. But always remember that the behaviors that may indicate illness in one child may be normal behaviors in another.

One or more of the following in a particular child should make an educarer suspect that an illness is present or developing. Some of these symptoms can be serious and need to be reported to the parents at once. Other symptoms need to be reported, but whether or not they are reported before the parents come to pick up the child depends on the severity of the symptoms and how they affect the child's total day.

General Appearance
1. Eyes dull and lackluster
2. Eyes watery or swollen
3. The eyes or lids pink or red

4. Discharge from *eyes*

5. Breathing heavy, labored, or wheezing

6. Offensive breath odor

7. Skin color pale or bluish

8. Skin red or flushed

9. Lips and nailbeds bluish color

10. Rash or sunburn present

11. Skin hot to the touch

12. Profuse perspiration when others find the room temperature comfortable

Figure 6–5
Handwashing Procedure

Adults

Wash hands upon arrival.
Wash hands **before** preparing food, eating, or feeding a child.
Wash hands **after**
—toileting self or a child
—handling body secretions (e.g., changing diapers, cleaning up a child who has vomited or spit up, wiping a child's nose, handling soiled clothing or other contaminated items)
Post signs to remind staff and children to wash their hands in the toilet room, the kitchen, and the area where diapers are changed.
Be sure that the hot water supplied to fixtures accessible to children does not exceed a maximum temperature of 115° F.

How to wash hands

Turn on water to a comfortable temperature. Check to be sure a paper towel is available.
Moisten hands with water and apply heavy lather of *liquid* soap.
Wash well under running water for approximately 15 seconds.
Pay particular attention to areas between fingers, around nail beds, under fingernails, and backs of hands.

Rinse well under running water for 30 seconds. Hold hands so that water flows from wrist to fingertips.
Dry hands with paper towel.
Use paper towel to turn off faucet; then discard towel.
Use hand lotion, if desired.

Infants/toddlers

Wipe hands with damp paper towel moistened with a liquid soap solution.
Wipe hands with paper towel moistened with clear water.
Dry hands with paper towel.
Turn off faucet with paper towel and discard.

Older children

Squirt a drop of liquid soap on children's hands.
Wash and rinse their hands in running water, directing flow from wrist to fingertips.
Dry hands with paper towel.
Turn off faucet with paper towel and discard.
Teach older children to carry out the procedure themselves. Supervise younger children in carrying out this handwashing procedure.

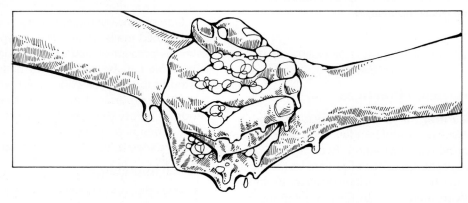

Reproduced with permission. *Healthy Young Children: A Manual for Programs.* Kendrick, Kaufmann, & Messenger, Eds. 1988. NAEYC.

13. Limping

14. Refusal to use some part of the body

15. Swollen areas, bumps, lumps, or red spots on head, body, or extremities

Behavior

1. Unusual irritability; has trouble getting along with others

2. Increased activity or unusual lethargy

3. Sleep disturbance; interrupted or restless sleep; inability to sleep

4. Extreme fatigue with or without excessive amount of sleeping

5. Unusual amount of crying, fussing, or whining

6. Seems to get hurt more often than usual; falls easily; bumps into things

7. Clings to parent or educarer

8. Drinks an unusual amount of liquids

Gastrointestinal

1. Vomiting/diarrhea

2. Poor or picky appetite or refusal to take food or bottle

3. Complaints of pain in abdomen

4. Intermittent loud crying with knees drawn up to abdomen (infants)

5. Blood in stool

6. Dark black tarry stools

Upper Respiratory

1. Fever

2. Persistent sneezing

3. Runny nose, crusting discharge or bleeding from nose

4. Coughing

5. Drainage from ears

6. Difficult or labored breathing

7. Difficulty in staying asleep because of obstructed breathing or cough

8. Rubbing or pulling ears

9. Turning head from side to side when lying down

10. Crying while trying to suck bottle

11. Difficulty in swallowing

12. Refusal of juice when child usually would like it

Genitourinary

1. Increased frequency of urination, sometimes with little urine volume

2. Complaint of pain with urination

3. Blood in urine

4. Vaginal discharge

5. Redness, irritation, or discharge in the area of the foreskin of the penis

Central Nervous System

1. Convulsions or seizures

2. Blackouts or loss of consciousness

3. Unequal strength on the two sides of the body

4. Projectile vomiting

Dental

1. Teeth emerging in other than usual area

2. Teeth turning dark

3. Refusal to nurse by infant, even though the child acts hungry until he or she starts sucking

It is important to report these findings to parents so that they can relate the symptoms to their pediatrician, thereby helping in making a quick and accurate diagnosis.

Management of Ill Children

If an adult does not feel well, what does he want? Peace and quiet, and perhaps a caring person to hold his hand, place a damp cloth on his fevered brow, and offer him a cool drink of water. Infants and toddlers have the same desires when they do not feel well. They want peace and

Figure 6–6
How to Change a Diaper

Check to be sure supplies you need are ready. **Place** paper or other disposable cover on diapering surface.
Pick up the child. If the diaper is soiled, hold the child away from you.

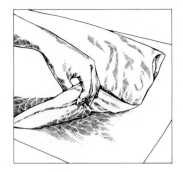

Lay the child on the diapering surface. **Never leave the child unattended.** If you use them, **put** on disposable gloves now.
Remove soiled diaper and clothes. Fold disposable diapers inward and reseal with their tapes.

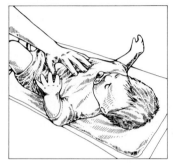

Put disposable diapers in a lined, covered step can. Put cloth diapers in a plastic bag securely tied, then put into a larger, labeled, plastic bag to go home. Do not put diapers in toilet. Bulky stool may be emptied into toilet.
Put soiled clothes in double, labeled, plastic bags to be taken home.

Clean the child's bottom with a moist disposable wipe. Wipe front to back using towelette only once. Repeat with fresh wipes if necessary. Pay particular attention to skin folds. Pat dry with paper towel. Do not use any kind of powder, as inhaling it can be dangerous. Use a skin care product only on parent request.
Dispose of the towelette or paper towel in a lined, covered step can.
If you used disposable gloves, discard them now.
Wipe your hands with a disposable wipe. **Dispose** of it in the lined, covered step can.

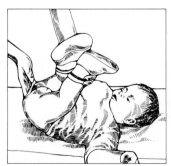

Reproduced with permission. *Healthy Young Children: A Manual for Programs.* Kendrick, Kaufmann, & Messenger, Eds. 1988. NAEYC

Figure 6–6

continuing

Diaper or dress the child. Now you can hold her or him close to you.

Wash the child's hands. Assist the child back to the group.

Remove disposable covering from the diapering surface.
Wash and rinse the area with water (use soap if necessary) and sanitize it
with bleach solution made fresh daily.

Wash your own hands thoroughly.

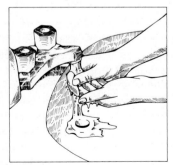

quiet, so we provide them with such a spot, away from the stimulation of their peers. They may want to sleep, so we provide a crib in a quiet spot. They may be alert enough to want to play, so we give them a toy or two or a favorite stuffed animal. They may want to be left alone, although I suspect the quiet presence of a caring person provides security and comfort.

All cases of suspected illness should be reported to the parents. Examples of signs and symptoms necessitating a recommendation for referral to a pediatrician include fever or chills, stuffy or running nose in combination with other symptoms, inflamed or itching eyes, enlarged cervical nodes or neck glands, frequent and persistent cough, difficulty in swallowing, chest pain, abdominal pain, change in rate and character of respiration, blood in stool or urine, or if the child just seems very sick.

Even when some of these signs are present, many educarers feel themselves competent to care for the child at the center or day-care home until the end of the day, and do not wish to "bother" the parent at work. But it is considerably more bother if the parent has to contact the pediatrician after office hours. It also is more expensive. If the child's symptoms or behaviors warrant a pediatrician's advice, by all means notify the parent as soon as possible so that arrangements can be made. This practice seems to be a comparatively minor consideration, but it is an example of a true partnership between educarers and parents.

Meanwhile, the child should be made as comfortable as possible, and no doubt should have his temperature taken. An infant's temperature is easily taken rectally without much fuss. It is difficult (impossible!) to get an accurate reading from a toddler with an oral thermometer, and the well-advertised fever strips have proved unreliable. One suggestion is to take the child's axillary (under the arm) temperature. This can be done by holding the child on your lap and looking at a book together. With an arm around the child in a friendly hug, the thermometer can be held under the child's arm with no problem.

If for some reason (such as an infected hangnail) the child needs to soak her hand in a water-based solution, turn the treatment into an episode of water play by supplying a few pouring utensils.

If a bottle-fed infant needs a liquid medication, give the baby an empty nipple to suck on, and then pour the medicine through the nipple. It will be swallowed almost before it is tasted.

Or, use a dropper or calibrated syringe (without the needle, of course) and squirt the fluid along the inside of the cheek instead of on the tongue, where it's easier for the child to spit out. Use the same technique for dropper-type vitamins. For toddlers, offer medicine mixed in with the applesauce or other "treat." I don't recommend Mary Poppins's "teaspoon of sugar," but both catsup and grape jelly mask the strong flavor of medicine quite well.

By using such approaches to ill children, the child's experience is nonthreatening and even pleasant at times. Also, these procedures will help decrease any anxiety about medical professionals.

When to Exclude Ill Children

It is advisable for each center or family day-care home to have a specific policy about restrictions of attendance in case of illness or illness symptoms. In general, a contagious disease (not a common cold or chicken pox), a rectal or axillary fever of 102°F, or vomiting and/or diarrhea for more than a day are sufficient causes for a child to be denied admission until the child is well and/or has clearance from a health consultant.

According to the American Academy of Pediatrics,

> There are very few illnesses for which children need to be excluded from day care. The center

should identify, in its written policy, those diseases which require exclusion until the contagious stage is past. To facilitate decisions by both parents and staff, the policy should specify certain symptoms that make keeping a child away from the center advisable. Diarrhea, vomiting, specific types of rashes, and fever should be mentioned as well as such signs of illness as pallor, irritability, and excessive sleepiness. The specific list will depend on state laws, local public health recommendations, and suggestions made by the medical consultant for the day care program. Programs which have staffing facilities to care for mildly ill children will be able to have more liberal policies than those with limited staffing and little space for ill children to receive the extra rest and supervision they require (1987, pp. 66–67).

Of course, most (if not all) of the infants and toddlers in group settings are there because there is no one at home. Some employers allow time off to the parent for the care of a sick child. If this is not possible (the majority of the cases today), centers or family day-care homes should provide a separate area away from the daily bustle, but observable by the educarer. Some communities provide a family day-care home for only sick children; some hospitals provide a "sick room" for young children in child care. Finding possible daytime care for sick children should be part of the preliminary planning for the health component of care and education.

Management of an Outbreak

There should be already in place a plan of action in case an infection spreads rapidly through a center or home in spite of all precautions. Outside medical resources should be contacted immediately for control measures, the starting of control measures, and for diagnostic tests of the involved children and others, who may have no observable symptoms.

> If containment of the outbreak (or the physical condition of the child) requires exclusion from the day care program, alternate care arrange-

ments should be implemented. . . . It must be emphasized that decisions concerning exclusion, alternate care, and readmission will be easier to make if plans are in place when the need for them arises. It is helpful, also, if the day care center has gathered information in advance concerning sources to cover or assist with payment for diagnosis, treatment, and alternative care (AAP, 1987, p. 72).

HEALTH-RELATED ISSUES

Health Requirements for Educarers

Educarers who have never been vaccinated for diphtheria, tetanus, and pertussis should receive these shots and also get a booster shot every 10 years. It is of the highest priority for all women of childbearing age to be immune to rubella, because rubella (or 3-day measles) has been proven to cause miscarriage and serious birth defects if contracted by a pregnant woman. "Child care workers, teachers and other individuals who spend a great deal of time around children should be particularly careful about keeping their immunizations up to date. They should also have annual flu shots" (Shelov, 1989, p. 48).

Preemployment examinations should include a physical evaluation and an assessment of the individual's emotional fitness to be a caregiver. These examinations should also be required of bus drivers, cooks, secretaries—anyone involved on a continuing basis in infant/toddler care and education.

The AAP (1987) suggests the following items should be included in a Staff Health Appraisal Form.

- Freedom from contagious disease
- History of childhood infectious diseases such as rubella and chicken pox
- Negative tuberculin test or, if positive, evidence of follow-up with a chest roentgenogram and evaluation for chemotherapy

- Immunization status: types, initial dates, dates of boosters or reimmunizations (record of tetanus booster within ten years)
- Conditions that might cause frequent absence from the job
- Conditions that might require emergency care
- Limitations affecting performance of day care work (e.g., allergy to art materials, skin conditions affected by frequent hand washing, inability to stay outdoors)
- Medications and special diet requirements
- Use of tobacco, alcohol, and drugs
- Hearing and visual acuity
- Evidence of mental and emotional fitness
- Results of special tests for transporters including color and depth perception and size of visual field (p. 21)

In addition to the preemployment information, the above information should be updated every 2 years or more often if the physician advises it. The same regulations for exclusion of sick children should apply to the adults who are in direct contact with the children.

Perhaps the following position statement will best describe the role of the adult while fulfilling the role of educarer in the health component of infant/toddler care and education.

If the wiping of runny noses is seen as a menial activity which nearly any person can perform, that activity can be delegated to the least-educated member of a care-giving staff. Very little attention will be paid to how nose wiping activity is carried out. It's quite likely that the nose will be wiped with a handkerchief, which is then put back in the caregiver's pocket (with no caregiver handwashing) and/or immediately used to wipe the next child's runny nose, thereby transmitting high doses of infectious agents from one child to the other. The wiping of runny noses doesn't have to be viewed as a "custodial" act. Instead it can be seen as an important public health measure, one which when done with an awareness of causes and control of infectious disease, can make a contribution to the reduction of disease in a community and to the prevention of the spread of viral and bacterial disease among the day care program's children. This preventive measure has implications for promoting the child's total development, since symptomatic viral and bacterial diseases may have negative implications for the total child (Pizzo & Aronson, 1976, pp. 16–17).

Health Education

For children and parents. Teaching about health is best accomplished by the example set by the center or family day-care home. The parents are "taught" by the emphasis placed on the preenrollment medical examination, the required immunizations, the admission procedures, and the care that is given their children in the environment designed to promote physical and mental health. Parents and their children learn that health care is a pleasant continuing experience, and not just "shots and drops."

Health-related routines and activities within the program begin to teach young children, even at the infant/toddler stage, the importance of personal health care. They learn about personal hygiene by the educarer's insistence on handwashing at the appropriate times (and the educarer's handwashing at these times, too). They learn about nutrition as they eat and drink a variety of foods that contain the daily nutrient requirements. They learn about dental care as the educarer first cleans their teeth, and then introduces a toothbrush at about 18 months of age. They learn about disease control by using disposable tissues for wiping or blowing noses, and by watching the educarer dispose of the used tissue. They learn about environmental sanitation when they use wastebaskets or trash cans, and when they observe someone spray the tables with disinfectant and vacuum the carpet after mealtime. They begin to learn that sleeping, eating, and elimination are somehow important as they see the educarer noting the occurrence of such activities. They develop calmer attitudes about minor accidents and injuries when these are handled calmly and pleasantly by an adult.

These routine happenings are the "curriculum" of health education for our youngest children. They also diminish fears of health-related activities that the children may have learned elsewhere. The parents also learn, as they observe or participate in the daily activities.

By providing health education in the infant/toddler setting, we decrease the numbers of preschool and school-age children who develop preventable physical health problems.

For the educaring persons. The AAP Manual titled *Health in Day Care* (1987) states that in most child care training, there is little attention given to the teaching of health, safety, and nutrition: "There is no textbook or specific set of materials that treats health, safety, and nutrition in day care adequately" (p. 94). The lack of information in the health field has been relieved by the recent publication by the National Association for the Education of Young Children titled *Healthy Young Children* (Kendrick, Kaufmann, & Messenger, 1988). This lack of attention also is the reason that this chapter on health, and the two following chapters on nutrition and safety, include more detailed information than has been previously found in one place.

In addition to the general lack of specific training information, the rate of staff turnover in child care is so high that education of the staff members must be continuous. On-the-job training is perhaps more effective than a series of lectures or a course, because learning is enhanced when the staff members have the opportunity to put into practice the information they have learned in the training. For instance, a demonstration of handwashing procedures (see Fig. 6–5) can be immediately put into practice by the educarer in washing her own hands, and the hands of the children.

Suggested topics for the health education of educarers include:

- Health assessment, including observation, screening, and evaluation of hearing, speech, vision, and dental problems
- Health records, including the collection, storing, and use of information
- Access to health-care services and information in the community, state, and nation
- Health policies and procedures
- Illness, including recognizing symptoms, managing the sick child, administering medication
- Infectious diseases, including immunization, transmission, prevention, and management

Sources for the above information are numerous, and may be identified by contacting local or state offices of Health and Human Services, the American Red Cross, the Visiting Nurse Association, and the Cooperative Extension Service. The state or local health department probably has many brochures and other printed materials from the American Academy of Pediatrics, as will a local pediatrician. Of course, the state standards for day care or child care frequently contain health information also, but individual states differ in their requirements. According to Morgan (1987), 36 states have some health training requirement for staff in a center "either health content for required training of all staff, or a First Aid training requirement for one staff member always on the premises" (p. 10–4). A recent review of the licensing standards for family day care providers reports that 23 states have no training requirement whatsoever for providers (The Children's Foundation, 1988). NAEYC (1988) firmly states that educarers must be trained in first aid and CPR (cardiopulmonary resuscitation).

SUMMARY

The health component of an infant/toddler setting is an essential part of any program. Indeed, if young children are not well cared for or protected from the consequences of their natural developmental behaviors and external conditions, there would be few children for whom to plan the developmental curriculum described in the preceding chapters.

Health goals for infants and toddlers (and older children) include both present and future well-being. They can be reached through educarers, parents, and community working together. Although the child's family bears the primary responsibility for the health of their children, the center or family day-care home plays an important helping role in meeting this responsibility.

In order to meet the essentials in this helping role, a health policy should be designed by professional health persons, child-care staff representatives, and parent representatives. The center or family day-care home implements the agreed-upon (written) policy. Implementation is begun by enforcing enrollment/admission requirements, and continued compliance with immunizations at the recommended ages after enrollment.

The ongoing provision of a health-promoting environment is a must. Personnel knowledgeable about health precautions and appropriate actions in case of illness or health emergency are also a must. Personnel must know the basic facts about infectious diseases, immunizations, symptoms indicating a health problem, and about procedures for the prevention of health problems and the management of health problems when they occur.

All licensing requirements about health in infant/toddler settings are either minimal or nonexistent, in spite of the importance of health concerns in group situations, and the vulnerability of very young children.

All parents want the best for their children, and every parent experiences heartbreak when his or her child is not doing well. Yet too many parents do not take the initiative to take their child to a pediatrician or another source of health care. We can, and should, encourage (or in some cases insist) that this be done. Parents of very young children in child care trust the educarers and confide in them because both the educarers and the parents care about the child's well-being. Persons in child care therefore have a unique opportunity in helping parents fulfill their hopes for their children. Educarers are not alone in this endeavor. There is a large group of professionals who are continually working to improve the quality of life for young children and their families. Educarers can

form the bridge between these experts and the parents of "their" children.

SUGGESTED ACTIVITIES AND QUESTIONS

1. Which of the national goals for child health are included in the goals for infant/toddler care and education? Select one goal and describe the steps necessary to meet this goal in an infant/toddler setting.

2. List the information you would use in responding to a parent who thinks immunizations are a waste of time and money, and are dangerous.

3. Start a health resources file. Collect materials from the various health agencies in your community and state. Informative and current brochures and lists may be ordered from:

American Academy of Pediatrics
141 Northwest Point Boulevard
Elk Grove Village, IL 60007
The brochure *You and Your Pediatrician* describes how to select a pediatrician. Send a self-addressed, stamped business-size envelope.

American Medical Association
535 N. Dearborn Street
Chicago, IL 60610
Provides brochures about many medical conditions and ethical issues.

American Academy of Family Physicians
8880 Ward Parkway
Kansas City, MO 64114
Has several brochures about selecting a family physician, preserving good health, and detecting medical conditions.

4. Make up a list of health-related questions, and interview a local pediatrician or pediatric nurse practitioner. Or invite a health professional to your class, and ask the questions from all the class members.

5. Make a list of arguments for and against keeping sick children in group care. Then list the necessary conditions for keeping sick children in group care.

6. Write for free brochure titled *Resources on Child Health* (1989). Order from:

Association for the Care of Children's Health
3615 Wisconsin Avenue N.W.
Washington, D.C. 20016

7. Write for listing of instructional materials about baby care and parenting. Order from:

J & J Baby Products Company
Consumer and Professional Services
Skillman, NJ 08554

SUGGESTED READINGS

American Academy of Pediatrics. Committee on Early Childhood Adoption, and Dependent Care. (1984). The pediatrician's role in promoting the health of a patient in day care. *Pediatrics, 74* (1), 157–158.

American Academy of Pediatrics. (1985). *Recommendations for day care centers for infants and children.* Evanston, IL: Author.

American Academy of Pediatrics. Committee on Early Childhood, Adoption and Dependent Care. (1987). S.R. Deitch, M.D. (Ed.), *Health in day care: A manual for health professionals.* Evanston, IL: Author.

American Academy of Pediatrics. Committee on Infectious Diseases. (1988). *Report of the Committee on Infectious Diseases* (ed. 21). Elk Grove Village, IL: Author.

American Academy of Pediatrics. Task Force on Pediatric AIDS. (1988, November). Pediatric guidelines for infection control of Human Immunodeficiency Virus (Acquired Immunodeficiency Virus) in hospitals, medical offices, schools, and other settings. *Pediatrics, 82,* 801–807.

American Academy of Pediatrics. (1989). *Choking prevention and first aid.* Elk Grove Village, IL: Author. (brochure)

Andersen, R. D., Bale, Jr., J. F., Blackman, J. A., & Murph, J. R. (1986). *Infections in children: A sourcebook for educators and child care providers.* Rockville, MD: Aspen.

Aronson, S. S. (1980). The health component of the child care program. In R. Neugebauer & R. Lurie (Eds.), *Caring for infants and toddlers: What works, what doesn't.* Vol. 1. Redmond, WA: Child Care Information Exchange.

Aronson, S. S. (1983, September). Health policies and procedures. *Child Care Information Exchange,* 14–16.

Aronson, S. S. (1984, October). Health and safety training for child care workers. *Child Care Information Exchange,* 25–28.

Aronson, S. S. (1987, March). Health concerns for caregivers—Infectious diseases and job stresses. *Child Care Information Exchange, 54,* 33–37.

Aronson, S. S. (1988, January). CMV and child care programs. *Child Care Information Exchange, 59,* 25–28.

Aronson, S. S. (1989). Ask Dr. Sue. *Child Care Information Exchange, 67,* 37–38.

Aronson, S., & Pizzo, P. (1977). Health and safety issues in day care. *FIDCR, Appropriateness Study State of the Art Paper.* Washington, DC: DHEW–Office for Planning and Evaluation.

Bax, M. (1981). The intimate relationship of health, development, and behavior in young children. In C. L. Brown (Ed.), *Infants at risk: Assessment and intervention.* Skillman, NJ: Johnson & Johnson.

Black, R., Dukes, A., Anderson, K., Wells, J., Sinclair, S., Gary, G., Hatch, M., & Gangaisa, E. (1981). Handwashing to prevent diarrhea in day-care centers. *American Journal of Epidemiology, 113* (4), 445–451.

The Child Infectious Diseases Study Group. Centers for Disease Control. (1985). Consideration of infectious diseases in day care centers. *Pediatric Infectious Diseases, 4* (2).

Child Welfare League of America. (1984). *Standards for day care services* (rev.). New York: Child Welfare League of America.

Committee on Psychosocial Aspects of Child and Family Health, 1985–1988. (1988). *Guidelines for health supervision II.* Elk Grove Village, IL: American Academy of Pediatrics.

Chu, A. (1988). Health and safety concerns in infant care. In A. Godwin & L. Schrag. (Eds.), *Setting up for infant care: Guidelines for centers and family day care homes.* Washington, DC: National Association for the Education of Young Children.

Denk-Glass, R., Laber, S. S., & Brewer, K. (1982). Middle ear disease in young children. *Young Children, 37* (6), 51–53.

DHHS, Office of the Secretary. (1980, July 17). Day care regulations. *Federal Register.*

Fauvre, M. (1988). Including young children with "new" chronic illnesses in an early childhood education setting. *Young Children, 43* (6), 71–77.

Fredericks, B., Hardman, B., Morgan, G., & Rogers, F. (1986). *A little bit under the weather.* Watertown, MA: Work/Family Directions.

Goodman, R., Osterholm, M., Granoff, D., & Pickering, L. (1984). Infectious diseases and child day care. *Pediatrics, 74* (1), 134–139.

Hansen, J. P., & Jeppson, E. S. (1986). *Seasons of caring: Curriculum guides for parents, educators, and health professionals.* Washington, DC: Association for the Care of Children's Health.

Healy, A., McAvearey, P., Von Huppel, C. S., & Jones, S. H. (1978). *Mainstreaming preschoolers: Children with health impairments.* (DHHS Publication No. [OHDS] 80–31111). Washington, DC: U.S. Government Printing Office.

Highberger, R., & Boynton, M. (1983). Preventing illness in infant/toddler day care. *Young Children, 38* (3), 3–8.

Kendrick, A. S., Kaufmann, R., & Messenger, K. P. (1988). *Healthy young children: A manual for programs.* Washington, DC: National Association for the Education of Young Children.

Lee, C., & Yeager, A. (1986). Infections in day care. *Current Problems in Pediatrics, 16,* 129–184.

Marotz, L. R., Rush, J. M., & Cross, M. Z. (1989). *Health, safety, and nutrition for the young child* (2nd ed.). Albany, NY: Delmar.

Meisels, S. J. (1985). *Developmental screening in early childhood: A guide* (rev. ed.). Washington, DC: National Association for the Education of Young Children.

Meisels, S. J., & Provence, S. (1989). *Screening and assessment: Guidelines for identifying young disabled and developmentally vulnerable children and families.* Washington, DC: National Center for Clinical Infant Programs.

National Association for the Education of Young Children. (1987). Lice aren't nice. *Young Children, 42* (3), 46.

North, A. F., Jr. (1972). *Day care 6: Health services. A guide for project directors and health personnel.* (a Head Start paperbound book)

Osterholm, M. T., Klein, J. O., Aronson, S. S., & Pickering, L. K. (Eds.). (1987). *Infectious diseases in child day care: Management and prevention.* Chicago: University of Chicago Press.

Raper, J., & Aldridge, J. (1988). What every teacher should know about AIDS. *Childhood Education, 64* (3), 146–149.

Rodgers, F. S., Morgan, G., & Fredericks, B. C. (1985). Caring for the ill child in day care. *Journal of School Health, 56,* 131–133.

Rubenstein, A. (1986). Schooling for children with acquired immune deficiency syndrome. *Journal of Pediatrics, 109,* 242–244.

Schmitt, B. D., M.D. (1987). *Your child's health: A pediatric guide for parents.* New York: Bantam. A *must* for every center or family day care.

U.S. Office of Human Development Services. Administration for Children, Youth and Families. *Head Start health services: Health coordination manual.* (DDHS Publication No. [OHDS] 84–31190). Washington, DC: U.S. Government Printing Office.

7

The Nutrition Component

What are little boys made of?
Snips and snails and puppy dog tails.
What are little girls made of?
Sugar and spice and everything nice.
                    Traditional rhyme

Most adults do not let children play with dangerous toys or equipment. Most adults keep poisons out of the reach of young children. Most adults protect children from obvious harm—*except* when it comes to feeding them. The nutritional component of a child-care program is of primary importance. Feeding children is not sufficient.

Our knowledge of the roles of various foods has been greatly enlarged since the period when it was believed that the sex of the unborn child was determined by the mother's diet. A lean diet (snips and snails and puppy dog tails) produced a son; a rich diet (sugar and spice and everything nice) produced a daughter. The mother's diet does have considerable effects on her expected child, but, so far as we know, sex determination is not one of them.

The total nutritional needs of children must be met each day. Therefore, the child-care program must provide the foods needed to supplement the food served at home. But the nutritional component includes much more than food service. The socialization and developmental needs of infants and very young children, as well as nutrition education for the children and their parents, also must be considered.

Therefore, even in centers large enough to hire a staff member whose sole responsibility is to purchase, prepare, and store food, each educarer is also a vital link in the delivery of the nutrition component of the care and protection curriculum. Regardless of center size, one person should have the prime responsibility for food service and its related factors, even if combining this with other educaring activities. In any case, the director should be directly involved in the supervision of food service, frequently to the extent of meal planning and food shopping. Each staff member should know the nutritional needs of children, the nutritional and psychological value of properly prepared and served

181

foods, and safe food practices. Ideally, training in nutrition and its many aspects should be a prerequisite for employment in a day-care delivery system. Realistically, this is seldom a requirement, except perhaps for the cook, but important information can be transmitted during in-service workshops or on-the-job training. Expert advice is readily available from the local representative of the Cooperative Extension Service programs. Frequently, faculty members from nearby colleges or universities will volunteer their services or will serve as consultants on a regular basis.

NUTRITION-RELATED DISORDERS

Malnutrition and Subnutrition

This country tends to react to the word malnutrition in terms of crisis: mass starvation, marasmus, and kwashiorkor make headlines and always seem to happen in someplace far away. A more accurate concept of malnutrition includes any functional impairment or physical condition that can be prevented or cured by improved nutrition. When so defined, instances of malnutrition exist in every society, whether it is technically advanced or newly developing. There are some 50 identified nutrients, and therefore there are a similar number of types of malnutrition, any of which might cause some measure of stunted physical growth, reduced resistance to disease, or general behavioral unresponsiveness.

There is an increasing amount of evidence from many parts of the world conclusively showing both a direct and indirect relationship of nutritional factors to intelligence and learning. There is even evidence that poor or "picky" eating during the first year of life is related to a depressed IQ score later on.

The period of rapid brain growth when brain cells rapidly multiply and grow takes place from about the second trimester of pregnancy to 24 months of age. The brain growth spurt in humans occurs in two general stages, the first during the second trimester, and the second from the third trimester of pregnancy through the normal period of breast feeding.

> The two stages overlap considerably, and many neurons are still multiplying even after birth. . . . Superimposed on the two stages of growth spurt are regional variations in brain development. Some sections of the brain develop earlier than others, and some develop quickly while others evolve more slowly. Throughout its growth spurt, the brain needs adequate nutrients in order to grow. Research findings in animals now indicate that severe malnutrition during this period can produce brain deficits which cannot be rectified nutritionally (Read, 1976. p. 12).

Although the unique human brain may not be this vulnerable throughout the growth spurt, evidence shows that it, like the brain of other animals, is probably more vulnerable to malnutrition throughout the growth spurt than at other times.

The relationship of nutrition to physical growth seems to be universally accepted. Even preschoolers have been told to eat their vegetables and drink their milk so that they can grow up big and strong. The relationship of nutrition to intellectual growth is more complex because of the multitude of interrelated environmental and genetic factors, and it is only in the last four decades that systematic investigations have been made. The War on Poverty and the resulting Head Start programs produced some direct clinical studies that supported the previous survey reports of the high incidence of unsatisfactory diets of young children from the economically disadvantaged segments of the population.

One of the best reviews of research evidence on the effects of malnutrition on learning and intelligence was included in the Congressional Record of the Senate as a supporting document for the Child Nutrition Act of 1972. A major portion of the summary statement follows:

> The evidence we have surveyed indicates strongly that nutritional factors at a number of

different levels contribute significantly to depressed intellectual level and learning failure. These effects may be produced directly as the consequences of irreparable alterations of the nervous system or indirectly as a result of ways in which the learning experiences of the developing organism may be significantly interfered with at critical points in the development course.

If one were to argue that a primary requirement for normal intellectual development and for formal learning is the ability to process sensory information and to integrate such information across sense systems, the evidence indicates that both severe acute malnutrition in infancy as well as chronic subnutrition from birth to the school years result in defective information processing. Thus by inhibiting the development of a primary process essential for certain aspects of cognitive growth malnutrition may interfere with the orderly development of experience and contribute to a suboptimal level of intellectual functioning.

Moreover, an adequate state of nutrition is essential for good attention and for appropriate and sensitive responsiveness to the environment. One of the most obvious clinical manifestations of serious malnutrition in infancy is a dramatic combination of apathy and irritability. The infant is grossly unresponsive to his surroundings and obviously unable to profit from the objective opportunities for experience present in his surroundings. This unresponsiveness characterizes his relation to people, as well as to objects. Behavioral regression is profound; and the organization of his functions are markedly infantalized. . . .

In children who are subnourished one also notes a reduction in responsiveness and attentiveness. In addition the subnourished child is easily fatigued and unable to sustain either prolonged physical or mental effort. Improvement in nutritional status is accompanied by improvements in these behaviors as well as in physical state.

It should not be forgotten that nutritional inadequacy may influence the child's learning opportunities by yet another route, namely, illness. Nutritional inadequacy increases the risk of infection, interferes with immune mechanisms, and results in illness which is both more gener-

alized and more severe. The combination of subnutrition and illness reduces time available for instruction and so by interfering with the opportunities for gaining experience disrupts the orderly acquisition of knowledge and the course of intellectual growth.

We have also pointed to intergenerational effects of nutrition upon mental development. The association between the mother's growth achievements and the risk to her infant is very strong. Poor nutrition and poor health in the mother when she was a girl result in a woman at maturity who has a significantly elevated level of reproductive risk. Her pregnancy is more frequently disturbed and her child more often of low birth weight. Such a child is at increased risk of neurointegrative abnormality and of deficient IQ and school achievement.

Despite the strength of the argument that we have developed, it would be tragic if one were now to seek to replace all the other variables— social, cultural, educational, and psychological—which exert an influence on intellectual growth with nutrition. Malnutrition never occurs alone, it occurs in conjunction with low income, poor housing, familial disorganization, a climate of apathy, ignorance and despair. The simple act of improving the nutritional status of children and their families will not and cannot of itself fully solve the problem of intellectual deficit and school failure. No single improvement in conditions will have this result. What must be recognized is that within our overall effort to improve the condition of disadvantaged children, nutritional considerations must occupy a prominent place, and together with improvements in all other facets of life including relevant and directed education, contribute to the improved intellectual growth and school achievement of disadvantaged children (Birch, 1972, p. S13458).

Malnutrition and chronic undernutrition are not unknown in our country. They may be less common than in the poorer, developing countries, but when they occur, the results are just as severe. Children between the age of 6 months and 3 years should be weighed every month. If there is no weight gain for 2 months in a row, there is something wrong. A regular monthly gain is the most important sign of a child's overall health and development.

It is quite possible that family day-care homes or centers in our country will never enroll a severely malnourished infant or toddler, but there are other nutrition-related health disorders that may occur more often and that we should work to prevent. In the United States there are four major health problems that are related to nutrition, and that may occur or have their beginning in early childhood: obesity, atherosclerosis, dental caries, and iron-deficiency anemia.

Obesity

Overnutrition is more prevalent than undernutrition in the United States. Not only is obesity physically unattractive, it is a significant nutritional disorder.

It is difficult to be specific about how much is "too much" food, because the amount of food that is barely adequate for one child may actually be excessive for another. There is no medically based definition of obesity, but in general terms, obesity is an excessive ratio of fat to fat-free body mass. Activity patterns, energy expenditures, metabolic rate, and age influence the adequacy of a diet for any one person. Neither parents nor educarers can be expected to scientifically determine the optimal adequate diet for any one child or group of children. Nutritionists and pediatricians have recommended amounts and types of food as well as meal patterns for children in various age groups. This information follows the discussion of the nutrition-related disorders.

The tendency for childhood obesity to persist into the adult years is well-known. Evidence suggests that overweight infants are more likely to become obese adults than are thin infants. The cultural belief that a fat baby is a healthy baby is not correct, and is really dangerous. If a baby puts on too much fat in the early months, the number of fat cells that will be carried around for the remaining life span may actually

increase. Along with an increase in fat, obesity puts children at risk for high blood pressure, respiratory diseases, diabetes, and a variety of orthopedic disorders, in addition to psychological and social problems (Obesity among children, 1987). According to Wishon, Bower, and Eller (1983), obesity is as much a health hazard as any other life-threatening disease.

The desire to overeat is tempting in the presence of an abundance of food (as many adults have learned). Many adults have also learned that permanent weight reduction is difficult and elusive. Overeating is a habit and "the earlier in life a habit—good or bad—is established, the more likely it is to persist; hence, the need to begin preventive efforts in infancy" (Fomon, 1977, p. 68).

Babies who are bottle-fed rather than breast-fed tend to gain weight more rapidly, perhaps because nursing mothers are not inclined to urge drinking "the last drop" when baby shows satisfaction and is reluctant to continue sucking. The educarer who is bottle-feeding the infant seems more inclined to insist on an empty bottle at the end of each feeding, regardless of baby's reluctance or even refusal. The amount of formula or milk in the bottle is somewhat arbitrary and may have little relationship to the amount that baby needs at any particular time. The same psychology applies to the feeding of "biekost" (foods other than milk or formula fed to infants). A clean plate is the goal, and parents and educarers alike engage in ludicrous antics to convince a child to eat "just one more bite." Food also has emotional connotations, and misinformed adults use food as a reward, a pacifier, an expression of love, or as a bribe, all of which encourage overeating. We should avoid the use of feedings as a response to *all* of a baby's distress signals. A drink of water, a back rub, or a snuggle with someone in a rocking chair are recommended pacifiers, and are noncaloric (Brasel, 1978).

It is currently fashionable to introduce biekost (solid food) as early as possible, even during the first month (thereby proving the infant is precocious), but there is no medical reason for introducing strained foods before the sixth month.

"Adequate intakes of human milk or a commercial infant formula meet all the known nutritional requirements of infants for the first 6 months of life, with the possible exception of vitamin D and fluoride in breast-fed infants" (AAP, 1985, p. 23). Commercially prepared foods are expensive, and their use may encourage overfeeding. Developmental readiness, not adult eagerness, should determine the time for introducing biekost.

The frequency of eating also appears to have implications for the prevention of obesity. Children under 3 years need nourishment five or six times a day. Their stomachs are small, but their energy needs are great.

Atherosclerosis

Atherosclerosis is a thickening of the inner wall of the arteries, which can cause clotting and block the flow of blood to the heart muscle. Atherosclerosis causes angina pectoris, heart attacks, and scarring of the heart muscle. Coronary artery disease has increased greatly because of (1) the universal dependence on the automobile and (2) overnutrition. It seems to run in families with a history of diabetes or high levels of cholesterol.

There is a current controversy about the advisability of modifying the diets of infants and young children for the purposes of decreasing the intake of total fat, saturated fatty acids, and cholesterol. Human milk, of course, is a rich source of these substances.

Many normal infants receive commercially prepared formulas for the first and sometimes the second year of life. These are relatively low in fatty acids and cholesterol. The formulas should be made with corn, soy, or other vegetable oil. Any other dietary considerations should be prescribed by the family physician and are not considered necessary for normally developing children at the time of this writing. A small minority of children have genetically based tendencies toward atherosclerosis, and dietary restrictions may be imposed by the family physician or pediatrician.

Dental Caries

Babies are born toothless, but there are two full sets of teeth, primary and permanent, developing in the gums. After birth, even before the teeth have erupted, the child should receive adequate amounts of calcium, phosphorus, and vitamins A, C, and D. These nutrients are well provided by formula or breast feeding, along with any supplements recommended by the child's pediatrician. An adequate source of dietary fluoride is also recommended. Formula-fed infants usually require no fluoride supplementation, assuming that powdered formula or concentrate is used and mixed with fluoridated water. The breast-fed infant should have extra fluoride whether or not the water is fluoridated.

Of course, one of the developmental highspots is the appearance of the first tooth (around 6 or 7 months), but even before then, baby's mouth should be kept clean by gently wiping with a bit of dampened gauze after each feeding. As soon as the first tooth appears, clean it with a damp gauze pad, optimally after every feeding, but at least once a day. When most of the primary teeth have come through, begin brushing. Use a small soft brush and a plain fluoride toothpaste.

These primary or "baby teeth" are temporary, and a popular myth holds that their care is not important, which may explain why so many older people wear dentures. Disregard of the primary teeth not only risks needless pain for the child and expense for the parents, but also endangers both the proper alignment and structural form of the developing teeth.

The American Society of Dentistry for Children has concluded that allowing a young child to nurse for long periods of time on milk, juices, or other sweetened liquids can have a destructive effect on the child's teeth, and that this destruction starts as soon as the primary teeth begin to erupt. If long nursing periods continue, the result is serious. Teeth will need crowns, the nerves or pulps will need treatment, and teeth may even have to be extracted because of extensive breakdown and infection. In addition, teeth affected by prolonged nursing remain highly susceptible to decay long after the nursing stops. This unfortunate condition is called "bottle mouth" or "nursing bottle caries." It is particularly unfortunate because it is easily preventable. The lactose naturally present in cow milk is probably not a major factor, but the sucrose and corn syrup solids in many infant formulas are the true culprits. Most destructive to teeth is the practice of bottle-feeding sweetened drinks or fruit juices. Once the teeth have erupted, bottle-feeding of any sweetened liquid, including formula, should be discontinued, particularly at nap or bedtime. Actually, any liquid other than water will cause dental caries if not swallowed immediately. Nursing bottle caries is most severe when the child is put to bed sucking on a bottle of milk or juice. The maxillary anterior teeth can be destroyed before the child is 1 year old. Therefore, not only should educarers *not* put a baby to bed with a bottle, but also they should caution parents about the nursing bottle syndrome.

One of the pervasive customs in the United States is eating between meals, and our choice of snacks has a definite relationship to dental caries, obesity, and, possibly, future atherosclerosis. One piece of sticky candy may coat the teeth with sugary substances for up to an hour. Snack choices should be made from fresh fruits and vegetables, nonsweetened enriched crackers, bread or cereals, cheeses, peanut butter, lean meats, and milk. Cakes, cookies, jams, and jellies are potential troublemakers. Pasteurized honey should *not* be given to children under 1 year of age because they are not able to neu-

tralize the botulism toxins naturally present. Honey is both safe and appropriate in the diet of a child older than 1 year. The suggested snacks in Table 7–1 are low in starch and sugar.

Most children do not have their first dental checkup until they are 2 or 3 years old at the earliest, and by then nursing bottle caries may have done irreparable damage. It is recommended that the first visit to a dentist, preferably a pedodontist, be made at 9 months of age. This recommendation can be made to the parents of infants in day care, along with the other recommendations about feeding procedures and immunizations.

An increasing number of dentists are recommending the addition of fluoride to formula or food, because human breast milk is low in fluoride, and baby formula and baby foods contain virtually no fluoride. Teeth start to form and harden before birth, and the enamel caps form in the first year.

Iron-Deficiency Anemia

Hemoglobin is the part of the red blood cell that carries oxygen to muscles, nerves, and organs. Iron-deficiency anemia occurs when the concentration of hemoglobin is below normal. In most countries, including the United States, low concentrations of hemoglobin are found most commonly in infants of low birth weight and in full-size infants between 6 and 24 months of age. National nutrition surveys have found that the majority of young children from all income levels receive intakes of iron less than the estimated requirement.

Neither cow's milk nor human milk contains much iron. About 15 quarts of cow's milk would have to be consumed each day to provide enough iron to meet the requirements of normal infants during the first year of life. Babies fed cow's milk should regularly receive an iron-fortified infant cereal or iron supplement. A daily serving of dry, precooked, iron-fortified infant cereals should be fed until 18 months of age. It

Table 7–1

Snack Foods Low in Starch and Sugar

Fruits (dried, fresh, or canned in own juice or light syrup)	Fresh vegetables	Protein food	Juices
Peeled apple wedges	Broccoli flowerets	Cheese cubes	Apple
Applesauce	Cabbage wedges	Cottage cheese	Apricot nectar
Apricots	*Carrot sticks or curls	Hard-cooked eggs	Cider
Banana chunks	*Cauliflowerets	Meat slices or cubes	Grapefruit
Berries	*Celery sticks, plain, or stuffed	Milk	Grape
Cherries (remove pits)	with peanut butter, cheese	Yogurt	Orange
Dates and figs	spread, or cottage cheese		Peach nectar
Grapefruit, orange, tangerine	Cucumber slices or sticks		Pineapple
sections (peel and remove	Green beans		Prune
seeds)	*Green pepper sticks		Tangerine
Grapes (seedless)	Lettuce leaves		Tomato
Melon cubes	Mushrooms		Vegetable or fruit
Peach wedges	Peas		combinations
Pear wedges	*Radishes		
Pineapple sticks	Romaine leaves		
Plums (remove pits)	Rutabaga strips		
Prunes (remove pits)	Spinach leaves		
	*Sweet potato strips		
	Tomato wedges or cherry		
	tomatoes		
	*Turnip strips		
	*Zucchini strips		

*Not suitable for infants unless cooked

is very possible that toddlers and preschool children also receive low intakes of iron. Perhaps there should also be moderate restrictions placed on intake of foods low in iron content. These include dairy products, unfortified bakery goods, candy, and soft drinks. Adequate intakes of iron can be provided with supplements, but an overdose can be very dangerous. It is always preferable to offer a more acceptable dietary selection. Meat, poultry, eggs, vegetables, fruits, and cereals are all sources of iron, but the iron from vegetables is generally less well absorbed than that from meats and fish.

A list of foods for infants and toddlers that contain worthwhile amounts of iron is contained in Table 7–2.

The amounts of iron absorbed by individuals consuming identical diets are influenced by age, sex, iron status, and physiological state.

Intestinal Parasites

From a purely nutritional standpoint, anything that feeds on what the child needs is a cause of serious concern. Intestinal parasites (worms that may grow to over a foot in length, with hundreds of them infesting one child) are native to the southeastern United States, and may occur in other areas where a warm moist climate is combined with a lack of sanitary toilet facilities, poor personal hygiene factors, overcrowding, and other poverty conditions. Round worms enter

Table 7–2
Foods containing worthwhile amounts of iron

Vegetables	Fruits	Meats and meat alternates
Asparagus	Apples	Beef
Beans—green,	(canned)	Veal
wax, lima	Berries	Pork
Broccoli	Dried fruits—	Poultry
Brussel sprouts	apricots,	Lamb and
Green leafy	dates, figs,	mutton
vegetables—beet	peaches,	Eggs
greens, collards,	prunes,	Legumes
kale, mustard	Plums, purple	
greens, spinach,	(canned)	
swiss chard,	Rhubarb	
turnip greens		
Peas, green		
Squash		
Sweet potatoes		
Tomatoes (canned)		
Tomato juice, paste,		
or puree		

the body through the mouth from objects such as toys, food, and hands that come into contact with soil contaminated by fecal waste from infected children. Hookworms enter the body by penetrating the soft skin between toes and fingers, and may live as long as 4 or 5 years in the small intestine. Barefoot infants and young children playing in contaminated soil are prime targets for parasitic invasion.

Educarers should need no other reason than this for frequent handwashing, both before and after diaper changing, and in connection with food preparation and service, regardless of geographic location. Child advocates in the trouble areas should give high priority to improvement of local sanitary conditions.

Toxic Foods

According to a report by the Natural Resources Defense Council (Cook & O'Malley, 1989), an apple or apple juice or applesauce may be putting children at serious risk of cancer and neurological damage. Pesticide residues are the culprit. The most damaging of the chemicals studied is daminozide (Alar), which is used to enhance the growth and appearance of red apples. This is frightening for all of us, and particularly for those of us who are responsible for feeding snacks and meals to young children. Every list of suggested snacks includes apples or apple juice; many nutritionists recommend apple juice as a substitute for artificially sweetened drinks. The NRDC study found that the average toddler drinks *a lot* of apple juice, and according to Whyatt, senior project scientist at the NRDC, "over a million preschoolers may have a risk nearly 1,000 times the EPA limit" (Cook & O'Malley, 1989, p. 16). The use of Alar as a pesticide was banned in November 1989 by the Environmental Protection Agency (Hymes, 1990). The best insurance against eating pesticides found on any produce is to wash all fresh fruits and vegetables in running water to remove debris and pesticide residues on the outside of the produce. The USDA Consumer Advisor (Silverman, 1989) does not recommend using soap or detergent. The wax coatings found on some cucumbers, peppers, and some apple varieties should be removed, as should the outer leaves on lettuce, cabbage, and other leafy vegetables (they may contain the most recent pesticide application) (Nielsen, 1989). Other recommendations are to buy domestically grown produce in season, to buy organically grown produce in season, to buy organically grown foods, and to use fewer processed foods.

The common ordinary egg, also, has been found to cause an alarming increase in bacterial food poisoning, which can be fatal to infants (as well as the elderly or those already weakened by illness). The egg is now added to the list of undercooked beef, pork, poultry, and raw dairy products as a possible carrier of Salmonella enteriditis. But we can control this food poisoning by buying grade A eggs that are refrigerated in the store, by storing them at a temperature below 40°F, and by thorough cooking. The yolk must be heated all the way through to destroy bacteria. Also, and this rule applies to the handling of raw meat and poultry as well as to raw eggs, wash dishes and utensils and your hands with hot soapy water immediately after handling (Weber, 1988).

Some foods are "toxic" for some children. The most usual food allergies for very young children are tomatoes, citrus fruits, onions, chocolate, and any drinks with caffeine. Some infants are allergic to cow's milk, usually before 12 months of age (Van Leuven, 1988). The association between food allergies and behavior disorders is not clear (Trites & Tryphonas, 1983).

NUTRIENTS AND GOOD NUTRITION

There is a popular belief, even among physicians, that children will choose nutritious foods when given a choice. This belief stems from the oft-quoted studies in the 1920s by Davis, who found that infants and toddlers, *when offered a variety of nutritious foods,* selected foods that were sufficient for growth and maintenance of health. The Great Depression of 1929 prevented Dr. Davis from her next study, which was to have offered children a choice between nutritious foods and nutrient-lacking foods. Although that study has never been done (to my knowledge), we now know that children are born with an innate preference for sweets. We therefore need to direct our children to healthful foods by offering as many nutritious choices as possible (Shaping budding tastes, 1987).

There are a few basic facts about food and nutrition that *every* provider of child care must know and put into practice. These include information about the essential nutrients and recommended meal patterns and practices for very young children.

Nutrients

The total nutrient needs of very young children are relatively low, but for children from 1 to 3 years of age the requirements for protein, calories, a number of minerals, and vitamins A, B, and E are about half those of adults, while calcium and vitamin C needs are about the same. Under the age of 4 years, children often need an iron supplement, because they require 50% more iron than is needed by an adult. Babies gain about 16 pounds during their first year, but only about 3 pounds between 12 and 24 months. Appetite diminishes after the first birthday, and many parents and caregivers become unnecessarily disturbed about decreased food intake and eating "problems."

In general terms, nutrients provide energy (expressed as calories), build and repair body parts, and help control body functions. There are six kinds of nutrients, usually categorized according to their uses in the human body. Each day each person needs a specific amount of each of the six nutrients, which include proteins, minerals, carbohydrates, fats, vitamins, and water.

Proteins. *Proteins* are the body's building blocks. They are essential for building and repairing all the body tissues, energy, and resisting diseases. Proteins (or their amino acids) are found in meat, fish, poultry, eggs, milk, cheese, nuts (not recommended before the age of 4), dried peas and beans, breads, and cereals.

Minerals. *Minerals* are needed to help build and repair all parts of the body. Four important mineral elements are:

1. *Calcium,* to build bones and teeth, to help make blood clot, and to help muscles and nerves work; milk is the best single source; other sources are milk products and deep green, leafy vegetables

2. *Phosphorus,* to build and repair all parts of the body, especially bones, teeth, nerves, and glands; found in milk, eggs, bran, and liver

3. *Iron,* to build red blood cells, which carry oxygen to all parts of the body; found in

liver, lean meat, egg yolk, enriched or whole grain bread and cereal, dried fruit, and green, leafy vegetables

4. *Iodine,* to help control the rate at which the body uses energy, and to prevent goiter; found in seafood and iodized salt

Carbohydrates. *Carbohydrates* are needed to furnish energy for physical and mental activities, as well as the energy needed in body processes such as respiration, circulation, and digestion. Carbohydrates are the sugars and starches, and are contained in breads, cereals, potatoes, corn, dried fruits, and any foods sweetened with sugar, such as syrup, jelly, and jam.

Fats. *Fats* furnish the body with energy and heat, and help keep the skin smooth and healthy. They come from both animal and vegetable sources, such as butter, margarine, cream, nuts, meat, salad oils, and cooking fats.

Vitamins. *Vitamins* are needed to promote growth and maintain health. They are nutrients, not medicine. A proper diet will provide adequate amounts of all the vitamins needed by any healthy child or adult. The vitamins are:

1. *Vitamin A,* to keep the skin smooth and healthy, to protect the mucous membranes from infection, and to help prevent nightblindness. Important sources of vitamin A are liver, egg yolk, butter, whole milk, cream, yellow fruits, and dark green and yellow vegetables

2. *Thiamine(vitamin B_1),* to help keep the nervous system healthy, to help keep the appetite and digestion normal, and to help change food into energy. Important sources are meats (especially pork), eggs, dried beans and peas, enriched and whole grain breads and cereals, and potatoes

3. *Riboflavin (vitamin B_2),* to help the cells use oxygen, to help eyes adjust to light, to help

keep the skin, tongue, and lips healthy. Important sources are meat, fish, poultry, eggs, ice cream, milk, and cheese

4. *Ascorbic acid (vitamin C),* to help make "cementing" materials that hold body cells together, to help keep the blood vessels healthy, and to help heal wounds and broken bones. Because the body does not store vitamin C, it must be supplied *daily* in the diet; important sources are citrus fruits (oranges, lemons, grapefruits, limes), tomatoes, raw cabbage, raw greens, cantaloupes, strawberries, green peppers, and potatoes

5. *Niacin,* to help keep the skin and nervous system healthy, to help keep the digestive tract healthy, and to promote growth. Important sources are meat, fish, poultry, milk, and enriched or whole grain bread and cereal

6. *Vitamin D* (the sunshine vitamin), to help build calcium and phosphorus into the hard material of bones; when the body is exposed to sunlight, vitamin D forms in the skin. Important food sources are fishliver oils and vitamin D milk

Water is essential to life, and some nutritionists classify it as a nutrient. Water regulates body temperature, aids in digestion, and helps rid the body of waste products.

The Child Care Food Program

The Child Care Food Program is one way of developing good eating habits and providing nutritious meals to the growing child. The program was established in 1975 through P.L. 94-105, and is administered by the U.S. Department of Agriculture, Food, and Nutrition Service, but the actual administering agencies and policies differ from state to state.

The program provides cash reimbursement and/or commodities for the provision of meals and snacks to institutions providing nonresiden-

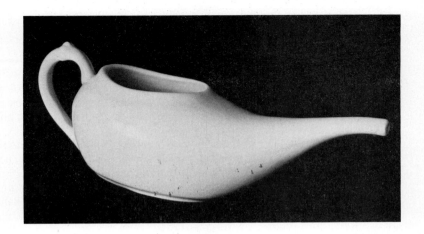

Porcelain baby feeder. (The University of Iowa Hospitals & Clinics, Iowa City, IA; c. 1870)

tial child care for children, such as child-care centers, family day-care homes, neighborhood and Head Start centers, and day-care centers for handicapped children. Subsidies are provided for two meals and one snack per day for children under 12 years old. The meals must meet USDA requirements, and the centers or home-based day-care homes must be licensed. Not only is the Child Care Food Program a nutrition program, it is a major source of support for child care, especially for family day care. For-profit day-care centers can participate only when at least 25% of their enrolled children are receiving benefits through the Social Services Program (AAP, 1985).

USDA meal patterns. Whether or not a particular program takes part in the Child Care

Food Program, the required meal patterns are excellent guidelines for meeting the nutrition needs of young children. These patterns for infants up to 12 months are in Table 7–3, and for children from 1 to 3 years in Table 7–4. Children under 3 years need food five or six times a day. Although their stomachs are small, their energy needs are great.

NUTRITION IN THE CHILD CARE PROGRAM

Infant Feeding

Milk or formula. Breast-feeding is possible for some infants in day care, and occasionally a mother is able to arrange her school or working schedule so that she can feed her child at the

Blown-into-a-mold baby bottle. (The University of Iowa Hospitals & Clinics, Iowa City, IA; c. 1870)

Table 7–3

The Child Care Food Program
Infant Meal Pattern Requirements

The first year of life is divided into three, 4-month age groupings with appropriate meal guidelines for each group. Although the meal pattern specifies breakfast, lunch, supper, and snack, this may not match each baby's feeding pattern. Babies seldom accept rigid eating schedules and may need to eat every 2 to 4 hours. Babies should be fed when hungry or "on demand."

There are ranges given for food portions to allow flexibility, based on each baby's appetite. Babies vary from day-to-day in the amounts they actually eat. The amounts listed are the *minimum* you must serve to meet requirements. You may serve larger portions to babies who want more than these amounts. Some babies may want less and should never be forced to finish what is in the bottle or what is spoon fed. Let babies determine how much they will eat and learn the individual cues each baby uses to show hunger or fullness.

Age of Baby by Month	Breakfast	Lunch and Supper	Snack
Birth through 3 months	4–6 fluid ounces (fl oz) breast milk[1] or formula[2]	4–6 fl oz breast milk[1] or formula[2]	4–6 fl oz breast milk[1] or formula[2]
4 months through 7 months	4–8 fl oz breast milk[1] or formula[2] 0–3 tablespoons (tbsp.) infant cereal[3] (optional)	4–8 fl oz breast milk[1] or formula[2] 0–3 tbsp. infant cereal[3] (optional) 0–3 tbsp. fruit and/or vegetable (optional)	4–6 fl oz breast milk[1] or formula[2]
8 months through 11 months	6–8 fl oz breast milk[1] or formula[2], or whole milk 2–4 tbsp. infant cereal[3] 1–4 tbsp. fruit and/or vegetable	6–8 fl oz breast milk[1] or formula[2], or whole milk 2–4 tbsp. infant cereal[3] *and/or* 1–4 tbsp. meat, fish, poultry, egg yolk, or cooked dry beans or peas, *or* 1–4 oz cottage cheese, cheese food, or cheese spread *or* ½–2 oz cheese 1–4 tbsp. fruit and/or vegetable	2–4 fl oz breast milk, formula[2], whole milk, or fruit juice[4] 0–½ slice bread or 0–2 crackers[5] (optional)

[1]Meals containing only breast milk are not reimbursable
[2]Iron-fortified infant formula
[3]Iron-fortified dry infant cereal
[4]Full-strength fruit juice
[5]Made from whole-grain or enriched meal or flour

Child Care Food Programs, requirements for meals. Section CCFP 226.21 FR January 22, 1980, Revised 7/89.

Table 7–4
Meal Patterns for Age 1 up to 3

Food Components	Breakfast	Lunch or Supper	Supplemental (Two of the four components.)
A. Milk			
Milk, fluid	½ cup[1]	½ cup[2]	½ cup[3]
B. Vegetables and Fruits			
Vegetable(s) and/or fruit(s); or full-strength vegetable or fruit juice or an equivalent quantity of any combination of vegetable(s), fruit(s), and juice	¼ cup		½ cup
C. Bread and Bread Alternates			
(Whole grain, enriched, or fortified)			
Bread;	½ slice	½ slice	½ slice
or cornbread, biscuits, rolls, muffins, etc.;	½ serving	½ serving	½ serving
or cold dry cereal; or cooked cereal;	¼ cup		¼ cup
or cooked pasta or noodle products;	¼ cup	¼ cup	¼ cup
or cooked cereal grains or an equivalent quantity of any combination of bread/ bread alternate	¼ cup	¼ cup	¼ cup
D. Meat and Meat Alternates			
lean meat/poultry/fish;		1 oz	½ oz
or cheese;		1 oz	½ oz
or eggs;		1 egg	½ egg
or cooked dry beans or peas;		¼ cup	⅛ cup
or peanut, soynut, other nut butters;		2 tbsp.	1 tbsp.
or peanuts, soynuts, tree nuts, or seeds;		½ oz[4]	½ oz
or yogurt (commercially prepared plain or sweetened and flavored yogurt, low-fat yogurt or nonfat yogurt);		1 oz or 2 tbsp.	2 oz or ¼ cup
or any equivalent quantity of any combination of the above meat/meat alternates			

Breakfast must include A, B, and C.
Lunch (or supper) must include A, B, C, and D.
Supplemental (snack) must include 2 of A, B, C, and D.
[1]as a beverage or on cereal, or both
[2]as a beverage
[3]as a beverage, on cereal, or both
[4]must be combined with another meat or meat alternate

Adapted from Child Care Food Program, requirements for meals. Section CCFP 226.21 FR January 22, 1980, Revised 7/89.

appropriate times. Any mother with the least inclination to do so should be encouraged, even though such feedings may ''upset'' the center routine. Indeed, there should be no routine in infant care that is so rigid that the rights of mother and child do not come first. Babies sometimes get hungry before mother has arrived, and there needs to be an agreement worked out between the mother and center staff as to the appropriate steps to take when this happens. Once nursing is well established, an occasional bottle feeding should not cause any problems. There is vigorous controversy about supplementing the diets of breast-fed infants with vitamin D, iron, and fluoride, and of course no one other than the parent and the pediatrician has the right to make this decision.

An iron-fortified, commercially prepared formula is a complete food for infants and requires no supplements of vitamins or minerals. Evaporated milk formulas are acceptable for infants younger than 6 months of age, with supplements of vitamin C and iron. Because of uncertain sterilization, however, preparation of single feedings is preferable to the preparing of all the feedings for a 24-hour period at one time.

"Solid" foods. Today most infants are introduced to foods other than milk or formula by 2 months of age, possibly because of social pressures and the pervasive attitude that earlier is always better. According to Fomon and Barness (1985), the starting of solid foods should be delayed until 5 or 6 months of age because of possible interference with established sound eating habits and the probable encouragement of overfeeding. The precautions about overfeeding stated earlier apply to both bottle-feeding and other foods. Feeding solid foods should be stopped at the earliest indication from the child of willingness to stop. Until the infant is able to sit with support and indicate desire for food by her actions feeding solid foods probably represents a type of forced feeding.

Iron-fortified cereal should be the first food introduced. When it has been accepted, other foods may be introduced, but not more than one or two during the same week. Below are additional tips for adding solid foods to a baby's diet:

1. Using a small spoon, place a little bit of strained food or cereal on the back of baby's tongue (but not so far back as to cause choking).

2. Expect baby to push out the food with her tongue; she needs time to get used to new tastes and textures.

3. Try one new food at a time and use it for several days before adding another. Watch for allergic reactions such as rash, diarrhea, coughing, or vomiting.

4. Try new foods when baby is hungry. A good time is in the middle of the morning.

5. *Cereals:* Until baby is at least 6 months old, use only rice, oat, or barley cereal. Measure 1 teaspoon of cereal and mix with 2 or 3 tablespoons of lukewarm formula and feed from a spoon (not in the bottle with the formula).

6. *Vegetables and fruits:* Add vegetables one at a time before adding fruits; start with milder vegetables such as squash, green peas, and green beans. Offer a new vegetable every 4 or 5 days; if baby will not eat it, wait a few days and try again. Introduce vegetables and fruits by serving ½ to 1 teaspoonful, gradually increasing the amount to 2 or 3 tablespoonfuls. When baby has a few teeth, the vegetables prepared for the older children (and adults) may be finely chopped.

7. *Meats and egg yolks:* Commercially available strained foods should be selected with care because there are wide variations in the amounts of total calories and of individual essential nutrients. It is preferable to scrape lean raw meat, form into a pattie, and cook in the top of double boiler until the meat is well done. When baby can handle chopped foods, meats may be baked, boiled, or broiled, and finely chopped.

8. *Storage:* Opened jars of baby food or center-prepared vegetables or fruits should be covered, dated, and refrigerated. The food should be used within 48 hours; raw fruit and meats should not be stored more than 1 day. Many servings of prepared foods may be frozen in ice cube trays and stored in freezer bags for up to 1 month. The need to strain center-prepared foods is temporary; just a few months is both beneficial for the baby, and cost-efficient for the caregiver.

Recommendations. Planners and providers of infant child care should be on the alert about major errors in feeding infants, which include:

- Too great dilution or too great caloric concentration of a formula
- A calorically inadequate diet because skim milk is being fed
- Hazard from nursing bottle caries
- An inadequate or excessive quantity of milk or formula consumed (less than 16 oz. or more than 32 oz. of milk or formula)
- Complete avoidance of certain food categories (e.g., an older infant who rarely eats fruits or vegetables)
- Inadequate facilities for food preparation and storage

- Excessive intake of fat-soluble vitamins
- Adherence to a special restrictive diet (especially if not under a physician's supervision)
- Pica [craving for unnatural foods] (Fomon, 1977, p. 12)

It sometimes seems that the infant's day revolves around eating, feeding, and related activities—diaper changing, hand and body washing, changing clothes, napping, and then the cycle begins again. These procedures consume much of the educarer's time, which is one of several reasons behind the recommended adult/child ratio of 1:3 for children from birth to 2 years of age. Although feeding times may be scheduled in the overall daily plan, this is an excellent example of the adage that "rules are made to be broken." Individual schedules should be determined by the individual babies themselves and should be adhered to. Soon each infant will settle into a fairly regular individual feeding schedule, so that educarers can then plan around it. Adults seem to be less accepting of individual needs and desires in this business of feeding than in any other component of child care (or parenting). Babies should not be forced into predetermined schedules designed for the adults' convenience.

Part of the group, but still prefers finger foods. (Early Childhood Education Center)

"Mass feeding" for toddlers.
(Kindercampus, Iowa City)

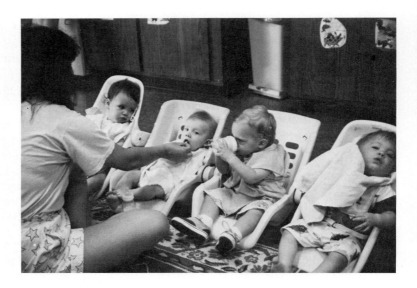

It also might seem more convenient to "bottle-prop" instead of holding the baby while feeding. However, adult convenience and infant group care are not compatible. Both the psychoanalytic theorists and the behavioral theorists would agree on the rule that holding the infant while bottle-feeding is highly desirable and even essential for the development of the sense of basic trust in the world, for laying the foundations of basic social relationships, and for learning about the world from early, repeated experiences. In addition to these important benefits, we now know that there are health complications "associated with the infant's drinking in a recumbent position and with falling asleep with a bottle of formula, milk, or juice in the mouth. The former may increase the incidence of otitis and the latter may result in the accelerated decay of teeth" (AAP, 1987, p. 23). If necessary, adults other than professional caregivers might be utilized during feeding times. Volunteers, senior citizens, the center's nurse, and high school or college students are examples of those who can come in at certain times and be assigned certain babies for feeding and holding. Ideally, however, each educarer assumes prime

responsibility for a small number of babies, and is the deliverer of all the routines as well as many of the social interactions to these same babies.

The infant should be held while being given food, as well as milk or formula, until able to sit with support at a table or high chair. Another way of handling this is to sit on the floor with your knees up and cradle the baby on your knees facing you. This frees both of your hands for spoon feeding, and gives excellent face-to-face contact between baby and caregiver.

Between 6 and 7 months of age a baby will delight in finger foods such as hard breads or dry cereals, and should be given the opportunity to drink from a cup. For a while, perhaps, the baby will insist on a bottle for milk but may accept juices or water from the cup.

Toddler Feeding and Eating

With a few modifications, toddlers eat just like older people, or at least like older people should. (One modification: oiling the toddler's face before spooning in pureed foods will make the wiping up easier.) Adults are often conscious of the aesthetics of eating: foods at certain temperatures; interesting combinations of texture and colors; and a variety of sauces and seasonings to tempt the appetite. Toddlers, apparently, could care less about the aesthetics of eating. Foods served at room temperatures are eaten in the same quantities as hot or cold ones. Young children do not insist upon a crisp salad with a soft entree. With the occasional exception of catsup, they want (or need) no added flavorings or seasonings. Toddlers should be easy to feed, and yet it is during this period, between 12 and 36 months of age, that eating "problems" appear.

Eating "problems". Some of the problems are in the minds of the adults. Toddlers apparently do not need as much food as infants, and we worry that they are not getting sufficient amounts of nutrients. However, a look at the average growth rates of young children shows that, while 1 year olds may have gained 14 to 16 pounds during the first year, 2 year olds will have gained only 3 or 4 pounds during the second year and, of course, their appetites diminish. An adult's insistence on eating more after the toddler indicates "no more" is not only wasteful of time and energy, but also soon changes a pleas-

ant experience into an emotionally charged experience resulting in frustration and even anger. If the child appears alert, happy, and curious, and is gaining some weight, there is no cause for concern. At the same time, the well-developing child is entering the period when a sense of autonomy seems to take priority, even over food, and the child's "No!" to food is an indication of this innate desire for self-assertion.

Very possibly, it is this same drive for autonomy that triggers finicky eating, the seemingly irrational selection of only certain foods or certain types or colors of foods, excluding all others. Usually these are temporary quirks, and they should be accepted and treated casually. However, the persistence of such quirks over a period of time suggests that a visit to the pediatrician might be in order. It is possible that some genetic influence has led to poor appetite or strong food preferences or aversions.

Unfortunately, even very young children soon learn that their eating behavior (or misbehavior) can be used to manipulate and control adults. It is very exciting to provoke anger and violent reactions in adults, and some young children seem to thrive on such activities. Mealtime should be one of the most enjoyable times

Conversation time during snack.
(Early Childhood Education Center)

of the day, but it may be the most upsetting. The choice is the educarer's. Young children are entitled to a pleasant mealtime the same as adults. Threats, rewards, and punishments should not be a part of the experience.

Meal planning. The meal patterns for children from birth to 36 months were presented in Tables 7–3 and 7–4. An example of their translation to actual menus for children 12 to 36 months is given in Table 7–5, which presents a plan for morning and afternoon snacks as well as for the main meal.

Evaluation. The following questions are useful in evaluating menus:

1. Are all components of the meal included?
2. Are serving sizes sufficient to provide young children the required quantity of: Meat or alternate or an equivalent? Two or more vegetables and/or fruits? Enriched or whole-grain bread or an equivalent? Fluid milk?
3. Are serving sizes planned?
4. Are other foods included to help meet the nutritional needs of young children and to satisfy appetites?
5. Are the combinations of food pleasing and acceptable to children?
6. Do meals include a good balance of: Color—in the foods themselves or as a garnish? Texture—soft, crisp, firm-textured; starchy, and other type foods? Shape—different sized pieces and shapes of foods? Flavor—bland and tart or mild and strong flavored foods? Temperature—hot and cold foods?
7. Are most of the foods and food combinations ones children have learned to eat?
8. Have children's cultural and ethnic food practices been considered?

Table 7–5
Meal plan for one week (12–36 months)

Monday	Tuesday	Wednesday	Thursday	Friday
AM snack				
Orange juice	Apricot nectar	Pineapple juice	Apple juice	Cranberry juice
Dry cereal	Oatmeal cookie	Peanut butter sandwich	Whole wheat crackers	Date bread/ margarine
noon meal				
Meat loaf	Scrambled eggs	Hamburger patty	Vegetable soup with noodles	Tuna casserole
Mashed potatoes	Stewed tomatoes	Scalloped potatoes	Cheese sandwich	Green beans
Carrots	Grits	Peas	Cherry tomatoes	Cornmeal muffin/ margarine
Bread/margarine	Bread/margarine	Bread/margarine	Bread/margarine	Milk
Apple sauce	Diced pears	Orange slices	Milk	
Milk	Milk	Milk		
PM snack				
Wheat crackers and cheese chunks	Apple slices with cheese spread	Dry cereal mix	Cottage cheese with pineapple chunks	Banana chunks
Milk	Milk	Milk	Milk	Milk

9. Are foods varied from day to day, week to week?

10. Are different kinds or forms of foods (fresh, canned, dried) included?

11. Are seasonal foods included?

Although young children do not appear to be at all impressed with variety in menus (for instance, banana chunks and milk are favorites day in and day out), menu planners rightfully seek diversity. One of the nutrition-related objectives for any group of children is the introduction of a variety of foods, not only to establish good eating habits, but also to ensure the supply of the essential nutrients. Sources of menu ideas may be found in the senior citizen and public school menus published in local newspapers, although the school menus are inclined to be overloaded with starches and carbohydrates. Excellent snack ideas can be found in the appetizer or hors d'oeuvres section of any cook book (the little hors d'oeuvres knives are ideal for children to spread their own bread or crackers; they are not sharp and just the right size for toddlers).

Little bits of wisdom can be easily learned from any cook in a toddler center, such as the following:

> Cheesespreads work on anything, from crackers to raw apple, potato, and turnip slices. Add oatmeal to all kinds of muffins and to meat loaf. Chinese celery is less stringy and more tasty than Pascal celery. Use flattened (rolled with a rolling pin) hamburger bun halves or refrigerator biscuits instead of English muffins for pizza. Peanut butter is easier and safer to eat if it has been whipped with butter or margarine: use two parts of peanut butter to one part of margarine. Use Grape-nuts or wheat germ in or on top of "everything" instead of nutmeats. Dentists frown on graham crackers (Early Childhood Education Center, University of Iowa).

As is true in all endeavors, experience is the best teacher, and many more practical suggestions may be obtained from interviews with persons involved in the daily preparation and meal service for very young children. There are also many printed materials available.

The Involvement of Children

Abilities of toddlers. Even though more food preparation activities are being included in preschools for 3- and 4-year-old children, adults are inclined to think that children under the age of 3 would just make a mess. Many cooks in centers do not want to be bothered and, of course, young children underfoot in a kitchen increases the risk of accidents and injuries. An alternative is to bring the foods and the appropriate utensils for cooking activities to the children's room. The term *cooking activities* in this instance includes all the steps necessary in the preparation and serving of foods, with or without the use of heat. The cooking-related activities that follow are listed in progressive order. Most 3 year olds are capable of mastering all of them.

1. Exploring cooking utensils (banging, nesting, putting away)

2. Exploring cooking utensils with water (cups, bowls, beaters, spoons, funnels)

3. Pouring dry ingredients (corn, rice)

4. Pouring wet ingredients (water)

5. Tasting fresh fruit and vegetables

6. Comparing tastes, textures, colors of fresh fruits and vegetables

7. Comparing tastes, textures, colors of fresh and canned fruits and vegetables

8. Dipping raw fruits and vegetables in dip or sauce

9. Scrubbing vegetables with brushes

10. Breaking or tearing lettuce; breaking or snapping beans; shelling peas

11. Stirring and mixing wet and dry ingredients

12. Measuring wet and dry ingredients (use rubber band to mark desired amount on container or measuring cup)

13. Placing toppings on pizza or snacks; decorating cookies or crackers that have been spread

14. Spreading bread or crackers

15. Pouring milk or juices to drink

16. Shaking (making butter from cream or coloring sugar or coconut)

17. Rolling with both hands (peanut butter balls, pieces of dough for cookies)

18. Juicing with a hand juicer

19. Peeling hard-cooked eggs, fruits

20. Cutting with dull knife (fruits, vegetables, cheese)

21. Beating with fork or eggbeater

"It tastes better when I do it."
(Early Childhood Education Center)

22. Grinding with hand grinder (apples, cranberries)

23. Kneading bread dough

24. Cleaning up

Participation in cooking-related activities helps to whet the appetite of even the most finicky eater. It is hard to imagine the number of children who have eaten something they helped to make, even though it was burned to a crisp. But other areas of development are also involved: concept development, basic motor skills, and even social-emotional development.

A suggested procedure. Involving young children in serving their main meal at the child care center also has benefits. A suggested procedure for 2 and 3 year olds to help with a family-style noon meal is described below.

Equipment Needed

1. Multishelved wheeled cart that holds (a) unbreakable bowls of food and large pitchers of milk, (b) serving utensils and individual spoons (and forks for the older children), (c) empty dishpan, (d) container for scraps and plate scraper

2. In classroom supply cupboard: (a) paper napkins, (b) paper towels or sponges, (c) paper plates, (d) plastic cups or glasses, (e) terrycloth bibs with Velcro fastening strips, and small pitchers

3. Trash container

4. Clean water supply

5. Child-sized tables and chairs (one for each group of five children and one adult)

Procedure

1. Children are engaged in group activity with adult(s) while another adult brings prepared cart from kitchen to classroom.

2. Adult adds plates, cups, and bibs to cart.

3. Adult places one napkin for each person on tables at appropriate places.

4. Child helpers volunteer or are chosen and come to the cart for supplies. Helper tasks include: (a) place plate by each napkin, (b) place cup or glass by each plate, (c) place spoon (and perhaps fork) by each plate, (d) put bib on each child's chair, (e) carry bowls of food to tables, (f) carry small pitchers of milk to tables.

5. When tables are ready, adults fasten bibs on children, and all are seated.

6. At each table adult passes or serves food, and all eat. Adult offers seconds or thirds.

7. At each table, adult initiates conversation about the attributes of the food, the morning's activities, plans for the afternoon, or whatever. Adult encourages language interaction among children (but it will mostly be adult-child or child-adult).

8. When the meal is finished, one adult goes to cart, a second adult stands by the supply of water. Children (a) bring plates and cups to be emptied by adult into plastic container, (b) put silverware and cups in dishpan for washing, (c) throw plates and napkins into trash container, (d) are de-bibbed by second adult, who rinses bib, uses it to wipe hands (and face when needed), and puts wet bib into laundry basket, (e) use paper towels for drying themselves, (f) run off to play!

9. Adult wheels cart back to kitchen.

In addition to the many learning possibilities, this procedure is smooth and efficient. No wonder the parents who join their children for lunch are amazed at the capabilities and good manners of their children. "But he would never eat that at home!" is a frequent comment.

An excellent source of information about the food preferences of very young children is, of course, the educarers in a child care program. Such a list is in Table 7–6. Note the absence of cookies and cupcakes. Indeed, the educarer commented that the children sometimes refused a cookie when one was offered.

Many adults have preconceptions about meal service, which may have no relationship whatsoever to what comes naturally to the young child. Adults prefer a variety of color and texture. Children may be perfectly happy with orange carrots, yellow-orange scrambled eggs, and orange gelatin. Adults also automatically assume that dessert follows the main course and that dessert depends on "cleaning one's plate." One infant-toddler educarer serves dessert (fruit, pudding, cookie, even ice cream) with the rest of the meal. In this instance, there is neither a temptation to bribe the child nor the likelihood that the child will accord undue importance to dessert.

Table 7–6
Favorite foods of infants and toddlers

Main dishes	Side dishes	Snacks
Macaroni with cheese	Green beans	Banana bread or muffins
Tacos and sloppy Joe's	Mashed potatoes	Yogurt
Meat loaf	Applesauce	Fresh fruit (except cantaloupe)
Hot dogs (without roll)	Jell-o	
Bologna (without bread)	Tater Tots	Hard boiled eggs with crackers
	Salad with Thousand Island or French dressing	Crackers and cheese
Soup (with lots of "stuff" in it)		Egg salad with crackers
Liver (with ketchup)	Sweet pickles	White or brown bread and butter
Ham loaf	Spiced apple rings	
Pizza	Lettuce	Graham crackers
Beef stew (lots of meat)*		
Salisbury steak*		
Tuna fish		
Egg salad		

*Overcook, so the meat breaks into small pieces.

Skills and Concepts

The list of beginning skills and concepts inherent in cooking-related activities is extensive. Some are readily apparent. All are essential skills and concepts for later learning and behaviors. For example, typical lists of academic readiness skills include: visual and auditory perception and discrimination, eye-hand coordination, oral language, and the association of print to meaning. What better vehicle for "readiness?" A few examples: peaches and oranges are similar in color and shape, but definitely different in taste and texture. Dishes may all be round, but differ in size and depth. Liquids bubble when they boil, and frozen liquids crackle when they start to melt. The child without eye-hand coordination will get meaningful practice when measuring and pouring liquids and brush-cleaning or cutting vegetables. Kneading and rolling dough uses the large muscles and coordination of both hands and arms. Using a knife to cut or spread requires a great deal of coordination. Mathematical concepts of sets and numbers, sequence and order, measurement, and time intervals are all parts of many food experiences. Oral language is also a part of the give-and-take of a food preparation experience. And even if the children are far too young to be expected to read, the visual display of a recipe or set of directions to which the educarer refers helps introduce the idea that print does have meaning and is useful. In no way am I suggesting an "academic" infant-toddler program, rather that beginning learning, understandings, and attitudes should be encouraged at the very earliest ages. They can be encouraged naturally in the course of daily activities.

Academic readiness is an important aspect of any early childhood program. In addition to readiness per se, there are basic nutritional concepts that adults can consciously teach and young children will unconsciously begin to learn. How do we consciously teach basic nutritional concepts to an infant or toddler? By modeling eating behavior (we *like and eat* everything that is served), by talking about our need for good food so that we can run and play and feel good, and by establishing a happy eating environment so that food becomes associated with pleasure as well as physical satisfaction.

Other teaching efforts will be directed to the parents of the children. As is true in most parent-center interactions, center personnel must tread softly. Parents think they know how to raise their children, and this is one of their rights. If we tell them they are not feeding their child correctly, we have probably lost the battle even before starting. If we include in our regular newsletter lists of suggested snacks, the program's menus, and sample recipes for food the children enjoy, most parents will start to compare their food habits with these suggestions. Possibly they will serve some of the suggested foods. It is hoped this kind of indirect instruction will initiate a dialogue and perhaps a parent-center meeting or workshop. Parents want the best for their children.

The nutrition concepts that we are striving to teach both children and parents are those developed by the Interagency Committee of Nutrition Education for Project Head Start (Head Start Bureau, 1961, p. 24), and are useful in any early childhood program.

1. Nutrition is the food you eat and how the body uses it.
    - We eat food to live, to grow, to keep healthy and well, and to get energy for work and play.
2. Food is made up of different nutrients needed for growth and health.
    - All nutrients needed by the body are available through food.
    - Many kinds and combinations of food can lead to a well-balanced diet.
    - No food, by itself, has all the nutrients needed for full growth and health.
    - Each nutrient has specific uses in the body.
    - Most nutrients do their best work in the body when teamed with other nutrients.

3. All persons, throughout life, have need for the same nutrients, but in varying amounts.
   - The amounts of nutrients needed are influenced by age, sex, size, activity, and state of health.
   - Suggestions for the kinds and amounts of food needed are made by trained scientists.
4. The way food is handled influences the amount of nutrients in food, its safety, appearance, and taste.
   - Handling means everything that happens to food while it is being grown, processed, stored, and prepared for eating.

Herr and Morse (1982) suggest a set of food and nutrition concepts that also can serve as guides for educarers in their work with very young children.

1. There is a wide variety of food.
2. Plants and animals are sources of food.
3. Foods vary in color, flavor, texture, smell, size, shape, and sound.
4. A food may be prepared and eaten in many different ways—raw, cooked, dried, frozen, or canned.
5. Good foods are important to health, growth, and energy.
6. Nutrition is how our bodies use the foods we eat for health, growth, and energy.
7. Food may be classified according to the following categories:

milk	vegetables
meat	breads
dried peas and beans	pastas
eggs	cereals, grains, and seeds
fruits	nuts

8. A good diet includes a wide variety of foods from each of the food categories.
9. There are many factors that influence eating:
   attractiveness of food
   method of preparation
   cleanliness/manners
   environment/atmosphere
   celebrations
10. We choose the foods we eat for many reasons:

availability and cost
family and individual habits
aesthetics
social and cultural customs
mass media influence (pp. 6–7).

Lesson Plans for Food Preparation Activities

It is unusual to find a "child" cookbook that includes activities specifically designed for children immediately after the infant stage, but toddlerhood is the right time to start. The following activities have proven successful with toddlers as one of the choices of table activities:

Crackers and/or fruit with cream cheese

Objectives

fine and gross motor coordination

socially acceptable behavior

Ingredients

softened cream cheese

fresh fruit (strawberries, peaches, etc.)

wheat crackers

paper towels or napkins

Equipment

4 table knives

2 bowls (one for cream cheese, one for fruit)

Procedure

(For 3 children and 1 adult.)

Children and adult wash hands.

One child passes a cracker to the others.

Each person spreads his cracker with cream cheese.

Each person adds fruit to his spread cracker.

When each cracker is ready, all may be eaten.

Napkins discarded, knives and bowls put in container for washing.

Wash hands.

Hard-Boiled Eggs

Objective

fine motor coordination

Ingredients

8 hard-boiled eggs

Equipment

4 table knives

4 paper towels or napkins

4 small bowls

1 tray

Procedure

(For 3 children and 1 adult.)

Children and adult wash hands.

Each one takes 2 eggs and puts them into his bowl.

With adult help, child cracks the egg on edge of bowl.

Child peels the eggs into the bowl, and sets peeled egg on paper towel.

Child cuts eggs in half, and puts the halves onto tray to save for lunch or snack (or eats one half, and saves the rest).

The adult helps only when needed, and also peels two eggs.

Paper towels and egg shells are discarded (or the shells saved for a craft project); knives are put into container for washing.

Wash hands.

Simple? Of course. But these and similar activities (decorating unbaked or baked gingerbread men, rolling banana chunks in juice and wheat germ) are the very beginnings of the nutrition component of infant/toddler care and education. They lead to concepts of identifying and comparing foods on the basis of color, taste, texture, smell, and sometimes sound. They also lay the groundwork for socially acceptable eating behaviors, in addition to acting ''grown-up.'' They supply another step toward the child's autonomy.

SUMMARY

The nutrition component of a child-care program is an integral part of the total care and protection curriculum. For many children, it is their program that supplies most or all of the essential nutrients.

Nutrition-related disorders most frequently found in American children are subnutrition, obesity, atherosclerosis, dental caries, iron-deficiency anemia, intestinal parasites, and problems caused by toxic foods. Information about the essential nutrients and their combinations in the basic food groups and resulting meal patterns has been detailed. An easy way to assess the nutritional adequacy of the foods eaten in a child-care program is by using the four basic food groups as a guide. For instance, the milk group provides calcium, phosphorus, protein, and some vitamins. Of all the foods commonly used, milk is the only supplier of calcium in amounts needed for building bone. The vegetable and fruit group is a gold mine of other minerals and vitamins. The meat group, with its alternatives, is the principal source of protein (along with the milk group), iron, and the B vitamins. The cereal group can be relied on as a supplemental source of protein, iron, and the B vitamins.

The actual feeding of the infants and toddlers and their eating are crucial activities. If they aren't eaten, the best planned menus will accomplish nothing except a waste of time and money.

In addition to the actual ingestion of recommended foods, there are other parts of the nutritional component. These include involving children in food preparation activities, teaching concepts and skills, and serving as information resources for the families of the children in our programs.

SUGGESTED ACTIVITIES AND QUESTIONS

1. The U.S. Department of Agriculture Child Care Food Program is an excellent source of free information about young children and their nutrition needs. If you write to their Washington D.C. address, they will send the name of the agency in your state which administers the program.

USDA Child Care Food Program
Food and Nutrition Services
500 12th Street, S.W.
Washington, DC 20402

2. For more information about food and pesticides, write to:

Mothers and Others for Pesticide Limits
P.O. Box 96641
Washington, DC 20090

3. Using the guidelines in Table 7–4, design a week's menus for a group of toddlers. Specify the time of year and make use of foods that are in season. Include morning and afternoon supplements as well as a main meal.

4. Make up the food shopping list for the meals and snacks you planned. Include amounts of food to be purchased and their current costs. You may assume that staples such as flour, sugar, seasonings, and so on are already available.

5. Design a parent newsletter containing nutrition information and suggested snacks and recipes for use at home. Include suggested ways of including toddlers in food preparation activities.

6. Write for materials about nutrition and dental care for infants and toddlers.

American Dental Association
211 E. Chicago Avenue
Chicago, IL 60611
Offers several brochures on dental health of children. Write for free catalog. Several titles are offered in Spanish.

American Dental Hygienists' Association
444 N. Michigan Avenue
Suite 3400
Chicago, IL 60611
The brochure *An Ounce of Prevention* answers questions about children's dental health care.

American Academy of Pediatric Dentistry
211 E. Chicago Avenue
Suite 1036
Chicago, IL 60611
Can provide a listing of their members who specialize in dentistry for children.

Food and Nutrition Information Center
National Agricultural Library, Room 304
Beltsville, MD 20705

SUGGESTED READINGS

American Academy of Pediatrics. Committee on Nutrition. (1985). *Pediatric Nutrition Handbook* (2nd ed.). Elk Grove Village, IL: Author.

American Academy of Pediatrics. Committee on Early Childhood, Adoption and Dependent Care. (1987). *Health in day care: A manual for health professionals.* (pp. 23–27). Elk Grove Village, IL: Author.

American Dental Association. (1976). *Care of children's teeth.* Chicago, IL: Author.

American Dental Association. (1983). *Nursing bottle mouth.* Chicago, IL: Author.

Aronson, S. (1980). Infant feeding policies. In R. Neugebauer & R. Lurie (Eds.), *Caring for infants and toddlers: What works, what doesn't.* Belmont, CA: Child Care Information Exchange.

Brunelle, D. A., & Dennis, S. (1989, Summer). A day in the life. *Child Health Talk,* 2–4.

Child Care Food Program Family Day Care Home Sponsors Directory. (1989). Englewood, CA: Wildwood Resources. (Lists administrative agencies for all 50 states). Order from:
Wildwood Resources
6143 South Willow Drive, Suite 320
Englewood, CA 80111

Children's Defense Fund. (1989). *A vision for America's future: An agenda for the 1990s: A Chil-*

dren's Defense budget. (pp. 38–43). Washington, DC: Author.

Dusto, H., & Olson, C. (1982). *Environments for eating, DNS 19, Nourishing and nurturing two-year-olds.* Ithaca, NY: Cornell University.

Eliason, C. F., & Jenkins, L. T. (1986). *A practical guide to early childhood curriculum.* Chapter 13, Nutrition and food experiences (229–268). Columbus, OH: Merrill.

Endres, J. B., & Rockwell, R. E. (1985). *Food, nutrition, and the young child* (2nd ed.). Columbus, OH: Merrill.

Finney, J. W. (1986). Preventing common feeding problems in infants and young children. *Pediatric Clinics North America, 33,* 775–778.

Fomon, S. J. (1974). *Infant Nutrition* (2nd ed.). Philadelphia, PA: Saunders. (Out of print, but a good library resource)

Fomon, S. J., et al. (1979). *Recommendations for feeding normal infants* (DHEW Publication No. [HSA] 79-5108). Washington, DC: U.S. Government Printing Office.

Graham, L., & Runyan, T. (1980). *Nutrition handbook for staff in child care centers.* Ames, IA: Iowa State University Research Foundation.

Herr, J., & Morse, W. (1982). Food for thought: Nutrition education for young children. *Young Children, 38* (1), 3–11.

Howard, R. B., & Winter, H. S. (1984). *Nutrition and feeding of infants and toddlers.* Boston: Little, Brown.

Ivens, B. J., & Weil, W. B. (1984). *Teddy bears and bean sprouts—The infant and vegetarian nutrition.* Fremont, MI: Gerber Products.

Kendrick, A. S., Kaufmann, R., & Messenger, K. P. (1988). *Healthy young children: A manual for programs* (pp. 151–171). Washington, DC: National Association for the Education of Young Children.

Lansky, V. (1974). *Feed me! I'm yours.* Deephaven, MN: Meadowbrook.

Leach, P. (1989). *Your baby & child: From birth to age five* (new ed.). (pp. 61–72; 122–137; 194–206; 291–304; 390–394). New York: Knopf. (Written for mothers, but has good information for educarers)

Marotz, L. R., Rush, J. M., & Cross, M. Z. (1989). *Health, safety, and nutrition for the young child* (2nd ed.). Albany, NY: Delmar.

Martin, S. (1987). Nutrition: Avenue for discovery learning. *Dimensions, 16* (2), 15–18.

Massachusetts Department of Public Health. (1984). *Infant feeding policy.* Boston, MA: Author.

National Academy of Early Childhood Program. (1984). *Accreditation criteria & procedures* (pp. 35–36; appendixes C and D). Washington, DC: National Association for the Education of Young Children.

Nutrition and feeding of infants and children under three in group day care. (1971). Washington, DC: U.S. Government Printing Office. DHEW Publication No. HM72-5606.

O'Brien, M., Herbert-Jackson, E. & Risley, T. R. (1978–79). *Menus for toddlers in day care,* parts 1–4. *Day Care and Early Education, 6* (1–4).

Pipes, P. L. (1985). *Nutrition in infancy and childhood* (2nd ed.). St. Louis, MO: Times Mirror/Mosby.

Stevens, J. H., & Baxter, D. H. (1981). Malnutrition and children's development. *Young Children, 36* (4), 60–71.

U.S. Department of Agriculture, Food and Nutrition Service. (1985). *A planning guide for food service in child care centers.* (FHS Publication No. 64). Washington, DC: U.S. Government Printing Office.

Vermont Department of Health, Nutrition Services. (1979). *Guidelines for feeding infants and young children.* Burlington, VT: Author.

Willis, J. (Sept., 1985). Good nutrition for the highchair set. *FDA Consumer, 19* (7), 5–7. (or DHHS Publication No. [FDA] 86-2208).

Wishon, P. M., Bower, R., & Eller, B. (1983). Childhood obesity: Prevention and treatment. *Young Children, 39* (1), 21–27.

8

The Safety Component

An ounce of prevention is worth a pound of cure.
Benjamin Franklin

All young children get their share of cuts, bruises, and even sprains in the course of growing up. Minor injuries, although upsetting at the moment, can usually be treated with a gentle swab of antiseptic, a bandage, and a soothing hug and kiss. Serious accidents, however, are another matter. No child should experience even one such accident. Serious accidents are avoidable; they occur because adults underestimate the child.

Current statistics show that the majority of accidents during the first few years of life occur in the child's home, but this finding may change as more and more young children are served by out-of-home care during the daytime hours. In addition, it has been impossible to get valid data about incidents and types of accidents and injuries in many day-care centers or homes, except on an individual basis, because of their independence and diversity. The usual sources of such statistics are the accident and liability insurance companies, but the issuance of such coverage for children (and staff) in noninstitu-

tionalized child-care centers and homes is a relatively new phenomenon, and is neither readily available nor affordable.

Countries with national health insurance plans have such records, and are justly proud of the statistics. In Sweden, for example, there are significantly fewer accidents at day-care centers than in the children's homes for the same children. This statement is particularly meaningful when we consider the long daytime hours children spend at the centers. The Swedish attention to safety is immediately evident to the visitor. Many pieces of equipment are made of large, multishaped, multicolored chunks of foam rubber that can be combined or folded into child-sized tables, chairs, or room dividers. Small items such as crayons and little toys and blocks are stored in natural woven baskets on uncluttered shelves. Tempered glass insets in the lower half of Dutch doors leading from the children's rooms to the adult kitchen and staff rooms enable children to watch but not be underfoot. To provide additional elements of

A bandage and a hug.
(Early Childhood Education Center)

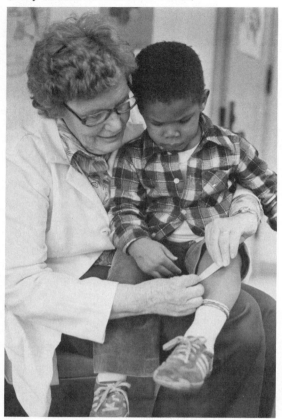

safety, door hinges are covered with smooth, vertical sheaths of molded plastic, so that little fingers cannot be smashed.

It may not be possible to design a completely accident-proof center or home, but it is possible to remove or prevent access to sources of injury. The goal is accident prevention through risk reduction.

Accidents will still happen in any group of children, but they will be the result of a child's actions (falling, bumping) rather than adult carelessness or lack of information.

An *accident* has been defined by the World Health Organization as "an event which is in-dependent of human willpower, caused by an external force, acts rapidly, and results in bodily or mental damage" (International Children's Center, 1979, p. 1).

A review of accident-related injuries in child care (Aronson, 1983) found that climbing equipment (for a very young child anything high is climbing equipment) accounted for more than twice as many injuries as the next most hazardous product (slides). An analysis of 1,324 accidents over a 42-month period at a university child-care center, serving 133 children from 6 weeks to 6 years of age, revealed that toddlers (13 to 24 months) had the highest average of injuries, most of them self-induced; that accidents peaked in mid-morning; and that September was the month with the highest accident rate. Although accidents were frequent, injuries were minor (Elardo, Solomons, & Snider, 1987).

Two major factors should be kept in mind when considering the safety of infants and toddlers. First, the young child is naturally active and very curious. However, a child's sense of balance and fear of danger do not develop until he matures and has some experience. Second, for the child an average indoor environment (home or center) is full of danger. Grown-ups can cope with staircases, hot stoves, cleaning agents, electric wires, and so on, but these can be very dangerous to children. We certainly do not want to stop a child from being active or curious, but we must create an environment in which he can be active safely.

Experience has shown that legislation about the risks in the environment is much more effective than education about the risks of injuries. Safety packaging is a good example.

Twenty years of poison control centers had no measurable beneficial effect on the frequency of accidental poisoning. Limiting baby aspirin to 36 per bottle, however, reduced aspirin poisoning by 50%. The subsequent introduction of safety packaging decreased childhood hospitalizations for aspirin poisoning by 90%. Similarly, years of safe-driving campaigns yielded no measurable benefit, yet seat belts have been shown to reduce auto fatalities by as much as 75% (Angle, 1980).

The leading causes of accidents to young children fall into the following five groupings:

1. Severe falls, blows, and cuts
2. Suffocation and strangulations
3. Ingestion of toxic substances
4. Drowning
5. Fires, burns, and electric shock

PREVENTION WITHIN THE CENTER OR FAMILY DAY-CARE HOME

Falls and Related Injuries

Falls. Deaths from falls in the toddler age group far exceed the number of the more sensational accidents by drowning or poisoning. Fortunately, although no child can be protected from all falls, most spills are fairly minor. Children fall from beds, cribs, and highchairs, on newly waxed or wet floors, on skidding throw rugs, and out of windows. Some educarers move cribs next to open windows for the "stimulation" of watching the fascinating world outside and apparently place total reliance on a screen latch that is not childproof. Children do not bounce when they fall. They may suffer skull fractures, brain damage, or dislocation or fractures of the extremities in addition to internal injuries. Remember that babies can climb on large toys left in a crib or playpen and fall over the railing. As soon as the baby can stand, the crib mattress should be put at its lowest position and the side rail locked at the highest position.

Almost half of the traumatic injuries of early childhood involve head injuries; the peak age is the second year of life. In addition to the potential for serious related physical or mental injury, emotional damage is very possible. The various hospital procedures—stitching up lacerations, taking radiographs, setting fractures and broken bones—are distress situations for little ones.

Children do not fall because educarers are "bad" educarers. They fall because educarers are not aware of or do not heed emerging patterns of development. New behaviors emerge rapidly during infancy and toddlerhood. Yesterday the baby lay on her back on the table, today she rolled over, *and off!* The peak age of incidence for all falls is between 12 and 36 months.

Severe blows. Sharp-edged furniture, open drawers, and easily overturned items such as lamps, flower pots, and other heavy items have been the frequent cause of severe blows to young children. Either eliminate these hazards, or keep a watchful eye on the children until they are old enough to use care in not causing an accident to themselves. (It is much easier and safer to get rid of the hazards.) Very young children must be kept out of the way of older children's active play on swings, seesaws, and slides.

Severe cuts. Sharp objects such as scissors, knives, razor blades, tools, and breakable objects must be removed from places where the child can reach them. Remember that children love to climb, and will climb using blocks or chairs or counter tops or shelves. The only safe place for these objects is behind a locked cupboard door!

Recommendations. Selected recommendations for the prevention of falls (and related accidents) in an infant-toddler center are as follows:

- Furniture and equipment should be sturdy and without sharp or splintered edges, loose parts, or toxic paint.
- Old equipment should be modified to meet the recommendations of the U.S. Consumer Product Safety Commission (CPSC); new equipment (cribs, highchairs, baby walkers)

should bear a label stating it meets the U.S. CPSC safety standards. All such equipment should be tip-proof.

- Floors should not be highly waxed; rugs should be skidproof. Floors and rugs should be easy to clean and cleaned daily.

- Stairs with more than three steps should have safety gates that open toward the exits. Stairways should have toddler-height hand rails on each side and should be well lighted and clear of any extraneous material.

- Cribs and playpens should not be placed by open windows; all openable windows should have sturdy screens or guards that have safety locks.

- Glass panels in doors should be made of tempered glass and clearly marked. Solid doors should have a lengthwise vertical inset of tempered glass. Dutch doors (or half-doors) are less likely than one-piece solid doors to cause accidents.

- The outdoor area should be fenced, and gates should have childproof locks (natural barriers such as dense shrubbery are not childproof); all parts of the area should be visible for supervision; there should be no holes in the ground (ditches, wells, etc.) into which children might fall.

- Outdoor equipment such as swings and climbing apparatus should be rigid, permanently anchored in the ground, and in good repair. Portable wading pools should be drained and upended when not in use.

- Concrete or asphalt surfaces should not be under climbing structures or swings. The most desirable surfaces for outdoor play areas are grass, artificial turf, and perhaps bark chips, with strips of hard surface for riding or pulling wheel toys.

- The outdoor area must be "policed" each time for broken glass or other hazards before children are allowed in the area.

- Very young children should be supervised by adults at all times, both indoors and outdoors.

Choking, Suffocation, and Strangulation

Choking. The sixth ranking cause of accidental death in the United States is foreign body obstruction of the airway or breathing passages. It ranks first as a cause of accidental death for infants below the age of 1 year. This is understandable, because curiosity is a driving force in infants, and is satisfied by mouthing the many small objects found on or near the floor or on reachable surfaces. Babies can choke on food-related objects such as bones, egg shells, peanut shells, and fruit skins and pits. Foreign bodies such as balloons, which are particularly lethal, beads, bobby pins, safety pins, coins, screws, and tacks are all potentially dangerous for infants. The following foods can be deadly to infants and other children under the age of 4: hard candies, hot dogs, raisins, nuts, raw carrots, corn, grapes, marshmallows, pop corn, and chewing gum.

A good rule-of-thumb is that objects less than 1½ inches wide or with removable parts less than 1½ inches wide should not be accessible to children under 2 years of age or who are still mouthing objects. A "choking tube" is useful in determining acceptable sizes of objects, and is available through many school supply stores or catalogs. A second rule-of-thumb is to restrict children from walking, running, or playing while they have food or anything else in their mouth.

Before putting an infant in the playpen or crib, or on the floor to play, check the area carefully. Keep buttons, beads, pins, screws, or anything small enough to fit into the baby's mouth safely out of reach. Small objects can get lodged in the throat and cut off the child's air supply or can puncture a vital organ if swallowed.

The most dangerous toys for a child under 3 years of age are those small enough to swallow. Do not let a young child play with marbles, small plastic toys, cars with easily detachable pieces, or stuffed animals and dolls with tiny button eyes or ornaments that the child can easily pull off. Balloons are a particular hazard. If the balloon bursts, a toddler could swallow all or part of it. Air in the child's throat can make the rubber "bubble up," causing asphyxiation. Swallowed balloons must be removed quickly, usually with surgery, to prevent the child from smothering.

If, in spite of precautions, an infant is choking and forcefully coughing, encourage the coughing and breathing by keeping him in an upright position, and verbally encourage the coughing.

> If an infant under one year of age chokes and is unable to breathe he is placed down over the rescuer's arm with head lower than trunk. The rescuer rests his forearm on his thigh. Four measured blows are rapidly delivered with the heel of the hand between the infant's shoulder blades. If breathing is not started, the infant is rolled over and four rapid compressions of the chest are performed as for CPR. . . . A choking child over one year of age should be placed on his back with the rescuer kneeling next to him and placing the heel of one hand on the child's abdomen in the midline between umbilicus and rib cage. A series of six to ten abdominal thrusts—Heimlich maneuver—(rapid inward and upward thrusts) should be applied until the foreign body is expelled. . . . If breathing is not started, open mouth with thumb over tongue and fingers wrapped around lower jaw. If a foreign body is seen it may be removed with a finger sweep (AAP, 1987, pp. 218–219).

In addition to a working knowledge of the correct procedures for choking incidents, educarers should know how to administer mouth-to-mouth ventilation and cardiopulmonary resuscitation. Both initial training and periodic updating should be a requirement for employment.

Suffocation and strangulation. One of the mixed blessings of our civilization is the almost universal use of plastic: plastic bags, plastic mattress covers, plastic baby pants. A plastic bag can be more dangerous than a poisonous snake. No one would place a child and a rattlesnake in the same crib, yet it is not unusual to leave pieces or bags of plastic film within the young child's reach. The resulting deaths are needless and tragic. An infant can suffocate in his crib with or without plastic. He cannot remove a pillow from his face, he cannot move his head from between the mattress and the side of the crib or carriage. The distance between the mattress and the crib or carriage side should be no more than the width of two adult fingers. An infant may also manage to wedge her head between the slats of a crib or playpen. Slat-to-slat distance should be no greater than 2⅜ inches, or about the width of three adult fingers.

The U.S. Consumer Product Safety Commission periodically releases warnings against products on the market that have a potential to cause death. A recent warning described stuffed animal mobiles designed to be suspended from the ceiling by means of three elastic cords and a cradle gym with an elastic cord strung with wooden beads and rings. The same release repeated a warning about two types of baby cribs that were designed so that an infant could trap her head between the corner post and the head or footboard and strangle. "If it's in the marketplace, it must be safe," is literally a death-defying assumption. The prevention of serious injury or loss of life caused by hazardous furniture and equipment is the direct responsibility of adults: those who manufacture them, and those who buy and use them.

One more avoidable accident: a baby old enough to hold a bottle can literally drown when put to bed with a bottle.

Ingestion of Toxic Substances

In the year 1450, the Court Apothecary in Scotland declared that "all persons are forbidden under the pain of treason to bring home poisons for any use by which Christian man or woman can take harm." Today public service messages and container labels offer repeated warnings to keep all potentially poisonous substances out of the reach of children. However, the problem of poisoning has persisted. More than 500,000 cases of accidental poisoning—at least one every minute of the day—occur in the United States each year. Over 50% of the victims of accidental poisonings in the area served by the poison control center at the University of Iowa are 1 and 2 year olds. This high percentage should not be surprising. Development from infancy to toddlerhood is accompanied by an increased accident potential. When infants have learned to coordinate eyes and hands, they reach, and they will reach for anything. Once they start to creep or crawl, they soon will be climbing. Everything is fair game for them to touch, mouth, and swallow, if small enough. They investigate under the sink, under the stairway, and behind and in the toilet. They go into closets and cupboards. The combination of the child's desire and ability to investigate and an unfriendly environment that contains substances that should not be investigated is explosive. Alarmingly, the majority of poisonings occur while the children are under the supervision of their parents or other responsible adults.

Common poisons. Poisons commonly found around the home, and frequently around a child-care center, include

- ammonia
- aspirin
- bleach
- cement and glue
- contraceptive pills
- deodorants
- depilatories
- detergents
- drain cleaner
- fabric softener
- floor wax
- hairspray
- headache remedies
- heart medicines
- insecticides
- iodine
- kerosene
- laxatives
- lighter fluid
- metal polish
- paint and paint thinner
- perfume
- permanent wave solutions
- reducing pills
- rodent poison
- room deodorizer
- rubbing alcohol
- rug cleaner
- shampoo
- shoe polish
- sleeping pills
- tranquilizers
- turpentine
- varnish
- vitamins
- washing soda

In addition to the above, many plants (over 700 species) have been identified as toxic substances. Lists of poisonous plants are constantly changing as new information is learned. There-

fore, instead of attempting to list these, the following list contains some common indoor plants that are safe for growing around young children.

- African violet
- Aluminum plant
- Begonia
- Boston fern
- Coleus
- Dracaena
- Hen-and-chickens
- Jade plant
- Peperomia
- Prayer plant
- Rubber plant
- Sensitive plant
- Snake plant
- Spider plant
- Swedish ivy
- Wandering Jew
- Wax plant
- Weeping fig

(AAP, 1987)

A nonpoisonous plant is not necessarily safe to eat, however, and eating too much of even a "safe" plant can make a child sick.

Role of the educarer. It is the adult who mismanages the environment, and it is the adult who frequently mismanages treatment. Many traditional treatments for the ingestion of poisons are useless and, even worse, they can compound and intensify the original damage. The time-honored procedure of using salt water to induce vomiting is both ineffective and potentially dangerous, as is giving doses of vinegar, citrus juices, oil, or milk of magnesia. Too few persons know that inducing vomiting might be the worst possible thing to do! Some substances can add to the irritation or burning of weakened digestive tract tissue as they are regurgitated.

Unfortunately, the antidote charts found in various locations (on drug store counters or in the popular magazines) are almost always out of date or inaccurate. Do not rely on them or on the "childproof" caps on bottles; they may be child-resistant, but are not necessarily childproof.

There is no reason or excuse for ignorance or misinformation about toxic substances; information and advice are readily available and free for the asking. Approximately 500 Poison Control Centers form a nationwide network designed to disseminate information to health professionals and lay persons, to treat poisoned victims, and to engage in continuing laboratory research. The local centers receive almost immediate current information by way of computer from the National Clearinghouse for Poison Control Centers, which analyzes all manufactured products and advises appropriate measures for their mismanagement. The Clearinghouse distributes materials to professional as well as lay persons.

Representative of their printed materials for lay persons are the following suggestions for poison-proofing homes and centers:

- All cleaners and household products in original safety-top containers out of reach in locked cabinets
- All household cleaning products stored in locked cabinets out of reach
- All cleaners and household products in original safety-top containers
- All bleaches, soaps, and detergents out of reach and in original containers
- All insect sprays, weed killers, gasoline and car products, turpentine, paints, and paint products in locked areas
- All plants out of reach
- All perfumes, cosmetics, mouthwashes, and powders out of reach
- All medications out of reach in locked cabinets

Educarers and other staff members may be conscientious and follow all of the above precautions, yet leave their purses or knapsacks containing medications, cosmetics, or pointed instruments (e.g., nail files) within easy reach of the children. The prevention of poisoning depends not so much on memorizing lists of rules, but on total awareness of possible risks and removing these risks from the child's environment.

If, in spite of precautions, a child does ingest a harmful substance—and many harmful substances are not labeled as poisonous—follow the directions below, *in the order given,* and *remain calm.*

1. *Do these things before you call someone:*
   a. Remove poisons from contact with eyes, skin, or mouth.

   (1) Eyes
      (a) Gently wash eyes with plenty of tap water for at least 5 minutes with the eyelids held open.
      (b) Do not allow the patient to rub the affected eye.
   (2) Skin
      (a) Wash the poison off the skin with large volumes of water.
      (b) Remove contaminated clothing.
   (3) Mouth: Remove all tablets, powder, plants, and so on, from patient's mouth. Examine for any burns, cuts, irritation, or unusual coloring.
   b. If exposed to gases or fumes:
   (1) Get the patient to fresh air.
   (2) Loosen clothing.
   (3) If not breathing, clear the airway and start mouth-to-mouth respiration. Continue until help arrives.
2. *Call for information about what to do next.* Call your doctor or the Poison Control Center. Don't hesitate to call even if you are unsure a poison was ingested. Provide your doctor or the Poison Control Center with the following information:
   a. Identify yourself and the patient. Give the patient's age and weight.
   b. Give your phone number so that you can be reached if your call is accidentally disconnected.
   c. Have the poison container available and read the label. Estimate the amount taken.
   d. *Remain calm.* There is always time to act. Your doctor or the Poison Center will give you instructions on what to do next.
3. *If instructed to induce vomiting:* Have syrup of ipecac available to induce vomiting.
   a. Syrup of ipecac can be purchased from a pharmacy without a prescription. It can be stored at room temperature for years. Keep 1 or 2 ounces available at all times.

    b. Recommended dosage for ipecac syrup:
      (1) Children 1 year old or less: 2 teaspoonfuls (10 ml)
      (2) Children over 1 year old: 1 tablespoonful (15 ml)
      (3) Adults: 2 tablespoonfuls (30 ml)
    c. Give the appropriate dose of ipecac with a few ounces of water or a favorite drink.
    d. If the patient has not vomited in 20 minutes, give another dose of syrup of ipecac and more liquids.
    e. *Do not waste time trying other ways to induce vomiting.*
4. *Never induce vomiting if:*
    a. Patient is unconscious.
    b. Patient is having a convulsion.
    c. A caustic (strong acid or alkali) was swallowed.
    d. A petroleum product was swallowed (gasoline, lighter fluids, cleaning products, furniture polish, etc.).
5. *If instructed to go to the hospital:*
    a. Take the poison and its container, plant, and so on to the hospital.
    b. Do not attempt any additional first aid unless your doctor or the Poison Control Center has instructed you to do so.

Remember:

- Keep calm if a poisoning has occurred.
- Do not delay in seeking advice.

To Avoid Poisoning:

- Keep all drugs and dangerous household chemicals locked up.
- Never place a dangerous chemical in a beverage container.
- Do not rely on childproof caps. They can frequently be opened by children.
- Do not store drugs in purses or drawers or in the medicine cabinet.
- Never call medicine candy.

Indoor pollutants. Although we have made great gains in the control of accidents and their resulting injuries, we are just beginning to concern ourselves about a newly documented cause of death and disability. This is a

> group of illnesses and developmental problems triggered or aggravated in children by releases of noxious gases, particulates, metals, fibers; the ingestion of toxins in food additives; radiation, including radon gas coming out of the earth in certain geographic areas and x-rays; and loud noise (Noyes, 1987, pp. 57–58).

These new hazards are dangerous. Their causative role may take years or generations to recognize and much longer to document (Lin-Fu, 1985). Besides inhaling pollutants, children absorb them through the gastrointestinal tract, and through the skin. Cigarette smoke can lead to persistent middle-ear ailments (a very common condition in very young children) and asthma and other respiratory diseases. The greater use of insulating materials has led to an increased concentration of pollutants inside. A heavier reliance on wood, coal, and kerosene as heating fuels may spew carbon monoxide and hydrocarbons. Gas cooking instead of electric cooking leads to increased respiratory illness before age 2. Young children who spend a good deal of time indoors are exposed to a variety of noxious chemicals: formaldehyde, asbestos, pesticides, radon, and lead. Even commonly used art materials contain dangerous agents.

The California Department of Health Services has prepared an arts and crafts guide for programs for young children, which advises avoiding the following substances and suggests acceptable alternatives:

Avoid	*Substitute*
Clay in dry form.	Clay in wet form
Prints, glazes, or finishes that contain lead or other metal pigments.	Water-based products.
Organic solvents and materials with fumes.	Water-based paints, glues, etc.
Commercial dyes.	Vegetable dyes.
Permanent markers.	Water-based markers.

Instant papier-mache or use of color print newspaper or magazines with water. Aerosol sprays. Powdered tempera paints.	Papier-mache made from black and white newspaper. Water-based materials. Liquid paints. (Aronson, 1988, p. 35)

Although we can never achieve a totally safe environment, we can decrease the amount and intensity of our indoor pollutants by keeping informed and acting on the information. Good sources of current information are

U.S. Consumer Product Safety Commission
Office of Information & Public Affairs
Washington, DC 20207

U.S. Environmental Protection Agency
Public Information Center, PM 211 B
401 M Street, SW
Washington, DC 20024

Allergens. There are some substances that are poisons for some but not all children. These substances are known as allergens and account for an estimated one-third of all chronic conditions in childhood. Noxious substances may be inhaled (dust, pollen, nasal sprays); may contact the skin (cosmetics, fabrics, metals); or may be injected through the skin (insect bites, some drugs). A few young children may be allergic to the very objects found in a well-equipped child-care environment: paint, glue, dress-up clothes, books, paper, stuffed or live animals, chalk, and plants.

A child who has puffy eyes, a runny nose, skin rash, or repeated sneezing/coughing episodes with no diagnosed cause may be suffering from an allergy that has not been identified. In such an instance we remove the plants and animals; we frequently launder any objects of fabric (including painting smocks, stuffed toys, dress-up clothes); we install a humidifier or air cleaner; we scrub floors and furniture and vacuum carpets frequently; and we use oil-based products, such as clay and marking pens, when available.

At the same time, educarers convey their suspicions of allergy to the child's parents and suggest they pursue the issue with their family doctor. The sooner an allergy is identified and remedial steps are taken, the better, because allergy is one causal factor of learning disabilities.

Insect bites can be soothed with cold applications and Calamine or similar lotion to relieve the itching. Shortness of breath and/or the eruption of rashlike hives may indicate an allergy to bee stings. These symptoms require the attention of a medical professional.

Drowning

Water is one of the most serious dangers for young children. The risk is increasing because more homes and more child-care centers have swimming or wading pools. A child should never be left alone in the bathtub, wading pool, or around open, frozen bodies of water. Drowning takes only seconds, and even shallow water is dangerous. As soon as children start to toddle or even crawl, you may be certain they will seek out water in the wading pool, swimming pool, storm sewers, and elsewhere. These areas must be securely fenced off or supervised. Remember, it only takes enough water to cover the nose and mouth to cause drowning.

Fires, Burns, and Electric Shock

Fires and burns. It is hoped that in any child-care setting matches and cigarette lighters as well as the pots and pans on the stove are totally inaccessible to young children. Even when children are protected from these obvious dangers, some educarers permit lighted candles on a birthday cake or in a Halloween jack-o'-lantern.

Infants and toddlers are at high risk of death or injury by fire because of their immobility and their dependence on adults. Roughly 10% of the population from birth to 5 years are injured or killed in fires each year, more than five times the percentage of children from 5 to 14 years of age.

Not all burns are fatal, but all burns are painful, and some cause permanent injury and scarring. Heat registers, radiators, hot water pipes, and floor furnaces should be guarded or insulated so that children cannot come in direct contact with them. Hot liquids or foods and hot appliances and their electric cords must be out of reach and carefully supervised. Hot water temperatures should not exceed 110° F at any outlet accessible to children. Temperature control mechanisms are readily available, and must be installed.

Electric shock. It is easier to prevent electric shock than it is to treat it. To a child, an electric outlet is a fascinating hole in the wall, just right for poking. Use childproof covers (or heavy electric tape) on unused electric outlets to keep out the baby's fingers and toys or other objects. To further safeguard against shock, have damaged appliances and frayed cords repaired promptly.

One of the most tragic—and avoidable—accidents occurs when a child mouths the end of an extension cord that is still plugged into the outlet. This can result in severe burning of the mouth and mucous membranes of the lips and tongue. The damage may not be recognizable immediately, but it is serious and irreparable. *Always* unplug a cord when it is not in use or, better yet, never use an extension cord whenever there are children under 5 years of age. Ideally, a center for young children will have wall outlets on a strip encircling the room at a height of 5 or 6 feet.

If a child does receive an electric shock, the first thing to do is to see if he is in contact with the live wire. If he is *not,* then remember an electric shock stops the victim's respiration and sometimes his heart, and can cause a severe burn. Give him artificial respiration immediately and treat his burns as soon as possible. Then call a doctor.

But if the child is still connected to the live wire, do not try to pull him away with your bare hands. The first thing to do is to shut off the current, or take out the cord from the wall plug.

Then use a dry stick or rubber gloves or a piece of cloth or newspaper to pull the wire away from the child. *Do not touch the child with your bare hands.* Then give artificial respiration or CPR immediately, and call the doctor. All electric burns must be evaluated by a physician (Children's Bureau, 1976).

Playspaces and Equipment (Indoor)

According to Jerome Bruner (1973), a baby needs a safe world where he or she is "encouraged to venture, rewarded for venturing his own acts, and sustained against distraction or premature interferences in carrying them out" (p. 8). Fifteen years later, that same thought was repeated by Greenman (1988) who said we need to "provide a safe enriched world for a group of tiny explorers and scientists devoid of any manners or sense of moral responsibility, a rich world to explore that sustains each child against distraction and learning interruption" (p. 50). Greenman suggests that the achievement of this safe enriched world is an example of "Mission Impossible."

The focus here is on a safe world for infants and toddlers. Many of the issues are identical to those in settings for preschool and older children, but some are specific to the developmental characteristics of the youngest children, who have little experience with the world of things and people, and who have little or no experience with their rapidly developing bodies and abilities.

Indoor playspaces. Young children fall, get cut, are electrocuted, are burned, take poisons or overdoses of medicine by mistake by the thousands every year and are injured, permanently crippled, or killed as a result. Yet almost all of these happenings can be prevented.

Even the youngest infants may manage to roll over or wriggle off a table or other high place if left unstrapped or untouched. But it is particularly when children begin to crawl that we must become aware of all the dangers around them.

Sharp objects and other dangerous things should be kept entirely out of reach. Certainly you should never leave medicines, cleaning solutions, fuel oils, paints and paint removers, chemicals, insect or animal poisons, sprays, weed killers, or any other possibly toxic materials or liquids anywhere that children might get at them. Even high places are not safe once children learn to climb, and they often learn overnight. The best rule is to keep all dangerous things under lock and key.

Accidents and poisonings in young children tend to happen most often when adults are occupied or preoccupied with other things. It is therefore important to develop the habit of always putting away dangerous materials immediately when you are finished using them (whether children are present or not), and always keeping them safely locked or guarded.

Equipment. The U.S. Consumer Product Safety Commission (1985) suggests the ABC's of a safe environment: A is for awareness of potential hazards in the child's environment; B is for the behavior of the educarer, and C is for caution when selecting and maintaining products for the child's environment. The Commission's Buyer's Guide (*The Safe Nursery: A Booklet to Help Avoid Injuries from Nursery Furniture and Equipment*) and their many Product Safety Fact Sheets should be referred to as new equipment is purchased, and as older equipment and furnishings are donated.

Parents and educarers should have a complete set of the Commission's publications relating to toys and equipment for young children. These publications may be obtained from:

United States Consumer Product Safety Commission
Room 336 B
5401 Westband Avenue
Bethesda, MD 20207

or any of their regional offices. The CPSC flyers and handbooks offer examples of outmoded and/or dangerous equipment. They are useful guides to designers of a reasonably safe environment. Other sources of concise information include the Committee on Accident and Poison Prevention of the American Academy of Pediatrics, and the state offices of the Cooperative Extension Service.

Protecting children from unsafe equipment and unsafe toys is the responsibility of everyone—the manufacturers, the buyers, and especially persons involved in child care and education.

Careful toy selection and proper supervision of children at play is still—and always will be—the best way to protect children from toy-related injuries (U.S. CPSC, 1988). When buying toys, look for and heed age recommendations, such as "*Not* recommended for children under three." Look for other safety labels including "Flame retardant/Flame resistant" on fabric products and "Washable/hygienic materials" on stuffed toys and dolls. New toys intended for children under 8 years of age should be free of sharp glass and metal edges (as regulated by the Federal Hazardous Substances Act and the Consumer Product Safety Act), but older toys (or imported toys) may break, exposing sharp edges or parts small enough to be swallowed or to become lodged in a child's windpipe, ears, or nose. Guard against removable small eyes and noses on stuffed toys and dolls, and small, removable squeakers on squeeze toys. All equipment and toys should be checked periodically for breakage and potential hazards. A damaged or dangerous toy should be thrown away or repaired immediately. Toys should be put away on shelves or in a toy box or chest to prevent trips or falls. The toy box itself can be a hazard if it does not have a lid that will stay open in any position to which it is raised.

Infant toys, such as rattles, squeeze toys, and teethers, should be large enough so they cannot enter and become lodged in an infant's throat and thus obstruct the airway. An infant's mouth and throat are extremely flexible and can stretch to hold larger shapes than one might expect. To date, the largest rattle known to have lodged in an infant's mouth/throat had an end

1⅝ inches in diameter. If you have any question about the size of a toy, throw it away. Even balloons, when uninflated or broken, can choke or suffocate if young children try to swallow them. More children have suffocated on uninflated balloons and pieces of broken balloons than on any other type of toy (U.S. CPSC, 1988).

PREVENTION OUTSIDE THE CENTER OR FAMILY DAY-CARE HOME

Passenger Safety

"Car accidents are the number one cause of death for children ages one to four, exceeding the combined death toll from polio, measles, rubella, mumps, chicken pox, whooping cough, and diphtheria" (Jones, 1988, p. 80). Every year 1,500 children under the age of 5 are killed, and another 60,000 are injured. As many as 71% of these deaths and 67% of these injuries could have been prevented with the *proper use* of a safety restraint (Kahane, 1986). The emphasis here is on the *proper use,* not on the restraints themselves, because since January 1, 1981, Federal Motor Vehicle Safety Standard (FMVSS) 213 has required that all children's car restraints sold in stores meet stringent requirements.

Although there are mandatory-use laws in all of the 50 states, many young children are either not buckled into child safety seats, or the buckling is done incorrectly. Because the anatomical structure of the infants and young children is not the same as an adult's, young children need specially designed restraint systems that help distribute crash forces over a large area of the body. Dual fastening of child and adult with the same seat belt actually may greatly compound the child's injuries in the case of a collision or near-collision. An appropriate restraint system does more than minimize injury, it keeps the child inside the vehicle. Fatal injuries are the usual result of being thrown clear of a vehicle. It must be noted, however, that up until now, no restraint system can protect a child from a side impact in a collision, and the best advice is to place any restraint in the center of the rear seat of the vehicle.

The following information about appropriate restraints has been adapted from publications of the U.S. Department of Transportation, National Highway Traffic Safety Administration, and is included here because of the important role educarers must play in educating parents and children about safe riding, as well as in establishing correct practices for the transportation of the children in their care.

Infants: birth to about 9–12 months. Protection for newborns should begin the first time they ride in a car, using an infant safety seat or a convertible seat in the infant position. When a convertible seat is in the infant position, it looks and functions exactly like an infant-only seat. Either of these seats cradles baby in a semi-reclining position, protects the infant with a harness, and is anchored to the car with the vehicle's safety belt. The seat *must face the rear of the car* so that the baby's strong back can absorb the forces of a crash. By the time a child is too big to face rearward comfortably, the chest and hips will be strong enough for the forward-facing position. When an infant-only seat is outgrown, a toddler seat must replace it.

Convertible seats: birth to about 4 years. Convertible seats recline and face rearward for infants, and can be changed to the frontfacing, nonreclining position for toddlers. When a convertible seat is in the toddler position, it looks and functions exactly like a toddler-only seat. The manufacturer's directions explain how to convert a seat from one position to another, how to rethread the harness, and how to reroute the car's lap belt through the seat in the toddler position. In addition, the instructions will explain when the child is big enough to require the toddler position.

Convertible seats save money because only one seat is needed as the child grows. But convertible models may be heavier and more difficult to move than infant-only and toddler-only seats. Some convertible seats have a tether that must be anchored if the seat is in the toddler position.

Toddler seats. Toddler seats are designed for children who can sit up without support. They can only be used forward-facing. Most contain a harness to protect a child's upper body, but a few seats use a shield system instead; some have both. It is important to attach the lap belt *exactly* as recommended by the manufacturer.

Booster seats. Booster seats are intended for older children who weigh 40 pounds or more. Most 3 year olds have reached this weight, and therefore booster seats belong in a program transporting children ages 2½ and over. Boosters elevate children so that the car's lap belts fit across their hips and pelvic bones, or the booster shield, rather than their stomachs. Booster seats and shields are preferred by childcare personnel because they are inexpensive, lightweight, adaptable to a wide range of child sizes, and take up the least amount of room (AAP, 1987).

Safety seats versus safety belts. Child safety seats are more effective than safety belts for small children. But when no safety seat is available, any child who can sit up unaided should be protected by a safety belt. Do not use the shoulder belt if it falls across the neck. Instead, use the lap belt only and fasten it snugly and as low as possible across a child's hips. The safest place to use safety belts is in the rear seat of the car.

Automatic safety belts and air bags. Automatic safety belts are not designed, and should not be used, to install child safety seats in a car. The shoulder-only automatic belts are designed to protect adults only. The lap/shoulder belts are not designed for infants or toddlers.

Air bags offer excellent frontal crash protection when used in combination with lap and shoulder safety belts.

The American Academy of Pediatrics regularly publishes information about infant/child safety seats. See the suggested activities at the end of the chapter for ordering information.

Common mistakes.

1. Infant and toddler seats: harness not fastened over child's shoulders, or too loosely fastened

2. Toddler seat: car belt is routed through the lowest section of frame

3. Infant and convertible seats: seat installed so infant faces front of car

4. Booster seat without shield: neither tether harness nor shoulder harness is used

One last word of caution: The instructions for correct installation and use are specific to each brand of safety device, and the information and ratings supplied by consumer organizations are based on correct usage only.

In addition to the appropriate use of child restraints, there are a few basic ''rules of the road.''

1. Continuing adult supervision for children getting in and out of a vehicle, always away from the street side

2. All children are securely and correctly fastened in before the motor is started

3. All car doors are locked before the motor is started. Many of the newer cars have locking devices that can be controlled from the driver's seat. Windows should also be locked in place

4. Children may never be left alone in a vehicle, whether the motor is running or not

5. When two or more children are in the vehicle, there should be at least one adult in addition to the driver

Pedestrian Safety

Automobiles and other vehicles also are the causes of injuries and deaths of child pedestrians.

Delivery and pick-up procedures. Of course, necessary precautions for the delivery and pick-up include having an adult in addition to the driver on the scene. The children should always be let out or picked up on the curb or protected side of the street. Sometimes the local police department or traffic authorities will help by placing restrictions on through traffic at or near the pick-up and delivery area. Markings for crosswalks, or signs announcing "stop," "loading area," or "children crossing" can alert the drivers in the vicinity.

When possible, the loading area should be off the street. When the specific location has been agreed on by parents and staff, there should be no deviations. Wherever the area, efforts should be made to encourage parents or other drivers to personally accompany the child inside, and to remove the child's outer clothing, and to transfer the child to the primary educarer. Not only is this procedure an effective safety precaution, it also frees staff members to welcome each child. Just as important, it ensures educarer-parent communication at the beginning of each day. If the procedure is reversed at the end of the day, a second opportunity is provided for the sharing of information.

Walking field trips. Simple but essential precautions must also be observed for walking field trips, which should be a frequent part of the program. Just because these children are in out-of-home care does not mean they are denied the pleasure of learning about the outside world. Walks close to traffic should be on the wide shoulders of highways, or on the sidewalks. Streets, highways, and country lanes should be crossed only at intersections protected by traffic lights, or at points with maximum visibility. The children must be kept in a group that is both led

and followed by adults. Various methods of grouping for safety include hand-holding pairs of children (not particularly reliable for toddlers); a long knotted rope with each child holding a knot (also not very reliable); or every two children holding the hands of an adult. In the Western European countries young children on field trips wear harnesses with an attached leash. This is both safe and practical, but their use has not been adopted in the United States.

Walking field trips provide excellent opportunities for involving parents or volunteers in order to achieve a safe adult/child ratio. Unfortunately, most infants and toddlers are in group care because their parents are not available during the day. Nonetheless, at least a few parents have been able to arrange their working schedules so that they can occasionally take part in their children's activities.

Ideally, walks in the immediate neighborhood will include no more than four children and two adults, thereby allowing time and opportunity to investigate an ant hill, or to watch mama bird feed her young ones. These "discovery" walks should be frequent. Walks with specific destinations, such as the grocery store or the library, have their place, but should not be the only field trips included in the program.

The pleasures of these walks should not be spoiled by constant behavior reminders. Educarers know that very young children lack impulse control, and that verbal directions are not always followed. The only guarantee of an accident-free experience is the optimal adult/child ratio of 1:2.

Playspaces and Equipment (Outdoor)

An outdoor playspace for young children is a safe, well-planned, fenced area. It is a learning place just as much as the indoor space. Its design and equipment should stimulate activities that promote social, emotional, and intellectual development, as well as physical growth and coordination. The outdoor playspace is also the location of serious accidents and injuries.

To plan for safety, one must know the ages, size, weight, abilities, characteristics, and interests of the children. We know the ages (infancy to 3 years old); the size (up to about 40 inches in length); and weight (up to about 45 pounds). Chapters 3, 4, and 5 in Part Two, the Developmental Curriculum, contained information about the characteristics, abilities, and interests of infants and toddlers.

Playground measures that reduce the risk of injury are similar to those for the indoor environment, in that all materials not meant to be tasted or swallowed should not be reachable. Outside, these include debris, glass, animal feces, and toxic plants. Equipment designed for climbing (this includes *all* equipment off the ground) should be no more than 3 feet high, should have railings, should have 6 or 7 feet of free space around them, should have secure anchoring devices that are submerged, and should be on top of 6 or more inches of cushiony material evenly spread out and not packed. Needless to say, there should be no sharp edges, loose bolts, or broken parts. Wooden structures and toys should be smooth and properly treated with nontoxic preservatives. Swing seats should be resilient (not wood or metal). The CPSC warns against "equipment with open-ended hooks, particularly S-hooks; moving parts which could pinch or crush fingers; sharp edges or rough surfaces; or rings with a diameter more than 5 inches but less than 10 inches, since they may entrap heads" (Fact Sheet No. 22).

One of the major problems in outdoor playspaces is that they are often used by children older than 3 years of age. If this is the case, "children should be segregated by developmental stage for play on gross motor apparatus to prevent younger children from being injured by imitating or encroaching on the more skillful play of older children" (AAP, 1987, p. 78).

Detailed technical guidelines governing construction, location, and installation of gross motor equipment and surfacing are found in *A Handbook for Public Playground Safety,* Volumes I and II (1981) of the Consumer Product Safety Commission. For suggestions on how to improve children's outdoor play spaces, see Frost (1986) and Esbensen (1987), as well as the AAP's *Health in Day Care* (1987).

Each specific detail is important, but most important of all is constant supervision by an adequate number of adults. No part of the playground must be obstructed from view, and the total playspace should be separated by barriers or fences from street traffic, thoughtless passersby, and unrestrained pets. The goal is *no accidents,* but realistically, there is no injury-proof playground. We can, however, supply an injury-resistant playground. Safety in an outside playspace is a complex matter.

EMERGENCY PREPAREDNESS AND PROCEDURES

Accidents will occur in the best of centers and homes even after all precautions have been taken. It is therefore important the educarers and day-care home providers (and parents) are proficient in the basic first aid procedures: how to control bleeding, how to administer artificial respiration, and how to administer CPR. Each staff member (educarer, cook, custodian, transporter) should also know the sources of emergency assistance, and the proper use of the items in the first aid kit. However, there is no substitute for professional medical advice.

Emergency Preparedness

Before an emergency occurs, arrangements should be made with the emergency room of your choice, and with one or two health professionals who are willing to be consulted on an emergency basis. An important part of emergency preparedness is the posting of related names, phone numbers, and addresses close to all the telephones. These include the police department, the fire department, the poison control center and the "emergency" doctor(s), and the emergency room.

Figure 8–1

CONSENT FOR MEDICAL/SURGICAL CARE/
EMERGENCY TREATMENT
AND CHILD'S MEDICAL INFORMATION

In presenting my son/daughter for diagnosis and treatment

Name: _____ for _____
      ☐ Mother   ☐ Father   ☐ Legal Guardian   ☐ Son   ☐ Daughter

of _____ years of age; hereby voluntarily consent to the rendering of such care, including diagnostic procedures, surgical and medical treatment, and blood transfusions, by authorized members of the hospital staff or their designees, as may in their professional judgment be necessary.

I hereby acknowledge that no guarantees have been made to me as to the effect of such examinations or treatment on child's condition.

I have read this form and I certify that I understand its contents.

We/I hereby give my consent to _____
                       (Name of Person/Agency)

who will be caring for our (my) child _____
                     (Name of Child)

for the period _____ to _____ to arrange for routine or emergency medical/surgical/dental care and treatment necessary to preserve the health of our (my) child.

We/I acknowledge that we are (I am) responsible for all reasonable charges in connection with care and treatment rendered during this period.

Each child's folder should contain the names and telephone numbers of the parents or guardians, and also of other persons to contact, in addition to the child's own pediatrician. Also, each child's folder should contain a signed *Consent for Medical/Surgical Care/Emergency Treatment* form and a *Consent for Transport of the Child for Emergency Treatment* form. These forms may be obtained from a physician or pediatrician. These signed forms can save precious time in the case of an emergency, because without these forms, many emergency room personnel will not treat minors unless their parent or guardian is present. A sample consent form is presented in Figure 8–1.

There is also a nationally recognized emergency treatment rule that allows the giving of medical care without parental approval. It applies to cases in which the child needs immediate treatment and the parents or guardian cannot be contacted with reasonable diligence (reasonable diligence takes time, and this is the reason for recommending a Consent-for-Treatment form); when any effort to secure approval would delay the treatment long enough to endanger the child's life or seriously worsen the condition; and when the parents or guardian have refused permission (usually for religious reasons), but the delay in securing a court order would have serious consequences for the child.

Figure 8–1 *continuing*

Name: _____   Family Physician: _____

Address: _____   Pediatrician: _____

_____   Surgeon: _____

Telephone No. _____   Orthopedist: _____

Name of Health Insurance Carrier: Child's Allergies, if any:

_____   _____

_____   Date of last tetanus booster _____

Group No. _____   Medicines Child is taking:

Agreement No. _____   _____

                                             _____

Signature: _____   _____

       Mother, Father or Legal Guardian   Date

Witness: _____   _____

                                             Date

IN CASE OF EMERGENCY I CAN BE REACHED AT _____

_____

A second physician's opinion is usually necessary in this last circumstance.

The American Academy of Pediatrics (1977) suggests procedures for telephone usage and emergency handling, found in Figure 8–2.

In the case of a serious medical emergency, the first step is to request emergency transportation. The second step is to call the hospital or other treatment facility to alert it to the nature of the emergency and to ask for advice. Only then, or after the child is receiving treatment, should the parents be notified. The emergency-procedure plan should be explained to both the educaring staff and the parents, and should be posted in a prominent location. Certain severe emergencies (including internal poisoning, skin or eye contact with corrosives, or neck or back injuries) require the immediate intervention of someone trained in first aid or emergency medical care. Necessary life-saving measures should be applied, and then the child should be transported promptly to the treatment center.

Fortunately, most injuries do not require such prompt action to save life or limb.

First Aid

Most injuries or hurts in an infant/toddler program can be ably cared for by a knowledgeable educarer. First aid should be given whenever

Figure 8–2

Suggested Guidelines for Telephone Usage and Handling Emergencies*

Nonemergency calls are handled most easily during the regular workday hours. Emergency care is available around the clock. If the receptionist promises a return call at a certain time and you are not called, do not hesitate to call again.

WHEN DO YOU PHONE?

1. When the child is acting sick—even though the signs and symptoms are vague.
2. If you are concerned by the way the child is acting, even if you can't explain why.

WHEN YOU TELEPHONE

When you telephone the doctor, usually a receptionist-secretary will receive your call. Be prepared to give:
1. Your name
2. Your telephone number
3. The patient's name and age
4. Your main concerns
5. If you believe the problem is an emergency, *say so!!*

   A pediatric nurse practitioner, a doctor or a nurse may return your call. In any case, have a pencil and paper ready and write down the instructions you receive.

When you telephone about an illness, be prepared to tell:
1. The patient's temperature
2. When did the patient become ill?
3. Symptoms such as:
   a. Vomiting and/or diarrhea—frequency of each in a given time period
   b. Urination—the last time
   c. Other—such as headache, sore throat, nasal congestion , cough, difficult breathing, irritability
   d. General appearances of the patient
   e. Any change from usual feeding pattern, particularly in infants
4. What treatment has been given?
5. Telephone number of your pharmacist
When you telephone about matters other than an illness, it will save time if you tell the receptionist the reason for your call so that the physician may have available when he calls back your account, laboratory results, names of physicians in other cities, etc.

IMMEDIATE CARE OF EMERGENCIES
Poisonings

1. Identify the product, if you can

*From American Academy of Pediatrics: Standards of child health care. ed. 3. Evanston, Ill. 1977. Copyright American Academy of Pediatrics, 1977.

necessary, and a written report of the accident and treatment should be given the parents or guardian when they come for the child at the end of the usual time period. Most injuries in infant toddler programs do not require immediate notification of the parents or guardian.

If the center has several staff members, one of them should assume the role of safety coordinator. In smaller centers or family day-care homes, the health coordinator may assume this additional responsibility. The safety coordinator should periodically inspect the premises, both indoors and out, develop and update procedures for emergency situations, and maintain a high quality first aid kit. The essentials for first

aid and health maintenance for children under 3 years of age are:

1. A quick-reference first aid manual (NAEYC recommends *A Sigh of Relief—The First Aid Handbook for Childhood Emergencies* by Green, 1984)
2. A First Aid Chart (from the American Red Cross or the American Academy of Pediatrics)
3. Towels and medicated liquid soap
4. Flashlight
5. Bandage scissors, splinter forceps, tweezers
6. Nail clippers

Figure 8–2
continuing

2. Estimate the maximum amount you think might have been ingested
3. Estimate the time of ingestion
4. Give any symptoms or unusual behavior
5. If you are unable to reach [the physician's] office promptly, phone without delay the Poison Information Center _____
6. Have *syrup of ipecac* available
   a. A small sealed bottle should be in every home where there are children in the one- to five-year-old age group. It may be obtained at any pharmacy without prescription.

Accidents

Laceration or "cut"

1. Apply direct pressure, then phone and report the problem
   a. Does it continue to bleed without pressure application?
   b. Does it gape open?

Burns

1. Immerse the part or apply cold water to area
2. Do not apply any salves, creams, butter, cooking oils to burn area

3. Report the extent of the injury
4. Wrap burn area in any clean sheeting or cloth, before transporting the patient to medical facility

Head injury

Many children fall and strike their heads. The injured, but not unconscious, patient cries out immediately following the injury and may vomit a few times. In such instances it is important to:
1. Permit the child to rest or even sleep
2. Observe the child closely, especially the color and breathing
3. *Do not* insist the patient remain awake

Two important do not's

1. *Do not* insist the patient remain awake
2. *Do not* move the patient to a medical facility prior to obtaining medical advice

Phone immediately for advice about the unconscious patient who neither cries out nor stirs following the injury.

7. Thermometers and storage containers
8. A measuring device for medications, such as a syringe, a calibrated measuring tube, or a medication spoon
9. Multiple pairs of rubber gloves
10. Ipecac syrup
11. Isopropyl alcohol
12. Sterile dressings, 2 × 2 and 3 × 3
13. Roller bandages and adhesive tape
14. Band-Aids, cotton balls, and cotton-tip applicators

The first-aid corner should also contain a step-on, covered, plastic-lined waste receptacle, and a locked medication storage place. If medicine needs to be refrigerated and must be stored where food is kept, it should be in a locked storage box in the refrigerator.

Some explanations and instructions for the use of these items will be needed by the non-health educarer(s), after which the educarers may use them for minor injuries, cuts, bruises, and an easily accessible foreign body in the eye.

Other Emergency Procedures

Emergency procedures for the evacuation of a building because of fires, extreme weather, or unexpected happenings must be posted at strategic points, and must be practiced monthly with the children (National Academy, 1984). This is a particular challenge with infants who may be napping. It is questionable if an infant, suddenly disturbed by a loud alarm and a sudden picking up from a sound sleep, will have any understanding of the drill. However, it is essential that educarers know exactly what to do in the case of a real problem. Perhaps a discussion with a representative of the fire department or licensing agency can be asked for suggestions about how to handle the practice drills, and a compromise may be reached.

Fire extinguishers and smoke detectors should be checked periodically, another responsibility of the person chosen as the safety coordinator.

The National Scene

A Congressional hearing was held in spring 1989 that was billed as the "first hearing ever held on the subject of protecting children from accidents." As one result, a bill was introduced to both the Senate and the House to require the Consumer Product Safety Commission to develop warning labels for all toys containing small parts. It is hoped the bill has become law by the time you read this. Two recent studies offer support for increased efforts to prevent injuries. In the first one (Chang, Lugg, & Nebedum, 1989), researchers found that 75% of accidents in day-care centers run by the Los Angeles school district could have been prevented with only a little bit of care. The second study (Salmi, Weiss, Peterson, Spengler, Sattin, & Anderson, 1989) suggests that many childhood deaths in rural areas may have been caused by a lack of adult supervision.

"ACCIDENTAL" INJURIES: CHILD ABUSE AND NEGLECT

Overview

Twenty-three causes of injury mortality in children ages 0–14 in the United States were analyzed by age, race, sex, and state of residence for the years 1980–85. Motor vehicles caused 37 percent of all injury-related deaths and were the leading cause of injury mortality in every group except children younger than one year, *for whom homicide was the leading cause.* (Waller, Baker, & Szocka, 1989, p. 310)

Infant homicide, often representing lethal cases of child abuse, is the most frequent cause of death for children under 1 year of age. According to the investigators at the Injury Prevention Center at Johns Hopkins University, many infant death certificates list *cause unknown,* so an accurate percentage cannot be established, but it is probably higher than the reported 17% of verified causes.

Some 2.25 million children were reported to be abused and/or neglected in 1987; more than 1,200 died. Their average age was *2 years old* (Erlanger, 1989).

The Child Abuse Prevention, Adoption, and Family Service Act, passed in April 1988 set spending levels for existing and expanded programs for the study, prevention, and treatment of family violence. Experts point out that while reports of child abuse went up 150% between 1980 and 1986, funding to attack the problem rose only 2%.

Child abuse is not a new phenomenon. In ancient times infants who did not *look* perfect were exposed to the elements and died of *natural causes.* In modern times infants and very young children who do not *behave* perfectly are subject to violence. Gold (1986) writes about parents who physically attack their own children when they cry, when they suck their thumb, when they are not toilet trained, when they wet the bed, when they throw a tantrum, when they use dirty words, when they spill their milk, and when they won't fall asleep.

Child abuse is not new. The newness is our societal concern for the "right of every child to a standard of living adequate for the child's physical, mental, spiritual, moral, and social development" (Defense for Children International, 1990, Article 27). Today child abuse and neglect (CAN) has been recognized as a family problem, a community problem, and a societal problem. Unfortunately it has also been a problem in some infant/toddler programs based in centers and in family day-care homes.

CAN in the Child-Care Setting

National attention was focused on the child-care setting as the result of Keyserling's 1972 report (*Windows on Day Care*). Two of her descriptions, one of a licensed center and the other of a licensed family day-care home, give some indication of the horrendous situations in these particular settings.

> This center should be closed! Absolutely filthy. Toilets not flushed, and smelly. Broken equipment and doors. Broken windows on lower level near back stairs and doors. Broken chairs and tables. No indoor play equipment. One paper towel used to wipe the faces and hands of all children. Kitchen very, very dirty (1972, p. 48).

This center had an enrollment of 35 children, from 2 to 5 years old. At the time of the visit, the only people in charge were 2 children, aged 10 and 12.

Some family day care is no better. The following description of a licensed family day-care home needs no comment.

> When Mrs.__ opened the door for us, we felt there were probably very few, if any, children in the house, because of the quiet. It was quite a shock, therefore, to discover about seven or eight children, one year old or under, in the kitchen. A few of them were in high-chairs, but most were strapped to kitchen chairs, all seemingly in a stupor.
> It wasn't until we were in the kitchen that we heard the noise coming from the basement. There we found over twenty children huddled in a too small, poorly ventilated, cement floor area. A TV with an apparently bad picture tube was their only source of entertainment or stimulation.
> When we went to look at the back yard, we passed through a porch, where we discovered, again, children, children and more children. The children were literally under our feet. Pathetically

enough, it was necessary for Mrs.__ to reprimand one child for stepping on another.

> Mrs.__ takes care of two families—six children—which the Bureau of Children's Services subsidizes. The other children (41, for a total of 47 children) she takes care of independently, receiving two dollars per day per child. She told us that she has been doing this for twenty years and seemed quite proud to be able to manage as well alone with no help (pp. 135–136).

Another report, not as dramatic but just as heart-breaking:

> Upon entering the infant room in a local day care center, a visitor sadly observed the following: nine babies in cribs, twelve one- and two-year-olds, and only one caregiver. After spending a few minutes with the infants, the visitor getting ready to leave felt a tug on her skirt. Looking down, she observed a tiny child who said, "Wanna go wif you!" (Mills, Matlock, & Herrell, 1988, p. 37).

Child abuse? Child neglect? No matter the definition, the urgent problem is to prevent such situations and to protect children.

Indications that abuse and neglect in child care are still major problems, as reported in the AAP *Health in Day Care* (1987), in Kendrick, Kaufmann, and Messenger, *Healthy Young Children* (1988), and in *Nursery Crimes* by Finkelhor, Williams, and Burns (1988).

The role of the educarer is three-fold: (1) prevention in the child-care setting; (2) prevention in the child's family, and (3) reporting of suspected child abuse and/or neglect.

Prevention in the Child-Care Setting

Employee screening. To date there is no reliable method for screening potential employees. Of course, preemployment screening is better than none at all. Thirty-three states were planning to, or did require, criminal records checks in centers in 1986, and 26 states were planning to, or did require, such checks for family day-care providers. In general, these checks are limited to only violent and/or sex-related crimes against children (Morgan, 1987). The effectiveness of these checks is open to question. However, all persons, not just those with direct responsibility for children, should be screened. Housekeepers, cooks, and transporters may be in frequent contact with the children. When the program is short-staffed, these persons may need to be with the children in order to meet the required child/staff ratio.

Child/staff ratio. Perhaps the best insurance against an abusive incident in a child-care setting is an appropriate child/staff ratio.

> Poorly staffed day care centers and family day care homes, where isolated caregivers are burdened with more children than they can manage, are more likely to have abuse occur than at adequately staffed facilities where stressful situations can be coped with more readily and other adults are present to observe the inappropriate behavior (AAP, 1987, p. 43).

The open-door policy. Another precaution (and a sign of a good quality program) is the *open-door* policy, wherein parents know they may always visit unannounced, and where the staff members know the parents have that right.

Prevention in the Child's Family

Preventive measures. Educarers are in a unique position to provide preventive services to the families they serve. In fact, it is possible that educarers are in a better position than anyone else to recognize possible indicators of family stress before a crisis situation develops. Every incident of child abuse and neglect has three components: the child, the abusing adult, and a crisis, whether actual or only perceived as such. The "crisis" is sometimes an insignificant but last straw.

Abusive parents are often isolated from caring persons or agencies, they move frequently from home to home, are usually young, and often unmarried. If they are married, they seem to have chosen a spouse who is not actively supportive in times when problems become overwhelming. Because of their lack of maturity and stability—and frequently because of their own history of being abused—their immediate response to stress is to strike out. Thus they strike out at someone who cannot strike back—a young child. Most child abusers are just plain people, not emotionally or mentally disturbed people, just plain people who momentarily succumb to the complexities of living. Most infants and toddlers in our day-care centers and homes are children of just plain people but people who are subject to more than their share of frustrations and stress.

Our current laws no longer prescribe punitive measures for child abusers but take a more compassionate and humanistic approach. Criminal penalties have been replaced by support services, and a vital support service, both before and after child abuse or neglect is discovered, can be offered by day-care homes and centers. A quality center or home recognizes the critical role of the parents in the child's development and creates opportunities for enhancing the amount and quality of family interaction with children both in the day-care setting and at the child's home. These opportunities include parent involvement in decision making, policy-setting, and daily operations. They also include both formal and informal individual parent-educarer conferences and group parent-center meetings, both educational and recreational.

Although the primary intent of such activities is not the prevention of child abuse and neglect, all of these activities can be considered prevention techniques. Educarers are frequently the first professional persons to have close daily contact with children and their families, and they are looked on as "experts" by young parents. Informal conversations between educarer and parent at pick-up and delivery time can be therapeutic for a parent under stress.

We should not underestimate the important therapeutic results, and the possible prevention of child abuse, derived from an educarer's sympathetic responses to a troubled parent. One parent said it this way:

> Twenty years ago I had spanked my own three year old boy with a hairbrush, hard enough to leave ridgemarks on his bottom. I don't remember what he did to trigger my anger, but in my mind I can still see those little bruises. . . . How wonderful it would have been if I could have called somebody, anybody, and talked normally about what I'd done. If only I could have aired my feelings and openly sought ways to help myself so that I could have understood episodes like those and defused them before they erupted. . . . (Wheat & Lieber, 1979, p. 5).

All parents need reassurance about their methods of child-rearing. There is no more conclusive proof of that statement than the number of advice books sold yearly and the number of related articles appearing monthly in the nonprofessional magazines.

Group meetings for parents can also be therapeutic. Just knowing that other parents face the same or similar (and sometimes worse) problems eases the anxiety, and no one is listened to more carefully than another parent who has faced the same problem and perhaps even solved it. However, there is little gained from a parent-educarer contact, and much lost, if the educarer assumes the role of all-knowing expert, shows horror at a parent's abusive feelings, or dictates rules and instructions for appropriate feelings and actions. Warm, open relationships between educarers and parents are just as essential as are warm relationships with children. There is no way to document the number of child abuse and neglect incidents that have been averted by sensitive adults, but it seems logical to assume that sensitivity and understanding can help avert many.

Center-parent partnership is an essential component in the delivery of early care and education. Detailed rationale, methods, and techniques are included in chapter 11.

The root causes of negligence in the care of children are even more difficult to pinpoint than are the causes of abuse. Even the term *neglect* cannot be defined with any degree of specificity. When is minimal care no longer even minimal? Neglect is the result of the absence of appropriate action. It implies not meeting the psychological or physical needs of children. Again, a sensitive educarer is alert to suspect conditions in the home through informal opportunities for parents and staff to learn and to share information, both in the center and through visits to the home.

Characteristics of abusive or neglectful parents. Educarers must also be alert to the possible characteristics of neglectful or abusive parents or guardians. Possible characteristics include:

1. Isolation of the family from any support system; discouragement by the family of others' attempts at social contacts

2. Reluctance to explain the child's injuries or condition (hunger, apathy, lack of appropriate clothing) or irrational or irrelevant explanations

3. Failure to obtain needed medical care for the child or constant changing of doctors or hospitals

4. Reliance on harsh punishment as the "only way" to make the child mind

5. Continuing criticism of the child; impatience toward the child's crying or other attention-seeking behaviors

6. Misuse of alcohol or drugs

7. Frequent disappearance (failure to pick up a child at the end of the day; failure to keep appointments)

8. Irrational, cruel, or sadistic behavior

Over a period of time, these characteristics will become apparent to educarers who are committed to the quality care and education of young children. Suspicions of child abuse and neglect need not depend on visible signs of injury; the visible evidence means that prevention techniques have not been successful in averting an incident.

Many communities have child abuse and neglect programs and parent support programs that include the services of lay health visitors, parent aides, respite/crisis child care, and emergency shelters. There is also a national organization, similar to Alcoholics Anonymous, called Parents Anonymous.

Reporting Suspected Child Abuse and Neglect

Mandatory reporting laws are in effect in each of the 50 states. However, individual states have different definitions of what must be reported. The National Committee for the Prevention of Child Abuse defines abuse as a "non-accidental injury or pattern of injuries to a child for which there is no 'reasonable' explanation" (Kendrick et al., 1988, p. 199).

Physical abuse. The most usual signs of physical abuse are bruises, welts, scars, fractured bones (sometimes not visible to the naked eye), burns, lacerations, and abrasions. Bruises are by far the most common, but a few bruises on the knees, shins, or even the forehead might be considered normal for a toddler. However, bruises on the back, thighs, buttocks, face, backs of the legs, or in the genital area should create suspicion of abuse.

If any injury is accidental, there should be some reasonable relationship between how the injury happened and the severity, type, and location of the injury. Could a fall from a highchair produce bruises in the genital area? Could a child who pushed a hot tea kettle off the stove have burns on the soles of her feet? Abusing parents are already on the defensive, and when asked for explanations of injuries, they may respond irrationally and illogically—or may claim ignorance of the whole thing.

Even when no physical injury is visible, a child's behavior may be the alerting cue to abuse. The abused child may shrink from adult contact, may become unduly apprehensive when other children cry or when the parent arrives at the end of the day, may demonstrate unusual extremes in behavior (withdrawal or aggression) that are outside the normal range of age-expected behaviors. Unusual behavior in an infant or toddler is a red flag—it means something is wrong. Because one of the several components of educaring is observation of children, any change in behavior should be readily noticed by an alert staff member.

Sexual abuse. Very young children (children under the age of 3 years) are also victims of sexual abuse. It is doubly hard to be objective about this type of abuse, but it cannot be ignored. Physical signs of sexual abuse include (1) difficulty in walking or sitting, (2) stained or bloody diapers or undergarments, (3) bruises, bleeding, or scabs in the genital area, and (4) the child's continued rubbing of the genital area. Not all states mention sexual abuse in their definitions of child abuse, but this is no excuse for permitting any suspected case to go unreported.

Emotional abuse. Physically abused or neglected children almost always are emotionally abused as well. The failure-to-thrive syndrome is one possible indicator, especially when the children begin to thrive when taken out of the home and into a treatment center. Other possible indicators include extremes in behavior: passivity, aggressiveness, perseverative rocking, thumb-sucking, or head-banging. The behavioral indicators exhibited by children who are emotionally abused and disturbed are quite similar, and it is the parent's attitude that offers clues to possible abuse. Parents of an emotionally *abused* child may either blame the child for the problem and related behaviors, or may completely ignore the problem and therefore see no need for help. The parents of an emotionally *disturbed* child are concerned and actively seek help.

Not all states include emotional abuse in their laws; it is the most difficult type to define and identify. Nonetheless, it is perhaps the type of abuse for which day-care personnel can be most helpful. Parents who consistently downgrade their children, consistently ignore them, or who fail to encourage their normal development are guilty of emotional abuse, whether so stated in the law or not. Many young parents do not know the psychological implications of such attitudes and treatment; many young or inexperienced parents do not know constructive approaches to child-rearing. There are diplomatic and non-threatening ways of offering suggestions and ideas to parents, and modeling appropriate educaring behavior is a good beginning. Parent involvement in the day-to-day program can easily lead to the discussion of alternative attitudes and approaches to children, after the parent has observed the educarer in action. Fundamentally, abusive and nonabusive parents have at least one thing in common: they all want to be good parents. Some of them just do not know how.

Child neglect. Child neglect can be defined as a parent's or educarer's failure to act, with such failure impeding the growth and development of the child. Physical neglect tends to be chronic, and all children in the family probably suffer from it. Emotional neglect and emotional abuse are closely related, and are so similar in their causes and manifestations that the terms are frequently used interchangeably. Neglect of an infant or toddler is suspected when the child is constantly hungry or even "steals" food from another; when she is consistently dirty and smelly; when he is listless and apathetic, and when medical or physical problems are not attended to.

Providers of child care and education are included among the list of mandatory reporters, so they no longer have the option of "choosing not to see." There is no legal or moral excuse for the following comments of a day-care provider.

Looking back, I can see . . . yes . . . there were clues. I should have known there was something

wrong. There were bruises on her arms and there was a wariness about her. We couldn't hug her or comfort her when she cried. She would draw back. The other staff and I didn't talk to each other about it. We didn't question the parents. We chose not to see (Abel, Alexander, & Smith, 1987, p. 18).

Policy Statements

Policy statements must include explicit procedures for taking care of and reporting the young child who is not called for within a reasonable time after the center has been closed for the day. Parents should be informed of these procedures. More than one youngster has been literally given to a day-care center without any announcement that this was going to happen. An example of a policy for late pick-up, and possible abandonment, follows. It is included in the parent manual of the Early Childhood Education Center (ECEC) at the University of Iowa, so that families cannot claim ignorance of the procedure.

Late pick-up.

The hours of the Center opening and closing must be respected. A late fee of $5.00 will be charged each time a child is picked up after closing time. Repeated late pick-ups will result in disenrollment of a child.

In the case of a regular scheduling conflict, the parent must make alternative arrangements for another adult to call for the child. However, children can be released *only* to parents or to individuals designated by parents *in writing* on the form "Release of Child to Adult Other Than Parent." Please update this form each semester.

In the rare instances when a parent or another designated individual is more than a few minutes late at the end of the session, staff members will initiate the following procedure:

1. Call the child's home and the parent's place of work;

2. If there is no parental response, call the adult(s) designated on the "Release of Child

to Adult Other Than Parent" form(s) to see if someone would come to get the child;

3. If no arrangement has yet been made for the child, call The University of Iowa Campus Police to request that they send a patrol car to the child's home to ascertain if a parent is at home but not answering the telephone;

4. If no arrangement has been made for the child by one hour after closing time, call the Iowa City Police (354-1800) to ask who from the Probation Office is on call;

5. Call the Probation Officer on call and notify him/her that it is possible that a child has been abandoned at the ECEC. (The chief probation officer has indicated that his office has legal authority to take custody of a child who is in emotional or physical danger or who is abandoned.)

6. An ECEC member must be with the child at *all times* until the probation officer or a designated adult arrives. If it is not possible for the ECEC staff member to wait with the child, another ECEC staff member should be contacted and asked to come to the ECEC. Under no circumstances should the child be taken from the ECEC, except by adults designated in writing by the parents or by the Probation Officer. The University of Iowa or Iowa City Police would also be able to take custody of the child in an emergency, but waiting in their facilities might cause the experience to be needlessly traumatic for the child.

7. The ECEC staff member should keep records of which of the above procedures were followed and at what time.

Other policies. If the child appears to need immediate attention, that is the first priority, but as soon as arrangements have been made for medical care, the suspicions must be reported. *Even when in doubt,* a report should be made, because although up to 50% of the families investigated as the result of a suspected child abuse report are not guilty of abuse as legally defined, they are in need of help and support

and are relieved to find a source of help. In actual practice, the legal requirement for reporting effectively addresses prevention as well as treatment.

Center policy should include statements about the procedures to follow when child abuse or neglect is suspected, and staff members and parents alike should know the policy before an incident occurs. Regardless of the number of children served and the number of educarers involved, one person should coordinate the child abuse and neglect activities. That person should establish and maintain relationships with the community agencies involved in the prevention and treatment of child abuse and neglect, such as state or local department of social services, county attorney, police or sheriff, and medical resources for treatment. The coordinator should

1. inform the other staff members regarding procedures for identifying and reporting suspected child abuse and neglect.

2. do the actual reporting of suspected cases to the appropriate agency.

3. discuss the reporting with the family when deemed necessary or desirable.

Reporting to the family is always advisable (reporting cannot be kept a secret for long), but the timing of notification requires a thoughtful decision based on previous knowledge and experience with the specific child and family. Abusive parents can become so enraged at the intrusion of the educarers that the life and welfare of the child may be further endangered. The reporting of suspected child abuse is an emotional trigger for all parties concerned.

The procedure varies from state to state, but more often than not, the departments of social services and law enforcement agencies are designated by law to receive the reports. State laws also differ in the information required, but the following items are generally included when possible:

1. Identity of the child; name, home address, age
2. Identity of the child's parents or other persons believed to be responsible for the child's care
3. Nature and extent of the child's injuries
4. Evidence of previous suspicious injuries
5. Name, age, and condition of other children in the home
6. Present location of the child
7. Name and address of the reporter

The report is first made orally, but a written report must be made as soon as possible. As soon as the oral report is made, the appropriate agency assumes the responsibility for the child and the child's family. This agency will advise the coordinator as to further action, if any, on the part of the center. Legally, the center's responsibility has been met by making the report, but if the center has continued contact with the child and family, its support can be vital in the rehabilitation.

Child abuse and neglect are no longer viewed as crimes for which adults must be punished; they are viewed as signals that the adults need help. Within that frame of reference, all the laws and all the agencies have as their primary goal the greatest possible protection of the child. In most cases, an intact family is considered the most protective situation. Termination of parental rights is a very last resort, considered only after every other measure has failed.

A Constructive Response

The following episode gives an indication of a coordinated response to one case of child abuse that was constructively resolved.

> This situation occurred in a small community of approximately six hundred people. The abuser was an eighteen year old mother with a small infant, the father was unemployed and the family

was new in the community and knew no one. The child had been admitted to the hospital because of severe injuries. It was obvious that the mother had no idea of how to take care of her baby, even diapering or bathing it. After discharge from the hospital the child was placed in a foster home in the same community with a very accepting foster mother. The real mother went every day to the foster home and took care of the baby under the foster mother's guidance. The mother accompanied the local health nurse on home visits and helped with the care given to other individuals. A job was obtained for the father. Both parents attended counseling at a mental health center nearby and the local church brought the parents into the church and town activities. Their loneliness was resolved. The child was returned to the home approximately eight months later (Solomons, cited in Lakin, Solomons, & Abel 1977, p. 103).

This is a beautiful example of coordinated community effort toward the realized goal of a well-functioning intact family.

Not only can child abuse/neglect cause death or major injury, it can do lasting harm in the resulting emotional and cognitive developmental disturbances. Infants learn unintended lessons when they are hit by their parents or educarers: (1) those who love you are also those who hit you; and (2) violence is permissible when other things don't work. These learnings are in addition to the imitative learning by which children model their behavior on the behavior of their significant adults (Strauss, Gelles, & Steinmetz, 1979). It is true that undesirable behavior is restrained faster and more completely the more violent the punishment. But more violence results in increased risks of negative and psychological and physical results, and at the extreme, even total passivity (Edfeldt, 1985).

It has been learned from studies of child development that young children go through various predictable phases. It is also recognized that some normal, age-appropriate behaviors annoy some adults, even to the extent of triggering child abuse. Infant/toddler educarers can make a difference if they are sensitive and supportive.

SUMMARY

Most accident-related injuries in child care are preventable. We know about the steps necessary to prevent accidents, and the present and emerging behavioral characteristics of young children. Infants wiggle and wriggle off elevated surfaces; they put all kinds of things into their mouths; they swallow any available liquid; and they have no sense of danger. Toddlers investigate, climb, open drawers and cupboards, suck or swallow objects and liquids, and move fast. Their enjoyment seems to come from imitating the actions of adults.

Efforts to eliminate child abuse and/or neglect in the child-care setting include the preemployment screening of all persons who will be in contact with the children; an optimal child/staff ratio; and an "open-door" policy. There are also attitudes and procedures for contacts with the families of the children that may supply support and understanding when needed.

It is required that educarers (and many others) report suspected cases of child abuse and/or neglect to the proper authorities. They no longer have the option of "choosing not to see."

Careful attention to the prevention of accidental and nonaccidental injuries will free the educarer to concentrate on the growth and development of the total child.

SUGGESTED ACTIVITIES AND QUESTIONS

1. Request copies of safety regulations or checklists from your state departments of education, public health, and health and human services. Also, a recommended checklist for site safety and playground equipment may be requested from:

Statewide Comprehensive Injury Prevention Program (SCIPP)
Department of Public Health
150 Tremont Street
Boston, MA 02111

2. Request a publication list from the U.S. Consumer Product Safety Commission, Office of Information & Public Affairs, Washington, DC 20207, as well as a packet of Product Safety Fact Sheets related to infants and toddlers.

3. Visit a family day-care home and a center-based program. Ask the educarer what safeguards are used to prevent accidents.

4. Interview a local social worker. Ask questions about mandatory reporting for educarers, and about the procedures followed after a report of suspected child abuse and/or neglect is received.

5. Describe ways in which an educarer can help prevent the abuse and/or neglect of children in an infant/toddler program.

6. Design a "safety tip" bulletin board based on the chapter information.

7. Order a single copy (multiple copies have a charge) of the current "Family Shopping Guide to Infant/Child Safety Seats" from:

American Academy of Pediatrics
Division of Publications
P.O. Box 927
Elk Grove Village, IL 60009-0927

SUGGESTED READINGS

Alexander, N. P. (1986). Child passenger safety: Getting it together. *Dimensions, 15* (1), 15–18.

American Academy of Pediatrics, Committee on Early Childhood, Adoption, and Dependent Care. (1987). *Health in day care: A manual for health professionals.* Elk Grove Village, IL: Author.

American Academy of Pediatrics. Committee on Psychosocial Aspects of Child and Family Health, 1985–88 (2nd ed.). (1988). *Guidelines for health supervision II* (especially pp. 27, 31, 35, 39, 42–43, 47, 51–52, 56, 60, 64). Elk Grove Village, IL: Author.

American Academy of Pediatrics. (1989). *1989 family shopping guide to infant/child safety seats.* (brochure). Elk Grove Village, IL: Author.

American Red Cross of Massachusetts Bay. (1986). *Health and safety for infants and children.* Boston: American Red Cross.

Aronson, S. (1988a, September). Chemical hazards in child care. *Child Care Information Exchange,* 33–37.

Aronson, S. (1988b). *First aid in child care settings.* Washington, DC: American Red Cross.

Aronson, S. S. (1988c). Safe, fun playgrounds. *Child Care Information Exchange, 61,* 35–40.

Aronson, S., & Pizzo, P. (1977). Health and safety issues in day care. *FIDCR Appropriateness Study State of the Art Paper.* Washington, DC: DHEW–Office for Planning and Evaluation.

Broadhurst, D., Edmunds, M., & MacDicken, R. A. (1979). *Early childhood programs and the prevention and treatment of child abuse and neglect.* Child Abuse and Neglect User Manual Series, DHEW Publication No. (OHDS) 79-30198. Washington, DC: U.S. Government Printing Office.

California Department of Health Services. (1986). *Program advisory with guidelines for safe use of art and craft materials.* Berkeley, CA: Author.

Dadd, D. L. (1986). *Nontoxic home: Protecting yourself from everyday toxics and health hazards.* Los Angeles: Jeremy P. Tarcher: distributed by St. Martin's Press, New York.

Eddowes, E. A. (1989). Safety in preschool programs. *Dimensions, 17* (2), 15–18.

Esbensen, S. (1987). *The early childhood playground: An outdoor classroom.* Ypsilanti, MI: High/Scope.

Ferguson, J. (1979). Creating growth—producing environments for infants and toddlers. In E. Jones (Ed.), *Supporting growth of infants, toddlers and parents.* Pasadena, CA: Pacific Oaks College.

Finkelhor, D., Williams, L. M., & Burns, N. (1988). *Nursery crimes: Sexual abuse in day care.* Newbury Park, CA: Sage Publications.

Frost, J. L. (1986). Children's playgrounds: Research and practice. In G. Fein & M. Rivkin (Eds.), *The young child at play: Reviews of research.* Vol. 4 (pp. 195–211). Washington, DC: National Association for the Education of Young Children.

Frost, J., & Klein, B. (1986). *Children's play and playgrounds.* Austin, TX: Playgrounds International.

Gillis, J., & Fise, M. E. R. (1986). *The childwise catalog: A consumer guide to buying the safest and best products for your children.* New York: Pocket Books.

Gold, S. J. (1986). *When children invite child abuse.* Eugene, OR: Fern Ridge Press.

Green, M. (1984). *A sigh of relief—The first aid handbook for childhood emergencies* (2nd ed.). New York: Bantam.

Greenman, J. (1988). *Caring spaces, learning places: Children's environments that work.* Redmond, WA: Exchange Press.

Jones, S. (1988). *Guide to baby products.* Mount Vernon, NY: Consumers Union.

Kane, D. N. (1986). *Environmental hazards to young children.* Phoenix: Oryx Press.

Kempe, C. H., & Helfer, R. E. (Eds.). (1980). *The battered child* (3rd ed.). Chicago: University of Chicago Press.

Kempe, R. S., & Kempe, D. H. (1984). *The common secret: Sexual abuse of children and adolescents.* New York: W. H. Freeman.

Koblinsky, S., & Behana, N. (1984). Child sexual abuse: The educator's role in prevention, detection, and intervention. *Young Children, 39* (6), 3–15.

Krugman, R. D. (1985). Preventing sexual abuse in day care: Whose problem is it anyway? *Pediatrics, 75,* 1150–1151.

Marotz, L. R., Rush, J. M., & Cross, M. Z. (1989). *Health, safety, and nutrition for the young child* (2nd ed.). Albany, NY: Delmar.

McIntire, M. S. (Ed.). (1980). *Handbook on accident prevention.* Hagerstown, MD: Harper & Row.

Meddin, B. J., & Rosen, A. L. (1986). Child abuse and neglect: Prevention and reporting. *Young Children, 41* (4), 26–30.

More on asbestos in play—Sand. (1986, November). *Child Health Alert,* P.O. Box 338, Newton Highlands, MA 02161.

Morris, S. (1989). Buying guide to tricycles. *Child Care Information Exchange,* (67), 11–15.

National Association for the Education of Young Children. (1986). *Toys: Tools for learning.* Washington, DC: Author.

National Highway Traffic Safety Administration. (1984). *We love you—Buckle up!* Washington, DC: Author. (Available from National Association for the Education of Young Children, 1834 Connecticut Avenue, N.W., Washington, DC 20009–5786)

Noyes, D. (1987). Indoor pollutants: Environmental hazards to young children. *Young Children, 42* (6), 57–65.

Prescott, E. (1984). The physical setting in day care. In J. T. Greenman & R. W. Fuqua (Eds.), *Making day care better.* New York: Teachers College Press.

Ruopp, R., Travers, J., & Goodrich, C. (1980). *Report of the National Day Care Study.* Cambridge, MA: Abt Associates.

Scott, D. K. (1985). Child safety seats—They work! *Young Children, 40* (4), 13–17.

Solomons, H. C., Lakin, J. A., Snider, B. C., & Paredes-Rojas, R. R. (1982). Is day care safe for Children? Accident records reviewed. *Children's Health Care, 10,* 90–93.

Steele, C., & Nauman, M. (1985). Infant's play on outdoor play equipment. In J. L. Frost & S. Sunderlin (Eds.), *When children play.* Wheaton, MD: Association for Childhood Education International.

Stewart, A. (1984). *Childproofing your home.* Reading, MA: Addison-Wesley.

Strickland, J., & Reynolds, S. (1989). The new untouchables: Risk management for child abuse in child care. *Child Care Information Exchange,* (65), 37–39.

U.S. Consumer Products Safety Commission. (1978). *Play happy, play safe.* Washington, DC: Author.

U.S. Consumer Product Safety Commission. (1981). *A handbook for public playground safety.* Vol. I and II. Washington, DC: U.S. Government Printing Office.

FOUR

The Educaring Environment

Suggestions for the developmental curriculum, and for the care and protection curriculum, did not include an emphasis on either the desirable physical facilities or the psychological climate that are a part of any infant/toddler program. The success of the appropriate activities that have been described is almost totally dependent on where they take place, and the manner in which they are introduced and continued.

Chapter 9 presents the physical and psychological dimensions of the environment, as well as suggested design features of both the indoor and outdoor space of the program.

Chapter 10 brings together the previous chapters in its presentation of both minimal and optimal qualifications for the educaring staff members, and describes the true meaning of educaring in action.

These two components of any program—the physical environment and the human environment—define the educaring environment.

9

The Physical and Experiential Environment

"The time has come," the walrus said, "to talk of many things."
Lewis Carroll

The growth and development of young children are influenced by the characteristics of their physical setting, both indoors and out-of-doors. This is particularly true for very young children who have limited control over their environment and who spend much of their time engaged in interaction with the physical, rather than the social environment (Parke, 1978; Weinstein & David, 1987).

In previous chapters, the here-and-now experiences have been targeted as the underlying foundation of what infants and toddlers know and do and feel and learn. The here-and-now is contained in two environments, the physical and the human. Both environments are the providers of stimulation, information, and affect.

This chapter contains the current thinking about the physical environment, its design, and its furnishings. Safety in the physical surroundings was treated at length in the preceding chapter. The "human" environment, the educarers, parents, and other persons who make the program work, will be presented in the next chapter.

ENVIRONMENTAL DIMENSIONS

Infants and toddlers are sensitive to all the qualitative aspects of a center: "its movements, sounds, volumes, textures, visual and kinesthetic vibrations, forms, colors, and rhythms" (Olds, 1987, p. 117).

Prescott (1984) describes the environment in terms of seven dimensions:

1. Open/closed
2. Simple/complex
3. High/low mobility
4. Large group/individual
5. Soft/hard
6. Intrusion/seclusion
7. Risk/safety

Open/Closed

The open/closed dimension may be used to rate materials, storage spaces, programs, the physical environment, and the whole center or family

A window to see the world.
(Early Childhood Education Center)

day-care home. Even the attitudes of the caregivers can be described as open or closed— open to exploration and experimentation, open to the wonder of emerging skills, open and warm in their relationships with the children and their families, and with other staff members. Open materials, of course, are those with a variety of uses or responses. Open storage means an orderly visible arrangement of toys and materials on shelves or in cupboards within a child's reach. The physical environment is open when it is uncluttered, but with a sense of organization, and with a clear traffic flow. I like to think that the whole program will be open to the world outside its walls. Infants and toddlers are intrigued by the world's sights and smells and sounds, and should have many outside experiences, in addition to windows to look out of.

Simple/Complex

This classification refers to the extent to which the play unit contains potential for active manipulation and alteration by children (Kritchevsky, Prescott, & Walling, 1969). A simple object has one obvious use or purpose and reacts in one predictable way. A jungle gym, a rocking horse, and a tricycle are examples of simple objects; they do not enable the child to manipulate or improvise.

A complex unit has subparts, or combines two essentially different play materials that allow the children to manipulate or improvise. An obstacle course is more complex than one bouncing beam or one slide. Cooking (or food preparation) is a complex activity, with its measuring,

A simple piece of equipment.
(Kindercampus, Iowa City)

A simple piece of equipment.
(Kindercampus, Iowa City)

combining, stirring, and pouring. Jones and Prescott (1978) state that increasing complexity is directly correlated to length of attention span, and that this is a worthwhile goal, particularly in an all-day program for young children.

High/Low Mobility

The mobility dimension is self-explanatory. It is used to describe the activities, equipment, and space that require large muscle movements (running, climbing), the small muscle movements (building with cube blocks), and hardly any movement (listening to a story or doing a puzzle).

High/low mobility also includes the ability of the child to move through space. For instance, a tricycle is a high mobility item (and is best used out-of-doors) whereas the circle games are low mobility, and are suitable for either indoors- or out-of-doors. They both use large muscle skills.

Large Group/Individual

An appropriately planned physical environment will suggest the social structure of the group. Knowing what we do about the characteristics of infants and toddlers, we do not plan total group activities (with the possible exception of eating and sleeping). Instead, we allow as much room as possible for individual exploration and experimentation, we provide "interest centers" as a way of organizing space, realizing that true social interaction at these age levels will just begin to occur as our children reach their third birthday. At this level, an "interest center" for infants might simply be a blanket or shag rug in front of a low horizontal mirror. For toddlers, a texture and/or color board mounted on the wall or the back of shelves, or a very simple housekeeping corner, meet the definition of *interest center*. The reading and listening corner for the sharing of books should serve a very few chil-

A complex unit. (Early Childhood Education Center)

dren at a time, so that the educarer can really individualize her storytelling or reading.

Soft/Hard

Montagu (1986) suggests that touch is the most critical sense for children under 3 years of age, because the skin is the largest organ of the body and is therefore a vital source of stimulation. Yet it has been observed that of the many senses, touch is the most neglected in nonresidential settings for children.

Prescott (1984) uses the degree of softness as a predictor of the quality of a child-care program, because it reflects the responsiveness of the environment to the children on a sensual-tactile level. Soft components include:

1. malleable materials such as clay or Play-doh
2. sand which the children can be in, either in a box or play area

3. "laps," teachers holding children
4. single-sling swings
5. grass that the children can be on
6. a large rug or carpeting indoors
7. water as an activity
8. very messy materials such as finger paint, clay, or mud
9. child/adult cozy furniture, such as rockers, couches, lawn swings
10. dirt to dig in
11. animals that can be held, such as guinea pigs, dogs, and cats (p. 52)

The younger the child, the more important is softness as a characteristic of the environment, both physical and human.

Intrusion/Seclusion

This dimension has to do with boundaries between people and things in the physical setting. It is closely related to the large group/individual dimension, in that the physical setting can allow children to be alone or in small groups or in continuous contact with all persons in the program. Room size and shape have some influence. Privacy (or seclusion) is more easily provided in an irregularly shaped large room. Many child-care centers or day-care homes do not have the opportunity to design their facility from the ground up, and must therefore rely on the arrangement of furniture and equipment to suggest a protected place. Jones (1977) suggests three ways of organizing space to provide some degree of seclusion:

1. Partially screened units: Activity tables or easels set against, or very close to walls, so that the visual input is minimized; one- or two-sided protection which functions to cut down on physical and/or visual intrusion.
2. Insulated units: Small areas which provide insulation or protection for a small group of children. . . . At least three-sided protection is provided by walls, low dividers, or other units.

High mobility. (Early Childhood Education Center)

3. Individual hide units: Cozy spaces, which usually have room for two children at the most, and where it is hard for the occupants to be seen (p. 15).

Protection from intrusion is a vital ingredient for the youngest children (and older ones, too). Particularly in a group setting for toddlers, there must be the place and opportunity for them to withdraw from the hustle and bustle of just being in a group. These children are just beginning to take tentative steps into their social world, and they need a place to retreat, or just to watch. In a family day-care home, the child can crawl into a big easy chair, or under the dining room table. Such "private corners" are often lacking in center care, but should be provided by the educarers. It is not difficult to arrange a secure "private" place. A large cardboard box, set on its side; a curtain in front of an empty shelf or cupboard; or a child-sized hole cut in the lower part of a cabinet—these will meet the need with little

or no expense. A bean bag chair can even meet the need for retreating, as well as providing softness and openness.

Risk/Safety

There is a happy medium in this dimension. Of course we plan a safe environment (see chapter 8), but we also sometimes remove all challenges in doing so. Young children love to experiment with their bodies in space (and have little sense of real danger). Young children must try out different ways of doing things, as an essential way of learning the best way. Adult-imposed rules are not foolproof, and even if heeded temporarily, will be forgotten as soon as the adult's attention turns elsewhere. When we "eliminate the booby traps such as sharp concrete edges that are covered up by sand, broken equipment, and poor placement of activities" (Prescott, 1984, pp. 54–55), we can minimize accidents

Low mobility. (Early Childhood Education Center)

without constant "don'ts." Facilitative supervision is the key.

Putting It All Together

The dimensions of activity settings for infants and toddlers are not a question of either-or, they are a question of degree. For instance, an appropriate setting should be more open than closed, although of course there are times when restraints or prohibitions must be used to limit or stop a child's actions. There should be many simple play units, but also a few with subparts or a combination of related materials. There should be opportunities for both high and low mobility: the appropriate balance will be determined by the characteristics of the children. Only rarely, if ever, will there be total group activities for the toddlers, but many provisions should be made for individual and parallel activities. The overall physical and psychological climate should be soft and not hard. There should be physical spaces for a toddler to withdraw from contact with other children (and adults) in order to facilitate his moving from an egocentric being to a social being. In our endeavors to keep children injury-free, we must not remove all challenges, because it is through meeting challenges head-on, that children (and adults) grow.

BASIC DESIGN FEATURES: INDOOR SPACES

Living and Learning Spaces

When either renovating a space for infants and toddlers, or planning a new space, there are certain architectural aspects that must be considered, such as space and density, the type of flooring, the availability of natural light, the placement of inner and outer doors, and the acoustics. Suggestions about these aspects of interior design are included with the hope that educarers can have some control over them.

Density. Space requirements for infants and toddlers in centers range from 20 to 50 square feet per child of child-usable space (in addition to space for hallways, kitchens, bathrooms, etc.). The most usual requirement is 35 square feet, but many centers have more space per child. Twenty-one states had no indoor space requirements for family day-care homes in 1986, but more states are adding these homes

in their licensing requirements each year (Morgan, 1987). It would appear that the 35-square-feet requirement is sufficient for an infant-toddler center, because the infants are not yet mobile. But "density is more than just the amount of available space; it is linked to the arrangement of that space and the types of resources available in that space as well" (Prescott, 1981, pp. 131–132). Only one of the studies about density and children has included children as young as 2 years of age. Rohe and Patterson (1974) observed more aggressive, destructive, and unoccupied behavior as the density increased, and more cooperative, constructive, and relevant participation as the amount of resources increased.

The activity room(s) should be large enough for large muscle activities and a feeling of openness, but not so large that toddlers feel lost or threatened. An open physical environment does not mean a big room with little in it besides children. It means open spaces, but also divided spaces. Dividers need be only 3 feet high: "thus

Small-group activity. (Early Childhood Education Center)

Individual (or one-to-one) activity. (Early Childhood Education Center)

an infant may experience a very divided space with alcoves and secluded corners while the caregiver experiences above the waist a largely open room" (Greenman, 1982a, p. 83). Even too-large rooms can be made visually comfortable by varying the floor surfaces and colors and heights. Raised platforms provide "watching" places and add visual interest to a large room. Small secluded or enclosed spaces allow infants and toddlers a few private moments. Almost anything 36 inches high can serve as a wall for a private nook: hollow block enclosures, large boxes or cardboard barrels, or even tables turned on one side with a blanket hanging down. A child-care program does not need a classroom; it needs a *living* room in the truest sense of the word.

Flooring. The kind of flooring influences the kind of program, and it is desirable to have a variety of flooring materials so that children can have the feeling of different kinds of spaces. Infants and toddlers (and preschool children) spend a good deal of time on the floor, so that while adults may take this part of the interior for granted, it is an area that is close to the heart and bodies of the children. The flooring should

be warm, resilient, easily cleaned and maintained, durable, and parts of it should be soundproofed. Choices include washable indoor-outdoor carpeting; vinyl treated linoleums, corks, asphalt tiles; wood, terrazo, or concrete; and area rugs and matting.

It is important to determine the needs of the children before deciding on the material to be used on the floors. For instance, the flooring beneath a crib might be washable carpeting in order to help with soundproofing. However, it would be highly desirable to have a vinyl-type covering on the floor if the babies are to be bathed in bathinettes or small tubs or fed in another part of the room. Carpeting that is subjected to a lot of water and/or food on it will tend to get soggy and develop a musty smell. One solution is to tape sheets of a plastic tarp to the carpet under the bathing, eating, and painting areas, using reinforced plastic duct tape for a secure fastening.

It is also important for an infant who is beginning to crawl to have a variety of textures on which to test some of his perceptual skills—the softness and warmth of a carpet or the hardness and cold of vinyl. One part of the floor should be elevated with one or two steps. Greenman

A soft environment. (Early
Childhood Education Center)

(1988) suggests using portable plywood carpeted platforms on lockable casters.

The contrast between a soft and hard flooring helps the toddlers and run-abouts in defining areas of quiet play and those for more noisy play. The area for books and individual listening might be defined by a throw rug (securely anchored) or carpeting; the area for block play with small hand wheel toys would be more efficient (but also noisier) if it were on a perfectly flat, smooth surface. For water play and easel painting, an easily cleanable surface is necessary. Some young children's centers have placed a drain in the appropriate place so that the floor may be hosed and squeegeed for easy maintenance.

Indoor carpeting as a floor covering is inexpensive and easy to maintain. However, dirty carpeting is not as noticeable as dirt on smooth surfaced floors and the tendency to have a build-up of dirt and dust with carpeting must be recognized.

Flooring may denote a particular area of activity, it may serve as part of the sensory experiences planned for the children, and it may serve as surface for construction, games, crawling, dancing, or resting.

> Infants require broad horizontal surfaces which accommodate them and adults comfortably . . . with boundaries that are quite distinct. Toddlers, on the other hand, need plenty of opportunity to roam freely, over moderate changes in level that offer some challenge in their balancing and walking skills. The ideal toddler environment, a "corralled open range," is an expansive, undulating horizontal surface, larger than that for infants, with clearly defined boundaries. (Weinstein & David, 1987, p. 124)

Wall coverings and display spaces. In an infant/toddler center, almost every inch of wall space has potential use for looking out (windows) and for looking in (a low horizontal mirror); for communicating both important and

Hardness. (Kindercampus)

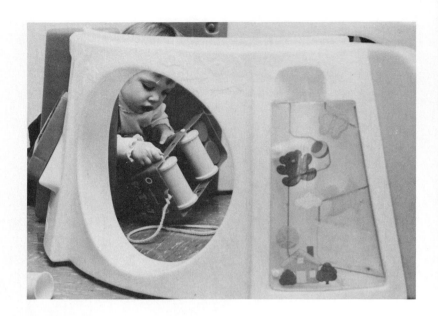

interest-arousing messages; for displaying pictures and children's art work; and for drawing and "writing." Walls can also support vertically mounted toys, grab bars for pulling up, texture and color boards, and mirrors and reflective surfaces at many heights. Walls can do much more than define the limits of a room.

Light, washable, nonpoisonous latex paints or heavy duty washable wallpapers should be used. Some centers have found laminated plywood veneer paneling (in light wood-tones) to be satisfactory and useful. Cork, tack-board, or styrofoam covered with burlap are appropriate for displaying pictures or art work. Displays are

Hard and soft. (Early Childhood Education Center)

A cozy space. (Early Childhood
Education Center)

at an appropriate level so the toddlers can see
and touch. For infants in cribs or play pens, flat
(nontoxic) pictures or designs may be fastened
to the wall or the crib-side. Hanging mobiles
should offer a horizontal view, not a vertical one
that adults are used to. Interest-arousing mobiles
may be hung over any place that the baby looks
up, including the diaper-changing surface.

The displays and messages for parents
should of course be at the adult eye-level. Warm
or neutral earth tones should be used for walls
and display spaces so as not to detract from the
displays themselves. There is an abundance of
color in the centers as a whole, and a background wall coloring serves as a balance.
Greenman (1988) agrees,

> Children's clothes provide color in motion, in ad-
> dition to the bright colors of toys, artwork, plastic
> furniture, pillows, and book covers. Designers,
> often unable to visualize the settings in action,

use too much color and graphics for accent walls.
The end result is a kaleidoscopic atmosphere that
cheers for a short time and wears on the individual for the other five to seven hours a day (p.
109).

The same comment might be made about
the designers of the multicolored, multidesign
carpets with children's games woven into the
fabric—they were not able to "visualize the settings in action."

Windows and ventilation. Windows play an
important part in the programs for young children, and serve adult needs as well. They open
the inside world to the wider world outside.
Changing weather and seasons, street and outdoor activities—these offer perceptual experiences. They are learning activities and a focus
for conversation. Younger children delight in
watching older children playing. Toddlers enjoy

a wide window seat as a place from which to view the world, or simply as a resting place, and adults need a way to observe children who are outside.

Windows in an early childhood center should have the following qualities:

- safety glass
- open and close easily
- don't leak water or air
- provide a view without glare
- can be opened without creating a draft
- have a surface that might be used for placement of art materials that could demonstrate opaqueness and transparency

Blinds, curtains, and shades are useful in controlling light and offer some acoustical protection in noisy areas. Awnings or a low overhanging roof can help control the glare of sunlight. Olds (1987) believes that daylight streaming through open windows may be critical to a child's health and overall development. The Scandinavians believe this so strongly that they bundle their babies in snowsuits and blankets and set their carriages outside for napping, regardless of the weather.

Open windows offer fresh air as well as daylight, and should be open whenever the outside temperature permits. Most licensing regulations specify an optimal indoor temperature in the range of 68° to 72°F, and some require this temperature down low, from 1 to 3 feet from the floor. Thermostats may be placed close to the floor but need to be protected from a toddler's curiosity and manipulation.

Doors. Doors are also the subject of local and state regulations as found in fire, safety, and/or health codes. Needless to say, they should open out, not in. If glass is used, it must be safety or plexiglass in order to reduce the number of children getting hit when the door opens. There is a possibility of breakage and cuts when window glass is used. A double dutch door, with plex-

iglass for the bottom half, is excellent for an inside room such as the bathroom or kitchen. If no provision has been made for an observation room, a one-way glass in a door or window can serve the purpose.

Door openings should be without sills, and should be large enough for a crib (and maybe a heavy-duty laundry cart) to pass through. Greenman (1984) writes of an ingenious solution to

> the problem of evacuating pre-walking children from a center in an emergency (or even when you just plain need to get everyone outside into the sunshine). They use a laundry cart—one of those 3 × 4 canvas wheeled carts that hotels and hospitals use for collecting linen. Up to six infants can be wheeled out safely (provided doors are wide enough) (p. 25).

At this caring center, the educarers give children frequent rides so that no infant is frightened when the carts are used in the monthly safety drills.

Even the placement of a doorknob deserves attention. In the infant room the knob could be placed high on the door for ease in going in and out when infants are being held. In a room for toddlers, the doorknob leading to the administrative offices or outside might be placed high for safety purposes. The door leading to the outdoor playspace should be placed so that the child has access and control.

Door locks may be necessary and should be in adult reach only. Locks must always be opened from the inside. The use of locks on closet or cupboard doors depends on what is stored, and on the program goals. Should the materials be accessible to the crawlers and toddlers and runabouts? Some things yes, some things no. Recessed pulls on cabinets will prevent children from bumping into knobs.

Lighting and electrical fixtures. Every room should have provision for some kind of artificial lighting, even though daylight may provide adequate light on certain days. The light should provide good illumination without glare, in addition to setting a mood for the room and the people in it. If possible, an expert in the lighting field should be consulted for guidance. Insufficient or glaring lights can cause eye fatigue or eye damage. Other important considerations should take into account the placement of windows (northern exposures are best) and the color of the walls and ceiling. It is also important to consider the lighting from all angles—what about the infants staring up at the ceiling? Can the lights be controlled for naps? Can the bulbs be changed easily?

Electrical outlets should be checked by local building and fire and electrical authorities. It is advisable to locate outlets at adult height, perhaps on an electrical strip running around the room. The low ones should be adequately protected for the safety of the children. Outlets are needed for cooking equipment, bottle-warmers, aquariums, vacuum cleaners, and so on. Some of the appliances that might be installed (such as a small refrigerator in the infants' room) might need heavy duty wiring. Extension cords and "octopi" put too much stress on the electrical system, in addition to being a serious safety risk for children under 5 years of age (see Electric Shock in chapter 8).

The staff should know where the breakers for the electrical system are located, and should be instructed in simple methods of cutting off the system. When new wiring is installed, the electrical box should be large enough for future expansion, and should be equipped with circuit breakers instead of fuses.

Color. Colors have different emotional qualities, and the response to color is highly individualized. The response is also age-related. New research on visual perception has revealed that infants in the first 9 months of life are more attracted to high-contrast black-and-white patterns than to pastel or bright primary colors. After this infant stage, however, color becomes very important. It gives messages, and in com-

bination with different lighting effects, can influence moods. Blues and greens are cool (or even cold) and nonstimulating; reds and oranges are exciting and hot. "Color can be used to visually divide space, and different areas of the environment can use color to project different emotional qualities" (Greenman, 1982b, p. 83). Perhaps red is best used on gross motor equipment, and green, blue, or white in quiet areas for story corners and napping. Overall, neutral shades should be used on walls and floors.

Acoustics. Noise levels are rarely included in state licensing standards, but they play an important role in the learnings and behaviors of both children and educaring persons. In general steady familiar background sounds do not distract attention. The goal is to reduce unnecessary noise, crying, and shouting. Sounds can be minimized with acoustical tile ceilings, carpeted floors, full draperies on large window spaces, fabric wall hangings, and fabric room dividers. Cork bulletin boards and upholstered furniture also help absorb sounds. A limited group size and the separation of activity centers are also elements of a good acoustical environment.

Activity centers. In addition to their acoustical benefits, activity centers (or interest centers) help in achieving some sense of order in a room with infants and toddlers and educarers and parents and practicum students and maybe a visiting fire fighter. Cataldo (1983) suggests the following interest areas for infants and toddlers: For infants, these include a rattle corner, a reaching center, a sensory corner, a manipulative area, an interaction-game area, an exercise mat, a water table, and a puppet theatre and doll house structure. Interest areas for toddlers include a creative corner, a music area, a construction center, a curiosity corner, an identity area, a simple playhouse, a problem-solving area, a sand table, a gymnastics area, and a play-dough table. Both infants and toddlers need a comfort corner, a library and book center, and a space for noting seasonal changes, holidays, and special events. Most important, both infants and toddlers need spaces for quiet and active play.

"Routine" Spaces

Kitchens. There will be days when the entire program seems to be devoted to food—preparing it, feeding it (or having it eaten), and cleaning up after meal or snack time. The hub of this activity is the kitchen, one of the most important rooms, and one from which children are frequently excluded. This may be necessary for safety reasons, especially in large centers, but it is not ideal. Prescott and David (1976) state,

> Some of the nicest moments which we have seen in day care are those where children could perch in safe places and watch, talk with or even help the cook. Good kitchen design can keep children safely away from dangerous areas and still not entirely close off contact between food preparation and the eating of food (p. 57).

Regulations concerning food preparation and storage usually focus on safety and health precautions, such as the following taken from the Iowa Licensing Standards for Child Care Centers (Iowa DHS, 1988):

1. Sufficient refrigeration space shall be provided for holding perishable foods at a maximum of 40 degrees F., and thermometers shall be maintained in the refrigerator.

2. Kitchens shall be clean, well lighted and ventilated, and free of rodents and insects.

3. Sanitary techniques shall be used in the preparation of all milk mixtures and other foods prepared in the center.

4. The person preparing meals must maintain good personal hygiene and appropriately covered hair while preparing food. Food shall not be handled by cooks with open sores or bandages on their hands unless wearing protective gloves.

5. A sufficient number of flytight, watertight garbage and rubbish containers shall be provided to properly store all material between collections. Containers must be maintained in a sanitary condition outside the building and away from the play area.

6. No chipped or cracked dishes shall be used.

7. Nondisposable dishes and silverware shall be properly cleaned by pre-rinsing or scraping, washing, sterilizing and air-drying. A dishwashing machine must provide a minimum wash temperature of 140 degrees F. For hand washing at least a two-compartment sink or comparable facility must be available. Tableware shall be either rinsed in water of a minimum of 180 degrees F. or rinsed in a chemical sanitizing agent and air-dried. No tableware shall be towel-dried (109.6 [5]).

The kitchen should be located close enough to the children's rooms so that the transporting of food can be done quickly and with a minimum of confusion (carts with trays are convenient for this purpose). It should also be located close to a convenient delivery area so that groceries may be easily delivered and refuse may be easily disposed of. Sometimes a pass-through directly to the children's rooms can be arranged from the kitchen. However, smells of cooking (which can be considered an advantage or disadvantage) and the clatter of dishes may be points to consider.

The kitchen may also serve as a demonstration center for parents in the preparation of foods for the family. If this is the case, there will need to be extra counter and floor space. Regardless of the size of the group of children and adults, and of the extent of food preparation and service, consultation with local health authorities is important.

Bathrooms. A diapering area in or near the play area is more convenient than in another room (i.e., the bathroom), and a diapering area in the infant crib room saves time and steps. But wherever the diapering is done, the area must contain everything within easy adult reach. Because of the danger of children falling, many educarers diaper on the floor—which "almost always results in very poor sanitation" (Greenman, 1988, p. 119). Diaper tables with rims and/or straps *may* reduce the risk of accidents, but the best insurance is to always keep one hand on the child.

Children's bathrooms should be located adjacent to the rooms where the children play, sleep, and/or eat, indoors and outdoors. Doors should be easily opened and probably will remain open for easy adult supervision. A half-wall between bathroom and activity room will facilitate supervision. Toilets and wash basins should be low enough for the children to use comfortably. Toilets that hang from the wall allow easy floor mopping. Seamless flooring, easily cleanable walls, and a tight seal between wall and floor are important for sanitation.

Although there is no perfect dispenser for paper towels, paper instead of cloth towels are recommended, and the dispenser must be child-reachable and child-usable. Personal wash cloths and personal toothbrushes should be labeled, used only by that child, and hung to dry in between use. Dust covers for the toothbrushes are required.

Napping areas. Many infant programs seem to "get by" without a separate crib room, but it is a must if infants and toddlers are both in the group. The rule is that a child should *never* share a crib or cot or mat or bedding with another child. Because few centers can afford continuous staffing of a crib room, a window to the playroom or an intercom can help maintain contact *if* the licensing agent agrees.

Adult Spaces

The amount of space needed for the educaring staff depends on the type of program, the hours of the program, and the number of children and adults. Minimum provisions include a place for personal belongings, an adult rest room, and a place to "get away" temporarily. No matter what the size, there needs to be office space with

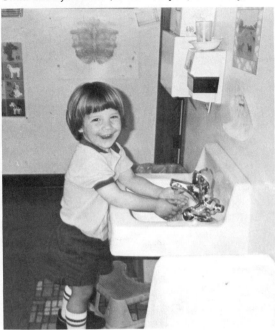

Child-sized facilities. (Kindercampus, Iowa City)

a desk, telephone, and file cabinets (for the children's records). A teacher's desk in the children's room takes up too much space, and creates a psychological climate directly opposed to the living-and-learning-together philosophy that is appropriate. The only piece of adult furniture in the rooms with children is an adult-sized rocking chair, which can be used for a moment or two for relaxation, but is primarily used as a haven for children (with or without an adult). It is a special treat for a child to sit in it and look at a picture book, or watch the others at a safe distance. At first, a young child is fascinated with all the child-sized furnishings, just the right size, but the immersion in a group of children may be frightening. In this case, even an empty big chair carries the message that there is a comforting adult nearby. Of course the educarer will take on her lap a child who asks for this either by words or behavior. However, when the educarer is too involved with the other children, then sitting in her chair is the next best thing.

Oblivious to the sounds around him. (Kindercampus, Iowa City)

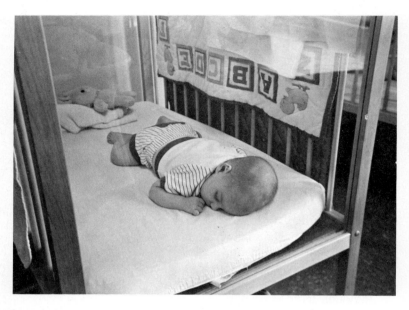

The center should have sufficient space to allow for efficient administration, staff and parent meetings, and comfort and privacy of both staff and parents. Ideally, there is a hospitality room with comfortable furniture, toys for children, and reading material for parents and other adults visiting the center. A pot of coffee and/or a supply of cold drinks add to the sense of welcome that should be fostered.

The director's office—discussing an equipment order.
(Kindercampus, Iowa City)

Also recommended is an observation space or room, equipped with one-way windows and an audio system. In practice, such a facility is found only in demonstration centers, usually sponsored by a college or university, for use in the preparation of educarers. However, it can prove to be very useful for in-service training of the center staff members, and for the parents of the children in the program. In any event, a pro-

gram should encourage visits, and provisions should be made, even if in the room(s) used by the children.

FURNISHING THE INDOOR SPACE

Furnishings and Equipment

Equipment, other than play materials, receives little attention from either licensing agencies or authors about infant/toddler programs, who usually focus on the activities of educaring or on the learning inherent in such activities. Perhaps it is assumed that we all know what very little children need, like cribs and mattresses and blankets and high chairs and tables and chairs and soft furniture and strollers. However, there are some few suggestions that might be new. For instance, high chairs take up floor space, whereas a car seat with a tray can be set any-where—on the floor, on tables, or on a shelf, and it serves the feeding-eating function adequately. Groups of small tables are more functional than one or two large tables; if there is a removable top for the water or sand table, the same floor space will serve several purposes. Of particular importance are the nurturing (or soft) objects. Greenman (1982b) lists them as soft furniture (couches, chairs, pillows, bean bag chairs); a water bed; mattresses, lofts, platforms, playpens, rocking chairs, swinging chairs, carpeted barrels, rugs, blankets, towels, baby carriers, cradles, and strollers. He explains his choices in the following way:

> Couches, armchairs, and rocking chairs create laps and soft places for babies. (Supervision is necessary for low mobility caregivers!) Pillows and mattresses in corners or on platforms create secure places for resting or watching. A playpen can be a planned, protected play space. Swingo-matic chairs are very useful, but fragile; hanging a swing from the ceiling or wall may fulfill the same purpose. Small rugs and blankets add softness and define space for a baby. Waterbeds, bean bag chairs and pillows have a give to them which is delightful and fascinating to babies. In-

Multi-age conversation. (Kindercampus, Iowa City)

fant carriers allow caregivers to do their work while nurturing a young infant (p. 98).

No prescribed list of materials or equipment can meet the needs and characteristics of the particular children in a particular setting for infants and toddlers. It is essential to observe the children, to get to know them, and to then purchase or make the objects that will serve them best. Keep in mind that good pieces of educaring equipment can be used in different ways, will encourage exploration, manipulation, and experimentation, will be fun (or at least comforting) to use, and are cleanable, durable, and safe.

Play Materials

Types of play equipment are seldom specified in licensing regulations for infants and toddlers. Willis and Ricciuti (1975) propose the following criteria for play equipment for infants and tod-

Figure 9–1

Some Good Toys & Activities for Young Children

Approximate age	What children are like	Types of good toys and worthwhile activities
Birth to 3 months	Begin to smile at people, coo Follow moving person or object with eyes Prefer faces and bright colors Reach, discover hands, kick feet, lift head Suck with pleasure Cry, but often are soothed when held Turn head toward sounds	Rattle, large rings, squeeze or sucking toys Lullabies, nursery rhymes, poems Bright pictures of faces hung so baby can see them Bells firmly attached to baby's wrist, ankle, booties Cardboard or vinyl books with high-contrast illustrations to stand in baby's view Brightly patterned crib sheets Mobile with parts visible from baby's position
4 to 6 months	Prefer parents and older siblings to other people Repeat actions that have interesting results Listen intently, respond when spoken to Laugh, gurgle, imitate sounds Explore hands and feet, put objects in mouth Sit when propped, roll over, scoot, bounce Grasp objects without using thumbs, bat at hanging objects Smile often	Soft doll, texture ball, socks with bright designs Toys that make noise when batted, squeezed, or mouthed Measuring spoons, teething toy Cloth, soft vinyl books with bright pictures to grasp, chew, & shake Pictures of faces covered in plastic, hung at child's level; unbreakable mirror Fingerplays, simple songs, peek-a-boo Socks with bright designs or faces
7 to 12 months	Remember simple events, form simple concepts Identify themselves, body parts, voices of familiar people Understand own name, other common words Say first meaningful words Explore, bang, or shake objects with hands Find hidden objects, put objects in and out of containers Sit alone Creep, pull themselves up to stand, walk May seem shy or become upset with strangers	All of the above *plus* Rag and baby dolls, stuffed animals, puppets Container for large beads, blocks, balls Nesting toy or plastic containers Board books to read, old magazines to tear Recordings of voices, animal sounds, music Wooden blocks, large soft blocks Water toys that float Rubber or large plastic balls Soft plastic or wood vehicle with wheels Games like peek-a-boo
1 to 1½ years	Imitate adult actions Speak and understand more words and ideas Enjoy stories	All of the above *plus* Surprise or music box Puzzles, 2 to 6 large pieces with knobs

Reproduced with permission. National Association for the Education of Young Children (1985). *Toys: Tools for learning.*

dlers (and they seem appropriate for children of all ages):

1. Toys should encourage action.

2. Play materials should respond to the baby's action.

3. The responsiveness of toys and play materials should be natural rather than "gimmicky."

4. A quality program includes both toys that encourage social interaction and those that can be used by a baby alone.

5. Toys should be chosen and placed to give babies choices as they pursue their own interests, but with the aim of channeling their efforts to use emerging skills.

6. Play materials should be versatile—that is,

Figure 9–1

continuing

1 to 1½ years (continued)	Experiment with objects Walk steadily, climb stairs Assert independence, but strongly prefer familiar people Recognize ownership of objects Develop friendships, but also play alone Are beginning to understand what adults want them to do, but do not yet have the ability to control themselves	Books/recordings with songs, rhymes, simple stories, & pictures Wide watercolor markers, nontoxic fat crayons, large blank paper Geometric, unit, or cardboard blocks People and animals, vehicles: wood or rubber Pounding bench Sand & water play: plastic measuring cups, boats, containers, washable doll Large cardboard box to crawl in Toys that jingle or move when used Kitchen cupboard of <u>safe</u> pots, pans, lids, and utensils.
1½ to 2 years	Solve problems Speak and understand even more Show pride in accomplishments, like to help with tasks Exhibit more body control, run Play more with others Begin pretend play	Self-help toys: sorting box, holes with pegs Large spools or beads to string Books with large colorful illustrations, short stories Soft dough clay, bells, drum Small broom, sponge, camera, pots & pans Shopping cart, wagon, steerable riding toy: toy telephone, washable doll
2 to 3½ years	Enjoy learning new skills Learn language rapidly Are always on the go Have some sense of danger Gain more control of hands and fingers Frustrated easily Act more independent, but are still dependent, too Act out familiar scenes	Wood puzzles with 4 to 20 pieces Pegboards, sewing cards, stacking toys, picture lotto, dominoes Picture story books, poems about familiar things Classical, folk, children's music Finger or tempera paint, ½" brushes, blunt scissors, white glue Unit blocks & accessories, wood train set with large pieces Hammer (13 oz steel shanked), soft wood, roofing nails, nailing block Triangle, wood block: texture- & sound-matching games Wagon or wheelbarrow, large rubber ball, riding toy Washable doll with a few clothes, doll bed Dress-up clothes: hats, shoes, shirts; hand puppet

they should lend themselves to a variety of uses.

7. Play materials should provide experience in a variety of modalities (pp. 58–62).

These criteria have been amply met by the listing in Figure 9–1.

Tentative conclusions about how play materials are related to mental development, as summarized by Bradley (1985), include:

1. There is a moderate correlation between the availability and use of toys and children's mental test scores beginning as early as the second year of life.

2. The relation between play materials and intelligence appears to be reciprocal, with brighter children eliciting more appropriate play materials to interact with.

3. Toys and other objects frequently serve as the focus of social encounters—more fully

social as the child matures. Such encounters afford numerous opportunities for direct and incidental learning (p. 139).

BASIC DESIGN FEATURES: OUTDOOR SPACE

Opposing Views

Infant/toddler group care and education is a relatively new phenomenon. Just as in former years when we adapted (by making smaller) the outdoor playgrounds and equipment of the elementary school for use by preschools, we are making the same adaptations for the very young. Full-page advertisements for playground equipment for toddlers appear in issues of *Child Care Information Exchange, Childhood Education, Dimensions,* and *Young Children.* They all picture structures made of aluminum or polyethylene or coated steel parts, and they claim to provide safe and fun ways for toddlers starting at 8 months to develop motor patterns and coordination skills and self-confidence. The equipment appears to be developmentally appropriate for motor development. It is also expensive.

A contrasting view of playground equipment has been expressed by Richard Dattner (1969), a landscape architect who calls traditional playgrounds "disaster areas."

> A playground should be like a small-scale replica of the world, with as many as possible of the sensory experiences to be found in the world in it. Experiences for *every* sense are needed, for instance: rough and smooth objects to look at and feel; light and heavy things to pick up; water and wet materials as well as dry things; cool materials and materials warmed by the sun; soft and hard surfaces; things that make sounds (running water) or that can be struck, plucked, plinked, etc.; smells of all varieties (flowers, bark, mud); shiny, bright objects and dull, dark ones; things both huge and tiny; high and low places to look at and from; materials of every type, natural, synthetic, thin, thick, and so on. The list is inexhaustible, and the larger the number of items that

are included, the richer and the more varied the environment for the child (p. 44).

Do you choose the manufactured plastic or metal units, or the "small-scale replica of the world"?

If we apply our knowledge of what infants and toddlers are like, what interests them, and if we remember our goals, we will be less dependent on manufactured products. Although most centers (or family day-care homes) are not located in the middle of a rolling meadow filled with wild flowers, fed by a babbling brook, and surrounded by trees, educarers *can* provide dirt mounds and digging places and running water and large sand pits and gardens.

What Is a Playground?

A playground is a place for a child to run, leap, shout, climb, splash, and find expression for his energy and ideas. Young children who spend most of their daylight hours in a child-care program have pressing needs for such a place.

The outdoor space should be used for much more than respite for the adult or as "recess" for the children. If the goal of the child care and education program is to expand a child's experience, to provide a wide range of activities, to develop the total child, then the importance of the playground cannot be neglected. Infants and toddlers are developing rapidly. As soon as they become mobile, they have special needs, some of which can be met better by outdoor activities and some of which can only be met outdoors. For large muscle development, a child needs plenty of room to tumble, jump, and climb. Certain equipment simply is not suitable for indoors, such as tricycles, climbing equipment, and swings. Other activities are simply more practical outdoors: mud, sand, and water play can be used with more freedom outside. Some activities take on new dimensions when outdoors. For example, water play indoors is quite different from splashing and wading outdoors, and caring for a terrarium indoors is a completely different experience from growing vegetables and flowers outdoors.

Playgrounds should provide the activities a child could engage in if he lived in the country. The obvious need of children is not just a place to play, but a total world to which he can respond (Friedberg, 1969).

Playground Design

Realistically, the outdoor play space for infants and toddlers is subject to space limitations, licensing requirements, geographical location, financial and other resources, and the creativity of the planners. There are some design principles that must be followed as closely as possible, given these constraints.

Seclusion and scale. Play areas should always have some form of containing boundary to define the area, to deter older children, and most important, to prevent the children from straying. Seclusion and scaling down to a child's size enable him to create a world of his own within the framework provided. However the area is planned, it should never be unprotected or placed in the middle of the older children's playspace. This sense of security and calm can be attained by careful planting and group shaping. Seats and comfortable surroundings are essential for the educarers and other adults.

Earth shaping. Small children adore climbing and sliding down, and full advantage should be taken of any difference of level. Ground shaping and artificial contoured mounds make good wind shields and barriers, and also serve as banks for rolling down and climbing up. Steps can be worked into these mounds, and there can be space at the bottom for a sand pit. The grade should be easy for the toddlers and runabouts to climb (and for them to roll down).

Surfacing and texture. No one has yet discovered the ideal surfacing for a small child's playground although a mixture of grass and paving seems an obvious compromise. The most pleasant surface, of course, is grass. Some wear and tear will occur, but new turf can be laid each year. The overmowing of grass destroys much that is pleasant to little children.

A combination of surfaces will provide various textures; playgrounds should have different textures in different areas.

Sand and water play. Sand play is much loved by little children; it is the perfect medium and gives endless pleasure. It should be kept pleasantly damp, so it can be made into pies or shaped into forms. There should be at least 20 inches depth of sand, and more if possible, to allow for digging and burrowing. The sand "box" should be large enough to accommodate several children, and should have some kind of low wall around it to prevent the sand from blowing away, and to provide a working space for children. Because playing with sand gives so much pleasure, some early childhood programs have included a large sand pit sunk in the floor of their indoor facility.

Water is one of the joys of childhood and has endless possibilities for play. An artificial brook may contain very little water and still provide for paddling, splashing, and sailing boats. But it needs access to clean water and a means of getting rid of surplus or contaminated water. A water hose is a good substitute—children can be showered in the hot weather, and can fill small containers, or a large basin for sailing boats and splashing. Plastic wading pools could even be set in the sand pit, if large enough. Sand and water make an entrancing mixture. Of course even shallow pools need close supervision.

The beauty of natural materials (water, sand, mud) lies in their versatility. There is no right or wrong way. Anything goes (Rubin et al., 1980).

Playground equipment. The traditional and somewhat ugly mechanical equipment is unnecessary for children under 3 years of age. Appropriate (and sufficient) equipment includes a low slide, a low climbing structure, baby or tire swings, a sand play area, a water play area, riding toys, push and pull toys, and soft large and small balls (Leavitt & Eheart, 1985). This basic equipment can be extended with "throwaways" such as low coffee tables, small chairs or hassocks, shelves, cupboards, benches, kitchen utensils and pots and pans, and large cardboard cartons or packing crates. A piece of rope can easily become a fireman's hose; a dish pan or bathtub can serve as a container for water.

Little children delight in creeping into small shelters and playing house. Little children delight in following a meandering path of stepping stones or sawed-off tree trunks. A ladder placed horizontally on a grassy area becomes a challenge for precision-stepping and balancing. Metal slides can be imbedded in a gently sloping mound of soil, with no danger of falling off the side. Stone or wood sculptures, often in abstract designs or shaped like larger-than-life-size animals can be used for climbing, crawling through, and riding.

These suggestions are offered as thought-starters, not as final answers or "recipes" for an infant/toddler playground. Manufactured equipment is readily available, expensive, and not nearly as satisfying as the result of creative thinking, some cooperation, and the use of natural and scrounged materials and equipment. One last thought: when they are outside, young children love playing in piles of leaves, rolling in the snow or grass, watching birds and airplanes, running after butterflies, jumping in puddles, digging in the dirt, and smelling the flowers. Outdoor time should be a joyous time.

SUMMARY

The physical and experiential environment, both indoors and out-of-doors influence the growth and development of young children. Dimensions of the environment, such as open/closed, refer not only to actual architectural features, but the arrangement of the furnishings, the attitudes of the educarers, and the whole program. The physical environment cannot be viewed as a separate entity, but as part of the comprehensive provision of educaring. The same can be said of the dimension soft/hard. The younger the child, the more important is softness a characteristic of both the physical and human environment.

Basic design features of indoor spaces include density, flooring, wall coverings and display spaces, windows and ventilation, doors, lighting and electrical fixtures, color, acoustics, and activity centers designed for infants and toddlers. Spaces for routines such as the kitchen, bathroom, and napping areas are essential areas that are sometimes overlooked in the excitement of planning activities and curriculum. Without detailed planning, these spaces and their related activities could prove disastrous. Just as important is the provision made for spaces for adults (educarers and others). Emphasis was placed on an adult-sized rocking chair, in addition to the more utilitarian provisions for a rest room, file cabinets for children's records, and so on.

Suggestions for furnishing and equipping the indoor environment once again emphasized the nurturing or soft dimension. A detailed list of good toys and activities for children from birth to 3½ years of age can serve as a guideline for children's characteristics and their appropriate toys and activities. Toys and other objects are more than play materials—they increasingly serve as the focus of social encounters that offer opportunities for direct and incidental learning.

The recommended outdoor play space for infants and toddlers goes far beyond the "put the swings here and the sandbox over there" approach. The recommended "furnishings" should be designed for as many sensory experiences as possible. The use of natural materials is far superior and much more appropriate than many of the metal units so frequently found on the playgrounds for preschool and elementary children. A playground was described as a place for a child to run, to leap, to shout, to climb, to splash, and to find expression for energy and ideas. The design features of the outdoor space include seclusion and scale, earth shaping, surfacing and texture, and the use of natural materials such as sand, water, and mud.

Elizabeth Prescott (1987) provides the inspiration for us to enlarge our views of physical environments for children. "Our attempts to design child-rearing spaces have, for the most part, been too narrow and timid. We think about climbing structures and child-sized furniture, but we do not think about the total child-rearing environment and its ultimate purpose" (p. 87).

SUGGESTED ACTIVITIES AND QUESTIONS

1. Obtain a copy of your state's licensing requirements for child-care centers and family day-care homes (if available). Note the requirements for physical facilities.
2. Visit a children's toy store or study catalogs and evaluate the toys recommended for the ages birth to 3 in terms of adult or child appeal, and in terms of developmental appropriateness.
3. Make a scale drawing of a floor plan for an infant-toddler activity room, including the placement of furniture and equipment. Incorporate the suggestions made in chapter 8 (The Safety Component) and in this chapter.
4. Make a scale drawing of an outdoor playspace. Include both manufactured and natural "furnishings."
5. What are the advantages and disadvantages of commercially produced large play equipment? What are the advantages and disadvantages of natural materials as play equipment? (Not all of these were included in the chapter.) Use your imagination.

SUGGESTED READINGS

Bechtel, R. B., Marans, R. B., & Michelson, W. (1987). Conclusions. In R. B. Bechtel, R. B. Marans, & W. Michelson (Eds.), *Methods in environmental and behavioral research.* New York: Van Nostrand.

Burtt, K. G., & Kalkstein, K. (1981). *Smart toys for babies from birth to two.* Cambridge, MA: Harper Colophon.

Dimond, E. (1979). From trust to autonomy: Planning day care space for infants and toddlers. In E. Jones (Ed.), *Supporting the growth of infants,*

toddlers, and parents. Pasadena, CA: Pacific Oaks College and Children's Center.

Esbensen, S. B. (1987). *The early childhood playground.* Ypsilanti, MI: High/Scope.

Ferguson, J. (1979). Creating growth producing environments for infants and toddlers. In E. Jones (Ed.), *Supporting the growth of infants, toddlers, and parents.* Pasadena, CA: Pacific Oaks College.

Fisher, J. J. (1986). *Toys to grow with: Infants & toddlers.* New York: Putnam.

Fisher, J. J. (1987). *More toys to grow with: Infants & toddlers.* New York: Putnam.

Goodson, D. B., & Bronson, M. B. (1985). *Guidelines for relating children's ages to toy characteristics.* Washington, DC: U.S. Consumer Product Safety Commission, Contract No. CPSC-85-1089.

Greenman, J. (1985). Babies get out: Outdoor settings for infant toddler play. *Beginnings 2* (2), 7–10.

Greenman, J. (1988). *Caring spaces, learning places: Children's environments that work.* Redmond, WA: Exchange Press.

Harms, T., & Clifford, R. M. (1980). *Early childhood environment rating scale.* New York: Teachers College Press, Columbia University.

Harms, T., & Clifford, R. (1989). *Family day care rating scale.* New York: Teachers College Press, Columbia University.

Herbert-Jackson, E., O'Brien, M., Porterfield, J., & Risley, T. R. (1977). *The infant center.* Baltimore: University Park Press.

Hill, D. M. (1977). *Mud, sand, and water.* Washington, DC: National Association for the Education of Young Children.

Hirsch, E. S. (Ed.). (1981). *The block book.* Washington, DC: National Association for the Education of Young Children.

Jones, E. (1977). *Dimensions of teaching learning environments II: Focus on day care.* Pasadena, CA: Pacific Oaks College.

Jones, E. (Ed.) (1979). *Supporting the growth of infants, toddlers, and parents.* Pasadena, CA: Pacific Oaks College.

Kaban, B. (1979). *Choosing toys for children*. New York: Schocken Books.

Kritchevsky, S., & Prescott, E. (1977). *Planning environments for young children: Physical space* (2nd ed.). Washington, DC: National Association for the Education of Young Children.

Lally, J. R., Provence, S., Szanton, E., & Weissbourd, B. (1987). Developmentally appropriate care for children from birth to age 3. In Bredekamp, S. (Ed.), *Developmentally appropriate practice in early childhood programs serving children from birth through age 8* (expanded edition) (pp. 17–33). Washington, DC: National Association for the Education of Young Children.

McGuinness, K. A., & Stokes, S. (1985). Caregivers and babies outdoors. *Beginnings 2* (2), 34–37.

McKee, J. S. (1986). Play materials and activities for children birth to 10 years. In J. S. McKee (Ed.), *Play: Working partner of growth*. Wheaton, MD: Association for Childhood Education International.

Mergen, B. (1982). *Play and playthings: A reference guide*. Westport, CT: Greenwood Press.

Miller, K. (1988). *The outside play and learning book*. Mt. Ranier, MD: Gryphon House.

Moyer, J. (Ed.). (1986). *Selecting educational equipment and materials for school and home*. Wheaton, MD: Association for Childhood Education International.

Olds, A. R. (1987). Designing settings for infants and toddlers. In C. S. Weinstein & T. G. David (Eds.), *Spaces for children*. New York: Plenum Press.

Oppenheim, J. F. (1984). *Kids and play*. New York: Ballantine.

Prescott, E. (1981). Relations between physical setting and adult/child behavior in day care. In S. Kilmer (Ed.), *Advances in Early Education and Day Care 2*, 129–158. Greenwich, CT: JAI Press.

Prescott, E. (1984). The physical setting in day care. In J. T. Greenman and R. W. Fuqua (Eds.), *Making day care better: Training, evaluation, and the process of change*. New York: Teachers College Press.

Provenzo, E., & Brett, A. (1983). *The complete block book*. Syracuse, NY: Syracuse University Press.

Roufberg, R. (1971). *Your child from two to five years*. Vol. 2. New York: The Learning Child.

Sheehan, R., & Day, D. (1975). Is open space just empty space? *Day Care and Early Education 3*, 10–13, 47.

Sponseller, D., & Lowrey, M. (1976). Designing a play environment for toddlers. In D. Sponseller (Ed.), *Play as a learning medium*. Washington, DC: National Association for the Education of Young Children.

Steele, C., & Nauman, M. (1985). Infant's play on outdoor equipment. In J. L. Frost & S. Sunderlin (Eds.), *When children play* (pp. 121–128). Wheaton, MD: Association for Childhood Education International.

Wachs, T. D. (1985). Toys as an aspect of the physical environment: Constraints and nature of relationship to development. *Topics in Early Childhood Special Education 5* (3), 31–46.

Wardle, F. (1980). Building a structure to facilitate toddler play. *Day Care and Early Education 8*, 20–24.

Weinstein, C., & David, T. (Eds.). (1987). *Spaces for children: The built environment and child development*. New York: Plenum.

Winter, S. (1985). Toddler play behaviors and equipment choices in an outdoor playground. In J. L. Frost & S. Sunderlin (Eds.), *When children play* (pp. 129–138). Wheaton, MD: Association for Childhood Education International.

Wortham, S. C. (1989). Outdoor play environments for infants and toddlers. *Day Care and Early Education, 16* (4), 28–30.

Wortham, S. C., & Wortham, M. R. (1989). Infant/toddler development and play. *Childhood Education, 65* (5), 295–299.

Yarrow, L. J., Rubinstein, J. L., & Pedersen, F. (1975). *Infant and environment: Early cognitive and motivational development*. New York: Wiley.

10

The Human Environment

When I approach a child, he inspires two sentiments—tenderness for what he is and respect for what he may become.

Louis Pasteur

Children need people in order to become human. Children discover what they can do and who they can become through observing and interacting with people older and younger than themselves. When the children are very young, they need very special kinds of people: educarers—and all the persons involved in an infant/toddler program should be educaring persons, not just the "teachers."

The act of educaring combines teaching and caring, and it is difficult if not impossible to separate the two functions in a well-qualified person or in a high quality program. For instance, when the adult uses words for items of clothing or body parts during diaper-changing, is she teaching or caring? When an adult talks about pictures or reads stories aloud, is she teaching or caring? When an adult places the child in a safety restraint device in a motor vehicle, explaining why it is necessary, is she teaching or caring? The truly human environment is an educaring environment.

The behaviors and attitudes of the educaring persons are determined by their conceptualizations about infants and toddlers. Can very young children actually learn anything, and if so, how? Does learning to talk just develop, or should it be taught, and if so, how? Is an infant/toddler program really just baby-sitting, or is it an opportunity for positive experiences that promote growth and development? Does the teaching part of educaring mean group lessons and teacher-directed activities, or just how *do* we teach babies?

The following episode clearly contrasts educaring (teaching and caring) with just custodial caring.

EPISODE 18

Chuck is in a highchair and has just finished his snack. The adult comes over to him holding a damp washcloth and says, "All finished, Chuck? Let's wash our hands." She wipes one hand, and uses the cloth to hide it, saying "Where's Chuck's hand?'' She removes the cloth, saying "There it is!'' Chuck watches intently, but gives no other observable reaction. The adult repeats the peek-a-boo game with the other hand. Then she hides just one finger, asking "Where's Chuckie's finger?'' Chuck is very attentive. He laughs, grabs the wash cloth and hides his own hand with it. He laughs again and whisks the cloth away when the adult asks, "Where's Chuckie's hand?'' "There it is—you like to play too.'' They laughed together. The adult removes the high chair tray, unbuckles the safety strap, and lifts Chuck in her arms. "Let's go to the bathroom,'' and they laugh again as they leave the scene.

Meanwhile, two high chairs down from Chuck's, another adult notices that Tina is finished with her snack. She gets a wash cloth, wipes Tina's hands and chin, removes the tray and belt, and carries Tina to the bathroom. There was no play, no language, no smile, no real human contact.

One must wonder if the second adult enjoyed babies, felt imposed on, or was having a bad day. Frequent bad days like this one can have disastrous effects on the babies, and should not happen. This particular center was a parent cooperative, and the second adult was one of the mothers who paid part of her child's fees by helping with the daily routines. Her attitudes and behaviors call for some gentle parent education about developmentally appropriate practices in the center, and in her own home.

It seems obvious that people are the critical element in any program serving infants and toddlers. The National Academy of Early Childhood Programs (1984) states it this way:

> The quality of the staff is the most important determinant of the quality of an early childhood program. Research has found that staff training in child development and/or early childhood education is related to positive outcomes for children such as increased social interaction with adults, development of prosocial behaviors, and improved language and cognitive development (p. 18).

CAREGIVING: THE REGULATIONS

Staffing Requirements

Child-staff ratios. For babies in center-based programs, a child-staff ratio of 4:1 has been set by more states than any other ratio. More than three-fourths of the states have ratios of 5:1 or lower for babies at age 6 months. For toddlers (age 1½) only 28 states have ratios of 5:1 or lower. More than half the states have set ratios at 10:1 for 3 year olds (Morgan, 1987).

The 1988 Family Day Care Licensing study indicates that 26 states have a 2:1 or 3:1 ratio for children under 24 months of age (The Children's Foundation, 1988). However, 11 states permit five or more babies with only one family day-care provider (Morgan, 1987).

The recommended child-staff ratios of the National Academy of Early Childhood Programs (1984) are 3:1 or 4:1 with no more than eight in a group of infants up to 12 months old; 3:1 or 4:1 or 5:1 with no more than 12 in a group of toddlers 12 to 24 months old; and 4:1, 5:1, or 6:1 with no more than 12 in a group of walkers 24 to 36 months old. The criteria include adult supervision of the children at all times.

Child-staff ratios affect child behavior, adult behavior, and child-care costs. An appropriate ratio is costly in terms of parent fees, but it is extremely important for the young child's growth and development. The final report of the National Day Care Study suggested that ratios are as important as group size for the infants and toddlers: low ratios "were associated with less overt distress and apathy on the part of children, less exposure to potential physical danger, and less management on the part of caregivers'' (Ruopp & Travers, 1982, p. 82).

Group size. Only 24 states have any regulation for group size in infant/toddler programs. The recommendations of the National Day Care Study (Ruopp, Travers, Glantz, & Coelen, 1979) for infants and toddlers include a child-staff ratio of 4:1, and a group size limit smaller than that for preschool children (only 18 states regulate group size for children 3 years and older).

The findings of the study led to the statement that both group size and child-staff ratio were linked to behavioral indicators of quality such as "the proportion of time which caregivers devote to developmental activities with children as opposed to management of children and routine tasks" (Abt Associates, 1979, p. 17). According to Bronfenbrenner (1979), the addition of another staff member would do more to increase opportunities for reciprocal adult-child activity than a reduction of group size. "During this early period, age-mates, as compared with adults, play a relatively minor role in the child's development, and it is only afterwards that the peer group becomes a potent force in the lives of young children" (p. 194).

Staff Qualifications

For center staff. Educational qualifications are minimal or nonexistent in the regulations of the majority of the states. As of 1986, 33 states required or were planning to require a criminal records check (Morgan, 1987). "Twenty-eight states require no training before teachers come to work at day care centers" (Children's Defense Fund, 1989, p. 58).

For family day-care providers. The report of the Children's Foundation (1988) includes training requirements for providers (27 states have some kind of training requirement that ranges from CPR or first aid to courses in child development); age requirements (most states require a provider to be at least 18 years of age); a physical exam and/or TB test (38 states); and a criminal record check, fingerprints, or Child Abuse Registry (37 states). "Twenty-eight states have such low expectations of family day care providers that they require neither training in child development nor any prior experience" (Children's Defense Fund, 1989, p. 58).

Comments. I hope each year will result in more stringent minimum requirements for per-

sons who have a considerable effect on the growth and development of a large number of the nation's very young children.

EDUCARING: BEYOND THE REGULATIONS

The Educaring Staff

A common assumption about adults in charge of young children is "the younger the child, the easier the job," and the less training is needed. Perhaps the almost universal use of the word *caregiver* has contributed to this misconception. The truth of the matter is "the younger the child, the harder the job," and a substantial amount of preservice and inservice training and education is required for an educarer in the true sense of the word. Ruopp et al. (1979) concluded that only one teacher characteristic was related to program effectiveness: the amount of early childhood training.

Staff training. The training of staff takes place in coursework, in supervised experiences, and through in-service staff meetings or workshops. Honig (1985) suggests the following components of staff training in order to achieve a high quality infant/toddler program:

1. Information about how infants and toddlers grow and develop
2. Information about the ecology of the environment (health, safety, aesthetics)
3. Understandings of positive communication techniques, including active listening skills;
4. Application of research findings

Additional topics, usually in inservice sessions, include the physical care of children including care of sick children, food and nutrition, learning activities and play, working with parents, child management, children with disabilities, first aid and CPR, and community resources. Many of the topics are addressed in sessions of conferences planned by the professional organizations that focus on early child care and/or education. Attendance at such conferences is highly recommended for any person as part of preservice activities and as in-service opportunities to expand knowledge and decision-making abilities.

The Child Development Associate (CDA) National Credentialing Program requires certain competencies to be mastered before the granting of the Child Development Associate Credential. Most, if not all, of these competencies become observable as the candidate puts into practice the knowledge gained in previous or ongoing training. In order to qualify for the credential, a person must be able to

1. establish and maintain a safe, healthy, learning environment
2. advance physical and intellectual competence
3. support social and emotional development and provide positive guidance
4. establish positive and productive relationships with families
5. ensure a well-run, purposeful program responsive to participant needs

6. maintain a commitment to professionalism (CDA National Credentialing Program, 1986, pp. 3–4).

These competencies are required for both infant/toddler caregivers in center-based programs, and for family day-care providers (CDA, 1985). According to Arnett (1989),

> The CDA credential is an important beginning in establishing a minimum level of competence for caregivers, but . . . there is virtually no research evidence comparing the competence of caregivers with the CDA credential with that of caregivers with no training. What little research has been conducted has relied on self-report measures of dubious value and validity. Child care advocates who urge the establishment of the CDA as a national minimum credential should reconsider until the worth of the credential is verified by research (p. 247).

Staff characteristics. Just as the children we serve are unique in their needs and abilities, so are their parents unique in their preferences for certain characteristics in the person(s) who will

Is the educarer someone the child will enjoy being with? (Early Childhood Education Center)

provide education and care to their child. The Office of Human Development Services (1980) suggests that parents decide which of the following characteristics they are particularly looking for.

Does the caregiver:

- appear warm and friendly?
- seem calm and gentle?
- seem to have a sense of humor?
- seem to be someone with whom you can develop a relaxed, sharing relationship?
- seem to be someone your child will enjoy being with?
- seem to feel good about herself and her job?
- have child-rearing attitudes and methods that are similar to your own?
- treat each child as a special person?
- understand what children can and want to do at different stages of growth?
- have the right materials and equipment on hand to help them learn and grow mentally and physically?
- patiently help children solve their problems?
- provide activities that encourage children to think things through?
- encourage good health habits, such as washing hands before eating?
- talk to the children and encourage them to express themselves through words?
- encourage children to express themselves in creative ways?
- have art and music supplies suited to the ages of all children in care?
- seem to have enough time to look after all the children in her care?
- help your child to know, accept, and feel good about him- or herself?
- help your child become independent in ways you approve?
- help your child learn to get along with and to respect other people, no matter what their backgrounds are?

- provide a routine and rules the children can understand and follow?
- accept and respect your family's cultural values?
- take time to discuss your child with you regularly?
- have previous experience or training in working with children?
- have a yearly physical exam and TB (and hepatitis) test?
- seem to enjoy cuddling your baby?
- care for your baby's physical needs such as feeding and diapering?
- spend time holding, playing with, talking to your baby?
- provide stimulation by pointing out things to look at, touch, and listen to?
- provide care you can count on so your baby can learn to trust her and feel important?
- cooperate with your efforts to toilet train your toddler?
- "child-proof" the setting so your toddler can crawl or walk safely and freely?
- realize that toddlers want to do things for themselves and help your child to learn to feed and dress him- or herself, go to the bathroom, and pick up his or her own toys?
- help your child learn the language by talking with him or her, naming things, reading aloud, describing what she is doing, and responding to your child's words (pp. 31–33)?

The "flavor" of these characteristics has been captured by Lally et al. (1987) in the following way:

Patient, warm adults are probably the most important factor in a developmentally appropriate program for infants and toddlers. From birth, children take an active role in their interaction with others. Adults who work well with children younger than age 3 are aware of the need to mesh their behaviors with each child's unique style of approaching people and objects (p. 25).

Does the educarer patiently help children solve their problems?
(Kindercampus, Iowa City)

Regardless of the quality and quantity of training given to the educarer(s), it is the one-to-one relationship between educarer and child that determines the quality of infant-toddler programs. This relationship is in a constant state of change. Each time the child takes another step toward independence, there is a corresponding change in the relationship. Stewart (1982) describes the most effective base for the educarer-child interaction as "flexibility and supportive informality" (p. 7). In order to be flexible, supportive, and informal, the educarer must be a responsive person who delights in the child's efforts to master something new, or to rehearse a previous mastery, no matter how insignificant in the adult's eyes. The organization of the program can either discourage or encourage this educaring relationship.

The Educaring Environment

Organization options. Infant/toddler groups are usually organized in one of two ways:

either the trained educarer is responsible for all the children, and is assisted by one or more persons of varying degrees of experience or training, or the total staff is collectively responsible for all the children. It is difficult in either situation to establish and maintain an educaring relationship.

A third organizational plan is gaining in popularity as more persons are becoming educarers, rather than teachers or caregivers. The plan is the primary caregiver system. The word *caregiver* is used in the following description, because the system has been publicized as primary caregiving, instead of primary educaring.

Primary caregiving. The assignment of children to primary caregivers, instead of the assignment of tasks (one person in charge of diapering, another in charge of naptime, etc.) is the best assurance that each child is intimately known by at least one educarer, and that each child has a familiar and therefore a significant other in the program. The maternal deprivation syndrome, which caused much concern during the 1950s and 1960s, was really caused by the deprivation of a significant person, whether mother or another person. A person is significant to an infant or toddler to the extent of the responsive interactions between the two. The problem of ensuring that each child has a significant other can be best solved by initiating the organizational plan of primary caregiving.

Considerations in assigning children to a specific primary caregiver include the match between the parents' time schedules and the caregiver's shift; the number of children already in the group; the age distribution of the primary children (there are advantages and disadvantages either way); a "good match"; and the timing of the child's entry and staff vacation schedule. The caregiver should be present at the intake interview to meet the parents and perhaps the child, and should also be part of the "welcoming committee" when the child arrives for the first time at the center.

The primary caregiver represents the program to the child and parent by performing five key roles:

- Communicator between parent and program and child and program

- Advocate in translating the individual needs and concerns of parents and children into action

- Caregiver during the routine care episodes, as well as a facilitator of language and motor and sensory exploration

- Teacher who provides developmentally appropriate activities and experiences either in a one-to-one group or in other groupings

- Monitor and evaluator who assesses the program's appropriateness for this child, and his responses to the day's happenings (Greenman, 1986)

The following description of a primary caregiving system was included in a parents' monthly newsletter, and was written by the well-trained "head teacher" of an infant-toddler program serving children from 2 weeks to 3 years of age. The center employed both part-time and full-time staff.

One essential element in the organization of an infant-toddler program is the relationship between the young child and his/her caregivers. Characteristics of caregivers play the greatest role in shaping the human environment. However, the human environment for infants and toddlers involves more than caregiver characteristics. The continuity and consistency of care in the child's day can offer security to a young child and help to develop that special attachment to a limited number of caregivers.

When we began to organize our infant-toddler program, several questions about the environment were of concern to us. These questions were:

- What type of caregiving arrangement would facilitate attachments to caregivers and provide for consistency and continuity of care?

- How should we organize our caregiving routines and responsibilities?

- How can each caregiver thoroughly know several children?

We chose to implement a plan for primary caregiving. Under this plan each staff person functions as a primary caregiver for one or two groups of children. These two groups were divided according to the ages and developmental levels of the children. Primary caregivers make the primary attachment to the children in their group. They are available for comfort, and the child and adult develop a close relationship. Parents can focus on the primary caregivers for communications about their child. The children within each group are more likely to interact and to depend on each other as the group spends special times together during the day.

The responsibilities of the primary caregivers are:

- to check the plexiglass chart for children in the group and keep it up to date. (We use this chart to communicate with parents and other staff about children's eating, napping, and toileting activities throughout the day.)

- to communicate with parents on a daily basis either verbally or by writing notes in the diary, or to be placed in individual cubbies.
- to check diapers and anticipate needs of the children (prepare bottles, baby food, any special diet or other considerations).
- to put children in their group down for their naps.
- to plan individual and group activities for the children.
- to assess the children at various stages of their development.
- to redesign the environment when necessary.

Initially we were concerned that dividing the children and caregivers into primary groups would segregate us during the day. We have avoided this problem by remaining flexible in implementing the primary caregiving arrangement. We interact with all the children and the children are encouraged to interact with each other. Thus a child will feel comfortable in the presence of another caregiver. This is important when one considers the staffing schedules for a ten-hour day, children's eating and napping schedules, as well as those times when children from both groups are together.

Here are examples of how our system has worked:

- When Rachel was three months old she began coming to the center. She had developed a strong attachment to her parents and was unhappy with a variety of caregivers—all so anxious to please her. By the second day we limited her interactions to a morning and afternoon caregiver. This helped Rachel adjust and offered her caregivers the opportunity to "read" her signals and wants.
- Gena and Sy are the oldest children in the group. They enjoy doing things together during the day. The toddler caregiver usually reads them a story or engages in a shared quiet-time activity with them just prior to nap. They both go into the sleeping room together. Gena walks with Sy to his crib and they say goodnight. Then Gena is put to sleep in her crib. This consistency in their napping routine by their caregiver has helped them develop an

attachment to one another as well as to their caregiver. It also offers security in knowing what to expect.

- After snack the children wash their hands and faces. Diapers need to be checked and changed before a teacher-directed activity begins for the toddlers. Some infants are being fed and a few infants and toddlers need to take their morning nap. The infant caregivers are working together to coordinate their caregiving efforts and the toddler caregivers are doing the same. When a caregiver from one group is not busy with her children, she will help the other groups' caregivers complete their routines and responsibilities. Thus our transition time from snack to activity time is smooth, well organized, and personal. Children have learned what to expect and are comforted by the consistency of the routine and of their interactions with caregivers.

We are always working on the organization of the room. The caregivers need to keep lines of communication open so they can function well within caregiving groups as well as learn how the groups can work together. Our satisfaction comes from observing positive changes in children. We feel that our program is a relaxed and warm environment and very homelike. (Rosenthal, 1979, pp. 1–2)

The key to a child's psychological development is trust: trust in the environment, trust in what might happen, and trust in a few significant adults. The primary caregiver system has been designed to establish and enhance baby's trust. The system has been adopted by the leading experts in the field. Honig & Lally (1981) recommend that each infant is assigned on entry a primary caregiver who is responsible for the important elements of the infant's care day, such as feeding, diapering, and sleeping. Godwin & Schrag (1988) recommend that each caregiver is responsible for no more than four infants. Hignett (1988) recommends that the child continue in the primary caregiver's care until he reaches age 3.

Realistically, this is rarely the case. The suggestions for the initial meeting between parent(s) and educarer, included in chapter 11 under Parent Conferences, are also appropriate for the transition from one educarer and location to another.

It is in this organizational plan that adult-child attachments are formed. As stated by the National Center for Clinical Infant Programs (1988),

> The formation of loving attachments in the earliest years of life creates an emotional "root system" for future growth and development. Every child needs a solid relationship with one or two people in the family. If part of the child's care occurs outside the family, the infant or toddler also needs a continuous, affectionate relationship with a main caregiver during the years of infancy and toddlerhood—a caregiver who cooperates with the family on behalf of the child (p. 5).

There appears to be almost unanimous approval for the primary caregiving system.

The child's human environment. The human environment includes more than the adults in the setting; there are other children.

If the infants and toddlers are in the same room or rooms, the age range is approximately 3 chronological years. The developmental age range may be considerably larger. It has been estimated that in any one kindergarten class for typical 5 year olds, the developmental range may be as large as 7 years. I know of no such determination for the normal birth to threes, but it is very possible that some threes will be operating on a 2-year-old level, and others at the 4-year-old level. This developmental range offers opportunities for rich experiences among the children themselves if there is ample provision made for individual and small group space. Distribution of staff is essential so that the toddlers and walkers receive their share of attention. It is easy to become so involved in the physical care routines of babies that the more independent toddlers are left on their own too

A toddler needs a continuous, affectionate relationship with a main caregiver. (Early Childhood Education Center)

much of the time. The model for a multi-aged group should resemble a family model, in that each child is an individual with equal rights and privileges. The rights of each include the appropriate quantity and quality of educaring. Its daily delivery differs because of differing developmental stages and needs. If the educarer insists on children sharing toys when such is not developmentally appropriate, little is gained and much is lost. One year olds and many 2 year olds may not approach others in a social mode on their own. They are engaged in the serious business of establishing an identity of their own (as well as learning to walk and talk). Even though these children are members of a group because they attend a group child-care program, there must always be an escape hatch for those children who wish or need it.

Making a plea for an escape hatch does not imply that children do not learn by observing one another. Mere observing is both stimulating and social, because it is a prerequisite for human interaction. When the little ones are ready to join in, they will do so on their own. Teacher intrusion is not necessary or desirable.

The custom of mainstream America is to have a space in the family home reserved for baby—either in a separate room or at least in a corner of the adult bedroom. Basically, this arrangement has met the adults' need for privacy and individuality. Psychological and physical space separating baby and primary caregiver is specific to this culture. It is not universally provided. A professor of pediatrics at Columbia Medical Center, and former director of the Institute for Exceptional Children at the Educational Testing Service in Princeton, suggests that this "cultural view of privacy and individuality has influenced the way we have conditioned our children's spatial needs" (Lewis & Harlan, 1981, p. 28). Baby learns from the periodic separation from adults that being alone is normal. Although the physical environment is not the focus here, we need to understand that these spatial arrangements teach baby a basic concept, that being alone sometimes is desirable. This does not

hinder baby's social development if the alone times are balanced by together times. Baby's innate curiosity needs will also counterbalance the learned need for privacy.

The child's social environment in the family, and the variety of emotions and moods resulting from family living are a necessary part of learning socialized behavior. The variety is unavoidable, and may be positive, unless carried to extremes. To help balance the variety instead of adding to it, the educaring team should work for consistency and continuity in behaviors toward one another and toward the children. Individual personalities need not be sacrificed, but there should be a commitment to agreed-upon policies, methods, and strategies that further each area of growth and development.

The young child in child care literally has two homes, but not two families. The child keeps primary family membership, regardless of the number of hours away from the family setting. The psychological adjustment to the two locations is sufficient challenge for him. It should not be compounded by either inconsistent behaviors by educarers or by undue intrusion into the child's personal space.

EDUCARING IN ACTION

Educaring Equals Responsive Caregiving and Teaching

There are two types of infant/toddler teachers. Some of these teachers have at their fingertips a large collection of activities and playthings designed to keep the children busy and happy. These persons can be described as practitioners. The other type of teacher is described as an educarer. An infant/toddler educarer:

- enjoys infants and toddlers
- is a sensitive observer who reads behavioral cues accurately, and responds to them appropriately
- engages in mutually satisfying interactions with the children (and the other educarers)

- is aware of materials, activities, and experiences that are developmentally appropriate
- knows when to initiate a new play activity or experience, and when to be physically close but not necessarily interacting with the child(ren)

The emphasis in educaring is on knowing when and how to respond to the universal needs and characteristics of children from birth to 3, and to the specific needs and characteristics of the children in the primary care group. The general needs and characteristics with their related responses are contained in Table 10–1. These are categorized as social-emotional, physical-behavioral, and cognitive.

There are overtones in any educaring interaction that are difficult to place in list form with much meaning. The adult-child interactions of touching, conversing, and playing are included as examples of educaring in action.

Touching Interactions

A nurturing, caring, responsive relationship with a baby is the cornerstone of the baby's optimal development. Lest anyone doubts the truth of this statement, please read the following excerpt from *Just a Touch of Nearness*.

It was a well-run hospital with a friendly and dedicated staff. The health care was the finest available anywhere. That's why it was such a shock when the hospital's newborn mortality rate showed a sudden increase. Perfectly healthy babies have died without apparent cause. Medical examiners were called in to study the phenomenon. They reviewed each case trying to find some clue. Tests were conducted, procedures reviewed and then reviewed again. There was nothing to explain the mysterious rise in infant deaths.

Then one day, one of the examiners made an off-hand observation about the nursery personnel: "You seem to be short-handed on the third shift," he said.

The hospital administrator explained that an elderly woman, a nurse's aide, had retired and not been replaced. "Mother Dora was something of a fixture around here," the executive explained. "She loved babies and took care of them as if they were her own. No baby cried for long without being picked up and cuddled and sung to when Dora was on duty."

Educaring in action.
(Early Childhood Education Center)

Table 10–1

Children's Needs and Characteristics, and Educaring Responses

	Child	**Educarer**
Social-emotional	Needs to feel sense of belonging	Establishes a close relationship that is caring and nurturing
		Is alert to child's needs for people and social experiences
		Includes child in group activities, either as spectator or as actual participant
	Likes to be with or near other children (sociocentric)	Provides opportunities to watch or join other children
	Is self-centered (egocentric)	Does not insist on group involvement, sharing behaviors, etc., that are beyond child's level of functioning
	Likes to be independent	Offers opportunities for child to do things for and by self; provides chances for child to assume responsibilities
		Provides materials and experiences that require initiative or problem-solving by child
	Needs adult guidance and support	Is accepting and appreciative of child's efforts
	Needs affection and praise	Gives child unlimited affection and appropriate praise; helps child learn socially acceptable ways of showing interest or affection.
	Has a good sense of humor	Plays with child; offers appropriate discrepancies in actions and words; laughs with child
	Is easily stimulated	Recognizes the fine line between enough and too much
	Is easily frustrated	Recognizes that a young child will persist only when successful, and may be able to handle only one or two failures with a task before giving up
		Provides challenges that match child's level of functioning
	Needs to experience success	Plans cumulative program of new experiences based on previous ones, so as to provide an appropriate match for the child's current level of functioning
	May have "unreasonable" fears of strangers or changes in environment or routine or activities	Understands that fearful children usually regress in their behavior; is soothing and supportive; shows love with body contact and quieting language
		Introduces changes slowly, one step at a time
	Is dependent on all adults, but very dependent on significant adults for social-emotional development	Is a "significant" adult by forming a close, nurturing, consistent relationship

Table 10–1

continuing

	Child	Educarer
Physical-behavioral	Is very active	Provides opportunities and space for free and vigorous movement
	Has developing control of large muscles; beginning control of fine muscles	Provides large muscle activities and equipment; gradually adds such activities as self-feeding, drawing, painting
	Tires easily	Adapts schedule to individual child's physiological needs
	Is highly susceptible to communicable diseases	Is alert to any change in child's usual behavior or appearance; is able to recognize early symptoms of child diseases; instills and enforces habits of cleanliness
		Expects irregular attendance at the center
	Has a small tummy	Provides meals on schedule, but snacks should always be available
	Is establishing handedness and eyedness	Provides activities and materials that require use of either or both hands
	Is far-sighted	Does not force near-vision activities; should let the child determine closeness
	Is progressing from nonverbal cry to verbal communication	Listens, responds, imitates; initiates "conversations"
	Is very dependent on adults for satisfying physical needs	Responds to needs with appropriate actions immediately or as soon as possible
Cognitive	Is intensely curious and eager to learn; learns by doing	Provides a wide variety of materials and experiences in an interesting environment; provides opportunities to explore, manipulate, and discover
		Eliminates safety hazards in the environment
		Allows time and space for individual explorations with only the necessary restrictions for the sake of safety
		Is alert for new signs of interest
		Knows progression of mental development and provides opportunities that match and stretch the child's behavior and thinking
	Has a very short attention span for other-initiated tasks	Allows time and freedom for self-initiated tasks that tend to encourage greater persistence
	Understands through sensorimotor experiences	Provides time and opportunity to experience many kinds of things and activities
	Enjoys "playful" experiences with language and activities	Smiles, laughs, enjoys, and adopts "playful" attitude toward routines and interactions
	Is dependent on all adults, but very dependent on significant adults for learning	Is a "significant" adult by forming a close, nurturing, consistent relationship; reinforces and encourages child's behaviors in all areas of functioning

When humans are not available . . .
(Kindercampus, Iowa City)

"And now?" asked the examiner.

"Well, the babies probably aren't held as much. Could it be . . . ?"

The next day a notice went up on the nursery bulletin board: Beginning today, all babies are to be held a minimum of ten minutes per hour.

And the problem went away.

Once we thought food and sleep and warmth were about all that babies needed to be healthy. Now we know that they need to be held, too. And so do we all, whether we are one day or one hundred years old.

> from the book *Just a Touch of Nearness* by Fred Bauer, C. R. Gibson, publisher. Copyright Fred Bauer 1985. Used by permission.

We send nonverbal messages to our children by how we touch them, and how frequently we touch them. Studies have shown that touch-deprived young children (not just young babies) frequently will fail to thrive. There seems to be a universal need to be touched. When humans are not available, the children will clasp inanimate objects such as blankets and teddy-bears to meet this need. Fred Rogers (of "Mr. Rogers' Neighborhood" on television) recognizes this need, as does the Smithsonian Institute in Washington. Mr. Rogers has granted their request, and has donated one of his bright red sweaters to the National Museum of American History as an important symbol of warmth and closeness and touch.

We all know that a touch can have a powerful effect on how we feel. Now we have learned that touch communicates feelings from one human being to another. We also have learned that touching can lay the emotional foundation necessary for learning and intellectual growth (Barnard & Brazelton, 1986). There is another bonus for frequent touching—at least one study shows that infants cry less when they are held throughout the day, and not just when they are crying.

When infants reach the stage of attaching to their significant persons (parents and educarers), the touching accessibility of these persons has a direct effect on future behavior. According to Biggar (1984), "rejection of physical contact by attachment figures . . . leads initially to increased approach efforts and eventually to anger and conflict" (p. 70).

There are opportunities for loving touches

No bottle propping, please. (Early Childhood Education Center)

throughout the program, but because much of the educarer's time is devoted to routine caregiving, feeding and diapering have been chosen as examples of opportunities for touching.

Feeding. Even babies who are able to hold their own bottles should be held in someone's arms. This is a special time for them to be close to an adult, preferably the primary caregiver. Willis and Ricciuti (1980) firmly state that "a program in which babies are not usually held when they have their bottles is probably in need either of more caregivers or a discussion of the importance of close one-to-one contact between babies and adults" (p. 81). The feeding experience is perhaps the most important opportunity for close body contact and responsive interaction between a child and an adult. Babies learn to trust the persons who are caring for them, who are holding them.

The primary caregiver should continue this one-to-one relationship even after baby has graduated to cup-drinking and finger foods, and is no longer physically held. Eating (or feeding) should be accompanied by pleasant human interactions. It is quite possible that these pleasant interactions might lessen the number of "eating problems" in the program (and at home). As the toddlers move to solid foods and self-feeding, the primary caregiver should remain with her assigned children. She knows their likes and dislikes, and their individual and sometimes unique eating styles.

Diapering. When the diaper of an active 6-month-old baby is changed by an educarer, the following growth and development experiences can occur:

- Motor activity—kicking vigorously when the caregiver removes confining clothes
- Cognitive activity—the caregiver's face disappears behind the diaper and reappears
- Language activity—caregiver and baby talk, coo, and laugh together
- Social activity—caregiver talks to the baby, laughs with him or her, touches the baby gently, responds to smiles and babbles
- Sensory experience—the feel of being free of clothes, the soft fresh dry feeling when a new diaper replaces the cold wet one (Willis & Ricciuti, 1980, p. 83)

Touch (or lack of touch) during diapering may even influence the infants' beginning ideas about sexuality, because of where they are not touched, or how others react when they are touched in certain places. A negative adult reaction to diaper changing may leave the impression that this covered-up part of the body must have something wrong about it. It can be the early beginning of many confusing messages about the body. How can something that feels so good (a dry bottom) cause such a reaction from someone who shows unconditional love at other times?

The following diaper-changing episode not only highlights the use of loving touches, but shows educaring in the true sense of the word. The child (Luther) is 3½ months old.

EPISODE 19

At 10:15 A.M. Luther's eyes open slowly. He holds them open for only a moment. A deep sigh follows. Then he rubs his face on the sheet. He stares a minute, and then begins to focus in. He lifts his head off the crib mattress, looking around. "Hey there, Luther, ready to get going?" asks the educarer. "Have a good rest?" she continues, as she offers a finger for a palm grasp. He grips her finger as she lowers the crib side with her free hand. "You took such a long nap, I'll bet your diapers are soaked. Let's take care of that right now." She snuggles close to his face and rubs noses. She hums a snatch of a song, then moves back. He makes a gurgling sound that she repeats. They "talk" face to face.

With one hand still gripped by the baby, she taps his nose with her free hand, "boop," and then runs her finger around his ear, down his neck, and under his chin. She gives his tummy a pat and says, "Okay, let's change those diapers. . . . "One snap, boop, boop, boop, there's that tummy," she says as she rubs his bare skin. Luther laughs. "Where are those feet?" she asks, as she pulls one leg out of his sleeper. "There it is," and the other leg is pulled out. Holding both legs at the ankles, she moves his legs in a running motion. "Look at those legs go!" She smiles. Holding both ankles in one hand, she raises his body, loosening and removing the damp diaper. She quickly slips a dry one under him, laying one end loosely over his front. She cleans the diaper area with a towelette, and again loosely replaces the diaper over him, allowing him to air-dry before fastening the diaper. "Better, huh? In go those toes, and snap, snap, snap, you're all fixed up and ready to go."

(Note: The rest of Luther's day at the center is described in chapter 12.)

Loving touches. Babies need their educarer's touches for comfort, for play, for feeding, for reassurances. Positive caring kinds of touches (including bear hugs) are as necessary to human existence as food when we are hungry and warmth when we are cold. Infants and toddlers, especially, need loving physical contact to assure them that all is right with their world. Educarers also know that "tactile and vestibular stimulation from physical contact with the caregiver enhances later cognitive development, but only for the first few months" (Fogel, 1986, p. 54). The infants are our main concern in this instance, but don't stop touching them after the infant stage.

Conversing Interactions

Although not conversation in the true sense, talking to children and reading aloud to children from the day of birth is highly recommended (Lamme, 1985). It is not the actual words nor the ideas that matter, it is the sound of the human voice using the language. Very young infants begin to learn the patterns, sounds, and rhythm of language when they hear and listen to the speech of their primary caregivers (parents and/or educarers). Infants observably react to the loudness, the pitch, and the emotional tones of the human voice, and they should therefore be read to and sung to and talked to. Educaring persons talk to the infant about what he is doing and what he is feeling, as well as about what they are going to do before they do it, while they are doing it, and after they have done it.

Hand and body movements (body English) and facial expressions help explain the meaning of the words. They also stimulate imitation, one of the most important fundamental activities for all future learning. When someone talks to the baby, the baby is also stimulated to respond vocally first with coos, then with laughter and babbles. *And* when the educarer repeats the sounds baby has made, two-way communication is started—the first conversation. Conversation and interest are sustained when the adult talks about things the child already has experienced, or about objects and events he can perceive. The basis of language development depends heavily on the development of object permanence. If the educarers provide enough "conversations" in the form of peek-a-boo, hide-the-toy, and other such games, they not only encourage the concept of the permanence of objects, but also the understanding and use of words that label and describe objects, people, and events (Honig, 1981).

The progression of conversations moves from mutual sound-making to meaningful verbal dialogue, as shown in Episode 20. Brian is 15 months old, and he and his peers are participating in water play outside the family day care home.

EPISODE 20

The day-care provider is holding a plastic gallon container from which she pours small amounts of water into each child's glass (also plastic). Sometimes she pours water into a large dishpan on the grass from which the children can scoop up water by themselves. Others are dipping large paint brushes into the pan of water and they are painting the steps, the air conditioner, the sidewalk, and various pieces of play equipment. The adult refers to the pan of water as "special water, just for painting."

Brian tries to put his paint brush into the gallon container. The educarer responds with "No, Brian. Let me pour the water into your glass. It will be easier to get the water on your brush. Hold your glass still, please, so I can pour into it. Oh, you did that nicely, Brian." Brian pours the water into the dishpan and turns back to the adult, saying, "Water." He pours the water into the dishpan and returns for more several times. At one point, he says, "More water." Still another time he says, "More water please," after hearing another child

use this phrase. The educarer responds with, "I like it when you say 'please,' Brian."

Almost adult conversation is used in the next episode, not because of the vocabulary of course, but because of the easy give-and-take of persons engaged in a group endeavor. The three girls are all about 30 months old.

EPISODE 21

Victoria has already started "cooking" in the play kitchen with Carol and Janelle. They giggle together as they noisily empty the child-sized cupboard of empty cans with picture labels, dishes, pots and pans, plastic food, silverware, and plates. Trisha, an aide credentialled as a CDA, approaches the noisy area and finds no direction in the dumping.

Trisha: What a messy kitchen you ladies keep! I'd never be able to find my way around in here. It's time to get these things put away. Victoria, use your bright eyes and pick out all the things that go in the refrigerator and put them there. Carol, you look for all the pans and put them on a convenient shelf. Janelle, you can put away the cans, and I'll help with the plates and spoons. (Victoria and Carol get busy putting their things away.)
Carol: I found a can with a picture of a tomato on the front.
Trisha: What do you suppose was in it?
Janelle: Tomato juice!
Trisha: You know, my tomato juice comes in a can like that too. It looks like the tallest can to me. I'll put it on the back of the shelf. Can you find another one the same size?
Janelle: This one is fat like that one. (She places a pear can on the shelf.) I found one that looks the same—we found two alike! (The two cans have the same diameter as the juice can, but are shorter. Trisha continues to motivate Janelle.)
Trisha: Let's find a can that had corn in it. (Janelle finishes putting the cans away, and the aide stacks the plates away.) What great

picker-uppers we are! The kitchen looks so clean. Look, Victoria put the yogurt in the refrigerator with the milk and eggs. What a good idea to keep the ice cream hard in the freezer. Carol, you put all the pans in the oven! That's where I put mine too, sometimes. But what's in that big pot on top of the stove?

Victoria: Stew. (Everyone has an imaginary taste.)

Janelle: Ick! I don't like stew!

Trisha: What do you like to eat?

Janelle: I like spaghetti!

Carol: Fried chicken!

Victoria: Hot dogs!

Trisha: I looked at the lunch menu and it says we'll be having something long, skinny, and white, with red sauce and brown meat, and Janelle really really loves it!

Victoria: Sgetti!

Carol: I can cook it. (She reaches for a can of corn. Janelle sits down at the table to feed a doll.)

Janelle: She's messy. (She wipes the doll's face with a cloth. The other two girls continue preparing dinner.)

(Note: The rest of Victoria's day at the center is described in chapter 12.)

These three 2½-year-old girls are cooperating, conversing, working, and playing. They are the result of responsive educaring, including high levels of adult-child verbal interactions.

McCartney, Scarr, Phillips, Grajeck, and Schwarz (1982) discovered that 3- and 4-year-old children who had attended infant/toddler programs that had been rated "good overall quality" but with low adult-child verbal interaction, were reported as more anxious, more aggressive, and hyperactive when compared to children in similar programs, except with high adult-child verbal interaction. This verbal interaction, this "conversation," should begin very early. Because today very young infants, sometimes only 1 or 2 weeks old, are spending time in nonmaternal care, it is necessary that their educarers know about and act on the impor-

tance of conversing long before the baby can respond vocally or verbally.

Playing Interactions

The very young infant is "playing" when he babbles, blows bubbles, and fingers his fingers, but play in the fullest sense is learned through imitation and interaction with people and things. This idea is reinforced by Oppenheim (1984), who describes the ideal first plaything for a baby.

- it moves (no switches, buttons, batteries, or wind-up keys required)
- it talks, makes music, plays back baby's first coos and calls
- it's cuddly (provides security and hours of pleasure)
- it's highly educational
- it's entertaining; encourages curiosity
- is composed of resilient, flexible, nontoxic, 100% natural materials
- it's a unique toy, crafted to meet the individual child's needs
- available only through private distribution*
  *To find nearest dealer, check your mirror (p. 16)

Although Oppenheim was writing for parents, these same qualities distinguish an educarer from a caregiver or teacher.

First games. Because the care and education of infants and toddlers in groups is still a fairly new part of our social scene (at least in this country), many of the suggestions for appropriate play activities have been in books for parents instead of for early childhood educators (or educarers). Brian and Shirley Sutton-Smith (1974) recommend the following sequence of games for the first 1½ years. They involve adult-child interactions in a playful situation.

- From birth to three months: imitate baby, make noises; alternate noises with baby (gurgles); "baby talk" (long vowels and high pitch); make clown faces; poke out your tongue; let baby pull your pinky

- Three to six months: make baby laugh; do gymnastics with baby (bounce on bed, turn upside down); blow raspberries on baby's body; play "pretend" walking, "pretend" standing; let baby pull your hair; play "This little pig"

- Six to twelve months: rough-house; give-and-take; play peek-a-boo; hide baby under a blanket; make baby laugh (sound, touch, social, and visual stimuli)

- One to two years: chase and be chased; hide a toy; empty and fill; play catch; have a tug-of-war

It is readily observable that the adult who wishes to encourage baby's play activities must be available, not just present. McCune (1986) writes, "Sit down beside the child on the floor, and try to observe and support the child's activities as much as possible, reacting when asked, playing when invited, and giving an occasional gentle suggestion or demonstration" (p. 53).

Pretend games. Pretending begins as early as the first birthday, and is in full bloom by the third birthday. During the first 2 years, however, children seem to pretend more frequently in the presence of a primary caregiver (parent or educarer) than when alone. Some persons suspect these little ones like the approval of an audience.

Early pretend play focuses on the simple substitution of pretend objects for real ones; it tends to be largely solitary; and the pretend objects must clearly resemble the real ones, in other words, toy stoves, toy dishes, toy cars, toy telephones. Pretend play is a move from total reliance on the here-and-now to objects and events that are not immediately present, and it has been suggested that it and imagination are basic to critical aspects of children's cognitive development (Piaget, 1962; Vygotsky, 1967).

What is the educarer's role? As noted above, just being there helps. But also educaring includes extending this kind of play by asking questions, suggesting new ideas, and perhaps even joining in (Saltz & Saltz, 1986). Educarers

need to be careful observers, and can encourage the play also by supplying related props.

Social games. The traditional view about social games and social interaction is that very young children have neither the capacity for nor interest in social interactions. As recently as the 1983 *Handbook of Child Psychology,* the following statement appeared: "Even though year-old babies smile and laugh at each other, the vast majority of their interactions are emotionally neutral. . . . There is no evidence that children are extensively sought out as social objects at this time" (Hartup, p. 115).

This observation may still be correct if two infants are placed at opposite corners of a mat on the floor, each with his own toys, and no adult encouragement or modeling in a typical research setting. However, if the two infants were placed near one another, facing each other, with only one toy, and the educarer encouraged mutual interest in the toy, and mutual manipulation of the toy, the groundwork of positive social interactions would be laid, and the infants would expand their social interests beyond the adult (Weltzer, 1985).

Certainly long before the end of the second year toddlers will be attracted to inanimate playthings and to their peers. Educarers not only support young children's interactions, but also create the atmosphere and the physical environment in which peer interactions can take place.

These examples of educaring in action— touching, conversing, playing—represent the kinds of attitudes and approaches that will enable our infants and toddlers to really bloom in a group setting. The very best stimulation activity is the responsive interaction between educarer and child.

THE EDUCARING TEAM

The educaring team makes up the adult human environment. This adult human environment largely determines what happens to the children and the adult-child interactions. Jorde-Bloom

(1988) of the National College of Education, suggests the following as characteristics of a high quality adult environment.

- friendly supportive staff who trust one another
- opportunities to learn new skills
- helpful feedback from the supervising person
- well-defined job descriptions and statements of policy
- opportunities for individuals to be innovative in their educaring behaviors (within the policies and philosophy of the program)
- shared commitment as to program philosophy, policy, and objectives.

In such a psychological climate, educarers are free to devote their thoughts and energies to the children in their primary group, and in the program. They are freed to establish what this whole book emphasizes—high quality adult-child relationships.

The requirement for well-defined job descriptions is essential in most organizational systems. However, in an infant/toddler program, neither job titles nor salaries nor previous educational levels will determine the type of work any member of the team may be asked to do. In any one day, the director or head educarer, the high school student, and the volunteer grandparent may each change diapers, bottle-feed a baby, read aloud to two or three toddlers, and/or supervise naptime. The typical job description may or may not be the best way to assign responsibilities and duties.

The adults involved in a center-based program will fit one of the following three categories: professionals (those who are trained and/or certified to work with young children); para-professionals (those who may have minimal or no training or who are receiving on-the-job training); and volunteers who may or may not have any training or experience. Paraprofessionals choose to work with infants and toddlers

Enter into the child's world.
(Kindercampus, Iowa City)

because they "love" them, and/or they want or need the experience for vocational or career plans. They usually work for very low pay. Volunteers choose to work with infants and toddlers, or to do things for the program, for no pay other than satisfaction and enjoyment. It's hoped the parents of a child (or children) enrolled in the program will volunteer their time and services whenever possible. Usually it is not possible for parents to serve during the center's hours of operation, but many very helpful activities can be done at home (making bibs) or on the weekend (painting the fence). Ways of including and involving parents will be suggested in more detail in the next chapter. Here the emphasis is on the educaring team involved in the day-to-day program for the children, which may or may not include parents as educaring volunteers.

Paraprofessionals should be present on a regular schedule, whether full-time or part-time. They may or may not be directly involved with the children, depending on the needs of the program, and their own qualifications and interests. Somehow there is always a need for an extra pair of hands (or arms), always a need for an extra lap, always a need for an educaring adult to interact with or to be with.

With or without well-defined job descriptions, a written list of guidelines for adult behaviors is useful. These guidelines could include such items as:

- when you are with a child, devote your entire attention to him/her
- always work toward developing the whole child, not just the good child or the smart child
- enter into the child's world, and follow through on what the child is doing, or what interests him
- model the behavior you want the child to adopt
- talk with the child, not at him; talk about what the child is looking at or doing, or talk about an object which you are holding

Table 10–2

Percentages of Caregiver Behaviors: Infants and Toddlers*

Behaviors	Infants (6–18 months)	Toddlers (19–30 months)
Child-directed		
Social interaction	26	25
Talks with children	24	25
Touches children	21	15
Cognitive-language stimulation	4	11
Management (of behavior)	2	4
Observes children	7	7
Non–child-directed		
Talks with adults	7	4
Administrative tasks	9	9

*Adapted from National Day Care Study (Abt, 1979).

- do not manipulate; flow with the child
- use loving touches and positive body contact.

These same kinds of suggestions might also be helpful to volunteers who "love" babies but who are not certain what to do with them. Of course, in the child's eyes, there is no difference between the professional staff, the paraprofessional staff, and the volunteers.

The National Day Care Study (Abt, 1979) includes the time percentages of categories of caregiver behaviors for infants (6 to 18 months) and toddlers (19 to 30 months), which are presented in Table 10–2. Few other positions require such a high percentage of concentration on and with children. One of the observations in a high quality infant-toddler center was that no educarer was able to function appropriately with children for an 8-hour stretch of time, even with coffee breaks. (Educarers should eat snack and lunch with their children.) Therefore, a full-day work schedule should include no more than 6 contact hours with the children. The other 2 hours can be profitably spent in record keeping,

planning, writing notes to parents, or even repairing a raggedy stuffed animal. An alert, un-
tired adult is necessary as the mediator who
structures the learning environment and the experiences for the children.

Perhaps the most important understanding
for all the educaring team members is about
their responsibility to the children. Their responsibility is not to *teach* something, because
the major accomplishments of the first 3 years
will emerge naturally in an educaring environment. Their responsibility is to provide a caring,
responsive human environment.

SUMMARY

The human environment, the adult-child interactions,
the adult-adult interactions—all are critical elements
in programs for very young children. The quality of
this environment depends on three factors: staff training, staff characteristics, and staff organization.

The licensing requirements about staff qualifications and child-staff ratios are less than satisfactory,
even in the states where they exist. The recommended child-staff ratios and group sizes are 3:1 or
4:1 with no more than eight in a group of infants up
to 12 months old; 3:1 to 5:1 with no more than 12 in
a group of toddlers 12 to 24 months old; and 4:1 to
6:1 with no more than 12 in a group of walkers 24 to
36 months old. These recommended ratios will make
it possible for the development of a one-to-one relationship between an adult and each child.

To facilitate this one-to-one relationship, a
primary caregiving organizational plan is recommended.

The major ingredient of the human environment
is educaring, the activity and approach of an adult
who combines responsive caregiving and responsive
teaching in ways that are developmentally appropriate for very young children. The emphasis is on knowing when and how to respond to the universal and
specific needs and characteristics of infants and
toddlers.

In addition to appropriate responsive actions on
the part of the educarer, the overtones of these actions
must be considered. Touch and body contact during
feeding and diapering are important, and change routine caregiving into educaring. Conversation with

young children is of prime importance, and starts long
before baby can respond verbally. Knowing when to
initiate play, and when not to intervene in play, is
another part of educaring.

The high quality adult-child interactions can best
occur in a high quality adult environment. Although
the persons working in an infant/toddler program
may have different training and experiential backgrounds, they make up an educaring team. The team
may include professionals, paraprofessionals, and
volunteers, some of whom may also have training or
experience. This team must work together to provide
a caring, responsive human environment.

SUGGESTED ACTIVITIES AND QUESTIONS

1. What are the benefits of a primary caregiving
   plan of organization? Are there disadvantages?

2. How would you explain the difference between
   a "caregiver" and an "educarer" to someone
   who is not studying early childhood education?

3. Visit an infant/toddler center-based program.
   Choose one adult or one child, and keep a running record of their one-to-one verbal interactions for the total of an hour. (You may want to
   observe for 3 minutes, record for 3 minutes, then
   observe again, etc.)

4. Visit a family day-care home that serves infants
   and/or toddlers. Keep a running record as described in question 3.

5. Compare your observations with those of your
   classmates. Discuss possible reasons for
   differences.

6. Some persons think that teachers are born, not
   trained. Do you agree?

SUGGESTED READINGS

Bos, B. (1983). *Before the basics: Creating conversations with children.* Roseville, CA: Turn-the-
Page Press.

Caldwell, B., & Richmond, J. (1968). A "typical day"
for the groups at the Children's Center (appendix B). In L. L. Dittmann (Ed.), *Early child care.*
New York: Atherton.

Cataldo, C. Z. (1984). Infant-toddler education: Blending the best approaches. *Young Children, 39* (2), 25–32.

CDA National Credentialing Program. (1985). *Family day care providers.* Washington, DC: Author.

CDA National Credentialing Program. (1986). *Infant/ toddler caregivers in center-based programs.* Washington, DC: Author.

Dittmann, L. (Ed.). (1984). *The infants we care for* (rev. ed.). Washington, DC: National Association for the Education of Young Children.

Dresden, J., & Myers, B. K. (1989). Early childhood professionals: Toward self-definition. *Young Children, 44* (2), 62–66.

Fogel, A. (1986). The role of adults in infant development: Implications for early childhood educators. In L. G. Katz (Ed.), *Current Topics in Early Childhood Education, 6,* 33–61.

Freeman, L. (1986). *Loving touches.* Seattle: Parenting Press.

Godwin, A., & Schrag, L. (Eds.). (1988). *Setting up for infant care: Guidelines for centers and family day care homes.* Washington, DC: National Association for the Education of Young Children.

Gonzalez-Mena, J. (1979). Quality adult-child relationships: A child's-eye view. In E. Jones (Ed.), *Supporting the growth of infants, toddlers and parents.* Pasadena, CA: Pacific Oaks College and Children's School.

Gonzalez-Mena, J., & Eyer, D. W. (1989). *Infants, toddlers and caregivers* (2nd ed.). Mountain View, CA: Mayfield.

Gordon, J. (1988, January). Separation anxiety: How to ask a family to leave your center. *Child Care Information Exchange,* 13–15.

Graham, T. L., & Camp, L. (1988). *Teaching terrific two's and other toddlers.* Atlanta: Humanics Press.

Harlow, H. (1971). *Learning to love.* New York: Ballantine Books.

Hauser-Cram, P. (1986, Spring). Backing away helpfully: Some roles teachers shouldn't fill. *Beginnings,* 18–20.

Hess, R. D., Price, G. C., Dickson, W. P., & Conroy, M. (1981). Different roles for mothers and teachers: Contrasting styles of child care. In S.

Kilmer (Ed.), *Advances in Early Education and Day Care, 2,* 1–28. Greenwich, CT: JAI Press.

Honig, A. S. (1978). Training caregivers to provide loving, learning experiences for babies. *Dimensions, 6,* 33–43.

Honig, A. S. (1984, Winter). Why talk to babies? *Beginnings,* 3–6.

Honig, A. S. (1986). Research in review: Stress and coping in children. In J. B. McCracken (Ed.), *Reducing stress in young children's lives* (pp. 142–167). Washington, DC: National Association for the Education of Young Children.

Honig, A. S. (1987). The Eriksonian approach: Infant-toddler education. In J. Roopnarine & J. Johnson (Eds.), *Approaches to early childhood education* (pp. 49–69). Columbus, OH: Merrill.

Honig, A. S. (1989). Quality infant-toddler caregiving: Are there magic recipes? *Young Children, 44* (4), 4–10.

Howes, C. (1989). Infant child care. *Young Children, 44* (6), 24–28.

Jorde-Bloom, P. (1988). *A great place to work: Improving conditions for staff in young children's programs.* Washington, DC: National Association for the Education of Young Children.

Karnes, M. B., Johnson, L. J., & Beauchamp, K. D. F. (1988). Enhancing essential relationships: Developing a nurturing affective environment for young children. *Young Children, 44* (1), 58–65.

Katz, L. G. (1980). Mothering and teaching: Some significant distinctions. In L. G. Katz (Ed.), *Current topics in early childhood education, 3.* Norwood, NJ: Ablex.

Lally, J. R., Provence, S., Szanton, E., & Weissbourd, B. (1987). Developmentally appropriate care for children from birth to age 3. In S. Bredekamp (Ed.), *Developmentally appropriate practice* (expanded ed.). Washington, DC: National Association for the Education of Young Children.

Leavitt, R., & Krause Eheart, B. (1985). *Toddler day care: A guide to responsive caregiving.* Lexington, MA: Lexington Books.

Lurie, R., & Neugebauer, R. (Eds.). (1982). *Caring for infants and toddlers: What works, what doesn't.* Vol. 2. Redmond, WA: Child Care Information Exchange.

Neugebauer, R., & Lurie, R. (Eds.). (1980). *Caring for infants and toddlers: What works, what doesn't.* Redmond, WA: Child Care Information Exchange.

Phillips, D. A. (Ed.). (1987). *Quality in child care: What does research tell us?* Washington, DC: National Association for the Education of Young Children.

Sale, J., & Torres, Y. (1979). *I'm not just a babysitter.* Pasadena, CA: Pacific Oaks College.

Schachter, F. F., & Strage, A. A. (1982). Adults' talk and children's language development. In S. G. Moore & C. R. Cooper (Eds.), *The young child: Reviews of research.* Vol. 3. Washington, DC: National Association for the Education of Young Children.

Schaffer, H. R. (1984). *The child's entry into a social world.* Orlando, FL: Academic Press.

Stern, D. (1985). *The interpersonal world of the infant: A view from psychoanalysis and developmental psychology.* New York: Basic Books.

Uzgiris, I. C. (1989). Infants in relation: Performers, pupils, and partners. In W. Damon (Ed.), *Child development today and tomorrow.* San Francisco: Jossey-Bass.

Weissbourd, B., & Musick, J. (Eds.). (1981). *Infants: Their social environments.* Washington, DC: National Association for the Education of Young Children.

Willis, A., & Ricciuti, H. (1980). Routine caregiving. In R. Neugebauer & R. Lurie (Eds.), *Caring for infants and toddlers: What works, what doesn't.* Vol. 1. Redmond, WA: Child Care Information Exchange.

Wittmer, D. S., & Honig, A. S. (1988). Teacher recreation of negative interactions with toddlers. In A. S. Honig (Ed.), Optimizing early child care and education [Special issue]. *Early Child Development and Care, 31,* 77–88.

Ziajka, A. (1981). *Prelinguistic communication in infancy.* New York: Praeger.

FIVE

Partnerships and Relationships

The theories and recommended methods and strategies offered in the previous four sections have incorporated the best knowledge to date about infant/toddler care and education—with one glaring exception. A main ingredient of a high quality program is its ongoing provision for parent involvement and participation, and its working together with parents in a true partnership.

Other partnerships are emerging or are already in existence, including the alliances with public education and with the business community.

Chapter 11 contains information about these three partnerships.

Chapter 12, which is probably the most enjoyable chapter of all, describes typical days in the lives of four infants and toddlers, three in a center-based program, and one in a family day-care home.

Chapter 13 includes guidelines for advocacy at the community, state, and federal levels, and describes exemplary advocacy organizations and efforts.

11

Parents, Public Education, and Business

We need a new manner of thinking if we are to survive.
Albert Einstein

There has been little attention given up until the present time to the effect of the relationships between parents and educarer(s), although there has been much attention given to their necessity and to descriptions of such relationships. Actually, there is little agreement about what parent involvement means, because it means many things to many people. But there is agreement that structuring realistic and meaningful parent involvement is a difficult procedure.

Two emerging partnerships, one with the public schools and the other with the business community, are growing in importance as we look at the entire early education picture. In some respects, these new alliances are causing controversy, and in some cases considerable alarm. Whether we agree with these new developments or not, it is important to be aware of them. If this trend continues, it will both enlarge and upgrade the profession and society's acceptance of nonmaternal infant/toddler care and education.

PARTNERSHIPS WITH PARENTS
The State of Affairs

Parent participation and involvement are especially important in programs for infants and toddlers. Why? Because infants and toddlers are physically and emotionally vulnerable. Their well-being should be monitored when care is provided outside the home. In addition, this is the age span during which disruptions in the continuity of care are most likely to be stressful for the child. Parents are the best sources of continuity, which means that the interface between the family and the educarer must be wide and must overlap; the transition between home and the program should be as smooth as possible.

Any visit to the local bookstore will reveal so many parent-advice publications that parents, particularly first-time parents, are easily overwhelmed. Not only is there a lot of information available, but there is much conflicting information. The infant/toddler program should be able to supply correct and relevant advice (or suggestions) to parents based on the latest research findings and expert opinion.

No matter what kind of child-care services or where they may be located, parent involvement is the key to quality. A child-care center or home is associated with superior care whenever parents are partners. One of the goals for infant/toddler programs (see chapter 1) is to meet the needs of parents, including sharing information about their child, about the program, and about community and government resources. This sharing not only is beneficial for the child's well-being, but actually strengthens the family. Brazelton (1984a) has written that "strengthening the family should be the major priority of any program directed to the care of infants from birth to two years" (p. 9).

The "Official" Roles of Parents

There are many parent roles in an infant/toddler program.

Licensing requirements from several states address some of them, including the right to visit and observe; the right to have written communications and parent meetings; the right to participate in the classroom; bicultural programming; and access to a complaint process. However, the licensing standards for family day-care homes in 24 states do not even mention parents; no mention is made in the licensing standards for centers in 14 states.

Only 18 states guarantee parents the right to visit their children's center, and only 11 guarantee parents the right to visit family day-care homes. Thirteen states require regular, frequent, and timely communication of information about the child between center staff and parents (Morgan, 1987).

It is true that licensing standards specify the bare minimum of requirements usually directed to health and safety measures, and include scant attention to program or other essential issues. Perhaps after reading the following information, you will be able to list the essential items about parents and their roles that *should* be included in licensing standards. Standards should reflect important developmental principles, but their implementation requires imagination for different parents and different children.

Nurturing, loving parents. (Early Childhood Education Center)

What Children Need

During the first years of life, there are five necessary basic parent orientations toward the child:

1. Being a *nurturing* parent—providing adequate food, shelter, and protection

2. Being a *loving* parent—cherishing the life of the child and making a patient investment in the child's future

3. Being an *enjoying* parent—finding focal points for interaction with the child that provide mutual satisfaction

4. Being a *teaching* parent, who understands enough about child development to become skillful as a mentor, and to sharpen the child's skills gradually as its capacity evolves

5. Being a *coping* parent, who knows how to seek help for developing skills that deal effectively with the inevitable vicissitudes of life (Hamburg, 1987, p. 2).

What Parents Need

The daily application of these necessary parent characteristics is based on individual strength *and* the availability of social support networks. For the families of very young children in nonmaternal care, one of these primary social supports is the infant/toddler program. In some cases, for example, single teenage mothers, supportive guidance may be needed and offered in each of these areas of parenting. In all cases, infant/toddler educarers have two very important, very specific responsibilities. The first is to foster early attachment to both the mother (or guardian) and the primary educarer. Solid attachment provides a secure base for exploration that in turn sustains curiosity, and leads to problem-solving capacity.

One of the crucial questions asked about infant/toddler programs in the 1960s and 1970s was whether or not such programs were detrimental to the child's emotional development or

attachment. The answer from the classic pioneer projects (Caldwell & Stedman, 1977; Caldwell, Wright, Honig, & Tannenbaum, 1970; Elardo & Caldwell, 1974; Fowler & Kahn, 1976; Keister, 1970; Lally & Honig, 1977) was *no,* if the educarers were nurturant, responsive adults, and the quality of care was high.

The second responsibility for infant/toddler educarers is to facilitate parent-child interactions so that parents become sensitive to the baby's cues and to appropriate responses, and in this way, share pleasure in this fundamental human relationship.

The child-care system should include a true partnership between the parents and their children's educarers. A really true partnership requires the coordination of child-rearing efforts, and a working together to help children make the smoothest transition from home to program to home again (Endsley & Bradbard, 1981). The achievement of such a partnership is more easily said than done.

Partnership Realities

Powell (1977, 1978, 1989) investigated the interpersonal relationships between caregivers and parents in 12 Detroit child-care centers with 80 caregivers serving 212 parents. He found that the child's family and the day-care centers functioned independently, and that there was a social distance between them. In another study of 50 families enrolled in a southwestern day-care center, Zigler and Turner (1982) found that although the center strongly encouraged parent visitation, observation, and participation, the parents spent an average of only 7.4 minutes per day in the center, primarily to deliver and call for their child(ren). Peters and his colleagues (Long, Peters, & Garduque, 1985; Peters & Benn, 1980) extended this question to the larger issue of home-child care continuity, with similar negative findings. The research reported by Phillips (1987) revealed that many educarers "harbor negative attitudes toward the parents whose children are in their care" (p. 124).

One of the reasons behind these negative attitudes is the observable unwillingness or reluctance for some parents to become involved in their children's programs. Indeed, some parents seem all too ready to turn over their child-rearing responsibilities to the educarers, who have studied child development and infant/toddler care and education, and who therefore "know more" than the parent. It is true that educarers support parents, but they do not assume the child-rearing responsibilities. Decisions about the time to introduce solid foods or to start toilet training (and how to do it), or techniques of behavior management are in the parents' domain. It is hoped parents and educarers reach a mutual decision about these and other child-rearing issues. Bromwich (1984) cautions us to always remember whose baby it is because when a parent feels in control, the parent will be more likely to take active responsibility.

In his 1977 study, Powell identified three major subgroups of day-care parents: dependent, independent, and interdependent. The dependent parents view the center or provider as a source of child development advice, and attempt to put into practice "what the teacher said." They view the educarer as the authority, and thereby subtly shift their responsibility. They may share some child-related information with the educarer(s), but they do not assume much initiative in decisions about their children.

The independent parents, on the other hand, assume that all the responsibility for child-rearing is theirs, and that the hours their children spend in nonmaternal care are benign, but have little important effect on their child. They assume that the staff do whatever they are supposed to do because they are in the business of caring for children. These parents may scan the parent bulletin board for announcements of available baby-sitting or outgrown clothes or furnishings for sale, but they see little reason for more than a hello and good-bye as they deliver and pick up their children. Indeed, they are annoyed by the rule that they must personally deliver and pick up. It is more convenient to use a carpool or center-supplied transportation.

> The interdependent parents, on the other hand, reflect considerable intersection between family and day-care centers; the two child-rearing systems function in an interdependent way. Interdependent parents have a high frequency of communication with caregivers, discuss parent/family related information, believe strongly that family information should be shared with caregivers, and believe that parents and caregivers should discuss child-rearing values (Powell, 1977, p. 18).

This interdependency should be the goal of all programs serving young children. It is not easily reached because of differing philosophies and because parents and educarers are always pressed for time. Interdependency and involvement are criteria for a high quality program. Howes (1987) studied centers serving children from 15 to 36 months of age, and found that in the high quality centers (determined by adult-child ratios, stability of educarers, and training of educarers), parents were "involved in the day-to-day life of the center, . . . were welcome in the classrooms, served on committees, and had some say in decision making. Parents were less involved in the low quality centers" (p. 84). Brazelton (1989) asserts that

> not only should parents be urged to participate actively in their babies' care, but child-care centers could provide opportunities for parent education, for peer support groups, and for the kind of nurturing support that formerly was provided by grandparents and aunts and uncles. Families and their small children could both benefit from such day care. Day care needn't split families. It could cement them and offer the backup for positive self-images both of parents and of their small children (p. 17).

It is the responsibility of the educarer(s) to initiate and maintain the interdependent network. This network is the result of carefully planned parent involvement.

STRATEGIES FOR PARENT INVOLVEMENT

Overview

Parent involvement has many dimensions that are dependent on the location of the program (center-based or home-based) and on the size of the program. It may be very informal and spontaneous, or it may be a required component of the infant/toddler program, and therefore somewhat more structured.

Many families do not want to be involved, other than coming to a conference or two. They just want a place where their child is safe, well-cared for, and happy for a few hours each day. Other families use child care as an extended family: they seek advice, they want to learn new skills, they enjoy family social activities, and they want to participate.

McKinney (1978, 1980) and Maraschiello (1981) found that in-class participation was the most popular with the parents; next popular were the parent meetings and policy planning sessions; and least popular were the social and fundraising activities. These data are from Head Start programs for 3 to 5 year olds, but they probably ring true for the parents of infants and toddlers.

In her 1986 review of research and practices in parent involvement, Becher summarized the effects of involvement as follows:

1. Parents develop more positive attitudes about the program and the program personnel.
2. Parents develop more positive attitudes about themselves as parents and increase their self confidence.
3. Parent-child relationships improve.
4. Parents use more positive forms of reinforcement.
5. If the involvement is continued in preschool and the early grades, the children increase their academic achievement and cognitive development.

Parent Conferences

The initial conference. The groundwork for parental involvement is laid after the parents and perhaps the child have visited the program and after the child has been enrolled but is not yet attending. A home visit by the educarer-to-be will help the parent feel more at ease, and will help the educarer begin to learn about the individuality of this child and this family. It can also help put the child at ease, as he sees mother and educarer together in familiar surroundings, and as educarer and child spend a few minutes playing with a toy brought from the program, and perhaps left with the child. Home visits are not always possible. When this is the case, it should be program policy that the child and parent (or guardian) both spend time together at the program so that the child becomes somewhat familiar with the new surroundings and the educarer from a psychologically secure position.

This initial visit provides the opportunity for the parent to tell about the accomplishments of her child, and what she hopes will be the next steps, and also for the educarer to explain how the program may help in these next steps. It is also the time to discuss the philosophy and policies of the program that are written in the Parent's Manual, which ideally was presented during the parent's visit to the program. Such a manual should contain a fairly formal collection of information and should include the following:

1. *General information*

    Calendar (open and closed days; hours of operation)
    Philosophy
    Purpose
    Developmental goals for the children
    The children and families served
    The staff
    Organization (multi-aged, primary caregiving, etc.)
    Funding (fees; other sources)

The Advisory Committee (if there is one)
Parent meetings and other participation
Health and safety policies

2. *Procedures*

Transportation and parking
Arrival and departure
Late pick-up policy
Payment of fees
Policy for temporary non-attendance
Parental termination of enrollment
Sick-child policy

3. *Daily program*

Time schedule
Clothing, including diapers
Food service
Birthdays (including the program's birth-
day) and other special events

4. *Forms to be signed by parent or guardian*

Release of child to adult other than parent
or guardian
Emergency treatment of a minor
Consent for field trips
Consent for photographs (useful in publicity, or sometimes research, or a book like
this one)
Health record and physical examination (to
be filled in by child's doctor)

Most if not all of these forms should be in
written form, even if the child is to be in a family
day-care home, in order to prevent misunderstandings, or in some cases, to prevent a crisis
situation, for example, emergency treatment in
case of an accident, or the child's pick-up by an
unauthorized person.

The information and the permission forms
in the manual may seem businesslike, particularly to first-time parents, but their impact may
be softened as the educarer talks about the items
and explains why they are necessary.

The educarer might also share some pictures of the children and activities, of family
events, and of the various staff members.

It is possible that the patterns of family life
in this family are in sharp contrast to the views
of the visiting educarer, but parents should be
approached in the same way children are approached, with respect and appreciation for individual differences. This means that no value
judgments are made about the homes or families
or the children, because value judgments get in
the way of acting in the best interests of the children. Katz (1980) recommends that educarers
focus on those aspects of the child's development that they actually do control, and not try
to change the family of the child, nor much of
the mother's behavior. Educarers should take
responsibility only for the time the child is in their
care (of course in the case of suspected child
abuse or neglect, the educarer is obligated to
make a report). Katz also cautions that educarers "who are unable to detach themselves optimally from their pupils and become too close
to them are likely to suffer emotional 'burnout' "
(p. 52).

Of course this initial visit gives the opportunity to express the hope (or requirement, if
that is the case) that all parents become involved
in some way. Evidence exists (Auerback, 1975;
Gray & Klaus, 1970; Levenstein, 1971, 1976;
Zigler & Turner, 1982; Zigler & Valentine, 1979)
that the more parents are involved in the activities of the child-care center and thus more involved in the shaping of their children's lives,
the more the children benefit from such
involvement.

In spite of these research findings (which
might be shared with the parent, or even included in the manual), and in spite of the conventional wisdom of child development experts
about the values of parent involvement, some
parents will become involved, some may choose
not to, and some may claim that they are unable
to do so, at least during the times their child is

in the program. Regardless of the parent's first decision, the educarer must at least create and maintain positive active communication with the parent(s) of each child in her care. It is hoped the initial meeting sets the stage for mutual trust and respect.

Scheduled conferences. After the child starts to attend the program, individual parent conferences with the primary educarer should be scheduled at least two times a year. During these conferences (and all other times, too) it is important to remember that although the educarer and parents are partners in guiding the development of the child they "share," it is the parents who are the senior partners. It is the parents who will continue to be responsible for their child's progress; it is the parents who will continue giving their support after the child leaves your program; and it is the parents whose

self-concept and feelings of security and worth are closely related to their hopes for their child(ren).

In order to make the most of the time spent in the conference, it is helpful if both the parent and the educarer have thought about what they want to talk about. Sending home a note asking the parents to think about (and perhaps write down) what they are especially interested in can be useful. The same idea applies to the educarer: "What I want to share, what I want to ask, how can I help?" The pages in the daily notebook (see Written Messages under Transition Communications) will be helpful as the educarer prepares for the conference.

Unscheduled conferences. Not all conferences are scheduled on a regular basis. Many are requested by either the parent or the educarer, and may be at any time, and as often as

Beginning of the day—from mother to primary educarer. (Early Childhood Education Center)

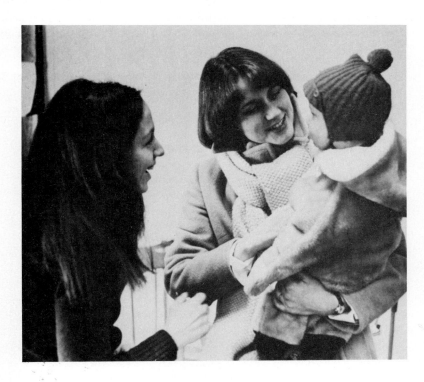

requested. They may be at the center or day-care home, perhaps during naptime, or at the child's home in the evening. Sometimes parents invite the educarer for the evening meal (a good indication of partnership) and then talk after the young one has been put to bed.

In all the parent conferences and other conversations educarers respect the fact that parents really do know their own children best, but they recognize that frequently help with behaviors related to group living may be needed (Gestwiki, 1987; Powell, 1989).

A good rule for all parent conferences, regardless of the age of the child, is to always begin with positive statements. When parents see their child's good points, their self-image as parents is reinforced. These self-images play an important part in how they feel and what they do. Infant/toddler educarers should realize that their comments about a very young child are probably the first professional evaluation the parents have had. If the educarer sees the child as a beautiful developing person, the parents will be-

gin to see him or her in the same way, and will take pride in knowing that this beautiful developing person is the result of good parenting.

Transition Communications

Delivery and pick-up. Most communication between parents and educarers occurs when the children are delivered and called for. It should be expected, or even required, that the children are personally delivered and called for by a parent or guardian. Carpool transportation or center-provided transportation should not occur in a program for children under 3 years of age. Examples of beneficial transition times are described in the "typical days" in the next chapter.

However, without some advance planning, even these daily contacts can easily become superficial and meaningless. "How did things go?" and "Thanks, see you tomorrow" have little communication (or partnership) value. Compare this with the following educarer's

End of the day—personal pick-up. (Early Childhood Education Center)

comment as the parent calls for her 6 month old after the very first day in group care.

> Wow, we should really have a celebration today. When I noticed how hard it was for her to say good-bye to you this morning, I realized this was the first time she's done that. That crying when you leave is a good sign that she loves you very much, that all your hard work these past few months has paid off and she's become attached to you. That's a very special day (Gestwicki, 1987, p. 250).

A major problem, of course, is that centers operate on an extended day basis, and few educarers can or should work more than 8 hours a day. If the primary educarer is present at the center's opening time (frequently 6:30 A.M.), the 8-hour day may be over before the children are called for. Split-shifts for educarers are one solution, but not a very good solution. Even if the primary educarer agreed to be present at the beginning and ending of each session, the responsibility for the child would rest on a non-primary caregiver for a major portion of the day. Some centers arrange to have aides on duty during the first and last hours of the day, with the primary caregiver there during the heart of the program. Of course, this too is unsatisfactory. Any split-shift arrangement is undesirable from the adult's view, and is very inadequate from the child's view. Rosenthal's recommendation (see chapter 10) of assigning one person in the morning (6:30 to 2:30 P.M.) and another in the afternoon (10:30 A.M. to 6:30 P.M.) as primary caregivers for the same group of children is a workable solution. It provides a time-overlap in the middle of the day, continuity of care for the child, and the opportunity for satisfactory communication with the parent(s).

Of course, the home provider usually spends longer than the 8-hour day, and this problem does not usually exist. Pence and Goelman (1987) found that the parents who use family day care speak more often with the educarers than those who use center-based care. They also found that these parents kept in touch with

Transition messages—wall chart and notebook. (Early Childhood Education Center)

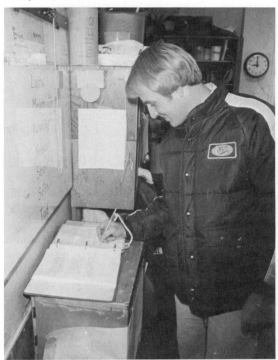

the provider after their children had left the family day-care home.

But in either place, the hurriedness of delivery and pick-up is usual, and therefore additional ways of communicating must be planned for.

Written messages. The transition communications can be more meaningful by referring to written notes recorded during the day. A large wall chart protected by Plexiglas serves two purposes. It contains a running account of each child's eating, sleeping, and toileting as a quick reference for the center staff. It also provides a quick summary of these items for the parent at the end of the day. This at-a-glance information frees the few minutes of face-to-face contact for the discussion of other relevant items.

In addition to the wall chart, a loose-leaf notebook should be readily available for both parents and educarers. Parents sign their children in on arrival and write any special news or questions (''Bobby's grandma arrived last night; she wants to visit the center this afternoon''; ''Cindy had a restless night''; ''I'd like to talk for a few minutes when I pick up Ruth''; or even ''Do you know any baby-sitters we could call when the new baby arrives?''). Examples of educarer's messages might be ''Johnnie really loves carrots''; ''Susie seems fussy—she might be coming down with something''; or ''Ralph took his first step today!'' This last item raises an interesting question. Should the educarer deprive the parents of the thrill of their child's first step? If you think not, perhaps a more appropriate notation might be ''Ralph is so close to taking his first step—maybe he'll do it tonight.'' Individual messages may also be placed in a child's cubby, so there is some degree of privacy.

If parents are rushed at the end of the day, and they usually are, they can get the news of their child's day from these written messages. Occasionally ''their'' educarer may be busy talking with other parents. This kind of message-writing also minimizes the disadvantages of more than one educarer for any one child.

Any announcement to all the parents (''Don't forget the potluck tomorrow night!'') can be written just once in bold letters at the top of the page-of-the-day.

These written messages help in furthering the interdependence of family and center.

Newsletters. Another procedure that works toward partnership is a newsletter. It is necessary in the center with more than one or two groups of children. It is not necessarily offered by family day-care providers because of the close relationships and contacts that are already in place. A newsletter can be only one page or several pages. It provides the opportunity for educaring and other staff members to express opinions, to make announcements, to suggest activities for home, to suggest appropriate snacks, and many other bits of information.

Each issue should include an article or news item from at least one of the parents.

Telephone calls. Although not a part of the initial transition communication system, telephone calls can play a major role in helping the parent who was particularly rushed at delivery time, or the new parent who is still unsure of herself. Ideally, a telephone with a direct line can be in each infant/toddler room, and both parents and educarers are able to call one another at any time during the day. Sometimes the parent questions are simple: ''Is he all right?'' ''Did he finish his bottle?'' These questions are ways in which the parent keeps in touch with her baby, and maybe help relieve some guilt about not being with him. If the parent's workplace allows personal calls, the parents will appreciate calls from the educarers also. The calls can give good messages most of the time, and are not limited to ''crisis'' situations.

Parent Meetings: Talking and Listening

Parent meetings can be mutually beneficial—or mutually deadening. Parent involvement in the planning and in the meeting itself will ensure a larger turnout than if the staff independently decides on the topic and presents the topic. Of course it helps if the child care and transportation are provided when necessary. Meetings that include slides or a videotape of the children are usually well attended. These shows offer the center staff the opportunity to insert a few words of wisdom related to the pictured events.

In addition to the center-to-parent meetings, parent-to-parent meetings have proved successful. These include a brief presentation by one parent on a specific aspect of parenting, followed by experience-sharing, and discussion, and light refreshments. The parents should choose the refreshments as well as the topic. If the traditional punch and cookies seem a little tame, there is no reason why beer and pretzels can't be served.

All kinds of topics may be suggested by the parents or the educarers or the other staff members. Frequent topics include:

- Health: immunizations, communicable diseases, care of teeth and gums, sources of free or inexpensive health care
- Nutrition: nutritious snacks, weaning and self-feeding, feeding "problems"
- Safety: car safety and restraint devices, accidental poisoning, water safety, safety in the home
- Toilet training
- Behavior and interpersonal relations: tantrums, sleep patterns, sibling jealousy, fear of strangers, attention-getting
- Sources of free information

These topics will vary, depending on the families being served.

Parent Meetings: Instead of Talking and Listening

Perhaps the most successful parent "meeting" is one in which the parents actually do something for the center, instead of just talking and listening. Don't hesitate to let your parents know if the center or day-care home needs help with a major project such as changing an empty room into an activity room, or building a sand box, or fencing in part of the outside play space for the infants to protect them from the more active toddlers. If the center or day-care provider supplies the lumber, the paint, the nails and other materials, and suggested plans for the construction (or let the parents draw up the plans and buy the materials), you can expect a large turnout on a day when the children's program is not in operation. Child care could be provided at no cost to the parents on this occasion. Mothers and staff might provide a pot-luck meal. There will be a lot of fun, a lot of kidding around, but also a real sense of accomplishment and involvement. Such activities are money-savers, also, which might mean a lower parent fee.

Some programs incorporate a pot-luck supper before the evening parent meeting. Parents bring their contribution in the morning when they deliver their child, and join their children for the evening meal. Once again, child care is provided during the meeting by some of the center personnel in familiar surroundings.

Other centers or homes plan purely social get-togethers, like an ice cream social, a pizza potluck, or a picnic for the children and their families, including siblings. A Saturday brunch (doughnuts, bagels, juice, and coffee) can be combined with an open house that features a book fair (with books for sale) and displays by the educarers.

Individual Participation

In-class. The door should always be open for parents to visit, to observe, or to become a temporary part of the ongoing program. Mothers who want to breast feed or offer a bottle to their baby should be given a comfortable chair and a quiet secluded place for them to be with their babies during this special time. "If parents feel that routines and regulations are not separating them from their baby, they will feel less possessive in their relation with a caregiver, and reassured that their baby's care is satisfactory" (Gestwicki, 1987, p. 250). Sometimes parents of toddlers have been able to arrange their schedules so they could occasionally join their children for the noon meal.

Of course, an extra lap is always appreciated, as is some one-to-one attention, not always available in a room of busy infants and toddlers. Programs can welcome senior citizens to the mutual benefit of all concerned. I know of one grampa who goes to an infant room every day "because the babies need me." He spends several hours in a rocking chair holding any baby who needs a little extra soothing. Somehow, his arms are always holding one or the other of the little ones, and he rocks them to sleep or to a state of calm. He feels needed, and he is needed. The babies need him.

A special time for mother and baby.
(Early Childhood Education Center)

One of the unfortunate characteristics of our society is that children have very little contact with older people. It is therefore recommended that senior citizens be included in the program on a regular basis, not just the yearly visit to the care center. Leichter (1974) writes that

> somehow we have to get the older people, grand-parents, widows and widowers, spinsters and bachelors, back close to growing children if we are to restore a sense of community, a knowledge of the past, and a sense of the future to today's children (p. 71).

Such encounters are mutually beneficial, and should be a part of every child's life from the beginning stages.

Out-of-class. There are always time-consuming chores connected with an infant/toddler program that do not need to be done on the site: typing notices or snack suggestions or newsletters; mending stuffed toys; making bibs or aprons or curtains; repairing toys; or even grocery shopping. Carpentry or cabinet-making projects may appeal to some.

The infant/toddler center or family day-care home can establish a lending library—toys, books, pamphlets, and magazines—that will need updating, and a system for keeping track of the items. An appreciated out-of-class activity is a collection of names of temporary day-time baby-sitters or family home providers who can provide care for children too sick to be at the center. Any infant/toddler program would have an abundant supply of photographs of the children and their activities—these could be organized in scrapbooks, labeled, and identified with a number so parents could order copies of special ones.

The parents and educarers might bring in newspaper clippings or magazine articles about young children or legislation or whatever. These might be made into a display or stapled to file folders so they could be checked out of the parent resource library.

These projects and others like them will help change a child-care program into a family support system. They take time, which is at a premium for the members of the staff. They can provide meaningful participation, and therefore involvement in the program when they are done by the parents.

Parents' Night Out

Centers or family home providers can add to the feeling of partnership by offering a monthly "night out," perhaps on a Saturday night from 7 P.M. to midnight. Only children enrolled in the center and their siblings may attend. The members of the staff are the baby-sitters for the evening. Children arrive in their sleepers or paja-

A multigenerational conversation.
(Kindercampus, Iowa City)

mas, clutching their teddy bears or dolls or blankets. They enjoy quiet times with stories or games, and are put to bed as they get sleepy, or when the parents have requested. Of course fees are charged, and the staff members are paid. According to the owners of one such program, "The center's reputation has been enhanced by offering this special service, which seems to add to the sense of togetherness for families and staff" (National Association for the Education of Young Children, 1986, p. 52).

Final Comments

It has been observed that when very young children are first enrolled in an infant/toddler program, their parents are usually highly motivated to become involved. Indeed, parents of infants and toddlers are more excited about a linkage with their care system than the parents of preschoolers. But as parents come to trust the staff (and perhaps to enjoy their daily freedom from baby's demands), they tend to shift more and more responsibility to the staff. We must watch for this, and actively prevent it.

As a conclusion to this discussion of parent involvement, there are two related statements expressed by two experts in the field: James Hymes, Jr., and T. Berry Brazelton. Their ideas are important.

> Beyond any question, when you work closely with parents you pay a price. You adjust to the other fellow's ideas, sometimes going faster and sometimes going at a slower pace than you desire. But there are rewards in working together that isolation could never bring. Teachers do gain. Parents gain. And the children are the real winners (Hymes, 1975, p. 4).

And from Dr. Brazelton,

> One of the most valuable aspects of a day-care center for small children is what it can mean to the families. It can become a focus in the community for many families who share similar concerns. Unless a center demands mutual participation from all its member families, it loses this value to them. As parents are forced to give to such a center, they begin to feel more responsibility and more involvement. . . . The parents gain through warmth of commitment, and the

young children benefit when their parents are right there making decisions that directly affect their daily lives. If parents allow themselves to be drawn away they begin to feel guilty and angry with themselves, at the same time longing for a closer touch with their children. Their unconscious response to such feelings will create a feeling of competition and hostility toward the caretakers in the center. This may come out in various ways, either as undermining the work of the center or as a kind of abdication of responsibility for this side of their children's care. It doesn't need to happen—if a day-care center presses the parent-child relationship as its major focus, rather than just care for the child (1974, pp. 179–180).

One last word about parent partnerships. Any baby who is apathetic, or who has extreme feeding problems or extreme sleep problems, or who is fearful and clingy in nonstressful situations, may be the child of a parent who needs help, one who may benefit from very close communication, and perhaps referral to a helping agency.

According to the American Adademy of Pediatrics (1988c), "disturbed" parenting may be caused by the individual parent's illness or vulnerability (physical or mental illness, mental retardation or educational deficiencies, personality disorder, alcoholism or drug abuse and addiction); lack of social or economic support systems (poverty, marital conflicts, unavailable social support); and excessive child-rearing responsibilities (chronically ill or disabled child, large family, multiple birth, difficult temperament in the child). Many of these conditions require the expertise of professionals other than the educarers, but "when a child has a significant relationship with another healthy adult, the development impact of a disturbed parent is lessened" (AAP, 1988c, p. 149).

EMERGING PARTNERSHIPS WITH PUBLIC EDUCATION

Historically, child care and early education have represented two distinct service strands, the for-

mer to help working parents, and the latter to emphasize children's cognitive growth and social competence. Therefore until quite recently, the state superintendents of schools, the state Boards of Education, and Congress expressed little interest in children under 5 years of age with the exception of children with disabilities or from impoverished living conditions. Today this interest is expanding at a rapid rate. Over 100 related bills were introduced to the 1987–1988 Congress. The thinking behind at least a few of these bills was prompted in part by pioneer programs in public school partnerships in California, Massachusetts, and Arkansas.

Pioneer Programs

The Children's Centers. California has led the country in its partnership between elementary schools and child care, starting in 1933. The Children's Centers are under the State Department of Education, and the school districts provide the space and some administrative services. Credentialed teachers are on the same salary schedule as the other public school teachers, and the credentialed early childhood teachers are represented by the largest of the city's teacher unions (Levine, 1978).

One example is the Pomona, California, Children's Center, which today provides child care and development services in a variety of settings to children aged 6 weeks to 14 years. The several components include the "School Age Parenting Infant Development" program, which provides child care to infants and toddlers of school-age parents who are finishing their high school education. There is provision also for teaching parenting skills to both parents and nonparents. The centers also provide year round child-care/development services to the infants, toddlers, preschool, and school-age children of parents who are working or in training during the day, evening, and on weekends. The centers are funded by Title XX Block grants, local taxes, and parent fees (Warger, 1988).

Brookline Early Education Project. One of the most famous and influential partnerships is the program known as BEEP. It was started in 1972, long before the current interest in public school involvement in programs for very young children. The rationale was based on the recognition that parents are the most influential teachers of their young children. It seemed

> that if schools were to form alliances with parents during the children's earliest years, child and family strengths could be recognized and potential weaknesses could be addressed, minimizing the exacerbation of serious educational problems. Parents and teachers could learn to communicate with each other before the tensions of academic concern surfaced (Pierson, Walker, & Tivnan, 1985, p. 74).

There were three interrelated components: (1) parent education and support, involving home visits, meetings, and child care during the meetings; (2) diagnostic monitoring, including physical, neurologic, and developmental assessments starting at 2 weeks and ending at kindergarten entry; and (3) education programs for children: starting at age 2, weekly playgroups; and for ages 3 and 4, a daily morning prekindergarten program. Extended day care was offered to the threes and fours also.

The goal of the 5-year project (from 1974 to 1979) was to reduce school-related difficulties; this goal was met (Pierson, Bronson, Dromey, Swartz, Tivnan, & Walker, 1983). The public school "took the lead in assuring (but not necessarily providing) resources for parent information and support, adequate health care, developmental assessments, optimum early child stimulation, case coordination, and advocacy" (Pierson et al., 1985, p. 82).

Center for Early Development and Education. This program, under the direction of Bettye M. Caldwell, is more generally referred to as the Kramer Project in Little Rock, Arkansas. Caldwell's overriding goal was to develop a uni-

fied early childhood–elementary school program. The components of the program, summarized from her article, "Kramer School— Something for Everybody" (1972), and other articles (1977; 1986a; 1989) were as follows:

1. A comprehensive early childhood program beginning infancy, with home intervention offered on a biweekly basis, or enrollment in the educational program offered on the premises of the Kramer Elementary School. Children were enrolled when they were 6 months of age. The program served 12 babies, 16 toddlers, and 20 to 25 in each age group of threes, fours, and fives. The program was in operation from 6:45 A.M. to 5:15 P.M., with planned instruction and activities from 8 A.M. to 3:30 P.M. The different age groups were together in the unplanned times, and frequently during the main part of the day. There were also many planned (and unplanned) occasions when the older brothers and sisters in the elementary grades joined in the early childhood events.

2. A dynamic elementary program offering continuity of developmental support. As a matter-of-fact, the elementary school became more and more "ungraded" as the project developed.

3. Extended day care for all the Kramer children who needed it, year-round, with the traditional day-care supports. Many primary age children took advantage of the before-and-after school program, and during school holidays and vacation times.

4. A broad research program in child development and education.

5. A comprehensive array of supportive family services, using two social workers, a school psychologist, and an aid. Activities included in these supplementary services: a toy-lending library, clothing sale and exchange, parent-teacher coffee hours, parent-education discussions, school-wide family functions,

and monthly meetings of a "parent sounding board" to call attention to any development within the community that might have relevance to the project.

6. An on-site training program for staff, including the elementary teachers.

7. Practicum and student teaching placements for early childhood and elementary students. Each student teacher was assigned to *each* of the four groups: babies and toddlers, threes-to-fives, primary, and upper elementary for periods of time.

8. A home intervention program for 150 infants and toddlers whose families lived outside the Kramer area.

Altogether, the project touched the lives of approximately 400 children and their families. The project was initially funded by a federal grant, with support from the University of Arkansas and the local school district. It kept going without the grant for a few years but unfortunately has not continued. However, Little Rock schools now have before- and after-school care for their primary children. The Kramer school was a "school for the future"; the 1970s could not adjust to such a total innovation. Caldwell wrote in 1984 "One of our biggest challenges in terms of linkages is to make peace with the public schools" (p. 6).

Recommendations for Partnerships

It was not until the late 1980s that State Superintendents of schools and State Boards of Education become seriously interested in nondisabled children under 5 years of age. They have been joined or motivated by the National Governors' Association, the National Committee of Economic Development, and the Congress of the United States.

Selected recommendations of the Committee for Economic Development (1987) include:

1. Keep pregnant teens and those with babies in school. Developing the skills that will help them get and keep decently paid jobs is the best deterrent to repeat pregnancies and a lifetime of dependency.

2. Emphasize parenting education. Programs should instruct teen mothers—and also young fathers who ought to share the responsibility of parenthood—in the physical and emotional care of their children.

3. Provide day care for young mothers in school, preferably on-site. The policy toward young mothers used to be that help ended at delivery. We now know that that approach only exacerbates the problem. It will be easier to keep young mothers in school if they can be near their children. This is also the best logistical solution because on-site facilities provide the ideal opportunity to use day care for ongoing parenting education and for providing a stimulating environment for infants and toddlers (p. 27).

The 1988 statement of the National Association of State Boards of Education includes the following recommendation:

We recommend that public schools develop partnerships with other early childhood programs and community agencies to build and improve services for young children and their parents (p. viii).

The Council of Chief State School Officers has discovered that

the dichotomy between nurturing and education has been blurred beyond distinction both because of the unprecedented societal changes affecting the very young and because we know good care for young children promotes learning and good learning experiences are caring and nurturing. We know that families never cease being teachers; we have also learned that teachers must consider the well-being of the children they teach (unpaged).

An article in Phi Delta Kappan states, "Community institutions of all sorts will have to shoulder their share of the responsibility for making high-quality early childhood programs widely available and readily accessible. And public schools must be partners in that effort"

(Mitchell, 1989, p. 672). Mitchell is codirector of the Public School Early Childhood Study sponsored by Bank Street College and Wellesley College, and her statement reflects the findings of that study.

The National Governors' Association (1989) called for a comprehensive approach to child development, beginning with prenatal care and followed by early education coordinated with affordable child care.

The Association for Supervision and Curriculum Development in its publication about early childhood programs in public schools (Warger, 1988) states "When the artificial distinction between education and care is removed, public schools can provide children with an experience-based program that incudes individual and group activities, structured and unstructured play, time for listening, sharing stories, resting, and the opportunity to be in a safe and stimulating environment for as long as their parents are at work" (p. 102).

These statements indicate a growing sense of the needs of children and families, and the recognition that our public education system should play an important role in meeting these needs. The early childhood community has long recognized these needs, but now we are hearing it from groups with no vested interest in working with young children. Perhaps Caldwell's "school for the future" will soon become a reality.

Current Exemplary Programs

There is substantial interest in interventions that directly focus on educating and supporting parents as the most important factor in their child's development. Three such programs, the Minnesota Early Childhood and Family Education program (ECFE), the Missouri Parents as Teachers Program, and the New Futures School, are examples of this interest.

Minnesota Early Childhood and Family Education Program. Since its beginning in 1974, the ECFE program has served thousands of families and their infants, toddlers, and pre-school-aged children. Funds come from state and local taxes, parent fees, in-kind contributions from the school district, and grants. The Department of Community Education, within the public school system, administers the program.

The program includes weekly classes for parents and children together, where they

> participate for 15 to 45 minutes in developmentally appropriate activities in an environment that fosters fun, exploration, and mutual learning. During the remainder of the time, parents go to a parent discussion group and children are cared for in the early childhood room. Parent group participation is voluntary and usually centers on discussion of specific interests (e.g., child development or special interests of the parents) (Warger, 1988, p. 120).

All the parents of children from birth to kindergarten age and expectant parents are eligible. The teachers are school district employees who are licensed and hold 4-year degrees. In 1988 there were over 300 ECFE programs in the state of Minnesota.

Missouri Parents as Teachers Program. An expansion of the BEEP under the direction of Burton White is the Parents as Teachers program in Missouri. It is a cooperative effort of the Missouri Department of Elementary and Secondary Education, and the local school districts. Mildred Winter, former state program director, has described the services of the program:

1. Information and guidance before the baby is born, to help first-time parents prepare themselves psychologically

2. Information about things to look for and expect in a growing child, and guidance in fostering language, cognitive, social, and motor skill development.

3. Periodic checkups of the child's educational and sensory (hearing and vision) development to detect possible problems or handicaps. If serious problems are discovered,

help is sought from other agencies or professionals

4. A parent resource center, located in a school building, which provides a meeting place for parents and staff, and facilities for child care during parent meetings

5. Monthly hour-long private visits in the home or at the center to individualize the education program for each family

6. Monthly group meetings with other new parents to share experiences and discuss topics of interest (Winter, 1985, p. 96)

The program started in 1981 in four school districts, and proved so successful that in 1984 the State Department of Education authorized funding for all the 543 school districts in the state. In 1987 the National Center for Parents as Teachers was established at the University of Missouri–St. Louis.

The Executive Evaluation Summary (1985) summarized the key findings of the project as follows:

• PAT children demonstrated advanced intellectual and language development.

• PAT children demonstrated significantly more aspects of positive social development than did comparison children.

• PAT parents were more knowledgeable about child-rearing practices and child development than were comparison parents.

• Traditional characteristics of "risk" were not related to a child's development at age 3.

Traditional measures of "risk" (parents' age and education, income, single-parent families, number of younger siblings, and amount of alternative care received) have little or no relationship to measures of intelligence, achievement, and language development. PAT parents and children performed well, regardless of socio-economic disadvantages and other traditional risk factors (p. 3).

• PAT staff were successful in identifying and intervening at "at-risk" situations.

• PAT participation positively influenced parents' perceptions of school districts.

• PAT parents had positive feelings about the program's usefulness.

The New Futures School. An increasing number of public schools, particularly in large urban school districts, offer parent education and child-care services to students who are parents (Marx, Bailey, & Francis, 1988). The alternative high school in the Albuquerque, New Mexico, public school system is designed to help school-age parents "make responsible, informed decisions, complete their education, have healthy babies, and become well adjusted and self-sufficient" (Committee for Economic Development, 1987, p. 30). It provides classes for young mothers both before and after the birth of their children, including vocational classes, as well as a full range of health and social services. There are three onsite child-care facilities that not only care for the infants and toddlers, but also provide the staff an opportunity to observe the parenting skills of the young mothers, give mothers time to breast feed, and give experience to all students in classes on child care and development.

Many school districts nation-wide have (or are establishing) such programs that have been shown to increase the possibilities for better lives of young mothers and their children. In general, the efforts to include young fathers have failed, because the fathers are not around. The number of these programs will probably increase as a result of provisions in the Family Support Act of 1988 (P.L. 100-485).

Perhaps public education (and the nation) are ready for an expanded concept of our public schools, as advocated by Edward Zigler.

The "School of the Twenty-First Century"

Edward Zigler is the director of the Bush Center in Child Development and Social Policy at Yale

University. He advocates the return to a "concept of the community school as a local center for all the social services required by the surrounding neighborhood" (Zigler, 1987, p. 38). He argues for a school-based approach to meet the seven criteria that must be met for a satisfactory child-care system to emerge:

1. The child care system must be reliable and stable. It must be tied to a major institution that is well-known throughout American society.

2. Every child should have equal access to child care, and all ethnic and socio-economic groups should be integrated as fully as possible.

3. The primary goal of the system is the optimal development of the children using the system. The quality of care is essential.

4. Child care of high quality should be readily accessible from early in pregnancy through the first 12 years of life.

5. Such programs should address the entire range of human development—not only cognitive development but also personality development and physical and mental health.

6. The child-care system should involve true partnership between parents and the children's caretakers.

7. We should do everything we can to train, upgrade the pay, and increase the status of those individuals who care for the nation's children (Hamburg, 1987, p. 16).

Zigler (1988) suggests a school-based approach to implement these principles and calls for the "School of the 21st Century." Under his proposal, the schools could (and should) add a second system to its traditional organization starting with kindergarten. This second system has several components:

1. A preschool for threes and fours with college-trained, certificated head teachers and staff personnel with less formal credentials (Child Development Associates and aides)

2. A network of family day-care homes in the neighborhood to serve the infants and children up to age 3 who need out-of-home care. These homes are under school sponsorship and regulation

3. On-site child care before and after school for children from 3 to 12 years of age; also onsite child care for the school vacation times for children who need it

4. Information and referral services

5. Home visits by school personnel for all the children (birth through age 12) in the area served by the school

Zigler's proposal "brings into focus the critical issue of an institutional basis for early intervention to foster child health and development" (Hamburg, 1987, p. 16).

In an interview reported in February, 1989, Zigler answered the question "Can the School of the 21st Century come into being without federal legislation?" in the following way:

It's happening as we talk. In January, the state of Connecticut began a pilot program of three 21st Century Schools, though here they're called Family Resource Centers: there's one in a rural community, one in a suburb and one in central Hartford. The public schools in Columbus, Ohio, are planning 21st Century Schools, starting with a few, then expanding. Other states are asking us to help them—North Carolina, Alabama, Florida (Span, 1989, p. 84).

Comment

The emerging partnership between public education and very early care and education is a phenomenon of the late 20th century. It has been shown that this partnership is beneficial and possible. It increases the probability that nonmaternal infant/toddler educaring will be looked on more positively in the future. It also opens many new employment opportunities.

PARTNERSHIPS WITH BUSINESS

It is now taken for granted that "most women of child-bearing age work and are going to continue to work while at the same time having babies and raising children" (Philip Morris, 1989, p. 3). Other findings of the Harris telephone poll (sponsored by Philip Morris) of over 4,000 individuals include:

- America in the late 1980s clearly feels deep concern about the way children are treated in society (p. 2).
- The number of working women with small children will be rising dramatically (p. 4).
- Parents are scrambling much of the time to put together a package of child-care arrangements (p. 5).
- A 90% majority of the entire adult population favors employers being encouraged to include parental leave as a standard part of benefits that parents, especially mothers, receive (p. 16).
- Precisely those who obviously may be least capable of having the wherewithal to cope at home with a new baby and yet do not want to jeopardize their job situation when they get back are precisely the ones who are most frightened about asking for parental leave or even about child-care help in the first place (pp. 15–16).

Experience has shown that child care cannot be sold as something good for children, or even good for children and families. Perhaps it can be sold as something that will help people get off welfare and become productive workers. For many poor parents, particularly poor single mothers, the lack of safe, affordable child-care options combined with existing welfare policies creates a climate in which it is better not to work. This situation keeps those on public assistance firmly entrenched within the welfare system (Committee for Economic Development, 1987). The business community is beginning to recognize the potential importance of child care and related services.

Employer Involvement

Pat Schroeder (U.S. Congresswoman from Colorado) has devoted special attention to child care and family issues during her tenure in Washington. She co-chaired the 1987–1988 Congressional Caucus for Women's Issues during its study of employer-sponsored child care.

In an effort to involve the nation's public policy leaders in the child-care debate, the Caucus asked members of Congress to identify the most innovative examples of employer-sponsored child-care programs in their districts. From the more than 160 employers who were identified, 19 were chosen as "pioneers," and 25 were chosen as "best on the block." In selecting the companies, the Child Care Challenge Advisory Panel looked at the degree of employer involvement in the establishment and operation of the child-care program, and if the program was established by employer innovation or employee request. The list of the pioneer and best-on-the-block companies, as well as other outstanding companies is in appendix F. Included here are descriptions of a few of the employer programs that include infants and/or toddlers. The descriptions have been summarized from the *Report on Employer-Sponsored Child Care Services* dated May 5, 1988.

America West Airlines (Arizona). America West (Arizona) initiated its child-care program in 1986. The company operates both a home-based care network and an on-site center for its employees. The home-based care program consists of a network of 20 homes that provide around-the-clock care. Careful screening is done to ensure high quality child care, from drug screening of caregivers to a home safety inspection by the county and fire departments. A maximum of four children is permitted in order to ensure quality care and supervision. The company provides toys, cribs, tables, chairs, and other equipment. The company subsidizes between 25% and 50% of the parents' weekly child care costs. (Note: In Congresswoman Schroeder's talk to the Commonwealth Club of California on March 3, 1989, she commented

> Airlines have young employees. If you are circling over San Francisco in the fog for two hours and the child care center closed two hours ago, you have a stressed-out crew. I as a passenger don't want a stressed-out crew, and the airlines don't want a stressed-out crew. We found airlines that went out and found day care homes where the time constraints weren't as serious. They trained the people, did background checks, withheld the money from the employees so there was no hassle with collection, and then made the day care workers part of the airline employee system with the same benefits for travel, etc., as the other employees. That worked "fantastically" (Schroeder, 1989, p. 108).

B & B Associates (Connecticut). The B & B child-care program was started in 1985, can serve up to 25 children, and cares for infants through the age 4. Young school children may be enrolled in the center on a part-time basis as space allows. Only one-quarter of the children enrolled are children of B & B employees. The rest come from the surrounding community. Employees at B & B are eligible for a 15% discount at the center. Parents are encouraged to visit the child-care center during the day. Parents cite the convenience of the center as a plus in their employment with B & B Associates.

Bank of America (California). The Bank of America Foundation developed a program in 1985 called the California Child Care Initiative in response to the shortage of licensed quality care in California. The program is funded through a public-private partnership of 33 organizations and is designed to recruit and train family day-care providers; to provide technical assistance to help them get licensed and into operation; and to provide ongoing support to help them stay in business. In its first year of operation, it helped 230 persons who provide care for over 1,000 children across the state.

Deaconess Medical Center (Washington). They opened their first child center in 1981, a second facility in 1987. Children of 165 families receive child-care services. The center is open from 6:00 A.M. until after midnight, seven days a week. Children from 1 month to 12 years old are eligible to be in the center. The center's fees are slightly under the average community rates, and 35% of the operational expenses are picked up by the hospital. Results from a survey of parents who work at the hospital indicated that many choose to work at the Deaconess Medical Center because of the child-care services available. The hospital management attributes a drop in absenteeism, increased recruitment, and improved employee morale and productivity to the availability of child-care services.

Dominion Bank (Virginia). As the result of an employee survey, the Dominion Bank opened an onsite child-care center in 1986. According to the president of the bank, the establishment of the center was more a response to economic and social realities than benevolence to its workers. As a result of having an onsite center, the bank has noticed significant drops in absenteeism, tardiness, and employee turnover. The center cares for children from 6 weeks to 5 years old and is licensed to serve 70 children. Parents are encouraged to visit their children at the center and to become involved with the center through a parents advisory committee, a newsletter, and field trips. Dominion Bank also provides 6 weeks of paid maternity leave to its employees and up to 4 months of unpaid leave.

Rockwell International (Iowa). The Rockwell Employees Child Development Centers were developed in response to employee concerns about the ability to find affordable, quality child care. The center, which opened in 1986, is licensed for 250 children, is the largest child-care center in Iowa, and is one of the largest in the country. Rockwell International runs several programs for its workers: a preschool-age care program for children from 6 weeks through 5 years old; a school-age child-care program that provides before- and after-school care for first through third graders, with transportation provided; and a summer youth activities program that serves children 6 through 14 years old. Rockwell International subsidizes 20% of the center's operating budget. The company initially invested close to $400,000 to open the center. Although the program has only been in operation for a short while, Rockwell International is convinced it has been a positive effect on employee recruiting, retention, morale, and productivity. The company also believes the child-care program sends a positive message about Rockwell International's overall concern and commitment to its employees.

Employer Benefits

Employers who have implemented child-care programs for their workers' benefit agree on one thing in particular, that the benefits in implementing the program far outweigh any costs incurred to get the program running. Employers also overwhelmingly agree that increased employee morale, productivity, loyalty, and retention are the by-products of the establishment of a child care program for their workers. The parent-employees agree. "They feel more secure about their children's care, and this translates into greater productivity and improved attitudes toward work and the workplace" (Magid, 1989, p. 440).

The companies that participated in the Caucus's study estimated that they save anywhere from $25,000 to $2 million each year with regard to employee turnover as a result of employer-supported child care.

Many companies use the opening of a child-care center or program as an opportunity to reach out to the surrounding community. A large number of the employer-sponsored centers serve families in the community as well as employees. This is true most particularly among college and university and hospital child-care programs. Employers recognize these services as a valuable community relations tool.

It can be noticed from the descriptions of these employer-sponsored programs (and others) that family-care benefits, not just child-care, have joined the business scene. At some large companies, elder-care benefits have "displaced child care as the prerequisite for recruiting and keeping the best and the brightest" (Perkin, 1989, p. F19). We in the early childhood profession must fight to retain and expand the progress that has been made for the partnership between business and child care, and not allow the children to be given second place.

A recently added family benefit (which *does* include young children) is the granting of up to 10 weeks of leave (unpaid, so far) to care for a sick child or parent.

Other Employer Innovations

A chain of supermarkets provides a baby-sitting service for its customers. One of them features a color TV, a VCR, an aquarium, art supplies and building blocks, as well as cars, trucks, and stuffed animals.

The new Colorado Convention Center in Denver has onsite child care for 50 young children, including infants.

A law firm in Washington, D.C., provides its employees an onsite backup child-care facility for times when their usual arrangements fall through. They insist that the parents have lunch with the children, who may not come more than 5 days in a row.

Companies with cafeterias and canteens are offering carry-out food service, ranging from salads to extensive evening meals, including full-course Thanksgiving dinners.

An increasing number of employers are creating programs that allow parents time off to care for sick children at home, or assistance in finding a caregiver to come to the house. The cost of the health aide is partially picked up by the companies.

At least three major companies are giving baby bonuses to each newborn or adopted child of their employees.

Company-supplied vouchers for child care, permanent part-time work, paid parental leaves, flexitime, job sharing, and telecommuting are recent innovations that are helping employees with young children. Some businesses are banding together in small consortiums to start joint child-care centers for their employees.

Schroeder (1989) found hospitals which said

> "We will take in infants, handicapped children, and children with problems. While we don't have the money to pay people, we will guarantee that any senior who volunteers will not have to pay the medicare deductible when they get sick." All sorts of seniors showed up and not one ever quit. If you are senior and you can go and rock a baby for three hours a day and never have to worry about medicare deductibles again, that's a win-win situation (p. 108).

Before we decide that the business community will solve the child care crisis, we need to be reminded of some realistic facts. Edward Zigler responded to a question about employers providing child care for their workers in the following way (Span, 1989):

> We should applaud the companies that are doing it, but the numbers tell you that it's not a viable solution. There are six million employers in this country; only 3,500 do anything at all about day care and most of that is information and referral services. The other problem is that businesses have cycles. When a firm gets into trouble, the first thing to be closed is the day care center. Families can't have that (p. 84).

Friedman (1989) states that only about 900 companies have created a child-care center, and two-thirds of these are sponsored by hospitals.

SUMMARY

Parent participation and involvement can result in a true partnership between parent and educarer. This is especially important in programs for infants and toddlers.

A young child needs a parent who is nurturing, loving, enjoying, teaching, and coping. A quality infant/toddler program will endeavor to create or enhance these qualities in each parent by its day-by-day interactions with parents, both planned and incidental. The major effects of parent involvement are that parents develop more positive attitudes about their child's program and the program personnel, and perhaps even more important, they develop more positive attitudes about themselves as parents and about their children.

Requirements and suggestions for effective partnerships include a variety of conferences, both scheduled and unscheduled; a variety of written communications from both parent and educarer; a written description of policies and procedures; telephone calls; and parent meetings, both semiformal and informal. Particular attention must be given to the daily interchanges at the transition times (delivery and pick-up). Parents should also be involved in in-class participation if their own schedule permits, and be given opportunities for out-of-class projects that are related to the program.

Two new partnerships are emerging that will have considerable impact on infant/toddler care and education. Public education is now openly admitting that what happens to children before the age of 5 years, and to their families, is important. Some schools have initiated programs that even include infants and toddlers. Three pioneer programs, one of which started in 1933, were perhaps influential in this new development. They are the Children's Centers in California, the Brookline Early Education Project in Massachusetts, and the Kramer School in Arkansas.

In the late 1980s strong statements about public education's involvement in early childhood programs were issued by the National Association of State Boards of Education, the Council of Chief State School Officers, the Association for Supervision and Curriculum Development, and Phi Delta Kappa (the professional educational organization). The National Governors' Association and the National Committee of Economic Development also recommend school involvement.

Current exemplary programs include the Minnesota Early Childhood and Family Education Program, the Missouri Parents as Teachers program, and the New Futures School. A proposal for the future has been made by Zigler in his "School of the 21st Century."

The nation's business community is also beginning to realize the benefits of implementing child care or related programs for their employee-parents. However most of the companies are involved in information and referral services, and not in directly providing child care.

SUGGESTED ACTIVITIES AND QUESTIONS

1. Write a set of standards about parent involvement in infant/toddler programs that should be a part of any licensing regulations.

2. Check recent issues of current magazines and newspapers for reports of school or business involvement in early childhood care and eduction programs, including programs for parents. Recent articles have appeared in the professional journals, but also in issues of *Parents, Working Woman, Working Mother, Newsweek, US News and World Report, Nation's Business, Fortune, Entrepreneur,* and *Changing Times. Ladies Home Journal, Good Housekeeping, McCall's,* and *Redbook* sometimes contain related articles.

3. Write to Consumer Information Center, Pueblo, CO 81009 for a copy of the Consumer Information Catalog (free). It lists articles and booklets available from over 30 agencies of the federal government, many of which are free. Educators, libraries, and other nonprofit groups who wish 25 copies of their quarterly catalog of consumer information may get on their mailing list. Many of the publications will be useful to educarers and to parents of young children.

4. Interview parents of an infant or toddler who is in a nonmaternal program. Ask what they expect of the program, and if their expectations have been met. In particular, ask questions about their relationships and involvement in the program.

5. Interview a director or an educarer in a center-based program, and a family day-care home pro-

vider, focusing on the activities that include parents.

SUGGESTED READINGS

Beck, R. (1982). Beyond the stalemate in child care public policy. In E. F. Zigler & E. W. Gordon (Eds.), *Day care: Scientific and social policy issues.* Boston: Auburn House.

Becker, R. M. (1986). Parent involvement: Research and practice. In L. G. Katz (Ed.), *Current topics in early childhood education, 6,* 85-122.

Bjorklund, G., & Burger, C. (1987). Making conferences work for parents, teachers, and children. *Young Children, 42* (2), 26–31.

Brazelton, T. B. (1984). Cementing family relationships. In L. L. Dittmann (Ed.), *The infants we care for* (rev. ed.). Washington, DC: National Association for the education of Young Children.

Brazelton, T. B. (1985). *Working and caring.* Reading, MA: Addison-Wesley.

Brazelton, T. B. (1989). *Families: Crisis and caring.* Reading, MA: Addison-Wesley.

Bromwich, R. (1984). *Working with parents and infants: An interactional approach.* Baltimore: University Park Press.

Burud, S., & Ranson, C. (1988). *Directory of corporate child care assistance programs.* Pasadena, CA: Child Care Benefits Consultants.

Caldwell, B. M. (1972). Kramer School—Something for everybody. In S. J. Braun & E. P. Edwards, *History and theory of early childhood education* (pp. 372–386). Worthington, OH: Jones. (Out of print, but check your library)

Caldwell, B. M. (1986). Day care and the public schools—Natural allies, natural enemies. *Educational Leadership, 44* (3), 34–39.

Caldwell, B. M. (1989). A comprehensive model for integrating child care and early education. *Teachers College Record, 90* (3), 404–414.

Caldwell, B., & Rorex, J. (1977). A day at the Kramer Baby House. In M. D. Cohen (Ed.), *Developing programs for infants and toddlers.* Washington, DC: Association for Childhood Education International.

Carter, M. (1984, Fall). Face-to-face communication: Understanding and strengthening the partnership. *Beginnings, 14–17.*

Core, M. (1982). Parent communication: Making the most of transition time. *Child Care Information Exchange, 26,* 33–39.

Dittmann, L. L. (1981). Where have all the mothers gone, and what difference does it make? In B. Weissbourd & J. S. Musick (Eds.), *Infants: Their social environments.* Washington, DC: National Association for the Education of Young Children.

Duff, R. E., Heinz, M. C., & Husband, C. L. (1978). Toy lending library: Linking home and school. *Young Children, 33* (4), 16–24.

Dusky, L. (1988). *The best companies for women.* New York: Simon & Schuster.

Elardo, P., & Caldwell, B. M. (1974). The Kramer adventure: A school for the future? *Childhood Education, 50* (3), 143–152.

Fenichel, E. S., & Eggbeer, L. (1989, September). Educating allies: Issues and recommendations in the training of practitioners to work with infants, toddlers and their families. *Zero to Three, 10* (1), 1–7.

Friedman, D. E. (1984). The challenge of employer-supported child care. In L. G. Katz (Ed.), *Current topics in early childhood education, 5,* 165–188.

Galinsky, E. (1986a). Contemporary patterns of child care. In N. Gunzenhauser & B. D. Caldwell (Eds.), *Group care for young children.* Skillman, NJ: Johnson & Johnson.

Galinsky, E. (1986b). How do child care and maternal employment affect children? *Child Care Information Exchange, 48,* 19–23.

Galinsky, E. (1988). Parents and teacher-caregivers: Sources of tension, sources of support. *Young Children, 43* (3), 4–12.

Galinsky, E., & Hooks, W. (1977). *The new extended family: Day care that works.* Boston: Houghton Mifflin.

Gordon, I. J. (1977). Parent education and parent involvement: Retrospect and prospect. *Childhood Education, 54* (2), 71–79.

Gordon, J. (1986, July). Childcare professionalism and the family. *Child Care Information Exchange,* 19–23.

Greenberg, P. (1989). Parents as partners in young children's development and education: A new American fad? Why does it matter? *Young Children, 44* (4), 61–75.

Greenman, J. (1989, February). Living in the real world. *Child Care Information Exchange,* (65), 25–27.

Greenspan, S., & Greenspan, N. T. (1989). *The essential partnership: How parents and children can meet the emotional challenges of infancy and childhood.* New York: Viking Penguin.

Hoffman, C. M. (1985). *Public education and day care.* Lancaster, PA: Technomic.

Honig, A. S. (1979). *Parent involvement in early childhood education* (rev. ed.). Washington, DC: National Association for the Education of Young Children.

Honig, A. S. (1982). Parent involvement in early childhood education. In B. Spodek (Ed.), *Handbook of research in early childhood education.* New York: Free Press.

Infants and toddlers away from their mothers? (1987). *Young Children, 42* (4), 40–42.

Ispa, J. M., Gray, M. M., & Thornburg, K. R. (1988). Parents, teachers, and day care children: Patterns of interconnection. *Journal of Research in Childhood Education, 3* (1), 76–84.

Kagan, S. L. (1989). The care and education of America's young children: At the brink of a paradigm shift? In F. J. Macchiarola & A. Gartner (Eds.), *Caring for America's children, 37* (2), 70–83. New York: The Academy of Political Science.

Kagan, S. L., & Zigler, E. F. (1987). Early schooling: A national opportunity? In S. L. Kagan & E. F. Zigler (Eds.), *Early schooling: The national debate.* New Haven: Yale University Press.

Kahn, A. J., & Kamerman, S. B. (1987). *Child care: Facing the hard choices.* Dover, MA: Auburn.

Kamerman, S. B., & Kahn, A. J. (1987). *The responsive workplace: Employers and a changing labor force.* New York: Columbia University Press.

Katz, L. G. (1980). Mothering and teaching—Some significant distinctions. In L. G. Katz (Ed.), *Current topics in early childhood education, 3,* 47–63.

Kristensen, N., & Billman, J. (1987). Supporting parents and young children: Minnesota Early Childhood Family Education Program. *Childhood Education, 63* (4), 276–282.

Levering, R., & Moskowitz, M. (1986). *The 100 best companies to work for in America.* New York: New American Library. (or 1987, New York: Signet)

Magid, R. Y. (1989). The consequences of employer involvement in child care. *Teachers College Record, 90* (3), 434–443.

McCracken, J. B. (1986). *So many goodbyes.* Washington, DC: National Association for the Education of Young Children.

Mernit, S. (1989, June). The newest in family-friendly benefits. *Working Mother, 12* (6), 64, 66–68.

Meservey, L. D. (1989). Handle with care: Strategies for retaining children in your program. *Child Care information Exchange,* (67), 21–24.

Multi-age caregiving (special issue). (1985). *Beginnings, 2* (1).

Muscari, A., & Morrone, W. W. (1989). *Child care that works.* New York: Doubleday.

Naisbitt, J., & Aburdene, P. (1985). *Reinventing the corporation: Transforming your job and your company for the new information society.* New York: Warner.

National Association for the Eduction of Young Children. (1988). *Employer-assisted child care resource guide* (rev. ed.). Washington, DC: Author.

National Governors' Association Committee in Human Resources and Center for Policy Research. (1987). *Focus on the first sixty months: A handbook of promising prevention programs for children zero to five years of age.* Washington, DC: National Governors' Association.

Parents and teachers (special issue). (1984, Fall). *Beginnings.*

Parent involvement (special issue). (1985). *Dimensions, 14* (1).

Peters, D., & Benn, J. (1980). Day care: Support for the family. *Dimensions, 9,* 78–82.

Powell, D. R. (1977). *The interface between families and child care programs: A study of parent-caregiver relationships.* Detroit: Merrill-Palmer Institute.

Powell, D. R. (1980). Toward a socioecological perspective of relations between parents and child care programs. In S. Kilmer (Ed.), *Advances in early education and day care, 1,* 203–226.

Powell, D. (1984). Enhancing the effectiveness of parent education. In L. Katz (Ed.), *Current topics in Early Childhood Education.* Vol. 5. Norwood, NJ: Ablex.

Powell, D. R. (1986). Parent education and support programs. *Young Children, 41,* 47–63.

Powell, D. R. (Ed.). (1988). Parent education in early childhood intervention: Emerging directions in theory, research and practice. *Advances in Applied Developmental Psychology.* Vol. 3. Norwood, NJ: Ablex.

Powell, D. R. (1989). *Families and early childhood programs.* Research Monograph Vol. 3. Washington, DC: National Association for the Education of Young Children.

Savage, J. (1989). Understanding the working parents' plight. *Day Care and Early Education, 16* (4), 42–43.

Scarr, S. (1984). *Mother care/Other care.* New York: Basic Books.

Span, P. (1989). Should neighborhood schools be child care centers, too? *Working Mother, 12* (2), 82, 84.

Travis, N. E., & Perreault, J. (1980). Day care as a resource to families. In L. G. Katz (Ed.), *Current topics in early childhood education, 3,* 127–137.

Vance, M. B., & Boals, B. (1985). The role of parents & caregivers: Nurturing infants. *Dimensions, 13* (2), 19–21.

Weissbourd, C. (1981). Supporting parents as people. In B. Weissbourd & J. Musick (Eds.), *Infants: Their social environments.* Washington, DC: National Association for the Education of Young Children.

Weider, S. (1989, September). Mediating successful parenting: Guidelines for practitioners. *Zero to Three, 10* (1), 21–22.

Wellesley College Center for Research on Women. (1989). *Learning together: A national directory of teen parenting and child care programs.* Wellesley, MA: Author.

Yogman, M. W., & Brazelton, T. B. (Eds.). (1986). *In support of families.* Cambridge, MA: Harvard University Press.

Zigler, E. F., & Goodman, J. (1982). The battle for day care in America: A view from the trenches. In E. F. Zigler & E. W. Gordon (Eds.), *Day care: Scientific and social policy issues.* Boston: Auburn House.

Zigler, E. F., & Weiss, H. (1985). Family support systems: An ecological approach to child development. In R. N. Rapoport (Ed.), *Children, youth, and families* (pp. 166–205). New York: Cambridge University Press.

12

Partnerships in Action

A teacher effects eternity; he can never tell where his influence stops.
Henry Brooke Adams

The principles and methods described in the preceding chapters apply to the best-funded and thoroughly staffed infant/toddler programs. They apply equally as well to any setting that is less than ideal, because children's needs are the same regardless of the quality of the program.

The application of these principles and methods is clearly shown in the following "typical days" in the lives of four "typical" young children in infant/toddler programs. The first three are enrolled in a licensed center-based program, funded by parent fees and the college of education at a midwestern university. The center is staffed by full-time professional early childhood educators, part-time graduate assistants, and a rotating group of student teachers. The fourth typical day takes place in a family day-care home in which the provider is a certificated early childhood educator. The program is funded by parent fees, state subsidies, and monies from the Child Care Food Program. It is a large family day-care home because there are

more than six children present for 2 or more hours at a time. Large family day-care homes in Iowa must be registered, and must meet minimum standards as specified by the Iowa Department of Human Services (The Children's Foundation, 1988).

The descriptions were written by the actual educarers, but all names are fictitious to protect the privacy of the adults and children alike. The photographs represent children of the appropriate gender and age.

These descriptions represent just one day in the national infant/toddler day-care picture, but the "issues, complexities, and nuances of the children's lives played out in these settings may illuminate the larger day care landscape" (Suransky, 1984, p. 54).

So that greater numbers of young children receive everything they deserve, the concluding chapter of this book contains an introduction to adult advocacy for children.

A DAY IN THE LIFE OF LUTHER
(3½-month-old boy)

SETTING: A day-care center for 84 children from 2 months to 60 months of age. The infant-toddler group serves children from 2 months to 3 years. It has two large playrooms connected by a nap room, and a bathroom. The infant room serves as the play and care center for 12 infants and young toddlers, with a staff of five. The room looks inviting. Its cheerfully painted walls are lined with colorful pictures. It has a feeling of spaciousness. At child's eye level, the space is broken up with a variety of shelving indicating areas of different uses. The shelves hold rattles, musical toys, dolls, cube blocks, and other age-appropriate materials. They also serve as supports for Busy Boxes, Cradle Gyms,

A baby is an inestimable blessing and a bother—
Mark Twain. (Early Childhood Education Center)

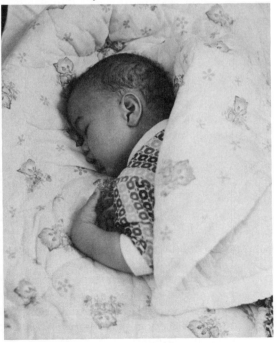

and mobiles. The lower sections of two walls are lined with long metal mirrors, mounted so that sitting infants can enjoy their images.

The floor is covered with indoor/outdoor carpet, with different spots temporarily covered with a soft blanket for the infants when they are placed on the floor. One area is covered with a patchwork of carpet samples of different colors and textures. The area under and around the tables used for eating and messy play is covered with a large, heavy-duty piece of plastic, securely taped to the carpet. Another strip of plastic on the floor is marked with the outlines of selected toys that are kept in the area, to encourage shape-matching activities.

A wooden platform fills a large bay window area. Its closely railed sides make it a safe, out-of-the-way spot for infants to observe the sights and sounds of the activities of the others without being underfoot. It is about 1½ feet off the floor, and the steps leading to it offer a practice spot for beginning stair climbers.

Adult-sized rocking chairs are in constant use, as a relaxing or comfort zone for adults and children. Two broad-based scooter chairs are available to provide mobility to beginning walkers.

Essential equipment, such as the large Plexiglas recordkeeping board, cases of diapers, a mountain of bibs, shelves of baby food and formula, a refrigerator, and a hotplate, are placed for easy access. Most important of all is the warm but animated atmosphere created by caring, knowledgeable adult staff members.

The center is open from 7:30 A.M. to 5:30 P.M. 5 days a week. Luther's day takes place on a Monday during the month of January.

7:25 A.M.: Luther arrives, warmly enveloped in his plaid bunting, in his daddy's arms.

Phil: His mama say he can eat rice cereal today.
Educarer: Good morning, Phil. So, Luther gets a little treat—I bet he will like that!

Phil: Harriet gave some to him over the weekend, but she say he don't use the spoon too good, and most of the food was all over his face.

Educarer: He will catch on to that spoon in no time. Does this mean that Luther will be getting other foods too?

Phil: Yeah, doctor say he can try one new food each week once his stomach gets used to the stuff. He say he should start with fruits and then try yellow vegetables, then mix in green vegetables and meats.

Educarer: That's great! Did you find that Luther was satisfied longer after feedings this weekend?

Phil: Harriet say that the solid food will fill him up better.

Educarer: Does he need less to drink? Will we be needing to think about changing the amount of formula?

Phil: For now he not eating enough to make a difference, he only getting a teaspoon down, but when he's eating more, he'll probably take less milk.

Educarer: That's great! I'll make a note on the daily chart (which hangs on the wall) that Luther will be starting on solid foods, and let the cook know so she'll be prepared. Just let us know what you'd like him to try next.

Phil: Oh yeah, Harriet say she thinks he'll eat better if you give him the cereal before his bottle.

Educarer: Sounds good, thanks.

Luther, who has slept through all this, is passed from his dad's arms to the educarer's. With a gentle stroke on his cheek, the educarer says good morning to the baby.

Educarer: I'll go unwrap him in his crib while you sign him in.

The educarer takes Luther to his crib in the nap room, lays him down, and unzips his bunting. She gently takes out each arm and then each leg; she makes a diaper check. He's damp. She raises the side of the crib and goes for the bucket of changing supplies.

Luther doesn't notice the quick exchange of diapers. He is rolled over on his tummy. The crib side is checked to be sure it is securely latched in the top position, even though Luther is only rolling from side to side in his sleep. The educarer takes the bunting and wet diaper with her and replaces the supply bucket on the shelf.

7:35 A.M.: Rejoining Phil in the playroom, she puts Luther's bunting in his own cubby. The diaper goes into a closed container in the bathroom. She washes her hands, and then records the diaper change and nap time on the daily board. Phil's check-in information says that Luther woke up at 5:45, when he had an 8-ounce bottle of formula.

Educarer: I see Luther slept late this morning.

Phil: Yeah, a big weekend, I guess.

Educarer: Phil, what about feeding times? And how much do you want him to have?

Phil: Harriet say Luther will get cereal two times a day for now. You can give it to him at lunch time, and she'll give it to him when he gets home. Let him have whatever he'll take.

Educarer: Sounds great, Phil. Thanks for the information. It really helps us when Harriet and you make this change for Luther over the weekend. We'll watch for any tummy troubles, but it sounds like he's doing fine. Thanks, Phil. Have a great day.

Phil: It's my day on the road, so if Luther has any problem you'll have to call Harriet at school.

Educarer: O.K. Bye.

7:40 A.M.: a quick peek at Luther shows he hasn't moved a muscle. He is checked periodically. He rests soundly, even though there are the sounds of other arrivals in the area.

10:00 A.M.: Luther is starting to be active in his sleep. He has rolled on his side and is sleeping with his head against the bumper: he turns his head from side to side and then is still. Another child cries, and Luther's eyes pop open but close again. The caregiver gives him a reassuring pat and pulls the blanket up around his body. His sleep is not as settled now. His lower lip quivers and his hand moves.

10:15 A.M.: Luther's eyes open slowly, but then fall closed. A deep sigh, he rubs his face on the sheet, and then they open again. He stares, and then begins to focus. A big yawn, and then he pushes his head off the sheet, looking.

Educarer: Hey there, Luther, are you ready to get going? (She maintains eye and voice contact as she walks over to the shelf for the diaper changing supplies.) Have a good rest? (She offers her finger, which he grips in his palm. She lowers the crib side with her free hand.) I'll bet your diapers are soaked. You took such a long nap. Let's take care of that right now.

She snuggles close to his face, humming a snatch of song. They touch nose to nose; she moves back a little; he makes a gurgling sound, which she imitates. They "talk" face to face. Luther is still gripping her hand. With the other, the caregiver taps his nose, says "Boop"; then she runs her finger around his ear, down his neck, under his chin, and down to his tummy. She gives his tummy a rub.

Educarer: Okay, let's change those diapers . . . One snap, boop, boop, boop . . . There's that tummy. (She rubs his bare skin. Luther laughs.) Where are those feet? (She pulls his legs out of his sleeper.) There they are. (She runs her hand down one leg to the ankle, then holds both legs at the ankles and moves them in a running motion.) Look at those legs go! (She smiles, and lifts his trunk to remove the wet diaper, immediately slipping a dry one under him, with one end over his tummy. She cleans the diaper area with a moist towelette, and moves the diaper end over him so he can air dry. She fastens the diaper.) In go those toes, and snap, snap, snap, you're ready to go. (She wipes her hands on a towelette, picks up Luther, slipping one hand under his shoulder blade and extending her fingers up to his neck and head. The other hand is under his bottom.) Up we go! (When he is secure on her shoulder, she picks up the supply bucket and the soiled diaper.) Let's go find all your friends.

The bucket is returned to its shelf and the diaper thrown in the container. Luther is set down on a blanket on the floor, while the edu-

carer washes her hands* and records the diaper change and wake-up time on the daily chart. She reviews the information already recorded: Up at 5:45, bottle at 5:50, nap from 7:30 to 10:15. She returns to Luther, and picks him up.

Educarer: Let's get something going for you—I bet you're going to be hungry real soon. (They go to the room refrigerator, take out the bottle with Luther's name on it, and put it in the bottle warmer.) Let's go visit for awhile until the milk is warm. (They walk over to a sunny corner of the room. Colorful posters are on the lower part of the walls, and two mobiles are hanging from the ceiling within the babies' visual range.)

10:25 A.M.: The educarer sits down on the floor with Luther on her lap facing her. She brings up her knees to form a V, and places the baby in the valley formed by her bent legs. They are joined by 16-month-old Melissa, who is carrying a teddy bear.

Educarer: Melissa, I think Luther would like to see your friend, Mr. Bear. Can you put him on Luther's tummy so he can see Mr. Bear's red tongue? Show me your red tongue, too. . . . There is it, just like Mr. Bear's. (The educarer draws Melissa close, with one arm around her waist. Melissa touches Luther's ear.) I like the way you are careful when you touch Luther. That's just the way I do it too, Melissa. Did that tickle? (Luther smiles and gazes at Melissa. His eyes turn back to the educarer when she begins to talk again.) Melissa, can you show Luther what you like to do with Mr. Bear? (Melissa firmly hugs the bear.) Oh, Melissa. I like hugs too. Will Bear hug me? (Melissa offers her furry friend, which the educarer places close to her heart.) Your bear is a good hugger, Melissa. Let's see what Luther thinks of his hugs. (Bear is snuggled face to face with Luther, who laughs as its soft body rubs his face and tummy.) So soft . . . Luther likes the way he

---

*Author's note: The changing surface and the sink handles need to be wiped with disinfectant.

feels when Bear hugs him too. Thanks for sharing Bear with Luther. You are a good sharing friend, Melissa.

10:40 A.M.: Luther is getting hungry.

Educarer: Melissa, thanks for talking to him while he had to wait. You helped him learn how to be a happy waiter. Do you think Bear would like something to eat too? (Melissa trots off to the play kitchen area, finds a Tyke Bike, and wheels off looking for some new excitement, leaving Bear and all thoughts of food.)

The educarer makes a quick diaper check (dry), picks up Luther, and together they go to the daily chart. She records ''dry at 10:40'' and rereads the feeding information. Another adult is there, and reaches over to take Luther, so that the educarer can wash her hands.

10:45 A.M.: Luther's educarer and he go to the shelf holding small bowls, feeding spoons, and a box of dry baby cereal. Luther is pacified by the educarer's tone of voice as she tells him what she is doing.

Educarer: Two tablespoons of cereal in the bowl . . . and let's get your bottle. (They settle down again on the floor, with Luther in the V of the educarer's legs, facing her. She tests the temperature of the formula, and pours a little into the bowl.) Ooo, you're going to love this cereal, Luther. (She takes his right hand in her left, strokes it, and guides it away from the cereal bowl. She puts a small bit of cereal in the spoon, and her mouth opens involuntarily as she brings the spoon toward Luther. His mouth forms a puckering circle as his tongue comes forward to suck. The educarer carefully guides the spoon to the back of his tongue and lays the cereal down the back of his throat.) Good stuff, huh? (He wrinkles his face in uncertainty. Food runs out of his mouth as he tries to work the corners of his mouth and chin with the edge of the spoon, and back in it goes.) Not too bad, old boy. (Several more small bites are eaten with the scoop and rescoop action. As another staff member passes by, Luther's educarer asks her to get a warm washcloth for them.)

11:10 A.M.: Luther takes two tablespoons of cereal and pushes the last bit out and gurgles.

Educarer: That all you want for now? (She cleans his face as best she can with the spoon and talks to him in low tones as they wait for the washcloth. Carefully she wipes his face with the warm cloth.) There you go. You look so nice. (She draws him near and nuzzles face to clean face. They pick up the bowl and towel and go to get the bottle. Luther gives a bubble as he is moved to her shoulder.) Feel better? (The still warm bottle is retrieved and is taken to a rocking chair where caregiver and baby make themselves comfortable.)

Luther is placed low in the crook of her arm, next to her heart. They make eye contact as she smiles to him and begins a rhythmic rock in the chair. Comfortable and secure, she offers the bottle to Luther by gently sliding it along his lower lip until he take it. His mouth opens reflexively and he sucks contentedly. With a big sigh his whole body heaves and he works intently on his bottle of formula.

His educarer watches as he drinks. Stroking his hand she sings quietly to him. He answers occasionally with a hum of contentment. A dribble of milk runs out of the corner of his mouth. The educarer moves the edge of his bib to catch the drip without disrupting his activity. Intent on sucking, Luther is still and relaxed. He and the adult enjoy the peaceful time together. She rocks and sings to enhance his concentration on sucking.

11:20 A.M.: Luther arches his back and wriggles, pushing the nipple away. He fusses as he wrinkles his face into a cry.

Educarer: What seems to be the problem? (She holds his bottle to see how many ounces he's taken. The bottle is two thirds empty.) Are you all done? (She moves him to her shoulder as she flips his bib so it is between him and her. She gently rocks as she pats from the base of his back up to his shoulders over and over again. He quiets as soon as she starts to rock. They rock as she pats—over and over again.

She wonders if maybe he is finished. They rock some more . . . up comes the bubble. She offers the bottle once again to be sure he's satisfied, and he settles in for the rest of the formula.)

11:35 A.M.: Once again the familiar rock, but he's now more attentive to the adult's face. She smiles and strokes his hand. The end of the bottle comes up as he sucks out the last drop. He stops sucking. His educarer moves him onto her lap so that he is facing her. She wipes around his mouth and checks his diaper.

Educarer: Let's see if you have another bubble. (She puts him to her shoulder. He burps and spits up a bit as she is putting him in position.) Hey, a good one—you got us both that time. (She gets up from the chair, puts the bottle and bib away and goes to the information board.) She writes:

11:00 2 T rice cereal
11:15 6 oz. formula
11:40 diaper change

11:40 A.M.: They go to his cubby for a fresh set of clothes, an 18″ by 18″ piece of white butcher paper, and the diaper-changing bucket. They settle down on the floor.

Educarer: You'll feel better as soon as we get those wet diapers off. (She centers him on the paper.) We'll make this quick since you just ate. (She quickly removes his sour-smelling suit while telling him all about what a good eater he had been, and how big he was going to be if he eats that well all the time. She replaces the soiled suit with a fresh one.) First one arm and then the other . . . (She puts on only the top half.) Now these diapers . . . (As she opens his diaper she finds him to be not only wet but soiled. She wipes him off as best she can with the diaper edges and rolls it into a ball. She then uses a towelette from the bucket to remove the rest.) There you go, and now a clean diaper. One, two, three. (The diaper is rolled up into the butcher paper, and the bucket goes back on the shelf. Luther is scooped up, along with the diaper and his soiled sleeper.)

11:45 A.M.: As they go across the room his educarer plans a place for him to play. She sees an infant seat and sits Luther in it. She angles it at a 60 degree angle so that his lunch will settle and he can play with the mobile that she will set him next to. With the seat belt fastened between his legs and around his waist she taps the mobile to catch his eye and helps him to get involved in it. Luther is full, clean, and happy, and is able to play on his own in a quiet prepared area while she puts the soiled diaper in a plastic bag, seals it, and throws it away. She rinses out the soiled outfit and puts it in a bag in the baby's cubby. She washes her hands with soap and water, and goes back to the information board.

11:50 A.M.: She notes on the chart "11:40 BM." Out of the corner of her eye she is watching Luther. The mirror lining the wall that he is sitting next to has captivated him. He stares expressionlessly at the baby in the mirror. The breeze moves the mobile and Luther is involved with it again, watching the colors and shapes move.

12:00 P.M.: A clean flannel blanket is spread out on the carpet, and is prepared with rattles and rocking toys. Luther's educarer sits next to his seat and loosens the strap. She lays him down on the blanket on his tummy moving the infant seat out of the way. She places the toys within his view and reach. Luther is so excited. His arms and legs fly as he arches his back to lift his head off the blanket. Back down . . . that's hard work, but up again they go for a second, over and over again.

While Luther is exercising, Travis brings a book over to the adult. He backs his way into her lap and gets comfortable. Luther gurgles to himself as he plays.

Luther is flinging his arms. He swipes his right ear again and again. The next time, much to his surprise, he finds a rattle. He startles at the sound. With a wild fling of his arm he knocks the rattle under his cheek.

Educarer: Better move the rattle for Luther, Travis. We wouldn't want him to fall on it. (She reaches over and moves the rattle into Luther's hand. She then initiates a roll by laying her arm behind his back and tipping him into her arm.) Over you go, (Once on his back Luther rediscovers the mobile with a squeal.) Travis, listen to the story that Luther is telling. Let's see if we can say it back to him.

Educarer and Travis: Ae, Ah, Ae, Ah (Luther quickly looks in their direction, and responds, "ah, ah, ah." The educarer puts Luther on her legs in the V sit.)

Educarer: Ah, Ah, Ah. (Luther responds. They exchange sounds, Luther waiting and watching his caregiver wide-eyed to see what will be next.) I've got your fingers. (She strokes her thumb against his fingers.) Let's take a walk up your arm. (As she walks her fingers up his arm, Luther begins to laugh.) Here's your neck and here's your chin, we'll skip right over that mouth . . . and there's that *nose*. (As she says "nose" she gathers him near and rubs noses and nuzzles with him. He giggles and laughs out loud.) Hey, did you hear that, Luther? (The educarer shakes the hand still gripping the rattle. He looks at the rattle. She reaches for another rattle and shakes it on the other side.) What a surprise. (He looks around to find it.) Let's try that again.

12:15 P.M.: Luther drops his rattle as he stretches and makes a large yawn. He wrinkles his face and fusses as he bats at his right ear.

Educarer: Are you getting tired? (She once again checks his diapers. They are dry.)

The educarer moves Luther to her shoulder, picks up the blanket and rattles, and stands up. She puts the toys in the "toys to be washed" bucket, the blanket in laundry basket, and marks the information chart that Luther's diapers were checked and found to be dry at 12:15. They find a rocking chair and sit.

Educarer: Hey, Luther, let's rock for a minute. (With Luther on her shoulder, she begins the slow rhythmic rock and gentle "heartbeat" pat on his back. She hums quietly to him. He is very tired. With a great sigh, his body quivers and he molds to her arms. They rock.)

12:25 P.M.: Sound asleep, Luther is placed in his crib. Again the educarer carefully lays him down on his tummy. "Sweet dreams," she whispers as she covers him with his blanket. She raises the crib side to the top and checks it, and goes to record his nap time on the information board. As she writes down the time, she anticipates another 2-hour rest for Luther. She checks on him frequently.

1:10 P.M.: Luther's sleep is less settled. He has kicked his blanket away. His arms and legs thrash as he seeks a comfortable position. The educarer replaces his blanket quietly and strokes his back gently to relax him.

1:15 P.M.: Luther whimpers as he rubs his nose back and forth on the sheet. Again he kicks away his blanket. A few more pats help Luther to relax again.

1:25 P.M.: Luther is just not comfortable. He whimpers again. His glassy eyes open unwillingly as he gathers a mournful cry. The educarer goes to his crib. Her voice is low and reassuring as she lowers the side of his crib to take him to a rocking chair to comfort him. He settles to her voice. Snuggled on her shoulder, they begin to rock. She notices how warm Luther's body feels next to hers. She presses her lips to his forehead . . . yes, he is warm. She decides that the nurse had better check him to see just how warm he is. A quick diaper check finds that Luther is still dry.

1:35 P.M.: The educarer looks over the information chart and records the newest information about Luther's nap and diaper. Luther, wrapped in his blanket, and his educarer are off to the nurse's office. Luther is very drowsy, and is relaxed on his educarer's shoulder as they reach the office.

Nurse: What nice bundle do you have there?
Educarer: Luther seems to be restless in his sleep and I thought he might have a temperature. He feels so warm. (The nurse takes Luther.)
Nurse: He does seem warm, doesn't he! Let's just check to see. (They disappear into a sup-

ply closet and return with a thermometer, jar of Vaseline, gauze pad, and fresh diaper. She takes Luther to the crib and lays him on his back. He stares blankly as she chats with him and loosens his sleeper.)

Educarer: His diaper was still dry when I got him up, and his last change was at 11:40.

Nurse: He looks like he's just getting up. (The nurse carefully holds his ankles to lift his bare bottom and insert the thermometer.) Has he been lying on his right ear? It looks a little red. (She continues to talk with him while she listens to the educarer's report.)

Educarer: He was fussing with it a little while he was playing, but nothing much. His dad said that he slept late this morning, but he fell asleep as usual on his ride to the center. He slept about an hour longer than he would ordinarily this morning, but was just great while he was awake to play. Did you notice on the information board that he started getting solids over the weekend?''

Nurse: The way this is rising, there's no doubt. It's to 102° already. We will call for his dad to pick him up. (The educarer goes to the nurse's desk to locate her emergency numbers card file for Phil's number.)

Educarer: Phil said that he was going to be on the road today, so we'll have to call Harriet at school. (She lays Luther's card on the desk. Luther is fussing and begins to whimper.)

Nurse: Well, he's up to 103.5°. I won't make him wait any longer. (She chats with him and reassures him all the while. The educarer moves to Luther's side and puts his diaper back on. The nurse gathers her equipment and goes to wash her hands.) He doesn't need to be sponged down, but he may like a bottle of water while he's waiting. (The caregiver quickly dresses Luther, blowing on his tummy and nestling with him as she fastens the last snap. Luther musters a smile, but drops to a tired stare immediately.)

2:00 P.M.: The nurse returns and places him on her shoulder.

Nurse: We'll give his mom a call. (The educarer goes to the kitchen for a bottle of water, while Luther rests in the nurse's arms. When

she returns Luther is watching the rattle in the nurse's hand while they rock.) His mom says that either she or Phil will be right here. She didn't leave a signed permission slip for Tylenol, so we'll just keep him cool and give him some water.

Educarer: He looks so comfortable with you, I'll go get his things together from the room. (The nurse offers Luther the bottle in the same comfortable way that his educarer does. Rocking slow and close, Luther sucks eagerly in a sleepy, stary state.)

2:15 P.M.: After 4 oz. of water, Luther is finding it very hard to keep his eyes open and has been lulled to sleep. The nurse moves him back to the crib to lay him down, but as she does he startles and whimpers. They rock again. His lips begin sucking action, so the nurse offers the bottle again. She strokes his brow and studies her docile patient, as they continue to rock. His sucking slows and stops . . . he hesitates . . . sucks again . . . he stops. His jaw quivers as he sighs and drops the bottle from his mouth. Luther is asleep. Again, the nurse takes him to the crib, but once more he fusses as he's lowered to the bed. They rock.

2:45 P.M.: Luther's dad appears at the door with the educarer. He has the bunting and a plastic bag with Luther's soiled suit. They have been discussing Luther's day.

Phil: She tellin' me here that Luther got a temp, and he not feelin' too good. Maybe he got that bug his big sister had last week.

Nurse: Thanks for coming, Phil. The girls were saying that he was fussing with that right ear, and it does look a little red. That may be some place for the doctor to start.

Phil: His sister had those ear troubles 'til she was three. Sure hope he don't get those. Harriet told the Doc we'd be there at 3:00, so we'd better get packed up. (While the nurse was chatting with Phil she had guided Luther into his bunting without arousing him.)

Nurse: There you go. We'll be anxious to hear what the doctor thinks. Hope that your evening goes well. Bye. (Luther, still sleeping, has ended his day at the day-care center.)

The important thing is not so much that every child should be taught as that every child should be given the wish to learn—John Lubbock. (Early Childhood Education Center)

A DAY IN THE LIFE OF TRAVIS (18-month-old boy)

SETTING: The same infant–young toddler room described in Luther's day. It also contains equipment and materials appropriate for beginning walkers. The colors, sights, and sounds suggest more "mature" uses of the same equipment; the variety of shelves that house toys also make play corners for dress-up and housekeeping play. There are also a water table for sensory exploration and two three-step slides for climbing, sliding, and imaginative play. Carpet samples are taped to a wall for texture and color discrimination. There are Velcro-covered balls for tossing. A shape-matching board is on another wall, which offers a vertical lotto game to be played with Velcro-backed matching shapes. There are milk carton blocks for stacking, diaper cartons for climbing in and out, and a small workbench holding large wooden nuts, bolts, and screws. A 3′ × 5′ chalkboard is mounted on one side of a room divider. Tape "highways" on the carpet suggest traffic patterns for cars and trucks. The platform area in the bay window overlooks a river, a parking lot, and an athletic field. A bookshelf containing cardboard and laminated picture books is readily accessible. Other shelves contain matching, sorting, stringing, building, and manipulating materials. There are both the security of familiar playthings and the adventure of the new.

Travis's day occurred during the springtime.

8:00 A.M.: Travis is delivered to the center by his mother, Connie. As they enter the playroom, they are both greeted.

Educarer: Good morning, Connie. Hey, Travis, what a nice smile you're wearing this morning! I'm glad to see you too!

Information is shared about Travis's evening that the educarers may need to know to help him through the day: a new word to reinforce, a scary thing to avoid, a rash to watch for, and a doctor's appointment to be made ready for. Routine information is noted for all the staff to share in a notebook, and the amount of sleep, meals, and any health problems are recorded on a Plexiglas chart mounted on the room wall in plain view for everyone.

Travis shares his adventures in coming to the center as his mother loosens the zipper tab so that he can unzip his jacket and hang it up. Mother shows her approval of his actions and also her positive feelings toward the center.

Connie: Thanks for helping. Looks like you're ready to play with your friends. (Connie picks him up for a kiss good-bye.) Have a nice day. (She smiles and puts him in the arms of the greeter who gives him a good morning squeeze and smile as they wave bye.)

8:05 A.M.: Across the room another staff member greets him, "Good morning, Travis, I'm glad to see you here today." Together he and his greeter survey the room.

Educarer: Well, what looks like fun today, Travis? I see Jimmy cooking in the kitchen, Betty is looking at books with Ann, Carol is drawing on the chalkboard, Bobby is playing with the Busy Box, Mike is riding in a wheelie chair, and I see Mary watching the buses outside. (The educarer lets Travis down.) No one is using the slide or balls right now. Would you like to roll a ball to me or help Tom in the house?

Travis: House.

Together they walk to the housekeeping corner. The adult picks up the receiver of the phone and sits down. After a brief conversation she says good-bye and hangs up. She then makes the phone ring, answers it, and hands it to Travis. "It's for you!" Travis excitedly says, "Hi" and hangs up. He laughs and rings the dial bell, calling over and over again. He continues exploring the phone and its bell, and even has a short chat with his mother. The educarer moves away unobtrusively. Travis remains captivated by his play, speaking in low tones, mostly to his mom, and dialing carefully over and again. After a time he takes the phone to a chair and sits down to continue his chat.

8:20 A.M.: Travis looks up as he hears the music of Ann's wind-up radio, and walks toward her with a smile on his face. He stops and looks at her, expecting her to give the toy to him. He then leans over and tries to take the toy out of her hands.

Educarer: Travis, Ann is using that radio; let's use our eyes and find another. (He continues to reach for the toy. The adult then tells him to look near the doll for another toy just like the one Ann is using. She tells him that Ann is playing with the toy to make him aware that he would either have to wait till she was through with it or look for another. Travis picks up the other radio. The educarer shows her approval.) Now you both have radios! Let's listen to their music.

Travis carefully holds the knob and twists the radio round and round to wind it up. He looks up contentedly as the music starts, and

carries it to the chalkboard where Carol (13 mo.) is drawing. He drops the radio by his side as he grasps the dangling string to the fat chunk of white chalk, and finds a drawing space on the board. He draws with large sweeping motions until his marks meet Carol's and they both laugh. Travis drops his chalk over the edge of the board and runs behind it to retrieve it. Delighted to find it, he runs back. Carol, charmed by his reappearance, laughs at his return. He continues ducking behind the divider and popping out in a peek-a-boo game with Carol, forgetting all about his vanished chalk.

As an educarer walks across the classroom she notices Tony (14 mo.) about to lose his balance. She scoops him up just in time in a drop-seat position with her hands under his bottom and the child's knees over her arm. She begins swinging him, singing, "Ding dong bell, kitty in the well." Immediately Kim, Travis, and Carol move to her. Tony is set down, safely rescued. The teacher gestures to the others to move to a place where they won't bump Mark, who was watching nearby. Each child has a turn singing "Ding dong bell, Travis in the well; ding dong bell, Tony in the well" until everyone has had enough turns.

Travis loves it, and requests over and over again, "Ding dong, ding dong, Travis's turn."

9:20 A.M.: After several turns the educarer notices that Travis' bottom seems warm. As he sits down at the end of a turn, she unobtrusively slips her finger down the waist of his diaper. It is wet.

Educarer: Hey, let's change those wet diapers, Travis, that will feel much better! (Together they walk to get the diaper bucket and a piece of butcher paper, then walk to an unoccupied place in the room. She lays the piece of paper on the floor and Travis lays himself on it. While she takes his pants off and changes him, she is still singing the Ding-dong song and he is singing his part too. She blows on his tummy as she pulls his pants up and they laugh.) All done! Thanks Travis. Let's go wash our hands. It's almost time for snack! You may carry the bucket if you like. It's nice to have you for a helper, Travis. Thanks. (They walk across the room to the bathroom area. Travis steps up to the sink.)

Educarer: Who's that fellow in the mirror? (She brushes his hair to one side with her hand.) Nice smile, huh? I see Travis!

Travis: See Janie. (He points in the mirror and turns to smile to Janie in person.)

Educarer: Hey, you can see me in the mirror, too, can't you! Neat! This is the way Travis washes, Travis washes, Travis washes . . . This is the way that Travis washes, *now* he's shiny clean! (The educarer leans over to mark the diaper change on the Plexiglas board.) You can dry your hands on the towel while I wash mine. Meet you at the snack table. (The educarer disinfects the changing surface and sink handles.)

9:50 A.M.: The cook brings snack into the room and places it on the counter. As soon as the children see the cook, they know it's time to go to the bathroom to wash their hands and then go to sit at the table. One adult takes the food to the table and passes it out. She tears off a paper towel placemat for each child and places a cracker spread with ham salad on each towel. Meanwhile the other adults are putting bibs on each of the children as they are helped into child-sized cube chairs. After the children and educarers are settled, juice is poured for all. During the whole process there is much conversation: "I see Jim is sitting next to Ann today. Mike, there is a chair by Freddie that no one is using, if you need a place to sit. Hey, you found it! I can tell you're ready for more crackers by the way you are showing me your empty hands, Carol."

Travis: Mo', mo' juice!

Educarer: Thanks for asking so nicely for more juice, Travis. I like that!

A plane flies overhead outside. Paul (21 mo.) screams, "Plane!"

Educarer: Did you hear a plane? Let's all listen, Paul hears something. (There is much giggling and excitement.) I can tell lots of us hear the plane. Thanks for telling us you heard the plane, Paul. You are a good listener! Planes go in the sky, not on the road like cars.

Paul: Mom plane.

Educarer: I remember when your mom went on the plane, Paul!

Travis: Mom.

Educarer: Oh, your mom has gone on a plane too, Travis?

Paul: Plane. (He points upward. The teacher gestures with her arms and eyes to listen again.)

Educarer: I don't hear it this time, it must be gone. (Paul drops the idea and continues eating.) I like the way Mike holds his cup with two hands. It really helps him hold on so he won't spill.

When the children are satisfied, they individually leave the table and find their way to the sink where there is an adult to help them clean up.

10:10 A.M.: In a quiet corner one of the educarers is gathering a group of four children. A large piece of posterboard is on the floor in front of them. It contains pictures of a candy cane, a bottle of baby lotion, a cup of coffee, a lemon, a flower, and a jar of peanut butter. Travis joins the group as the adult begins to speak.

Educarer: You're just in time to help us match some smells. Come and join us. (She offers each child a sealed canister with holes in in the top.) We are going to discover what is inside the can without using our eyes. How can we do that? (Two children bring up their cans to their noses.) That's right, we're going to use our noses. (She sniffs her can.) Tami, would you show us the picture of what is inside your can? We'll watch. (Tami leans over and places her can on the picture of the baby lotion bottle.) Tami thinks her can smells like baby lotion. Will you give each of us a smell too? (Tami holds her can out to the others and they agree.) Thanks, Tami. Let's see if Travis can show us which picture shows the smell in his can. (Travis puts his canister on the picture of the peppermint stick, and runs off to play. He goes back to the snack table and watches the adult who is washing it off.)

Educarer: Oh, would you like to wash too?

Travis: Wash too.

Educarer: Okay, I'll get a cloth for you too, Travis. I like to have a helper. (The adult wets several cloths knowing there will be more volunteers.) There you go. I want you to wash off this red chair, Travis. Mike, you do the blue one over there. Thanks guys! (The washcloths and helpers scatter to other areas. The cover of *Early Bird* catches Travis's eye as he washes the bookshelf. He drops the washcloth and takes the book to an educarer sitting nearby. He backs up and lands in her lap.)

Educarer: Thanks for sharing this book with me, Travis. I like this one too. Oh, look Travis, show me where Early Bird is . . . yes, he's just waking up from a good rest, isn't he? Can you stretch like Early Bird? Let's do it. (Travis stretches, but reaches up for the educarer's arm and quickly pulls it back down to hold the book.) And look! What is he doing in this picture?

Travis: Eat.

Educarer: Yes, he's eating his breakfast with his mom and dad—just like you do! (Paul comes over to show them a truck he's using.) Travis, look at the truck Paul is using. What kind of truck are you driving, Paul?

Paul: Milk. (Paul answers after a glance at the book, which shows a milkman. Travis meanwhile is making himself more comfortable lying back in the nest he has made of the educarer's lap.)

Educarer: Hey, Early Bird likes milk for his breakfast, doesn't he, Travis? There's a spot right next to me if you'd like to see this book with us, Paul. Neat, now we can all see the book. (A squeeze for Travis reassures him of his safe place.) Let's see what happens next. (The two boys laugh as they point to the pictures.)

10:40 A.M.: When Paul and Travis notice some children getting sweaters on, they jump up and run to their cubbies.

Travis: 'Side, 'side.

Educarer: Sure, I'll get your sweater so *you* can go outside too, Travis. (One staff member has moved to the door and is singing, "If you're ready and you know it, clap your hands . . . ," while the others are getting ready to go.)

An adult has prepared the playground with Tyke Bikes, wagons, balls, and trucks for the sandbox. One educarer leads the five children out and another follows.

Travis heads straight for the stationary climbers. He climbs to the top of one of the two pieces of climbing apparatus. The educarer is very attentive, standing next to him and talking with him about his actions directly. She comments to Travis, using his name, about how high he is and how he had managed to climb up unassisted. The tone of her voice is very warm and enthusiastic; her physical proximity seems also to lend security (although at no time does she actually touch or move to support him while he is at the top of the climber).

When Travis is ready to climb down, he looks to the educarer for assistance. While talking with him about the action as it takes place, she helps Travis by guiding his foot to the next lowest rung. At no time does she take major control of the child's movement, but acts merely as a guide to assure him of his actions. Although not at all verbal during the activity, he never appears to be apprehensive and seems to enjoy the climbing and interacting with the adult.

He runs across the playground where three or four children have gathered in a loose circle to play with several rubber and textured balls. The educarer talks with Jimmy and Ann about the ball she has, describing its shape, color, size (relative to a smaller textured ball), and its bouncing action. She then encourages Jimmy to roll the ball to Ann and back again, talking about their actions and the movement of the ball all the while. When Travis joins the group, he proceeds to roll over in an awkward but complete somersault. The educarer is delighted with this action, and, encouraging him to tumble again, says, "Travis can roll just like a ball." Ann and Jimmy continue to roll the ball back and forth, with occasional bounces in between. Travis rolls over and over until time to go inside.

11:20 A.M.: One adult takes three children inside, but Travis and Mike stay out a few minutes longer, in order to give the inside educarer a chance to help each of her children take their sweaters off and put them away, get a drink, wash their hands and have their diapers changed. Travis, Mike, and their educarer come in.

Another educarer is sitting on the floor waiting for them with colored shape blocks and cards with one or two corresponding shapes. Those interested move to her quiet corner. At one point, Travis picks up all the cards and starts to leave the area with them. The adult says quietly that he should leave the cards there. After a slight hesitation, he gives the cards to her, and she puts them in the box.

Educarer: Thanks, Travis, now the other kids can use them too. (Jimmy reaches for the box of cards and Travis becomes very excited. He repeats "No" to Jimmy several times and moves the box away from him. The adult suggests to Travis that he could share them with his friends. Her tone is calm and nonthreatening. He doesn't appear to understand. After about a minute, he leaves the area and the cards behind, appearing to forget his original interest.)

Another educarer, seeing that Travis was having problems finding something to do, focuses her attention on him for awhile. She picks out a hat from some play clothes and puts it on.

Educarer: Travis, can you see a hat to wear?
Travis: No.
Educarer: Come here, Travis. Show me what you have there? Hey, that's a frog!
Travis: Yep.
Educarer: What does he say?
Travis: Ribbet! (Travis has fun repeating "ribbet," and during the conversation the educarer picks him up and sits with him on her lap, rocking in a chair. After talking about the frog she begins singing a song to which there are hand motions. She shows him the motions so that he can follow along, which he does on several parts.)

11:40 A.M.: After a few minutes he is relaxed and ready for a rest.

Educarer: You feel so relaxed, Travis, I bet you're ready for a nap. Can you say goodnight to your friends? (An adult sitting close by says goodnight to Travis. His diaper is checked (dry) as he is carried into the nap room. He reaches for his blanket as he sits on his crib.)
Educarer: Do you want your shoes off or on? (Travis rolls over with his shoes on and his blanket is tucked around him. The caregiver pats him on the back and kisses him.)
Educarer: Night-night, Travis. Have a good rest. See you after your sleep. (His crib side is raised and the caregiver leaves.)

The adult checks frequently to be sure he has fallen asleep quickly and to be there when he wakes up. Travis usually sleeps for 2 hours at this time (late morning).

1:10 P.M.: Travis wakes and is brought back into the big room from his nap. He is still sleepy, and stands in one spot by the door. The educarer gets up from her chair and goes over to welcome him with a hug.

Educarer: Hi, Travis, how are you today? Oh, Oh. We need to change your diaper before we have our lunch. (He stands still while she gets the white butcher paper and the pail full of clean diapers and changing supplies, then lies down by himself on the paper on the floor. The educarer kneels down to begin changing him. She bends over very close to his face.)
Educarer: I'll bet those dirty diapers are uncomfortable, aren't they? We will get rid of them and make you feel good. (She tickles Travis and he smiles.)

All the while she is changing his pants, she talks to him constantly, giving him little pats and tickles during the process. She talks about what she is doing during the different steps of changing. Travis lies quietly, watching her face and smiling appropriately. He says nothing. When the process is completed and the educarer has washed her hands, together they straighten his clothes, comb his hair, and sit down in the rocking chair by the windows.

Educarer: It seems like you're still tired. Let's rock a minute. (He responds by smiling, hugging, and nodding his head. When the educarer finishes rocking him, he gives her another hug, and Travis runs off to play, wide awake.) I'm glad you're ready to play.

1:20 P.M.: Lunch had been kept warm for those children who were sleeping while the other older children had eaten. The plates of food had been set on the table with glasses of milk, and the late-risers came over to eat. Travis makes his way to the bathroom to wash his hands and seats himself at the table. Again an adult helps put on bibs and sits with the children to keep them company while they eat.

There are four children seated around the table enjoying their lunch. Travis soon decides that he has had enough to eat. He leaves the table and goes to the bathroom to wash his hands.

Educarer: There's that guy in the mirror again!

1:35 P.M.: Travis notes an adult taping together large diaper cartons for the children to play in. He wants to help, and she is happy to have some help. He puts the tape randomly on the boxes.

Educarer: Hey, Travis, you are doing a nice job. (He appears pleased.) Will you please throw these scraps in the wastebasket? (He rushes over to the wastebasket to toss in the scraps and rushes back to her.) Thank you, Travis. You are a good helper. (Travis is truly interested in what she is doing.) I'm making a train for you and your friends to play in. (He is very anxious to have a part in every one of the educarer's movements. She comments positively about each of his movements. He continues to tape and carry scraps to the wastebasket until the project is over. He then gets into the boxes, and the educarer sits down to watch and talk with him.) All aboard, here you go! Choo-choo-choo. (Travis choo-choo's along. The educarer sings "Down by the station" and Travis laughs.)

Travis quickly busies himself. He leaves the boxes and disappears into the housekeeping corner. After a few minutes he returns with an armful of cans, puts them in the box train and returns to the kitchen. He works silently until he has filled the large box with smaller boxes, dolls, and toys. Other children walk by and help themselves to the refound treasures, without bothering him. He continues to fill the car. When the car is filled to his satisfaction, he sits down in the next car and chooses a purse to open, close, and study.

1:55 P.M.: The playroom door opens and the nurse, dressed in a white lab coat, walks in carrying a glass containing several labeled vials of medication. She walks over to Travis, smiling, and stands watching his play for a minute or two. She bends down and tells him that it is time for his medicine. He opens his mouth as she pours the pink liquid in. He takes it readily.

Nurse: Thanks. Travis, you drank it down to the last drop! (She picks up a plate.) Where are you going with all your cargo? (He smiles and goes back to his work. The nurse pauses for a few more minutes on her knees as the children play.)

From the collection of toys Travis pulls out a duck puppet. Gary, 22 months, sees it and comes over. He stands and looks until he finds a puppet, too. Gary puts his hand in his puppet. "Cock-a-doodle-do!" he says to the duck. Travis picks up his puppet, puts it on his hand, and tries a "quack." An educarer nearby enhances their interaction by singing "Old *McGary* had a rooster . . ." and "old *McTravis* had a duck . . ." letting Gary and Travis do the animal sounds. The boys look at each other, laugh, and run to the window.

Travis: (pointing to the river): Ish—wa—wa. (Gary laughs.)

2:15 P.M.: The boys spot the masking tape circle on the rug. Travis goes over to stamp on it. He runs around and around the circle until he falls, but gets up laughing. Around some more and down again!

An adult turns a record on and invites the children to come listen to the music: to move fast when the music makes them feel like going fast, and slowly when it makes them feel like going slowly. The music begins and each child moves in his own way. Everyone smiles and enjoys feeling the music. They jump, roll, twirl, and just stand still; one by one they leave the group until only the educarer remains.

2:30 P.M.: Travis has slipped away to the infants' corner. He is sitting and studying the Busy Box, silently showing the nearby infant how each activity works. The educarer thanks him for showing Mark (4 mo.) how it moves, and reassures him that soon Mark will be doing it for himself now that he has shown him how. The educarer explains that she is getting ready to give the baby a bottle of formula.

Educarer: If you'd like to help, you could come over and sit in the rocking chair with us. (Travis makes his way into the chair with a helping hand, and carefully holds the baby's bottle, studying the baby's fingers.) You used to be tiny like Mark, didn't you, Travis? And I'll bet you drank from a bottle too! I like the way you are careful with his fingers, Travis. You are a good helper. Mark is smiling. He likes you too!

2:45 P.M.: Travis soon loses interest and crawls down to explore other parts of the room. He sits for a moment. The educarer sitting by a large mat of pictures catches his eye.

Educarer: Travis, can you find the picture that shows how you came to the center today? (Travis jumps to his feet and runs to the picture board. He sorts through the pile of 3″ × 5″ laminated cardboard matching pieces and picks out the picture of a bus and of red sneakers.) Hey, Travis. Okay! I rode a yellow bus today. We both rode on the bus.

Travis sits down and matches the picture of the sneakers, a teddy bear, and a book. The educarer slips away, and sets a large ball of play dough on the table. Travis looks up, drops the picture cards, and goes off to investigate. Other children notice the play dough, and a few join Travis and the adult at the table. As each one sits down, the educarer gives out a glob of dough to manipulate.

Educarer: My dough feels cold. How does yours feel? My dough feels soft now. I'm going to pat it. (As she pats it she sings a pat-a-cake song. Some of the children imitate her, others feel, tear, and squeeze the dough. Now that they are started, she comments on what they are doing.) Travis, I like the way you are patting yours so softly. (He smiles, looks up and says "cake," and looks over to see what the other children are doing. As Ann begins to put the play dough in her mouth the educarer quickly intervenes, asking Ann to show her how she can pound the play dough. As children lose interest they leave and go to the bathroom to wash their hands.)

2:55 P.M.: The snack that usually is served at the play dough table has been taken out to the playground because it was such a nice day. After the children wash their hands they are taken outside. A blanket has been spread under a tree for a picnic. Bananas and a thermos of milk are enjoyed along with the breeze.

Educarer: I'll start to open your banana, and *you* can peel it down. Here you go. If you need some help let me know. I like the way you are holding the bottom of yours, Travis. As soon as you are finished, put the peel part in this trash can and I'll give you a towel for your fingers and mouth. You are good helpers. Thank you.

Travis trots over to the rabbit hutch. He squats down to look at the bunny, his fingers entwined in the mesh cage. Suddenly he dashed to the corner of the playground, grabs a handful of grass, and rushes back to the cage. He throws the grass against the cage. Some of it goes in, and he dashes back for more.

3:10 P.M.: Meanwhile, Travis's mother has come to the playroom to pick him up for his doctor appointment. She reads the daily information on the Plexiglas chart. An educarer approaches as she is gathering Travis's belongings in his cubby.

Educarer: Hi, Connie. How did your day go? Travis really got involved putting toys in the cardboard train. You'll have to ask him about it tonight. He's just had a snack, so he should be in good spirits for the doctor. Hope all goes well. See you tomorrow.

A DAY IN THE LIFE OF VICTORIA
(30-month old girl)

SETTING: The toddler playroom is colorful and includes components that appeal to sight, touch, and sounds. The large windows are low enough for the children to look out at the world. They are dressed with muslin curtains that have been handprinted by the children. The walls are lined with artwork from the day before. Each child has a cubby for personal belongings. The shelves of free choice materials are low and open, and in-

vite curious hands and eyes with well-arranged toys.

The room is divided into active and less active play areas. Today the large motor area contains the postman's Tyke Bike "delivery cars" and a large portable climber with an attached slide. The quieter area contains a drawing station, a bookcase filled with picture books, a toy mailbox, action posters of the postman sorting and delivering mail and other related tasks. There is also a housekeeping corner with empty food containers, pots and pans, doll babies, cribs, and table and chairs. Another corner of the room has clothes racks holding child-sized costumes of many varieties, as well as dress-up hats, shoes, dresses, pants, and shirts. A full-length mirror is hung on the wall. A chalkboard the length of one side of the room is mounted just off the floor and is equipped with white chalk fastened to long strings. A privacy cave lines the other wall, made by removing cupboard doors and replacing them with flannel blankets hang-

The world is so full of a number of things, I'm sure we should all be as happy as kings—Robert Louis Stevenson (Early Childhood Education Center)

ing down over the openings for easy entrance and exit. An adult-sized rocking chair completes the list of furnishings. There are 12 children enrolled in the group, with usual attendance of about 9 or 10. There are four educarers.

The time of the year is early fall.

8:15 A.M.: Victoria appears at the open playroom door. She is greeted by her educarer.

Educarer: Good morning! You must have fast feet today, Victoria. I don't see your dad. Is he taking Sissy to her room first?

Victoria seems eager to join the other 11 children who are already busy. She surveys the situation as she waits for her dad. She spots two boys sitting in an $8' \times 10' \times 15''$ box filled with rice that is permanently placed on the floor. The inner sides of the box are lined with action posters of farm life and animals. Ben, wearing a railroad engineer's cap, is busy scooping a tractor and wagon full of rice. Ron is intent on setting up a fence around a barn for rubber animals. Sam, Allan, and Susie scoot by the doorway, "double-footing" their Tyke Bikes in an aimless rush. Victoria reaches down to pick up Sam's hard hat, which had fallen off as he made a wide turn in front of her.

8:20 A.M.: Victoria's dad has now arrived, and Victoria points out her vegetable print from yesterday, hanging on the wall.

Victoria: See, Daddy? I used a carrot.
Father: I like the red color, Victoria. It will look real nice on the wall of your room at home. (She and her dad go to her cubby, where she takes off her sweater and hangs it on the hook. Her dad puts a record on the cubby shelf.) Victoria would like to share her new disco record if she could.
Educarer: Sure, Victoria, I'll bet the kids would like to boogie while we get ready for lunch. We'll keep the record in your cubby until we need it. You help me remember, Okay? (Victoria smiles.)

8:25 A.M.: Carol and Janelle spot Victoria and her dad and race over, squealing, to the new

arrival. The three laugh and grab each other happily.

Janelle: We both have stripes, don't we? (She points out their striped turtleneck shirts.)
Victoria: Yeah-a-ah. (She is pleased at this bond of friendship. Carol offers Victoria a doll like the one she is holding.)
Carol: Here's yours. (Victoria accepts the doll. Victoria hugs her dad's leg, says goodbye, and scampers off with Carol and Janelle to the housekeeping corner.)
Father: Sissy has an ear infection and has to go to the doctor at 11:00. I'll stop in to see Victoria then.
Educarer: Could you have lunch with us? We'll be eating around 11:50.
Father: Thanks. Sounds good. I'll try to, if we are back from Sissy's appointment.

8:35 A.M.: Victoria has already started "cooking" in the kitchen with Carol and Janelle. They giggle together as they noisily empty the cupboard of cans with picture labels, dishes, pots and pans, realistic plastic food, wooden spoons, and food containers. Tricia, a teacher's aide, approaches the noisy area and finds no direction in the dumping.

Tricia: What a messy kitchen you ladies keep! I'd never be able to find my way around in here. It's time to get these things put away. Victoria, you use your bright eyes and pick out all the things that go in the refrigerator and put them there. Carol, you look for all the pans and put them on a convenient shelf. Janelle, you can put away the cans, and I'll help with the plates and spoons. (Victoria and Carol got busy putting their things away.)
Carol: I found a can with a picture of a tomato on the front.
Tricia: What do you suppose was in it?
Janelle: Tomato juice!
Tricia: You know, my tomato juice comes in a can like that too. It looks like the tallest can to me. I'll put it on the back of the shelf. Can you find another one the same size?
Janelle: This one is fat like that one. (She places a pear can on the shelf.) I found one

that looks the same—we found two alike! (The two cans have the same diameter as the juice can, but are shorter. Tricia continues to motivate Janelle.)

Tricia: Let's find a can that had corn in it. (Janelle finishes putting the cans away, and the aide stacks the plates away.) What great picker-uppers we are! The kitchen looks so clean. Look, Victoria put the yogurt in the refrigerator with the milk and eggs. What a good idea to keep the ice cream hard in the freezer. Carol, you put all the pans in the oven! That's where I put mine too, sometimes. But what's in that big pot on top of the stove?''

Victoria: Stew. (Everyone has an imaginary taste.)

Janelle: Ick! I don't like stew!

Tricia What do you like to eat?

Janelle: I like spaghetti!

Carol: Fried chicken!

Victoria: Hot dogs.

Tricia: I looked at the lunch menu and it says we'll be having something long, skinny, and white, with red sauce and brown meat, and Janelle really really loves it!

Victoria: Sgetti!

Carol: I can cook it. (She reaches for a can of corn. Janelle sits down at the table to help a doll.)

Janelle: She's messy. (She wipes the doll's face with a cloth. The other two girls continue preparing dinner.)

9:35 A.M.: Victoria looks around and announces that she needs to go potty.

Tricia: Thanks for reminding me, Victoria. Ben, Ron, do you need to go to the bathroom too? (Ben, Ron, and Victoria scoot to the door.)

Educarer: Let's pretend we're helicopters. (She sings as they walk together down the hallway.) Propellers on the helicopters go around and around. (The children chime in.) Not up front and not behind, but right on top of the plane you'll find. Propellers on a helicopter go around and around. (They go into the bathroom, a large open space with a row of child-sized toilets and sinks. Ron and Ben stand in front of the same toilet; Victoria tries to unfasten her belt.)

Educarer: Have a new belt on your jeans today, Victoria?

Victoria: Ya. My mom said I could undo it myself. (After several futile attempts, she looks up.)

Educarer: How about a helping hand? (She loosens the fastener by taking it out of the hole and making the belt into a large loop in the buckle.) Now you try. (Victoria pulls it out with satisfaction.) There you go, it just needed to be looser. (The boys are finished, and Ron is trying to pull up his jeans with his underwear still at his knees.) Remember to pull up those white underpants, Ron. There you go . . . now your jeans will fit right over them. Good job! (Ben flushes the toilet and goes to the sink to wash his hands. He turns on the water in both sinks full force. Ron giggles.) You two will not be comfortable in wet shirts. (The teacher turns down the water and hands them the soap. She sings as the boys wash their hands.) Over and under, inside and out, look how they're shiny clean. (As they towel their hands dry, the teacher notices that Victoria is working on a bowel movement.) Look at those guys in the mirror. (Ben is still wearing the engineer's cap and smiles at his image.)

Ben: I see you too. (He turns to look at the adult's face.)

Educarer: You know, Ben, with that hat on you look a lot like the farmer in the picture in the rice box. He has something else on his face. Kinda black, right above his lip.

Ron: A moustache! Like my dad.

Educarer: Ben, do you know anyone who wears a moustache?

Ben: Uncle Bill. (He gazes at himself in the mirror.)

Educarer: Where would one look good on you? (Ron and Ben both point to their upper lips. They turn and head for the door.) You'll need to wait for Victoria and me.

Victoria is working on her belt, having wiped herself, flushed the toilet, and gotten her clothes in place.

Educarer: Did your mom say you should buckle it too?

Victoria: Yeah, she showed me. (Victoria slowly manages to thread the strap through the buckle and latches the prong on the first hole. With a smile of accomplishment, she goes to the sink, with belt sagging, to wash her hands. Four more children with another educarer appear at the door, and Victoria's group trots down the hall to their room.)

9:40 A.M.: While they were in the bathroom, the cook had delivered the morning snack. An assistant educarer had prepared the table, with Carol placing a napkin and a cup at each place. The remaining children go to the playroom sink to wash their hands and sit down at the table.

Educarer: I see Jon is ready for snack. (She initiates conversation while waiting for the others to be seated.) Today we're going to have something that is yellow and long and grows on trees, and monkeys like to eat them. (Several children yell "Bananas!" Sam is trying to sit in the same chair that Susie is settled into.) Sam, you need to look for a chair no one is using. Susie is sitting in that one. Can you find the yellow one next to Jim? Thanks, that works better. Today these bananas are going to have a special taste, if you like. (The teacher holds up six small plastic bags, each half filled. Two contain graham cracker crumbs, two granola, and two coconut.) When you finish peeling your banana, you can shake it up in one of these bags, and give your banana a new taste. The teacher puts a pinch of crumbs on each napkin.) How do you think it will taste if you use this bag?

Janelle: It tastes like crackers.

Educarer: Mmmm, it does taste like graham crackers. If you like that taste, you may want to shake your banana in this bag. Let's use our noses to guess what is this white stuff. (She passes around the opened bag of coconut. Victoria says she likes the way it smells. All the children are given a pinch to taste.) This grows on a tree in a large brown nut. It's coconut.

The adult continues in the same manner with the granola. She then gives each child a

banana half to peel, and asks which taste they want on their banana. Another educarer passes a bowl of milk for banana-dipping, and then zips up the seal as each child puts in the banana. Each one shakes his or her own. Half glasses of milk are poured after the children finish shaking. A third educarer records the bathroom information while the children concentrate on their snack. Victoria asks for, and is given, another banana half.

10:10 A.M.: As soon as the individual children finish, they leave the table. Victoria starts to get up.

Educarer: Victoria, you need to stay in your chair until you are finished chewing. It's not a good idea to play while you are chewing. Thanks. (Victoria is now finished. She puts her milk glass in the dish tub, and scoops her banana peelings and napkin into the wastebasket. She then goes to the sink to wash her hands and wipe her mouth.)

10:15 A.M.: She surveys the room looking for the "bathroom" educarer, who is making impromptu paper moustaches for Ben and a few others. Victoria joins them. "Me, too," she says as she waits for her moustache. She puts it on her lip and crowds for a spot at the long mirror. Satisfied, she turns to see some children watching the fish in the aquarium, some children in dress-up clothes, and some looking at books in the book corner. She discovers Janelle and Carol pretending to sleep in the bottom of the climbing apparatus. They giggle as Victoria wedges her way between them. The three stretch and lie still. Carol makes a snoring sound. They pop up, giggling. Down again, and silence. Carol snores and they shriek with delight, again and again. Victoria reaches out to get a doll and tucks it close beside her. Allan decides to join them. He climbs up and stands on the ledge above them, stamping his feet. The girls giggle, and he repeats his noise-making.

Victoria: Get down, Allan. (He refuses and stomps again. The girls protest, and a teacher's attention is attracted.)

Educarer: It looks like Allan is your alarm clock, girls. Allan, is that the way your mom wakes you up in the morning? (Allan smiles.)
Allan: No—she says "Wake up!"
Educarer: Those girls are sleeping now. How do you think they would like to be waked up?
Allan: R-r-ring wake up! (The girls sit up laughing; Allan laughs. The girls lie down again; the sequence is repeated over and over. Allan slides down the slide to get a moustache, and the girls continue to chatter in their private place.)

The table has been cleared and is being readied for an activity. Bottles of liquid starch and liquid soap, a stack of washcloths, a stack of paper squares, a dishpan of water, and a crayon are grouped at the educarer's spot. The educarer places a paint shirt on the back of each chair and quietly announces, "If anyone would like to mix colors, come over and find a chair." Five children hurry over. Victoria leaves Carol and Janelle to take care of the doll baby and joins the group. The children put on their smocks. The adult makes a puddle of the starch, soap, and powdered tempera paint in front of each artist. Victoria's eyes follow closely the whole procedure, and then she puts her right hand in the blue and her left hand in the yellow, and swirls them around.

Victoria: Hey, I'm two colors! (She holds up her hands.)
Educarer: You look as blue as the sky over here and as yellow as our bananas over here! (Victoria laughs and claps her hands.) Let's see what happens when you put your blue hand in the yellow. It's green! (Victoria stirs the two colors together. Then she "prints" on the table top with her hands, mixes some more, smoothes it, and even runs her fingers through it in a finger-painting motion.) Would you like another color? (Victoria nods and the educarer adds red tempera to the puddle. Victoria mixes it in.)
Victoria: Ooo, this is icky color. (The educarer adds some white tempera.)
Educarer: Does that make it a color you like better? Maybe you would like to start over.

(Victoria smiles. They both wipe up the murky puddle from Victoria's spot on the table. Both rinse off their hands in the tub of water, and the procedure starts again. Victoria chooses yellow and white, and she is soon smoothing the two colors from side to side, and apparently is enjoying the smooth wetness of the mixture. The other children are making hand prints or paper prints [pressing a sheet of paper down on their puddles]; some are scaring each other with their gooey hands.)

10:40 A.M.: As the children tire of the activity, each one is given a washcloth to wipe their table area before washing their hands. Victoria is fascinated with her yellow hands and covers them back and front with paint.

Victoria: I'm all yellow.
Educarer: Victoria, if you were all yellow, you'd be a . . . ? ("Big Bird," volunteers the orange person in the next chair, "and I'm an orange bird!" Victoria and the "orange bird" laugh, and then Victoria hiccups.) Would you like a drink of water, Victoria? (she hiccups again, and they both laugh. Victoria dips her hands in the tub and wipes them on a washcloth. Another adult offers her a cup of water.) That should get rid of those hiccups. (Victoria drinks it down in a large gulp, and gives a big sigh, which the adult imitates. Victoria sighs again—they both laugh.) Hey, Victoria, you did it! You got rid of your hiccups! (Victoria announces "I'm done," and the educarer gives her a cloth to wipe up the yellow puddle on the table.)

10:50 A.M.: Ron, who is looking out the window, spots a garden tractor mowing the field below. Victoria drops the cloth, wipes her hands on her pants, and runs to the window with some others. One of the boys proudly announces that his dad can drive a tractor. The group watches the methodical movements of the tractor, and they talk about where to drive a tractor, its uses, how it is different from, and like, a car, and places where they have seen a tractor. This lively discussion continues until the tractor disappears in a grove of trees. The sound is still audible, and Bob is certain another one is coming. The educarer sees that the art table has been cleared and cleaned, and silently communicates to another staff member, who moves to the cubby area.

Educarer: Maybe we could see the tractor better if we watch it from the playground. Go get your sweaters on and I'll meet you at the door. (All the children run to get their sweaters, and go to the door where the educarer is waiting.) She sings. "If you're ready and you know it, clap your hands; if you're ready and you know it, clap your hands, if you're ready and you know it, your clapping will really show it; if you're ready and you know it, clap your hands." (She continues with "tap your head" and "jump up and down" until all the children and educarers are ready to go.)

Victoria holds onto Ron's hand, and they all go to the playground, with two adults leading and one following the last child. The educarers remind the children to listen for the tractor sound as they approach the playground. The area had been prepared. Today the environment includes the open playhouse, tricycles, chalk for drawing, and crepe paper streamers tied to a tree. The children head for the sound of the tractor while they continue to share their own knowledge of tractors. Karen and Valerie choose a paper streamer, and run to the hiding place inside the concrete culvert. Victoria joins them and buzzes around the culvert, pretending to be an airplane. Soon there are three airplanes buzzing noisily around the yard, with streamers flying. They "land" by the playhouse and start to eat their sand cake and drink, which is passed out to them, drive-up style. "Hi, Sissy," Victoria shouts as she sees her sister in another part of the play yard. She rushes over for a quick hug, and then back to the drive-in for service. The tricyclists whiz by, some stopping for a pie, and then off again.

One educarer draws a hopscotch design with the chalk. Victoria notices it, goes over, and asks about it. The adult looks around for a stone while she answers.

Educarer: It's hopscotch. I'll show you how, and then you can do it. (The educarer hops down the board.) One foot, two feet, one foot, two feet . . . Watch this! (She whizzes around at the end. They both laugh, and she starts back.) I don't want to step on a line . . . now you. (Victoria jumps on—bump, bump, bump down the board, using two feet each time. She goes straight on, back to her playhouse friends.)

11:30 A.M.: It's time to go inside. The group leaves the play yard a third at a time so that each child will have the chance to go to the bathroom and wash hands before lunch. Victoria is part of the last group.

Aide: Need any help with your belt, Victoria?
Victoria: No, I can. (She works at it, needing just a little help. With clean hands, Victoria joins the others on the rug for group time. She wants to sit right next to the educarer and pushes her way to the front. The educarer has two children on her right, two on her left, and one right in front of her.)
Aide: It doesn't look like there's a space right here, Victoria. You'll need to find a place where no one is sitting. (Victoria turns and sits at the edge of the circle, immediately saying "I can't see" even before she is seated. The educarer acknowledges her concern.) You'll need to move your body til you can . . . and I'll hold the book very high.

The book is a favorite one, *A Whistle for Willie*. The educarer begins by showing the cover to the children.

Educarer: What do you suppose this book is about? (The group answers, "A dog!") Does anyone know this dog's name?
Carol: "Willie."
Educarer: Do you remember this boy's name? (The teacher points to Peter.)
Carol: Peter.
Educarer: I guess Carol has read this book before! Do you know what Peter wanted to learn how to do?
Carol: Whistle.

The adult asks if any of the children can whistle, and apparently no one can. She continues by saying that as they listen to the story, they can try, just like Peter did. She opens the book and begins reading. She points out the pictures, and the children are engrossed. In the story, Peter tries and tries to whistle. Each time he tries, the educarer and the children try. She asks how they feel when they can't whistle, and the children respond with deep frowns. As the story continues, Victoria's sad expression brightens when Peter produces his whistle. The story ends.

Educarer: Wasn't that a good story? Let's try to whistle again. (There are no whistlers in the group.) Well, I guess we'll just have to try and try and try like Peter. And some day we'll be able to whistle too.

The children had been so attentive that the educarer asks if they would like to read the story to her, and there is a rousing "Yeah." She holds the book up high.

Educarer: This is a story called . . .
Children: Whistle for Willie. (She opens to the first page.)
Educarer: What's going on here? (She listens to the many answers.) Yes, Peter is feeling sad because he can't whistle and he wants to learn. (She recaps each page, as the children tell her what is happening.)

When the story is almost finished, Victoria's special educarer hands the record jacket to Victoria, and signals to the group educarer that she has put the record on the player.

Educarer: You sure are good story readers. I like the way you remembered all about Peter and Willie. I can tell you like that story. We can read it again someday. But today, Victoria brought a surprise for us. Victoria, can you tell us? (Victoria stands up and shows the jacket to her disco record.)
Educarer: Can you tell us about your record? Look at the picture . . . do you think that is a Winnie-the-Pooh record? ("No!" is the group response, accompanied by giggles.) Well, what should we do to find out what kind of a record it is?
Victoria: We can hear it.

Educarer: Good idea. (She walks over to the record player and turns it on. Lively music fills the room, and everyone laughs.) Let's boogie. (She moves to the music. Victoria joins in, dancing wildly. Everyone jumps and runs and moves to the music with much joy. When the first song ends, the educarer picks up the needle.) Whew, I'm pooped! (The children stop too. She asks if they want to dance some more, and they all say "Yeah!" Again the room is filled with much activity and music.)*

11:55 A.M.: An aide appears and indicates that lunch is ready. At the end of the next song, the group educarer stops the record and announces that lunch is ready, and that they can disco over to eat. The music starts again, and the children parade over to the lunch tables.

Educarer: Victoria, I'd like you to sit in this red chair today. (Victoria sits down in front of a plate containing spaghetti, tossed salad, French bread, and applesauce. Bibs are put on the children, and they all start to eat eagerly.) You all look kinda warm . . . what have you been up to?
Allan: We were dancing!
Educarer: We dance all the time, but I never saw you look so warm before. Was there something different about the music?
Victoria: Yeah, it's disco!
Educarer: Oh, I love to disco. (The conversation continues about dancing, partners, and different kinds of dancing, and then shifts to remembering the tractor event of the morning.)

Victoria asks for more spaghetti and salad. Gradually the other children finish, and announce "All done." When Victoria finishes her lunch, she washes her hands and face, takes off the bib, and goes back to the play area. During the children's lunch, an educarer had brought the dress-up clothes—costumes, hats, shoes, long dresses, jackets and gloves—to the center of the rug. Many of the children are dressing.

---

*Author's note: There may be mixed feelings about such an exciting activity right before a meal. A more quiet activity is generally recommended.

Victoria chooses her favorite apricot taffeta dress and yellow high-heeled shoes. She asks if they could dance some more. The educarer responds that she is all dressed up for dancing and asks what she would like to hear. She holds up four record jackets.

Victoria: Disco!
Educarer: Well, okay, but we'll need to keep it pretty low.

The music starts, and the music corner is soon filled with dressed-up disco dancers who are wiggling and giggling. The dancers soon slow down, and the adult changes the record to a more quiet one. Victoria yawns a big yawn and sits down.

Educarer: Victoria, you look like you are ready for your rest. I'll get your record so you can put it back in your cubby while you put your beautiful dress back in the dress-up box. (Victoria undresses herself, puts the dress and shoes away, and goes to the bathroom. The adult follows.) Good idea. I'm glad you remembered you might need to go. Would you like to put that special belt in your cubby with your record? It will feel better if you don't wear it while you rest. (Victoria and her educarer head toward her cubby. Victoria places the record and her belt in her cubby.)
Educarer: Now your daddy will know just where to find it when it's time to go home. Thanks. (Hand in hand, Victoria and her special educarer walk into the sleeping area and to the cot with Victoria's name on it. The adult lowers it to the sleeping position and Victoria takes off her shoes and reaches for her blanket. She clambers onto the cot. The educarer spreads the blanket over her and gives her a special hug.)
Educarer: Sweet dreams, Victoria. (She rubs Victoria's back gently; Victoria closes her eyes momentarily and then opens them.)
Victoria: Can we play the record again?
Educarer: Sure, the kids will like that. (Victoria settles again and drops off to sleep. She sleeps soundly for 2 hours.)

3:20 P.M.: Victoria awakens and sits up on her cot. "Ready to wake up?" asks the aide who is sitting in the rocker nearby. Victoria stretches and smiles sleepily. The aide motions to her.

Aide: Bring your shoes and I can help you put them on. (Victoria gathers her shoes and one sock . . . She looks around and finds the other one in a ball under her cot. The aide smiles, and boosts Victoria onto her lap.) You look like you had a good rest . . . but your feet must have gotten too hot. Look at those toes! (Victoria smiles as the aide rubs her feet to give a friendly wake-up squeeze.) Do you want me to help with your socks, or do you want to do it? (Victoria pulls out the toe of the balled sock. She gives two giant tugs, and the socks are on.) Good. Put your sneakers on and I'll tie them for you. (Victoria is ready to go.) Hey, we need to find your belt. Now where did we leave it?
Victoria: It's in my cubby.
Aide: Oh, yes, I'll get your belt and meet you in the bathroom.
Victoria: Is Carol playing?
Aide: No, she's still resting. But Ben and Joanna and Sam are ready to play.

Once in the bathroom, Victoria goes directly to the toilet and takes care of herself, including pulling up her pants. The aide is waiting with the belt.

Aide: Here you go . . . round and round we go, one loop, two loops, three loops, four loops, five loops! (The aide tucks in her shirt and buckles the belt.) There you are, ready to find your friends. (Victoria bounces into the playroom.)

3:40 P.M.: Valerie and Janelle are tearing pictures out of magazines and taping them to the mirror, with a teacher's help. Sam is looking at a picture book. Ben and Joanna are shelling soybean pods at the science table. Victoria spots a "beauty parlor," which was not there before. An area semi-enclosed with floor-length mirrors is decorated with pictures of beauticians, barbers, hairstyles, and other magazine pictures. A hair dryer is secured to a round table in the center, and a customer's chair is backed up to it, holding a doll ready for care. The counter is filled with the necessities: brushes, combs, empty shampoo bottles, hair bonnets, rollers, capes, faucet spray attachments, and wigs. Victoria puts on a blonde wig, inspects herself in a mirror, and goes over to the hair dryer chair.

Carol is up! Off goes Victoria to join her. With an exchange of hugs and excited chatter, Victoria leads Carol to the "surprise." She places Carol under the dryer, but Carol gets up to investigate the area for herself. Both girls put on hair bonnets, and they begin to rearrange the chairs and wash the doll's hair. More children arrive after their naps, and the beauty parlor is a busy place. The end of Allan's hair sprayer hits Victoria's arm.

Victoria: It isn't nice to hit. (Victoria is scowling: Allan appears surprised. He rubs up next to her arm, looking sympathetic.) Victoria orders Carol: "Don't let Allan hit me again!" (The two girls turn away with disgust.)

In one corner children are lined up in front of a mirror where an educarer is offering shaving cream and tongue-depressor razors to bibbed customers. Victoria and Carol are intrigued by the fragrance.

Educarer: You two ready for a shave? (The girls laugh and run over to the window, where an educarer is sharing a book with Janelle. The book is all about feet. The girls wiggle their feet when the adult asks, "Where are your feet?" and "Can you feel with your feet?")
Victoria: I feel wet grass with my feet.
Educarer: I like the way that feels too, Victoria. What can you feel, Janelle?
Janelle: I feel wet grass, too.
Educarer: Do you feel anything else?
Janelle: I feel my socks. I have one, two.

Victoria jumps up and starts to sing "Put your left foot in, put your left foot out." Carol and Janelle join in with "and you shake it all about. You do the hokey pokey and you turn yourself around—that's what it's all about—Hey!" The adult is smiling and clapping to their music. The girls grin back, and go off together to the snack table. The other children join them. Placed on the table are six small bowls of peanut butter, with two spreaders for each bowl. The crackers are passed and the cranberry juice is poured. Conversation centers on the beauty parlor/barber shop. Snack is finished, and each child throws the napkin and paper cup away, and washes hands. The table of cleared of snack.

4:15 P.M.: An educarer sits at the table, and in front of her are a sweet potato, a white potato, and a carrot; a pitcher of water, paper towels, and a knife.

Educarer: Anyone who wants to help can come over and find a chair that no one else is sitting in. (Five children hurry over and sit down. The teacher holds up a potato.) What's this? Where do potatoes grow—on a tree? (A chorus of "No!") On a bush? (Again no.) Well, where?
Sam: In the ground.
Educarer: Thanks, Sam. How do you get them? (Sam shrugs his shoulders.) You have to dig them with a shovel. Here's another kind of potato—a sweet potato. (She then holds up the carrot.) What's this? ("A carrot!") Where does it grow? ("In the ground.")
Victoria: You pull it.
Educarer: That's right. The potatoes and the carrot all grow in the ground, don't they? (The vegetables are passed around and each child touches and sniffs them.) What color is this potato? (A fast answer: "Brown.") What color is it inside? (No answer.) What color are mashed potatoes?
Janelle: White.
Educarer: Well, if we cut up this potato to make mashed potatoes, what color do you think the inside will be? Let's cut it open with our knife and look inside. (Silence while the teacher cuts.)

Janelle: It's white. (Victoria is watching quietly.)

Educarer: Would anyone like a taste? (The teacher offers a small piece to each child. Sam spits his out and says, "Ick!" Victoria makes a face, and Carol asks for more. They all volunteer how they fix potatoes at home, and which kind is their favorite.)

The educarer then holds up the carrot and follows the same procedure. She then holds up the sweet potato, asks the questions about the color inside, and asks how can they find out. "Cut it" is the answer. She does, and they are surprised to see that it is orange, just like the carrot. After samples of the sweet potato are passed around, the educarer says she would like to grow some plants, and asks if the children think they could grow a carrot or a potato plant. They say yes.

Educarer: What will we need? (No response.) What do you do at home to make plants grow?
Sam: Water 'em.
Educarer: Yes, so I think we can do an experiment with water. Let's put this potato half in the jar of water, and we'll look at it every day to see if anything happens. Would you like to grow a plant too? (The chorus of yeses is gratifying. Each child is given a small cup with his or her name printed on it, and carrot pieces are passed around. Victoria pops hers into her mouth.) That's for your cup, Victoria! (The adult gives her another one. Water is poured into each cup.) Where should we put them so they will grow?
Janelle: Sun. (The children are directed to the window ledge, and each cup is set down so that the name labels are visible.)
Educarer: We will check each day to see if the plants are changing. We'll put them right next to our bean seeds. Can you guess how they will change?
Sam: It will grow.
Educarer: Yes, we need to watch the bottom part. We might see the little tiny hairs that make roots. We can watch our bean seeds and our carrot starts every day. Thanks for helping.

4:35 P.M.: The gardeners are taken to the bathroom to clean up and get ready to go outside to play. The yard offers the same playhouse and tricycles. In addition, there are bowls of soap bubbles and blowers, on a wooden bench. Several empty diaper cartons are on the ground, arranged in a train. An aide is helping a few children cut out the doors and windows of the train cars. Victoria watches the train activities, but then goes to the bubble-blowing activity. She and Janelle blow bubbles and then chase after them. Janelle's mother appears at the playground gate. She and Janelle say goodbye to the group and go into the room for Janelle's things. Other moms and dads appear to pick up their children. Victoria is eying the gate frequently as she and the remaining children pick up the playground for another day. They tramp inside, and several get drinks of water. Victoria appears to be feeling unhappy, and her educarer notices.

Educarer: Would you like to sit on my lap for a minute? Can you choose a book to share? (Victoria brings a book and snuggles on the adult's lap. The book is a favorite one, and the educarer asks Victoria to tell the story as the pages are turned. Instead, Victoria asks, "What's happening on this page?" They both laugh, and Victoria responds to her own questions with silly answers. In a minute, Victoria remembers her record, leaves the lap for the record player.)
Victoria: Can we hear my record? (Victoria gets the record from her cubby, and joins the aide at the record player. She watches the aide put the needle down, and soon the room is filled with music and enthusiastic dancers.)

5:10 P.M.: The door opens and Victoria's dad appears. Victoria runs over for a hug.

Father: Is that your record I hear?
Victoria: Yeah. (She begins to bounce. They are joined by a teacher.)
Educarer: The kids have really enjoyed Victoria's record today. We listened to it at lunch time, too.

Dad: Sorry I missed lunch, but Sissy's doctor's appointment took longer than I expected.

Educarer: No one mentioned it to Victoria, so maybe you can do it another day. (While this conversation is going on, another educarer has helped Susie choose a different record, and has given Victoria's to her.) Thanks for sharing this with us today.

Victoria and her dad clear her cubby, and dad notices the beauty shop equipment.

Father: That looks like fun. Did you play there? (Victoria and her dad leave to pick up Sissy, chatting about Victoria's day.)

A DAY IN THE LIFE OF SALLY
(12-month-old girl)

SETTING: A Day in the Life of Sally (a 12-month-old girl) takes place in a family day-care home in a small town. The child-care provider in this home offers child care for five children plus three of her own—5½-year-old Melanie, 8-year-old Rachael and 11½-year-old Annie. The five other children come from families who live in the country nearby: Justin, age 4½ years and Derek, age 4 months, are brothers; Peter, age 4 years and Jimmy, age 18 months, are also brothers. Sally is the only child in her family.

Sally was almost 5 months old when she first came to this family day-care home. She had been in another day-care home from the time she was 2 months old. Sally's parents made the change because the previous provider was no longer offering child care due to family obligations. Sally made the transition fairly easily and has developed a close relationship with her current care provider, as well as with the other children at the day-care home.

The main play area of the family day-care home is located on the lower level of a ranch style house in a quiet neighborhood. It is a convenient location for the families who use it. When children arrive with their parent(s), they enter through a side door without knocking. They hang jackets in a hall closet at the top of

Don't worry when you stumble—remember a worm is the only thing that can't fall down—Henry Thoreau. (Early Childhood Education Center)

the stairs or place them in the child's basket on a shelf at a preschool eye level, at the bottom of the stairs. As they enter the play area, they are each greeted by the child care provider.

The physical environment of the play area can be described as follows: It features a large carpeted room of about 520 sq. ft. (40 × 13) which is divided into interest areas. There are cribs and playpens placed at the far end of the room for an infant-toddler sleeping area, and there are several cots with sheets, pillows, and blankets for use by older toddlers and preschoolers. A tall shelf unit acts as a room divider to decrease distractions in the sleeping area. This shelf and other shelves in the room contain various kinds of toys appropriate for children aged from infancy to about 8 years of age. Included are large hard plastic trucks and cars; puzzles (wooden and other); stuffed animals and dolls; a large variety of plastic foods, dishes, pots, and pans; "little people," buildings, and vehicles; books (cardboard, laminated, and others); manipulatives; large and small farm animals; a toy telephone; pounding box; blocks; musical instruments; and several tubs filled with baby-type toys—good for chewing and sucking, which are easily washable. Some toys are easily reached by the children, while others can only be reached with adult help. A housekeeping area is equipped with child-sized wooden sink, stove, refrigerator, cupboard, table, and chairs.

A changing table (a cabinet that previously served as an examination table in a doctors' office) is equipped with colorful baskets labeled with infants' names, which contain diapers, extra clothes, ointments, and wipes. A closed storage area under the table holds extra blankets, sheets, and changes of clothes. The changing table has a hard surface that is easily wiped clean with a disinfecting solution. A pillow is available to support a baby's head during changing. A wooden adult-sized rocking chair is close by, as is an infant wind-up swing.

A television set is recessed in the wall, at the eye level of young children. A colorful hard plastic junior gym is in the center of a large motor area, along with a Tike Bike and a riding dog.

A sofa is located near the entrance to the room and serves as a comfortable place for children and adults to relax. The eating area is nearby. A plastic covering is taped to the floor under two high chairs and a 2' × 4' child-height table. This table is also used for creative art activities and projects, as well as for small motor activities and table games. A breakfast bar serves as an out-of-children's-reach surface for journals, notebooks, paper plates, and cups, and as a serving center for food. At mealtimes food is carried on a tray from the kitchen (located upstairs) and placed on this bar until served. There are high shelves and a telephone nearby.

The day begins for the family day-care provider shortly before the children arrive, as she organizes baby food, cereal, juice, milk, bowls, spoons and small cups on a tray for the children's breakfast.

Sally's day takes place in the late springtime.

7:55 A.M.: Sally arrives at the day-care home just before 8:00. Jimmy, Peter, Derek, and Justin have already arrived. When Sally and her mom enter the play area, Sally's feet begin to wiggle. They both are cheerfully greeted by the child-care provider, Ms. Lisa. "Good morning Sally. Good morning Teresa." (Sally's mom.) Sally smiles in recognition. Teresa says, "Sally may be extra tired today. She's been up since before 6:00! She ate some Cheerios with milk and had some apple juice." Sally reaches for Ms. Lisa and gives her a big squeeze around the neck as she rests her head on her shoulder. In a moment she moves to get down. She is greeted by 18-month-old Jimmy who gives her a hug, a kiss, and a "Hi, Sally." Sally responds with a hug but soon her hands start waving and bump into Jimmy's face. Jimmy squirms but is not upset. Sally and Jimmy both walk over to the table to see an "animal sounds barn" toy. Sally's mom and Ms. Lisa exchange more information about Sally's previous evening and morning. Teresa says "Good-bye" to Sally several times before Sally turns from her play for a quick wave "Bye-bye." (Sally does not usually fuss when her mother leaves. She has developed a close, secure relationship with her caregiver. She is also secure in her relationship with her mother, so separation is apparently not a problem.)

8:05 A.M.: Sally begins to protest as Jimmy dominates the animal sounds toy. Jimmy pulls the toy away and Sally cries, putting her thumb into her mouth. She stops in several seconds. Ms. Lisa offers her a flower rattle. "Here Sally!" She takes her thumb out of her mouth, holds the rattle and looks at it. Ms. Lisa helps her hold it so she can see herself in the small mirror on the rattle. "Look at Sally!" Sally pulls the rattle close to her face as she turns her head to the side to look. "That's Sally in the mirror!" Sally smiles and relaxes as Ms. Lisa holds her. She hugs tightly for several seconds.

8:10 A.M.: The caregiver's oldest daughter (11½ years old) comes bounding into the room to "check things out." She greets Jimmy and offers him a hug. He happily responds. She notices Sally, goes over and reaches for her affectionately, saying, "My Sal, my Sal." Sally snuggles closer to Ms. Lisa, but soon relaxes and lets Annie take her. Annie carries Sally over to a small, green plastic box containing little people. "Here Sal, put the people in this box," indicating a larger red plastic box. Sally moves "people" from one box to the other. Annie says, "Bye Sal-Sal, bye Jim-Jim," as she leaves the play area to finish getting ready for school.

8:20 A.M.: Ms. Lisa puts Sally in the high chair and securely buckles her in. Sally sits quietly while a bib is put on her. "Sally, are you hungry this morning? Here is a yummy piece of toast for you." Sally is also offered a few dry Cheerios and sips of milk and orange juice from a "sipper" cup. She sometimes reaches for the cup and says "Uh." Jimmy is sitting in a high chair next to hers. She reaches for a piece of toast on his tray, which he willingly offers to her. Ms. Lisa notices and substitutes Jimmy's toast with a fresh piece. In a few minutes Sally begins to drop Cheerios onto the floor, one by one. This is a clue that breakfast is over. Sally's hands and face are wiped with a moist, sturdy paper towel. She fusses and pulls her hands away. Ms. Lisa calls her name gently, kisses her hand, and smiles. Sally's hands relax, and she laughs while Ms. Lisa quickly finishes wiping her hands and face. When Ms. Lisa takes Sally out of the high chair, Sally puts her arms around her neck and squeezes, saying, "Eeee." "Sally, that's such a nice hug." Sally notices a muppet on the TV (Sesame Street) and points to it. "That's Cookie Monster. He likes to eat Cookies. He's a very soft and friendly monster," explains Ms. Lisa.

8:40 A.M.: Sally loses interest in Cookie Monster. She gets down and walks over to the housekeeping area where Justin, Melanie, and Peter are gathering dishes. Justin picks her up with his arms around her tummy and "hauls" her away. She returns and is moved away again. Because she is still unsteady on her feet, she falls down. She cries and goes over to Ms. Lisa. Ms. Lisa picks her up. Sally lays her head on Ms. Lisa's shoulder, and her thumb goes into her mouth, and her crying stops. She is held and comforted for several more minutes.

8:50 A.M.: An odor is noticed. Before going to the changing table, Ms. Lisa gets a small duck-shaped rattle from the box marked "baby toys." (Babies this age often do not like having diapers changed. The toy is helpful for Sally to hold, suck on, shake, distracting her so her diapering will go smoothly.) Sally is playing with the rattle as she lays on the changing table. "Can you shake it, Sally?" She shakes it and it falls to the floor. "Oh, oh," Sally says. "The rattle fell on the floor. Here Sally, you can hold this one," as Ms. Lisa hands her a ring of plastic keys. Ms. Lisa continues to talk to her as she finishes changing the diaper. She notices that Sally has a slight rash. Sally turns her body to the side to reach for the baby wipes. Ms. Lisa quickly picks her up. "All done. Now your diaper is dry." Sally smiles. They go to the sofa to sit and put Sally's pants on. "This foot goes in this leg. This foot goes in the other leg. Sally's pants are on. Yeah!" Sally begins to struggle to get down, and Ms. Lisa quickly finishes and lets her get down to play.

9:00 A.M.: As Sally walks across the room, Jimmy comes by and bumps into her. She falls down on her bottom and begins to fuss. Ms. Lisa says, "Oh, oh. Sally fell down. You're okay now Sally!" She stops fussing and goes off to play. (Sally spends the next half hour or so going from one area to another—climbing, exploring, and interacting with other children.) She reaches for a horse that Justin has loaded onto a wooden truck, and Justin says, "No, no." Sally stops and watches Justin for a minute. She says "Umm" and toddles off to the climber. Here she climbs up and slides down several times before rejoining the others in the housekeeping area. They have neatly piled the small table with dishes and play food. Sally begins to push food to the floor. Melanie objects and picks her up with her arms around her tummy and carries her over to a shelf with the animal sounds barn toy. Melanie says, in a sweet inviting voice, "Here Sally. Play with this. See the cow. It says moo." Sally begins playing with the top cow and Melanie returns to her play with Justin and Peter in the housekeeping area.

Sally loses interest in the toy. She walks over to the eating area and picks up a tiny piece of paper from the floor. Ms. Lisa takes it away from her without incident. (When Sally crawled, she often had wads of paper in her mouth that were found by both her mother at home and by her caregiver. Since she has begun to walk, she doesn't seem to notice paper on the floor so easily because it's not at eye level.) Soon Sally goes to the child-sized table that *is* at her eye level, and picks up a cup that had been left there. Ms. Lisa removes the cup before the orange juice is spilled.

Sally notices a riding toy dog, climbs onto it, and pushes herself backward with her feet while making a motor sound. She bounces several times. She rubs her hand across the smooth face of the toy, says "ahh," then continues making motor sounds. Ms. Lisa acknowledges Sally's play with positive comments about what she is doing.

As Sally tires of the riding toy, she is off to climb on a nearby chair. Jimmy climbs onto the riding toy and riding away. Sally doesn't notice. A chair is a new challenge for her, and takes her entire attention. She gets on, gets off, gets on, sits down, stands up, and giggles with her accomplishment. Today she discovers another challenge as she climbs from the chair onto the low table. Ms. Lisa moves her back to the chair, "Sally, you may sit on this chair. Look, Jimmy, Sally is sitting on a chair." Jimmy walks over and begins to push her as he tries to get onto the chair too. Sally begins to fuss, and Ms. Lisa redirects Jimmy by putting a four-piece puzzle

on the table. "Here Jimmy, can you put the tractor in this empty space?" Jimmy turns his attention to the puzzle. Sally continues to explore as Ms. Lisa attends to the needs of other children. Ms. Lisa may offer a new play food to Justin, Melanie, and Peter who are playing in the housekeeping area. She may play a short game of peek-a-boo with Jimmy. She may give Derek a bottle of formula, or she may record information in a child's Day-Care Journal. A journal is kept for each family that comes to the day-care home. It is a spiral notebook with a plastic cover. Parents may take this journal home at the end of each day in order to review their child's day, or they may choose to take it home only on weekends, or just periodically.

Several entries are made in Sally's journal:

1. 8:15 Breakfast—ate 1 toast triangle, few dry Cheerios, 2 oz. o.j., 2 oz. milk. Sally is doing very well feeding herself.
2. 8:50 chg. wet/BM (loose consistency; slight diaper rash—Desitin applied.) Sally learned a new "trick" today—she climbed onto the table from a chair!

(In a family day-care home, there are many things to attend to along with taking care of children's needs. A home day-care provider is the administrator-director, teacher, nurse, nutritionist-cook, record-keeper, and janitor. Nutritious snacks and meals have to be prepared by the provider during the day, while maintaining a safe, positive atmosphere for the children. When children are playing happily and independently, the provider can begin lunch preparations. These preparations can be stopped to attend to a fussy baby who needs a bottle or to help resolve a conflict that has arisen between two preschoolers.)

9:30 A.M.: Sally has approached Ms. Lisa several times in the last 10 minutes showing signs of fussiness. A quick diaper check shows that she is still dry. Sally is cuddled on her caregiver's shoulder with her thumb in her mouth, and is then gently laid in her crib and covered with a soft, cozy blanket. "Good night Sally. Have a nice rest." (Sally's crib is located in a room right next to the napping area of the playroom. This arrangement works best because she is easily distracted by the other children.)

9:40 A.M.: Sally is sleeping peacefully in her crib. Four-month-old Derek is also asleep. This is a good time to offer a creative art activity or small manipulatives to the older children. Today the children use soft homemade blue playdough. As they pound, stretch, roll, pinch, and poke, there is discussion of how blue the sky is today, that Jimmy is wearing a blue shirt, and that the picture Peter drew with magic markers has lots of blue in it. Melanie announces that blue begins with "b."

Derek begins to fuss and Ms. Lisa goes to his crib. He usually wakes up about 10:00, ready for a bottle. His brother Justin announces "I want to feed Derek." Melanie also wants to help. Justin and Melanie begin to argue over who will feed Derek. "You both may have a turn holding and feeding him. Justin, I know you like to feed your brother and you do a great job. Melanie likes to help too and she may." (Derek's mother is very tolerant about the older children helping care for him. She has always allowed Justin to hold his brother and play with him. As a result, the brothers are very comfortable with each other and have a close relationship. Ms. Lisa has not seen any serious signs of jealousy from Justin.) Melanie and Justin each have a turn feeding Derek. Ms. Lisa supervises closely to be sure Derek is comfortable and safe.

10:30 A.M.: Sally is still asleep. (She usually sleeps 1 to 2 hours in the morning.) It is a beautiful spring day, and the children and caregiver want to spend some time outside. Ms. Lisa asks Melanie, Justin, Peter, and Jimmy to pick up the play dough and other toys in the room so they can go outside. Peter refuses to help, but the other three begin to put the toys on the shelves. Ms. Lisa goes to Sally's crib and gently calls her name to awaken her. She wakes up quickly but fusses. She lays her head on Ms. Lisa's shoulder as she is carried to the changing table. Sally has

a loose stool again and her rash is worse than before. The loose stool is recorded in her journal. The changing table is cleaned with a disinfecting solution and the caregiver washes her hands thoroughly.

10:45 A.M.: Melanie, Peter, and Justin go upstairs ahead of the others. Melanie asks, "Can I use the green tractor first?" Jimmy and Sally climb the stairs while Ms. Lisa follows with Derek in an infant seat. They go out the side door onto a screened porch. Derek is placed inside a playpen in his infant seat so he can observe all the activities going on. Jimmy and Sally go out to the yard. Sally walks across the grassy yard, and stumbles as she goes down a slight hill. She is not hurt, and gets back up and continues walking toward a toddler push toy. (Sally walked at 11 months, which is a little earlier than the average. Because she has only been walking for 4 weeks, she is still quite unsteady and loses her balance easily. Walking on the uneven ground is good practice for her. She seems to prefer walking instead of crawling to get where she's going.) Melanie, Justin, Peter, and Jimmy are playing a hide-and-find game. Ten plastic colored blocks from a sort box are hidden in various places around the yard. It is Justin's turn to hide the blocks. He says, "Don't look. Everyone cover your eyes." Jimmy covers his eyes with his hands in imitation of Peter. Everyone looks and laughs. He laughs too. Sally gets involved in the game when she picks up a yellow block from the ground and puts it into the box. Everyone says, "Yeah, Sally." She smiles and toddles away. Jimmy claps his hands and says "yeah" too.

11:15 A.M.: Sally and Jimmy play on the screened porch with the door to the outside locked, while Ms. Lisa finishes lunch preparations. (The children are within hearing distance.) Today's lunch is homemade macaroni and cheese, green beans, saltines with peanut butter, peach slices, and milk. The food is placed on a tray along with appropriate utensils.

11:30 A.M.: Ms. Lisa goes to the porch to get the children. Derek is carried down the stairs and placed in an infant swing to wait. Sally is carried down also, and Jimmy follows, crawling down backward. Sally and Jimmy are secured in their highchairs; their hands are wiped with a soapy, wet paper towel, and they are given a peanut butter cracker. Ms. Lisa goes upstairs to get the rest of the food and to call the three preschoolers to lunch. They go to the downstairs bathroom to wash their hands while the food is being served. Sally is given a plate of food with small servings of macaroni and cheese, green beans, and peaches cut into small pieces. She is also given a small spoon that she does not really use for eating, but just holds in her left hand while she eats with her right hand. (Sally has only recently become competent with eating finger foods. Just several weeks ago it was necessary to provide either a jar of baby food as a supplement or to puree the table food with a baby food grinder. Foods such as applesauce and soup still have to be fed to her. Today's menu works well for Sally because everything can be eaten with her fingers.) A cup of milk with a sipper lid is offered to Sally. She handles this very well by herself. She is allowed ample time to finish her lunch with help when necessary. After the preschoolers finish, the table is cleared, and Sally is cleaned up and taken out of the high chair.

12:00 P.M.: Sally is ready to play. She goes to the climber, crawls through a space underneath, climbs up to the platform, and slides down. She does it again. (Just 4 weeks ago Sally did not have the physical skills to do this. She would try to climb but would easily fall. Because she has started walking, she practices all her newly learned skills just as eagerly as an athlete practicing for the Olympics. She is becoming very capable in controlling her own body.) Ms. Lisa has put a Raffi tape into the tape player. Jimmy begins to dance, and Sally walks over to watch him. Ms. Lisa says, "Do you want to dance too?" The three older children join them. In a minute or so Sally wanders off to push the empty baby swing and then heads for the stairs. Ms. Lisa notices this and quickly stops Sally.

"No, Sally. You may not climb on the stairs." She puts a pressure gate at the stairway entrance. (It is important to note here that this 12-month-old baby has an abundance of energy. She goes from place to place very quickly and is interested in everything that catches her eye. This can be a very frustrating experience for the caregiver. It takes a tremendous amount of patience to maintain a positive, safe environment for Sally while providing appropriate experiences for younger and older children too. The advanced physical abilities of Sally add to the difficulty of caring for her. The attachment that had taken place between the caregiver and baby during the preceding months is essential in getting them through these sometimes difficult times.)

12:30 P.M.: Ms. Lisa is feeding a bottle to Derek. Sally crawls up onto the sofa where they are sitting, and reaches for the bottle. "Sally would you like to help me feed Derek?" Sally grabs the bottle and tries to pull it away several times. She cries when Ms. Lisa does not let her have the bottle. Ms. Lisa asks Justin to help feed his brother while she gets a cup of juice for Sally. When Sally is offered the cup, she pushes it away and fusses. Ms. Lisa takes her to the rocking chair for some soothing rocking. Justin announces that Derek has finished his bottle, and he doesn't want to hold him anymore. By now Sally is comforted and wanders off to play as Ms. Lisa continues taking care of Derek. (Sally has been off the bottle for several weeks now. If she gets very fussy and wants a bottle, Ms. Lisa gives her one. The desire for the bottle occurs less frequently than it did even 2 weeks ago. When she is tired and sees another baby having a bottle, she is more likely to want one too.)

1:00 P.M.: It's naptime for everyone. Jimmy is changed and laid in his crib. Justin and Peter go to the bathroom and then to their cots, which have been set up in the playroom. Melanie, the caregiver's daughter, goes upstairs to her own bedroom where she sleeps or rests. After changing Sally, Ms. Lisa puts her in her crib. A few baby toys are placed in there for her to play with because she doesn't usually fall to sleep immediately. Ms. Lisa puts a lullaby tape into the player to provide soothing background music. Derek starts to fuss now, which means he is sleepy too. He is changed, given his pacifier, and laid in his crib on his tummy. He uses his arms to push himself up so he can look around. Ms. Lisa puts his pacifier back into his mouth and gently pats his back until he relaxes and he is soon asleep. All the children sleep for 2 to 3 hours today, but this is not the case every day.

3:15 P.M.: Ms. Lisa's two school-age daughters (Rachael and Annie) arrive home from school, and come to the children's room.

3:30 P.M.: Eighteen-month-old Jimmy wakes up first. Annie greets him, "Hi, Jim-Jim." He reaches for her and gives her a hug. Annie offers to take him outside to play on the swing. A little later she takes him for a short walk.

3:45 P.M.: Sally is awake. Ms. Lisa gets her out of her crib to change her. She has another loose stool. Ointment is used on the rash and this is recorded in her journal.

Ms. Lisa sits down with Sally to put her shoes on, but she begins to stiffen her body and arch her back in protest. "Sally, I need to put your shoes on you." She sings, "Where is Sally? Where is Sally? Right here on my lap." Sally relaxes a little as Ms. Lisa holds onto her tightly as she puts her shoes on. Sally is very eager to get down to play.

4:00 P.M.: Justin, Peter, and Melanie are awake now and anticipating snack. Ms. Lisa instructs them to wash their hands and go to their places at the table, while she buckles Jimmy and Sally in their high chairs. Snack today includes bite-sized crackers with sour cream dip and apple juice. Sally is given a plain cracker that she holds between her thumb and forefinger. Ms. Lisa offers her another cracker with dip. When she feels the dip, she drops the cracker, looks at it, picks it up to taste it and looks at it again, and puts it back into her mouth to eat it. She notices Ms. Lisa pouring juice. She begins kicking her feet, reaches for a cup and says, "Uh, uh." "Sally, do you want some juice?" Sally puts her

thumb in her mouth and waits patiently for her juice.

4:20 P.M.: Sally has finished her snack, as have the other children. Everyone is cleaned up and ready for the end of the day activities. "Sesame Street" is playing on the TV. Jimmy and Peter sit down to watch for several minutes. Melanie and Justin go outside with Annie. Derek is still sleeping. Sally continues her explorations much like she did in the morning. She practices her climbing skills on the little gym, a chair, the bottom step, and in and out of a car seat. Sally is a very busy girl.

4:45 P.M.: Ms. Lisa is sitting at the small table with Sally on her lap. The children are playing with a toy pots and pans set consisting of three plastic pots, a lid, and a spoon. Peter is making stew in one pot, and Sally is holding a lid. "Sally, can you put the lid on this pan?" She tries and succeeds. "Yeah, Sally." The others join in with "Yeah, Sally," too. She smiles with her accomplishment. Eight-year-old Rachael joins them. She says, "Is it good Jimmy?" He pretends to drink from the pot and says, "Umm." Peter offers stew to Ms. Lisa, and Rachael brings the animal sounds barn to the table for Sally. "See Sally. This is a horse." All the children want to play and Rachael helps them take turns. Ms. Lisa quickly checks on Melanie and Justin, who are still outside with Annie.

5:00 P.M.: Teresa arrives to pick Sally up. She says, "Hi, Sally. Hi Sally." Sally notices her, laughs, and walks in the other direction playing a come-and-get-me game. Ms. Lisa picks her up and carries her to Teresa. Sally is holding a plastic play spoon in her hand. Ms. Lisa says, "Sally had a very busy day! She learned a new trick today—she discovered that she can climb from the chair onto the table!" They both smile about this. They review the notes in the journal. "Sally's stools were very loose and they are causing a rash." Teresa says, "She's been having loose stools at home too. Maybe I should call the doctor." "That sounds like a good idea. That way we will know if we should watch what she eats." They discuss this further. Ms. Lisa tucks the journal into Sally's diaper bag, while Teresa tries to take the toy spoon from Sally, who is holding on tight. Teresa reaches into the diaper bag to find one of Sally's own toys, and Sally reaches for her own toy as Ms. Lisa takes the other toy.

As Teresa and Sally go up the stairs, they wave bye-bye. "Bye, Sally. Have a nice evening with your mommy and daddy. I'll see you tomorrow." And so another day in the life of Sally in her home day-care has ended.

A concluding statement by the provider. A home day-care situation for infants and toddlers has several unique features to offer. These include a homelike setting where natural daily activities take place, a small group size that can include all the children from a family, the consistency of a single caregiver, flexible and part-time hours, close to a child's own home, and sometimes a cost break to parents.

In the homelike setting, the child's care can be provided in a fairly unstructured fashion to meet individual needs of the child in a family atmosphere. A home day care offers a small group size that can include brothers and sisters who spend their day together just as they would if they were at home with mom and dad. A 4-year-old boy can help with the care of his baby brother by feeding him and playing with him. There is ample opportunity for them to be together, so a special relationship can develop. An older sister might join them after her day at school.

The consistency of a single caregiver seems to offer a tremendous boost to an infant or toddler. The person who greets the child in the morning is also the one who says "bye-bye" at the end of the day. This is a big plus in the life of a baby. It is a special ingredient that can only be offered in home day care.

Flexible hours are more easily offered in a home day care. A child who needs care at 5:30 A.M. can be accommodated, as can a child who needs evening or overnight care. A home caregiver should carefully consider her own family

obligations before offering after-hour, or part-time care, but these are possibilities.

Family day-care homes are usually in residential neighborhoods, and therefore offer the children care close to their own homes. This is convenient for the parents. It also means that a child in after-school care can play close to home and school.

A family day-care may be able to charge lower fees than a center-based program, because of lower overhead expenses. However, the quality care of an infant is both labor intensive and vital; it depends on the consistency of the caregiver. It is hoped parents will be willing to pay a reasonable fee for child care in order to motivate the provider to stay in business for a period of time. Research has shown that very young children should not be moved from one caregiver to another, at least before their third birthday. Although this is not always possible, it is a goal to work for.

Operating a home day-care business is a valuable career option for anyone who has met the requirements for a CDA credential or for a degree in early childhood education. The advantages include being at home for your own children, and providing a valuable service for other children and their families as you put into practice the skills of the profession.

CONCLUDING REMARKS

It is true that many infants and toddlers are not receiving the high quality educaring described in the four typical days. However, such educaring is possible, as shown in the examples, when the educaring staff is well-trained and committed to delivering a high quality service to children and families.

The issue of quality received much professional attention during the 1980s, and resulted in the following publications that serve as guidelines for educaring environments and activities.

1. *Early Childhood Environment Rating Scale* by Harms and Clifford

2. *Family Day Care Rating Scale* by Harms and Clifford

3. *Infant/Toddler Environment Rating Scale* by Harms, Clifford, and Cryer

4. *Child Development Associate* credentials for family day care and infant/toddler care from the CDA National Credentialing Program

5. *Developmentally Appropriate Care for Children from Birth to Age 3* by Lally, Provence, Szanton, and Weissbourd. This is the first part of NAEYC's *Developmentally Appropriate Practice in Early Childhood Programs Serving Children from Birth through Age 8* (expanded ed.) (1987), edited by Bredekamp.

6. Accreditation criteria and procedures of the National Academy of Early Childhood Programs

7. The draft report of the APHA/AAP project to develop national health and safety standards (Cohen, 1989) or the finalized version.

SUGGESTED ACTIVITIES

1. Observe a full day in an infant/toddler center, and in a family day-care home serving infants and toddlers. Select one child in each, and write a running account of his or her day. Using this account list examples of high quality and low quality educaring. Share the descriptions and lists with your classmates, and compile a master list of developmentally appropriate practices for infant/toddler educarers.

2. Observe a full day in an infant/toddler center, and in a family day-care home serving infants and toddlers. Write a running account of the activities of the primary educarer in each situation. Share your descriptions with your classmates, and compile a list of guidelines for educaring activities in either setting.

3. Write to your State Department of Human Services, asking for a copy of licensing requirements for infant/toddler programs, both in centers and in family or group day-care homes (or contact your county DHS office).

4. Interview the licenser from the local DHS. Ask questions about the nonmaternal provisions for infants and/or toddlers in the local community.

5. Write to the National Association for Family Day Care, P.O. Box 71268, Murray, UT 84107 for list of publications and a sample copy of their newsletter.

6. The Bush Center in Child Development and Social Policy has developed a National Family Day Care Project resource clearinghouse. Write for information.

The Bush Center in Child Development and Social Policy
Yale University
P.O. Box 11A, Yale Station
New Haven, CT 06520–7447

SUGGESTED READINGS

Caldwell, B., & Rorex, J. (1977). A day at the Kramer Baby House. In M. D. Cohen (Ed.), *Developing programs for infants and toddlers*. Washington, DC: Association for Childhood Education International.

CDA National Credentialing Program. (1985). *Family day care providers: Child Development Associate assessment system and competency standards*. Washington, DC: Author.

CDA National Credentialing Program. (1986). *Infant/toddler caregivers in center-based programs: Child Development Associate assessment system and competency standards*. Washington, DC: Author.

Cohen, H. J. (Chair of the APHA/APA Project to develop National Health and Safety Standards). (1989). *Draft report of the technical report on children with special needs*. New York: Albert Einstein College of Medicine of Yeshiva University.

Harms, T., & Clifford, R. (1980). *Early Childhood Environment Rating Scale*. New York: Teachers College Press.

Harms, T., & Clifford, R. (1989). *Family Day Care Rating Scale*. New York: Teachers College Press.

Harms, T., Clifford, R., & Cryer, D. (1990). *Infant/Toddler Environment Rating Scale.* New York: Teachers College Press.

Lally, J. R., Provence, S., Szanton, E., & Weissbourd, B. (1987). Developmentally appropriate care for children from birth to age 3. In S. Bredekamp (Ed.), *Developmentally appropriate practice in early childhood programs serving children from birth through age 8* (expanded ed.). Washington, DC: National Association for the Education of Young Children.

National Academy of Early Childhood Programs. (1984). *Accreditation criteria & procedures.* Washington, DC: National Association for the Education of Young Children.

Roemer, J. (1989). *Two to four from 9 to 5: The adventures of a daycare provider.* New York: Harper & Row.

Sale, J. S. (1971). *I'm not just a sitter. . .* Pasadena, CA: Pacific Oaks College.

13

Advocacy for Children and Families

The journey of a thousand miles begins with a single step.
-Lao-Tzu
(Chinese philosopher, 6th Century B.C.)

Children are totally dependent on adult caring and adult advocacy because children cannot vote, lobby or make campaign contributions, or write laws or editorials. Responsible citizens all over the world who are concerned about the welfare of children (and the related future of the world), developed the *UN Convention on the Rights of the Child.* In our country, many persons and many organizations have not waited for the United States ratification of the *Convention,* and have already become outspoken advocates for children and their families. At the present time, however,

> national and local institutions have not yet become responsive to families' need for support as they address the normal, developmental challenges of child rearing. In all other industrial countries—in Europe and Asia, for example— there are institutionalized support systems for young families. They provide flexible schedules for working mothers, for example, and arrangements for substitute child care. The U.S. has not been sensitive to families' needs, nor is it a child-oriented society (Brazelton, 1989, pp. 14–15).

Throughout the 1970s and early 1980s there were five unsuccessful attempts to pass comprehensive child-care legislation. The reasons for failure had little to do with child care, but involved states' rights issues, the separation of church and state, the fear of new taxes, and the general state of the economy. These same issues are being debated, either openly or disguised in other language, as we enter the 1990s. Even the corporate-supported child-care programs have been established for reasons far beyond the best interests of the child. Business is getting involved because child and family programs have had a positive effect on employee recruitment, retention, and productivity.

Child care is a political issue, and advocacy is the way to influence the political process (Caldwell, 1987). Currently there seem to be only three sets of people within the triangle of the day-care trilemma: parents, educarers, and children. The triangle needs to be expanded by drawing in employers, government at all levels, private and public agencies, foundations, public education, religious groups, organized labor, and the United Way. Such partnerships can provide financial and social support. Financial support would ensure the stable funding of good quality day-care programs at prices affordable to families. Social support is needed to promote awareness of child-care issues, to help parents develop child-care consumer skills, to identify problems and promote public policy changes to improve child care, and to view child care as a basic necessity to today's families. Quality child care is not simply an issue for parents. It is an issue for our society as a whole, because good quality child care is a sound investment in our future.

Community-Level Advocacy

Until recently, child advocates have looked to the federal government for assistance in meeting child-care needs. Now we have learned that "politicians have viewed family issues as worth

mentioning in speeches but not worth addressing in policy" (Schroeder, 1989, p. 10). Today, although the role of the federal government is important (Title IV—A of the Social Security Act, The Child Care Food Program, and the Family Support Act [passed in October, 1988, and to be operating by October, 1990]), it is clear that the government will not and cannot solve the problem alone. It is necessary for communities to mobilize all levels and kinds of support—local business and industry, community service organizations, volunteer agencies, and concerned citizens, as well as the early childhood community. Today many community agencies are involved with families, particularly families with problems, but this involvement usually comes when the child is 3 years or older.

It is true that our main responsibility is to offer direct services to children and families, but one important way to meet this responsibility is to work for policies that promote children's

Every child has the right to adequate nutrition, housing, recreation, and medical services; the right to free primary education; the right to special treatment education, and care if handicapped; and protection from any form of discrimination regardless of race, color, sex, religion, or nationality—UN Convention on the Rights of the Child, adopted 1989. (Early Childhood Education Center)

growth and development. How? We can protest conditions as they are or as they are proposed, such as

- "Keep off the grass" signs in a city park
- "No children allowed" policies in rental housing
- The closing of the free medical clinic because of lack of volunteers
- The refusal of the high school to operate a child-care center for babies of teenage mothers who need to finish their schooling
- The cutbacks in funding of the Department of Human Services, resulting in increased case loads for child care licensers and/or monitors
- The rezoning of land next to your center, so that industry (with its pollution) can move in

As individuals, we can

- survey toy shops for war toys
- watch the Saturday morning children's programs, and write a reaction letter to the TV station
- write a letter to the editor responding to an article or event
- use radio call-in shows
- join a professional group
- participate in "The Week of the Young Child" (NAEYC)
- invite city officials (and state representatives) to visit your program
- educate parents about the characteristics of quality programs, about community resources in place, and community resources that should be in place
- join with parents and colleagues in attending a state legislator's town meeting
- speak at the local school board meeting about developmentally appropriate practices for young children
- work to organize a resource and referral agency to provide information to parents by maintaining up-to-date listings of available

educarers, their location, ages served, and fees charged. The R & R agency should not recommend, but could limit their list to the licensed or registered centers and family day-care homes (Making the most, 1987). Corsini et al. (1988) suggest that the role of the R & R agency be expanded to assist providers with financial matters and to provide training for professional development. Some R & R agencies include toy-lending libraries and resource libraries for parents and educarers.

It is obvious that these suggested activities are not specifically directed to the infant/toddler years, but they are directly related to the early childhood years. The result of such activities will lead to the recognition that infant/toddler educarers are also child-and-family advocates, and this recognition will lead to an increased awareness and appreciation of our efforts for the very youngest children.

The main message here is that infant/toddler educarers should not only join in advocacy efforts under way, but should also seek out new ways to become recognized as advocates for children and their families. Just one example will illustrate how to take the initiative at a time of an apparently unrelated happening.

> In one community a fire broke out in a licensed family day care home that enrolled more than 10 children. (There is usually a limit of 6.) Local advocates, who for years had been trying to limit the number of children in group care, used the opportunity to talk with reporters about their issue. Several stories followed that examined state and local licensing requirements and the need for legislative change (Goffin & Lombardi, 1988, p. 61).

State-Level Advocacy

The responsibility for many programs has been moved from the federal to the state level, so advocates can make an important impact by focusing on state activities. Five steps to successful advocacy are:

1. Get acquainted with state decision-makers.

2. Know your facts (both statistical and your personal knowledge).

3. Share your expertise (write letters and ask for a response; send telegrams, mailgrams or telephone; visit legislators at the State Capitol or when they are home; prepare a "fact sheet").

4. Maintain contact in and outside the legislative process. Send newsletters, pictures of your program; make the legislator an honorary board member.

5. Join with others (state or local networks; state professional organizations) (Lombardi & Goffin, 1986).

To become effective advocates, we must learn how to lobby. Lobbying may sound intimidating, but "it is nothing more than getting the right information to the right people at the right time" (Wilkins & Blank, 1986, p. 71). Remember, we are not alone. Involve the parents by distributing flyers about the proposed state budget, and ask them to call their legislators as lobbyists for child care in the budget, and also as lobbyists for increased wages for educaring staff. What is good for early childhood personnel (higher wages or appropriate adult-child ratios) is good for children and their families. Caldwell (1987) is firm in her opinion that

> There is no way that it can be good for children to be cared for by persons who are overworked, underpaid, and underappreciated; who cannot afford to play an important role in the lives of children of other people without causing their own children to suffer economic privation; who constantly have to defend the validity of what they do to persons who at best consider them inconsequential and at worst harmful. In short, there can be no effective advocacy for children without including advocacy for those who help care for and education them (p. 30).

National-Level Advocacy (Governmental)

Members of Congress do not receive many individually written letters expressing opinions on vital issues; therefore, they are apt to pay considerable attention to the ones they receive. Representatives are human beings, regardless of their high offices, and are more reachable than many of us suppose.

The most effective way to write to your members of Congress is to compose your own letter, in your own words. Identify the subject clearly, state the reason for writing and include how the issue would affect you, your family, your community, and/or children and families. Be reasonable, and do not threaten. (I won't vote for you unless. . . .) Ask them to state their positions on the issue in their replies. Thank your legislators for their consideration of your opinion, for their reply (in advance), and for past actions on particular issues with which you agree.

The proper forms for addressing the representatives are as follows:

For U.S. Senators
    The Hon. _____
    United States Senate
    Washington, D.C. 20510
    Dear Senator _____

For U.S. Representatives
    The Hon. _____
    House of Representatives
    Washington, D.C. 20515

Guidelines for Legislation

The National Association for the Education of Young Children (1987) has adopted a position statement titled *Guidelines for Developing Legislation Creating or Expanding Programs for Young Children,* which suggests the following questions to ask about new legislation:

Provision of program standards to assure quality programs
1. Does the legislation spell out a process for developing and effectively implementing standards that ensure the safety and well-being of the children served, while promoting their healthy development?
    a. If the process is the state's licensing system, does the licensing office have ade-

quate staffing to handle the expansion and are the standards adequate to accomplish the purposes of the legislation?

b. If the process is *not* licensing because programs may be delivered primarily through public agencies, does the legislation include wording to assure that the new programs will be at least equal to or surpass in quality programs licensed by the state?

c. When standards are developed, does the legislation assure that program standards address each of the following areas:
   - staff qualifications,
   - parent role,
   - group size and staff-child ratios,
   - discipline, and
   - developmentally appropriate practice?

d. Does the legislation assure that there will be a system for implementing the standards that include monitoring and inspections?

2. Does the legislation require that an advisory committee, composed in part of members with early childhood expertise, approve the program standards once developed?

3. Does the legislation assure that the appropriate use of evaluation instruments and procedures are addressed within the program standards?

a. Are decisions regarding enrollment, retention, and placement in special classes based primarily on observations by parents and qualified professionals, rather than on a single test score?

b. Is developmental assessment of children's progress and achievement used to plan curriculum, identify children with special needs, communicate with parents, and evaluate the program's effectiveness?

Parental access and involvement

1. Does the legislation provide opportunities for families to make informed choices concerning the program they want for their child? (e.g., Can parents choose either home-based child care or a center-based program? Can parents choose a school near their work site as well as near their home?)

2. Does the legislation assure the establishment of close ties between program staff and children's families?

a. Are staff required to inform parents or guardians of the program's philosophy and operating procedures?

b. Are parents provided with ongoing opportunities to discuss their children's needs and progress with program staff?

c. Are parent representatives included as members of pertinent advisory groups?

d. Do parents have unrestricted access to the program facility?

3. Does the legislation make provision for a variety of family needs, including those of working families, by allowing the funding of full-day programs (covering the average parent's working day) as well as part-day programs?

Eligibility for service

1. Is the long-term goal of the legislation to provide services to all children? If the legislation or available resources restrict service provision, is the target group the most needy?

2. Will the legislation extend eligibility to previously unserved or underserved groups (e.g., teenage parents, families who would be poor without subsidized early childhood programs)?

3. Does the legislation facilitate a socioeconomic mix of children in programs through the use of such mechanisms as sliding fee scales and other funding sources?

Linkages and coordination

1. Does the legislation provide the administering agency flexibility to fund a variety of public and private community agencies that demonstrate the ability to provide high quality early childhood services?

2. Does the legislation encourage or require programs to make linkage with other funding sources in order to serve more children (e.g., in-kind contributions, parent fees, coordinative agreements, and matching funds from private and public sources)?

3. Does the legislation encourage collaboration among the various agencies whose programs affect young children and their families (e.g., legislative creation of an Interagency Committee or other such mechanism to assure coordination of service provision for young children and their families)?

4. Does the legislation contribute to the overall

provision of services for young children and
avoid duplicating existing public or private
programs?

Provision of professional expertise

1. Does the legislation require programs to employ persons with early childhood professional expertise at all stages of development
and implementation and does it assure adequate compensation for those who work with
young children?
2. Are advisory groups that include members of
the early childhood profession as well as parent and community representatives legisla-
tively created at both the state and program
level?
3. Are the staff responsible for implementation
in the administering agency and at the program level required to have specialized training related to the age of children served and
work experience with this age group?

Funding

1. Will the legislation provide adequate funds
per child to assure program quality and permit adequate compensation for staff?
2. Are funds to continued effort to meet
standards?
3. Will the legislation provide for increased
funding reflective of the cost of living? (Reprinted by permission of NAEYC, 1987, pp.
44–45).

Grass Roots Advocacy

While waiting for national action instead of political rhetoric, concerned persons have established action groups and massive lobbying
efforts.

The Child Care Action Campaign
(CCAC). Founded by Elinor Guggenheimer,
the Campaign is fighting for a nationwide child-
care system to relieve the guilt and worry of
working mothers who must work. In February,
1989, the Campaign led a nationwide survey,
with the results as follows:

- Over 75 percent of 150,000 respondents believe the federal government must do more to
meet the child-care needs of families.

- Over 62 percent feel businesses should play a
key role.
- More than 93 percent pushed for parental
leave to take care of a newborn, newly
adopted, or sick child, without fear of losing
one's job (Family Matters, 1989, p. 58).

These results were sent to the president and
many members of Congress for their consideration when writing legislation. The CCAC has
also approached Labor Department officials,
because it will take more than a federal law to
solve the day-care problem.

Long-range goals of CCAC include the

establishment of a National Child Care Office,
expansion of the Head Start program, job-pro-
tected parental leave, use of public schools as
child-care facilities, and subsidies or tax credits
for parents using day care and businesses that
provide it for employers (Gannett News Service,
May 26, 1989).

The Family Resource Coalition (FRC).
This coalition's mission is to build support and
resources within communities that strengthen
and empower families, enhance the capacities
of parents, and foster the optimal development
of children. This national coalition provides
leadership by developing resources for programs, by affecting public policies, and by
increasing the public understanding of and
commitment to families (Family Resource
Coalition, 1989).

The coalition itself is an umbrella organization consisting of a diversity of support programs for low-income families. Although the focus is not on infant/toddler care and education
per se, providing such a program is frequently
a basic need in order to allow families the time
and freedom to increase their possibility of self-
sufficiency. Almost all advocacy for children efforts have recognized the necessity of including
advocacy for families. FRC President, Bernice
Weissbourd, states, "We believe that children
cannot be seen as separate and distinct from the
family, nor the family as separate and distinct

from the community in which it lives'' (*Our story*, Family Resource Coalition, n.d.).

Parent Action. Child and family advocate Bernice Weissbourd, pediatrician T. Berry Brazelton, and singer Stevie Wonder are three of the founders and chairpersons of Parent Action, a new (1989) national voice for American families. It is one of the many divisions of the Family Resource Coalition. Top priorities are improved child-care services, a national parental leave policy, and expanded family-support programs. Parent Action is designed to enable parents to take their concerns directly to the nation's legislators.

Children's Defense Fund (CDF). ''The Children's Defense Fund exists to provide a strong and effective voice for the children of America who cannot vote, lobby, or speak for themselves'' (Children's Defense Fund, 1990, cover page). The Fund's endeavors focus on programs and policies that affect large numbers of children and their families. Several states have established their own CDF Offices. Their president, Marian Wright Edelman, is a frequent keynote speaker at national conferences, and is responsible for the annual analyses of the federal budget in terms of children's needs.

The Child Care Employee Project. This project released its findings of the National Child Care Staffing Study in October, 1989, and presented them to the House Select Committee on Children, Youth, and Families. The major findings (as expected) were the very low wages for early childhood educators, and that better quality centers had higher wages for teaching staff, lower teaching staff turnovers, better educated and trained staff, and more teachers caring for fewer children. It is hoped our legislators will realize the critical importance of a trained and stable educaring work force as they confront the on-going debates about what is best for children in nonmaternal child care.

SUMMARY

Very young children are totally dependent on the adults who make decisions about their well-being. It is very clear that many groups of concerned citizens and legislators have become aware of the absolute necessity of providing quality nonmaternal education and care to all children who need it. It will be many years before each and every child will receive what we now know is essential for the future of our society. The child and family advocacy movement will be successful only when there is a ground swell of grassroots support. The committed infant/toddler educarer must become a committed advocate for the things we all believe in.

SUGGESTED ACTIVITIES

1. Write for list of publications about the National Child Care Staffing Project.

   Child Care Employee Project
   P.O. Box 5603
   Berkeley, CA 94705

2. Request information about the Family Resource Coalition and its several programs, including Parent Action.

   Family Resource Coalition
   230 N. Michigan Avenue
   Suite #1625
   Chicago, Illinois 60601

3. Request advocacy materials from:

   National Association for Family Day Care
   Box 71268
   Murray, Utah 84107

4. The Department of Health and Human Services issued proposed regulations for the Family Support Act of 1988 in April, 1989. All states were required to adapt their own welfare reform efforts to comply with the federal regulations. Contact your local or state DHHS office to learn the decisions that have been reached in your state.

5. Look for conditions in your community that are not in the best interest of children, and discuss possible strategies to bring about their improvement. Join with your classmates and/or others and use one of the strategies.

6. Conduct a survey of parents with young children in your community, asking about their child-care needs and their solutions. If their needs are not being met satisfactorily, write a letter explaining your findings to your city officials.

7. Check your newspaper and the news magazines for information about proposed legislation related to children and/or families at the state and national levels. Select one of the advocacy strategies suggested in the chapter, and put it into operation. (This should be an on-going activity for all educarers.)

SUGGESTED READINGS

Allen, E. K. (1983). Children, the Congress and you. *Young Children, 38* (2), 71–75.

Almy, M. (1985). New challenges for teacher education. *Young Children, 40 (6),* 10–11.

Beck, R. (1979). *It's time to stand up for your children: A parent's guide to child advocacy.* Washington, DC: Children's Defense Fund.

Bing, S. R., & Richart, D. W. (1987). *Fairness is a kid's game: A background paper for child advocates.* Indianapolis: The Lilly Endowment, Inc. Available from Kentucky Youth Advocates, Inc., 2024 Woodford Pl., Louisville, KY 40205.

Blank, H. (1989). Child care and welfare reform: New opportunities for families. *Young Children, 44* (4), 28–30.

Briggs, P. (1985). The early childhood network: We work together for young children. *Young Children, 40* (5), 54–55.

Bronfenbrenner, U., & Weiss, H. B. (1983). Ecological perspectives on child and family policy. In E. F. Zigler (Ed.), *Children, families, and government.* New York: Cambridge University Press.

Cahill, B. F. (1986). Training volunteers as child advocates. *Child Welfare, 65,* 545–553.

Caldwell, B. (1983). How can we educate the American public about the child care profession? *Young Children, 38* (3), 11–17.

Caldwell, B. (1986). Professional child care: A supplement to parental care. In N. Gunzenhauser & B. M. Caldwell (Eds.), *Group care for young children.* Somerville, NJ: Johnson & Johnson Baby Products.

Caldwell, B. (1987, March). Advocacy is everybody's business. *Child Care Information Exchange,* (54), 29–32.

Children's Defense Fund. (published yearly). *A children's defense budget: An analysis of the FY 19 [ ] federal budget and children.* Washington, DC: Author. (122 C St. N.W., Washington, DC 20001)

Children's Defense Fund. (1987). *Child care: The time is now.* Washington, DC: Author.

Children's Defense Fund. (1989). *A vision for America's future.* Washington, DC: Author.

Children's Defense Fund. (1990). *S.O.S. America!* Washington, DC: Author.

The common good: Social welfare and the American future. (1989). New York: Ford Foundation.

Corsini, D. A., Wisensale, S., & Caruso, G. A. (1988). Family day care: System issues and regulatory models. *Young Children, 43* (6), 17–23.

Family Resource Coalition. (1989). *Programs that serve families at risk.* Chicago: Author.

Fennimore, B. S. (1989). *Child advocacy for early childhood educators.* New York: Teachers College Press.

Fink, J., & Sponseller, D. (1977, March). Practicing for child advocacy. *Young Children, 32* (3), 49–54.

Forgione, P. D., Jr. (1980). Early childhood policymaking: Inputs, processes and legislative outputs. *Education and Urban Society, 12* (2), 227–239.

Freeman, M. (1986). *Called to act: Stories of child care advocacy in our churches.* New York: Child Advocacy Office, Division of Church and Society, National Council of the Churches in the U.S.A. (475 Riverside Dr., New York, NY 10115–0050)

Fried, M. (1983). Coalition building for children. *Young Children, 38* (4), 77–80.

Goffin, S. G. (1988). Putting our advocacy efforts into a new context. *Young Children, 43* (3), 42–56.

Goffin, S. G., & Lombardi, J. (1988). *Speaking out: Early childhood advocacy.* Washington, DC: National Association for the Eduction of Young Children.

Goodnow, J. J., & Burns, A. (1982). Factors affecting policies in early childhood education: An Australian case. In L. G. Katz (Ed.), *Current Topics in Early Childhood Education.* Vol. 5. Norwood, NJ: Ablex.

Grotberg, E. (1980). The roles of the federal government in regulation and maintenance of quality child care. In S. Kilmer (Ed.), *Advances in early education and day care, 1,* 19–45.

Halpern, R. (1987). Major social and demographic trends affecting young families: Implications for early childhood care and education. *Young Children, 42* (6), 34–40.

Hofferth, S. L., & Phillips, D. A. (1987). Child care in the United States, 1970 to 1985. *Journal of Marriage and the Family, 49,* 559–571.

Hostetler, L. (1981). Child advocacy: Your professional responsibility? *Young Children, 36* (3), 3–8.

Hostetler, L. (1983, March/April). How-to guide for advocates. *Child Care Information Exchange,* (30), 25–29.

Hayes, C. D. (1982). *Making policies for children: A study of the federal process.* Washington, DC: National Academy Press.

How to lobby for child care. (1985, May). *Child Care Information Exchange,* (43), 9–10.

Hunt, A. (1988). From solo to chorus: Child advocacy in Tennessee. *Dimensions, 16* (4), 23–26.

Jensen, M. A., & Chevalier, Z. W. (Eds.). (1990). *Issues and advocacy in early education* (especially ch. 2: Advocacy for the Professional and the Profession, and ch. 13: Advocacy: Influencing policy and regulations). Needham, MA: Allyn & Bacon.

Jorde, P. (1986). Early childhood education: Issues and trends. *The Educational Forum, 50,* 172–181.

Kagan, S. L. (1988, May). Dealing with our ambivalence about advocacy. *Child Care Information Exchange,* (61), 31–34.

Kagan, S., Powell, D., Weissbourd, B., & Zigler, E. (Eds.). (1987). *America's family support programs.* New Haven, CT: Yale University Press.

Kipnis, K. (1987). How to discuss professional ethics. *Young Children, 42* (4), 26–30.

Lande, J. S. Scarr, S., & Gunzenhauser, N. (Eds.). (1989). *Caring for children: Challenge to America.* Hillsdale, NJ: Lawrence Erlbaum.

League of Women Voters. (n.d.). *When you write to Washington: A guide to citizen action.* Washington, DC: Author.

Levine, C. (Ed.). (1988). *Programs to strengthen families: A resource guide* (rev. ed.). Chicago: Family Resource Coalition.

Lombardi, J. (1986). Training for public policy and advocacy. *Young Children, 41* (4), 65–69.

Lombardi, J. (1987). Improving child care for infants and toddlers. *Dimensions, 15* (3), 26–27.

Lombardi, J. (1988). Now more than ever. . . . It is time to become an advocate for better child care. *Young Children, 43* (5), 41–43.

Lombardi, J., & Goffin, S. G. (1986). Child advocacy at the state level: Strategies for success. *Dimensions, 14* (2), 15–18.

Macchiarola, F. J., & Gartner, A. (1989). *Caring for America's children.* New York: The Academy of Political Science.

Making the most of new child care funds. (1987, January). *CDF Reports,* 4–5.

Mills, B. C., Matlock, J. R., & Herrell, A. L. (1988). Infant care: Does anybody care? *International Journal of Early Childhood, 20* (2), 36–45.

Modigliani, K. (1986). But who will take care of the children? Child care, women, and devalued labor. *Journal of Education, 168* (3), 46–49.

Montessori, S. (1985, May). How to lobby for child care. *Child Care Information Exchange,* (43), 9–10.

Morgan, G. (1983). Practical techniques for change. *Journal of Children in Contemporary Society* (Special issue: Childcare: Emerging issues), *15* (4), 91–103.

Morgan, G. (1984). Change through regulation. In J. T. Greenman & R. W. Fuqua (Eds.), *Making day care better: Training, evaluation, and the process of change.* New York: Teachers College Press.

National Association for the Education of Young Children. (1981). NAEYC advocacy strategies: The care of infants and toddlers. *Young Children, 36* (2), 51–55.

National Association for the Education of Young Children. (1984). *NAEYC position statements on child care and family day care regulation.* Washington, DC: Author.

National Association for the Education of Young Children. (1987). Guidelines for developing legislation creating or expanding programs for young children. *Young Children, 42* (3), 43–45.

NAEYC Position statement on licensing and other forms of regulation of early childhood programs in centers and family day care homes. (1987). *Young Children, 42* (5), 64–68.

National Center for Clinical Infant Programs. (1988). *Who will mind the babies?* (2nd ed.). Washington, DC: Author.

Nelson, J. R., Jr. (1982). The politics of federal day care regulation. In E. F. Zigler & E. W. Gordon (Eds.), *Day care: Scientific and social policy issues.* Boston: Auburn House.

Nickel, P. S., & Delany, H. (1985). *Working with teen parents: A survey of promising approaches.* Chicago: Family Resource Coalition.

Oakes, M. (Ed.). (1987). *Your legislative guide to child advocacy.* Washington, DC: National PTA.

Orton, R. E., & Langham, B. (1980). What is government's role in quality day care? In S. Kilmer (Ed.), *Advances in early education and day care, 1,* 47–62.

Phillips, D. (1987). From a tattered patchwork quilt to whole cloth: Child care advocacy for 1987. *Dimensions, 16* (1), 18–10, 23.

Phillips, D. A., & Lande, J. (1988, January). The politics of child care. *Child Care Information Exchange,* (59), 9–12.

Schroeder, P. (1989). *Champion of the great American family.* New York: Random House.

Suransky, V. P. (1984). *The erosion of childhood.* Chicago: University of Chicago Press.

Tyler-Wilkins, A., & Blank, H. (1987). Building a child care coalition and giving it power. In *Child Care America: Project guidelines and resources for community organization and outreach activity* (pp. 67–77). (A National Project of the Public Television Outreach Alliance). Available from NAEYC.

Weiser, M. G. (1982). Public policy: For or against children and families: An international perspective. *Childhood Education, 58* (4), 227–234.

Whitebrook, M., & Ginsburg, G. (Eds.). (1984). *Just working with kids: Preparing early childhood teachers to advocate for themselves and others.* Berkeley, CA: Child Care Employee Project. (P.O. Box 5603, Berkeley, CA, 94705)

Wilkins, A., & Blank, H. (1986). Child care: Strategies to move the issue forward. *Young Children, 42* (1), 68–72.

Young, K. T., & Zigler, E. (1986). Infant and toddler day care: Regulations and policy implications. *American Journal of Orthopsychiatry, 56,* 43–55.

Zigler, E. (1986). The family resource movement: No longer the country's best secret. *Family Resource Coalition Report, 5* (3), 9–12.

Zigler, E., & Finn, M. (1981a). From problem to solution: Changing public policy as it affects children and families. *Young Children, 36* (4), 31–32, 55–59.

Zigler, E., & Finn, M. (1981b). A vision of child care in 1980s. In L. A. Bond & J. M. Jaffe (Eds.), *Facilitating infant and early child development.* Hanover, NH: University Press of New England.

Zigler, E. F., & Gordon, E. W. (1982). *Day care: Scientific and social policy issues* (esp. chs. 15–22, 24). Boston: Auburn House.

Zill, N. (1988). *Basic facts about the use of child care and preschool services by families in the U.S.* Washington, DC: Child Trends.

Appendixes

A

Education of the Handicapped Act Amendments of 1986, Part H.

PART H—HANDICAPPED INFANTS AND TODDLERS

FINDINGS AND POLICY

SEC. 671. (a) FINDINGS.—The Congress finds that there is an urgent and substantial need—

(1) to enhance the development of handicapped infants and toddlers and to minimize their potential for developmental delay,

(2) to reduce the educational costs to our society, including our Nation's schools, by minimizing the need for special education and related services after handicapped infants and toddlers reach school age,

(3) to minimize the likelihood of institutionalization of handicapped individuals and maximize the potential for their independent living in society, and

(4) to enhance the capacity of families to meet the special needs of their infants and toddlers with handicaps.

(b) POLICY.—It is therefore the policy of the United States to provide financial assistance to States—

(1) to develop and implement a statewide, comprehensive, coordinated, multidisciplinary, interagency program of early intervention services for handicapped infants and toddlers and their families,

(2) to facilitate the coordination of payment for early intervention services from Federal, State, local, and private sources (including public and private insurance coverage), and

(3) to enhance its capacity to provide quality early intervention services and expand and improve existing early intervention services being provided to handicapped infants, toddlers, and their families.

DEFINITIONS

SEC. 672. As used in this part—

(1) The term "handicapped infants and toddlers" means individuals from birth to age 2, inclusive, who need early intervention services because they—

(A) are experiencing developmental delays, as measured by appropriate diagnostic instruments and procedures in one or more of the following areas: Cognitive development, physical development, language and speech development, psychosocial development, or self-help skills, or

(B) have a diagnosed physical or mental condition which has a high probability of resulting in developmental delay.

Such term may also include, at a State's discretion, individuals from birth to age 2, inclusive, who are at risk of having substantial developmental delays if early intervention services are not provided.

363

(2) "Early intervention service services" are developmental services which—

(A) are provided under public supervision,

(B) are provided at no cost except where Federal or State law provides for a system of payments by families, including a schedule of sliding fees,

(C) are designed to meet a handicapped infant's or toddler's developmental needs in any one or more of the following areas:

(i) physical development,

(ii) cognitive development,

(iii) language and speech development,

(iv) psycho-social development, or

(v) self-help skills,

(D) meet the standards of the State, including the requirements of this part,

(E) include—

(i) family training, counseling, and home visits,

(ii) special instruction,

(iii) speech pathology and audiology,

(iv) occupational therapy,

(v) physical therapy,

(vi) psychological services,

(vii) case management services,

(viii) medical services only for diagnostic or evaluation purposes,

(ix) early identification, screening, and assessment services, and

(x) health services necessary to enable the infant or toddler to benefit from the other early intervention services,

(F) are provided by qualified personnel, including—

(i) special educators,

(ii) speech and language pathologists and audiologists,

(iii) occupational therapists,

(iv) physical therapists,

(v) psychologists,

(vi) social workers,

(vii) nurses, and

(viii) nutritionists, and

(G) Are provided in conformity with an individualized family service plan adopted in accordance with section 677.

(3) The term "developmental delay" has the meaning given such term by a State under section 676(b)(1).

(4) The term "Council" means the State Interagency Coordinating Council established under section 682.

GENERAL AUTHORITY

SEC. 673. The Secretary shall, in accordance with this part, make grants to States (from their allocations under section 684) to assist each state to develop a statewide, comprehensive, coordinated, multidisciplinary, interagency system to provide early intervention services for handicapped infants and toddlers and their families.

GENERAL ELIGIBILITY

SEC. 674. In order to be eligible for a grant under section 673 for any fiscal year, a State shall demonstrate to the secretary (in its application under section 678) that the State has established a State Interagency Coordinating Council which meets the requirements of section 682.

CONTINUING ELIGIBILITY

SEC. 675. (a) FIRST TWO YEARS.—In order to be eligible for a grant under section 673 for the first or second year of a State's participation under this part, a State shall include in its application under section 678 for that year assurances that funds received under section 673 shall be used to assist the state to plan, develop, and implement the statewide system required by section 676.

(b) THIRD AND FOURTH YEAR.—(1) In order to be eligible for a grant under section 673 for the third or fourth year of a State's participation under this part, a State shall include in its application under section 678 for that year information and assurances demonstrating to the satisfaction of the Secretary that—

(A) the State has adopted a policy which incorporates all of the components of a statewide system in accordance with section 676 or obtained a waiver from the Secretary under paragraph (2),

(B) funds shall be used to plan, develop, and implement the statewide system required by section 676, and

(C) such statewide system will be in effect no later than the beginning of the fourth year of the State's participation under section 673, except that with respect to section 676(b)(4), a State need only conduct multidisciplinary assessment, develop individualized family service plan, and make available case management services.

(2) Notwithstanding paragraph (1), the Secretary may permit a State to continue to receive assistance under section 673 during such third year even if the State has not adopted the policy required by paragraph (1)(A) before receiving assistance if the State demonstrates in its application—

(A) that the State has made a good faith effort to adopt such a policy,

(B) the reasons why it was unable to meet the timeline and the steps remaining before such a policy will be adopted, and

(C) an assurance that the policy will be adopted and go into effect before the fourth year of such assistance.

(c) FIFTH AND SUCCEEDING YEARS.—In order to be eligible for a grant under section 673 for a fifth and any succeeding year of a State's participation under this part, a State shall include in its application under section 678 for that year information and assurances demonstrating to the satisfaction of the Secretary that the State has in effect the statewide system required by section 676 and a description of services to be provided under section 676(b)(2).

(d) EXCEPTION—Notwithstanding subsections (a) and (b), a State which has in effect a State law, enacted before September 1, 1986, that requires the provision of free appropriate public education to handicapped children from birth through age 2, inclusive, shall be eligible for a grant under section 673 for the first through fourth years of a State's participation under this part.

REQUIREMENTS FOR STATEWIDE SYSTEM

SEC. 676. (a) IN GENERAL.—A statewide system of coordinated, comprehensive, multidisciplinary, interagency programs providing appropriate early intervention services to all handicapped infants and toddlers and their families shall include the minimum components under subsection (b).

(b) MINIMUM COMPONENTS.—The stateside system required by subsection (a) shall include, at a minimum—

(1) a definition of the term "developmentally delayed" that will be used by the State in carrying out programs under this part.

(2) timetables for ensuring that appropriate early intervention services will be available to all handicapped infants and toddlers in the State before the beginning of the fifth year of a State's participation under this part,

(3) a timely, comprehensive, multidisciplinary evaluation of the functioning of each handicapped infant and toddler in the State and the needs of the families to appropriately assist in the development of the handicapped infant or toddler,

(4) for each handicapped infant and toddler in the State, an individualized family service plan in accordance with section 677, including case management services in accordance with such service plan,

(5) a comprehensive child find system, consistent with Part B, including a system for making referrals to service providers that includes timeliness and provides for the participation by primary referral sources.

(6) a public awareness program focusing

on early identification of handicapped infants and toddlers,

(7) a central directory which includes early intervention services, resources, and experts available in the State and research and demonstration projects being conducted in the State,

(8) a comprehensive system of personnel development,

(9) a single line of responsibility in a lead agency designated or established by the Governor for carrying out—

(A) the general administration, supervision, and monitoring of programs and activities receiving assistance under section 673 to ensure compliance with this part,

(B) the identification and coordination of all available resources within the State from Federal, State, local and private sources,

(C) the assignment of financial responsibility to the appropriate agency,

(D) the development of procedures to ensure that services are provided to handicapped infants and toddlers and their families in a timely manner pending the resolution of any disputes among public agencies or service providers,

(E) the resolution of intra- and interagency disputes, and

(F) the entry into formal interagency agreements that define the financial responsibility of each agency for paying for early intervention services (consistent with State law) and procedures for resolving disputes and that include all additional components necessary to ensure meaningful cooperation and coordination,

(10) a policy pertaining to the contracting or making of other arrangements with service providers to provide early intervention services in the State, consistent with the provisions of this part, including the contents of the application used and the conditions of the contract or other arrangements,

(11) a procedure for securing timely reimbursement of funds used under this part in accordance with section 681(a),

(12) procedural safeguards with respect to programs under this part as required by section 680, and

(13) policies and procedures relating to the establishment and maintenance of standards to ensure that personnel necessary to carry out this part are appropriately and adequately prepared and trained, including—

(A) the establishment and maintenance of standards which are consistent with any State approved or recognized certification, licensing, registration, or other comparable requirements which apply to the area in which such personnel are providing early intervention services, and

(B) to the extent such standards are not based on the highest requirements in the State applicable to a specific profession or discipline, the steps the State is taking to require the retraining or hiring of personnel that meet appropriate professional requirements in the State, and

(14) a system for compiling data on the number of handicapped infants and toddlers and their families in the State in need of appropriate early intervention services (which may be based on a sampling of data), the number of such infants and toddlers and their families served, the types of services provided (which may be based on a sampling of data), and other information required by the Secretary.

INDIVIDUALIZED FAMILY SERVICE PLAN

SEC. 677. (a) ASSESSMENT AND PROGRAM DEVELOPMENT.—Each handicapped infant or toddler and the infant or toddler's family shall receive—

(1) a multidisciplinary assessment of unique needs and the identification of services appropriate to meet such needs, and

(2) a written individualized family service plan developed by a multidisciplinary team, including the parent or guardian, as required by subsection (d).

(b) PERIODIC REVIEW.—The individualized family service plan shall be evaluated once a year and the family shall be provided a review of the plan at 6-month intervals (or more often where appropriate based on infant and toddler and family needs).

(c) PROMPTNESS AFTER ASSESSMENT.— The individualized family service plan shall be developed within a reasonable time after the assessment required by subsection (a)(1) is completed. With the parent's consent, early intervention services may commence prior to the completion of such assessment.

(d) CONTENT OF PLAN.—The individualized family service plan shall be in writing and contain—

(1) a statement of the infant's or toddler's present levels of physical development, cognitive development, language and speech development, psychosocial development, and self-help skills, based on acceptable objective criteria,

(2) a statement of the family's strengths and needs relating to enhancing the development of the family's handicapped infant or toddler,

(3) a statement of the major outcomes expected to be achieved for the infant and toddler and the family, and the criteria, procedures, and timeliness used to determine the degree to which progress toward achieving the outcomes are being made and whether modifications or reviews of the outcomes or services are necessary,

(4) a statement of specific early intervention services necessary to meet the unique needs of the infant or toddler and the fam-

ily, including the frequency, intensity, and the method of delivering services,

(5) the projected dates for initiation of services and the anticipated duration of such services,

(6) the name of the case manager from the profession most immediately relevant to the infant's and toddler's or family's needs who will be responsible for the implementation of the plan and coordination with other agencies and persons, and

(7) the steps to be taken supporting the transition of the handicapped toddler to services provided under part B to the extent such services are considered appropriate.

STATE APPLICATION AND ASSURANCES
SEC. 678. (a) APPLICATION.—Any State desiring to receive a grant under section 673 for any year shall submit an application to the Secretary at such time and in such manner as the Secretary may reasonably require by regulation. Such an application shall contain—

(1) a designation of the lead agency in the State that will be responsible for the administration of funds provided under section 673,

(2) information demonstrating eligibility of the State under section 674,

(3) the information or assurances required to demonstrate eligibility of the State or the particular year of participation under section 675, and

(4)(A) information demonstrating that the State has provided (i) public hearings, (ii) adequate notice of such hearings, and (iii) an opportunity for comment to the general public before the submission of such application and before the adoption by the State of the policies described in such application, and (B) a summary of the public comments and the State's responses,

(5) a description of the uses for which funds will be expended in accordance with this part and for the fifth and succeeding

fiscal years a description of the services to be provided,

(6) a description of the procedure used to ensure an equitable distribution of resources made available under this part among all geographic areas within the State, and

(7) such other information and assurances as the Secretary may reasonably require by regulation.

(b) STATEMENT OF ASSURANCES.—Any State desiring to receive a grant under section 673 shall file with the Secretary a statement at such time and in such manner as the Secretary may reasonably require by regulation. Such statement shall—

(1) assure that funds paid to the State under section 673 will be expended in accordance with this part,

(2) contain assurances that the State will comply with the requirements of section 681,

(3) provide satisfactory assurance that the control of funds provided under section 673, and title to property derived therefrom, shall be in a public agency for the uses and purposes provided in this part and that a public agency will administer such funds and property,

(4) provide for (A) making such reports in such form and containing such information as the Secretary may require to carry out the Secretary's functions under this part, and (B) keeping such records and affording such access thereto as the Secretary may find necessary to assure the correctness and verification of such reports and proper disbursement of Federal funds under this part,

(5) provide satisfactory assurance that Federal funds made available under section 673 (A) will not be commingled with State funds, and (B) will be so used as to supplement and increase the level of State and local funds expended for handicapped infants and toddlers and their families and in no case to supplant such State and local funds,

(6) provide satisfactory assurance that such fiscal control and fund accounting procedures will be adopted as may be necessary to assure proper disbursement of, and accounting for, Federal funds paid under section 673 to the State, and

(7) such other information and assurances as the Secretary may reasonably require by regulation.

(c) APPROVAL OF APPLICATION AND ASSURANCES REQUIRED.—No State may receive a grant under section 673 unless the Secretary has approved the application and statement of assurances of that State. The Secretary shall not disapprove such an application or statement of assurances unless the Secretary determines, after notice and opportunity for a hearing, that the application or statement of assurances fails to comply with the requirements of this section.

USES OF FUNDS

SEC. 679. In addition to using funds provided under section 673 to plan, develop, and implement the statewide system required by section 676, a State may use such funds—

(1) for direct services for handicapped infants and toddlers that are not otherwise provided from other public or private sources, and

(2) to expand and improve on services for handicapped infants and toddlers that are otherwise available.

PROCEDURAL SAFEGUARDS

SEC. 680. The procedural safeguards required to be included in a statewide system under section 676(b)(12) shall provide, at a minimum, the following:

(1) The timely administrative resolution of complaints by parents. Any party aggrieved by the findings and decision regarding administrative complaint shall have the right to bring a civil action with respect to the complaint, which action may be

brought in any State court of competent jurisdiction or in a district court of the United States without regard to the amount in controversy. In any action brought under this paragraph, the court shall receive the records of the administrative proceedings, shall hear additional evidence at the request of a party, and, basing its decision on the preponderance of the evidence, shall grant such relief as the court determines is appropriate.

(2) The right to confidentiality of personally identifiable information.

(3) The opportunity for parents and a guardian to examine records relating to assessment, screening, eligibility determinations, and the development and implementation of the individualized family service plan.

(4) Procedures to protect the rights of the handicapped infant and toddlers whenever the parents or guardian of the child are not known or unavailable or the child is a ward of the State, including the assignment of an individual (who shall not be an employee of the State agency providing services) to act as a surrogate for the parents or guardian.

(5) Written prior notice to the parents or guardian of the handicapped infant or toddler whenever the State agency or service provider proposes to initiate or change or refuses to initiate or change the identification, evaluation, placement, or the provision of appropriate early intervention services to the handicapped infant or toddler.

(6) Procedures designed to assure that the notice required by paragraph (5) fully informs the parents or guardian, in the parents' or guardian's native language, unless it clearly is not feasible to do so, of all procedures available pursuant to this section.

(7) During the pendency of any proceeding or action involving a complaint, unless the State agency and the parents or guardian otherwise agree, the child shall continue to receive the appropriate early intervention services currently being provided or if applying for initial services shall receive the services not in dispute.

PAYOR OF LAST RESORT

SEC. 681. (a) NONSUBSTITUTION.—Funds provided under section 673 may not be used to satisfy a financial commitment for services which would have been paid for from another public or private source but for the enactment of this part, except that whenever considered necessary to prevent the delay in the receipt of appropriate early intervention services by the infant or toddler or family in a timely fashion, funds provided under section 673 may be used to pay the provider of services pending reimbursement from the agency which has ultimate responsibility for the payment.

(b) REDUCTION OF OTHER BENEFITS.—Nothing in this part shall be construed to permit the State to reduce medical or other assistance available or to alter eligibility under title V of the Social Security Act (relating to maternal and child health) or title XIX of the Social Security Act (relating to medicaid for handicapped infants and toddlers) within the State.

STATE INTERAGENCY COORDINATING COUNCIL

SEC. 682. (a) ESTABLISHMENT.—(1)Any State which desires to receive financial assistance under section 673 shall establish a State Interagency Coordinating Council composed of 15 members.

(2) The Council and the chairperson of the Council shall be appointed by the Governor. In making appointments to the Council, the Governor shall ensure that the membership of the Council reasonably represents the population of the State.

(b) COMPOSITION—The Council shall be composed of—

(1) at least 3 parents of handicapped infants or toddlers or handicapped children aged 3 through 6, inclusive,

(2) at least 3 public or private providers of early intervention services,

(3) at least one representative from the State legislature,

(4) at least one person involved in personnel preparation, and

(5) other members representing each of the appropriate agencies involved in the provision of or payment for early intervention services to handicapped infants and toddlers and their families and others selected by the Governor.

(c) MEETINGS.—The Council shall meet at least quarterly and in such places as it deems necessary. The meetings shall be publicly announced, and, to the extent appropriate, open and accessible to the general public.

(d) MANAGEMENT AUTHORITY.—Subject to the approval of the Governor, the Council may prepare and approve a budget using funds under this part to hire staff, and obtain the services of such professional, technical, and clerical personnel as may be necessary to carry out its functions under this part.

(e) FUNCTIONS OF COUNCIL.—The Council shall—

(1) advise and assist the lead agency designated or established under section 676(b)(9) in the performance of the responsibilities set out in such section, particularly the identification of the sources of fiscal and other support for services for early intervention programs, assignment of financial responsibility to the appropriate agency, and the promotion of the interagency agreements,

(2) advise and assist the lead agency in the preparation of applications and amendments thereto, and

(3) prepare and submit an annual report to the Governor and to the Secretary on the status of early intervention programs for handicapped infants and toddlers and their families operated within the State.

(f) CONFLICT OF INTEREST.—No member of the Council shall cast a vote on any matter which would provide direct financial benefit to that member or otherwise give the appearance of a conflict of interest under State law.

(g) USE OF EXISTING COUNCILS.—To the extent that a State has established a Council before September 1, 1987, that is comparable to the Council described in this section, such Council shall be considered to be in compliance with this section. Within 4 years after the date the State accepts funds under section 673, such State shall establish a council that complies in full with this section.

FEDERAL ADMINISTRATION

SEC. 683. Sections 616, 617, and 620 shall, to the extent not inconsistent with this part, apply to the program authorized by this part, except that—

(1) any reference to a State educational agency shall be deemed to be a reference to the State agency established or designated under section 676(b)(9),

(2) any references to the education of handicapped children and the education of all handicapped children and the provision of free public education to all handicapped children shall be deemed to be a reference to the provision of services to handicapped infants and toddlers in accordance with this part, and

(3) any reference to local educational agencies and intermediate educational agencies shall be deemed to be a reference to local service providers under this part.

ALLOCATION OF FUNDS

SEC. 684. (a) From the sums appropriated to carry out this part for any fiscal year, the Secretary may reserve 1 percent for payments to Guam, American Samoa, the Virgin Islands, the Republic of the Marshall Islands, the Federated States of Micronesia, the Republic of Palau, and the Commonwealth of the Northern Mariana Islands in accordance with their respective needs.

(b)(1) The Secretary shall make payments to the Secretary of the Interior according to the need for such assistance for the provision of early intervention services to handicapped infants and toddlers and their families on reservations serviced by the elementary and secondary schools operated for Indians by the Department of the Interior. The amount of such payment for any fiscal year shall be 1.25 percent of the aggregate of the amount available to all States under this part for that fiscal year.

(2) The Secretary of the Interior may receive an allotment under paragraph (1) only after submitting to the Secretary an application which meets the requirements of section 678 and which is approved by the Secretary. Section 616 shall apply to any such application.

(c)(1) For each of the fiscal years 1987 through 1991 from the funds remaining after the reservation and payments under subsections (a) and (b), the Secretary shall allot to each State an amount which bears the same ratio to the amount of such remainder as the number of infants and toddlers in the State bears to the number of infants and toddlers in all States, except that no State shall receive less than 0.5 percent of such remainder.

(2) For the purpose of paragraph (1)—

(A) the terms "infants" and "toddlers" mean children from birth to age 2, inclusive, and

(B) the term "State" does not include the jurisdictions described in subsection (a).

(d) If any State elects not to receive its allotment under subsection (c)(1), the Secretary shall reallot, among the remaining States, amounts from such State in accordance with such subsection.

AUTHORIZATION OF APPROPRIATIONS

SEC. 685. There are authorized to be appropriated to carry out this part $50,000,000 for fiscal year 1987, $75,000,000 for fiscal year 1988, and such sums as may be necessary for each of the 3 succeeding fiscal years.

Developmental Milestones of Children from Birth to Age 3

	Interest in Others	Self-awareness	Motor Milestones and Eye-hand Skills
The Early Months (birth through 8 months)	Newborns prefer the human face and human sound. Within the first 2 weeks, they recognize and prefer the sight, smell, and sound of the principal caregiver. Social smile and mutual gazing is evidence of early social interaction. The infant can initiate and terminate these interactions. Anticipates being lifted or fed and moves body to participate. Sees adults as objects of interest and novelty. Seeks out adults for play. Stretches arms to be taken.	Sucks fingers or hand fortuitously. Observes own hands. Places hand up as an object comes close to the face as if to protect self. Looks to the place on body where being touched. Reaches for and grasps toys. Clasps hands together and fingers them. Tries to cause things to happen. Begins to distinguish friends from strangers. Shows preference for being held by familiar people.	The young infant uses many complex reflexes; searches for something to suck; holds on when falling; turns head to avoid obstruction of breathing; avoids brightness, strong smells, and pain. Puts hand or object in mouth. Begins reaching toward interesting objects. Grasps, releases, regrasps, and releases object again. Lifts head. Holds head up. Sits up without support. Rolls over. Transfers and manipulates objects with hands. Crawls.

Language Development/ Communication	Physical, Spatial, and Temporal Awareness	Purposeful Action and Use of Tools	Expression of Feelings
Cries to signal pain or distress. Smiles or vocalizes to initiate social contact. Responds to human voices. Gazes at faces. Uses vocal and nonvocal communication to express interest and exert influence. Babbles using all types of sounds. Engages in private conversations when alone. Combines babbles. Understands names of familiar people and objects. Laughs. Listens to conversations.	Comforts self by sucking thumb or finding pacifier. Follows a slowly moving object with eyes. Reaches and grasps toys. Looks for dropped toy. Identifies objects from various viewpoints. Finds a toy hidden under a blanket when placed there while watching.	Observes own hands. Grasps rattle when hand and rattle are both in view. Hits or kicks an object to make a pleasing sight or sound continue. Tries to resume a knee ride by bouncing to get adult started again.	Expresses discomfort and comfort pleasure unambiguously. Responds with more animation and pleasure to primary caregiver than to others. Can usually be comforted by familiar adult when distressed. Smiles and activates the obvious pleasure in response to social stimulation. Very interested in people. Shows displeasure at loss of social contact. Laughs aloud (belly laugh). Show displeasure or disappointment at loss of toy. Expresses several clearly differentiated emotions: pleasure, anger, anxiety or fear, sadness, joy, excitement, disappointment, exuberance. Reacts to strangers with soberness or anxiety.

	Interest in Others	Self-awareness	Motor Milestones and Eye-hand Skills
Crawlers and Walkers (8 to 18 months)	Exhibits anxious behavior around unfamiliar adults. Enjoys exploring objects with another as the basis for establishing relationships. Gets others to do things for child's pleasure (wind up toys, read books, get dolls). Shows considerable interest in peers. Demonstrates intense attention to adult language.	Knows own name. Smiles or plays with self in mirror. Uses large and small muscles to explore confidently when a sense of security is offered by presence of caregiver. Frequently checks for caregiver's presence. Has heightened awareness of opportunities to make things happen, yet limited awareness of responsibility for own actions. Indicates strong sense of self through assertiveness. Directs actions of others (e.g., "Sit there!"). Identifies one or more body parts. Begins to use *me, you, I.*	Sits well in chairs. Pulls self up, stands holding furniture. Walks when led. Walks alone. Throws objects. Climbs stairs. Uses marker on paper. Stoops, trots, can walk backward a few steps.
Toddlers and 2 Year Olds (18 months to 3 years)	Shows increased awareness of being seen and evaluated by others. Sees others as a barrier to immediate gratification. Begins to realize others have rights and privileges. Gains greater enjoyment from peer play and joint exploration. Begins to see benefits of cooperation. Identifies self with children of same age or sex. Is more aware of the feelings of others. Exhibits more impulse control and self-regulation in relation to others. Enjoys small-group activities.	Shows stong sense of self as an individual, as evidenced by "NO" to adult requests. Experiences self as a powerful, potent, creative doer. Explores everything. Becomes capable of self-evaluation and has beginning notions of self (good, bad, attractive, ugly). Makes attempts at self-regulation. Uses names of self and others. Identifies six or more body parts.	Scribbles with marker or crayon. Walks up and down stairs. Can jump off one step. Kicks a ball. Stands on one foot. Threads beads. Draws a circle. Stands and walks on tiptoes. Walks up stairs one foot on each step. Handles scissors. Imitates a horizontal crayon stroke.

Note: This list is not intended to be exhaustive. Many of the behaviors indicated here will happen earlier or later for individual infants. The chart suggests an approximate time when a behavior might appear but it should not be rigidly interpreted.

Often, but not always, the behaviors appear in the order in which they emerge. Particularly for younger infants the behaviors listed in one domain overlap considerably with several other developmental domains. Some behaviors are placed under more than one category to emphasize this interrelationship.

Language Development/ Communication	Physical, Spatial, and Temporal Awareness	Purposeful Action and Use of Tools	Expression of Feelings
Understands many more words than can say. Looks toward 20 or more objects when named. Creates long babbled sentences. Shakes head no. Says 2 or 3 clear words. Looks at picture books with interest, points to objects. Uses vocal signals other than crying to gain assistance. Begins to use *me, you, I*.	Tries to build with blocks. If toy is hidden under one of three cloths while child watches, looks under the right cloth for the toy. Persists in a search for a desired toy even when toy is hidden under distracting objects such as pillows. When chasing a ball that rolled under sofa and out the other side, will make a detour around sofa to get ball. Pushes foot into shoe, arm into sleeve.	When a toy winds down, continues the activity manually. Uses a stick as a tool to obtain a toy. When a music box winds down, searches for the key to wind it up again. Brings a stool to use for reaching for something. Pushes away someone or something not wanted. Feeds self finger food (bits of fruit, crackers). Creeps or walks to get something or avoid unpleasantness. Pushes foot into shoe, arm into sleeve. Partially feeds self with fingers or spoon. Handles cup well with minimal spilling. Handles spoon well for self-feeding.	Actively shows affection for familiar persons: hugs, smiles at, runs toward, leans against, and so forth. Show anxiety at separation from primary caregiver. Shows anger focused on people or objects. Expresses negative feelings. Shows pride and pleasure in new accomplishments. Shows intense feelings for parents. Continues to show pleasure in mastery. Asserts self, indicating strong sense of self.
Combines words. Listens to stories for a short while. Speaking vocabulary may reach 200 words. Develops fantasy in language. Begins to play pretend games. Defines use of many household items. Uses compound sentences. Uses adjectives and adverbs, Recounts events of the day.	Identifies a familiar object by touch when placed in a bag with two other objects. Uses "tomorrow," "yesterday." Figures out which child is missing by looking at children who are present. Asserts independence: "Me do it." Puts on simple garments such as cap or slippers.	When playing with a ring-stacking toy, ignores any forms that have no hole. Stacks only rings or other objects with holes. Classifies, labels, and sorts objects by group (hard versus soft, large versus small). Helps dress and undress self.	Frequently displays aggressive feelings and behaviors. Exhibits contrasting states and mood shifts (stubborn versus compliant). Shows increased fearfulness (dark, monsters, etc). Expresses emotions with increasing control. Aware of own feelings and those of others. Shows pride in creation and production. Verbalizes feelings more often. Expresses feelings in symbolic play. Shows empathic concern for others.

Reprinted with permission, Lally, J. R., Provence, S., Szanton, E., & Weissbourd, B. (1986). Developmentally appropriate care for children from birth to age 3. In S. Bredekamp (Ed.), *Developmentally appropriate practice*. Washington, DC: National Association for the Education of Young Children.

Normal Language Development—Expected Sequence and Approximate Age Norms

Age in months (approx.)	Pragmatics	Phonology	Grammar Morphology-syntax	Semantics
1	Gazing, crying, "comfort sounds"	Begins to play with pitch change		
3	Laughs, smiles when played with: looks at speaker; sometimes responds to a speaker by vocalizing	Vocalizes two or more syllables		
6	Babbles and smiles at a speaker; stops (begins turn taking) when someone speaks	Babbles four or more syllables at one time; plays at making noises; labial (/p/, /b/, /m/) consonants emerge; vowels		

Age in months (approx.)	Pragmatics	Phonology	Grammar Morphology-syntax	Semantics
8	Plays "peek-a-boo" and "pat-a-cake"; listens to adult conversations; turns toward speaker; understands gesture	Intonation patterns for questions and commands; jargon includes vowels and consonants (five or more of each)	(No real words, but vocalizing sounds as if it is a sentence or question)	Recognizes names of some common objects
10	Follows simple commands; enjoys clapping to music; begins to "send message" by pointing	Uses a varied jargon, with pitch and rhythm		Says "first" words; tries to imitate words
12	Responds to manner and attitude of speaker (for example, joy, anger, or hurry)	Consonant-vowel and consonant-vowel-consonant jargon	"Holophrastic speech" (one word stands for a whole sentence)	Uses two or more words; learns new words every few days
12 to 18	Follows one- and two-step directions	Imitates noises and speech sounds	Some begin to use two-word sentences	Recognizes and points to many familiar objects; learns new words almost daily
18 to 24	Jargon and some echolalia; "dialogue" uses speech to get attention: "asks" for help	Uses /p/. /b/, /m/, /h/, /t/, and vowels	Two- to three-word sentences but omits articles and most modifiers; begins to use personal pronouns; "telegraphic speech"	Says 10 to 20 words at 18 months, but some say as many as 200 words by 24 months; understands many more

Continued

Age in months (approx.)	Pragmatics	Phonology	Grammar Morphology-syntax	Semantics
24 to 36	At 2, speech is not used for social control, but at 2½, demands and attempts control By 3, language is linguistically and contextually contingent, and 70% of speech is intelligible, although articulation errors are still common. Short sentences (three to four words) are common. All vowels are correct, but /r/, /s/, /ch/, /j/, /v/, /l/, /x/ are often incorrectly spoken. Vocabulary ranges to as many as 1,000 words. Sentence types include agent-action, action-object, and agent-object.	Many begin to use additional consonants; add /f/, /k/, /d/, /w/, /g/; vowels 90% intelligible	By 2½ grammatical morphemes begin to appear: -ing (present progressive) -s and -es (plurals) -ed (past tense) a, an, the (articles) my and 's (possessives) auxiliary verbs prepositions	Recognizes names and pictures of most common objects; understands 500 words

Age in months (approx.)	Pragmatics	Phonology	Grammar Morphology-syntax	Semantics
36 to 48	Social control; whispers; tells name; "explains" what happened; asks questions; sustains topic; systematic changes in speech depend on the listener; some role-playing; metalinguistic awareness (ability to think about language and comment on it); "hints" at things through smiles and gestures as well as words	All vowels correct; although many children articulate most consonants accurately, articulation errors on the following are still within "normal range": /l/, /r/, /s/, /z/, /sh/, /ch/, /j/, /th/; pitch and rhythm variations similar to adults, but this age enjoys extremes— yells and whispers	Expands noun phrases with tense, gender, and number; conjugates "to be" correctly; uses pronouns, adjectives, and plurals; near age 4, begins using longer and more compound and complex sentences; begins to interrelate clauses (uses and, because, when, and then)	Vocabulary grows rapidly; actively seeks to learn new words; likes to "experiment" and makes many charming errors; continues process of differentiating lexical types, knows between 900 and 1,000 words
48 to 60	Seeks information constantly; "why" is a favorite; becomes aware of behavior listeners attend to; begins to grasp relevance	Begins to use stress contours; pitch changes purposefully; articulation errors still common, but diminishing; nonfluency not unusual; blends difficult	Uses comparatives (big, biggest); uses all sentence types, including relative clauses; grammar approximates that of adults	Size of vocabulary varies widely with experiences; many know 2,000 or more words

Reprinted with permission. Cook, R. E., Tessier, A., & Armbruster, V. B. (1987). *Adapting early childhood curricula for children with special needs* (2nd ed.). Columbus, OH: Merrill.

A Sampling of Infant Toddler Assessment Techniques

Battelle Developmental Inventory
AUTHOR: Battelle Memorial Institute
PUBLISHER: DLM Teaching Resources, One DLM Park, P.O. Box 4000, Allen, TX 75002
AGES: Birth to 8 years
REQUIRED RESPONSES: Verbal and non-verbal
ADMINISTRATION: Individually by teacher
SCORING: Easy
DESCRIPTION: This developmental inventory is a multifactored assessment based on observations, parent interviews, and structured testing in the personal-social, adaptive, motor, communication, and cognitive domains. Separate test booklets for each domain allow independent assessment by various professionals. It is appropriate for both handicapped and nonhandicapped, and is useful in depicting child progress.
SCORES: Age equivalents, percentile ranks, and standard scores
OTHER CONSIDERATIONS: The technical information presented is extensive and the manuals are well organized. More validity data is becoming available.
Brigance Diagnostic Inventory Early Development
AUTHOR: A. H. Brigance
PUBLISHER: Curriculum Associates, Inc., 5 Esquire Road, North Billerica, MA 01862-2589

AGES: Up to 7 years
REQUIRED RESPONSES: Nonverbal and verbal
ADMINISTRATION: Individually by teacher or trained paraprofessional either in its entirety or by individual skills, as needed
SCORING: Easy
DESCRIPTION: This criterion-referenced inventory allows the teacher to determine developmental levels in the areas of psychomotor, self-help, communication, general knowledge, and comprehension and academic skills.
SCORES: Developmental ages
OTHER CONSIDERATIONS: It includes developmental record books providing systematic, graphic performance records. Results are readily translated into sequential, individualized lessons. Validity data is not reported in the manual.
Carolina Developmental Profile
AUTHORS: D. L. Lillie and G. L. Harbin
PUBLISHER: Kaplan Corporation, 2596 Viceroy Drive, Winston-Salem, NC 27103
AGES: 2 years to 5 years
REQUIRED RESPONSES: Verbal and non-verbal
ADMINISTRATION: Individually by teacher at several different times
SCORING: Easy
DESCRIPTION: This is a criterion-referenced checklist that includes gross motor, fine motor,

visual perception, receptive, and expressive language. It is designed to provide a profile of what a child can and cannot do.

SCORES: Developmental ages

OTHER CONSIDERATIONS: It can be used in conjunction with the Developmental Task Instruction System also developed by Lillie.

Comprehensive Identification Process (CIP)

AUTHOR: R. R. Zehrback

PUBLISHER: Scholastic Testing Service, Inc., 480 Meyer Road, Bensenville, IL 60106

AGES: 2 years to 5½ years

REQUIRED RESPONSES: Verbal and nonverbal

ADMINISTRATION: Individually by teacher or trained paraprofessional in 30 to 45 minutes. Specialists are recommended for the vision, hearing, and speech and language subtests.

SCORING: Easy to moderately difficult

DESCRIPTION: This screening test samples cognitive-verbal, fine motor, gross motor, speech, language, social-affective, hearing, and visual development.

SCORES: The following three-part system is used to rate the items: pass, evaluate, and refer or rescreen

OTHER CONSIDERATIONS: Children are screened individually at different stations. Parents' opinions are considered.

Denver Developmental Screening Test

AUTHORS: W. K. Frankenburg, J. B. Dodds, and A. Fandal

PUBLISHER: Ladoca Project and Publishing Foundation, East 51st Avenue and Lincoln Street, Denver, CO 80216

AGES: 1 month to 6 years

REQUIRED RESPONSES: Verbal and nonverbal

ADMINISTRATION: Individually by teacher or trained paraprofessional in 15 to 20 minutes

SCORING: Items are scored as passed, failed, refused, or no opportunity. Developmental levels are obtained.

OTHER CONSIDERATIONS: The forms and manual have been translated into Spanish. "The test significantly under refers children"

(Casto & Biro, 1989, p. 51).

Developmental Activities Screening Inventory (DASI-II)

AUTHOR: R. F. DuBose and M. B. Langley

PUBLISHER: Teaching Resources Corporation, 50 Pond Park Road, Hingham, MA 02043

AGES: Birth to 6 years

REQUIRED RESPONSES: Nonverbal

ADMINISTRATION: Individually by teacher in 20 to 40 minutes. Instructions may be given either visually or verbally.

SCORING: Easy

DESCRIPTION: The 55 test items assess fine-motor control, cause-effect relationships, associations, number concepts, size discriminations, and sequencing.

SCORES: Developmental level and quotient

OTHER CONSIDERATIONS: Tasks can be adapted for use with the visually impaired. Simple remedial programs are suggested in the test manual. Has been used successfully with multihandicapped children. "There are not enough data on it to validate its usefulness" (Casto & Biro, 1989, p. 51).

Developmental Indicators for the Assessment of Learning (DIAL-R)

AUTHORS: C. Mardell-Czudnowski and D. Goldenberg

PUBLISHER: Childcraft Education Corporation, 20 Kilmer Road, Edison, NJ 08817

AGES: 2 years to 6 years

REQUIRED RESPONSES: Verbal and nonverbal

ADMINISTRATION: Individually by teacher or trained paraprofessional in 25 to 30 minutes

SCORING: Easy

DESCRIPTION: Areas within this revised prekindergarten screening test include gross motor, fine motor, concepts communication, and social and emotional development.

SCORES: Scaled scores and functional level

OTHER CONSIDERATIONS: Strengths and weaknesses can be recorded on a profile sheet. It is necessary to be cautious when scoring the articulation items. "This is a team-based screening test with weak predictive validity. The Communications/Language section would tend to under refer children for further evaluation in this area'' (Casto & Biro, 1989, p. 51).

Developmental Profile
AUTHORS: G. D. Alpern and T. J. Boll
PUBLISHER: Psychological Development Publications, 7150 Lakeside Drive, Indianapolis, IN 46278
AGES: 6 months to 12 years
REQUIRED RESPONSES: Rater responses
ADMINISTRATION: Individually rated from direct observation or interview of parents in 30 to 40 minutes
SCORING: Easy
DESCRIPTION: This test is designed to screen quickly for competencies in physical, self-help, social, academic, and communication development.
SCORES: Age norms
OTHER CONSIDERATIONS: Allows for administration, scoring, and interpretation by people without specific training in psychological testing.

Early-LAP: The Early Learning Accomplishment Profile
AUTHORS: E. M. Glover, J. Preminger, and A. Sanford
PUBLISHER: Kaplan Press, 2596 Viceroy Drive, Winston-Salem, NC 27103
AGES: Birth to 36 months
REQUIRED RESPONSES: Nonverbal and verbal
ADMINISTRATION: Individually by teacher or trained paraprofessional
SCORING: Easy
DESCRIPTION: This is a revised version of the Learning Accomplishment Profile for infants. It is a developmental checklist for assessing behaviors in gross motor, cognitive, fine motor, language, self-help, and social emotional growth.
OTHER CONSIDERATIONS: The checklist format generates appropriate instructional objectives and task analysis programming.

Peabody Picture Vocabulary Test (PPVT-R)
AUTHORS: L. M. Dunn and L. M. Dunn
PUBLISHER: American Guidance Service, Publishers' Building, Circle Pines, MN 55014
AGES: 2 years to adult
REQUIRED RESPONSES: Nonverbal
ADMINISTRATION: Individually by teachers in 10 to 20 minutes.
SCORING: Easy
DESCRIPTION: This test requires the child to hear a cue word and to point to the one picture out of four that corresponds best to the perceived word. It is a test of hearing vocabulary and receptive language.
SCORES: Percentile ranks, age equivalents, and stanines
OTHER CONSIDERATIONS: A child must have adequate hearing, sight, some degree of motor coordination, and understanding of standard English to respond appropriately. It is primarily a test of receptive vocabulary.

The Portage Guide to Early Education
AUTHORS: Portage Preschool Project
PUBLISHER: CESA 12, Box 564, Portage, WI 53901
AGES: Up to 6 years
REQUIRED RESPONSES: Nonverbal and verbal
ADMINISTRATION: Individually by teacher or trained paraprofessional in approximately 30 minutes
SCORING: Easy
DESCRIPTION: This criterion-referenced checklist assesses behaviors in five developmental areas: cognitive, self-help, motor, language, and socialization.
SCORES: Developmental levels in years
OTHER CONSIDERATIONS: This checklist combines items from a number of developmental scales and originated as part of the Portage Project, a home-based early intervention program. Each skill is referenced to a card that describes how to teach the skill assessed.

Background Information

1. Child's name _____ _____
                            last   first   middle   Name used
2. Sex _____Date of birth _____Birthplace _____
3. Father's name _____Occupation _____
   Business telephone _____
4. Mother's name _____Occupation _____
   Business telephone _____
5. Home address _____Telephone _____
6. What are your goals for your child's attendance at the center? (Include goals for your child and for yourself.) _____
   _____
   _____

Home relationships

7. Who resides with child in the home? (Please give birthdates of other children.)

Name	**Birthdate**
_____	_____
_____	_____
_____	_____

8. Describe the relationships of the child to others in the home.
   a. Responsibility for care of the child:
   b. Sibling relationships:
   c. Discipline used and child's reaction:
   d. Child's status in the family:
   e. Does your child have a pet?
9. What activities does your child particularly enjoy?
   What activities do you particular enjoy doing with your child?
10. How self-sufficient is your child in dressing in indoor and outdoor clothes?

Description of child

11. How would you describe your child's personality and temperament?
12. How does your child comfort himself/herself?
13. How does he/she react to anger or frustration?
14. Does your child have any particular fears? If so, please describe.
15. How has your child reacted to change or to separation from parents?

Social development

16. What group contacts has the child had? (Include description of the type of play, ages of children; also former day-care experiences.)

Language development

17. Describe the sequence, rate of growth, vocabulary.

Additional information

18. Add any other information that would be of help in understanding your child (e.g., play patterns, behavior patterns, interests, handicaps.)

19. Describe meal times, food preferences, parental attitudes and methods, self-sufficiency of child, food allergies, etc.

    In case of special diets please describe completely.

    How self-sufficient is your child in eating?

Sleeping

20. Please describe regularity, amount, need for naps and usual schedule, specific problems and methods for handling.

Elimination

21. Please describe methods and timing of toilet training, parental attitudes, treatment of accidents, position, special words, responsibility.

    Describe any problems the center might have connected with elimination.

Filled out by_____

Date_____

*Adapted from form used by the Early Childhood Education Center, University of Iowa

Selections by the Congressional Caucus for Women's Issues

PIONEER AWARD RECIPIENTS

American West Airlines (Arizona)
American Express (New York)
American Savings and Loan (California)
Ameritrust (Ohio)
Bank of America (California)
Caltech, Jet Propulsion Laboratory (California)
Dominion Bank (Virginia)
Fel-Pro Incorporated (Illinois)
Gulf & Western/Paramount Pictures Corporation (California)
Hoffman-La Roche (New Jersey)
International Ladies Garment Workers Union, Local 23–25 (New York)
Levi Strauss and Company (California)
Merck and Company (New Jersey)
Mountain Bell (Colorado)
Nyloncraft, International (Indiana)
Polaroid Corporation (Massachusetts)
Rouse and Associates (Maryland)
Stride Rite Corporation (Massachusetts)
Zale Corporation (Texas)

BEST ON THE BLOCK

B & B Associates (Connecticut)
Blytheville Air Force Base (Arkansas)
City and County of Denver (Colorado)
Deaconess Medical Center (Washington)
Grieco Brothers Inc. (Massachusetts)
Johnson Wax (Wisconsin)
Kingston-Warren Corporation (New Hampshire)
Kitchens of Sara Lee (Iowa)
Lomas & Nettleton Financial Corporation
National Bureau of Standards (Maryland)
Pacific Mutual Life Insurance Co. (California)
Pennsylvania Blue Shield (Pennsylvania)
Riverside Methodist Hospital (Ohio)
Rockwell International (Iowa)
Spartanburg Regional Medical Center (South Carolina)
State of California, Dept. of Personnel Administration (California)
The Bureau of National Affairs, Inc. (Maryland)
Trammell Crow Company/Turnpike Children's Center, Inc. (Texas)
Tysons Corner Play and Learn (Virginia)
University of Maine at Fort Kent (Maine)
Northern Maine Medical Center (Maine)
University of Puerto Rico (Puerto Rico)
University of Southern Maine (Maine)
Valley View Professional Care Center (Kansas and Connecticut)
Young Company, Phoenix Memorial Hospital (Arizona)

OTHER OUTSTANDING PROGRAMS

First Atlanta Bank (Georgia)
Campbell Soup Company (New Jersey)
International Business Machines
Mervyn's (California and Nevada)
Proctor and Gamble
The Prudential Insurance Company (New Jersey)
Steelcase, Inc. (Michigan)
Lincoln National Bank (Indiana)

University of California at Los Angeles (California)
Union Bank (California)
Dupont (Delaware)
Northlake Foods
Colorado Place (built by Southmark Corp.)

Report on employer-sponsored child care services (1988). Washington, DC: The Congressional Caucus for Women's Issues.

References

Abel, C., Alexander, R., & Smith, B. (1987). *Protecting Iowa's children: A training manual for mandatory reporters of child abuse*. Iowa City: University of Iowa.

Abt Associates. (1979). *Final report of the National Day Care Study: Children at the center*. Cambridge, MA: Author.

American Academy of Pediatrics. Committee on Standards of Child Health Care. (1977). *Standards of child health care* (3rd ed.). Evanston, IL: Author.

American Academy of Pediatrics. (1980). *An agenda for America's children*. Evanston, IL: Author.

American Academy of Pediatrics. Committee on Nutrition. (1985). *Pediatric nutrition handbook* (2nd ed.). Elk Grove Village, IL: Author.

American Academy of Pediatrics. Committee on Early Childhood, Adoption and Dependent Care. (1987). S. R. Deitch, M. D. (Ed.). *Health in day care: A manual for health professionals*. Evanston, IL: Author.

American Academy of Pediatrics. (1988a). *Guidelines for health supervision* (2nd ed.). Elk Grove Village, IL: Author.

American Academy of Pediatrics. Task Force on Pediatric AIDS. (1988b). Pediatric guidelines for infection control of Human Immunodeficiency Virus (Acquired Immunodeficiency Virus) in hospitals, medical offices, schools, and other settings. *Pediatrics, 82,* 801–807.

American Academy of Pediatrics. Committee on Infectious Diseases. (1988c). *Report of the Committee on Infectious Diseases* (ed. 21). Elk Grove Village, IL: Author.

American Academy of Pediatrics. (1989). *Temper tantrums: A normal part of growing up*. (brochure). Elk Grove Village, IL: Author.

Ames, L. B. (1952). The sense of self of nursery school children as manifested by their verbal behavior. *Journal of Genetic Psychology, 81,* 193–232.

Andersen, R. D., Bale, J. F., Jr., Blackman, J. A., & Murph, J. R. (1986). *Infections in children: A sourcebook for educators and child care providers*. Rockville, MD: Aspen.

Anderson, S., & Messick, S. (1974). Social competency in young children. *Developmental Psychology, 10* (2), 282–293.

Angle, C. R. (1980). Behavior and psychological aspects of accident prevention. In M. S. McIntire (Ed.), *Handbook on accident prevention* (pp. 99–106). Hagerstown, MD: Harper & Row.

Anselmo, S. (1987). *Early child development: Prenatal through age eight*. Columbus, OH: Merrill.

Appleton, T., Clifton, R., & Goldberg, S. (1975). The development of behavioral competence in infancy. In F. D. Horowitz (Ed.), *Review of child development research*. Vol. 4. Chicago: University of Chicago Press.

Aries, P. (1962). *Centuries of childhood*. New York: Random House.

Arnett, J. (1989). Issues and obstacles in the training of caregivers. In J. S. Lande, S. Scarr, & N. Gunzenhauser (Eds.), *Caring for children: Challenge to America.* Hillsdale, NJ: Lawrence Erlbaum.

Arnold, A. (1971). *Teaching your child to learn.* Englewood Cliffs, NJ: Prentice-Hall.

Aronson, S. S. (1980). The health component of the child care program. In R. Neugebauer & R. Lurie (Eds.), *Caring for infants and toddlers: What works, what doesn't.* Vol. 1. Redmond, WA: Child Care Information Exchange.

Aronson, S. (1982). Health and safety in the child care program—An update. In R. Lurie & R. Neugebauer (Eds.), *Caring for infants and toddlers: What works, what doesn't.* Vol. 2. Redmond, WA: Child Care Information Exchange.

Aronson, S. S. (1983). Injuries in child care. *Young Children, 38* (6), 19–20.

Aronson, S. (1988, September). Chemical hazards in child care. *Child Care Information Exchange,* 33–37.

Auerbach, A. (1975). Parent's role in day care. *Child Care Quarterly 4* (3), 180–187.

Azrin, N. H., & Foxx, R. M. (1981). *Toilet training in less than a day.* New York: Pocket Books.

Baker, B. R. (1989). Learning experiences through fingerplays. *Day care and Early Education, 16* (3), 21–26.

Barker, R. (1968). *Ecological psychology: Concepts and methods for studying the environment of human behavior.* Stanford, CA: Stanford University Press.

Barnard, K., & Brazelton, T. B. (1986). *Touch—The language of love.* Skillman, NJ: Johnson & Johnson Baby Products Company.

Barness, L. A. (1985). Infant feeding: Formula, solids. In *The Pediatric Clinics of North America.* Philadelphia: Saunders.

Bates, E. (1976). Pragmatics and sociolinguists in child language. In D. Morehead & A. Morehead (Eds.), *Language deficiency in children: Selected readings.* Baltimore: University Park Press.

Bates, L., & Learned, J. (1954). Age changes in kaleidoblock response. *Journal of Genetic Psychology, 84–85,* 237–270.

Bauer, F. (1985). *Just a touch of nearness.* Norwalk, CN: C. R. Gibson.

Becher, R. M. (1986). Parent involvement: Research

and practice. In L. G. Katz (Ed.), *Current topics in early childhood education, 6,* 85–122.

Bell, S., & Ainsworth, M. (1972). Infant crying and maternal responsiveness. *Child Development, 43,* 1171–1190.

Belsky, J. (Ed.). (1982). *In the beginning: Readings on infancy.* New York: Columbia University Press.

Belsky, J. (1986). Infant day care: A cause for concern? *Zero to three, 6* (5), 1–9.

Berg, B. J. (1989, July). My Blankie and me. *Parents, 64* (7), 94–98, 100.

Berman, C., & Szanton, E. (Eds.). (1989). *The intent and spirit of P. L. 99–457: A sourcebook.* Washington, DC: National Center for Clinical Infant Programs.

Berrueta-Clement, J. R., Schweinhart, L. J., Barnett, W. S., Epstein, A. S., & Weikart, D. P. (1984). *Changed lives: The effects of the Perry Preschool Program on youths through age 19* (Monographs of the High/Scope Educational Research Foundation No. 8). Ypsilanti, MI: High/Scope Press.

Bettelheim, B. (1987). *A good enough parent: A book on child-rearing.* New York: Vintage.

Biggar, M. L. (1984). Maternal aversion to mother-infant contact. In C. C. Brown (Ed.), *The many facets of touch.* Skillman, NJ: Johnson & Johnson Baby Products Company.

Birch, H. G. (1972, August 14). Malnutrition, learning and intelligence. *Congressional Record-Senate, S12355.*

Bjorklund, G. (1978). *Planning for play.* Columbus, OH: Merrill.

Blass, E. M., Ganchrow, J. R., & Steiner, J. E. (1984). Classical conditioning in newborn humans 2–48 hours of age. *Infant Behavior and Development, 7,* 223–235.

Bloom, B. S. (1964). *Stability and change in human characteristics.* New York: John Wiley & Sons.

Bloom, L., & Lahey, M. (1978). *Language development and language disorders.* New York: Wiley.

Blow, S. E. (1985). *The songs and music of Friedrich Froebel's mother play.* New York: D. Appleton.

Borke, H. (1972). Chandler and Greenspan's "Ersatz Egocentrism: A rejoinder. *Developmental Psychology, 7,* 107–109.

Bowlby, J. (1951). Maternal care and mental health. *Bulletin of the World Health Organization, 3,* 355–534.

Bowlby, J. (1982). *Attachment and loss* (2nd ed.). New York: Basic Books.

Bowlby, J. (1985). The nature of a child's tie to his mother. *International Journal of Psychoanalysis, 39,* 350–373.

Bradley, R. H. (1985). Play materials and intellectual development. In C. C. Brown & A. W. Gottfried (Eds.), *Play interactions: The role of toys and parental involvement in children's development* (pp. 31–36). Pediatric Round Table 11. New York: Johnson & Johnson Baby Products.

Brasel, J. (1978). Infantile obesity. *Dialogues in Infant Nutrition, 1* (4), 1–4.

Braun, S. J., & Edwards, E. P. (1972). *History and theory of early childhood education.* Belmont, CA: Wadsworth.

Brazelton, T. B. (1974). *Toddlers and parents: A declaration of independence.* New York: Dell.

Brazelton, T. B. (1978). Foreward. In E. B. Thoman & S. Trotter (Eds.), *Social responsiveness in infants.* Pediatric Round Table 2. New York: Johnson & Johnson Baby Products.

Brazelton, T. B. (1979). Infant learning. *Options in Education Program* No. 202, Part 1. Washington, DC: National Public Radio and the Institute for Educational Leadership.

Brazelton, T. B. (1984a). Cementing family relationships. In L. L. Dittmann (Ed.), *The infants we care for* (rev. ed.). Washington, DC: National Association for the Education of Young Children.

Brazelton, T. B. (1984b). Introduction. In C. C. Brown (Ed.), *The many facets of touch: The foundation of experience: Its importance through life, with initial emphasis for infants and young children.* Skillman, NJ: Johnson & Johnson Baby Products.

Brazelton, T. B. (1987). *What every baby knows.* Reading, MA: Addison-Wesley.

Brazelton, T. B. (1989, March). Nurturing the nurturers. *World Monitor,* 14–17.

Bredekamp, S. (Ed.). (1986). *Developmentally appropriate practice.* Washington, DC: National Association for the Education of Young Children.

Bredekamp, S. (Ed.). (1987). *Developmentally appropriate practice in early childhood programs serving children from birth through age 8* (expanded ed.). Washington, DC: National Association for the Education of Young Children.

Breger, L. (1974). *From instinct to identity: The development of personality.* Englewood Cliffs, NJ: Prentice-Hall.

Bremner, R. H. (Ed.). (1970). *Children and youth in America: A documentary history.* Vol. 1. Cambridge, MA: Harvard University Press.

Bretherton, I., & Bates, E. (1979). The emergence of intentional communication. *New Directions for Child Development, 4,* 81–100.

Bridges, K. M. B. (1933). A study of social development in social infancy. *Child Development, 4,* 36–49.

Brody, S., & Axelrod, S. (1970). *Anxiety and ego formation in infancy.* New York: International Universities.

Bromwich, R. M. (1977). Stimulation in the first year of life? A perspective on infant development. *Young Children, 32* (2), 71–82.

Bromwich, R. (1984). *Working with parents and infants.* Baltimore: University Park Press.

Bronfenbrenner, U. (1978). Who needs parent education? *Teachers College Record, 70* (4), 767–787.

Bronfenbrenner, U. (1979). *The ecology of human development.* Cambridge, MA: Harvard University Press.

Bruner, J. S. (1973). Organization of early skilled action. *Child Development, 44,* 1–111.

Bruner, J. S. (1977). Early social interaction and language acquisition. In H. R. Schaeffer (Ed.), *Studies in mother-infant interaction* (pp. 271–290). London: Academic Press.

Buhler, C. (1933). The social behavior of children. In C. Murchison (Ed.), *Handbook of child psychology.* Worcester, MA: Clark University.

Burtt, K. G., & Kalkstein, K. (1981). *Smart toys for babies from birth to two.* New York: Harper & Row.

Butler, D. (1983). *Babies need books.* New York: Atheneum.

Butler, I. G. (1973). Enep'ut: A hot idea from the Eskimos. *Day Care and Early Education, 1* (1), 15–18.

Caldwell, B. M. (1972). Kramer School—Something for everybody. In S. J. Braun & E. P. Edwards, *History and theory of early childhood education* (2nd ed.) (pp. 372–386). Worthington, OH: Jones.

Caldwell, B. M. (1977). Aggression and hostility in young children. *Young Children, 32* (2), 4–13.

Caldwell, B. M. (1984). What is quality child care? *Young Children, 39* (3), 3–8.

Caldwell, B. M. (1986a). Day care and the public schools—Natural allies, natural enemies. *Educational Leadership, 44* (3), 34–39.

Caldwell, B. M. (1986b). Professional child care: A supplement to parental care. In N. Gunzenhauser & B. M. Caldwell (Eds.), *Group care for young children: Considerations for child care and health professionals, public policy makers, and parents* (pp. 3–13). Skillman, NJ: Johnson & Johnson Baby Products.

Caldwell, B. (1987, March). Advocacy is everybody's business. *Child Care Information Exchange,* (54), 29–32.

Caldwell, B. M. (1988). It's not nice to bite. *Working Mother, 11* (11), 138, 140.

Caldwell, B. M. (1989). A comprehensive model for integrating child care and early childhood education. *Teachers College Record, 90* (3), 404–414.

Caldwell, B., & Richmond, J. (1968a). The Children's Center in Syracuse, New York. In L. L. Dittmann (Ed.), *Early child care* (pp. 326–358). New York: Atherton Press.

Caldwell, B., & Richmond, J. (1968b). A "typical day" for the groups at the children's center. In L. L. Dittmann (Ed.), *Early child care* (pp. 373–377). New York: Atherton Press.

Caldwell, B., & Rorex, J. (1977). A day at the Kramer Baby House. In M. D. Cohen (Ed.), *Developing programs for infants and toddlers.* Washington, DC: Association of Childhood Education International.

Caldwell, B. M., & Stedman, D. J. (Eds.). (1977). *Infants' education: A guide for helping handi-capped children in the first three years.* New York: Walker.

Caldwell, B. M., Wright, C., Honig, A. S., & Tannenbaum, J. (1970). Infant day care and attachment. *American Journal of Orthopsychiatry, 40* (37), 397–412.

Cartwright, S. (1988). Play can be the building blocks of learning. *Young Children, 43* (5), 44–47.

Caruso, D. A. (1988). Play and learning in infants: Research and implication. *Young Children, 42* (6), 63–70.

Castelle, K. (1990). *In the child's best interest: A primer on the U.N. Convention on the Rights of the Child* (3rd ed., adopted text). East Greenwich, RI: Foster Parents Plan International; New York: Defense for Children International–USA.

Casto, G., & Biro, P. (1989). Selected infant and preschool screening tests, appendix II. In S. J. Meisels & S. Provence, *Screening and assessment: Guidelines for identifying young disabled and developmentally vulnerable children and their families.* Washington, DC: National Center for Clinical Infant Programs.

Cataldo, C. Z. (1983). *Infant and toddler programs: A guide to very early childhood education.* Reading, MA: Addison-Wesley.

Cazden, C. (Ed.). (1981). *Language in early childhood education* (rev. ed.). Washington, DC: National Association for the Education of Young Children.

CDA National Credentialing Program. (1985). *Family day care providers: Child Development Associate assessment system and competency standards.* Washington, DC: Author.

CDA National Credentialing Program. (1986). *Infant/toddler caregivers in center-based programs: Child Development Associate assessment system and competency standards.* Washington, DC: Author.

Center for Disease Control. (1985). Education and foster care for children infected with human T-lymphotropic virus type III/lymphadenopathy-associated virus. *Morbidity and Mortality Weekly Report, 34,* 517–521.

Chandler, M. J., & Greenspan, S. (1972). Ersatz egocentrism: A reply to H. Borke. *Developmental Psychology, 7,* 104–106.

Chang, A., Lugg, M. M., & Nebedum, A. (1989). Injuries among preschool children enrolled in day-care centers. *Pediatrics, 8* (2), 272–277.

Chess, S. (1987). Comments: Infant day care: A cause for concern. *Zero to Three, 7* (3), 24–25.

Child Care Employee Project. (1989). *National child care staffing study.* Berkeley, CA: Author.

Child Care Food Program (Final Rule). *Federal Register,* Jan. 22, 1980. (revised July 1989)

Child Welfare League of America. (1984). *Standards for day care services (rev.)* New York: Author.

Children's Bureau. (1976). *Young children and accidents in the home.* (DHEW Publication No. [OHD] 76–30034). Washington, DC: U.S. Government Printing Office.

Children's Defense Fund. (1988). *A Children's defense budget.* Washington, DC: Author.

Children's Defense Fund. (1989). Child care. In *A vision for America's future* (pp. 55–65). Washington, DC: Author.

Children's Defense Fund. (1990). S. O. S. America! Washington, DC: Author.

The Children's Foundation. (1988). *1988 Family day care licensing study.* Washington, DC: Author.

Christie, J. F. (1983). The effects of play tutoring on young children's cognitive performance. *Journal of Educational Research, 76,* 326–330.

Clarke-Stewart, A. (1989). When mother goes to work. In A. Campbell (Ed.), *The opposite sex.* Topsfield, MA: Salem House.

Cohen, H. J. (Chair of the APHA/AAP Project to develop National Health and Safety Standards). (1989). *Draft report of the technical panel on children with special needs.* New York: Albert Einstein College of Medicine of Yeshiva University.

Coleman, J. S., & others. (1966). *Equality of educational opportunity.* Washington, DC: U.S. Government Printing Office.

Committee for Economic Development, Research and Policy Committee. (1987). *Children in need: Investment strategies for the educationally disadvantaged.* New York: Author.

Convention on the Rights of the Child. (1990). Appendix II in K. Castelle, *In the child's best interest: A primer on the U.N. Convention on the Rights of the Child* (3rd ed., adopted text). East Greenwich, RI: Foster Parents Plan International and New York: Defense for Children Inter-National–USA.

Cook, R. E., Tessier, A., & Armbruster, V. B. (1987). *Adapting early childhood curricula for children with special needs* (2nd ed.). Columbus, OH: Merrill.

Cook, S., & O'Malley, A. (1989). Forbidden fruit. *Family Circle, 102* (5), 14–17.

Coopersmith, S. (Ed.). (1975). *Developing motivation in young children.* San Francisco: Albion.

Copple, C., DeLisi, R., & Sigel, I. (1982). Cognitive development. In B. Spodek (Ed.), *Handbook of research in early childhood education* (pp. 3–26). New York: Free Press.

Corsini, D. A., Wisensale, S., & Caruso, G. (1988). Family day care: System issues and regulatory models. *Young Children, 43* (6), 17–23.

Council for Early Childhood Professional Recognition. (1986). *Child Development Associate assessment system and competency standards.* Washington, DC: Author.

Council of Chief State School Officers. (1988). *Early childhood and family education: Foundations for success.* Washington, DC: Author.

Cratty, B. J. (1982). Motor development in early childhood: Critical issues for researchers in the 1980s. In B. Spodek (Ed.), *Handbook of Research in Early Childhood Education* (pp. 27–46). New York: Free Press.

Cullinan, B. E. (1989). Literature for young children. In D. S. Strickland & L. M. Morrow (Eds.), *Emerging literacy: Young children learn to read and write.* Newark, DE: International Reading Association.

Cunnington, P., & Buck, A. (1965). *Children's costume in England.* New York: Barnes & Noble.

Darwin, C. (1859). *The origin of the species.* London: Murray.

Darwin, C. (1873). *Expression of the emotions in man and animals.* New York: Appleton.

Dattner, R. (1969). *Design for play.* Cambridge, MA: MIT Press.

Day, M. C., & Parker, R. K. (Eds.). (1977). *The pre-

school in action (2nd ed.). Boston: Allyn & Bacon.

DeCasper, A., & Carstens, A. (1981). Contingencies of stimulation: Effects of learning and emotion in neonates. *Infant Behavior and Development, 4,* 19–35.

Defense for Children International. (1988). *Text of draft Convention on the Rights of the Child following the UN Working Group meeting of 28 November–9 December, 1988.* Geneva, Switzerland: Author.

Department of Public Instruction. (1985). *Rules of special education.* Des Moines, IA: Author.

Derman-Sparks, L., & A. B. C. Task Force. (1989). *Anti-bias curriculum. Tools for empowering young children.* Washington, DC: National Association for the Education of Young Children.

Dinsmore, K. E. (1988). Baby's first books: A guide to the selection of infant literature. *Childhood Education, 64* (4), 215–219.

Dinsmore, K. E. (1989). The fallacies and dangers of baby exercise programs. *Focus on infancy, 1* (3), 1–2. (ACEI Division for Infancy)

Discipline: Are tantrums normal? (1988). *Young Children, 43* (6), 35–40.

Dittmann, L. L. (Ed.). (1984). *The infants we care for* (rev. ed.). Washington, DC: National Association for the Education of Young Children.

Eastman, P. (1989). Babies don't need workouts. *Working Mother, 3,* 46.

Edfeldt, A. W. (1985, June). *Swedish research and theory on violence towards children.* Paper presented at the United States–Sweden Joint Seminar on Physical and Sexual Abuse of Children, Satra Bruk, Sweden.

Elardo, P., & Caldwell, B. (1974, January). The Kramer adventure: A school for the future? *Childhood Education, 50* (3), 143–152.

Elardo, R., Solomons, H. C., & Snider, B. C. (1987). An analysis of accidents at a day care center. *American Journal of Orthopsychiatry, 57,* 60–65.

Elkind, D. (1988). Play. *Young Children, 43* (3), 2.

Endsley, R. C., & Bradbard, M. R. (1981). *Quality day care: A handbook of choices for parents and caregivers.* Englewood Cliffs, NJ: Prentice-Hall.

Erikson, E. (1964). *Childhood and society* (rev. ed.). New York: Norton.

Erlanger, S. (1989). Horror at home: The tragedy of family violence. *Family Circle, 102* (5), 78–83, 98–100.

Esbensen, S. (1987). *The early childhood playground: An outdoor classroom.* Ypsilanti, MI: High/Scope.

Executive Evaluation Summary: New Parents as Teachers Project. (1985). Missouri Department of Elementary & Secondary Education.

Family matters (1989, July). *Ladies' Home Journal, 106* (7), 58.

Family Resource Coalition. (1989). *Programs that serve families at risk.* Chicago: Author.

Fauvre, M. (1988). Including young children with "new" chronic illnesses in an early childhood education setting. *Young Children, 43* (6), 71–77.

Fein, G. G. (1979). Echoes from the nursery: Piaget, Vygotsky, and the relationship between language and play. *New Directions for Child Development* (6), 1–14.

Feldman, R. E. (1975). Teaching self-control and self-expression via play. In S. Coopersmith (Ed.), *Developing motivation in young children.* San Francisco: Albion.

Fenson, L. (1985). The developmental progression of exploration and play. In C. C. Brown & A. W. Gottfried (Eds.), *Play interactions: The role of toys and parental involvement in children's development* (pp. 31–36). Pediatric Round Table 11. New York: Johnson & Johnson Baby Products.

Feshback, S. (1970). Aggression. In P. H. Mussen (Ed.), *Carmichael's manual of child psychology.* New York: John Wiley & Sons.

Finkelhor, D., Williams, L. M., & Burns, N. (1988). *Nursery crimes: Sexual abuse in day care.* Newbury, CA: Sage Publications.

Fisher, J. (Ed.). (1988). *Johnson and Johnson from baby to toddler.* New York: Perigree Books.

Flavell, J. (1963). *The developmental psychology of Jean Piaget.* Princeton, NJ: Van Nostrand.

Fogel, A. (1986). The role of adults in infant development: Implications for early childhood educators. In L. Katz (Ed.), *Current Topics in Early Childhood Education, 6,* Norwood, NJ: Ablex.

Fomon, S. J. (1974). *Infant nutrition* (2nd ed.). Philadelphia: Saunders.

Fomon, S. J. (1977). *Nutritional disorders of children: Prevention screening, and follow-up.* (DHEW Publication No. [HSA] 77–5104). Washington, DC: U.S. Government Printing Office.

Fomon, S. J., & others. (1979). *Recommendations for feeding normal infants* (DHEW Publication No. [HSA] 79–5108). Washington, DC: U.S. Government Printing Office.

Food and Nutrition Service, U. S. Department of Agriculture. (1976). *A planning guide for good service in child care centers* (FNS–64). Washington, DC: U.S. Government Printing Office.

Food and Nutrition Service, U.S. Department of Agriculture. (1980). *Food buying guide for child care centers* (FNS–108). Washington, DC: U.S. Government Printing Office.

Forbes, D. (1978). Recent research on children's social cognition: A brief review. *New Directions for Child Development* (1), 123–139.

Forman, G. E., & Hill, F. (1984). *Constructive play: Applying Piaget in the preschool* (rev. ed.). Menlo Park, CA: Addison-Wesley.

Fowler, W. (1980). *Infant and child care: A guide to education in group settings.* Boston: Allyn & Bacon.

Fowler, W., & Khan, N. (1976). *A follow-up investigation of the later development of infants in enriched group care.* Urbana, IL: ERIC Clearinghouse on Early Childhood Education. (ERIC Document Reproduction Service No. ED 093 506)

Friedberg, M. P. (1969). *Playgrounds for city children.* Washington, DC: Association for Childhood Education International.

Friedman, D. E. (1989). The corporation as a family resource. *Family Resource Coalition Report, 8* (1), 14–15.

Froebel, F. (1879). *Mother-Play and nursery songs. With notes to mothers.* (Tr. from the German). Boston: Lee.

Froebel, F. (1887). *The education of man: The art of education, instruction, and training.* New York: D. Appleton. (Original work published 1826)

Frost, J. L. (1986). Children's playgrounds: Research and practice. In G. Fein & M. Rivkin (Eds.), *The young child at play. Reviews of Research.* Vol 4. Washington, DC: National Association for the Education of Young Children.

Frost, J. L., & Klein, B. L. (1979). *Children's play and playgrounds.* Boston: Allyn & Bacon.

Gannett News Service. (1988, October 7). Iowa City: *Iowa City Press Citizen,* 5C.

Gannett News Service. (1989, May 26). Child care campaign calls for more action. Iowa City: *Iowa City Press Citizen.*

Gardner, H. (1985). *Frames of mind: The theory of multiple intelligences.* New York: Basic Books.

Garvey, C. (1977). *Play.* Cambridge, MA: Harvard University Press.

Garvey, C. (1984). *Children's Talk.* Cambridge, MA: Harvard University Press.

Geismar-Ryan, L. (1986). Infant social activity: The discovery of peer play. *Childhood Education, 63* (1), 24–29.

Genishi, C. (1986). Acquiring language and communicative competence. In C. Seefeldt (Ed.), *Early childhood curriculum: A review of current research* (pp. 75–106). New York: Teachers College Press.

Gerber, M. (1981). What is appropriate curriculum for infants and toddlers? In B. Weissbourd & J. Musick (Eds.), *Infants: Their social environments* (pp. 77–85). Washington, DC: National Association for the Eduction of Young Children.

Gesell, A. (1923). *The preschool child.* New York: Macmillan.

Gesell, A. (1940a). *The first five years of life.* New York: Harper & Row.

Gesell, A. (1940b). *Gesell development schedules.* New York: Psychological Corporation.

Gesell, A., & Ilg, F. L. (1943). Infant and child in the culture of today. New York: Harper.

Gestwicki, C. (1987). *Home, school and community relations: A guide to working with parents.* Albany, NY: Delmar.

Gewirtz, J. L. (1971). Stimulation, learning, and motivation principles for day care settings. In E. H. Grotberg (Ed.), *Day care: Resources for deci-*

sions. Washington, DC: Office of Economic Opportunity.

Glazer, S. M. (1989). Oral language and literacy development. In D. S. Strickland & L. M. Morrow (Eds.), *Emerging literacy: Young children learn to read and write.* Newark, DE: International Reading Association.

Glubok, S. (Ed.). (1969). *Home and child life in colonial days.* New York: Macmillan.

Gober, B. E., & Franks, B. D. (1988, September). Physical and fitness education of young children. *Journal of Physical Education, Recreation and Dance, 57–61.*

Godwin, A., & Schrag, L. (Eds.). (1988). *Setting up for infant care: Guidelines for centers and family day care homes.* Washington, DC: National Association for the Education of Young Children.

Goelman, H. (1986). The language environments of family day care. In S. Kilmer (Ed.), *Advances in Early Education and Day Care, 4,* 153–179.

Goffin, S. G., & Lombardi, J. (1988). *Speaking out: Early childhood advocacy.* Washington, DC: National Association for the Education of Young Children.

Gold, S. J. (1986). *When children invite child abuse.* Eugene, OR: Fern Ridge Press.

Gonzalez-Mena, J., & Eyer, D. W. (1980). *Infancy and caregiving.* Palo Alto, CA: Mayfield.

Gordon, I. J. (1973). A home learning center approach to early stimulation. In J. L. Frost (Ed.), *Revisiting early childhood education: Readings* (pp. 98–122). New York: Holt, Rinehart & Winston.

Gordon, I. J. (1975). *The infant experience.* Columbus, OH: Merrill.

Gordon, I. J., Guinagh, B., & Jester, R. E. (1977). The Florida Parent Education Infant and Toddler Programs. In M. C. Day & R. K. Parker (Eds.), *The preschool in action* (2nd ed.) (pp. 97–127). Boston: Allyn & Bacon.

Gordon, I. J., & Lally, J. R. (1967). *Intellectual stimulation for infants and toddlers.* Gainsville, FL: University of Florida, Institute for the Development of Human Resources.

Gray, S., & Klaus, R. (1970). The early training pro-

ject: A seventh year report. *Child Development, 4,* 909–924.

Green, M. (1984). A sigh of relief—the first aid handbook for childhood emergencies (2nd ed.). New York: Bantam.

Greenberg, P. (1987). Ideas that work with young children. What is curriculum for infants in family day care (or elsewhere?). *Young Children, 42* (5), 58–62.

Greenman, J. (1982a). Designing infant/toddler environments. In R. Lurie & R. Neugebauer (Eds.), *Caring for infants and toddlers: What works, What doesn't.* Vol. 2. Redmond, WA: Child Care Information Exchange.

Greenman, J. (1982b). Furnishing the infant/toddler environment. In R. Lurie & R. Neugebauer (Eds.), *Caring for infants and toddlers: What works, what doesn't.* Vol. 2. Redmond, WA: Child Care Information Exchange.

Greenman, J. (1984, Summer). Worlds for infants and toddlers: New ideas. *Beginnings, 21–25.*

Greenman, J. (1986). Primary caregiver systems. *Caring for infants and toddlers, 1* (3), 9–12.

Greenman, J. (1988). *Caring spaces, learning places: Children's environments that work.* Redmond, WA: Exchange Press.

Greenman, J., & Fuqua, R. (1984). *Making day care better: Training, evaluation and the process of change.* New York: Teachers College Press.

Grotberg, E. H. (Ed.). (n.d.). *200 years of children.* Washington, DC: U.S. Department of Health, Education and Welfare.

Group for the Advancement of Psychiatry. (1973). *The joys and sorrows of parenthood.* New York: Scribner's Sons.

Grusec, J. E. (1974). Power and the internalization of self-denial. *Child Development, 45,* 248–251.

Guide for state action: Early childhood & family education. (1988). Washington, DC: Council of Chief State School Officers.

Halliday, M. A. K. (1975). *Learning how to mean: Exploration in the development of language.* London: Edward Arnold.

Hamburg, D. A. (1987). *Fundamental building blocks of early life.* New York: Carnegie Corporation.

Harms, T., & Clifford, R. (1980). *Early Childhood*

Environment Rating Scale. New York: Teachers College Press.

Harms, T., & Clifford, R. (1989). *Family Day Care Rating Scale.* New York: Teachers College Press.

Hartup, W. H. (1982). Peer relations. In C. B. Kopp & J. B. Krakow (Eds.), *The child: Development in a social context.* Reading, MA: Addison-Wesley.

Hartup, W. W. (1983). Peer relations. In P. H. Mussen (Ed.), *Handbook of child psychology.* Vol. 4. New York: Wiley & Sons.

Havighurst, R. J. (1952). *Developmental tasks and education* (2nd ed.). New York: David McKay.

Hayward, H. C. (1987). A mediational teaching style. *The thinking teacher: Cognitive education for young children, 4* (1), 1–6.

Head Start Bureau. (1967). *Nutrition: Better eating for a head start.* (DHEW Publication No. [OHDS] 76–31009). Washington, DC: U.S. Government Printing Office.

Herr, J. & Morse, W. (1982). Food for thought: Nutrition education for young children. *Young Children, 38* (1), 3–11.

Hignett, W. F. (1988). Infant/toddler day care, yes; but we'd better make it good. *Young Children, 44* (1), 32–33.

Hill, E. (1980). *Where's Spot?* New York: Putnam.

Hill, E. (1981). *Spot's first walk.* New York: Putnam.

Hill, E. (1982). *Spot's birthday party.* New York: Putnam.

Hill, E. (1984). *Spot goes to school.* New York: Putnam.

Hill, E. (1985). *Spot goes to the beach.* New York: Putnam.

Hill, E. (1986). *Spot goes to the circus.* New York: Putnam.

Hill, E. (1987a). *Spot's first picnic.* New York: Putnam.

Hill, E. (1987b). *Spot goes to the farm.* New York: Putnam.

Hirsch, E. S. (Ed.). (1984). *The block book.* Washington, DC: National Association for the Education of Young Children.

Hoffman, M. L. (1972). *Symposium on development of altruism.* Paper presented at the annual con-ference of the American Psychological Association, Honolulu, HI.

Honig, A. S. (1976). The training of infant care providers. *Voice for Children, 9* (1), 12–17.

Honig, A. S. (1981). Recent infancy research. In B. Weissbourd & J. S. Musick (Eds.), *Infants: Their social environments.* Washington, DC: National Association for the Education of Young Children.

Honig, A. S. (1982). Meeting the needs of infants. In R. Lurie & R. Neugebauer (Eds.), *Caring for infants and toddlers: What works, what doesn't.* Vol. 2 (pp. 9–16). Redmond WA: Child Care Information Exchange.

Honig, A. S. (1985). High quality infant/toddler care. *Young Children, 41* (1), 40–46.

Honig, A. S. (1990). Infant/toddler education issues: Practices, problems, and promises. In C. Seefeldt (Ed.), *Continuing issues in early childhood education.* Columbus, OH: Merrill.

Honig, A. S., & Lally, J. R. (1981). *Infant caregiving: A design for training.* New York: Syracuse University Press.

Horowitz, F. D. (1969). Learning, developmental research and individual differences. In L. P. Lipsitt & H. W. Reese (Eds.), *Advances in child development and behavior.* Vol. 4. New York: Academic Press.

Howes, C. (1987). Quality indicators in infant and toddler child care: The Los Angeles study. In D. A. Phillips (Ed.), *Quality in child care: What does research tell us?* Research Monographs of the National Association for the Education of Young Children, 1, 81–88.

Hunt, J. McV. (1961). *Intelligence and experience.* New York: Ronald.

Huntington, D. S., Provence, S., & Parker, R. K. (1973). *Day Care 2: Serving infants.* (DHEW Publication No. OCD 73–14). Washington, DC: U.S. Government Printing Office.

Hymes, J. L., Jr. (1975). *Effective home-school relations* (rev. ed.). Carmel, CA: Hacienda Press.

Hymes, J. L., Jr. (1990). *The year in review: A look at 1989.* Washington, DC: National Association for the Education of Young Children.

Illnesses in day care children require more hospitalizations. (1989, June). *Index: Child Care, 1,* 8.

Ingram, D. (1976). *Phonological disability in children.* London: Edward Arnold Publishers.

International Children's Center. (1979). *Prevention of accidents in childhood.* Geneva: Author.

Iowa Department of Human Services. (1988). *Child day care centers and preschool licensing standards and procedures.* Des Moines, IA: Author.

Iowa Department of Public Instruction. (1985). *Rules of special education.* Des Moines, IA: Author.

Jalongo, M. R. (1987). Do security blankets belong in the preschool? *Young Children, 42* (3), 3–8.

Jalongo, M. R. (1989). *Young children and picture books: Literature from infancy to six.* Washington, DC: National Association for the Education of Young Children.

Johnson, G. (1986). Food sensitivity. *Child Care Center, 1* (2), 45–47.

Johnson, H. (1933). *The art of block building.* New York: Day.

Johnson, H. M. (1936). *School begins at two.* New York: New Republic.

Johnson, H. M. (1972). *Children in "the nursery school."* New York: Agathon. (Originally published in 1928)

Johnson, J. E., Christie, J. F., & Yawkey, T. D. (1987). *Play and early childhood development.* Glenview, IL: Scott, Foresman.

Johnson, J. E., Ershler, J., & Lawton, J. T. (1982). Intellective correlates of preschoolers' spontaneous play. *Journal of General Psychology, 106,* 115–122.

Jones, E. (1977). *Dimensions of teaching-learning environments: Handbook for teachers.* Pasadena, CA: Pacific Oaks College.

Jones, E., & Prescott, E. (1978). *Dimensions of teaching—Learning environments–II. Focus on day care.* Pasadena, CA: Pacific Oaks College.

Jones, S. (1988). *Guide to baby products.* Mount Vernon, NY: Consumer Union.

Jorde-Bloom, P. (1988). *A great place to work: Improving conditions for staff in young children's programs.* Washington, DC: National Association for the Education of Young Children.

Kagan, J. (1971). *Change and continuity in infants.* New York: John Wiley & Sons.

Kahane, C. J. (1986, February). *An evaluation of child passenger safety: The effectiveness and benefits of safety seats* (Report DOT HS 806 890). Washington, DC: U.S. Department of Transportation, National Highway Traffic Safety Administration.

Kamii, C., & DeVries, R. (1978). *Physical knowledge in preschool education.* Englewood Cliffs, NJ: Prentice-Hall.

Karnes, M. B., & Zehrback, R. R. (1977). Educational intervention in the home. In M.C. Day & R. K. Parker (Eds.), *The preschool in action* (2nd ed.) (pp. 75–94). Boston: Allyn & Bacon.

Katz, L. G. (1980). Mothering and teaching—Some significant distinctions. In L. G. Katz (Ed.), *Current topics in early childhood education, 3,* 47–63.

Katz, L. (1988). What should young children be doing? *American Educator, 12,* 28–33, 44.

Keister, M. E. (1970). *"The good life" for infants and toddlers.* Washington, DC: National Association for the Education of Young Children.

Kendrick, A. S., Kaufmann, R., & Messenger, K. P. (1988). *Healthy young children: A manual for programs.* Washington, DC: National Association for the Education of Young Children.

Kessen, W. (1965). *The child.* New York: John Wiley & Sons.

Keyserling, M. D. (1972). *Windows on day care.* New York: National Council of Jewish Women. (ERIC Document Reproduction Service No. ED 063 027)

Klaus, M. H., & Kennell, J. H. (1976). *Maternal-Infant bonding.* St. Louis: Mosby.

Klaus, M. H., & Kennell, J. H. (1982). *Parent-Infant Bonding* (2nd ed.). St. Louis: Mosby.

Knoblock, H., & Pasamanick, B. (1974). *Gesell and Armatruda's developmental diagnosis* (3rd ed.). New York: Harper & Row.

Kritchevsky, S., & Prescott, E. (1977). *Planning environments for young children: Physical space* (2nd ed.). Washington, DC: National Association for the Education of Young Children.

Kritchevsky, S., Prescott, E. & Walling, L. (1969). *Planning environments for young children: Physical space.* Washington, DC: National Association for the Education of Young Children.

Kuczaj, S. A. (1985). Language play. *Early child development and care, 19,* 53–67.

Kunhardt, D. (1940). *Pat the bunny.* Racine, WI: Western.

Kunhardt, E. (1984). *Pat the cat.* Racine, WI: Western.

Lakin, J., Solomons, G. & Abel, C. (1977). *Child abuse and neglect: A self-instructional text for Head Start personnel.* (DHEW Publication No. [OHDS] 78–31102). Washington, DC: U.S. Government Printing Office.

Lally, J. R., & Honig, A. S. (1977). The Family Development Research program. In M. C. Day & R. K. Parker (Eds.), *The preschool in action* (2nd ed.) (pp. 151–194). Boston: Allyn & Bacon.

Lally, J. R., Provence, S., Szanton, E., & Weissbourd, B. (1987). Developmentally appropriate care for children from birth to age 3. In S. Bredekamp (Ed.), *Developmentally appropriate practice in early childhood programs serving children from birth through age 8* (expanded ed.). Washington, DC: National Association for the Education of Young Children.

Lamb, M. E. (1977). Father-infant and mother-infant interaction in the first year of life. *Child Development, 48,* 167–181.

Lamb, M. E., & Campos, J. J. (1982). *Development in infancy: An introduction.* New York: Random House.

Lamme, L. (1985). *Growing up reading.* Washington, DC: Acropolis Books.

Languis, M., Sanders, T., & Tipps, S. (1980). *Brain and learning: Directions in early childhood education.* Washington, DC: National Association for the Education of Young Children.

Larcom, L. (1889). *A New England girlhood.* Boston: Houghton Mifflin.

Leach, P. (1981). *Your baby and child from birth to age five.* New York: Knopf.

Leavitt, R. L., & Eheart, B. K. (1985). *Toddler day care: A guide to responsive caregiving.* Lexington, MA: Lexington Books.

Leichter, H. J. (Ed.). (1974). *The family as educator.* New York: Teachers College Press.

Levenstein, P. (1971). *Verbal interaction project: Aiding cognitive growth in disadvantaged mother-child home program.* Final report. Freeport, NY: Family Service Association of Nassau County.

Levenstein, P. (1976). Cognitive development through verbalized play: The mother-child home program. In J. S. Bruner, A. Jolly, & K. Sylva (Eds.), *Play: Its role in development and evolution.* New York: Basic Books.

Levenstein, P. (1977). The Mother-Child Program. In M. C. Day & R. K. Parker (Eds.), *The preschool in action* (2nd ed.) (pp. 27–49). Boston: Allyn & Bacon.

Levine, J. A. (1978). *Day care and the public schools.* Newton, MA: Education Development Center.

Levine, R. A. (1974). Parental goals: A cross-cultural view. In H. J. Leichter (Ed.), *The family as educator* (pp. 52–65). New York: Teachers College Press.

Lewis, M., & Brooks-Gunn, J. (1979). Toward a theory of social cognition: The development of self. In I. C. Uzgiris (Ed.), Social interaction and communication during infancy. *New directions for child development.* No. 4. San Francisco: Jossey-Bass.

Lewis, M., & Harlan, E. (1981, February). Space. *Mother's Manual,* 28–30.

Lin-Fu, J. S. (1985). Forward. In D. N. Kane, *Environmental hazards to young children.* Phoenix: Oryx.

Loevinger, J. (1976). *Ego development: Conceptions and theories.* San Francisco: Jossey-Bass.

Lombardi, J., & Goffin, S. G. (1986). Child advocacy at the state level: Strategies for success. *Dimensions, 14* (2), 15–18.

Long, R., Peters, D. L., & Garduque, L. (1985). Continuity between home and day care: A model for defining relevant dimensions of child care. In I. Siegel (Ed.), *Advances in applied developmental psychology.* Vol. 1. Norwood, NJ: Ablex.

Lourie, R. S. (1973). The roots of violence. *Early Child Development and Care, 2,* 1–12.

Magid, R. Y. (1989). The consequences of employer involvement in child care. *Teachers College Record, 90* (3), 434–443.

Mahalski, P. A. (1983). The incidence of attachment objects and oral habits of bedtime in two longitudinal samples of children aged 1.5 to 7 years.

Journal of Child Psychology and Allied Disciplines, 24 (2), 283–295.

Mahler, M., & Pine, F. (1975). *The psychological birth of the infant.* New York: Basic Books.

Making the most of new child care funds. (1987, January). *CDF Reports,* 4–5.

Maraschiello, R. (1981). *Evaluation of prekindergarten Head Start program 1979–1980.* (Technical Summary Report No. 8132). Philadelphia: Philadelphia School District, Office of Research and Evaluation. (ERIC Document Reproduction Service No. ED 206 637)

Marx, F., Bailey, S., & Francis, J. (1988). *Child care for the children of adolescent parents: Findings from a national survey and case studies.* Working paper No. 184, Wellesley College Center for Research on Women, Wellesley, MA.

Maslow, A. H. (1943). A theory of human motivation. *Psychological Review, 50,* 370–396.

Maudry, M., & Nekula, M. (1939). Social relations between children of the same age during the first two years of life. *Journal of Abnormal and Social Psychology, 27,* 243–269.

McAfee, O. (1967). The right words. *Young Children, 23,* 74–78.

McCartney, K., Scarr, S., Phillips, D., Grajeck, S., & Schwarz, J. C. (1982). Environmental differences among day care centers and their effects on children's development. In E. F. Zigler & E. W. Gordon (Eds.), *Day care: Scientific and social policy issues* (pp. 126–151). Boston: Auburn House.

McClearn, G. E. (1964). Genetics and behavior development. In M. L. Hoffman & L. W. Hoffman (Eds.), *Review of child development research* (Vol. 1) (pp. 433–480). New York: Russell Sage Foundation.

McCune, L. (1986). Symbolic development in normal and atypical infants. In G. Fein & M. Rivkin (Eds.), *The young child at play: Reviews of research.* Vol. 4. Washington, DC: National Association for the Education of Young Children.

McDonald, D. T., & Simons, G. M. (1989). *Musical growth and development: Birth through six.* New York: Schirmer.

McGraw, M. (1954). Maturation of behavior. In L. Carmichael (Ed.), *Manual of child psychology.* New York: Wiley.

McKinney, J. (1978). *Study of parent involvement in early childhood programs.* Philadelphia, PA: Philadelphia School District, Office of Research and Evaluation. (ERIC Document Reproduction Service No. ED 164 134)

McKinney, J. (1980). *Evaluation of parent involvement in early childhood programs 1979–1980.* Philadelphia: Philadelphia School District, Office of Research and Evaluation. (ERIC Reproduction Service No. ED 204 388)

McNeill, D. (1970). *The acquisition of language.* New York: Harper & Row.

Mead, G. (1934). *Mind, self and society.* Chicago: University of Chicago Press.

Mediax Associates. (1980). *Head Start profiles of program effects on children.* Newsletter, Issue III. Westport, CT: Mediax.

Meltzoff, A. N., & Moore, M. K. (1977). Imitation of facial and manual gestures by human neonates. *Science, 198,* 75–78.

Meyerhoff, M. K., & White, B. L. (1986). New parents as teachers. *Educational Leadership, 44* (2), 42–46.

Miller, K. (1984). Some toddlers bite when they are frustrated. *Conference Materials, Caring for Infants and Toddlers.* Redmond, WA: Child Care Information Exchange.

Mills, B., Matlock, J. & Herrell, A. (1988). Infant care—Does anybody care? *International Journal of Early Childhood, 20* (2), 336–345.

Mitchell, A. (1989). Old baggage, new visions: Shaping policy for early childhood programs. *Phi Delta Kappan, 70* (9), 664–672.

Montagu, A. (1986). *Touching: The human significance of the skin* (3rd ed.). New York: Harper & Row.

Moore, R. S., et al. (1975). *Influences on learning in early childhood: A literature review.* Berrien Springs, MI: Hewitt Research Center. (ERIC Document Reproduction Service No. Ed. 144 711)

Moore, S. G. (1982). Prosocial behavior in the early years: Parent and peer influences. In B. Spodek (Ed.), *Handbook of Research in Early Childhood Education* (pp. 65–81). New York: Free Press.

Morgan, G. (1987). *The national state of child care regulation 1986.* Watertown, MA: Work/Family Directions.

Murphy, L. B. (1956). *Colin—A normal child.* New York: Basic Books.

Murphy, L. B. (1962). *The widening world of childhood.* New York: Basic Books.

Murphy, L. B. (1968). Assessment of infants and young children. In L. L. Dittmann (Ed.), *Early child care: The new perspectives* (pp. 107–138). New York: Atherton Press.

Murphy, L. B., Heider, G. M., & Small, C. T. (1986). Individual differences in infants. *Zero to Three, 7* (2), 1–8.

Murphy, L. B. & Leeper, E. M. (1976). From "I" to "we." *Caring for children.* No. 8. Washington, DC: U.S. Government Printing Office.

Murphy, L. G., & Moriarty, A. E. (1976). *Vulnerability, coping, and growth.* New Haven, CT: Yale University Press.

Musick, J., & Householder, J. (1986). *Infant development: From theory to practice.* Belmont, CA: Wadsworth.

Mussen, P. H. (Ed.). (1970). *Carmichael's manual of child psychology* (3rd ed.). New York: John Wiley & Sons.

Mussen, P. H. (Ed.). (1983a). *Handbook of child psychology.* Vol. 2. *Infancy and developmental psychobiology.* New York: John Wiley.

Mussen, P. H. (Ed.). (1983b). *Handbook of child psychology.* Vol. 3. *Cognitive Development.* New York: Wiley.

Mussen, P. H. (Ed.). (1983c). *Handbook of child psychology.* Vol. 4. *Socialization, personality, and social development* (4th ed.). New York: Wiley.

National Academy of Early Childhood Programs. (1984). *Accreditation criteria & procedures.* Washington, DC: National Association for the Education of Young Children.

National Academy of Early Childhood Programs. (1985). *Guide to accreditation.* Washington, DC: National Association for the Education of Young Children.

National Association of Children's Hospitals and Related Institutions. (1989). *Profile of child health in the United States.* Alexandria, VA: Author.

National Association for the Education of Young Children. (1985). *Toys: Tools for learning.* Washington, DC: Author.

National Association for the Education of Young Children. (1986). Parents' night out and child safety seats. *Young Children, 41* (6), 52.

National Association for the Education of Young Children. (1987). Guidelines for developing legislation creating or expanding programs for young children. *Young Children, 42* (3), 43–45.

National Association for the Education of Young Children. (1989). New guidelines in HIV infection (AIDS) announced for group programs. *Young Children, 44* (2), 51.

National Association of State Boards of Education. (1988). *Right from the start.* Alexandria, VA: Author.

The National Center for Clinical Infant Programs. (1986). *Infants can't wait.* Washington, DC: Author.

National Center for Clinical Infant Programs. (1988). *Who will mind the babies?* (2nd ed.). Washington, DC: Author.

National Governors' Association Committee on Human Resources and Center for Policy Research and the Council of State Governments. (1987). *Focus on the first sixty months The next steps.* Washington, DC: National Governors' Association.

National Governors' Association. (1989). *America in transition: Report of the task force on children.* Washington, DC: Author.

National Institute of Neurological and Communicative Disorders and Stroke (1977). *Learning to talk.* (DHEW Publication No. N1H 77–43). Washington, DC: U.S. Government Printing Office.

Nelson, C. (1988). Infant movement. *Journal of Physical Education, Recreation and Dance,* 57–61.

Nielsen, S. (1989, June). Pesticides & fruit: Ways to lower your risks. *Good Housekeeping, 208* (12), 241–242.

North, A. F., Jr. (1973). *Day care 6. Health Services.* Washington, DC: U.S. Government Printing Office.

Noyes, D. (1987). Indoor pollutants: Environmental hazards to young children. *Young Children, 42* (6), 57–65.

Obesity among children: It's growing bigger. (November, 1987). *Tufts University Diet & Nutrition Letter, 7.*

O'Donnell, P. (1969). *Motor and haptic learning.* Sioux Falls, SD: Adapt Press.

Office of Human Development Services. (1980). *A parents' guide to day care.* (DHHS Publication No. [OHDS] 80–30254). Washington, DC: U.S. Government Printing Office.

Olds, A. R. (1987). Designing settings for infants and toddlers. In C. S. Weinstein & T. G. David (Eds.), *Spaces for children.* New York: Plenum Press.

Oppenheim, J. F. (1984). Kids and play (chs. 1–4). New York: Ballantine.

Osgood, C. E. (1957). Motivational dynamics of language behaviors. In M. R. Jones (Ed.), *Nebraska Symposium on Motivation.* Lincoln, NE: University of Nebraska Press.

Osofsky, J. D. (Ed.). (1979). *Handbook of infant development.* New York: Wiley.

Our story. (n.d.). Chicago: Family Resource Coalition.

Parke, R. D. (1978). Children's home environments. In I. Altman & J. F. Wohlwill (Eds.), *Children and the environment.* New York: Plenum Press.

Parten, M. B. (1932). Social participation among preschool children. *Journal of Abnormal and Social Psychology, 27,* 243–269.

Pence, A. R., & Goelman, H. (1987). Silent partners: Parents of children in three types of day care. *Early Childhood Research Quarterly, 2,* 103–118.

Perkin, C. A. (1989, June 4). Help for workers who care for their parents. *New York Times,* p. F19.

Pestalozzi, J. H. (1898). *How Gertrude teaches her children* (2nd ed.). (L. Holland & F. Turner, Trans.). Syracuse, NY: Bardeen. (Original work published 1801)

Peters, D., & Benn, J. (1980). Day care: Support the family. *Dimensions, 9,* 78–82.

Pflaum-Connor, S. (1978). *The development of language and reading in young children* (2nd ed.). Columbus, OH: Merrill.

Philip Morris Companies. (1989). *Family survey II: Child care.* New York: Philip Morris Companies.

Phillips, D. A. (1987). Epilogue. In D. A. Phillips (Ed.), *Quality in child care: What does research tell us?* Research Monographs of the National Association for the Education of Young Children, *1,* 121–126.

Phillips, D., McCartney, K., Scarr, S., & Howes, C. (1987). Selective review of infant day care research: A cause for concern! *Zero to three, 7* (3), 18–21.

Piaget, J. (1952). *The origins of intelligence in children.* New York: International Universities Press. (Originally published 1936)

Piaget, J. (1954). *The construction of reality in the child.* New York: Basic.

Piaget, J. (1962). *Play, dreams, and imitation in childhood.* New York: Norton. (Originally published 1946)

Piaget, J. (1967). *Biology and knowledge.* Chicago: University of Chicago Press.

Pierson, D. E., Bronson, M. B., Dromey, E., Swartz, J. P., Tivnan, T., & Walker, D. K. (1983). The impact of early education, measured by classroom observations and teacher ratings of children in kindergarten. *Evaluation Review, 7* (2), 191–216.

Pierson, D. E., Walker, D. K., & Tivnan, T. (1985). A school-based program from infancy to kindergarten for children and their parents. In F. M. Hechinger (Ed.), *A better start: New choices for early learning.* New York: Walker.

Pizzo, P., & Aronson, S. S. (1976). *Concept paper on health and safety issues in day care.* Mimeo. Washington, DC: United States Department of Health, Education, and Welfare.

Platt, W. (1974). Policy making and international studies in educational evaluations. *Phi Delta Kappan, 55* (7).

Powell, D. R. (1977). *The interface between families and child care programs: A study of parent-caregiver relationships.* Detroit: Merrill-Palmer Institute.

Powell, D. R. (1978). The interpersonal relationship between parents and caregivers in day care settings. *American Journal of Orthopsychiatry, 48,* 680–689.

Powell, D. R. (1989). *Families and early childhood programs.* Research Monograph Vol. 3. Washington, DC: National Association for the Education of Young Children.

Prescott, E. (1981). Relations between physical setting and adult/child behavior in day care. In S. Kilmer (Ed.), *Advances in Early Education and Day Care, 2,* 129–158. Greenwich, CT: JAI Press.

Prescott, E. (1984). The physical setting in day care. In J. T. Greenman & R. W. Fuqua (Eds.), *Making day care better: Training, evaluation, and the process of change.* New York: Teachers College, Columbia University.

Prescott, E. (1987). The environment as organizer of intent in childcare settings. In C. S. Weinstein & T. G. David (Eds.), *Spaces for children: The built environment and child development.* New York: Plenum Press.

Prescott, E., & David, T. G. (1976). *The effects of the physical environment on day care.* Pasadena, CA: Pacific Oaks College. (Also Document No. 156–356, ERIC Document Reproduction Service)

Press, B. K., & Greenspan, S. I. (1985). Ned and Dan: The development of a toddler friendship. *Children Today, 14* (2), 24–29.

Radke-Yarrow, M., Zahn-Waxler, C., & Chapman, M. (1983). Children's prosocial dispositions and behavior. In P. H. Mussen (Ed.), *Handbook of child psychology.* Vol. 4. *Socialization, personality, and social development* (4th ed.) (pp . 469–545). New York: Wiley.

Raper, J., & Aldridge, J. (1988). What every teacher should know about AIDS. *Childhood Education, 64* (3), 146–149.

Read, M. S. (1976). *Malnutrition, learning and behavior.* (DHEW Publication No. [NIH] 76–1036). Bethesda, MD: U.S. Government Printing Office.

Reilly, A. P. (Ed.). (1980). *The communication game: Perspectives on the development of speech, language and non-verbal communication skills.* Pediatric Round Table 4. New York: Johnson & Johnson Baby Products.

Report on employer-sponsored child care services. (1988). Washington, DC: The Congressional Caucus for Women's Issues.

Rheingold, H. L., Hay, D. F., & West, M. J. (1976). Sharing in the second year of life. *Child Development, 47,* 1148–1158.

Rivkin, M. S. (1986). The teacher's place in children's play. In G. Fein & M. Rivkin (Eds.), *The young child at play. Reviews of Research, 4,* 213–217. Washington, DC: National Association for the Education of Young Children.

Robertson, A. (1982). Day care and children's responsiveness to adults. In E. F. Zigler & E. W. Gordon (Eds.), *Day care: Scientific and social policy issues* (pp. 152–173). Boston: Auburn House.

Robinson, C. H., & Lawler, M. R. (1982). *Normal and therapeutic nutrition.* New York: Macmillan.

Roedell, W. C., Slaby, R. G., & Robinson, H. B. (1976). *Social development in young children.* Washington, DC: U.S. Government Printing Office.

Rohe, W., & Patterson, A. H. (1974). The effects of varied levels of resources and density on behavior in a day care center. In R. C. Moore (Ed.), *Man-Environment interactions: Evaluations and applications, 12.* Washington, DC: Environmental Research Association.

Rose, D. H., & Slater, A. M. (1983). Infant recognition memory following brief stimulation exposure. *British Journal of Developmental Psychology, 2* (1), 1–2.

Rosenthal, J. (1979). Primary care giving: An important element of a quality infant-toddler program. *Early Childhood Education Newsletter, 2* (1), 1–2.

Rousseau, J. J. (1893). *Emile, or treatise on education*

(W. Payne, Trans.). New York: D. Appleton. (Original work published 1762)

Rousseau, J. J. (1957). *The social contract* (C. Frankel, Trans.). New York: Hafner. (Original work published 1762)

Rubenstein, J. L., & Howes, C. (1979). Caregiving and infant behavior in day care and in homes. *Developmental Psychology, 15,* 1–24.

Rubin, K. H., Fein, G. G., & Vandenberg, B. (1983). Play. In E. H. Mussen (Ed.), *Handbook of child psychology.* Vol. 4. *Socialization, personality, and social development* (4th ed.) (pp. 693–774). New York: Wiley.

Rubin, R. R., Fisher, J. J., & Doering, S. G. (1980). *Your toddler.* New York: Macmillan.

Rubin, Z. (1980). *Children's friendships.* Cambridge, MA: Harvard University Press.

Rudolph, M. (1973). *From hand to head.* New York: McGraw-Hill.

Ruff, H. (1984). Infants' manipulative exploration of objects: Effect of age and object characteristics. *Developmental Psychology, 20,* 9–20.

Ruff, H., McCarton, C., Kurtzberg, D., & Vaugh, H. G. (1984). Preterm infants' manipulative explorations of objects. *Child Development, 55,* 1116–1173.

Roupp, R. R., & Travers, J. (1982). Janus faces day care: Perspectives on quality and cost. In E. F. Zigler & E. W. Gordon (Eds.), *Day care: Scientific and social policy issues.* Boston: Auburn House.

Ruopp, R., Travers, J., Glantz, F., & Coelen, O. (1979). *Children at the center: Summary findings and their implications.* Final report of the National Day Care Study. Vol. 1. Cambridge, MA: Abt Associates.

Safford, P. L. (1989). *Integrated teaching in early childhood.* White Plains, NY: Longman.

Salmi, L. R., Weiss, H. B., Peterson, P. L., Spengler, R. F., Sattin, R. W., & Anderson, H. A. (1989). Fatal farm injuries among young children. *Pediatrics, 83* (2), 267–271.

Saltz, E., Dixon, D., & Johnson, J. (1977). Training disadvantaged preschoolers on various fantasy activities: Effects on cognitive functioning and impulse control. *Child Development, 48,* 367–380.

Saltz, R., & Saltz, E. (1986). Pretend play training and its outcomes. In G. Fein & M. Rivkin (Eds.), *The young child at play: Reviews of research* (Vol. 4) (pp. 155–173). Washington, DC: National Association for the Education of Young Children.

Sameroff, A. J., & Cavanagh, P. J. (1979). Learning in infancy: A developmental perspective. In J. D. Osofsky (Ed.), *Handbook of infant development* (pp. 344–392). New York: Wiley.

Samples, R. E. (1975). Serving intrinsic motivation in early education. In S. Coopersmith (Ed.), *Developing motivation in young children.* San Francisco: Albion.

Samples, R. (1976). *The metaphoric mind.* Menlo Park, CA: Addison-Wesley.

Schaefer, E. S., & Aaronson, M. (1977). Infant education research project: Implementation and implications of a home tutoring project. In M. C. Day & R. K. Parker (Eds.), *The preschool in action* (2nd ed.) (pp. 52–71). Boston: Allyn & Bacon.

Schmitt, B. D. (1980). The child with nonaccidental trauma. In C. Kempe & R. Helfer (Eds.), *The battered child.* Chicago: University of Chicago Press.

Schmitt, B. D. (1987). *Your child's health: A pediatric guide for parents.* New York: Bantam.

Schroeder, P. (1989, March 13). Childcare legislation: Can Congress and the White House work together? *The Commonwealth, 83* (11), 106–109.

Schroeder, P. (1989). *Champion of the great American family.* New York: Random House.

Sears, R. R., Macoby, E. E., & Levin, H. (1957). *Patterns of child rearing.* Evanston, IL: Row, Peterson.

Select Committee on Nutrition and Human Needs. (1977). *Dietary goals for the United States* (ed. 2). Washington, DC: U.S. Senate.

Shaping budding tastes. (1987, March). *Tufts University Diet & Nutrition Letter,* 1–2.

Shelov, S. P. (MD, FAAP). (Aug. 1989). Complete guide to immunization. *Working Mother, 12* (8), 44–48.

Silverman, E. (1989, August). Vegetables & soap. *Good Housekeeping. 209* (2), 148.

Silverstein, R. (1989). A window of opportunity: P. L. 99–457. In C. Berman & E. Szanton (Eds.), *The intent and spirit of P. L. 99–457: A sourcebook*. Washington, DC: National Center for Clinical Infant Programs.

Skeels, H. M. (1966). Adult status of children with contrasting early life experiences: A follow-up study. *Monographs of the Society for Research in Child Development, 31* (3, Serial No. 105), 1–65.

Smart, M. S., & Smart, R. C. (1978). *Infants* (2nd ed.). New York: Macmillan.

Smilansky, S. (1968). *The effects of sociodramatic play on disadvantaged pre-school children*. New York: Wiley.

Solomons, H., & Elardo, R. (1989). Bite injuries at a day care center. *Early Childhood Research Quarterly, 4,* 89–96.

Span, P. (1989). Should neighborhood schools be child care centers, too? *Working Mother, 12* (2), 82, 84.

Spodek, B. (Ed.). (1982). *Handbook of Research in Early Childhood Education*. New York: Free Press.

Sponseller, D. (1982). Play and early education. In B. Spodek (Ed.), *Handbook of Research in Early Childhood Education* (pp. 215–241). New York: Free Press.

Sroufe, L. A. (1979). Socioemotional development. In J. D. Osofsky (Ed.), *Handbook of infant development* (pp. 462–516). New York: Wiley.

State of California. (1987). *Manual of policies and procedures: Day care centers*. Health and Welfare Agency, Department of Social Services.

Steele, B. (1980). Psychodynamic factors in child abuse. In C. Kempe & R. Helfer (Eds.), *The battered child* (3rd ed.). Chicago: The University of Chicago Press.

Stewart, I. S. (1982). The real world of teaching two-year-old children. *Young Children, 37* (5), 3–13.

Stolz, L. M. (1978). The Kaiser Service Centers. In J. L. Hymes, Jr., *Living history interviews*. Book 2. Carmel, CA: Hacienda Press.

Strauss, M. A., Gelles, R. J. & Steinmetz, S. K. (1979). *Behind closed doors: Violence in the American family*. New York: Doubleday.

Strickland, D. S., & Taylor, D. (1989). Family storybook reading: Implications for children, families, and curriculum. In D. S. Strickland & L. M. Morrow (Eds.), *Emerging literacy: Young children learn to read and write*. Neward, DE: International Reading Association.

Suransky, V. P. (1984). *The erosion of childhood*. Chicago: University of Chicago Press.

Suskind, D., & Kittel, J. (1989). Clocks, cameras, and chatter, chatter, chatter: Activity boxes as curriculum. *Young Children, 44* (2), 46–50.

Sutton-Smith, B., & Sutton-Smith, S. (1974). *How to play with your children (and when not to)*. New York: Hawthorn.

Thoman, E. B., & Browder, S. (1987). *Born dancing: How intuitive parents understand their baby's unspoken language and natural rhythms*. New York: Harper & Row.

Thomas, A., Chess, S., & Birch, H. G. (1980). *Behavioral individuality in early childhood*. New York: Greenwood. (Reprint of the 1963 edition, published by New York University Press)

Thomas, A., Chess, S. Birch, H. G. & Hertzig, M. E. (1963). *Behavioral individuality in early childhood*. New York: New York University Press.

Thomas, A., Chess, S., Birch, H. G., Hertzig, M. E., & Korn, S. (1983). *Behavioral individuality in early childhood*. New York: New York University Press.

Travers, R. M. W. (1985). *Training human intelligence: Developing exploratory and aesthetic skills*. Holmes Beach, FL: Learning Publications.

Trites, R. L., & Tryphonas, H. (1983). Food additives: The controversy continues. *Topics in Early Childhood Special Education, 3* (2), 43–47.

Trumpp, C. E., & Karasic, R. (1983). Management of communicable diseases in day care centers. *Pediatric Annals, 12* (3).

Uhde, A. P. (1983). Socio-Dramatic play: A creative experience. *Dimensions, 12* (1), 15–18.

Ulich, R. (1954). *Three thousand years of educational wisdom* (2nd ed.). Cambridge, MA: Harvard University Press.

U.S. Consumer Product Safety Commission. (1979). *Fact sheet No. 22: Playground equipment.* Washington, DC: Author.

U.S. Consumer Product Safety Commission. (1981). *A handbook for public playground safety.* Vols. I and II. Washington, DC: U.S. Government Printing Office.

U.S. Consumer Product Safety Commission. (1985). *The safe nursery.* Washington, DC: Author.

U.S. Consumer Product Safety Commission. (1988). *Think toy safety.* Washington, DC: Author.

U.S. Consumer Product Safety Commission. (n.d.). *Fact sheet No. 22.* Washington, DC: Author.

U.S. National Commission on the International Year of the Child. (1980). *Report to the President.* Washington, DC: Author.

Van Leuven, N. (1988). *Food to grow on: A parent's guide to nutrition.* Pownal, VT: Storey Communications.

de Villiers, P. A., & de Villiers, J. G. (1979). *Early language.* Cambridge, MA: Harvard University Press.

Vygotsky, L. S. (1967). Play and its role in the mental development of the child. *Soviet Psychology, 12,* 62–76.

Vygotsky, L. S. (1976). Play and its role in the mental development of the child. In J. S. Bruner, A. Jolly, & K. Sylva (Eds.), *Play: Its role in development and evolution* (pp. 537–554). New York: Basic Books.

Walker, A. E., Baker, S. P., Szocka, A. (1989). Childhood injury deaths: National analysis and geographic variations. *American Journal of Public Health, 79* (3), 310–315.

Warger, C. (Ed.). (1988). *Public school early childhood programs.* Alexandria, VA: Association for Supervision and Curriculum Development.

Watson, J. B., & Watson, R. R. (1928). *The psychological care of the infant and child.* New York: Norton.

Wattenberg, W. W., & Clifford, C. (1964). Relation of self concepts to beginning achievement in reading. *Child Development, 35* (35), 461–467.

Weber, L. (1988, August). Everyday foods that can make you very sick. *Good Housekeeping,* 187–188.

Weikart, P. S. (1985). *Movement plus music.* Ypsilanti, MI: High/Scope Press.

Weinstein, C., & David, T. (Eds.). (1987). *Spaces for children: The built environment and child development.* New York: Plenum.

Weir, R. (1962). *Language in the crib.* The Hague: Mouton.

Weltzer, H. (1985). Teaching infants infant-infant social interaction. *Early Child Development and Care, 20,* 145–155.

Wheat, P., & Lieber, L. (1979). *Hope for the children.* Minneapolis: Winston.

White, B. L. (1972). Fundamental early environmental influences on the development of competencies. In M. E. Meyer (Ed.), *Third symposium on learning: Cognitive learning.* Bellingham, WA: Western Washington State College Press.

White, B. L. (1975). *The first three years of life.* Englewood Cliffs, NJ: Prentice-Hall.

White, B. L. (1979). Infant learning. *Options in Education Program* No. 202, Part II. Washington, DC: National Public Radio and the Institute for Educational Leadership.

White, B. L. (1980). The knowledge base: The development of intelligence. Part II. *Newsletter of the Center for Parent Education, 11* (4).

White, B. L. (1985). *The first three years of life* (rev. ed.). New York: Simon & Schuster.

White, B. L. (1988a). *Educating the infant and toddler.* Lexington, MA: Lexington Books.

White, B. L. (1988b). The Missouri New Parents as Teachers Project. In B. L. White, *Educating the infant and toddler* (pp. 155–232). Lexington, MA: Lexington Books.

White, B. L. & Watts, J. C. (1973). *Experience and environment: Major influences on the development of the young child.* Vol. 1. Englewood Cliffs, NJ: Prentice-Hall.

White House Conference on Food, Nutrition and Health. (1969). *Final report (1970).* Washington, DC: U.S. Government Printing Office.

White, R. W. (1968). Motivation reconsidered: The concept of competence. In Almy, M. (Ed.), *Early childhood play: Selected readings related to cognition and motivation* (pp. WITE-1A–WITE-37A). New York: Simon & Schuster.

Wilkins, A., & Blank, H. (1986). Child care: Strategies to move the issue forward. *Young Children, 42* (1), 68–72.

Willis, A., & Ricciuti, H. (1975). *A good beginning for babies: Guidelines for group care.* Washington, DC: National Association for the Education of Young Children.

Willis, A., & Ricciuti, H. (1980). Routine caregiving. In R. Neugebauer & R. Lurie (Eds.), *Caring for infants and toddlers: What works, what doesn't* Vol. 1. Redmond, WA: Child Care Information Exchange.

Winter, M. (1985). Parents as first teachers. In F. M. Hechinger (Ed.), *A better start: New choices for early learning.* New York: Walker.

Wishon, P. M., Bower, R., & Eller, B. (1983). Childhood obesity: Prevention and treatment. *Young Children, 39* (1), 21–27.

Woodcock, L. P. (1941). *Life and ways of the two-year-old.* New York: E. P. Dutton.

World Health Organization. (1962). *Deprivation of maternal care: A reassessment of its effects.* Geneva: Author.

Yarrow, L. J. (1979). Historical perspectives and future directions in infant development. In J. D. Osofsky (Ed.), *Handbook of infant development* (pp. 897–917). New York: Wiley.

Yawkey, T. D., & Pellegrini, A. D. (1984). *Child's play: Developmental and Applied.* Hillsdale, NJ: Erlbaum.

Zaichkowsky, L. D., Zaichkowsky, L. B., & Martinek, T. J. (1980). *Growth and development: The child and physical activity.* St. Louis: Mosby.

Zigler, E. F. (1973). Project Head Start: Success or failure? *Learning, 1,* 43–47.

Zigler, E. F. (1987). Formal schooling for four-year-olds? No. In S. L. Kagan & E. F. Zigler (Eds.), *Early schooling: The national debate.* New Haven: Yale University Press.

Zigler, E. (1988, May, April). Solving the child care crisis. *Missouri Schools,* 6–10.

Zigler, E. F., & Turner, P. (1982). Parents and day care workers: A failed partnership? In E. F. Zigler & E. W. Gordon (Eds.), *Day care: Scientific and social policy issues* (pp. 174–182). Boston: Auburn House.

Zigler, E., & Valentine, J. (1979). *Project Head Start: A legacy of the War on Poverty.* New York: Free Press.

Name Index

Subject Index